KU-522-978

The
Oxford Book
Of Seventeenth Century
Verse

The Oxford Book Of Seventeenth Century Verse

Chosen by

H. J. C. Grierson

and

G. Bullough

Oxford

At the Clarendon Press

Oxford University Press, Ely House, London W. 1

GLASGOW NEW YORK TORONTO MELBOURNE WELLINGTON
CAPE TOWN SALISBURY IBADAN NAIROBI LUSAKA ADDIS ABABA
BOMBAY CALCUTTA MADRAS KARACHI LAHORE DACCA
KUALA LUMPUR SINGAPORE HONG KONG TOKYO

FIRST PUBLISHED 1934
REPRINTED 1938, 1942, 1946, 1951, 1958, 1966, 1968

PRINTED IN GREAT BRITAIN

PREFACE

THIS book, like others of the series, takes the seventeenth century 'in its simplest meaning' and with as little overlapping as possible. Donne's early, that is most of his secular poems, might justifiably have been included in Sir Edmund Chambers's *Book of Sixteenth Century Verse*, if a claim for a share of Campion's poems might have been put in by the editors of this volume. Some such overlapping, dove-tailing, is imperative unless a selection is to lose altogether its dominant character. Campion's songs are among the most finished examples of Elizabethan song composed immediately to be set to music. Donne's 'Songs and Sonets', not alone in virtue of their content and 'wit', but in their rhythms, their suggestion of speech rather than song (the occasional medial pause, 'the sense variously drawn out from line to line' in stanzas of elaborate construction, the difficult clusters of consonants troublesome to a singer), mark a new fashion in poetry, a shifting of the centre of gravity not confined to those who may be called 'metaphysical' poets from the form of poetry to its content, from a poetry which, in Sir Edmund Chambers's phrase, 'plays upon the coloured surface of things' to one that with varying degrees of sincerity and effectiveness, 'draws from the wells'. For not all those who played with thoughts (to use Scott's description) as the Elizabethans had played with words did so under the impulse of a deeper vein of thought, a more passionate and sincere inspiration. But some did; and the greater body of seventeenth-century verse, whether the tragedies of Shakespeare and Webster, or 'metaphysical' poetry, or poetry that is still Spenserian and allegorical (the Fletchers and others), or classical (Jonson, Milton, even Herrick) is, if not 'sicklied o'er' yet troubled, and made at times to sound 'a harsh and dolorous note', by the intrusion of the intellect, a spirit of inquiry impatient of traditional, conventional sentiment. Even in flattering a mistress our poets will seek a novel way of approach.

That all this did not make for a poetry of such immediate pure delight as that of Spenser and the Elizabethans is evident from the judgement passed on it by contemporaries, as Drummond and Milton, and by the fate that overtook much of it for the greater part of two centuries. In the earliest anthology of English poetry which in the 'eighties' of last century came into the hands of one of the present editors, *Ward's English Poets*, the seventeenth century was represented in the main by Jonson, Milton, Herrick, and Dryden, with a few selections from some of the least characteristic poets—Drummond, songs from the dramatists, Browne, Carew, and certain precursors of the century that was to follow, Cowley, Waller, Denham, and Davenant. The 'metaphysicals' were hardly represented, and the Anglican and Roman religious poets were slumped together and represented by some fifteen poems or short extracts. In the *Golden Treasury* it was not very different. Donne appears only as the author of a poem which he did not write. Herbert is represented by a single poem; Vaughan by two, and a verse from another; Crashaw by a few lines from one poem. Our immediate reference is to the 1890 edition—there was some later infiltration.

Palgrave's chief and best guide was Tennyson, on whose fine ear the metres of the 'metaphysicals' must have grated as did those of his friend Browning; and a distinguished poet of our own day has in a recent lecture indicated clearly that his judgement is more in agreement with that of Tennyson than with that of the admirers of Donne. Into the merits of these judgements, and the question of whether 'wit', the play of thought, is or is not the intruder in poetry which Steele and Mr. Housman have adjudged it, whether 'simile and metaphor are things inessential to Poetry' or, as Aristotle thought, the mark of genius, the incommunicable gift, this is not the place to enter on at length. Certainly the poets of the seventeenth century, from Shakespeare in his great tragedies (which though not represented here are of this period, and more akin alike in diction, wit, and verse to the poetry of Donne and his fellows than has always been recognized), and Chapman and Fulke Greville and John Donne to Milton and Cowley and Dryden, deemed poetry a fit vehicle for the play of thought. And the test of such poetry must be, not the value or interest or ingenuity of the thought in itself, but its fitness to suggest, express, communicate a mood of feeling. If we are to judge by the sense abstractly we shall condemn equally Lovelace when he sings:

> Each step trod out a lover's thought
> And the ambitious hopes he brought,
> Chain'd to her brave feet with such arts,
> Such sweet command, and gentle awe,
> As when she ceas'd we sighing saw
> The floor lay pav'd with broken hearts;

and Steele when he commends his mistress by declaring that 'to love her is a liberal education'; and Wordsworth when he tells us that

> One impulse from a vernal wood
> May teach us more of man,
> Of moral evil and of good
> Than all the sages can.

The poetical value of such statements is not dependent on their truth, scientific or philosophical, but their fitness to convey the feeling that inspired them, the conviction they communicate of having come warm from the heart and imagination of the poet; that, and the charm of the words and rhythms in which they are conveyed. If one cannot get over the ingenuity or foolishness of the first ('to love and to be wise is given to no man') or the evident want of philosophic truth in the last, then one had better leave poetry alone and turn one's attention to science and philosophy, for the truth of poetry is truth of feeling not of statement.

It is, then, as poetry that the tormented and at times monstrous wit of Donne; the passionate conceits and hyperboles of Shakespeare and Carew and Crashaw; the playful and serious fancies of Herrick and Marvell; the homely and pious turns of thought and fancy in Herbert and other religious poets; the high reasoning of Milton; the eloquent compliments and virile argument of Dryden must ultimately be judged. The present editors' guide in selection has been quite simply their individual reaction to the element of poetry which each piece contains in fuller or lesser measure. That in the opinion of some readers we shall be judged to have erred by inclusion and omission goes without saying.

We have had a wide field to survey—printed volumes, music books, and manuscript collections; and human memory and judgement are alike fallible.

The order of the poems has been determined by the experience of our publishers of what is most practical. Personally we should have wished to divide the poems of Milton and Dryden, placing the earlier pieces near the middle and their later poems at the end, closing our survey on Dryden. But a chronological sequence following the birth-dates of authors has undoubted advantages in a series made by different editors.

Textually this book is something of an experiment. We have endeavoured wherever possible to give authoritative versions, in many cases from miscellanies and song-books, in many from first editions, in some from the last editions published within the lifetime of their authors. Our aim has been to provide a text preserving as far as might be the characteristics of the original and yet intelligible to the general reader. The problem was to find some *via media* between complete modernization in spelling and punctuation, and a transcription of all the varied forms used by seventeenth-century poets and printers. The latter course would have resulted in a collection of usages which might have proved invaluable to serious students, since it would have illustrated the important changes in spelling and punctuation occurring during the period. But the book is not intended merely for the specialist, so a simple process of transcription would not suffice. On the other hand it was felt that a total modernization was less essential in dealing with this, than with the previous century, that it would dissipate something of the distinctive flavour of the poetry, and that it would occasionally cause actual falsification—in cases, for example, of unusual pronunciation, or where a poet made use of eye-rhyme. And although no all-embracing laws of punctuation may be drawn, yet a particular consistency is often noticeable, so that to eliminate the apostrophe of elision from Donne and Cowley, to remove the medial pointing from Chapman's *Iliad*, to substitute the modern logical for the more rhetorical pointing of Shakespeare's day, would be to ignore unnecessarily technical symbols of considerable interest and significance. We leave our survey of a century's printed verse, acknowledging the advantages of the new regularity prevalent after the Restoration, but fortified in our respect for the frequent vigour and subtlety of the earlier punctuation.

Among the current forms with which we were faced may be mentioned the following:

redundant final 'e'; internal mute 'e'; 'y' for modern 'i' (wayte, dye, lye); 'i' for 'y' (plaies, plaid); 'e' for 'a' (cleere, deer); 'i' for 'e' and 'e' for 'i' (pincel, Squirril, peece, Beere (Bier)); 'u' for 'o' (bloud, droupe); 'u' for 'w' (floures); 'w' for 'u' (clowd, asswage); 'ei' for 'ie' (greife); 'ea' for 'a' (Heark!); 'a' for 'ea' (hart); 'oa' for 'o' (smoake); 'ck' or 'que' for 'c' or 'k' (rustick, musique, thinck); the doubling of consonants (legg, becomming, Eccho, Carrols); the omission of one element of a double consonant (ratling, babling, madnes, wel); the absence of the apostrophe; 't' for 'd' (wisht).

The occasional presence of such forms in a word or a line of verse should not handicap any reader after the first moment or two. But a thickset accumulation of them through whole stanzas and poems might prove a serious obstacle to the inexperienced. To obviate this, while preserving the general characteristics of the original texts, we evolved a flexible procedure. We have not 'modernized', but where words or lines might seem ugly to modern eyes, or where difference in usage might lead to ambiguity, we have substituted simpler forms, always taking care (we believe) that the substituted form *was actually in use during the seventeenth century*, that verbal music is unspoiled, and that individual peculiarities are as far as possible retained. Hence we have not always dropped the redundant 'e', or put 'pieces', 'clear', 'assuage', 'echo', 'smoke'. Our guide has been the appearance of the words in their context, and the ease with which the average intelligent reader might understand them. But we have doubled the final consonant in words like 'madnes' and 'wel'; given 'I'll', 'We'll', for 'Ile', 'I'l', 'Wele', 'W'el', &c.; 'o'er' for 'ore', 'o're', 'oer', &c.; 'ne'er' for 'nere', &c.; inserted the apostrophe in 'here's', 'it's', &c.; and given the form 'than' instead of the usual 'then', except in rhymes.

In this way we have tried to avoid the pitfalls of complete modernization and the imposition of a standard form where there was no standard. With the original punctuation we have interfered very little, only occasionally removing an apparent irrelevance or ambiguity by the omission or addition of a point—again with an eye on seventeenth-century practice.

Beyond an occasional variant and the explanation of a word in a footnote we have not gone in the direction of annotations, for (a full commentary being out of the question) it seemed better to fill our space with texts rather than to make by arbitrary selection what must have proved an inadequate commentary. Of many important authors (Donne, Milton, Butler, &c.)

there are in existence fully annotated texts. The general reader will often find that a difficulty is more apparent than real, especially as he becomes familiar with the range of thought and wit within which poets of the century move in the main, the sources literary or realistic from which they drew their imagery.

The dates following poems are those of the first editions. When the text is taken from another source this is indicated; but it should have been noted that Cowley's poems are printed from the first collected edition of 1668, except where a return to the text of the first edition is indicated.

The fact that our selection includes extracts from longer poems differentiates it from many others which select only lyrical poems. While the limits of our final scheme do not allow us to make individual acknowledgements, we have, as is customary, consulted the work of our predecessors, though we have always gone to the original source before making our choice and deciding on a text. Selections consulted by us include those of Ward, Palgrave, Saintsbury, Bullen, and Oliphant; and, of more recent works, Mr. Fellowes's *English Madrigal Verse*, Mr. William Kerr's *Restoration Verse*, Mr. Massingham's *Seventeenth Century English Verse*, *Metaphysical Lyrics and Poems* by H. J. C. G., and the *Elizabethan Lyrics* and *Seventeenth Century Lyrics* of Mr. Norman Ault, with his specially full collections, dates, and notes. We are also much indebted to an analysis of a large number of Madrigal Books, Song Books, Catch Books, Wit Collections, Drolleries, &c., made by Mr. A. K. Das Gupta of the University of Calcutta when working at Edinburgh University for the degree of Ph.D. We hope that this work will shortly be published.

We should like to acknowledge the help we have received, in the matter of inclusion and rejection, from Sir E. K. Chambers and from Miss Gwyneth Lloyd Thomas, Girton College, Cambridge; in preparing of texts and proof-reading, from Mrs. Bullough; Professor Dickins, the University, Leeds; Mr. John Purves, Lecturer in Italian, the University, Edinburgh; Mr. H. Harvey Wood, Lecturer in English, the University, Edinburgh; and Mr. Frank D. Simpson, I.C.S. (ret.), who checked the text of various poems from MSS. in the British Museum.

H. J. C. GRIERSON
G. BULLOUGH

FULK GREVILLE, LORD BROOKE

1554–1628

1

Sonnet lxxxvii

WHEN as Mans life, the light of human lust,
In socket of his earthly lanthorne burnes,
That all this glory unto ashes must,
And generation to corruption turnes;
Then fond desires that onely feare their end,
Doe vainely wish for life, but to amend.
But when this life is from the body fled,
To see it selfe in that *eternall Glasse*,
Where time doth end, and thoughts accuse the dead,
Where all to come, is one with all that was;
Then living men aske how he left his breath,
That while he lived never thought of death.

Cælica, 1633

2

Sonnet lxxxviii

MAN, dreame no more of curious mysteries,
As what was here before the world was made,
The first Mans life, the state of Paradise,
Where heaven is, or hell's eternall shade,
For Gods works are like him, all infinite;
And curious search, but craftie sinnes delight.

The Flood that did, and dreadfull Fire that shall,
Drowne, and burne up the malice of the earth,
The divers tongues, and *Babylons* downe-fall,
Are nothing to the man's renewed birth;
First, let the Law plough up thy wicked heart,
That Christ *may come, and all these types depart.*

When thou hast swept the house that all is cleare,
When thou the dust hast shaken from thy feete,
When God's All-might doth in thy flesh appeare,
Then Seas with streames above the skye doe meet;
  For *Goodnesse onely doth God comprehend,*
  Knowes what was first, and what shall be the end.

Cælica, 1633

3 *Sonnet xciv*

MEN, that delight to multiply desire,
Like tellers are that take coyne but to pay,
Still tempted to be false with little hire,
Blacke hands except, which they would have away:
  For where power wisely Audits her estate,
  The Checquer Mens best recompense is hate.

The little Maide that weareth out the day,
To gather flow'rs still covetous of more,
At night when she with her desire would play,
And let her pleasure wanton in her store,
  Discernes the first laid underneath the last,
  Wither'd, and so is all that we have past.

Fix then on good desires, and if you finde
Ambitious dreames or feares of over-thwart;
Changes, temptations, bloomes of earthly minde,
Yet wave not, since earth-change hath change of smart;
  For lest Man should thinke flesh a seat of blisse,
  God workes that his joy mixt with sorrow is.

Cælica, 1633

Checquer *Warwick MS.*; Exchequer *1633*.
earthly *Warwick MS.*; earthy *1633*.

FULK GREVILLE, LORD BROOKE

4 *Sonnet xcvii*

ETERNALL Truth, almighty, infinite,
Onely exiled from man's fleshly heart,
Where ignorance and disobedience fight,
In hell and sinne, which shall have greatest part:
When thy sweet mercy opens forth the light,
Of Grace which giveth eyes unto the blind,
And with the Law even plowest up our sprite
To faith, wherein flesh may salvation finde:
Thou bidst us pray, and wee doe pray to thee,
But as to power and God without us plac'd,
Thinking a wish may weare out vanity,
Or habits be by miracles defac'd.
One thought to God wee give, the rest to sinne,
Quickely unbent is all desire of good,
True words passe out, but have no being within,
Wee pray to *Christ*, yet helpe to shed his blood;
For while wee say *beliefe*, and feele it not,
Promise amends, and yet despaire in it,
Heare *Sodom* judg'd, and goe not out with *Lot*,
Make Law and Gospell riddles of the wit:
We with the *Jewes* even *Christ* still crucifie,
As not yet come to our impiety.

Cælica, 1633

5 *Sonnet xcix*

DOWNE in the depth of mine iniquity,
That ugly center of infernall spirits,
Where each sinne feels her owne deformity,
In these peculiar torments she inherits,
Depriv'd of human graces, and divine,
Even there appeares this *saving* God of mine.

And in this fatall mirrour of transgression,
Shewes man as fruit of his degeneration,
The errour's ugly infinite impression,
Which beares the faithlesse downe to desperation;
  Depriv'd of humane graces and divine,
  Even there appeares this *saving God* of mine.

In power and truth, Almighty and eternall,
Which on the sinne reflects strange desolation,
With glory scourging all the Spirits infernall,
And uncreated hell with unprivation;
  Depriv'd of humane graces, not divine,
  Even there appeares this *saving God* of mine.

For on this spirituall Crosse condemned lying,
To paines infernall by eternall doome,
I see my Saviour for the same sinnes dying,
And from that hell I fear'd, to free me come;
  Depriv'd of humane graces, not divine,
  Thus hath his death rais'd up this soule of mine.

Cælica, 1633

6 *Sonnet ciii*

O FALSE and treacherous *Probability*,
Enemy of truth, and friend to wickednesse;
With whose bleare eyes opinion learnes to see,
Truth's feeble party here, and barrennesse.

When thou hast thus misled Humanity,
And lost obedience in the pride of wit,
With reason dar'st thou judge the Deity,
And in thy flesh make bold to fashion it.

Vaine thought, the word of Power a riddle is,
And till the vayles be rent, the flesh newborne,
Reveales no wonders of that inward blisse,
Which but where faith is, every where findes scorne;
Who therfore censures God with fleshly sprite,
As well in time may wrap up infinite. *Cælica*, 1633

7 *Sonnet cv*

THREE things there be in Mans opinion deare,
Fame, many *Friends*, and *Fortunes* dignities:
False visions all, which in our sense appeare,
To sanctifie desires Idolatry.

For what is *Fortune*, but a wat'ry glasse?
Whose chrystall forehead wants a steely backe,
Where raine and stormes blowe all away that was,
Whose ship alike both depths and shallowes wracke.

Fame againe, which from blinding power takes light,
Both *Cæsar's* shadow is, and *Cato's* friend,
The child of humour, not allyed to right,
Living by oft exchange of winged end.

And many *Friends*, false strength of feeble mind,
Betraying equals, as true slaves to might;
Like *Ecchoes* still send voyces down the wind,
But never in adversity finde right.

Then Man, though vertue of extremities
The middle be, and so hath two to one,
By Place and Nature constant enemies,
And against both these no strength but her owne,
Yet quit thou for her, Friends, Fame, Fortune's throne;
Divels there many be, and Gods but one. *Cælica*, 1633

sprite, *MS.*; spirit, *1633*. blowe *MS.*; beare *1633*.

8 *Of Human Learning*

THE chiefe Use then in man of that he knowes,
Is his paines taking for the good of all,
Not fleshly weeping for our owne made woes,
Not laughing from a Melancholy gall,
Not hating from a soule that overflowes
With bitternesse, breath'd out from inward thrall:
But sweetly rather to ease, loose, or binde,
As need requires, this fraile fall'n humane kinde.

Yet *Some seeke knowledge, meerely to be knowne*,
And idle Curiositie that is;
Some but to *sell*, not freely to bestow,
These gaine and spend both time, and wealth amisse,
Embasing Arts, by basely deeming so;
Some to build others, which is Charity,
But these to build themselves, who wise men be.

And to conclude, whether we would erect
Our selves, or others by this choice of Arts;
Our chiefe endeavour must be to effect
A sound foundation, not on sandy parts
Of light Opinion, Selfenesse, Words of men,
But that *sure rocke of truth*; *Gods Word, or Penne.*

Next that we doe not overbuild our states,
In searching secrets of the Deity,
Obscurities of Nature, casualtie of Fates;
But measure first our own Humanity,
Then on our gifts impose an equall rate,
And so seeke wisedome with sobriety:
Not curious what our fellowes ought to doe,
But what our owne creation bindes us to.

Lastly, we must not to the world erect
Theaters, nor plant our Paradise in dust,
Nor build up *Babels* for the Divels elect;
Make temples of our hearts to God we must;
  And then, as *Godlesse wisedomes follies be,*
  So are his heights our true Philosophie.

With which faire cautions, Man may well professe
To studie God, whom he is borne to serve;
Nature, t' admire the greater in the lesse;
Time, but to learne; our selves we may observe,
  To humble us: Others, to exercise
  Our love and patience, wherein Duty lies.

Lastly, the truth and good, to love and doe them:
The error, onely to destroy, and shunne it;
Our hearts in generall will lead us to them,
When gifts of Grace, and Faith have once begun it.
  For without these, the minde of man growes numbe,
  The body darkenesse, to the soule a tombe.

Thus are true Learnings in the humble heart
A *Spirituall worke*, raising Gods Image, rased
By our transgression; a *well-framed art*,
At which the world, and error stand amazed;
A *Light divine*, where man sees joy, and smart
Immortall, in this mortall body blazed;
  A *wisdome*, which *the Wisedome* us assureth
  With hers even to the sight of God endureth.

Hard Characters (I grant) to flesh and blood,
Which in the first perfection of creation
Freely resign'd the state of being good,
To know the evill, where it found privation;

And lost her being, ere she understood
Depth of this fall, paine of *Regeneration*:
  'By which she yet must raise herselfe againe,
  Ere she can judge all other knowledge vaine.'

Of Humane Learning, 1633 (stanzas 143–51)

9

Chorus Primus
Wise Counsellors

HONOR in chief, our Oath is to uphold,
That by no trafficke it be bought or sold.
Else looke what brings that dainty *Throne-worke* downe,
Addes not, but still takes something from a Crowne.
Profit, and her true Mine, Frugality,
Incident likewise to our Office be:
As husbanding the Scepters spreading right,
To stretch itself, yet not grow infinite;
Or with Prerogative to Tyrannize,
Whose workes prove oft more absolute than wise.
Not mastering Lawes, which Freedom interrupt;
Nor moulding Pulpits, which is to corrupt,
And help Change in; *whose vanity still tends*
To worke immortal things to mortall ends.
But our part is to keep the Justice free,
As equall peising liberality;
Which both contents the People that receives,
And Princely giver more enabled leaves.
Likewise with *forraigne States* we keep respect
By diligence, which seldom findes neglect.
In Treaties still concluding mutuall good;
Since *no one byas'd Contract ever stood.*

In Complements we strive to hold such measure,
That outward forme consume not inward treasure.
For betwixt Man, and Man; twixt Kings and Kings
Our place should offer well-digested things.
Else as those Crudities, which doe remaine
Within the body, all Complexions staine:
So doth advantage betweene State and State,
Though finely got, yet prove unfortunate:
And oft Disorder-like in government,
Leave even those that prosper, discontent.

Mustapha, 1633

10

Chorus Tertius

Of Time: Eternitie

TIME

WHAT meane these mortall children of mine owne,
Ungratefully, against me to complaine,
That all I build is by me overthrowne?
Vices put under to rise up againe?
That on my wheeles both Good, and Ill doe move;
The one beneath, while th' other is above?

Day, Night, Houres, Arts, All; God, or Men create,
The world doth charge me, that I restlesse change;
Suffer no being in a constant state:
Alas! Why are my revolutions strange
Unto these Natures, made to fall, or clime,
With that sweet *Genius*, ever-moving *Time*?

What Wearinesse; what lothsome Desolations
Would plague these life and death-begetting Creatures?
Nay what absurdity in my Creations
Were it, if *Time-borne* had *Eternall* features;
  This nether Orbe, which is Corruptions Sphere,
  Not being able long one shape to beare.

Could Pleasure live? Could Worth have reverence?
Lawes, Arts, or Sects (meere probabilities)
Keepe up their reputation in Mans sense,
If Noveltie did not renew his eyes;
  Or *Time* take mildly from him what he knew,
  Making both me, and mine, to each still new?

Daughter of Heaven am I; but God, none greater;
Pure like my Parents; life, and death of Action;
Author of ill successe to every creature
Whose pride against my Periods makes a faction:
  With me who goe along, rise while they be;
  Nothing of mine respects Eternitie.

Kings! why do you then blame me, whom I choose,
As my Annointed, from the Potters ore;
And to advance you made the People lose,
While you to me acknowledged your power?
  Be confident *all Thrones subsist in me:*
  I am the measure of Felicitie.

. . . . .

I bring the Truth to light; detect the Ill;
My Native greatnesse scorneth bounded wayes;
Untimely Power a few dayes ruine will;
Yea, Worth it selfe falls, till I list to raise.
  The Earth is mine: of earthly things the care
  I leave to Men, that like them, earthly are.

. . . . .

Not Kings, but I, can *Nemesis* send forth,
The judgments of Revenge, and Wrong, are mine:
My Stampes alone doe warrant reall Worth;
How doe untimely Vertues else decline?
  For Sonne, or Father, to destroy each other,
  Are bastard deeds, where *Time* is not the mother.

Such is the worke this State hath undertaken,
And keepes in Clouds; with purpose to advance
False counsells; in their selfe-craft justly shaken,
As grounded on my slave and shaddow, *Chance.*
  Nay more; *My childe* Occasion *is not free*
  To bring forth good, or evill, without me.

And shall I for revealing this misdeed,
By tying Future to the Present ill,
Which keepes disorders wayes from happie speed;
Be guiltie made of Man's *still-erring* will?
  Shall I, that in my selfe still golden am,
  By their Grosse metall, beare an Iron name?

No; Let Man draw, by his owne cursed Square,
Such crooked lines, as his fraile thoughts affect;
And, like things that of nothing framed are,
Decline unto that Centre of defect:
  I will disclaime his downfall, and stand free,
  As native rivall to *Eternitie.*

ETERNITIE

What meanes this New-borne childe of Planets' motion?
This finite Elfe of Mans vaine acts, and errors?
Whose changing wheeles in all thoughts stirre commotion?
And in her owne face, onely, beares the Mirror.
  A Mirror in which, since *Time* tooke her fall,
  Mankinde sees Ill increase; no Good at all.

Because in your vast mouth you hold your Tayle,
As coupling Ages past with times to come;
Doe you presume your Trophees shall not fayle,
As both Creation's Cradle, and her Tombe?
  Or for beyond your selfe you cannot see,
  By dayes, and houres, would you *Eternall* be?

Time is the weakest worke of my Creation,
And, if not still repayr'd, must straight decay:
The Mortall take not my true constellation,
And so are dazzled, by her nimble sway,
  To thinke her course long; which if measur'd right,
  Is but a Minute of my Infinite.

A Minute which doth her subsistence tye;
Subsistencies which, in not being, be:
Shall is to come; and *Was* is passed by;
Time present cements this Duplicitie:
  And if one must, of force, be like the other,
  Of Nothing is not Nothing made the mother?

Why strives *Time* then to parallell with me?
What be her types of longest lasting glory?
Arts, Mitres, Lawes, Moments, Supremacie,
Of Natures erring *Alchymie* the storie:
  From Nothing sprang this point, and must, by course,
  To that confusion turne againe, or worse.

For she, and all her mortall off-springs, build
Upon the moving Base of selfe-conceit:
Which constant forme can neither take, nor yeeld;
But still change shapes, to multiply deceit:
  Like playing *Atomi*, in vaine contending,
  Though they beginning had, to have no ending.

FULK GREVILLE, LORD BROOKE

I, that at once see *Time's* distinct progression;
I, in whose bosome *Was*, and *Shall*, still be;
I, that in Causes worke th' Effects Succession,
Giving both Good, and Ill, their destinie;
  Though I bind all, yet can receive no bound;
  But see the finite still it selfe confound.

Time! therefore know thy limits, and strive not
To make thy selfe, or thy works *Infinite*,
Whose Essence only is to write, and blot:
Thy Changes prove thou hast no stablish't right.
  Governe thy mortall Sphere, deale not with mine:
  Time *but the servant is of Power Divine.*

Blame thou this present State, that will blame thee;
Brick-wall your errors from one, to another;
Both faile alike unto *Eternitie*,
Goodnesse of no mixt course can be the mother.
  Both you, and yours doe covet states *Eternall*;
  Whence, though pride end, your pains yet be Infernall.

Ruine this Masse; worke Change in all Estates,
Which, when they serve not me, are in your power:
Give unto their corruption doomes of Fate;
Let your vast wombe your *Cadmus*-men devoure.
  The Vice yeelds scope enough for you, and hell,
  To compasse ill ends by not doing well.

. . . .

Crosse your owne steps; hasten to make, and marre;
With your Vicissitudes please, displease your owne:
Your three light wheeles of sundry fashions are,
And each, by others motion, overthrowne.
  Doe what you can: Mine shall subsist by Me:
  I am the measure of *Felicitie*.

Mustapha, 1633

11 *Chorus Quintus*
Tartarorum

VAST *Superstition*! Glorious stile of Weaknesse!
Sprung from the deepe disquiet of Man's passion,
To desolation, and despaire of Nature:
Thy texts bring Princes' Titles into question:
Thy Prophets set on worke the sword of Tyrants:
They manacle sweet Truth with their distinctions;
Let Vertue blood; teach Crueltie for Gods sake;
Fashioning one God, yet him of many fashions,
Like many-headed Error, in their Passions.
Mankinde! Trust not these *Superstitious* dreames;
Feare's Idoles, Pleasure's Relikes, Sorrowe's Pleasures.
They make the willful hearts their holy Temples;
The Rebells unto Government their Martyrs.
No: Thou childe of false miracles begotten!
False Miracles, which are but ignorance of Cause,
Lift up the hopes of thy abjected Prophets:
Courage and Worth abjure thy painted Heavens.
Sicknesse, thy blessings are; Miserie, thy triall;
Nothing, thy way unto eternall being;
Death, to salvation; and the Grave to Heaven.
So Blest be they, so Angel'd, so Eterniz'd
That tie their senses to thy senseless glories,
And die, to cloy the after-age with stories.
Man should make much of Life, as *Nature's table*,
Wherein she writes the Cypher of her glorie.
Forsake not Nature, nor misunderstand her:
Her mysteries are read without Faith's eye-sight:
She speaketh in our flesh; and from our Senses
Delivers downe her wisdomes to our Reason.

If any man would breake her lawes to kill,
Nature doth, for defence, allow offences.
She neither taught the Father to destroy;
Nor promis'd any man, by dying, joy.

Mustapha, 1633

12

Chorus Sacerdotum

OH wearisome Condition of Humanity!
Borne under one Law, to another bound:
Vainely begot, and yet forbidden vanity;
Created sicke, commanded to be sound:
What meaneth Nature by these diverse Lawes?
Passion and Reason, selfe-division cause:
Is it the marke or Majesty of Power
To make offences that it may forgive?
Nature herselfe doth her owne selfe defloure,
To hate those errours she her selfe doth give.
For how should man thinke that, he may not doe
If Nature did not faile, and punish too?
Tyrant to others, to her selfe unjust,
Onely commands things difficult and hard;
Forbids us all things which it knowes is lust,
Makes easie paines, unpossible reward.
If Nature did not take delight in blood,
She would have made more easie wayes to good.
We that are bound by vowes, and by Promotion,
With pompe of holy Sacrifice and rites,
To teach beliefe in good and still devotion,
To preach of Heaven's wonders, and delights:
Yet when each of us in his own heart lookes,
He findes the God there, farre unlike his Bookes.

Mustapha, 1633

GEORGE CHAPMAN

1559–1634

13 From 'Homer's Iliads' (1611)

(i)

Poetry and Learning

A PRINCES statue, or in Marble carv'd,
Or steele, or gold, and shrin'd (to be preserv'd)
Aloft on Pillars, or Pyramides,
Time into lowest ruines may depresse:
But, drawne with all his vertues in learn'd verse,
Fame shall resound them on Oblivions hearse,
Till graves gaspe with her blasts, and dead men rise.
No gold can follow, where true Poesie flies.

Then let not this Divinitie in earth
(Deare Prince) be slighted, as she were the birth
Of idle Fancie, since she workes so hie:
Nor let her poore disposer (Learning) lie
Still bed-rid. Both which, being in men defac't,
In men (with them) is Gods bright image rac't.
For, as the Sunne, and Moone, are figures given
Of his refulgent Deitie in Heaven:
So, Learning, and her Lightner, Poesie,
In earth present his fierie Majestie.
Nor are Kings like him, since their Diademes
Thunder, and lighten, and project brave beames;
But since they his cleare vertues emulate,
In Truth and Justice imaging his State,
In Bountie, and Humanitie since they shine;
Than which, is nothing (like him) more divine:

rac't: ras'd, eras'd.

Not Fire, not Light; the Sunnes admired course;
The Rise, nor Set of Starres; nor all their force
In us, and all this Cope beneath the Skie;
Nor great *Existence*, term'd his Treasurie.
Since not, for being greatest, he is blest;
But being Just, and in all vertues best.
  What sets his Justice, and his Truth, best forth,
(Best Prince) then use best; which is Poesies worth.

The Epistle Dedicatory, lines 62–93

(*ii*)

The Trojans outside the Walls

THIS speech all Trojans did applaud; who from their traces loos'd
Their sweating horse; which severally with headstalls they repos'd,
And fastned by their chariots; when others brought from towne,
Fat sheepe and oxen, instantly; bread, wine; and hewed downe
Huge store of wood: the winds transfer'd, into the friendly skie,
Their suppers savour; to the which, they sate delightfully,
And spent all night in open field; fires round about them shin'd;
As when about the silver Moone, when aire is free from wind,
And stars shine cleare; to whose sweete beames, high prospects, and the brows
Of all steepe hills and pinnacles, thrust up themselves for showes;

Ignes Troianorum astris similes.

And even the lowly vallies joy, to glitter in their sight,
When the unmeasur'd firmament, bursts to disclose her light,
And all the signes in heaven are seene, that glad the shepheards heart;
So many fires disclos'd their beames, made by the Trojan part,
Before the face of *Ilion*; and her bright turrets show'd.
A thousand courts of guard kept fires: and every guard allow'd
Fiftie stout men, by whom their horse, eate oates and hard white corne,
And all did wilfully expect, the silver-throned morne.

Book 8, lines 480–97

(iii)

Sarpedon's Speech

AS ye see, a mountaine Lion fare;
Long kept from prey: in forcing which, his high mind makes him dare,
Assault upon the whole full fold: though guarded never so
With well-arm'd men, and eager dogs; away he will not go,
But venture on, and either snatch, a prey, or be a prey:
So far'd divine *Sarpedons* mind, resolv'd to force his way
Through all the fore-fights, and the wall: yet since he did not see
Others as great as he, in name, as great in mind as he:
He spake to *Glaucus*: *Glaucus*, say, why are we honor'd more
Than other men of *Lycia*, in place? with greater store
Of meates and cups? with goodlier roofes? delightsome gardens? walks?
More lands, and better? so much wealth, that Court and countrie talks

Sarpedons speech to Glaucus, never equalled by any (in this kind) of all that have written.

Of us, and our possessions; and every way we go,
Gaze on us as we were their Gods? this where we dwell, is so:
The shores of *Xanthus* ring of this; and shall not we exceed,
As much in merit, as in noise? Come, be we great in deed
As well as looke; shine not in gold, but in the flames of fight;
That so our neat-arm'd-*Lycians*, may say; See, these are right
Our kings, our Rulers; these deserve, to eate, and drinke the
best;
These governe not ingloriously: these, thus exceed the rest,
Do more than they command to do. O friend, if keeping backe
Would keepe backe age from us, and death; and that we
might not wracke
In this lifes humane sea at all: but that deferring now
We shun'd death ever; nor would I, halfe this vaine valour
show,
Nor glorifie a folly so, to wish thee to advance:
But since we must go, though not here; and that, besides the
chance
Propos'd now, there are infinite fates, of other sort in death,
Which (neither to be fled nor scap't) a man must sinke
beneath:
Come, trie we, if this sort be ours: and either render thus,
Glorie to others, or make them, resigne the like to us.

Book 12, lines 303–32

(*iv*)

Achilles shows himself in the Battle by the Ships

ALL this (said she) we know,
And wish, thou onely wouldst but show, thy person to
the eyes
Of these hot *Ilians*, that (afraid, of further enterprise)

The *Greeks* may gaine some litle breath. She woo'd, and he was won,
And straite *Minerva* honor'd him; who *Joves* shield clapt upon
His mightie shoulders; and his head, girt with a cloud of gold,
That cast beames round about his browes. And as when armes enfold
Simile. A citie in an Isle; from thence, a fume at first appeares,
(Being in the day) but when the Even, her cloudie forehead reares,
Thicke show the fires, and up they cast, their splendor, that men nigh
Seeing their distresse, perhaps may set, ships out to their supply:
So (to shew such aid) from his head, a light rose, scaling heaven.
And forth the wall he stept and stood; nor brake the precept given
By his great mother (mixt in fight,) but sent abroad his voice,
Which *Pallas* farre off echoed; who did betwixt them hoise
Simile. Shrill Tumult to a toplesse height. And as a voice is heard
With emulous affection, when any towne is spher'd
With siege of such a foe, as kills, mens minds; and for the towne
Makes sound his trumpet: so the voice, from *Thetis* issue throwne,
Won emulously th'eares of all. His brazen voice once heard,
The minds of all were startl'd so, they yeelded; and so fear'd
The faire-man'd horses, that they flew, backe, and their chariots turn'd,
Presaging in their augurous hearts, the labours that they mourn'd

A litle after; and their guides, a repercussive dread
Tooke from the horrid radiance, of his refulgent head;
Which *Pallas* set on fire with grace. Thrice great *Achilles* spake;
And thrice (in heate of all the charge) the *Trojans* started backe.
Twelve men, of greatest strength in *Troy*, left with their lives exhal'd,
Their chariots and their darts, to death, with his three summons call'd.
And then the *Grecians* spritefully, drew from the darts the corse,
And hears'd it, bearing it to fleete. His friends, with all remorse
Marching about it. His great friend, dissolving then in teares,
To see his truly-lov'd return'd, so hors'd upon an hearse,
Whom with such horse and chariot, he set out safe and whole;
Now wounded with unpittying steele, now sent without a soule,
Never againe to be restor'd, never receiv'd but so;
He follow'd mourning bitterly. The Sunne (yet farre to go)
Juno commanded to go downe; who in his powres despight,
Sunke to the Ocean; over earth, dispersing sodaine Night.
And then the *Greeks*, and *Trojans* both, gave up their horse and darts.

Juno commands the Sunne to go downe before his time.

Book 18, lines 169–207

(*v*)

The Death of Hector

THUS deaths hand clos'd his eyes;
His soule flying his faire limbs, to hell; mourning his destinies,
To part so with his youth and strength. Thus dead; thus *Thetis* sonne,

His prophecie answer'd: Die thou now; when my short thred is spunne,
I'll beare it as the will of *Jove*. This said, his brazen speare,
He drew, and stucke by: then his armes (that all embrewed were)
The Greeks admiration of Hectors person being slaine.
He spoil'd his shoulders off. Then all, the *Greeks* ran in to him,
To see his person; and admir'd, his terror-stirring limb:
Yet none stood by, that gave no wound, to his so goodly forme;
When each to other said: O *Jove*, he is not in the storme,
He came to fleete in, with his fire; he handles now more soft.
O friends, (said sterne *Æacides*) now that the gods have brought
Achilles to the Grecians.
This man thus downe; I'll freely say, he brought more bane to *Greece*,
Than all his aiders. Trie we then, (thus arm'd at every peece,
And girding all *Troy* with our host) if now their hearts will leave
Their citie cleare; her cleare stay slaine; and all their lives receave;
Or hold yet, *Hector* being no more. But why use I a word
Of any act, but what concernes, my friend? dead, undeplor'd,
Unsepulcher'd; he lies at fleete, unthought on; never houre
Shall make his dead state, while the quicke, enjoyes me; and this powre,
To move these movers. Though in hell, men say, that such as die,
Oblivion seiseth; yet in hell, in me shall *Memorie*
Hold all her formes still, of my friend. Now, (youths of *Greece*) to fleete
Beare we this body; *Pæans* sing; and all our navie greete

my friend] Patroclus.

With endlesse honor; we have slaine, *Hector*, the period
Of all *Troys* glorie; to whose worth, all vow'd, as to a god.
  This said; a worke, not worthy him, he set to: of both feete,
He bor'd the nerves through, from the heele, to th'ankle; and
    then knit
Both to his chariot, with a thong, of whitleather; his head
Trailing the center. Up he got, to chariot; where he laid
The armes repurchac't; and scourg'd on, his horse, that freely
    flew.
A whirlewind made of startl'd dust, drave with them, as they
    drew;
With which were all his black-browne curls, knotted in
    heapes, and fil'd.
And there lay *Troys* late Gracious; by *Jupiter* exil'd
To all disgrace, in his owne land, and by his parents seene.
  When (like her sonnes head) all with dust, *Troys* miserable
    Queene,
Distain'd her temples; plucking off, her honor'd haire; and
    tore
Her royall garments, shrieking out. In like kind, *Priam* bore
His sacred person; like a wretch, that never saw good day,
Broken, with outcries. About both, the people prostrate lay;
Held downe with *Clamor*; all the towne, vail'd with a cloud
    of teares.
Ilion, with all his tops on fire, and all the massacres,
Left for the *Greeks*, could put on lookes, of no more overthrow
Than now fraid life.

Achilles tyranny to Hector's person, which we lay on his fury, and love to his slaine friend, for whom himselfe living, sufferd so much.

Priam and Hecubas miserable plight for Hector.

Book 22, lines 313–56

(*vi*)

Priam and Achilles

Priam enters Achilles tent.

THIS said; he high *Olympus* reacht, the king then left his coach
To grave *Idæus*, and went on; made his resolv'd approach:
And enter'd in a goodly roome; where, with his Princes sate
Jove-lov'd *Achilles*, at their feast; two onely kept the state
Of his attendance, *Alcymus*, and Lord *Automedon*.
At *Priams* entrie; a great time, *Achilles* gaz'd upon
His wonder'd-at approch; nor eate: the rest did nothing see,
While close he came up; with his hands, fast holding the bent knee
Of *Hectors* conqueror; and kist, that large man-slaughtring hand,
Simile. That much blood from his sonnes had drawne; And as in some strange land,
And great mans house; a man is driven, (with that abhorr'd dismay,
That followes wilfull bloodshed still; his fortune being to slay
One, whose blood cries alowde for his) to pleade protection
In such a miserable plight, as frights the lookers on:
In such a stupefied estate, *Achilles* sate to see,
So unexpected, so in night, and so incrediblie,
Old *Priams* entrie; all his friends, one on another star'd,
To see his strange lookes, seeing no cause. Thus *Priam* then prepar'd
Priam to Achilles. His sonnes redemption: See in me, O godlike *Thetis* sonne,
Thy aged father; and perhaps, even now being outrunne
With some of my woes; neighbour foes, (thou absent) taking time
To do him mischiefe; no meane left, to terrifie the crime

Of his oppression; yet he heares, thy graces still survive,
And joyes to heare it; hoping still, to see thee safe arrive,
From ruin'd *Troy*: but I (curst man) of all my race, shall live
To see none living. Fiftie sonnes, the Deities did give,
My hopes to live in; all alive, when neare our trembling shore
The *Greeke* ships harbor'd; and one wombe, nineteene of those sons bore.
Now *Mars*, a number of their knees, hath strengthlesse left; and he
That was (of all) my onely joy, and *Troyes* sole guard; by thee
(Late fighting for his country) slaine; whose tender'd person, now
I come to ransome. Infinite, is that I offer you,
My selfe conferring it; expos'd, alone to all your oddes:
Onely imploring right of armes. *Achilles*, feare the gods,
Pitie an old man, like thy sire; different in onely this,
That I am wretcheder; and beare, that weight of miseries
That never man did: my curst lips, enforc't to kisse that hand
That slew my children. This mov'd teares; his fathers name did stand
(Mention'd by *Priam*) in much helpe, to his compassion;
And mov'd *Æacides* so much, he could not looke upon
The weeping father. With his hand, he gently put away
His grave face; calme remission now, did mutually display
Her powre in eithers heavinesse; old *Priam*, to record
His sonnes death; and his deaths man see, his teares, and bosome pour'd
Before *Achilles*. At his feete, he laid his reverend head.
Achilles thoughts, now with his sire, now with his friend, were fed.
Betwixt both, *Sorrow* fill'd the tent. But now *Æacides*,
(Satiate at all parts, with the ruth, of their calamities)

Start up, and up he rais'd the king. His milke-white head and
beard,
Achilles remorse of Priam.
With pittie he beheld, and said; Poore man, thy mind is scar'd,
With much affliction; how durst, thy person thus alone,
Venture on his sight, that hath slaine, so many a worthy sonne,
And so deare to thee? thy old heart, is made of iron; sit
And settle we our woes, though huge; for nothing profits it.
Cold mourning wastes but our lives heates. The gods have
destinate,
That wretched mortals must live sad. Tis the immortall state
Of Deitie, that lives secure. Two Tunnes of gifts there lie
In *Joves* gate; one of good, one ill, that our mortalitie,
Maintaine, spoile, order: which when *Jove*, doth mixe to any
man;
One while he frolicks, one while mourns. If of his mournfull
Can
A man drinks onely; onely wrongs, he doth expose him to.
Sad hunger, in th'abundant earth, doth tosse him to and fro,
Respected, nor of gods, nor men. The mixt cup *Peleus*
dranke,
Even from his birth, heaven blest his life; he liv'd not that
could thanke
The gods for such rare benefits, as set forth his estate.
He reign'd among his *Myrmidons*, most rich, most fortunate.
And (though a mortall) had his bed, deckt with a deathlesse
Dame.
And yet with all this good, one ill, god mixt, that takes all
name
From all that goodnesse; his Name now, (whose preservation
here,
Men count the crowne of their most good) not blest with
powre to beare

One blossome, but my selfe: and I, shaken as soone as blowne.
Nor shall I live to cheare his age, and give nutrition
To him that nourisht me. Farre off, my rest is set in *Troy*,
To leave thee restlesse, and thy seed. Thy selfe, that did enjoy,
(As we have heard) a happie life: what *Lesbos* doth containe,
(In times past being a blest mans seate:) what the unmeasur'd
    maine
Of *Hellespontus*, *Phrygia* holds; are all said to adorne
Thy Empire; wealth, and sonnes enow: but when the gods
    did turne
Thy blest state to partake with bane; warre, and the bloods
    of men,
Circl'd thy citie, never cleare. Sit downe and suffer then;
Mourne not inevitable things; thy teares can spring no deeds
To helpe thee, nor recall thy sonne: impatience ever breeds
Ill upon ill; makes worst things worse; and therefore sit.

Book 24, lines 414–96

14 *From 'Homer's Odyssey' (1614)*

(*i*)

Praise of Homer

GEO. CHAPMAN *Humbly celebrates this New-Yeares sight with discoverie of that long hidden Relict, for whose presentment Macedon would have given a kingdom; Homer revived:*

THAT he to his unmeasur'd mightie Acts,
Might adde a Fame as vast; and their extracts,
In fires as bright, and endlesse as the starres,
His brest might breathe; and thunder out his wars.
But that great Monarks love of fame and praise,
Receives an envious Cloud in our foule daies:

For since our Great ones, cease themselves to do
Deeds worth their praise; they hold it folly too
To feed their praise in others. But what can
(Of all the gifts that are) be given to man,
More precious than *Eternitie* and *Glorie*,
Singing their praises, in unsilenc't storie?
Which No blacke Day, No Nation, nor no Age;
No change of Time or Fortune, Force, nor Rage,
Shall ever rase? All which, the Monarch knew,
Where *Homer* liv'd entitl'd, would ensew:
——*Cuius de gurgite vivo*
Ex Angeli Politiani Ambra. *Combibit arcanos vatum omnis turba furores &c.*
From whose deepe Fount of life, the thirstie rout
Of Thespian Prophets, have lien sucking out
Their sacred rages. And as th' influent stone
Of Father *Joves* great and laborious Sonne,
Lifts high the heavie Iron; and farre implies
The wide Orbs; that the Needle rectifies,
In vertuous guide of every sea-driven course,
To all aspiring, his one boundlesse force:
So from one *Homer*, all the holy fire,
That ever did the hidden heate inspire
In each true Muse, came cleerly sparkling downe,
And must for him, compose one flaming Crowne.
He, at *Joves* Table set, fills out to us,
Cups that repaire Age, sad and ruinous;
And gives it Built, of an eternall stand,
With his all-sinewie Odyssæan hand.
Shifts Time, and Fate; puts Death in Lifes free state;
And Life doth into Ages propagate.
He doth in Men, the Gods affects inflame;
His fuell Vertue, blowne by *Praise* and *Fame*:

And with the high soules, first impulsions driven,
Breakes through rude Chaos, Earth, the Seas, and Heaven.
The Nerves of all things hid in Nature, lie
Naked before him; all their Harmonie
Tun'd to his Accents; that in Beasts breathe Minds.
What Fowles, what Floods, what Earth, what Aire, what
    Winds,
What fires Æthereall; what the Gods conclude
In all their Counsels, his Muse makes indued
With varied voices, that even rockes have mov'd.
And yet for all this, (naked Vertue lov'd)
Honors without her, he, as abject, prises;
And foolish Fame, deriv'd from thence, despises.

From the Dedication

(*ii*)

The Sacrifice

THE rosie-fingerd morne, no sooner shone,
But up he rose, tooke aire, and sat upon
A seate of white, and goodly polisht stone,
That such a glosse as richest ointments wore
Before his high gates; where the Counsellor
That matcht the Gods (his Father) us'd to sit:
Who now (by Fate forc't) stoopt as low as it.
And here sate *Nestor*, holding in his hand
A Scepter; and about him round did stand
(As early up) his sonnes troope; *Perseus*,
The God-like *Thrasimed*, and *Aretus*,
Echephron, *Stratius*; the sixt and last
Pisistratus; and by him (halfe embrac't

Still as they came) divine *Telemachus*;
To these spake *Nestor*, old *Gerenius*:

. . . . .

The forme of the Sacrifice. This said; not one, but in the service held
Officious hand. The Oxe came led from field;
The Souldiers troopt from ship; the Smith he came,
And those tooles brought, that serv'd the actuall frame,
His Art conceiv'd; brought Anvile, hammers brought,
Faire tongs, and all, with which the gold was wrought.
Minerva likewise came, to set the Crowne
On that kind sacrifice, and mak't her owne.
Then th'old Knight *Nestor* gave the Smith the gold,
With which he strait did both the hornes infold;
And trimm'd the Offering so, the Goddesse joy'd.
About which, thus were *Nestors* sonnes employ'd:
Divine *Echephron*, and faire *Stratius*,
Held both the hornes: the water odorous,
In which they washt, what to the rites was vow'd,
Aretus (in a caldron, all bestrow'd
With herbes and flowres) serv'd in from th'holy roome
Where all were drest; and whence the rites must come.
And after him, a hallow'd virgin came,
That brought the barley cake, and blew the flame.
The axe, with which the Oxe should both be fel'd
And cut forth, *Thrasimed* stood by, and held.
Perseus the vessell held, that should retaine
The purple licour of the offering slaine.
Then washt, the pious Father: then the Cake
(Of barley, salt, and oile made) tooke, and brake.
Askt many a boone of *Pallas*; and the state
Of all the offering, did initiate.

In three parts cutting off the haire, and cast
Amidst the flame. All th'invocation past,
And all the Cake broke; manly *Thrasimed*
Stood neare, and sure; and such a blow he laid
Aloft the offring; that to earth he sunke,
His neck-nerves sunder'd, and his spirits shrunke.

Book 3, lines 547–61, 577–610

(*iii*)

Ulysses in the Waves

THIS said; he (begging) gather'd clouds from land;
Frighted the seas up; snatcht into his hand,
His horrid Trident; and aloft did tosse
(Of all the winds) all stormes he could engrosse.
All earth tooke into sea with clouds; grim *Night*
Fell tumbling headlong from the cope of Light.
The East and Southwinds justl'd in the aire;
The violent *Zephire*, and *North*-making faire,
Roll'd up the waves before them: and then, bent
Ulysses knees; then all his spirit was spent.
In which despaire, he thus spake: Woe is me!
What was I borne to? man of miserie?
Feare tells me now, that all the Goddesse said,
Truths selfe will author; that *Fate* would be paid
Griefes whole summe due from me, at sea, before
I reacht the deare touch of my countries shore.
With what clouds *Jove*, heavens heightned forehead binds?
How tyrannize the wraths of all the winds?
How all the tops, he bottomes with the deepes?
And in the bottomes, all the tops he steepes?
Thus dreadfull is the presence of our death.

Thrice foure times blest were they that sunke beneath
Their Fates at *Troy*; and did to nought contend,
But to renowme *Atrides* with their end?
I would to God, my houre of death, and Fate,
That day had held the power to terminate;
When showres of darts, my life bore undeprest,
About divine *Æacides* deceast.
Then had I been allotted to have died,
By all the Greeks, with funerals glorified;
(Whence *Death*, encouraging good life, had growne)
Where now I die, by no man mourn'd, nor knowne.
  This spoke; a huge wave tooke him by the head,
And hurl'd him o'er-boord: ship and all it laid
Inverted quite amidst the waves; but he
Farre off from her sprawl'd, strow'd about the sea:
His Sterne still holding, broken off; his Mast
Burst in the midst: so horrible a blast
Of mixt winds strooke it. Sailes and saile-yards fell
Amongst the billowes; and himselfe did dwell
A long time under water: nor could get
In haste his head out: wave with wave so met
In his depression; and his garments too,
(Given by *Calypso*) gave him much to do,
Hindring his swimming; yet he left not so
His drenched vessell, for the overthrow
Of her nor him; but gat at length againe
(Wrestling with *Neptune*) hold of her; and then
Sate in her Bulke, insulting over Death;
Which (with the salt streame, prest to stop his breath)
He scap't, and gave the sea againe; to give
To other men.

. . . . . .

While this discourse he held;
A curst Surge, gainst a cutting rocke impel'd
His naked bodie, which it gasht and tore;
And had his bones broke, if but one sea more
Had cast him on it. But she prompted him, *Pallas.*
That never fail'd; and bad him no more swim
Still off and on; but boldly force the shore,
And hug the rocke, that him so rudely tore.
Which he, with both hands, sigh'd and claspt; till past
The billowes rage was; which scap't; backe, so fast
The rocke repulst it, that it reft his hold,
Sucking him from it, and farre backe he roll'd.
And as the *Polypus*, that (forc't from home
Amidst the soft sea; and neare rough land come
For shelter gainst the stormes that beate on her
At open sea, as she abroad doth erre)
A deale of gravill, and sharpe little stones,
Needfully gathers in her hollow bones:
So he forc't hither, (by the sharper ill, *Per asperiora vitare lævia.*
Shunning the smoother) where he best hop't, still
The worst succeeded: for the cruell friend,
To which he cling'd for succour, off did rend
From his broad hands, the soaken flesh so sore,
That off he fell, and could sustaine no more.
Quite under water fell he; and, past Fate,
Haplesse *Ulysses*, there had lost the state
He held in life; if (still the grey-ey'd Maid,
His wisedome prompting) he had not assaid
Another course; and ceast t'attempt that shore;
Swimming, and casting round his eye, t'explore
Some other shelter. Then, the mouth he found
Of faire *Callicoes* flood; whose shores were crown'd

With most apt succors: Rocks so smooth, they seem'd
Polisht of purpose: land that quite redeem'd
With breathlesse covers, th' others blasted shores.
The flood he knew; and thus in heart implores:
King of this River! heare; what ever name
Makes thee invokt: to thee I humbly frame
My flight from *Neptunes* furies; Reverend is
To all the ever-living Deities,
What erring man soever seekes their aid.
To thy both flood and knees, a man dismaid
With varied sufferance sues. Yeeld then some rest
To him that is thy suppliant profest.
  This (though but spoke in thought) the Godhead heard;
Her Current strait staid; and her thicke waves clear'd
Before him, smooth'd her waters; and just where
He praid, halfe drown'd; entirely sav'd him there.
  Then forth he came, his both knees faltring; both
His strong hands hanging downe; and all with froth
His cheeks and nosthrils flowing. Voice and breath
Spent to all use; and downe he sunke to Death.
The sea had soakt his heart through: all his vaines,
His toiles had rackt, t'a labouring womans paines.

Ω'δεε of ὀδυνω *á partu doleo.*

Book 5, lines 370–420, 560–613

(*iv*)

Nausicaa

THE servants then (commanded) soone obaid
Fetcht Coach, and Mules joyn'd in it. Then the Maid
Brought from the chamber her rich weeds, and laid
All up in Coach: in which, her mother plac't
A maund of victles, varied well in taste,
And other junkets. Wine she likewise fill'd

Within a goat-skin bottle, and distill'd
Sweete and moist oile into a golden Cruse,
Both for her daughters, and her handmaids use;
To soften their bright bodies, when they rose
Clens'd from their cold baths. Up to Coach then goes
Th'observed Maid: takes both the scourge and raines;
And to her side, her handmaid strait attaines.
Nor these alone, but other virgins grac't
The Nuptiall Chariot. The whole Bevie plac't;
Nausicaa scourg'd to make the Coach Mules runne;
That neigh'd, and pac'd their usuall speed; and soone,
Both maids and weeds, brought to the river side;
Where Baths for all the yeare, their use supplied.
Whose waters were so pure, they would not staine;
But still ran faire forth; and did more remaine
Apt to purge staines; for that purg'd staine within,
Which, by the waters pure store, was not seen.
These (here arriv'd,) the Mules uncoacht, and drave
Up to the gulphie rivers shore, that gave
Sweet grasse to them. The maids from Coach then tooke
Their cloaths, and steept them in the sable brooke.
Then put them into springs, and trod them cleane,
With cleanly feet; adventring wagers then,
Who should have soonest, and most cleanly done.
When having throughly cleans'd, they spred them on
The floods shore, all in order. And then, where
The waves the pibbles washt, and ground was cleare,
They bath'd themselves; and all with glittring oile,
Smooth'd their white skins: refreshing then their toile
With pleasant dinner, by the rivers side.
Yet still watcht when the Sunne, their cloaths had dried.
Till which time (having din'd) *Nausicae*

With other virgins, did at stool-ball play;
Their shoulder-reaching head-tires laying by.
Nausicae (with the wrists of Ivory)
The liking stroke strooke; singing first a song;
(As custome orderd) and amidst the throng,
Made such a shew; and so past all was seene;
Simile. As when the Chast-borne, Arrow-loving Queene,
Along the mountaines gliding; either over
Spartan Taygetus, whose tops farre discover;
Or *Eurymanthus*; in the wilde Bores chace;
Or swift-hov'd Hart; and with her, *Joves* faire race
(The field Nymphs) sporting. Amongst whom, to see
How farre *Diana* had prioritie
(Though all were faire) for fairnesse; yet of all,
(As both by head and forehead being more tall)
Latona triumpht; since the dullest sight,
Might easly judge, whom her paines brought to light;
Nausicaa so (whom never husband tam'd)
Above them all, in all the beauties flam'd.
But when they now made homewards, and array'd;
Ordring their weeds, disorder'd as they plaid;
Mules and Coach ready; then *Minerva* thought,
What meanes to wake *Ulysses*, might be wrought,
That he might see this lovely sighted maid,
Whom she intended, should become his aid:
Bring him to Towne; and his returne advance.
Her meane was this, (though thought a stool-ball chance)
The Queene now (for the upstroke) strooke the ball
Quite wide off th'other maids; and made it fall
Amidst the whirlpooles. At which, out shriekt all;
And with the shrieke, did wise *Ulysses* wake.

Book 6, lines 101–69

GEORGE CHAPMAN

(*v*)

Scylla and Charybdis

OF these two spitefull Rocks, the one doth shove
Against the height, of heaven her pointed brow.
A blacke cloud binds it round, and never show
Lends to the sharp point: not the cleare blew skie
Lets ever view it. Not the *Sommers* eye;
Not fervent *Autumnes*. None, that Death could end
Could ever scale it; or if up, descend;
Though twenty hands and feete he had for hold:
A polisht ice-like glibnesse doth enfold
The rocke so round, whose midst, a gloomie cell
Shrowds, so farre Westward, that it sees to hell.
From this, keepe you as farre, as from his bow
An able yong man can his shaft bestow.
For here, the whuling *Scylla*, shrowds her face:
That breathes a voice, at all parts, no more base
Than are a newly-kitn'd kitlings cries;
Her selfe a monster yet, of boundlesse size;
Whose sight would nothing please a mortals eyes;
No nor the eyes of any God, if he
(Whom nought should fright) fell foule on her; and she
Her full shape shew'd. Twelve foule feete beare about
Her ugly bulke. Sixe huge long necks lookt out
Of her ranke shoulders: every necke, doth let
A ghastly head out: every head; three set
Thicke thrust together, of abhorred teeth;
And every tooth stucke with a sable death.
She lurkes in midst of all her denne; and streakes
From out a ghastly whirle-poole, all her necks;
Where, (gloating round her rocke) to fish she falles;

And up rush Dolphins, Dogfish; somewhiles, Whales,
If got within her, when her rapine feeds;
For ever-groning *Amphitrite* breeds
About her whirlepoole, an unmeasur'd store;
No Sea-man ever boasted touch of shore
That there toucht with his ship; but still she fed
Of him, and his. A man for every head
Spoiling his ship of. You shall then descrie
The other humbler Rocke, that moves so nie,
Your dart may mete the distance. It receaves
A huge wilde Fig-tree, curl'd with ample leaves;
Beneath whose shades, divine *Charybdis* sits
Supping the blacke deepes. Thrice a day her pits
She drinking all dry; and thrice a day againe,
All, up she belches; banefull to sustaine.
When she is drinking, dare not neare her draught,
For not the force of *Neptune*, (if once caught)
Can force your freedome. Therefore in your strife
To scape *Charybdis*, labour all, for life
To row neare *Scylla*; for she will but have
For her sixe heads, sixe men; and better save
The rest, than all make offerings to the wave.

Book 12, lines 122–72

(*vi*)

The End of the Suitors

AND now, man-slaughtering *Pallas* tooke in hand
Her Snake-fring'd shield, and on that beam took stand
In her true forme, where Swallow-like she sat.
And then, in this way of the house and that:
The wooers (wounded at the heart with feare)

Fled the encounter: As in Pastures, where
Fat Herds of Oxen feede, about the field
(As if wilde madnesse their instincts impell'd)
The high-fed Bullockes flye: whom in the Spring
(When dayes are long) Gadbees, or Breezes sting.
  Ulysses and his sonne, the Flyers chas'd;
As when with crooked Beakes and Seres, a cast
Of hill-bred Eagles, cast off at some game,
That yet their strengths keepe; But (put up) in flame
The Eagles stoopes; From which, along the field
The poore Fowles make wing: this and that way yield
Their hard-flowne Pinions: Then, the clouds assay
For scape or shelter; their forlorne dismay
All spirit exhaling, all wings strength to carry
Their bodies forth; and (truss'd up) to the Quarry
Their Faulconers ride in, and rejoyce to see
Their Hawkes performe a flight so fervently;
So (in their flight) *Ulysses* with his Heire,
Did stoope and cuffe the wooers, that the aire
Broke in vaste sighes: whose heads, they shot and cleft;
The Pavement boyling with the soules they reft.

Book 22, lines 379-404

JOSHUA SYLVESTER

1563-1618

15 *Autumnus*

WHEN the Leaves in Autumn wither,
  With a tawny tanned Face,
Warpt and wrinkled-up together,
Th' Years late Beauty to disgrace:

There thy Life's Glass maist thou finde thee,
Green now, gray now, gone anon;
Leaving (Worldling) of thine Own,
Neither Fruit, nor Leaf behind thee.

Spectacles (*Works*, 1621)

16 *Omnia Somnia*

GO, silly Worm, drudge, trudge, and travell,
Despising Pain;
So Thou maist gain
Some Honour, or some Golden Gravell:
But Death the while (to fill his number)
With sudden Call
Takes thee from All,
To prove thy Daies but Dream and Slumber.

Mottoes (*Works*, 1621)

17 *Sonnet*

THEY say that shadowes of deceased ghosts
Doe haunt the houses and the graves about,
Of such whose lives-lamp went untimely out,
Delighting still in their forsaken hostes:
So, in the place where cruell love doth shoote
The fatall shaft that slew my loves delight,
I stalke and walke and wander day and night,
Even like a ghost with unperceived foote.
But those light ghosts are happier far than I,
For, at their pleasure, they can come and goe
Unto the place that hides their treasure, so,
And see the same with their fantastick eye.
Where I (alas) dare not approach the cruell
Proud Monument, that doth inclose my Jewell.

Posthumi (Sonnet 16) (*Works*, 1641)

ANONYMOUS

18 (*Beware fair Maide*)

BEWARE fair Mayde of muskie courtiers oathes,
Take heed what gifts and favours you receive,
Let not the fading glosse of silken clothes
Dazell your vertue, or your fame bereave.
For loose but once the hold you have of grace,
Who'll e'er respect your fortune or your face.

Each greedy hand will strive to catch the flowre
When none regards the stalke it growes upon,
Each creature seekes the fruite still to devoure
But leave the tree to fall or stand alone.
Yet this advise, faire creature, take of me,
Let none take fruit, unlesse he take the tree.

Beleeve no oathes, nor much protesting men,
Credit no vowes, nor no bewayling songs,
Let Courtiers sweare, forsweare, and sweare againe;
Their hearts do live ten Regions from their tongues.
For when with oathes they make thy heart to tremble
Believe them least, for then they most dissemble.

Beware lest Caesar do corrupt thy minde
Or fond Ambition sell thy modesty.
Say though a king thou ever courteous finde
He cannot garden thy virginitie.
Begin with king, to subject you will fall,
From Lord to Lackey, and at last to all.

Brit. Mus. MS. 10309 and 25707. *Ascribed to Joshua Sylvester*

19

LOVERS conceits are like a flattring glasse,
That makes the lookers fairer than they are,
Who pleas'd in their conceits contented passe;
Such one was mine, who thought there was none faire,
None witty, modest, vertuous but she,
But now I finde the glasse abused me.

Brit. Mus. MS. 10309 f. 143

20 *Greatness*

THOU wouldst be greate and to such height wouldst rise
That all might know thee: thou all despise.
Alas! thou knowst not, what full blessings flow
To those that strive to keepe themselves below.
We fooles that gaze on great ones and admire
Their outward light, feele not their inwarde fire.
Our eyes behold them followed and attired
Like Gods on earth: but were our mindes inspired
To see them when these clouds are overblowne,
They are but wretches when they are alone.
Try such a one if he dare blesse his sight
With beames of peace, and contemplations hight.
Clean thoughts, selfe-knowledge, and retirednesse
Means sent from heaven, to make our sufferings lesse
While in this life we turne our painful wheeles,
Become his heavie torments: then he feeles
His greefes, his feares, his errors, his unrest
Attending on him; and his owne rackt breast
Sitting as Judge is forced to declare
Those happie who most far from greatness are.

These things like spirits haunt, and curse his wayes,
Though armd with circling pompe, and spells of prayse.
They check his pride, they interrupt delight,
They give him restless dayes, and sleeplesse nights;
They breed such paines as damned soules endure.
Who neither can nor will release procure,
Who sees his steps with snares compassd round
All paths uncertaine, and no passage found,
His journey forwards daunger, his returne
Disgrace, and daunger, vaine it is to mourne
His lucklesse entrance to the fatall plaine,
For should some messenger of heavenly grace
Instruct, and guide him in this doubtful waye
He in the pride and pleasure still would staye,
And in his glorious aping takes content,
Though he abhor th' ensuinge punishment.
O blinded men who borne to endlesse paine
Find ev'ry hour just reason to complaine
Of this corrupted house wherein you dwell,
What strange enchaunter, armd straight from hell
Hath thus bewitcht you with distracting charmes
To seeke new arts to increase your native harmes?
Is't not enough that inward fell debate
Disturb you in your most retyred state?
That you like banisht wretches in a land
Dry, and unfruitful as the parching sand,
Where reason gainst as manie monsters fights
As you have senses, passions, appetites,
But you must boldly raise yourselves on high
To be the marke of every envious eye,
To climbe to cares by smooth and brittle staires
Where he is happie that at first despaires.

ANONYMOUS

When you look upwards; then you see no bounds,
A dreadful depth when you behold the grounds.
To gaine the bitter and tormented hate
Of those that liv'd in equall hope and state,
To whose vext mindes all your commodities
Seem losses, all your honours injuries;
To live base slaves to your unconstant friends,
Drawne by their own (and those, insatiate) ends;
Whose faults are made your Crimes, while they remaine
Free from your woes though partners of your gaine:
To please your selves as if you could be blest
By joyes depending on anothers breast,
Who in a moment can your glories drowne
And make you wretches by one cloudie frowne.
The man that rashly plants his comforts here
Let him not death, nor strife, nor torments feare.
His state is proofe against the dreadful curse
Of blastinge tongues; no mischiefe can be worse.
Infernal feendes, whom from your hideous den
God lets you loose to punish sinfull men,
Choose for your weapons neither swords nor fires,
Nor hot infections; but extreme desires
Of Courtly greatness, and t'augment their paine
Teach the fit wayes their fruitlesse scope t' obtaine.

Brit. Mus. MS. 25707

MICHAEL DRAYTON

1563–1631

21 *To Himselfe and The Harpe*

AND why not I, as hee
That 's greatest, if as free?
(In sundry strains that strive,
Since there so many be)
Th' old *Lyrick* kind revive?

I will, yea, and I may;
Who shall oppose my way?
For what is he alone,
That of himselfe can say,
Hee's Heire of *Helicon*?

APOLLO, and the Nine,
Forbid no Man their Shrine,
That commeth with hands pure;
Else be they so divine,
They will not him indure.

For they be such coy Things,
That they care not for Kings,
And dare let them know it;
Nor may he touch their Springs,
That is not borne a Poet.

The *Phocean* it did prove,
Whom when foule Lust did move,
Those Mayds unchast to make,
Fell, as with them he strove,
His Neck and justly brake.

Pyreneus, *King of* Phocis, *attempting to ravish the Muses.*

That instrument ne'er heard,
Strooke by the skilfull Bard,
  It strongly to awake;
But it th' infernalls scar'd,
  And made Olympus quake.

Sam. lib. 1. cap. 16.

As those Prophetike strings
Whose sounds with fiery Wings,
  Drave Fiends from their abode,
Touch'd by the best of Kings,
  That sang the holy Ode.

So his, which Women slew,
And it int' Hebrus threw,
  Such sounds yet forth it sent,
That Bacchus to weepe that drew,
  As downe the Streame it went.

. . . .

The Ancient British *Priests* so called of their abode in woods.

The *Druides* imbrew'd
With Gore, on Altars rude
  With Sacrifices crown'd,
In hollow Woods bedew'd,
  Ador'd the Trembling sound.

Pindar *Prince of the* Greeke lyricks, *of whom* Horace: Pindarum quisquis studet, &c. Ode 2. lib. 4.

Though wee be All to seeke,
Of PINDAR that Great *Greeke*,
  To Finger it aright,
The Soule with power to strike,
  His hand retayn'd such Might.

Horace *first of the* Romans *in that kind.*

Or him that *Rome* did grace
Whose Ayres we all imbrace,
  That scarcely found his Peere,
Nor giveth PHŒBUS place,
  For Strokes divinely cleere.

The *Irish* I admire,
And still cleave to that Lyre, *The* Irish *Harpe.*
  As our Musike's Mother,
And thinke, till I expire,
  APOLLO 's such another.

. . . .

To those that with despight
Shall terme these Numbers slight,
  Tell them their Judgement 's blind,
Much erring from the right,
  It is a Noble kind.

Nor is't the Verse doth make,
That giveth, or doth take,
  'Tis possible to clyme,
To kindle, or to slake,
  Although in SKELTON's Ryme. *An old* English *Rymer.*

Odes, 1619

22 *The Sacrifice to Apollo*

PRIESTS of APOLLO, sacred be the Roome,
For this learn'd Meeting: Let no barbarous Groome,
  How brave soe'er he bee,
  Attempt to enter;
  But of the Muses free,
  None here may venter;
This for the *Delphian* Prophets is prepar'd:
The prophane Vulgar are from hence debar'd.

And since the Feast so happily begins,
Call up those faire Nine, with their Violins;

They are begot by JOVE,
Then let us place them,
Where no Clowne in may shove,
That may disgrace them:
But let them neere to young APOLLO sit;
So shall his Foot-pace over-flow with Wit.

Where be the Graces, where be those fayre Three?
In any hand they may not absent bee:
They to the Gods are deare,
And they can humbly
Teach us, our Selves to beare,
And doe things comely:
They, and the Muses, rise both from one Stem,
They grace the Muses, and the Muses them.

Bring forth your Flaggons (fill'd with sparkling Wine)
Whereon swolne BACCHUS, crowned with a Vine,
Is graven, and fill out,
It well bestowing,
To ev'ry Man about,
In Goblets flowing:
Let not a Man drinke, but in Draughts profound;
To our God PHŒBUS let the Health goe Round.

Let your Jests flye at large; yet therewithall
See they be Salt, but yet not mix'd with Gall:
Not tending to disgrace,
But fayrely given,
Becoming well the place,
Modest, and even;
That they with tickling Pleasure may provoke
Laughter in him, on whom the Jest is broke.

Or if the deeds of HEROES ye rehearse,
Let them be sung in so well-ord'red Verse,
 That each word have his weight,
 Yet runne with pleasure;
 Holding one stately height,
 In so brave measure,
That they may make the stiffest Storme seeme weake,
And dampe JOVES Thunder, when it lowd'st doth speake.

And if yee list to exercise your Vayne,
Or in the Sock, or in the Buskin'd Strayne,
 Let Art and Nature goe
 One with the other;
 Yet so, that Art may show
 Nature her Mother;
The thick-brain'd Audience lively to awake,
Till with shrill Claps the Theater doe shake.

Sing Hymnes to BACCHUS then, with hands uprear'd,
Offer to Jove, who most is to be fear'd;
 From him the Muse we have,
 From him proceedeth
 More than we dare to crave;
 'Tis he that feedeth
Them, whom the World would starve; then let the Lyre
Sound, whilst his Altars endlesse flames expire.

Odes, 1619

23 *To the Virginian Voyage*

YOU brave Heroique minds,
 Worthy your Countries Name;
 That Honour still pursue,
 Goe, and subdue,
Whilst loyt'ring Hinds
Lurke here at home, with shame.

Britans, you stay too long,
Quickly aboard bestow you,
  And with a merry Gale
  Swell your stretch'd Sayle,
With Vowes as strong,
As the Winds that blow you.

Your Course securely steere,
West and by South forth keepe,
  Rocks, Lee-shores, nor Shoales,
  When EOLUS scowles,
You need not feare,
So absolute the Deepe.

And cheerfully at Sea,
Successe you still intice,
  To get the Pearle and Gold,
  And ours to hold,
VIRGINIA,
Earth's onely Paradise.

Where Nature hath in store
Fowle, Venison, and Fish,
  And the Fruitfull'st Soyle,
  Without your Toyle,
Three Harvests more,
All greater than your Wish.

And the ambitious Vine
Crownes with his purple Masse,
  The Cedar reaching hie
  To kisse the Sky,
The Cypresse, Pine
And use-full Sassafras.

To whome, the golden Age
Still Natures lawes doth give,
  No other Cares that tend,
  But Them to defend
From Winters rage,
That long there doth not live.

When as the Lushious smell
Of that delicious Land,
  Above the Seas that flowes,
  The cleere Wind throwes,
Your Hearts to swell
Approaching the deare Strande.

In kenning of the Shore
(Thanks to God first given,)
  O you the happy'st men,
  Be Frolike then,
Let Cannons roare,
Frighting the wide Heaven.

And in Regions farre
Such Heroes bring yee foorth,
  As those from whom We came,
  And plant Our name,
Under that Starre
Not knowne unto our North.

And as there Plenty growes
Of Lawrell every where,
  APOLLO's Sacred tree,
  You may it see,
A Poets Browes
To crowne, that may sing there.

Thy Voyages attend
Industrious HACKLUIT,
  Whose Reading shall inflame
  Men to seeke Fame,
And much commend
To after-times thy Wit.

Odes, 1619

24 *An Ode written in the Peake*

THIS while we are abroad,
  Shall we not touch our Lyre?
Shall we not sing an ODE?
  Shall that holy Fire,
In us that strongly glow'd,
  In this cold Ayre expire?

Long since the Summer layd
  Her lustie Brav'rie downe,
The Autumne halfe is way'd,
  And BOREAS 'gins to frowne,
Since now I did behold
  Great BRUTES first builded Towne.

Though in the utmost *Peake*,
  A while we doe remaine,
Amongst the Mountaines bleake
  Expos'd to Sleet and Raine,
No Sport our Houres shall breake,
  To exercise our Vaine.

What though bright PHŒBUS Beames
  Refresh the Southerne Ground,
And though the Princely *Thames*

With beautious Nymphs abound,
And by old *Camber's* Streames
Be many Wonders found;

Yet many Rivers cleare
Here glide in Silver Swathes,
And what of all most deare,
Buckston's delicious Bathes.
Strong Ale and Noble Cheare,
T' asswage breeme Winters scathes.

Those grim and horrid Caves,
Whose Lookes affright the day,
Wherein nice Nature saves,
What she would not bewray,
Our better leasure craves,
And doth invite our Lay.

In places farre or neere,
Or famous, or obscure,
Where wholesome is the Ayre,
Or where the most impure,
All times, and every-where,
The Muse is still in ure.

Odes, 1619

25

To His Coy Love

A Canzonet

I PRAY thee leave, love me no more,
Call home the Heart you gave me,
I but in vaine that Saint adore,
That can, but will not save me:

These poore halfe kisses kill me quite;
  Was ever man thus served?
Amidst an Ocean of Delight,
  For Pleasure to be sterved.

Shew me no more those Snowie Brests
  With Azure Riverets branched,
Where whilst mine Eye with Plentie feasts,
  Yet is my Thirst not stanched.
O TANTALUS, thy Paines ne'er tell,
  By me thou art prevented;
'Tis nothing to be plagu'd in Hell,
  But thus in Heaven tormented.

Clip me no more in those deare Armes,
  Nor thy Life's Comfort call me;
O, these are but too pow'rfull Charmes,
  And doe but more inthrall me.
But see how patient I am growne,
  In all this coyle about thee;
Come nice Thing, let thy Heart alone,
  I cannot live without thee. *Odes*, 1619

26 *To the Cambro-Britains and their Harpe, his Ballad of* AGINCOURT

FAIRE stood the Wind for *France*,
When we our Sayles advance,
Nor now to prove our chance,
    Longer will tarry;
But putting to the Mayne,
At *Caux*, the Mouth of *Seine*,
With all his Martial Trayne,
    Landed King HARRY.

And taking many a Fort,
Furnish'd in Warlike sort,
Marcheth tow'rds *Agincourt*,
    In happy howre;
Skirmishing day by day,
With those that stop'd his way,
Where the *French* Gen'rall lay,
    With all his Power.

Which in his Hight of Pride,
King Henry to deride,
His Ransome to provide
    To the King sending.
Which he neglects the while,
As from a Nation vile,
Yet with an angry smile,
    Their fall portending.

And turning to his Men,
Quoth our brave Henry then,
Though they to one be ten,
    Be not amazed.
Yet have we well begunne,
Battels so bravely wonne,
Have ever to the Sunne,
    By Fame beene raysed.

And, for my Selfe (quoth he),
This my full rest shall be,
England ne'er mourne for Me,
    Nor more esteeme me.

Victor I will remaine,
Or on this Earth lie slaine,
Never shall Shee sustaine,
    Losse to redeeme me.

Poiters and *Cressy* tell,
When most their Pride did swell,
Under our Swords they fell,
    No lesse our skill is,
Than when our Grandsire Great,
Clayming the Regall Seate,
By many a Warlike feate,
    Lopp'd the *French* Lillies.

The Duke of *Yorke* so dread,
The eager Vaward led;
With the maine, HENRY sped,
    Among'st his Hench-men.
EXCESTER had the Rere,
A Braver man not there,
O Lord, how hot they were,
    On the false *French-men*!

They now to fight are gone,
Armour on Armour shone,
Drumme now to Drumme did grone,
    To heare, was wonder;
That with the Cryes they make,
The very Earth did shake,
Trumpet to Trumpet spake,
    Thunder to Thunder.

Well it thine Age became,
O Noble ERPINGHAM,
Which didst the Signall ayme,
  To our hid Forces;
When from a Medow by,
Like a Storme suddenly,
The *English* Archery
  Stuck the *French* Horses,

With *Spanish* Ewgh so strong,
Arrowes a Cloth-yard long,
That like to Serpents stung,
  Piercing the Weather;
None from his fellow starts,
But playing Manly parts,
And like true *English* hearts,
  Stuck close together.

When downe their Bowes they threw,
And forth their Bilbowes drew,
And on the French they flew,
  Not one was tardie;
Armes were from shoulders sent,
Scalpes to the Teeth were rent,
Downe the *French* Peasants went,
  Our Men were hardie.

This while our Noble King,
His broad Sword brandishing,
Downe the *French* Hoast did ding,
  As to o'er-whelme it;

And many a deepe Wound lent,
His Armes with Bloud besprent,
And many a cruell Dent
Bruised his Helmet.

GLOSTER, that Duke so good,
Next of the Royall Blood,
For famous *England* stood,
With his brave Brother;
CLARENCE, in Steele so bright,
Though but a Maiden Knight,
Yet in that furious Fight,
Scarce such another.

WARWICK in Bloud did wade,
OXFORD the Foe invade,
And cruell slaughter made,
Still as they ran up;
SUFFOLKE his Axe did ply,
BEAUMONT and WILLOUGHBY
Bare them right doughtily,
FERRERS and FANHOPE.

Upon Saint CRISPIN's day
Fought was this Noble Fray,
Which Fame did not delay,
To *England* to carry;
O, when shall *English* Men
With such Acts fill a Pen,
Or *England* breed againe,
Such a King HARRY?

Odes, 1619

27 *To my most dearly-loved friend* Henry Reynolds *Esquire, of Poets and Poesie*

MY dearely loved friend how oft have we,
In winter evenings (meaning to be free,)
To some well-chosen place us'd to retire;
And there with moderate meate, and wine, and fire,
Have past the howres contentedly with chat,
Now talk'd of this, and then discours'd of that,
Spoke our owne verses 'twixt our selves, if not
Other mens lines, which we by chance had got,
Or some Stage pieces famous long before,
Of which your happy memory had store;
And I remember you much pleased were,
Of those who lived long agoe to heare,
As well as of those of these latter times,
Who have inricht our language with their rimes,
And in succession, how still up they grew,
Which is the subject, that I now pursue;
For from my cradle, (you must know that) I,
Was still inclin'd to noble Poesie,
And when that once *Pueriles* I had read,
And newly had my *Cato* construed,
In my small selfe I greatly marveil'd then,
Amongst all other, what strange kinde of men
These Poets were; And pleased with the name,
To my milde Tutor merrily I came,
(For I was then a proper goodly page,
Much like a Pigmy, scarse ten yeares of age)
Clasping my slender armes about his thigh.
O my deare master! cannot you (quoth I)
Make me a Poet, doe it if you can,

And you shall see, I'll quickly bee a man.
Who me thus answered smiling, boy quoth he,
If you'll not play the wag, but I may see
You ply your learning, I will shortly read
Some Poets to you; *Phœbus* be my speed,
To't hard went I, when shortly he began,
And first read to me honest *Mantuan*,
Then *Virgils Eglogues*; being entred thus,
Me thought I straight had mounted *Pegasus*,
And in his full Careere could make him stop,
And bound upon *Parnassus*' bi-clift top.
I scorned your ballet then though it were done
And had for Finis, *William Elderton*.
But soft, in sporting with this childish jest,
I from my subject have too long digrest,
Then to the matter that we tooke in hand,
Jove and *Apollo* for the *Muses* stand.
 That noble *Chaucer*, in those former times,
The first inrich'd our *English* with his rimes,
And was the first of ours, that ever brake,
Into the *Muses* treasure, and first spake
In weighty numbers, delving in the Mine
Of perfect knowledge, which he could refine,
And coyne for current, and as much as then
The *English* language could expresse to men,
He made it doe; and by his wondrous skill,
Gave us much light from his abundant quill.
 And honest *Gower*, who in respect of him,
Had only sipt at *Aganippas* brimme,
And though in yeares this last was him before,
Yet fell he far short of the others store.

ballet: ballad.

When after those, foure ages very neare,
They with the *Muses* which conversed, were
That Princely *Surrey*, early in the time
Of the Eight *Henry*, who was then the prime
Of *Englands* noble youth; with him there came
Wyat; with reverence whom we still doe name
Amongst our Poets; *Brian* had a share
With the two former, which accompted are
That times best makers, and the authors were
Of those small poems, which the title beare,
Of Songs and Sonnets, wherein oft they hit
On many dainty passages of wit.

. . . . . .

Grave morrall *Spencer* after these came on
Than whom I am perswaded there was none
Since the blind *Bard* his *Iliads* up did make,
Fitter a taske like that to undertake,
To set downe boldly, bravely to invent,
In all high knowledge surely excellent.
The noble *Sidney* with this last arose,
That *Heroe* for numbers, and for Prose.
That throughly pac'd our language as to show,
The plenteous *English* hand in hand might goe
With *Greek* or *Latine*, and did first reduce
Our tongue from *Lilly's* writing then in use;
Talking of Stones, Stars, Plants, of fishes, Flyes,
Playing with words, and idle Similies,
As th' *English*, Apes and very Zanies be,
Of every thing, that they doe heare and see,
So imitating his ridiculous tricks,
They spake and writ, all like meere lunatiques.

. . . . . .

Neat *Marlow* bathed in the *Thespian* springs
Had in him those brave translunary things,
That the first Poets had, his raptures were,
All ayre, and fire, which made his verses cleere,
For that fine madnes still he did retaine,
Which rightly should possesse a Poets braine.

. . . . .

Shakespeare, thou hadst as smooth a Comicke vaine,
Fitting the socke, and in thy naturall braine,
As strong conception, and as Cleere a rage,
As any one that trafiqu'd with the stage.
Amongst these *Samuel Daniel*, whom if I
May speake of, but to censure doe denie,
Onely have heard some wisemen him rehearse,
To be too much *Historian* in verse;
His rimes were smooth, his meeters well did close,
But yet his manner better fitted prose:
Next these, learn'd *Johnson*, in this List I bring,
Who had drunke deepe of the *Pierian* spring,
Whose knowledge did him worthily prefer,
And long was Lord here of the Theater,
Who in opinion made our learn'st to sticke,
Whether in Poems rightly dramatique,
Strong *Seneca* or *Plautus*, he or they,
Should beare the Buskin, or the Socke away.
Others againe here lived in my dayes,
That have of us deserved no lesse praise
For their translations, than the daintiest wit
That on *Parnassus* thinks, he highst doth sit,
And for a chaire may mongst the Muses call,
As the most curious maker of them all;
As reverend *Chapman*, who hath brought to us,

Musæus, *Homer*, and *Hesiodus*
Out of the Greeke; and by his skill hath reard
Them to that height, and to our tongue endear'd,
That were those Poets at this day alive,
To see their bookes thus with us to survive,
They would think, having neglected them so long,
They had bin written in the *English* tongue.

. . . . .

But if you shall
Say in your knowledge that these be not all
Have writ in numbers, be inform'd that I
Only my selfe, to these few men doe tye,
Whose works oft printed, set on every post,
To publique censure subject have bin most;
For such whose poems, be they ne'er so rare,
In private chambers, that incloistered are,
And by transcription daintyly must goe;
As though the world unworthy were to know,
Their rich composures, let those men that keepe
These wonderous reliques in their judgement deepe;
And cry them up so, let such Peeces bee
Spoke of by those that shall come after me,
I passe not for them: nor doe meane to run,
In quest of these, that them applause have wonne.

Elegies upon Sundry Occasions, 1627

28 *(The Queen's Chariot)*

HER Chariot ready straight is made,
Each thing therein is fitting layde,
That she by nothing might be stayde,
For naught must be her letting,

Foure nimble Gnats the Horses were,
Their Harnasses of Gossamere,
Flye Cranion her Chariottere,
  Upon the Coach-box getting.

Her Chariot of a Snayles fine shell,
Which for the colours did excell:
The faire Queene *Mab*, becoming well,
  So lively was the limming:
The seate the soft wooll of the Bee;
The cover, (gallantly to see)
The wing of a pyde Butterflee,
  I trow t'was simple trimming.

The wheeles compos'd of Crickets bones,
And daintily made for the nonce,
For feare of ratling on the stones,
  With Thistle-downe they shod it;
For all her Maydens much did feare,
If *Oberon* had chanc'd to heare,
That *Mab* his Queene should have bin there,
  He would not have abode it.

She mounts her Chariot with a trice,
Nor would she stay for no advice,
Untill her Maydes that were so nice,
  To wayte on her were fitted,
But ranne her selfe away alone;
Which when they heard there was not one,
But hasted after to be gone,
  As she had beene diswitted.

Hop, and *Mop*, and *Drop* so cleare,
Pip, and *Trip*, and *Skip* that were,
To *Mab* their Soveraigne ever deare:
  Her speciall Maydes of Honour;
Fib, and *Tib*, and *Pinck*, and *Pin*,
Tick, and *Quick*, and *Jill*, and *Jin*,
Tit, and *Nit*, and *Wap*, and *Win*,
  The Trayne that wayte upon her.

Upon a Grasshopper they got,
And what with Amble, and with Trot,
For hedge nor ditch they spared not,
  But after her they hie them.
A Cobweb over them they throw,
To shield the winde if it should blowe,
Themselves they wisely could bestowe,
  Lest any should espie them.

From Nymphidia, 1627

29 *From The Sixt Nimphall*

CLEERE had the day bin from the dawne,
  All chequerd was the Skye,
Thin Clouds like Scarfs of Cobweb Lawne
Vayld Heaven's most glorious eye.
The Winde had no more strength than this,
That leasurely it blew,
To make one leafe the next to kisse,
That closely by it grew.
The Rills that on the Pebbles playd,
Might now be heard at will;
This world they onely Musick made,
Else everything was still.

The Flowers like brave embraudred Girles,
Lookt as they much desired,
To see whose head with orient Pearles,
Most curiously was tyred;
And to it selfe the subtle Ayre,
Such soverainty assumes,
That it receiv'd too large a share
From natures rich perfumes.

Muses Elizium, 1630

30 *From the Second Song from Polyolbion*

TO these, the gentle South, with kisses smooth and soft,
Doth in her bosome breathe, and seemes to court her oft.
Besides, her little Rills, her in-lands that doe feed,
Which with their lavish streames doe furnish everie need:
And Meads, that with their fine soft grassie towels stand
To wipe away the drops and moisture from her hand.
And to the North, betwixt the fore-land and the firme,
Shee hath that narrow Sea, which we the *Solent* tearme: (The Solent.)
Where those rough irefull Tides, as in her Straits they meet,
With boystrous shocks and rores each other rudely greet:
Which fiercelie when they charge, and sadlie make retreat,
Upon the bulwarkt Forts of *Hurst* and *Calsheot* beat, (Two Castles in the Sea.)
Then to *South-hampton* runne: which by her shores supplide
(As *Portsmouth* by her strength) doth vilifie their pride;
Both, Roads that with our best may boldlie hold their plea,
Nor *Plimmouths* selfe hath borne more braver ships than they;
That from their anchoring Bayes have travailed to finde
Large *Chinas* wealthie Realms, and view'd the either *Inde*,
The pearlie rich *Peru*; and with as prosperous fate,
Have borne their ful-spred sailes upon the streames of *Plate*:

Whose pleasant harbors oft the Sea-mans hope renue,
To rigge his late-craz'd Barke, to spred a wanton clue;
Where they with lustie Sack, and mirthful Sailers songs,
Defie their passed stormes, and laugh at *Neptunes* wrongs:
The danger quite forgot wherein they were of late;
Who halfe so merrie now as Maister and his Mate?
And victualling againe, with brave and man-like minds
To Sea-ward cast their eyes, and pray for happie winds.

Polyolbion, 1613

31 *From the Third Song from Polyolbion*

AWAY yee barb'rous Woods; How ever yee be plac't
On Mountaines, or in Dales, or happily be grac't
With floods, or marshie* fells, with pasture, or with earth
By nature made to till, that by the yeerely birth
The large-bay'd Barne doth fill, yea though the fruitfulst ground.
For, in respect of *Plaines*, what pleasure can be found
In darke and sleepie shades? where mists and rotten fogs
Hang in the gloomie thicks, and make unstedfast bogs,
By dropping from the boughs, the o'er-grown trees among,
With Caterpillers kells, and duskie cobwebs hong.
The deadlie Screech-owle sits, in gloomie covert hid:
Whereas the smooth-brow'd *Plaine*, as liberallie doth bid
The Larke to leave her Bowre, and on her trembling wing
In climing up tow'rds heaven, her high-pitcht Hymnes to sing
Unto the springing Day; when gainst the Sunnes arise
The earlie Dawning strewes the goodly Easterne skies
With Roses every where: who scarcelie lifts his head
To view this upper world, but hee his beames doth spred

The *Plaine* of *Salisburies* speech in defence of all *Plaines*.
*Boggy places. A word frequent in *Lancashire*.

Upon the goodlie *Plaines*; yet at his Noonesteds hight,
Doth scarcelie pierce the Brake with his farre-shooting sight.

. . . .

O three times famous Ile, where is that place that might
Be with thy selfe compar'd for glorie and delight,
Whilst *Glastenbury* stood? exalted to that pride,
Whose Monasterie seem'd all other to deride?
O who thy ruine sees, whom wonder doth not fill
With our great fathers pompe, devotion, and their skill?
Thou more than mortall power (this judgement rightly wai'd)
Then present to assist, at that foundation lai'd;
On whom for this sad waste, should Justice lay the crime?
Is there a power in Fate, or doth it yeeld to Time?
Or was their error such, that thou could'st not protect
Those buildings which thy hand did with their zeale erect?
To whom didst thou commit that monument, to keepe,
That suffreth with the dead their memory to sleepe?
Joseph of *Arimathea.* §. When not great *Arthurs* Tombe, nor holy *Josephs* Grave,
From sacriledge had power their sacred bones to save;
He who that God in man to his sepulchre brought,
Or he which for the faith twelve famous battels fought.
What? Did so many Kings do honor to that place,
For Avarice at last so vilely to deface?
For rev'rence, to that seat which hath ascribed beene,
Trees yet in winter bloome, and beare their Summers greene.

The wondrous tree at *Glastenbury.*

Polyolbion, 1613

32 *From the Thirteenth Song from Polyolbion*

WHEN *Phœbus* lifts his head out of the Winters wave,
No sooner doth the Earth her flowerie bosome brave,
At such time as the Yeere brings on the pleasant Spring,
But Hunts-up to the Morne the feath'red *Sylvans* sing:

And in the lower Grove, as on the rising Knole,
Upon the highest spray of every mounting pole,
Those Quirristers are pearcht with many a speckled breast.
Then from her burnisht gate the goodly glittring East
Gilds every lofty top, which late the humorous Night
Bespangled had with pearle, to please the Mornings sight:
On which the mirthfull Quires, with their cleere open throats,
Unto the joyfull Morne so straine their warbling notes,
That Hills and Valleys ring, and even the ecchoing Ayre
Seemes all compos'd of sounds, about them every where.
That Throstell, with shrill Sharps; as purposely he song
T'awake the lustlesse Sunne; or chyding, that so long
He was in coming forth, that should the thickets thrill:
The Woosell neere at hand, that hath a golden bill;
As Nature him had markt of purpose, t'let us see
That from all other Birds his tunes should different bee:
For, with their vocall sounds, they sing to pleasant May;
Upon his dulcet pype the Merle doth onely play.
When in the lower Brake, the Nightingale hard-by,
In such lamenting straines the joyfull howres doth ply,
As though the other Birds shee to her tunes would draw.
And, but that Nature (by her all-constraining law)
Each Bird to her owne kind this season doth invite,
They else, alone to heare that Charmer of the Night
(The more to use their eares) their voyces sure would spare,
That moduleth her tunes so admirably rare,
As man to set in Parts, at first had learn'd of her.

Of all Birds, only the Black-bird whistleth.

33 *From the same*

*Of hunting, or Chase.

OF all the Beasts which we for our * veneriall name,
The Hart amongst the rest, the Hunters noblest game:
Of which most Princely Chase sith none did ere report,
Or by description touch, t'expresse that wondrous sport
(Yet might have well beseem'd th' ancients nobler Songs)
To our old *Arden* heere, most fitly it belongs:
Yet shall shee not invoke the Muses to her ayde;
But thee *Diana* bright, a Goddesse and a mayd:
In many a huge-growne Wood, and many a shady Grove,
Which oft hast borne thy Bowe (great Huntresse) us'd to rove
At many a cruell beast, and with thy darts to pierce
The Lyon, Panther, Ounce, the Beare, and Tiger fierce;
And following thy fleet Game, chaste mightie Forrests Queene,
With thy disheveld Nymphs attyr'd in youthfull greene,
About the Launds hast scowr'd, and Wastes both farre and neere,
Brave Huntresse: but no beast shall prove thy Quarries heere;
Save those the best of Chase, the tall and lusty Red,
The Stag for goodly shape, and statelinesse of head,

A description of hunting the Hart.

Is fitt'st to hunt at force. For whom, when with his hounds
The laboring Hunter tufts the thicke unbarbed grounds
Where harbor'd is the Hart; there often from his feed
The dogs of him doe find; or thorough skilfull heed,

*The tract of the foote.

The Huntsman by his* slot, or breaking earth, perceaves,
Or entring of the thicke by pressing of the greaves
Where he hath gone to lodge. Now when the Hart doth heare
The often-bellowing hounds to vent his secret laire,
He rouzing rusheth out, and through the Brakes doth drive,
As though up by the roots the bushes he would rive.

And through the combrous thicks, as fearefully he makes,
Hee with his branched head, the tender Saplings shakes,
That sprinkling their moyst pearle doe seeme for him to weepe;
When after goes the Cry, with yellings lowd and deepe,
That all the Forrest rings, and every neighbouring place:
And there is not a hound but falleth to the Chase.
Rechating with his horne, which then the Hunter cheeres, One of the Measures in winding the horne.
Whilst still the lustie Stag his high-palm'd head up-beares,
His body showing state, with unbent knees upright,
Expressing (from all beasts) his courage in his flight.
But when th' approaching foes still following he perceives,
That hee his speed must trust, his usual walke he leaves;
And o'er the Champaine flies: which when th' assembly find,
Each followes, as his horse were footed with the wind.
But beeing then imbost, the noble stately Deere
When he hath gotten ground (the kennell cast arear)
Doth beat the Brooks and Ponds for sweet refreshing soyle:
That serving not, then proves if he his scent can foyle,
And makes amongst the Heards, and flocks of shag-wooll'd Sheepe,
Them frighting from the guard of those who had their keepe.
But when as all his shifts his safety still denies,
Put quite out of his walke, the wayes and fallowes tryes.
Whom when the Plow-man meets, his teame he letteth stand
T'assaile him with his goad: so with his hooke in hand,
The Shepheard him pursues, and to his dog doth halloo:
When, with tempestuous speed, the hounds and Huntsmen follow;
Until the noble Deere through toyle bereav'd of strength,
His long and sinewy legs then fayling him at length,
The Villages attempts, enrag'd, not giving way
To any thing hee meets now at his sad decay.

The cruell ravenous hounds and bloody Hunters neer,
This noblest beast of Chase, that vainly doth but feare,
Some banke or quick-set finds: to which his haunch oppos'd,
He turnes upon his foes, that soone have him inclos'd.
The churlish throated hounds then holding him at bay,
And as their cruell fangs on his harsh skin they lay,
With his sharp-poynted head he dealeth deadly wounds.
The Hart weepeth at his dying: his teares are held to be precious in medicine.
The Hunter, coming in to helpe his wearied hounds,
He desperatly assailes; until opprest by force,
He who the Mourner is to his owne dying Corse,
Upon the ruthlesse earth his precious teares lets fall.

Polyolbion, 1613

34 *From the Twentieth Song from Polyolbion*

A WORLD of mightie Kings and Princes I could name,
From our god *Neptune* sprung; let this suffice, his fame
Incompasseth the world; those Starres which never rise,
Above the lower South, are never from his eyes:
As those againe to him doe every day appeare,
Continually that keepe the Northerne Hemisphere;
Who like a mightie King, doth cast his Watched robe,
Farre wider then the land, quite round about the Globe.
Where is there one to him that may compared be,
That both the Poles at once continually doth see;
And Gyant-like with heaven as often maketh warres;
The Ilands (in his power) as numberlesse as Starres,
He washeth at his will, and with his mightie hands,
He makes the even shores, oft mountainous with Sands:
Whose creatures, which observe his wide Emperiall seat,
Like his immeasured selfe, are infinite and great.

Polyolbion, 1622

35 *From the Two and Twentieth Song from Polyolbion*

TH' EARLE *Douglasse* for this day doth with the *Percies* stand,
To whom they *Berwicke* gave, and in *Northumberland*
Some Seigniories and Holds, if they the Battell got,
Who brought with him to Field full many an angry *Scot*,
At *Holmdon* Battell late that being overthrowne,
Now on the King and Prince hop'd to regaine their owne;
With almost all the power of *Cheshire* got together,
By *Venables* (there great) and *Vernon* mustred thether.
The Vaward of the King, great *Stafford* tooke to guide.
The Vaward of the Lords upon the other side,
Consisted most of *Scots*, which joyning, made such spoyle,
As at the first constrain'd the *English* to recoyle,
And almost brake their Rankes, which when King *Henry* found,
Bringing his Battell up, to reinforce the ground,
The *Percies* bring up theirs, againe to make it good.
Thus whilst the either Host in opposition stood,
Brave *Douglasse* with his spurres, his furious Courser strake,
His Lance set in his rest, when desperatly he brake
In, where his eye beheld th' Emperiall Ensigne pight,
Where soone it was his chance, upon the King to light,
Which in his full carreere he from his Courser threw;
The next *Sir Walter Blunt*, he with three other slew,
All armed like the King, which he dead sure accounted;
But after when hee saw the King himselfe remounted:
This hand of mine, quoth he, foure Kings this day hath slaine,
And swore out of the earth he thought they sprang againe,

The high courage of *Douglasse* won him that addition of *Doughty Douglasse*, which after grew to a Proverbe.

Or Fate did him defend, at whom he onely aym'd.
When *Henry Hotspurre*, so with his high deeds inflam'd,
Doth second him againe, and through such dangers presse,
That *Douglasse* valiant deeds he made to seeme the lesse,
As still the people cryed, A *Percy Espirance*.
The King which saw then time, or never to advance
His Battell in the Field, which neere from him was wonne,
Ayded by that brave Prince, his most couragious sonne,
Who bravely coming on, in hope to give them chase,
It chanc'd he with a shaft was wounded in the face;
Whom when out of the fight, his friends would beare away,
He strongly it refus'd, and thus was heard to say,
Time never shall report, Prince *Henry* left the field,
When *Harry Percy* staid, his traytrous sword to weeld.
Now rage and equall wounds, alike inflame their bloods,
And the maine Battels joyne, as doe two adverse floods
Met in some narrow Arme, shouldring as they would shove
Each other from their path, or would their bankes remove.
The King his traytrous foes, before him downe doth hew,
And with his hands that day, neere fortie persons slue:
When conquest wholly turnes to his victorious side,
His power surrounding all, like to a furious tyde;
That *Henry Hotspurre* dead upon the cold earth lyes,
Stout *Wor'ster* taken was, and doughtie *Douglasse* flyes.
Five thousand from both parts left dead upon the ground,
Mongst whom the kings fast friend, great *Staffords* coarse
was found;
And all the Knights there dubb'd the morning but before,
The evenings Sunne beheld there sweltred in their gore.

Polyolbion, 1622

SIR HENRY WOTTON

1568–1639

36 *A Hymn to my God in a night of my late Sicknesse*

OH *thou great Power*, in whom I move,
For whom I *live*, to whom I *die*,
Behold me through thy beams of *love*,
Whilst on this *couch* of *tears* I lye;
And Cleanse my sordid *soul* within,
By thy *Christs Blood*, the *bath* of sin.

No hallowed Oyls, no grains I need,
No rags of Saints, no purging fire,
One rosie drop from *David's* Seed
Was worlds of Seas, to quench thine Ire.
O precious Ransome! which once paid,
That *Consummatum est* was said.

And said by *him*, that said no more,
But seal'd it with his sacred Breath.
Thou then, that hast dispung'd my score,
And dying, wast the death of Death;
Be to me now, on thee I call,
My Life, my Strength, my Joy, my All.

Reliquiæ Wottonianæ, 1651 (text 1672)

37 *On his Mistress, the Queen of Bohemia*

YOU meaner *Beauties* of the *Night*,
That poorly satisfie our *Eyes*
More by your *number*, than your *light*,
You *Common people* of the *Skies*;
What are you when the *Sun* shall rise?

You curious Chanters of the Wood,
That warble forth *Dame Natures* layes,
Thinking your *Voices* understood
By your weak *accents*; what 's your praise
  When *Philomel* her voice shall raise?

You *Violets*, that first appear,
By your *pure purple mantles* known,
Like the proud *Virgins* of the *year*,
As if the *Spring* were all your own;
  What are you when the *Rose is blown*?

So, when *my Mistress* shall be *seen*
In *Form* and *Beauty* of her *mind*,
By *Vertue* first, then *Choice a Queen*,
Tell me, if *she* were not design'd
  Th' *Eclipse* and *Glory* of her kind?

Reliquiæ Wottonianæ, 1651 (text 1672)

38 *Upon the sudden Restraint of the Earl of Somerset, then falling from favour*

DAZZLED thus with height of place,
  Whilst our Hopes our wits Beguile,
No man marks the narrow space
'Twixt a Prison and a Smile.

Then since Fortunes favours fade,
You that in her arms do sleep,
Learn to swim and not to wade;
For the Hearts of Kings are deep.

But if Greatness be so blind,
As to trust in Towers of *Air*,
Let it be with Goodness lin'd,
That at least the Fall be fair.

Then though darkened you shall say,
When Friends fail and Princes frown,
Vertue is the roughest way,
But proves at night a *Bed of Down.*

Reliquiæ Wottonianæ, 1651 (text 1672)

39 *The Character of a Happy Life*

HOW *happy* is he born and taught,
That serveth not anothers *will*?
Whose *armour* is his *honest thought*,
And simple *truth* his utmost *skill*?

Whose *passions* not his *masters* are,
Whose *soul* is still prepar'd for *death*;
Unti'd unto the *World* by care
Of *publick fame*, or *private breath*.

Who *envies* none that *chance* doth *raise*,
Nor *vice* hath ever understood;
How deepest wounds are giv'n by *praise*,
Nor rules of *State*, but rules of *good*.

Who hath his *life* from *rumours freed*,
Whose *conscience* is his strong *retreat*:
Whose *state* can neither *flatterers feed*,
Nor *ruine* make *Oppressors* great.

Who *God* doth late and early pray,
More of his *grace* than *gifts* to lend:
And entertains the harmless day
With a *Religious Book*, or Friend.

This man is freed from servile bands,
Of hope to rise, or *fear* to fall:
Lord of himself, though not of *Lands*,
And having *nothing*, yet hath *all*.

Reliquiæ Wottonianæ, 1651 (text 1672)

40 *On a* Bank *as I sate a* Fishing

A description of the Spring

AND now all *Nature* seem'd in *love*;
The lusty *sap* began to move;
New *juice* did stir th'embracing *Vines*;
And *Birds* had drawn their *Valentines*:
The *jealous Trout*, that low did lie,
Rose at a well-dissembled *flie*:
There stood my Friend, with patient skill
Attending of his trembling *quill*.
Already were the *Eaves* possest
With the swift *Pilgrims* daubed nest.
The *Groves* already did rejoyce
In *Philomels* triumphing *voice*.
The *showers* were short, the *weather* mild,
The morning fresh, the evening smil'd.
Jone takes her neat-rub'd Pale, and now
She trips to milk the Sand-red *Cow*;
Where for some sturdy foot-ball *Swain*,
Jone strokes a *sillabub* or twain.

The *Fields* and *Gardens* were beset
With *Tulip*, *Crocus*, *Violet*:
And now, though late, the *modest Rose*
Did more than half a blush disclose.
Thus all look'd *gay*, all full of *chear*,
To welcome the New-livery'd *year*.

Reliquiæ Wottonianæ, 1651 (text 1672)

41 *Upon the death of Sir* Albert Morton'*s Wife*

HE first deceas'd; She for a little tri'd
To live without him: lik'd it not, and di'd.

Reliquiæ Wottonianæ, 1651 (text 1672)

42 *A Dialogue betwixt God and the Soul*

Imitatio Horatianæ Odes 9. lib. 3 donec gratus eram tibi

Soul. WHILST my *Souls* eye beheld no light
But what stream'd from thy gracious sight,
To me the worlds greatest King,
Seem'd but some little vulgar thing.

God. Whilst thou prov'dst pure; and that in thee
I could glass all my Deity:
How glad did I from Heaven depart,
To find a lodging in thy heart!

Soul. Now Fame and Greatness bear the sway,
('Tis they that hold my prisons Key:)
For whom my soul would die, might she
Leave them her Immortalitie.

God. I, and some few pure Souls conspire,
And burn both in a mutual fire,
For whom I'ld die once more, ere they
Should miss of Heavens eternal day.

Soul. But Lord! what if I turn again,
And with an adamantine chain,
Lock me to thee? What if I chase
The world away to give thee place?

God. Then though these souls in whom I joy
Are *Seraphins*, Thou but a toy,
A foolish toy, yet once more I
Would with thee live, and for thee die.

Ignoto

Reliquiæ Wottonianæ, 1651 (text 1672)

43 *De Morte*

MANS life's a Tragedy: his mothers womb
(From which he enters) is the tyring room;
This spacious earth the Theater; and the Stage
That Country which he lives in: Passions, Rage,
Folly, and Vice are Actors: The first cry
The Prologue to th' ensuing Tragedy.
The former act consisteth of dumb shows;
The second, he to more perfection grows;
I'th third he is a man, and doth begin
To nurture vice, and act the deeds of sin:
I'th fourth declines; i'th fifth diseases clog
And trouble him; then Death's his Epilogue.

Ignoto

Reliquiæ Wottonianæ, 1651 (text 1672)

SIR ROBERT AYTON

1570–1638

44

(I lov'd thee once)

I LOV'D thee once, I'll love no more,
Thyne be the grief as is the blame,
Thou art not what thou wast before,
What reason I should be the same?
Hee that can love unlov'd againe
Hath better store of love than braine,
God send mee love my debts to pay,
While unthrifts fooles their love away.

Nothing could have my love o'erthrowne
If thou had still continu'd myne,
Nay if thou had remain'd thyne owne
I might perchance have yet been thyne,
But thou thy freedome did recall
That it thou might elsewhere inthrall,
And then how could I but disdaine
A Captives Captive to remaine?

When new desires had conquer'd thee
And chang'd the object of thy will,
It had been Lethargie in mee,
Noe constancy, to love thee still
Yea it had been a sin to go
And prostitute affection soe,
Since wee are taught noe prayers to say
To such as must to others pray.

Yet doe thou glory in thy choice,
Thy choice of his good fortune boast,
I'll neither grieve nor yet rejoice
To see him gaine what I have lost;
 The hight of my disdaine shall be
 To laugh at him, to blush for thee,
 To love thee still, but goe no more
 A begging at a beggars door.

British Museum (Add. MS. 10308)

45 *To his Forsaken Mistresse*

I DO confesse th' art smooth and fair,
 And I might ha' gone neer to love thee,
Had I not found the slightest pray'r
That lip could move, had pow'r to move thee.
But I can let thee now alone,
As worthy to be lov'd by none.

I do confess th' art sweet, yet find
Thee such an Unthrift of thy Sweets;
Thy favours are but like the wind,
Which kisseth ev'ry thing it meets:
And since thou canst with more than one,
Th' art worthy to be kiss'd by none.

The morning Rose that untouch'd stands,
Arm'd with her briars, how sweet she smells!
But pluck'd, and strain'd through ruder hands,
Her sweets no longer with her dwells;
But Scent and Beauty both are gone,
And Leaves fall from her one by one.

Such Fate ere long will thee betide,
When thou hast handled been a while,
With sere Flow'rs to be thrown aside;
And I shall sigh when some will smile,
To see thy love to ev'ry one
Hath brought thee to be lov'd by none.

Playford, *Select Ayres and Dialogues*, 1659

46 *(When thou did thinke I did not love)*

WHEN thou did thinke I did not love
Then thou did dote on mee,
Now when thou finds that I doe prove
As kinde as kinde can bee,
Love dyes in thee.

What way to fyre the Mercurie
Of thy Inconstant mynde?
Methinkes it were good policie
For mee to turne unkinde
To make thee kinde,

Yet will I not good nature strayne
To buy at soe greate cost,
That which before I doe obtaine
I make accompt almost
That it is lost.

And though I might myselfe excuse
By Imitating thee,
Yet will I noe examples use
That may bewray in mee
Lightness to bee.

But since I gave thee once my heart
  My constancy shall show
That though thou play the woman's part
  And from a friend turns foe,
    Men doe not soe.

British Museum (Add. MS. 10308)

47 *Upon a Diamond cut in forme of a heart set with a Crowne above, and a bloody dart piercing it sent in a New-yeares gift*

THOU sent to mee a heart was Crown'd
I thought it had been thine,
But when I saw it had a wound
I knew the heart was Mine.
A bounty of a strange conceate
To give myne owne to mee,
And give it in a worse Estate
Than it was giv'n to thee.
The heart I sent it had noe paine,
It was intire and sound,
But thou did send it back againe
Sick of a deadly wound.
Oh Heavens how would you use a heart
That should Rebellious be,
When you undoe it with a dart
That yieldes itselfe to thee?
Yet wish I it had noe more paine
Than from the wound proceedes;
More for the sending back againe
Than for the wound it bleedes.
Envy will say some misdesert
Hath caus'd thee turn 't away,

And where it was thy fault, thy Art
The blame on it will lay.
Yet thou dost know that noe defect
In it thou couldst reprove,
Thou only fear'd it should infect
Thy loveless heart with love,
A crime which if it could commit
Would so indear 't to thee
That thou would rather harbour it
Than send it back to mee.
Yet keepe it still, or if poore heart
It hath been thine too long,
Send mee it back as free from smart
As it was free from wrong.

British Museum (Add. MS. 10308)

48 (*Wrong not sweete Empress of my heart*)

WRONG not sweete Empress of my heart
The merit of true passion
Pretending that he feeles no smart
That sues for no compassion,
Since if my plaints come not t' approve
The conquest of thy beautie,
It comes not from defect of love
But from excess of duty.
For knowing that I sue to serve
A sainte of such perfection
As all desire but none deserve
A place in her affection,
I rather chuse to want reliefe
Than venter the revealing,

Where glory recommends the griefe
  Dispayre distrusts the healing.
Thus those desires which aime too high
  For any mortal lover
When reason cannot make them die
  Discretion doth them cover.
Yet when discretion bids them leave
  The plaints which they should utter,
Then thy discretion may perceive
  That silence is a suitor.
Silence in love bewrays more woe
  Than words though never so witty,
A beggar that is dumbe you knowe
  Doth merit double pity.
Then wrong not deare heart of my heart
  My true though secret passion,
He merits most that hides his smart
  And sues for no compassion.

British Museum (Add. MS. 10308)

THOMAS MIDDLETON AND WILLIAM ROWLEY

1570?–1627 1585?–1642?

49 *Song*

TRIP it Gipsies, trip it fine,
  Shew tricks and lofty Capers;
At threading Needles we repine,
    And leaping over Rapiers.
Pindy Pandy rascall toyes,
    We scorne cutting Purses,
Tho we live by making noyse,
    For cheating none can curse us.

Over High-wayes, over low,
And over Stones and Gravell,
Tho we trip it on the Toe,
And thus for Silver travell;
Tho our Dances waste our backs,
At night fat Capons mend them;
Eggs well brew'd in Butter'd-sack,
Our Wenches say befriend them.

Oh that all the World were mad,
Then should we have fine Dancing,
Hobby horses would be had,
And brave Girles keepe a prancing.
Beggars would on Cock-horse ride,
And Boobies fall a roaring,
And Cuckolds, tho no Hornes be spied,
Be one another goring.

Welcome Poet to our Ging,
Make Rimes, we'll give thee reason,
Canary Bees thy braines shall sting,
Mull-sack did ne'er speake Treason.
Peter-see-me shall wash thy nowle,
And Malligo Glasses fox thee,
If Poet thou tosse not bowle for bowle
Thou shalt not kisse a Doxie.

From The Spanish Gipsie, 1653. Act 3, Sc. 1

Ging: gang. Peter-see-me: *Pedro Ximenes*, a sweet Spanish wine. Malligo: Malaga. fox: intoxicate.

JOHN CHALKHILL

fl. 1600

50 *Rhotus on Arcadia*

ARCADIA was of old (said he) a State
Subject to none but their own Laws and Fate:
Superior there was none, but what old age
And hoary hairs had rais'd; the wise and sage,
Whose gravity, when they were rich in years,
Begat a civil reverence more than fears
In the well-manner'd people; at that day
All was in common, every man bare sway
O'er his own Family; the jars that rose
Were soon appeas'd by such grave men as those:
This mine and thine, that we so cavil for,
Was then not heard of; he that was most poor
Was rich in his content, and liv'd as free
As they whose flocks were greatest, nor did he
Envy his great abundance, nor the other
Disdain the low condition of his Brother,
But lent him from his store to mend his state;
And with his love he quits him, thanks his fate,
And taught by his example, seeks out such
As wants his help, that he may do as much.
Their Laws, e'en from their childhood, rich and poor
Had written in their hearts by conning o'er
The Legacies of good old men, whose memories
Out-live their Monuments: the grave advice
They left behind in writing; this was that
That made *Arcadia* then so blest a State,
Their wholesome Laws had linkt them so in one,
They liv'd in peace and sweet communion.

Peace brought forth plenty, plenty bred content,
And that crown'd all their pains with merriment.
They had no foe, secure they liv'd in Tents,
All was their own they had, they paid no rents;
Their Sheep found cloathing, Earth provided food,
And Labour drest them as their wills thought good.
On unbought Delicates their Hunger fed,
And for their Drink the swelling Clusters bled:
The Vallies rang with their delicious strains,
And pleasure revell'd on those happy Plains,
Content and Labor gave them length of days,
And Peace serv'd in delight a thousand ways.
The golden Age before *Deucalion*'s Flood
Was not more happy, nor the folk more good.
But Time that eats the Children he begets,
And is less satisfied the more he eats,
Led on by Fate that terminates all things,
Ruin'd our State, by sending of us Kings:
Ambition (Sins first-born) the bane of State,
Stole into men, puffing them up with hate
And emulous desires; Love waxes cold,
And into Iron freeze the age of Gold.
The Laws contempt made cruelty step in,
And stead of curbing animated Sin,
The Rich man tramples on the Poor man's back,
Raising his Fortunes by his Brothers wrack.
The wronged Poor necessity 'gan teach,
To live by Rapine, stealing from the Rich.
The Temples, which Devotion had erected
In honor of the Gods, were now neglected.
No Altar-smoaks with sacrificed Beasts,
No Incense offer'd, no Love-strength'ning Feasts.

Men's greedy Avarice made Gods of Clay,
Their Gold and Silver: Field to Field they lay,
And House to House; no matter how 'twas got,
The hand of Justice they regarded not.
Like a distemper'd Body Fever-shaken,
When with combustion every Limb is taken:
The Head wants ease, the heavy Eyes want sleep,
The beating Pulse no just proportion keep;
The Tongue talks idly, reason cannot rule it,
And the Heart fires the Air drawn in to cool it.
The Palate relisheth no meat, the Ears
But ill affected with the sweets it hears.
The Hands deny their aid to help him up,
And fall, as to his lips they lift the cup.
The Legs and Feet disjoynted, and useless,
Shrinking beneath the burden of the Flesh.

From *Thealma and Clearchus*, 1683

JOHN DONNE

1573–1631

51 ### *The Good-morrow*

I WONDER by my troth, what thou, and I
Did, till we lov'd? were we not wean'd till then?
But suck'd on countrey pleasures, childishly?
Or snorted we in the seaven sleepers den?
T'was so; But this, all pleasures fancies bee.
If ever any beauty I did see,
Which I desir'd, and got, t'was but a dreame of thee.

And now good morrow to our waking soules,
Which watch not one another out of feare;
For love, all love of other sights controules,
And makes one little roome, an every where.
Let sea-discoverers to new worlds have gone,
Let Maps to others, worlds on worlds have showne,
Let us possesse one world, each hath one, and is one.

My face in thine eye, thine in mine appeares,
And true plaine hearts doe in the faces rest,
Where can we finde two better hemispheares
Without sharpe North, without declining West?
What ever dies, was not mixt equally;
If our two loves be one, or, thou and I
Love so alike, that none doe slacken, none can die.

Songs and Sonnets, 1633

52 *The Canonization*

FOR Godsake hold your tongue, and let me love,
  Or chide my palsie, or my gout,
My five gray haires, or ruin'd fortune flout,
  With wealth your state, your minde with Arts improve,
    Take you a course, get you a place,
    Observe his honour, or his grace,
Or the Kings reall, or his stamped face
  Contemplate, what you will, approve,
  So you will let me love.

Alas, alas, who's injur'd by my love?
  What merchants ships have my sighs drown'd?
Who saies my teares have overflow'd his ground?

When did my colds a forward spring remove?
When did the heats which my veines fill
Adde one more to the plaguie Bill?
Soldiers finde warres, and Lawyers finde out still
Litigious men, which quarrels move,
Though she and I do love.

Call us what you will, wee are made such by love;
Call her one, mee another flye,
We'are Tapers too, and at our owne cost die,
And wee in us finde the'Eagle and the Dove.
The Phœnix riddle hath more wit
By us, we two being one, are it.
So to one neutrall thing both sexes fit,
Wee die and rise the same, and prove
Mysterious by this love.

Wee can die by it, if not live by love,
And if unfit for tombes and hearse
Our legend bee, it will be fit for verse;
And if no peece of Chronicle wee prove,
We'll build in sonnets pretty roomes;
As well a well-wrought urne becomes
The greatest ashes, as halfe-acre tombes,
And by these hymnes, all shall approve
Us *Canoniz'd* for Love:

And thus invoke us; You whom reverend love
Made one anothers hermitage;
You, to whom love was peace, that now is rage;
Who did the whole worlds soule contract, and drove

Into the glasses of your eyes
(So made such mirrors, and such spies,
That they did all to you epitomize,)
Countries, Townes, Courts: Beg from above
A patterne of your love!

Songs and Sonnets, 1633

53

Lovers infinitenesse

IF yet I have not all thy love,
Deare, I shall never have it all,
I cannot breathe one other sigh, to move,
Nor can intreat one other teare to fall,
And all my treasure, which should purchase thee,
Sighs, teares, and oathes, and letters I have spent,
Yet no more can be due to mee,
Than at the bargaine made was ment,
If then thy gift of love were partiall,
That some to mee, some should to others fall,
Deare, I shall never have Thee All.

Or if then thou gavest mee all,
All was but All, which thou hadst then;
But if in thy heart, since, there be or shall,
New love created bee, by other men,
Which have their stocks intire, and can in teares,
In sighs, in oathes, and letters outbid mee,
This new love may beget new feares,
For, this love was not vowed by thee.
And yet it was, thy gift being generall,
The ground, thy heart is mine, what ever shall
Grow there, deare, I should have it all.

Yet I would not have all yet,
Hee that hath all can have no more,
And since my love doth every day admit
New growth, thou shouldst have new rewards in store;
Thou canst not every day give me thy heart,
If thou canst give it, then thou never gavest it:
Loves riddles are, that though thy heart depart,
It stayes at home, and thou with losing savest it:
But wee will have a way more liberall,
Than changing hearts, to joyne them, so wee shall
  Be one, and one anothers All.

Songs and Sonnets, 1633

54 *Song*

SWEETEST love, I do not goe,
  For wearinesse of thee,
Nor in hope the world can show
  A fitter Love for mee;
    But since that I
Must dye at last, 'tis best,
To use my selfe in jest
  Thus by fain'd deaths to dye;

Yesternight the Sunne went hence,
  And yet is here to day,
He hath no desire nor sense,
  Nor halfe so short a way:
    Then feare not mee,
But beleeve that I shall make
Speedier journeys, since I take
  More wings and spurres than hee.

JOHN DONNE

O how feeble is mans power,
 That if good fortune fall,
Cannot adde another houre,
 Nor a lost houre recall!
  But come bad chance,
And wee joyne to'it our strength,
And wee teach it art and length,
 It selfe o'er us to'advance.

When thou sigh'st, thou sigh'st not winde,
 But sigh'st my soule away,
When thou weep'st, unkindly kinde,
 My lifes blood doth decay.
  It cannot bee
That thou lov'st mee, as thou say'st,
If in thine my life thou waste,
 Thou art the best of mee.

Let not thy divining heart
 Forethinke me any ill,
Destiny may take thy part,
 And may thy feares fulfill;
  But thinke that wee
Are but turn'd aside to sleepe;
They who one another keepe
 Alive, ne'er parted bee.

Songs and Sonnets, 1633

55 *Aire and Angels*

TWICE or thrice had I loved thee,
  Before I knew thy face or name;
So in a voice, so in a shapelesse flame,
Angells affect us oft, and worship'd bee;
  Still when, to where thou wert, I came,
Some lovely glorious nothing I did see.
  But since my soule, whose child love is,
Takes limmes of flesh, and else could nothing doe,
  More subtile than the parent is,
Love must not be, but take a body too,
  And therefore what thou wert, and who,
    I bid Love aske, and now
That it assume thy body, I allow,
And fixe it selfe in thy lip, eye, and brow.

Whilst thus to ballast love, I thought,
And so more steddily to have gone,
With wares which would sinke admiration,
I saw, I had loves pinnace overfraught,
  Ev'ry thy haire for love to worke upon
Is much too much, some fitter must be sought;
  For, nor in nothing, nor in things
Extreme, and scatt'ring bright, can love inhere;
  Then as an Angell, face and wings
Of aire, not pure as it, yet pure doth weare,
  So thy love may be my loves spheare;
    Just such disparitie
As is twixt Aire and Angells puritie,
'Twixt womens love, and mens will ever bee.

Songs and Sonnets, 1633

56 *The Anniversarie*

ALL Kings, and all their favorites,
All glory of honors, beauties, wits,
The Sun it selfe, which makes times, as they passe,
Is elder by a yeare, now, than it was
When thou and I first one another saw:
All other things, to their destruction draw,
Only our love hath no decay;
This, no to morrow hath, nor yesterday,
Running it never runs from us away,
But truly keepes his first, last, everlasting day.

Two graves must hide thine and my corse,
If one might, death were no divorce.
Alas, as well as other Princes, wee,
(Who Prince enough in one another bee,)
Must leave at last in death, these eyes, and eares,
Oft fed with true oathes, and with sweet salt teares;
But soules where nothing dwells but love
(All other thoughts being inmates) then shall prove
This, or a love increased there above,
When bodies to their graves, soules from their graves remove.

And then wee shall be throughly blest,
But wee no more, than all the rest;
Here upon earth, we'are Kings, and none but wee
Can be such Kings, nor of such subjects bee.
Who is so safe as wee? where none can doe
Treason to us, except one of us two.

inmates, i.e. lodgers.

True and false feares let us refraine,
Let us love nobly, and live, and adde againe
Yeares and yeares unto yeares, till we attaine
To write threescore: this is the second of our raigne.

Songs and Sonnets, 1633

57

Twicknam garden

BLASTED with sighs, and surrounded with teares,
Hither I come to seeke the spring,
And at mine eyes, and at mine eares,
Receive such balmes, as else cure every thing;
But O, selfe traytor, I do bring
The spider love, which transubstantiates all,
And can convert Manna to gall,
And that this place may thoroughly be thought
True Paradise, I have the serpent brought.

'Twere wholsomer for mee, that winter did
Benight the glory of this place,
And that a grave frost did forbid
These trees to laugh, and mocke mee to my face;
But that I may not this disgrace
Indure, nor yet leave loving, Love let mee
Some senslesse peece of this place bee;
Make me a mandrake, so I may groane here,
Or a stone fountaine weeping out my yeare.

Hither with christall vyals, lovers come,
And take my teares, which are loves wine,
And try your mistresse Teares at home,
For all are false, that taste not just like mine;
Alas, hearts do not in eyes shine,

Nor can you more judge womans thoughts by teares,
  Than by her shadow, what she weares.
O perverse sexe, where none is true but shee,
  Who 's therefore true, because her truth kills mee.

Songs and Sonnets, 1633

58 *The Dreame*

DEARE love, for nothing lesse than thee
Would I have broke this happy dreame,
    It was a theame
For reason, much too strong for phantasie,
Therefore thou wakd'st me wisely; yet
My Dreame thou brok'st not, but continued'st it,
Thou art so truth, that thoughts of thee suffice,
To make dreames truths; and fables histories;
Enter these armes, for since thou thoughtst it best,
Not to dreame all my dreame, let's act the rest.

As lightning, or a Tapers light,
Thine eyes, and not thy noise wak'd mee;
    Yet I thought thee
(For thou lovest truth) an Angell, at first sight,
But when I saw thou sawest my heart,
And knew'st my thoughts, beyond an Angels art,
When thou knew'st what I dreamt, when thou knew'st when
Excesse of joy would wake me, and cam'st then,
I must confesse, it could not chuse but bee
Prophane, to thinke thee any thing but thee.

Coming and staying show'd thee, thee,
But rising makes me doubt, that now,
    Thou art not thou.
That love is weake, where feare's as strong as hee;

'Tis not all spirit, pure, and brave,
If mixture it of *Feare*, *Shame*, *Honor*, have.
Perchance as torches which must ready bee,
Men light and put out, so thou deal'st with mee,
Thou cam'st to kindle, goest to come; Then I
Will dreame that hope againe, but else would die.

Songs and Sonnets, 1633

59 *A Valediction: of weeping*

LET me powre forth
My teares before thy face, whil'st I stay here,
For thy face coines them, and thy stampe they beare,
And by this Mintage they are something worth,
For thus they bee
Pregnant of thee;
Fruits of much griefe they are, emblems of more,
When a teare falls, that thou falst which it bore,
So thou and I are nothing then, when on a diverse shore.

On a round ball
A workeman that hath copies by, can lay
An Europe, Afrique, and an Asia,
And quickly make that, which was nothing, *All*,
So doth each teare,
Which thee doth weare,
A globe, yea world by that impression grow,
Till thy teares mixt with mine doe overflow
This world, by waters sent from thee, my heaven dissolved so.

O more than Moone,
Draw not up seas to drowne me in thy spheare,
Weepe me not dead, in thine armes, but forbeare
To teach the sea, what it may doe too soone;
Let not the winde
Example finde,
To doe me more harme, than it purposeth;
Since thou and I sigh one anothers breath,
Who e'er sighes most, is cruellest, and hastes the others death.

Songs and Sonnets, 1633

60

The Message

SEND home my long strayd eyes to mee,
Which (Oh) too long have dwelt on thee;
Yet since there they have learn'd such ill,
Such forc'd fashions,
And false passions,
That they be
Made by thee
Fit for no good sight, keep them still.

Send home my harmlesse heart againe,
Which no unworthy thought could staine;
But if it be taught by thine
To make jestings
Of protestings,
And crosse both
Word and oath,
Keepe it, for then 'tis none of mine.

Yet send me back my heart and eyes,
That I may know, and see thy lyes,
And may laugh and joy, when thou
    Art in anguish
    And dost languish
        For some one
        That will none,
Or prove as false as thou art now.

Songs and Sonnets, 1633

61 *A nocturnall upon S. Lucies day,*
Being the shortest day

TIS the yeares midnight, and it is the dayes,
  Lucies, who scarce seaven houres herself unmaskes,
  The Sunne is spent, and now his flasks
  Send forth light squibs, no constant rayes;
    The worlds whole sap is sunke:
The generall balme th'hydroptique earth hath drunk,
Whither, as to the beds-feet, life is shrunke,
Dead and enterr'd; yet all these seeme to laugh,
Compar'd with mee, who am their Epitaph.

Study me then, you who shall lovers bee
At the next world, that is, at the next Spring:
  For I am every dead thing,
  In whom love wrought new Alchimie.
    For his art did expresse
A quintessence even from nothingnesse,
From dull privations, and leane emptinesse:
He ruin'd mee, and I am re-begot
Of absence, darknesse, death; things which are not.

every: a very *some editions*.

All others, from all things, draw all that's good,
Life, soule, forme, spirit, whence they beeing have;
  I, by loves limbecke, am the grave
  Of all, that's nothing. Oft a flood
    Have wee two wept, and so
Drownd the whole world, us two; oft did we grow
To be two Chaosses, when we did show
Care to ought else; and often absences
Withdrew our soules, and made us carcasses.

But I am by her death, (which word wrongs her)
Of the first nothing, the Elixer grown;
  Were I a man, that I were one,
  I needs must know; I should preferre,
    If I were any beast,
Some ends, some means; Yea plants, yea stones detest,
And love; All, all some properties invest;
If I an ordinary nothing were,
As shadow, a light, and body must be here.

But I am None; nor will my Sunne renew.
You lovers, for whose sake, the lesser Sunne
  At this time to the Goat is runne
  To fetch new lust, and give it you,
    Enjoy your summer all;
Since shee enjoyes her long nights festivall,
Let mee prepare towards her, and let mee call
This houre her Vigill, and her Eve, since this
Both the yeares, and the dayes deep midnight is.

Songs and Sonnets, 1633

62 *The Apparition*

WHEN by thy scorne, O murdresse, I am dead,
And that thou thinkst thee free
From all solicitation from mee,
Then shall my ghost come to thy bed,
And thee, fain'd vestall, in worse armes shall see;
Then thy sicke taper will begin to winke,
And he, whose thou art then, being tir'd before,
Will, if thou stirre, or pinch to wake him, thinke
Thou call'st for more,
And in false sleepe will from thee shrinke,
And then poore Aspen wretch, neglected thou
Bath'd in a cold quicksilver sweat wilt lye
A veryer ghost than I;
What I will say, I will not tell thee now,
Lest that preserve thee; and since my love is spent,
I'had rather thou shouldst painfully repent,
Than by my threatnings rest still innocent.

Songs and Sonnets, 1633

63 *A Valediction: forbidding mourning*

AS virtuous men passe mildly away,
And whisper to their soules, to goe,
Whilst some of their sad friends doe say,
The breath goes now, and some say, no:

So let us melt, and make no noise,
No teare-floods, nor sigh-tempests move,
T'were prophanation of our joyes
To tell the layetie our love.

Moving of th'earth brings harmes and feares,
  Men reckon what it did and meant,
But trepidation of the spheares,
  Though greater farre, is innocent.

Dull sublunary lovers love
  (Whose soule is sense) cannot admit
Absence, because it doth remove
  Those things which elemented it.

But we by a love, so much refin'd,
  That our selves know not what it is,
Inter-assured of the mind,
  Care lesse, eyes, lips, and hands to misse.

Our two soules therefore, which are one,
  Though I must goe, endure not yet
A breach, but an expansion,
  Like gold to aiery thinnesse beate.

If they be two, they are two so
  As stiffe twin compasses are two,
Thy soule the fixt foot, makes no show
  To move, but doth, if the'other doe.

And though it in the center sit,
  Yet when the other far doth rome,
It leanes, and hearkens after it,
  And growes erect, as that comes home.

Such wilt thou be to mee, who must
  Like th'other foot, obliquely runne;
Thy firmness makes my circle just,
  And makes me end, where I begunne.

Songs and Sonnets, 1633

makes my circle] drawes my circle *one MS*.

64 *The Extasie*

WHERE, like a pillow on a bed,
A Pregnant banke swell'd up, to rest
The violets reclining head,
Sat we two, one anothers best.
Our hands were firmely cimented
With a fast balme, which thence did spring,
Our eye-beames twisted, and did thred
Our eyes, upon one double string;
So to'entergraft our hands, as yet
Was all the meanes to make us one,
And pictures in our eyes to get
Was all our propagation.
As 'twixt two equall Armies, Fate
Suspends uncertaine victorie,
Our soules, (which to advance their state,
Were gone out,) hung 'twixt her, and mee.
And whil'st our soules negotiate there,
Wee like sepulchrall statues lay;
All day, the same our postures were,
And wee said nothing, all the day.
If any, so by love refin'd,
That he soules language understood,
And by good love were growen all minde,
Within convenient distance stood,
He (though he knew not which soule spake,
Because both meant, both spake the same)
Might thence a new concoction take,
And part farre purer than he came.
This Extasie doth unperplex
(We said) and tell us what we love,

Wee see by this, it was not sexe,
  Wee see, we saw not what did move:
But as all severall soules containe
  Mixture of things, they know not what,
Love, these mixt soules, doth mixe againe,
  And makes both one, each this and that.
A single violet transplant,
  The strength, the colour, and the size,
(All which before was poore, and scant,)
  Redoubles still, and multiplies.
When love, with one another so
  Interinanimates two soules,
That abler soule, which thence doth flow,
  Defects of lonelinesse controules.
Wee then, who are this new soule, know,
  Of what we are compos'd, and made,
For, th'Atomies of which we grow,
  Are soules, whom no change can invade.
But O alas, so long, so farre
  Our bodies why doe wee forbeare?
They are ours, though they are not wee, Wee are
  The intelligences, they the spheare.
We owe them thankes, because they thus,
  Did us, to us, at first convay,
Yielded their forces, sense, to us,
  Nor are drosse to us, but allay.
On man heavens influence workes not so,
  But that it first imprints the ayre,
So soule into the soule may flow,
  Though it to body first repaire.
As our blood labours to beget
  Spirits, as like soules as it can,

Because such fingers need to knit
  That subtile knot, which makes us man:
So must pure lovers soules descend
  T'affections, and to faculties,
Which sense may reach and apprehend,
  Else a great Prince in prison lies.
To'our bodies turne wee then, that so
  Weake men on love reveal'd may looke;
Loves mysteries in soules doe grow,
  But yet the body is his booke.
And if some lover, such as wee,
  Have heard this dialogue of one,
Let him still marke us, he shall see
  Small change, when we'are to bodies gone.

Songs and Sonnets, 1633

65 *The Funerall*

WHO ever comes to shroud me, do not harme
    Nor question much
That subtile wreath of haire, which crowns my arme;
The mystery, the signe you must not touch,
    For 'tis my outward Soule,
Viceroy to that, which then to heaven being gone,
    Will leave this to controule,
And keepe these limbes, her Provinces, from dissolution.

For if the sinewie thread my braine lets fall
    Through every part,
Can tye those parts, and make mee one of all;
These haires which upward grew, and strength and art

Have from a better braine,
Can better do'it; Except she meant that I
By this should know my pain,
As prisoners then are manacled, when they'are condemn'd to die.

What e'er shee meant by'it, bury it with me,
For since I am
Loves martyr, it might breed idolatrie,
If into others hands these Reliques came;
As 'twas humility
To afford to it all that a Soule can doe,
So, 'tis some bravery,
That since you would save none of mee, I bury some of you.

Songs and Sonnets, 1633

66 *The Blossome*

LITTLE think'st thou, poore flower,
Whom I have watch'd sixe or seaven dayes,
And seene thy birth, and seene what every houre
Gave to thy growth, thee to this height to raise,
And now dost laugh and triumph on this bough,
Little think'st thou
That it will freeze anon, and that I shall
To morrow finde thee falne, or not at all.

Little think'st thou poore heart
That labour'st yet to nestle thee,
And think'st by hovering here to get a part
In a forbidden or forbidding tree,

And hop'st her stiffenesse by long siege to bow:
Little think'st thou,
That thou to morrow, ere that Sunne doth wake,
Must with this Sunne, and mee a journey take.

But thou which lov'st to bee
Subtile to plague thy selfe, wilt say,
Alas, if you must goe, what's that to mee?
Here lyes my businesse, and here I will stay:
You goe to friends, whose love and meanes present
Various content
To your eyes, eares, and tongue, and every part.
If then your body goe, what need you a heart?

Well then, stay here; but know,
When thou hast stayd and done thy most;
A naked thinking heart, that makes no show,
Is to a woman, but a kinde of Ghost;
How shall shee know my heart; or having none,
Know thee for one?
Practise may make her know some other part,
But take my word, shee doth not know a Heart.

Meet mee at London, then,
Twenty dayes hence, and thou shalt see
Mee fresher, and more fat, by being with men,
Than if I had staid still with her and thee.
For Gods sake, if you can, be you so too:
I would give you
There, to another friend, whom wee shall finde
As glad to have my body, as my minde.

Songs and Sonnets, 1633

67

The Relique

WHEN my grave is broke up againe
Some second ghest to entertaine,
(For graves have learn'd that woman-head
To be to more than one a Bed)
And he that digs it, spies
A bracelet of bright haire about the bone,
Will he not let'us alone,
And thinke that there a loving couple lies,
Who thought that this device might be some way
To make their soules, at the last busie day,
Meet at this grave, and make a little stay?

If this fall in a time, or land,
Where mis-devotion doth command,
Then, he that digges us up, will bring
Us, to the Bishop, and the King,
To make us Reliques; then
Thou shalt be a Mary Magdalen, and I
A something else thereby;
All women shall adore us, and some men;
And since at such time, miracles are sought,
I would have that age by this paper taught
What miracles wee harmelesse lovers wrought.

First, we lov'd well and faithfully,
Yet knew not what wee lov'd, nor why,
Difference of sex no more wee knew,
Than our Guardian Angells doe;
Coming and going, wee
Perchance might kisse, but not between those meales;
Our hands ne'er toucht the seales,

Which nature, injur'd by late law, sets free:
These miracles wee did; but now alas,
All measure, and all language, I should passe,
Should I tell what a miracle shee was.

Songs and Sonnets, 1633

68 *The Prohibition*

TAKE heed of loving mee,
At least remember, I forbade it thee;
Not that I shall repaire my'unthrifty waste
Of Breath and Blood, upon thy sighes, and teares,
By being to thee then what to me thou wast;
But, so great Joy, our life at once outweares,
Then, lest thy love, by my death, frustrate bee,
If thou love mee, take heed of loving mee.

Take heed of hating mee,
Or too much triumph in the Victorie.
Not that I shall be mine owne officer,
And hate with hate againe retaliate;
But thou wilt lose the stile of conquerour,
If I, thy conquest, perish by thy hate.
Then, lest my being nothing lessen thee,
If thou hate mee, take heed of hating mee.

Yet, love and hate mee too,
So, these extreames shall neithers office doe;
Love mee, that I may die the gentler way;
Hate mee, because thy love is too great for mee;
Or let these two, themselves, not me decay;
So shall I, live, thy Stage, not triumph bee;
Lest thou thy love and hate and mee undoe,
To let mee live, O love and hate mee too.

Songs and Sonnets, 1633

69 *A Lecture upon the Shadow*

STAND still, and I will read to thee
A Lecture, Love, in loves philosophy.
These three houres that we have spent,
Walking here, Two shadowes went
Along with us, which we our selves produc'd;
But, now the Sunne is just above our head,
We doe those shadowes tread;
And to brave clearnesse all things are reduc'd.
So whilst our infant loves did grow,
Disguises did, and shadowes, flow,
From us, and our cares; but, now 'tis not so.

That love hath not attain'd the high'st degree,
Which is still diligent lest others see.

Except our love at this noone stay,
We shall new shadowes make the other way.
As the first were made to blinde
Others; these which come behinde
Will worke upon our selves, and blind our eyes.
If our love faint, and westwardly decline;
To me thou, falsly, thine,
And I to thee mine actions shall disguise.
The morning shadowes weare away,
But these grow longer all the day,
But oh, loves day is short, if love decay.

Love is a growing, or full constant light;
And his first minute, after noone, is night.

Songs and Sonnets, 1635

70 *Elegie v. His Picture*

HERE take my Picture; though I bid farewell,
Thine, in my heart, where my soule dwells, shall dwell.
'Tis like me now, but I dead, 'twill be more
When wee are shadowes both, than 'twas before.
When weather-beaten I come backe; my hand,
Perhaps with rude oares torne, or Sun-beams tann'd,
My face and brest of haircloth, and my head
With cares rash sodaine hoarinesse o'erspread,
My body'a sack of bones, broken within,
And powders blew staines scatter'd on my skinne;
If rivall fooles taxe thee to'have lov'd a man,
So foule, and coarse, as, Oh, I may seeme than,
This shall say what I was: and thou shalt say,
Doe his hurts reach mee? doth my worth decay?
Or doe they reach his judging minde, that hee
Should now love lesse, what hee did love to see?
That which in him was faire and delicate,
Was but the milke, which in loves childish state
Did nurse it: who now'is growne strong enough
To feed on that, which to disused tastes seemes tough.

Elegies, 1633

71 *Elegie xii. His parting from her*

SINCE she must go, and I must mourn, come Night,
Environ me with darkness, whilst I write:
Shadow that hell, unto me, which alone
I am to suffer when my Love is gone.
Alas, the darkest Magick cannot do it,
Thou and greate Hell to boot are shadows to it.
Should *Cinthia* quit thee, *Venus*, and each starre,
It would not forme one thought dark as mine are.

I could lend thee obscureness now, and say,
Out of my self, There should be no more Day,
Such is already my felt want of sight,
Did not the fires within me force a light.
Oh Love, that fire and darkness should be mixt,
Or to thy Triumphs soe strange torments fixt?
Is't because thou thy self art blind, that wee
Thy Martyrs must no more each other see?
Or tak'st thou pride to break us on the wheel,
And view old Chaos in the Pains we feel?
Or have we left undone some mutual Right,
Through holy fear, that merits thy despight?
No, no. The fault was mine, impute it to me,
Or rather to conspiring destinie,
Which (since I lov'd for forme before) decreed,
That I should suffer when I lov'd indeed:
And therefore now, sooner than I can say,
I saw the golden fruit, 'tis rapt away.
Or as I had watcht one drop in a vast stream,
And I left wealthy only in a dream.
Yet Love, thou'rt blinder than thy self in this,
To vex my Dove-like friend for my amiss:
And, where my own sad truth may expiate
Thy wrath, to make her fortune run my fate:
So blinded Justice doth, when Favorites fall,
Strike them, their house, their friends, their followers all.
Was't not enough that thou didst dart thy fires
Into our blouds, inflaming our desires,
And made'st us sigh and glow, and pant, and burn,
And then thy self into our flame did'st turn?
Was't not enough, that thou didst hazard us
To paths in love so dark, so dangerous:

And those so ambush'd round with houshold spies,
And over all, thy husbands towring eyes
That flam'd with oylie sweat of jealousie:
Yet went we not still on with Constancie?
Have we not kept our guards, like spie on spie?
Had correspondence whilst the foe stood by?
Stoln (more to sweeten them) our many blisses
Of meetings, conference, embracements, kisses?
Shadow'd with negligence our most respects?
Varied our language through all dialects,
Of becks, winks, looks, and often under-boards
Spoke dialogues with our feet far from our words?
Have we prov'd all these secrets of our Art,
Yea, thy pale inwards, and thy panting heart?
And, after all this passed Purgatory,
Must sad divorce make us the vulgar story?
First let our eyes be riveted quite through
Our turning brains, and both our lips grow to:
Let our armes clasp like Ivy, and our fear
Freeze us together, that we may stick here,
Till Fortune, that would rive us, with the deed
Strain her eyes open, and it make them bleed:
For Love it cannot be, whom hitherto
I have accus'd, should such a mischief doe.
Oh Fortune, thou'rt not worth my least exclame,
And plague enough thou hast in thy own shame.
Do thy great worst, my friend and I have armes,
Though not against thy strokes, against thy harmes.
Rend us in sunder, thou canst not divide
Our bodies so, but that our souls are ty'd,
And we can love by letters still and gifts,
And thoughts and dreams; Love never wanteth shifts.

JOHN DONNE

I will not look upon the quickning Sun,
But straight her beauty to my sense shall run;
The ayre shall note her soft, the fire most pure;
Water suggest her clear, and the earth sure.
Time shall not lose our passages; the Spring
How fresh our love was in the beginning;
The Summer how it ripened in the eare;
And Autumn, what our golden harvests were.
The Winter I'll not think on to spite thee,
But count it a lost season, so shall shee.
And dearest Friend, since we must part, drown night
With hope of Day, burthens well borne are light.
Though cold and darkness longer hang somewhere,
Yet *Phoebus* equally lights all the Sphere.
And what he cannot in like Portions pay,
The world enjoyes in Mass, and so we may.
Be then ever your self, and let no woe
Win on your health, your youth, your beauty: so
Declare your self base Fortunes Enemy,
No less by your contempt than constancy:
That I may grow enamoured on your mind,
When my own thoughts I there reflected find.
For this to th'comfort of my Dear I vow,
My Deeds shall still be what my words are now;
The Poles shall move to teach me ere I start;
And when I change my Love, I'll change my heart;
Nay, if I wax but cold in my desire,
Think, heaven hath motion lost, and the world, fire:
Much more I could, but many words have made
That, oft, suspected which men would perswade;
Take therefore all in this: I love so true,
As I will never look for less in you. *Elegies*, 1669

72 *Epithalamion made at Lincolnes Inne*

THE Sun-beames in the East are spred,
Leave, leave, faire Bride, your solitary bed,
No more shall you returne to it alone,
It nurseth sadnesse, and your bodies print,
Like to a grave, the yielding downe doth dint;
You and your other you meet there anon;
Put forth, put forth that warme balme-breathing thigh,
Which when next time you in these sheets will smother,
There it must meet another,
Which never was, but must be, oft, more nigh;
Come glad from thence, goe gladder than you came,
To day put on perfection, and a womans name.

Daughters of London, you which bee
Our Golden Mines, and furnish'd Treasurie,
You which are Angels, yet still bring with you
Thousands of Angels on your mariage daies,
Help with your presence and device to praise
These rites, which also unto you grow due;
Conceitedly dress her, and be assign'd,
By you, fit place for every flower and jewell,
Make her for love fit fewell
As gay as Flora, and as rich as Inde;
So may shee faire, rich, glad, and in nothing lame,
To day put on perfection, and a womans name.

And you frolique Patricians,
Sonnes of these Senators, wealths deep oceans,
Ye painted courtiers, barrels of others wits,
Yee country men, who but your beasts love none,
Yee of those fellowships whereof hee's one,

Of study and play made strange Hermaphrodits,
Here shine; This Bridegroom to the Temple bring.
Loe, in yon path which store of straw'd flowers graceth,
The sober virgin paceth;
Except my sight faile, 'tis no other thing;
Weep not nor blush, here is no griefe nor shame,
To day put on perfection, and a womans name.

Thy two-leav'd gates faire Temple unfold,
And these two in thy sacred bosome hold,
Till, mystically joyn'd, but one they bee;
Then may thy leane and hunger-starved wombe
Long time expect their bodies and their tombe,
Long after their owne parents fatten thee.
All elder claimes, and all cold barrennesse,
All yeelding to new loves bee far for ever,
Which might these two dissever,
All wayes all th'other may each one possesse;
For, the best Bride, best worthy of praise and fame,
To day puts on perfection, and a womans name.

Oh winter dayes bring much delight,
Not for themselves, but for they soon bring night;
Other sweets wait thee than these diverse meats,
Other disports than dancing jollities,
Other love tricks than glancing with the eyes,
But that the Sun still in our halfe Spheare sweates;
Hee flies in winter, but he now stands still.
Yet shadowes turne; Noone point he hath attain'd,
His steeds nill bee restrain'd,
But gallop lively downe the Westerne hill;
Thou shalt, when he hath runne the worlds half frame,
To night put on perfection, and a womans name.

The amorous evening starre is rose,
Why then should not our amorous starre inclose
  Her selfe in her wish'd bed? Release your strings
Musicians, and dancers take some truce
With these your pleasing labours, for great use
  As much wearinesse as perfection brings;
    You, and not only you, but all toyl'd beasts
Rest duly; at night all their toyles are dispensed;
But in their beds commenced
    Are other labours, and more dainty feasts;
She goes a maid, who, least she turne the same,
To night puts on perfection, and a womans name.

Thy virgins girdle now untie,
And in thy nuptiall bed (loves altar) lye
  A pleasing sacrifice; now dispossesse
Thee of these chaines and robes which were put on
T'adorne the day, not thee; for thou, alone,
  Like vertue'and truth, art best in nakednesse;
    This bed is onely to virginitie
A grave, but, to a better state, a cradle;
Till now thou wast but able
  To be what now thou art; then that by thee
No more bee said, *I may be*, but, *I am*,
To night put on perfection, and a womans name.

Even like a faithfull man content,
That this life for a better should be spent,
  So, shee a mothers rich style doth preferre,
And at the Bridegroomes wish'd approach doth lye,
Like an appointed lambe, when tenderly
  The priest comes on his knees t'embowell her;
    Now sleep or watch with more joy; and O light

Of heaven, to morrow rise thou hot, and early;
This Sun will love so dearely
        Her rest, that long, long we shall want her sight;
Wonders are wrought, for shee which had no maime,
To night puts on perfection, and a womans name.

Epithalamions, 1633

73 *Satyre iii*

KINDE pitty chokes my spleene; brave scorn forbids
Those teares to issue which swell my eye-lids;
I must not laugh, nor weepe sinnes, and be wise,
Can railing then cure these worne maladies?
Is not our Mistresse faire Religion,
As worthy of all our Soules devotion,
As vertue was to the first blinded age?
Are not heavens joyes as valiant to asswage
Lusts, as earths honour was to them? Alas,
As wee do them in meanes, shall they surpasse
Us in the end, and shall thy fathers spirit
Meete blinde Philosophers in heaven, whose merit
Of strict life may be imputed faith, and heare
Thee, whom hee taught so easie wayes and neare
To follow, damn'd? O if thou dar'st, feare this;
This feare great courage, and high valour is.
Dar'st thou ayd mutinous Dutch, and dar'st thou lay
Thee in ships woodden Sepulchers, a prey
To leaders rage, to stormes, to shot, to dearth?
Dar'st thou dive seas, and dungeons of the earth?
Hast thou couragious fire to thaw the ice
Of frozen North discoueries? and thrice
Colder than Salamanders, like divine
Children in th'oven, fires of Spaine, and the line,

Whose countries limbecks to our bodies bee,
Canst thou for gaine beare? and must every hee
Which cryes not, Goddesse, to thy Mistresse, draw,
Or eate thy poysonous words? courage of straw!
O desperate coward, wilt thou seeme bold, and
To thy foes and his (who made thee to stand
Sentinell in his worlds garrison) thus yeeld,
And for forbidden warres, leave th'appointed field?
Know thy foes: The foule Devill (whom thou
Strivest to please,) for hate, not love, would allow
Thee faine, his whole Realme to be quit; and as
The worlds all parts wither away and passe,
So the worlds selfe, thy other lov'd foe, is
In her decrepit wayne, and thou loving this,
Dost love a withered and worne strumpet; last,
Flesh (it selfes death) and joyes which flesh can taste,
Thou lovest; and thy faire goodly soule, which doth
Give this flesh power to taste joy, thou dost loath.
Seeke true religion. O where? Mirreus
Thinking her unhous'd here, and fled from us,
Seekes her at Rome; there, because hee doth know
That shee was there a thousand yeares agoe,
He loves her ragges so, as wee here obey
The statecloth where the Prince sate yesterday.
Crantz to such brave Loves will not be inthrall'd,
But loves her onely, who at Geneva is call'd
Religion, plaine, simple, sullen, yong,
Contemptuous, yet unhansome; As among
Lecherous humors, there is one that judges
No wenches wholsome, but course country drudges.
Graius stayes still at home here, and because

to be quit: to be free of

Some Preachers, vile ambitious bauds, and lawes
Still new like fashions, bid him thinke that shee
Which dwells with us, is onely perfect, hee
Imbraceth her, whom his Godfathers will
Tender to him, being tender, as Wards still
Take such wives as their Guardians offer, or
Pay valewes. Carelesse Phrygius doth abhorre
All, because all cannot be good, as one
Knowing some women whores, dares marry none.
Gracchus loves all as one, and thinkes that so
As women do in divers countries goe
In divers habits, yet are still one kinde,
So doth, so is Religion; and this blind-
nesse too much light breeds; but unmoved thou
Of force must one, and forc'd but one allow;
And the right; aske thy father which is shee,
Let him aske his; though truth and falshood bee
Neare twins, yet truth a little elder is;
Be busie to seeke her, beleeve mee this,
Hee's not of none, nor worst, that seekes the best.
To adore, or scorne an image, or protest,
May all be bad; doubt wisely; in strange way
To stand inquiring right, is not to stray;
To sleepe, or runne wrong, is. On a huge hill,
Cragged, and steep, Truth stands, and hee that will
Reach her, about must, and about must goe;
And what the hills suddenness resists, winne so;
Yet strive so, that before age, deaths twilight,
Thy Soule rest, for none can worke in that night.
To will, implyes delay, therefore now doe:
Hard deeds, the bodies paines; hard knowledge too
The mindes indeavours reach, and mysteries

Are like the Sunne, dazling, yet plaine to all eyes.
Keepe the truth which thou hast found; men do not stand
In so ill case here, that God hath with his hand
Sign'd Kings blank-charters to kill whom they hate,
Nor are they Vicars, but hangmen to Fate.
Foole and wretch, wilt thou let thy Soule be tyed
To mans lawes, by which she shall not be tryed
At the last day? Oh, will it then boot thee
To say a Philip, or a Gregory,
A Harry, or a Martin taught thee this?
Is not this excuse for mere contraries,
Equally strong? cannot both sides say so?
That thou mayest rightly obey power, her bounds know;
Those past, her nature, and name is chang'd; to be
Then humble to her is idolatrie.
As streames are, Power is; those blest flowers that dwell
At the rough streames calme head, thrive and do well,
But having left their roots, and themselves given
To the streames tyrannous rage, alas, are driven
Through mills, and rockes, and woods, and at last, almost
Consum'd in going, in the sea are lost:
So perish Soules, which more chuse mens unjust
Power from God claym'd, than God himselfe to trust.

Satyres, 1633

74 *To the Countesse of* Bedford
On New-yeares day

THIS twilight of two yeares, not past nor next,
Some embleme is of mee, or I of this,
Who Meteor-like, of stuffe and forme perplext,
Whose *what*, and *where*, in disputation is,
If I should call mee *any thing*, should misse.

I summe the yeares, and mee, and finde mee not
  Debtor to th'old, nor Creditor to th'new;
That cannot say, My thankes I have forgot,
  Nor trust I this with hopes, and yet scarce true
  This bravery is, since these times shew'd mee you.

In recompence I would show future times
  What you were, and teach them to'urge towards such.
Verse embalmes vertue; and Tombs, or Thrones of rimes,
  Preserve fraile transitory fame, as much
  As spice doth bodies from corrupt aires touch.

Mine are short-liv'd; the tincture of your name
  Creates in them, but dissipates as fast,
New spirits: for, strong agents with the same
  Force that doth warme and cherish, us doe wast;
  Kept hot with strong extracts, no bodies last:

So, my verse built of your just praise, might want
  Reason and likelihood, the firmest Base,
And made of miracle, now faith is scant,
  Will vanish soone, and so possesse no place,
  And you, and it, too much grace might disgrace.

When all (as truth commands assent) confesse
  All truth of you, yet they will doubt how I,
One corne of one low anthills dust, and lesse,
  Should name, know, or expresse a thing so high,
  And not an inch, measure infinity.

I cannot tell them, nor my selfe, nor you,
  But leave, lest truth b'endanger'd by my praise,
And turne to God, who knowes I think this true,
  And useth oft, when such a heart mis-sayes,
  To make it good, for, such a praiser prayes.

Hee will best teach you, how you should lay out
His stock of *beauty*, *learning*, *favour*, *blood*;
He will perplex security with doubt,
And cleare those doubts; hide from you,'and shew you good,
And so increase your appetite and food;

Hee will teach you, that good and bad have not
One latitude in cloysters, and in Court;
Indifferent there the greatest space hath got;
Some pitty'is not good there, some vaine disport,
On this side sinne, with that place may comport.

Yet he, as hee bounds seas, will fixe your houres,
Which pleasure, and delight may not ingresse,
And though what none else lost, be truliest yours,
Hee will make you, what you did not, possesse,
By using others, not vice, but weakenesse.

He will make you speake truths, and credibly,
And make you doubt, that others doe not so:
Hee will provide you keys, and locks, to spie,
And scape spies, to good ends, and hee will show
What you may not acknowledge, what not know.

For your owne conscience, he gives innocence,
But for your fame, a discreet warinesse,
And though to scape, than to revenge offence
Be better, he showes both, and to represse
Joy, when your state swells, *sadnesse* when 'tis lesse.

From need of teares he will defend your soule,
Or make a rebaptizing of one teare;
Hee cannot, (that 's, he will not) dis-inroule
Your name; and when with active joy we heare
This private Gospell, then 'tis our New Yeare.

Letters to Severall Personages, 1633

75 *Letter to Sir H. Wotton at his going Ambassador to Venice*

AFTER those reverend papers, whose soule is
Our good and great Kings lov'd hand and fear'd name,
By which to you he derives much of his,
And (how he may) makes you almost the same,

A Taper of his Torch, a copie writ
From his Originall, and a faire beame
Of the same warme, and dazeling Sun, though it
Must in another Sphere his vertue streame:

After those learned papers which your hand
Hath stor'd with notes of use and pleasure too,
From which rich treasury you may command
Fit matter whether you will write or doe:

After those loving papers, where friends send
With glad griefe, to your Sea-ward steps, farewell,
Which thicken on you now, as prayers ascend
To heaven in troupes at'a good mans passing bell:

Admit this honest paper, and allow
It such an audience as your selfe would aske;
What you must say at Venice this meanes now,
And hath for nature, what you have for taske:

To sweare much love, not to be chang'd before
Honour alone will to your fortune fit;
Nor shall I then honour your fortune, more
Than I have done your honour wanting it.

But 'tis an easier load (though both oppresse)
  To want, than governe greatnesse, for wee are
In that, our owne and onely businesse,
  In this, wee must for others vices care;

'Tis therefore well your spirits now are plac'd
  In their last Furnace, in activity;
Which fits them (Schooles and Courts and Warres o'erpast)
  To touch and test in any best degree.

For mee, (if there be such a thing as I)
  Fortune (if there be such a thing as shee)
Spies that I beare so well her tyranny,
  That she thinks nothing else so fit for mee;

But though she part us, to heare my oft prayers
  For your increase, God is as neere mee here;
And to send you what I shall begge, his staires
  In length and ease are alike every where.

Letters to Severall Personages, 1633

76 *From 'Of the Progresse of the Soule' The second Anniversarie* (1612)

(i)

Contemplation of our state in our deathbed

THINKE then, my soule, that death is but a Groome,
Which brings a Taper to the outward roome,
Whence thou spiest first a little glimmering light,
And after brings it nearer to thy sight:
For such approaches doth heaven make in death.
Thinke thy selfe labouring now with broken breath,

And thinke those broken and soft Notes to bee
Division, and thy happyest Harmonie.
Thinke thee laid on thy death-bed, loose and slacke;
And thinke that, but unbinding of a packe,
To take one precious thing, thy soule from thence.
Thinke thy selfe parch'd with fevers violence,
Anger thine ague more, by calling it
Thy Physicke; chide the slacknesse of the fit.
Thinke that thou hear'st thy knell, and think no more,
But that, as Bells cal'd thee to Church before,
So this, to the Triumphant Church, calls thee.
Thinke Satans Sergeants round about thee bee,
And thinke that but for Legacies they thrust;
Give one thy Pride, to'another give thy Lust:
Give them those sinnes which they gave thee before,
And trust th'immaculate blood to wash thy score.
Thinke thy friends weeping round, and thinke that they
Weepe but because they goe not yet thy way.
Thinke that they close thine eyes, and thinke in this,
That they confesse much in the world, amisse,
Who dare not trust a dead mans eye with that,
Which they from God, and Angels cover not.
Thinke that they shroud thee up, and think from thence
They reinvest thee in white innocence.
Thinke that thy body rots, and (if so low,
Thy soule exalted so, thy thoughts can goe,)
Think thee a Prince, who of themselves create
Wormes which insensibly devoure their State.
Thinke that they bury thee, and thinke that rite
Laies thee to sleepe but a Saint Lucies night.

Text 1633. Lines 85–120

(ii)

The soules ignorance in this life and knowledge in the next

POORE soule, in this thy flesh what dost thou know?
Thou know'st thy selfe so little, as thou know'st not,
How thou didst die, nor how thou wast begot.
Thou neither know'st, how thou at first cam'st in,
Nor how thou took'st the poyson of mans sinne.
Nor dost thou, (though thou know'st, that thou art so)
By what way thou art made immortall, know.
Thou art too narrow, wretch, to comprehend
Even thy selfe: yea though thou wouldst but bend
To know thy body. Have not all soules thought
For many ages, that our body'is wrought
Of Ayre, and Fire, and other Elements?
And now they thinke of new ingredients,
And one Soule thinkes one, and another way
Another thinkes, and 'tis an even lay.
Knowst thou but how the stone doth enter in
The bladders cave, and never breake the skinne?
Know'st thou how blood, which to the heart doth flow,
Doth from one ventricle to th'other goe?
And for the putrid stuffe, which thou dost spit,
Know'st thou how thy lungs have attracted it?
There are no passages, so that there is
(For ought thou know'st) piercing of substances.
And of those many opinions which men raise
Of Nailes and Haires, dost thou know which to praise?
What hope have wee to know our selves, when wee
Know not the least things, which for our use be?
Wee see in Authors, too stiffe to recant,
A hundred controversies of an Ant;

And yet one watches, starves, freezes, and sweats,
To know but Catechismes and Alphabets
Of unconcerning things, matters of fact;
How others on our stage their parts did Act;
What *Cæsar* did, yea, and what *Cicero* said.
Why grasse is greene, or why our blood is red,
Are mysteries which none have reach'd unto.
In this low forme, poore soule, what wilt thou doe?
When wilt thou shake off this Pedantery,
Of being taught by sense, and Fantasie?
Thou look'st through spectacles; small things seeme great
Below; But up unto the watch-towre get,
And see all things despoyl'd of fallacies:
Thou shalt not peepe through lattices of eyes,
Nor heare through Labyrinths of eares, nor learne
By circuit, or collections to discerne.
In heaven thou straight know'st all, concerning it,
And what concernes it not, shalt straight forget.

Text 1633. Lines 254–300

(iii)

Our companie in the next world

UP, up, my drowsie Soule, where thy new eare
Shall in the Angels songs no discord heare;
Where thou shalt see the blessed Mother-maid
Joy in not being that, which men have said.
Where she is exalted more for being good,
Than for her interest of Mother-hood.
Up to those Patriarchs, which did longer sit
Expecting Christ, than they'have enjoy'd him yet.

Up to those Prophets, which now gladly see
Their Prophesies growne to be Historie.
Up to th'Apostles, who did bravely runne
All the Suns course, with more light than the Sunne.
Up to those Martyrs, who did calmly bleed
Oyle to th'Apostles Lamps, dew to their seed.
Up to those Virgins, who thought, that almost
They made joyntenants with the Holy Ghost,
If they to any should his Temple give.

Text 1633. Lines 339–355

77 *La Corona*

D*EIGNE at my hands this crown of prayer and praise,*
Weav'd in my low devout melancholie,
Thou which of good, hast, yea art treasury,
All changing unchang'd Antient of dayes;
But doe not, with a vile crowne of fraile bayes,
Reward my muses white sincerity,
But what thy thorny crowne gain'd, that give mee,
A crowne of Glory, which doth flower alwayes;
The ends crowne our workes, but thou crown'st our ends,
For, at our end begins our endlesse rest;
The first last end, now zealously possest,
With a strong sober thirst, my soule attends.
'Tis time that heart and voice be lifted high,
Salvation to all that will is nigh.

Divine Poems 1633

78

Annunciation

SALVATION to all that will is nigh;
That All, which alwayes is All every where,
Which cannot sinne, and yet all sinnes must beare,
Which cannot die, yet cannot chuse but die,
Loe, faithfull Virgin, yeelds himselfe to lye
In prison, in thy wombe; and though he there
Can take no sinne, nor thou give, yet he'will weare
Taken from thence, flesh, which deaths force may try.
Ere by the spheares time was created, thou
Wast in his minde, who is thy Sonne, and Brother;
Whom thou conceiv'st, conceiv'd; yea thou art now
Thy Makers maker, and thy Fathers mother;
Thou'hast light in darke; and shutst in little roome,
Immensity cloysterd in thy deare wombe.

Divine Poems, 1633

79

Nativitie

IMMENSITIE cloysterd in thy deare wombe,
Now leaves his welbelov'd imprisonment,
There he hath made himselfe to his intent
Weake enough, now into our world to come;
But Oh, for thee, for him, hath th'Inne no roome?
Yet lay him in this stall, and from the Orient,
Starres, and wisemen will travell to prevent
Th'effect of *Herods* jealous generall doome.
Seest thou, my Soule, with thy faiths eyes, how he
Which fills all place, yet none holds him, doth lye?
Was not his pity towards thee wondrous high,
That would have need to be pittied by thee?
Kisse him, and with him into Egypt goe,
With his kinde mother, who partakes thy woe.

Divine Poems, 1633

80

Temple

WITH his kinde mother who partakes thy woe,
Joseph turne backe; see where your child doth sit,
Blowing, yea blowing out those sparks of wit,
Which himselfe on the Doctors did bestow;
The Word but lately could not speake, and loe,
It sodenly speaks wonders, whence comes it,
That all which was, and all which should be writ,
A shallow seeming child, should deeply know?
His Godhead was not soule to his manhood,
Nor had time mellow'd him to this ripenesse,
But as for one which hath a long taske, 'tis good,
With the Sunne to beginne his businesse,
He in his ages morning thus began
By miracles exceeding power of man.

Divine Poems, 1633

81

Crucifying

BY miracles exceeding power of man,
Hee faith in some, envie in some begat,
For, what weake spirits admire, ambitious, hate;
In both affections many to him ran,
But Oh! the worst are most, they will and can,
Alas, and do, unto the immaculate,
Whose creature Fate is, now prescribe a Fate,
Measuring selfe-lifes infinity to'a span,
Nay to an inch. Loe, where condemned hee
Beares his owne crosse, with paine, yet by and by
When it beares him, he must beare more and die:
Now thou art lifted up, draw mee to thee,
And at thy death giving such liberall dole,
Moyst, with one drop of thy blood, my dry soule.

Divine Poems, 1633

82 *Resurrection*

M*OYST with one drop of thy blood, my dry soule*
Shall (though she now be in extreme degree
Too stony hard, and yet too fleshly,) bee
Freed by that drop, from being starv'd, hard, or foule,
And life, by this death abled, shall controule
Death, whom thy death slue; nor shall to mee
Feare of first or last death, bring miserie,
If in thy little booke my name thou enroule,
Flesh in that long sleep is not putrified,
But made that there, of which, and for which 'twas;
Nor can by other meanes be glorified.
May then sinnes sleep, and deaths soone from me passe,
That wak't from both, I againe risen may
Salute the last, and everlasting day.

Divine Poems, 1633

83 *Ascention*

S*ALUTE the last and everlasting day,*
Joy at the uprising of this Sunne, and Sonne,
Yee whose just teares, or tribulation
Have purely washt, or burnt your drossie clay;
Behold the Highest, parting hence away,
Lightens the darke clouds, which hee treads upon,
Nor doth hee by ascending, show alone,
But first hee, and hee first enters the way.
O strong Ramme, which hast batter'd heaven for mee,
Mild Lamb, which with thy blood, hast mark'd the path;
Bright Torch, which shin'st, that I the way may see,
Oh, with thy owne blood quench thy owne just wrath,
And if thy holy Spirit, my Muse did raise,
Deigne at my hands this crowne of prayer and praise.

Divine Poems, 1633

JOHN DONNE

84

Holy Sonnets

i

THOU hast made me, and shall thy worke decay?
Repaire me now, for now mine end doth haste,
I runne to death, and death meets me as fast,
And all my pleasures are like yesterday;
I dare not move my dimme eyes any way,
Despaire behind, and death before doth cast
Such terrour, and my feeble flesh doth waste
By sinne in it, which it t'wards hell doth weigh;
Only thou art above, and when towards thee
By thy leave I can looke, I rise againe;
But our old subtle foe so tempteth me,
That not one houre my selfe I can sustaine;
Thy Grace may wing me to prevent his art,
And thou like Adamant draw mine iron heart.

Divine Poems, 1633

ii

AS due by many titles I resigne
My selfe to thee, O God; first I was made
By thee, and for thee, and when I was decay'd
Thy blood bought that, the which before was thine;
I am thy sonne, made with thy selfe to shine,
Thy servant, whose paines thou hast still repaid,
Thy sheepe, thine Image, and, till I betray'd
My selfe, a temple of thy Spirit divine;
Why doth the devill then usurpe on mee?
Why doth he steale, nay ravish that's thy right?
Except thou rise and for thine owne worke fight,
Oh, I shall soone despaire, when I doe see
That thou lov'st mankind well, yet wilt'not chuse me,
And Satan hates mee, yet is loth to lose mee.

Divine Poems, 1633

iii

O MIGHT those sighes and teares returne againe
Into my breast and eyes, which I have spent,
That I might in this holy discontent
Mourne with some fruit, as I have mourn'd in vaine;
In mine Idolatry what showres of raine
Mine eyes did waste? what griefs my heart did rent?
That sufferance was my sinne; now I repent;
'Cause I did suffer I must suffer paine.
Th'hydroptique drunkard, and night-scouting thiefe,
The itchy Lecher, and self-tickling proud
Have the remembrance of past joyes, for reliefe
Of coming ills. To (poore) me is allow'd
No ease; for, long, yet vehement griefe hath beene
Th'effect and cause, the punishment and sinne.

Divine Poems, 1633

iv

OH my blacke Soule! now thou art summoned
By sicknesse, deaths herald, and champion;
Thou art like a pilgrim, which abroad hath done
Treason, and durst not turne to whence hee is fled,
Or like a thiefe, which till deaths doome be read,
Wisheth himselfe delivered from prison;
But damn'd and hal'd to execution,
Wisheth that still he might be imprisoned.
Yet grace, if thou repent, thou canst not lacke;
But who shall give thee that grace to beginne?
Oh, make thy selfe with holy mourning blacke,
And red with blushing, as thou art with sinne;
Or wash thee in Christs blood, which hath this might
That being red, it dyes red soules to white.

Divine Poems, 1633

v

I AM a little world made cunningly
Of Elements, and an Angelike spright,
But black sinne hath betraid to endlesse night
My worlds both parts, and (oh) both parts must die.
You which beyond that heaven which was most high
Have found new sphears, and of new lands can write,
Poure new seas in mine eyes, that so I might
Drowne my world with my weeping earnestly,
Or wash it, if it must be drown'd no more:
But oh it must be burnt! alas the fire
Of lust and envie have burnt it heretofore,
And made it fouler; Let their flames retire,
And burne me O Lord, with a fiery zeale
Of thee and thy house, which doth in eating heale.

Divine Poems, 1633

vi

THIS is my playes last scene, here heavens appoint
My pilgrimages last mile; and my race
Idly, yet quickly runne, hath this last pace,
My spans last inch, my minutes latest point,
And gluttonous death, will instantly unjoynt
My body, and soule, and I shall sleepe a space,
But my'ever-waking part shall see that face,
Whose feare already shakes my every joynt:
Then, as my soule, to'heaven her first seate, takes flight,
And earth-born body, in the earth shall dwell,
So, fall my sinnes, that all may have their right,
To where they'are bred, and would presse me, to hell.
Impute me righteous, thus purg'd of evill,
For thus I leave the world, the flesh, the devill.

Divine Poems, 1633

vii

AT the round earths imagin'd corners, blow
Your trumpets, Angells, and arise, arise
From death, you numberlesse infinities
Of soules, and to your scattred bodies goe,
All whom the flood did, and fire shall o'erthrow,
All whom warre, dearth, age, agues, tyrannies,
Despaire, law, chance, hath slaine, and you whose eyes,
Shall behold God, and never taste deaths woe.
But let them sleepe, Lord, and mee mourne a space,
For, if above all these, my sinnes abound,
'Tis late to aske abundance of thy grace,
When wee are there; here on this lowly ground,
Teach mee how to repent; for that's as good
As if thou'hadst seal'd my pardon, with thy blood.

Divine Poems, 1633

viii

IF faithfull soules be alike glorifi'd
As Angels, then my fathers soule doth see,
And adds this even to full felicitie,
That valiantly I hells wide mouth o'erstride:
But if our mindes to these soules be descry'd
By circumstances, and by signes that be
Apparent in us, not immediately,
How shall my mindes white truth by them be try'd?
They see idolatrous lovers weepe and mourne,
And vile blasphemous Conjurers to call
On Jesus name, and Pharisaicall
Dissemblers feigne devotion. Then turne
O pensive soule, to God, for he knowes best
Thy true griefe, for he put it in my breast.

Divine Poems, 1633

ix

IF poysonous mineralls, and if that tree,
Whose fruit threw death on else immortall us,
If lecherous goats, if serpents envious
Cannot be damn'd; Alas; why should I bee?
Why should intent or reason, born in mee,
Make sinnes, else equall, in mee more heinous?
And mercy being easie, and glorious
To God, in his sterne wrath why threatens hee?
But who am I, that dare dispute with thee
O God? Oh! of thine only worthy blood,
And my teares, make a heavenly Lethean flood,
And drowne in it my sinnes blacke memorie;
That thou remember them, some claime as debt,
I thinke it mercy, if thou wilt forget.

Divine Poems, 1633

x

DEATH be not proud, though some have called thee
Mighty and dreadfull, for, thou art not soe,
For, those, whom thou think'st, thou dost overthrow,
Die not, poore death, nor yet canst thou kill mee.
From rest and sleepe, which but thy pictures bee,
Much pleasure, then from thee much more must flow,
And soonest our best men with thee doe goe,
Rest of their bones, and soules deliverie.
Thou art slave to Fate, Chance, kings, and desperate men,
And dost with poyson, warre, and sicknesse dwell,
And poppie, or charmes can make us sleepe as well,
And better than thy stroake; why swell'st thou then?
One short sleepe past, wee wake eternally,
And death shall be no more; death, thou shalt die.

Divine Poems, 1633

xi

SPIT in my face you Jewes, and pierce my side,
Buffet, and scoffe, scourge, and crucifie mee,
For I have sinn'd, and sinn'd, and onely hee,
Who could do no iniquitie, hath dyed:
But by my death can not be satisfied
My sinnes, which passe the Jewes impiety:
They kill'd once an inglorious man, but I
Crucifie him daily, being now glorified.
Oh, let mee then, his strange love still admire:
Kings pardon, but he bore our punishment.
And *Jacob* came cloth'd in vile harsh attire
But to supplant, and with gainfull intent:
God cloth'd himselfe in vile mans flesh, that so
Hee might be weake enough to suffer woe.

Divine Poems, 1633

xii

WHY are wee by all creatures waited on?
Why doe the prodigall elements supply
Life and food to mee, being more pure than I,
Simple, and further from corruption?
Why brook'st thou, ignorant horse, subjection?
Why dost thou bull, and bore so seelily
Dissemble weaknesse, and by'one mans stroke die,
Whose whole kinde, you might swallow and feed upon?
Weaker I am, woe is me, and worse than you,
You have not sinn'd, nor need be timorous.
But wonder at a greater wonder, for to us
Created nature doth these things subdue,
But their Creator, whom sin, nor nature tyed,
For us, his Creatures, and his foes, hath dyed.

Divine Poems, 1633

xiii

WHAT if this present were the worlds last night?
Marke in my heart, O Soule, where thou dost dwell,
The picture of Christ crucified, and tell
Whether that countenance can thee affright,
Teares in his eyes quench the amasing light,
Blood fills his frownes, which from his pierc'd head fell.
And can that tongue adjudge thee unto hell,
Which pray'd forgivenesse for his foes fierce spight?
No, no; but as in my idolatrie
I said to all my profane mistresses,
Beauty, of pitty, foulnesse onely is
A signe of rigour: so I say to thee,
To wicked spirits are horrid shapes assign'd,
This beauteous forme assures a pitious minde.

Divine Poems, 1633

xiv

BATTER my heart, three person'd God; for, you
As yet but knocke, breathe, shine, and seeke to mend;
That I may rise, and stand, o'erthrow mee,'and bend
Your force, to breake, blowe, burn and make me new.
I, like an usurpt towne, to'another due,
Labour to'admit you, but Oh, to no end,
Reason your viceroy in mee, mee should defend,
But is captiv'd, and proves weake or untrue.
Yet dearely'I love you, and would be loved faine,
But am betroth'd unto your enemie:
Divorce mee, untie, or breake that knot againe,
Take mee to you, imprison mee, for I
Except you'enthrall mee, never shall be free,
Nor ever chaste, except you ravish mee.

Divine Poems, 1633

xv

WILT thou love God, as he thee! then digest,
My Soule, this wholsome meditation,
How God the Spirit, by Angels waited on
In heaven, doth make his Temple in thy brest.
The Father having begot a Sonne most blest,
And still begetting, (for he ne'er begonne)
Hath deign'd to chuse thee by adoption,
Coheire to'his glory,'and Sabbaths endlesse rest.
And as a robb'd man, which by search doth finde
His stolne stuffe sold, must lose or buy'it againe:
The Sonne of glory came downe, and was slaine,
Us whom he'had made, and Satan stolne, to unbinde.
'Twas much, that man was made like God before,
But, that God should be made like man, much more.

Divine Poems, 1633

xvi

FATHER, part of his double interest
Unto thy kingdome, thy Sonne gives to mee,
His joynture in the knottie Trinitie
Hee keepes, and gives to me his deaths conquest.
This Lambe, whose death, with life the world hath blest,
Was from the worlds beginning slaine, and he
Hath made two Wills, which with the Legacie
Of his and thy kingdome, doe thy Sonnes invest.
Yet such are thy laws, that men argue yet
Whether a man those statutes can fulfill;
None doth; but all-healing grace and spirit
Revive againe what law and letter kill.
Thy lawes abridgement, and that last command
Is all but love; Oh let this last Will stand!

Divine Poems, 1633

xviii

SHOW me deare Christ, thy spouse, so bright and clear.
What! is it She, which on the other shore
Goes richly painted? or which robb'd and tore
Laments and mournes in Germany and here?
Sleepes she a thousand, then peepes up one yeare?
Is she selfe truth and errs? now new, now outwore?
Doth she, and did she, and shall she evermore
On one, on seaven, or on no hill appeare?
Dwells she with us, or like adventuring knights
First travaile we to seeke and then make Love?
Betray kind husband thy spouse to our sights,
And let myne amorous soule court thy mild Dove,
Who is most trew, and pleasing to thee, then
When she'is embrac'd and open to most men.

Westmoreland MS.

85 *Goodfriday, 1613. Riding Westward*

LET mans Soule be a Spheare, and then, in this,
The intelligence that moves, devotion is,
And as the other Spheares, by being growne
Subject to forraigne motions, lose their owne,
And being by others hurried every day,
Scarce in a yeare their naturall forme obey:
Pleasure or businesse, so, our Soules admit
For their first mover, and are whirld by it.
Hence is't, that I am carryed towards the West
This day, when my Soules forme bends toward the East.
There I should see a Sunne, by rising set,
And by that setting endlesse day beget;
But that Christ on this Crosse, did rise and fall,

Sinne had eternally benighted all.
Yet dare I'almost be glad, I do not see
That spectacle of too much weight for mee.
Who sees Gods face, that is selfe life, must dye;
What a death were it then to see God dye?
It made his owne Lieutenant Nature shrinke,
It made his footstoole crack, and the Sunne winke.
Could I behold those hands which span the Poles,
And turne all spheares at once, peirc'd with those holes?
Could I behold that endlesse height which is
Zenith to us, and our Antipodes,
Humbled below us? or that blood which is
The seat of all our Soules, if not of his,
Made dirt of dust, or that flesh which was worne
By God, for his apparell, ragg'd, and torne?
If on these things I durst not looke, durst I
Upon his miserable mother cast mine eye,
Who was Gods partner here, and furnish'd thus
Halfe of that Sacrifice, which ransom'd us?
Though these things, as I ride, be from mine eye,
They'are present yet unto my memory,
For that looks towards them; and thou look'st towards mee,
O Saviour, as thou hang'st upon the tree;
I turne my backe to thee, but to receive
Corrections, till thy mercies bid thee leave.
O thinke mee worth thine anger, punish mee,
Burne off my rusts, and my deformity,
Restore thine Image, so much, by thy grace,
That thou may'st know mee, and I'll turne my face.

Divine Poems, 1633

turne all spheares] tune 1633–69.

86 *A Hymn to Christ, at the Authors last going into Germany*

IN what torne ship soever I embarke,
That ship shall be my embleme of thy Arke;
What sea soever swallow mee, that flood
Shall be to mee an embleme of thy blood;
Though thou with clouds of anger do disguise
Thy face; yet through that maske I know those eyes,
Which, though they turne away sometimes,
They never will despise.

I sacrifice this Iland unto thee,
And all whom I lov'd there, and who lov'd mee;
When I have put our seas twixt them and mee,
Put thou thy sea betwixt my sinnes and thee.
As the trees sap doth seeke the root below
In winter, in my winter now I goe,
Where none but thee, th'Eternall root
Of true Love I may know.

Nor thou nor thy religion dost controule,
The amorousnesse of an harmonious Soule,
But thou would'st have that love thy selfe: As thou
Art jealous, Lord, so I am jealous now,
Thou lov'st not, till from loving more, thou free
My soule: Who ever gives, takes libertie:
O, if thou car'st not whom I love
Alas, thou lov'st not mee.

Seale then this bill of my Divorce to All,
On whom those fainter beames of love did fall;
Marry those loves, which in youth scattered bee
On Fame, Wit, Hopes (false mistresses) to thee.

Churches are best for Prayer, that have least light:
To see God only, I goe out of sight:
And to scape stormy dayes, I chuse
  An Everlasting night.

Divine Poems, 1633

87 *Hymne to God my God, in my sicknesse*

SINCE I am coming to that Holy roome,
  Where, with thy Quire of Saints for evermore,
I shall be made thy Musique; As I come
  I tune the Instrument here at the dore,
  And what I must doe then, thinke here before.

Whilst my Physitians by their love are growne
  Cosmographers, and I their Mapp, who lie
Flat on this bed, that by them may be showne
  That this is my South-west discoverie
  Per fretum febris, by these streights to die,

I joy, that in these straits, I see my West;
  For though their currents yeeld returne to none,
What shall my West hurt me? As West and East
  In all flat Maps (and I am one) are one,
  So death doth touch the Resurrection.

Is the Pacifique Sea my home? Or are
  The Easterne riches? Is *Jerusalem*?
Anyan, and *Magellan*, and *Gibraltare*,
  All streights, and none but streights, are wayes to them,
  Whether where *Japhet* dwelt, or *Cham*, or *Sem*.

We thinke that *Paradise* and *Calvarie*,
  Christs Crosse, and *Adams* tree, stood in one place;
Looke Lord, and finde both *Adams* met in me;
  As the first *Adams* sweat surrounds my face,
  May the last *Adams* blood my soule embrace.

So, in his purple wrapp'd receive mee Lord,
  By these his thornes give me his other Crowne;
And as to others soules I preach'd thy word,
  Be this my Text, my Sermon to mine owne,
  Therefore that he may raise the Lord throws down.

Divine Poems, 1635

88 *A Hymn to God the Father*

WILT thou forgive that sin, where I begun,
  Which is my sin, though it were done before?
Wilt thou forgive those sinns through which I runn
  And doe them still, though still I doe deplore?
    When thou hast done, thou hast not done,
      for I have more.

Wilt thou forgive that sin, by which I'have wonne
  Others to sin, and made my sin their dore?
Wilt thou forgive that sin which I did shunne
  A yeare or twoe, but wallowed in a score?
    When thou hast done, thou hast not done,
      for I have more.

I have a sin of feare that when I have spun
  My last thred, I shall perish on the shore;
Sweare by thy self that at my Death, thy Son
  Shall shine as he shines nowe, and heretofore;
    And having done that, thou hast done,
      I have noe more.

Trinity College, Dublin, MS.

BEN JONSON

1573–1637

89 *To William Camden*

CAMDEN, most reverend head, to whom I owe
All that I am in arts, all that I know.
(How nothing 's that!) to whom my countrey owes
The great renowne and name wherewith she goes.
Than thee the age sees not that thing more grave,
More high, more holy, that shee more would crave.
What name, what skill, what faith hast thou in things!
What sight in searching the most antique springs!
What weight, and what authority in thy speech!
Man scarce can make that doubt, but thou canst teach.
Pardon free truth, and let thy modesty,
Which conquers all, be once overcome by thee.
Many of thine this better could, than I,
But for their powers, accept my piety.

Epigrammes, 1616 (xiv)

90 *On My First Daughter*

HERE lies to each her parents' ruth,
Mary, the daughter of their youth:
Yet, all heaven's gifts, being heaven's due,
It makes the father less to rue.
At sixe months end, she parted hence
With safety of her innocence;
Whose soule Heaven's Queen (whose name she beares)
In comfort of her mother's teares,
Hath plac'd amongst her Virgin-traine:
Where, while that sever'd doth remaine,
This grave partakes the fleshly birth,
Which cover lightly, gentle earth.

Epigrammes, 1616 (xxii)

91 *To John Donne*

DONNE, the delight of Phœbus, and each *Muse*,
 Who, to thy one, all other braines refuse;
Whose every work, of thy most early wit,
 Came forth example, and remaines so, yet:
Longer a knowing, than most wits do live;
 And which no affection praise enough can give!
To it, thy language, letters, arts, best life,
 Which might with halfe mankind maintaine a strife;
All which I meant to praise, and, yet, I would;
 But leave, because I cannot as I should!

Epigrammes, 1616 (xxiii)

92 *On His First Sonne*

FAREWELL, thou child of my right hand, and joy;
 My sinne was too much hope of thee, lov'd boy,
Seven yeeres thou'wert lent to me, and I thee pay,
 Exacted by thy fate, on the just day.
O, could I lose all father, now. For why
 Will man lament the state he should envie?
To have so soone scap'd worlds, and fleshes rage,
 And, if no other miserie, yet age?
Rest in soft peace, and, ask'd, say here doth lye
 BEN. JONSON his best piece of *poetrie*.
For whose sake, hence-forth, all his vowes be such,
 As what he loves may never like too much.

Epigrammes, 1616 (xlv)

93 *To Francis Beaumont*

HOW I doe love thee, Beaumont, and thy *Muse,*
  That unto me dost such religion use!
How I doe feare my selfe, that am not worth
  The least indulgent thought thy pen drops forth!
At once thou mak'st me happie, and unmak'st;
  And giving largely to me, more thou tak'st.
What fate is mine, that so it selfe bereaves?
  What art is thine, that so thy friend deceives?
When even there, where most thou praisest mee,
  For writing better, I must envie thee.

Epigrammes, 1616 (lv)

94 *To Thomas Lord Chancellor*

WHIL'ST thy weigh'd judgements, EGERTON, I heare,
  And know thee, then, a judge, not of one yeare;
Whil'st I behold thee live with purest hands;
  That no affection in thy voice commands;
That still th'art present to the better cause;
  And no lesse wise, than skilfull in the lawes;
Whil'st thou art certaine to thy words, once gone,
  As is thy conscience, which is alwayes one:
The *Virgin,* long since fled from earth, I see,
  T' our times return'd, hath made her heaven in thee.

Epigrammes, 1616 (lxxiv)

95 *On Lucy Countesse of Bedford*

THIS morning, timely rapt with holy fire,
  I thought to forme unto my zealous *Muse,*
What kinde of creature I could most desire,
  To honor, serve, and love; as *Poets* use.

I meant to make her faire, and free, and wise,
  Of greatest blood, and yet more good than great;
I meant the day-starre should not brighter rise,
  Nor lend like influence from his lucent seat.
I meant shee should be curteous, facile, sweet,
  Hating that solemne vice of greatnesse, pride;
I meant each softest vertue, there should meet,
  Fit in that softer bosome to reside.
Onely a learned, and a manly soule
  I purpos'd her; that should, with even powers,
The rock, the spindle, and the sheeres controule
  Of destinie, and spin her owne free houres.
Such when I meant to faigne, and wish'd to see,
  My *Muse* bade, *Bedford* write, and that was shee.

Epigrammes, 1616 (lxxvi)

96 *To Edward Allen* (*Alleyne*)

IF *Rome* so great, and in her wisest age,
  Fear'd not to boast the glories of her stage,
As skilful Roscius, and grave Æsope, men,
  Yet crown'd with honors, as with riches, then;
Who had no lesse a trumpet of their name,
  Than Cicero, whose every breath was fame:
How can so great example dye in me,
  That Allen, I should pause to publish thee?
Who both their graces in thy selfe hast more
Out-stript, than they did all that went before:
And present worth in all dost so contract,
  As others speak, but only thou dost act.
Weare this renowne. 'Tis just, that who did give
  So many *Poets* life, by one should live.

Epigrammes, 1616 (lxxxix)

97 *To Lucy, Countesse of Bedford, with Mr. Donnes Satyres*

LUCY, you brightnesse of our spheare, who are
  Life of the *Muses* day, their morning Starre!
If works (not th'authors) their own grace should look,
  Whose poems would not wish to be your book?
But these, desir'd by you, the maker's ends
  Crowne with their own. Rare poems aske rare friends.
Yet, *Satyres*, since the most of mankind bee
  Their un-avoided subject, fewest see:
For none e'er tooke that pleasure in sins sense,
  But, when they heard it tax'd, tooke more offence.
They, then, that living where the matter is bred,
  Dare for these Poemes, yet, both aske, and read,
And like them too; must needfully, though few,
  Be of the best: and 'mongst those, best are you;
Lucy, you brightnesse of our spheare, who are
  The *Muses* evening, as their morning-starre.

Epigrammes, 1616 (xciv)

98 *To Sir Henrie Savile upon his Translation of Tacitus*

IF, my religion safe, I durst embrace
  That stranger doctrine of PYTHAGORAS,
I should beleeve, the soule of TACITUS
  In thee, most weighty SAVILE, liv'd to us:
So hast thou rendred him in all his bounds,
  And all his numbers, both of sense, and sounds.
But when I read that speciall piece, restor'd,
  Where NERO falls, and GALBA is ador'd,

To thine owne proper I ascribe then more;
  And gratulate the breach, I griev'd before:
Which *Fate* (it seemes) caus'd in the historie,
  Onely to boast thy merit in supply.
O, would'st thou adde like hand, to all the rest!
  Or, better worke! were thy glad countrey blest,
To have her storie woven in thy thred;
  MINERVAES loome was never richer spred.
For who can master those great parts like thee,
  That liv'st from hope, from feare, from faction free;
That hast thy breast so cleere of present crimes,
  Thou need'st not shrinke at voyce of after-times;
Whose knowledge claymeth at the helme to stand;
  But, wisely, thrusts not forth a forward hand,
No more than SALUST in the *Romane* state!
  As, then, his cause, his glorie emulate.
Although to write be lesser than to doo,
  It is the next deed, and a great one too.
We need a man that knowes the severall graces
  Of historie, and how to apt their places;
Where brevitie, where splendor, and where height,
  Where sweetnesse is required, and where weight;
We need a man, can speake of the intents,
  The councells, actions, orders, and events
Of state, and censure them: we need his pen
  Can write the things, the causes, and the men.
But most we need his faith (and all have you)
  That dares nor write things false, nor hide things true.

Epigrammes, 1616 (xcv)

99 *Inviting a Friend to Supper*

TO-NIGHT, grave sir, both my poore house, and I
  Doe equally desire your companie:
Not that we thinke us worthy such a guest,
  But that your worth will dignifie our feast,
With those that come; whose grace may make that seeme
  Something, which, else, could hope for no esteeme.
It is the faire acceptance, Sir, creates
  The entertaynment perfect: not the cates.
Yet shall you have, to rectifie your palate,
  An olive, capers, or some better sallad
Ushring the mutton; with a short-leg'd hen,
  If we can get her, full of eggs, and then,
Limons, and wine for sauce: to these, a coney
  Is not to be despair'd of, for our money;
And, though fowle, now, be scarce, yet there are clerkes,
  The skie not falling, thinke we may have larkes.
I'll tell you of more, and lye, so you will come:
  Of partrich, pheasant, wood-cock, of which some
May yet be there; and godwit, if we can:
  Knat, raile, and ruffe too. How so e'er, my man
Shall reade a piece of VIRGIL, TACITUS,
  LIVIE, or of some better booke to us,
Of which wee'll speake our minds, amidst our meate;
  And I'll professe no verses to repeate:
To this, if ought appeare, which I not know of,
  That will the pastrie, not my paper, show of.
Digestive cheese, and fruit there sure will bee;
  But that, which most doth take my *Muse*, and mee,
Is a pure cup of rich *Canary*-wine,
  Which is the *Mermaids*, now, but shall be mine:

Of which had Horace, or Anacreon tasted,
  Their lives, as doe their lines, till now had lasted.
Tabacco, *Nectar*, or the *Thespian* spring,
  Are all but Luthers beere, to this I sing.
Of this we will sup free, but moderately,
  And we will have no *Pooly*, or *Parrot* by;
Nor shall our cups make any guiltie men:
  But, at our parting, we will be, as when
We innocently met. No simple word,
  That shall be utter'd at our mirthfull board,
Shall make us sad next morning: or affright
  The libertie, that wee'll enjoy to-night.

Epigrammes, 1616 (ci)

100 *To Mary Lady Wroth*

Madame, had all antiquitie been lost,
  All history seal'd up, and fables crost;
That wee had left us, nor by time, nor place,
  Least mention of a *Nymph*, a *Muse*, a *Grace*,
But even their names were to bee made anew,
  Who could not but create them all, from you?
He, that but saw you weare the wheaten hat,
  Would call you more than Ceres, if not that:
And, drest in shepherd's tire, who would not say:
  You were the bright Oenone, Flora, or *May*?
If dancing, all would cry th' *Idalian* Queene,
  Were leading forth the Graces on the greene:
And, armed to the chase, so bare her bow
  Diana 'alone, so hit, and hunted so.
There 's none so dull, that for your style would aske,
  That saw you put on Pallas' plumed caske:

Or, keeping your due state, that would not cry,
  There JUNO sate, and yet no Peacock by.
So are you *Nature's Index*, and restore
I' your selfe, all treasure lost of th'age before.

Epigrammes, 1616 (cv)

101 *Epitaph on Salathiel Pavy a Child of Queen Elizabeth's Chappel*

WEEPE with me all you that read
  This little storie:
And know, for whom a teare you shed,
  Death's selfe is sorry.
'Twas a child, that so did thrive
  In grace, and feature,
As *Heaven* and *Nature* seem'd to strive
  Which own'd the creature.
Yeeres he numbred scarce thirteene
  When *Fates* turn'd cruell,
Yet three fill'd *Zodiackes* had he beene
  The stages jewell;
And did act (what now we moane)
  Old men so duely,
As, sooth, the *Parcæ* thought him one,
  He plai'd so truely.
So, by error, to his fate
  They all consented;
But viewing him since (alas, too late)
  They have repented.
And have sought (to give new birth)
  In baths to steepe him;
But, being so much too good for earth,
  Heaven vowes to keepe him.

Epigrammes, 1616 (cxx)

102 *Epitaph on Elizabeth, L.H.*

WOULD'ST thou heare, what man can say
  In a little? Reader, stay.
Underneath this stone doth lye
  As much beauty, as could dye:
Which in life did harbour give
  To more vertue, than doth live.
If, at all, she had a fault,
  Leave it buried in this vault.
One name was ELIZABETH,
  Th'other let it sleep with death:
Fitter, where it dyed to tell,
  Than that it liv'd at all. Farewell.

Epigrammes, 1616 (cxxiv)

103 *To William Roe*

ROE (and my joy to name) th'art now, to go
  Countries, and climes, manners, and men to know,
T'extract, and choose the best of all these knowne,
  And those to turne to blood, and make thine owne.
May winds as soft as breath of kissing friends,
  Attend thee hence; and there, may all thy ends,
As the beginnings here, prove purely sweet,
  And perfect in a circle always meet.
So, when we, blest with thy returne, shall see
  Thy selfe, with thy first thoughts, brought home by thee,
We each to other may this voyce inspire;
  This is that good ÆNEAS, pass'd through fire,
Through seas, stormes, tempests: and imbarqu'd for hell,
  Came back untouch'd. This man hath travail'd well.

Epigrammes, 1616 (cxxviii)

104 *To Penshurst*

THOU art not, PENSHURST, built to envious show,
  Of touch, or marble; nor canst boast a row
Of polish'd pillars, or a roofe of gold:
  Thou hast no lantherne, whereof tales are told;
Or staire, or courts; but stand'st an ancient pile,
  And these grudg'd at, art reverenc'd the while.
Thou joy'st in better markes, of soyle, of ayre,
  Of wood, of water: therein thou art faire.
Thou hast thy walkes for health, as well as sport:
  Thy *Mount*, to which the *Dryads* doe resort,
Where PAN, and BACCHUS their high feasts have made,
  Beneath the broad beech, and the chest-nut shade;
That taller tree, which of a nut was set,
  At his great birth, where all the *Muses* met.[1]
There, in the writhed barke, are cut the names
  Of many a SYLVANE, taken with his flames,
And thence, the ruddy *Satyres* oft provoke
  The lighter *Faunes*, to reach thy *Ladies oke*.
Thy copse, too, nam'd of GAMAGE, thou hast there,
  That never failes to serve thee season'd deere,
When thou would'st feast, or exercise thy friends.
  The lower land, that to the river bends,
Thy sheepe, thy bullocks, kine, and calves doe feed:
  The middle grounds thy mares, and horses breed.
Each banke doth yeeld thee conies; and the tops
  Fertile of wood, ASHORE, and SYDNEY's copse,
To crowne thy open table, doth provide
  The purpled pheasant, with the speckled side:

[1] Sir Philip Sidney.

The painted partrich lyes in every field,
  And, for thy messe, is willing to be kill'd.
And if the high swolne *Medway* faile thy dish,
  Thou hast thy ponds, that pay thee tribute fish,
Fat, aged carps, that runne into thy net.
  And pikes, now weary their owne kinde to eat,
As loth, the second draught or cast to stay,
  Officiously, at first, themselves betray.
Bright eeles, that emulate them, and leape on land,
  Before the fisher, or into his hand.
Then hath thy orchard fruit, thy garden flowers,
  Fresh as the ayre, and new as are the houres.
The early cherry, with the later plum,
  Fig, grape, and quince, each in his time doth come;
The blushing apricot, and woolly peach
  Hang on thy walls, that every child may reach.
And though thy walls be of the countrey stone,
  They'are rear'd with no mans ruine, no mans grone,
There's none, that dwell about them, wish them downe;
  But all come in, the farmer, and the clowne:
And no one empty-handed, to salute
  Thy lord, and lady, though they have no sute.
Some bring a capon, some a rurall cake,
  Some nuts, some apples; some that thinke they make
The better cheeses, bring 'hem; or else send
  By their ripe daughters, whom they would commend
This way to husbands; and whose baskets beare
  An embleme of themselves, in plum, or peare.
But what can this (more than expresse their love)
  Adde to thy free provisions, farre above
The neede of such? whose liberall boord doth flow,
  With all that hospitalitie doth know!

Where comes no guest, but is allow'd to eate,
  Without his feare, and of thy Lords owne meate:
Where the same beere, and bread, and selfe-same wine,
  That is his Lordships, shall be also mine.
And I not faine to sit (as some, this day,
  At great mens tables) and yet dine away.
Here no man tells my cups; nor, standing by,
  A waiter doth my gluttony envy:
But gives me what I call, and lets me eate;
  He knowes, below, he shall finde plentie of meate,
Thy tables hoord not up for the next day.
  Nor, when I take my lodging, need I pray
For fire, or lights, or livorie: all is there;
  As if thou, then, wert mine, or I raign'd here:
There 's nothing I can wish, for which I stay.
  That found King JAMES, when hunting late this way,
With his brave sonne, the Prince, they saw thy fires
  Shine bright on every harth as the desires
Of thy *Penates* had been set on flame,
  To entertayne them; or the countrey came,
With all their zeale, to warme their welcome here.
  What (great, I will not say, but) sodayne cheare
Did'st thou, then, make 'em! and what praise was heap'd
  On thy good lady, then! who, therein, reap'd
The just reward of her high huswifery;
  To have her linnen, plate, and all things nigh,
When shee was farre: and not a roome, but drest,
  As if it had expected such a guest!
These, PENSHURST, are thy praise, and yet not all.
  Thy lady's noble, fruitfull, chaste withall.
His children thy great lord may call his owne:
  A fortune in this age but rarely known.

They are, and have beene taught religion: Thence
  Their gentler spirits have suck'd innocence.
Each morne, and even, they are taught to pray,
  With the whole houshold, and may, every day,
Reade, in their vertuous parents noble parts,
  The mysteries of manners, armes, and arts.
Now, PENSHURST, they that will proportion thee
  With other edifices, when they see
Those proud, ambitious heaps, and nothing else,
  May say, their lords have built, but thy lord dwells.

The Forrest, 1616

105 *Song—To Celia*

COME my CELIA, let us prove,
  While wee may, the sports of love;
Time will not be ours for ever:
He, at length, our good will sever.
Spend not then his gifts in vaine.
Sunnes that set, may rise againe:
But, if once wee lose this light,
'Tis, with us, perpetuall night.
Why should we deferre our joyes?
Fame, and rumor are but toyes.
Cannot we delude the eyes
Of a few poore houshold spyes?
Or his easier eares beguile,
So removed by our wile?
'Tis no sinne, loves fruit to steale,
But the sweet theft to reveale:
To bee taken, to be seene,
These have crimes accounted beene.

The Forrest, 1616

106 *That Women are but Mens Shaddows*

FOLLOW a shaddow, it still flies you,
  Seeme to flye it, it will pursue:
So court a mistris, she denies you;
  Let her alone, she will court you.
Say, are not women, truly, then,
  Styl'd but the shaddows of us men?
At morne, and even, shades are longest;
  At noone, they are or short, or none:
So men at weakest, they are strongest,
  But grant us perfect, they're not knowne.
Say, are not women truly, then,
  Styl'd but the shaddows of us men?

The Forrest, 1616

107 *To Celia*

DRINKE to me, onely, with thine eyes,
  And I will pledge with mine;
Or leave a kisse but in the cup,
  And I'll not looke for wine.
The thirst, that from the soule doth rise,
  Doth aske a drink divine:
But might I of JOVE's *Nectar* sup,
  I would not change for thine.
I sent thee, late, a rosie wreath,
  Not so much honoring thee,
As giving it a hope, that there
  It could not withered bee.
But thou thereon did'st onely breath,
  And sent'st it backe to mee:
Since when it growes, and smells, I sweare,
  Not of it selfe, but thee.

The Forrest, 1616

108 *To Heaven*

GOOD, and great God, can I not thinke of thee,
  But it must, straight, my melancholy bee?
Is it interpreted in me disease,
  That, laden with my sinnes, I seeke for ease?
O, be thou witnesse, that the reines dost know,
  And hearts of all, if I be sad for show,
And judge me after: if I dare pretend
  To ought but grace, or ayme at other end.
As thou art all, so be thou all to mee,
  First, midst, and last, converted one, and three;
My faith, my hope, my love: and in this state,
  My judge, my witnesse, and my advocate.
Where have I beene this while exil'd from thee?
  And whither rap'd, now thou but stoop'st to mee?
Dwell, dwell here still: O, being every-where,
  How can I doubt to finde thee ever, here?
I know my state, both full of shame, and scorne,
  Conceiv'd in sinne, and unto labour borne,
Standing with feare, and must with horror fall,
  And destin'd unto judgement, after all.
I feele my griefs too, and there scarce is ground,
  Upon my flesh t'inflict another wound.
Yet dare I not complaine, or wish for death
  With holy Paul, lest it be thought the breath
Of discontent; or that these prayers bee
  For weariness of life, not love of thee.

The Forrest, 1616

109 *An Angel Describes Truth*

UPON her head she weares a crowne of starres,
Through which her orient hayre waves to her waist,
By which beleeving *mortalls* hold her fast,
And in those golden chordes are carried even,
Till with her breath she blowes them up to heaven.
She weares a robe enchas'd with eagles eyes,
To signifie her sight in *mysteries*;
Upon each shoulder sits a milke-white dove,
And at her feet doe witty serpents move:
Her spacious armes doe reach from *East* to *West*,
And you may see her heart shine through her breast.
Her right hand holds a *sunne* with burning rayes,
Her left a curious bunch of golden kayes,
With which *Heaven* gates she locketh, and displayes.
A christall mirror hangeth at her brest,
By which men's consciences are search'd, and drest:
On her coach-wheeles *hypocrisie* lies rackt;
And squint-eyd *slander*, with *vaine-glory* backt
Her bright eyes burne to dust: in which shines fate.
An *angell* ushers her triumphant gait,
Whilst with her fingers fans of starres shee twists,
And with them beates backe *Error*, clad in mists.
Eternall *Unitie* behind her shines
That *fire*, and *water*, *earth*, and *ayre* combines.
Her voyce is like a trumpet lowd, and shrill,
Which bids all sounds in *Earth*, and *Heav'n* be still.
And see! descended from her chariot now,
In this related pompe shee visits you.

The Barriers (*Hymenaei*, Part 2), 1606

110 (*Slow, slow, fresh fount*)

SLOW, slow, fresh fount, keepe time with my salt teares;
Yet slower, yet, O faintly gentle springs:
List to the heavy part the musique beares,
Woe weepes out her division, when shee sings.
Droope herbs, and flowres;
Fall griefe in showres;
Our beauties are not ours:
O, I could still
(Like melting snow upon some craggie hill,)
drop, drop, drop, drop,
Since natures pride is, now, a wither'd daffodill.

Cynthias Revels, 1600

111 *Hymn to Diana*

QUEENE, and *Huntresse*, chaste, and faire,
Now the *Sunne* is laid to sleepe,
Seated in thy silver chaire,
State in wonted manner keepe:
HESPERUS intreats thy light,
Goddesse, excellently bright.

Earth, let not thy envious shade
Dare it selfe to interpose;
CYNTHIAS shining orbe was made
Heaven to cleere, when day did close:
Blesse us then with wished sight,
Goddesse, excellently bright.

Lay thy bow of pearle apart,
And thy cristall-shining quiver;
Give unto the flying hart
Space to breathe, how short soever:
Thou that mak'st a day of night,
Goddesse, excellently bright.

Cynthias Revels, 1600

112 *Song*

STILL to be neat, still to be drest,
As you were going to a feast;
Still to bee powdred, still perfum'd:
Lady, it is to be presum'd,
Though Arts hid causes are not found,
All is not sweet, all is not sound.

Give me a look, give me a face,
That makes simplicity a grace;
Robes loosely flowing, hayre as free:
Such sweet neglect more taketh me,
Than all th' adulteries of Art;
They strike mine eyes, but not my heart.

The Silent Woman, 1609

113 *A Hymne to God the Father*

HEARE mee, O God!
A broken heart,
Is my best part:
Use still thy rod,
That I may prove
Therein, thy Love.

BEN JONSON

If thou hadst not
    Beene stern to mee.
    But left me free.
I had forgot
    My selfe and thee.

For sin's so sweet,
    As minds ill bent
    Rarely repent,
Untill they meet
    Their punishment.

Who more can crave
    Than thou hast done:
    That gav'st a Sonne,
To free a slave?
    First made of nought;
    With All since bought.

Sinne, Death, and Hell,
    His glorious Name
    Quite overcame,
Yet I rebell,
    And slight the same.

But, I'll come in,
    Before my losse,
    Me farther tosse,
As sure to win.
    Under his Crosse.

Underwoods, 1641

114

A Song

OH doe not wanton with those eyes,
  Lest I be sick with seeing;
Nor cast them downe, but let them rise,
  Lest shame destroy their being:
O, be not angry with those fires,
  For then their threats will kill me;
Nor looke too kind on my desires,
  For then my hopes will spill me;
O, doe not steepe them in thy Teares,
  For so will sorrow slay me;
Nor spread them as distract with feares,
  Mine owne enough betray me.

Underwoods, 1641

115

An Ode. To himselfe

WHERE do'st thou carelesse lie
  Buried in ease and sloth:
Knowledge, that sleepes, doth die;
  And this Securitie,
  It is the common Moth,
That eats on wits, and Arts, and destroyes them both.

Are all th' *Aonian* springs
  Dri'd up? lyes *Thespia* wast?
Doth *Clarius* Harp want strings,
  That not a Nymph now sings!
  Or droop they as disgrac't,
To see their Seats and Bowers by chattring Pies defac't.

If hence thy silence be,
As 'tis too just a cause;
Let this thought quicken thee,
Minds that are great and free,
Should not on fortune pause,
'Tis crowne enough to vertue still, her owne applause.

What though the greedie Frie
Be taken with false Baytes
Of worded Balladrie,
And thinke it Poesie?
They die with their conceits,
And only piteous scorne, upon their folly waites.

Then take in hand thy Lyre,
Strike in thy proper straine,
With *Japhets* line, aspire
Sols Chariot for new fire,
To give the world againe:
Who aided him, will thee, the issue of *Joves* braine.

And since our Daintie age,
Cannot indure reproofe,
Make not thy selfe a Page,
To that strumpet the Stage,
But sing high and aloofe,
Safe from the wolves black jaw, and the dull Asses hoofe.

Underwoods, 1641

116 *To the immortall memorie, and friendship of that noble paire, Sir Lucius Cary and Sir H. Morison*

The Turne [1]

BRAVE Infant of *Saguntum*, cleare
Thy coming forth in that great yeare,
When the Prodigious *Hannibal* did crowne
His rage, with razing your immortall Towne.
Thou, looking then about,
Ere thou wert halfe got out,
Wise child, did'st hastily returne,
And mad'st thy Mothers wombe thine urne.
How summ'd a circle didst thou leave man-kind
Of deepest lore, could we the Center find!

The Counter-turne

Did wiser Nature draw thee back,
From out the horrour of that sack,
Where shame, faith, honour, and regard of right
Lay trampled on; the deeds of death, and night,
Urg'd, hurried forth, and hurld
Upon th' affrighted world:
Sword, fire, and famine, with fell fury met;
And all on utmost ruine set;
As, could they but lifes miseries fore-see,
No doubt all Infants would returne like thee.

[1] Turne, Counter-turne, Stand: the strophe, antistrophe, and epode of the regular Pindaric Ode.

The Stand

For, what is life, if measur'd by the space,
Not by the act?
Or masked man, if valu'd by his face,
Above his fact?
Here's one out-liv'd his Peeres,
And told forth fourescore yeares;
He vexed time, and busied the whole State;
Troubled both foes, and friends;
But ever to no ends:
What did this Stirrer, but die late?
How well at twentie had he falne, or stood!
For three of his four-score, he did no good.

The Turne

Hee entred well, by vertuous parts,
Got up and thriv'd with honest arts:
He purchas'd friends, and fame, and honours then,
And had his noble name advanc'd with men:
But weary of that flight,
Hee stoop'd in all mens sight
To sordid flatteries, acts of strife,
And sunke in that dead sea of life
So deep, as he did then death's waters sup;
But that the Corke of Title buoy'd him up.

The Counter-turne

Alas, but *Morison* fell young:
Hee never fell, thou fall'st my tongue.
Hee stood, a Souldier to the last right end,
A perfect Patriot, and a noble friend,

But most a vertuous Sonne.
All Offices were done
By him, so ample, full, and round,
In weight, in measure, number, sound,
As though his age imperfect might appeare,
His life was of Humanitie the Spheare.

The Stand

Goe now, and tell out dayes summ'd up with feares,
And make them yeares;
Produce thy masse of miseries on the Stage,
To swell thine age;
Repeat of things a throng,
To shew thou hast beene long,
Not liv'd; for life doth her great actions spell,
By what was done and wrought
In season, and so brought
To light: her measures are, how well
Each syllable answer'd, and was form'd, how faire;
These make the lines of life, and that's her aire.

The Turne

It is not growing like a tree
In bulke, doth make man better bee;
Or standing long an Oake, three hundred yeare,
To fall a logge, at last, dry, bald, and seare:
A Lillie of a Day,
Is fairer farre, in May,
Although it fall, and die that night;
It was the Plant, and flowre of light.
In small proportions, we just beauties see:
And in short measures, life may perfect bee.

bald] bold, *Underwoods*.

The Counter-turne

Call, noble *Lucius*, then for Wine,
And let thy lookes with gladnesse shine:
Accept this garland, plant it on thy head,
And thinke, nay know, thy *Morison* '*s* not dead.
He leap'd the present age,
Possest with holy rage,
To see that bright eternall Day:
Of which we *Priests*, and *Poets* say
Such truths, as we expect for happy men,
And there he lives with memorie; and *Ben*.

The Stand

Johnson, who sung this of him, ere he went
Himselfe to rest,
Or taste a part of that full joy he meant
To have exprest,
In this bright *Asterisme*:
Where it were friendships schisme,
(Were not his *Lucius* long with us to tarry)
To separate these twi-
Lights, the *Dioscuri*;
And keepe the one halfe from his *Harry*.
But fate doth so alternate the designe,
Whilst that in heav'n, this light on earth must shine.

The Turne

And shine as you exalted are;
Two names of friendship, but one Starre:
Of hearts the union. And those not by chance
Made, or indenture, or leas'd out t'advance

The profits for a time.
No pleasures vaine did chime,
Of rimes, or riots, at your feasts,
Orgies of drinke, or fain'd protests:
But simple love of greatnesse, and of good;
That knits brave minds, and manners, more than blood.

The Counter-turne

This made you first to know the Why
You lik'd, then after, to apply
That liking; and approach so one the t'other
Till either grew a portion of the other:
Each stiled by his end,
The Copie of his friend.
You liv'd to be the great surnames,
And titles, by which all made claimes
Unto the Vertue. Nothing perfect done,
But as a CARY, or a MORISON.

The Stand

And such a force the faire example had,
As they that saw
The good, and durst not practise it, were glad
That such a Law
Was left yet to Man-kind;
Where they might read, and find
Friendship, indeed, was written, not in words:
And with the heart, not pen,
Of two so early men,
Whose lines her rolls were, and records.
Who, ere the first downe bloomed on the chin,
Had sow'd these fruits, and got the harvest in.

Underwoods, 1641

117 *Chorus*

SPRING all the *Graces* of the age,
And all the *Loves* of time;
Bring all the pleasures of the stage,
And relishes of rime:
Adde all the softnesses of Courts,
The lookes, the laughters, and the sports,
And mingle all their sweets, and salts,
That none may say, the Triumph halts.

Neptunes Triumph, 1624

118 *To the memory of my beloved, the Author, Mr. William Shakespeare: and what he hath left us*

TO draw no envy (*Shakespeare*) on thy name,
Am I thus ample to thy Booke, and Fame:
While I confesse thy writings to be such,
As neither *Man*, nor *Muse*, can praise too much.
'Tis true, and all mens suffrage. But these wayes
Were not the paths I meant unto thy praise:
For seeliest Ignorance on these may light,
Which, when it sounds at best, but eccho's right;
Or blinde Affection, which doth ne'er advance
The truth, but gropes, and urgeth all by chance:
Or crafty Malice, might pretend this praise,
And thinke to ruine, where it seem'd to raise.
These are, as some infamous Baud, or whore,
Should praise a Matron. What could hurt her more?
But thou art proofe against them, and indeed
Above th' ill fortune of them, or the need.
I, therefore will begin. Soule of the Age!
The applause! delight! the wonder of our Stage!

My *Shakespeare*, rise; I will not lodge thee by
 Chaucer, or *Spenser*, or bid *Beaumont* lye
A little further, to make thee a roome:
 Thou art a Moniment, without a tombe,
And art alive still, while thy Booke doth live,
 And we have wits to read, and praise to give.
That I not mixe thee so, my braine excuses;
 I meane with great, but disproportion'd *Muses*,
For, if I thought my judgement were of yeeres,
 I should commit thee surely with thy peeres,
And tell, how farre thou didst our *Lily* out-shine,
 Or sporting *Kid*, or *Marlowes* mighty line,
And though thou hadst small *Latine*, and lesse *Greeke*,
 From thence to honour thee I would not seeke
For names; but call forth thundring *Æschilus*,
 Euripides, and *Sophocles* to us,
Paccuvius, *Accius*, him of *Cordova* dead,
 To life againe, to heare thy Buskin tread,
And shake a Stage: Or, when thy Sockes were on,
 Leave thee alone, for the comparison
Of all, that insolent *Greece*, or haughtie *Rome*
 Sent forth, or since did from their ashes come.
Triumph, my *Britaine*, thou hast one to showe,
 To whom all Scenes of *Europe* homage owe.
He was not of an age, but for all time!
 And all the *Muses* still were in their prime,
When like *Apollo* he came forth to warme
 Our eares, or like a *Mercury* to charme!
Nature her selfe was proud of his designes,
 And joy'd to weare the dressing of his lines!
Which were so richly spun, and woven so fit,
 As, since, she will vouchsafe no other Wit.

The merry *Greeke*, tart *Aristophanes*,
Neat *Terence*, witty *Plautus*, now not please;
But antiquated, and deserted lye
As they were not of Natures family.
Yet must I not give Nature all: Thy Art,
My gentle *Shakespeare*, must enjoy a part.
For though the *Poets* matter, Nature be,
His Art doth give the fashion. And, that he,
Who casts to write a living line, must sweat,
(Such as thine are) and strike the second heat
Upon the *Muses* anvile: turne the same,
(And himselfe with it) that he thinkes to frame;
Or for the lawrell, he may gaine a scorne,
For a good *Poet's* made, as well as borne.
And such wert thou. Looke how the fathers face
Lives in his issue, even so, the race
Of *Shakespeares* minde, the manners brightly shines
In his well turned, and true-filed lines:
In each of which, he seemes to shake a Lance,
As brandish't at the eyes of Ignorance.
Sweet Swan of *Avon*! what a sight it were
To see thee in our waters yet appeare,
And make those flights upon the bankes of *Thames*,
That so did take *Eliza*, and our *James*!
But stay, I see thee in the *Hemisphere*
Advanc'd, and made a Constellation there
Shine forth, thou Starre of *Poets*, and with rage,
Or influence, chide, or cheere the drooping Stage;
Which, since thy flight from hence, hath mourn'd like night,
And despaires day, but for thy Volumes light.

First Folio of Shakespeare, 1623

119 *Ode (to himself)*

COME leave the loathed stage,
And the more loathsome age:
Where pride and impudence (in faction knit)
Usurpe the chaire of wit!
Indicting, and arraigning every day
Something they call a Play.
Let their fastidious, vaine
Commission of the braine
Run on, and rage, sweat, censure, and condemn:
They were not made for thee, lesse thou for them.

Say, that thou pour'st them wheat,
And they will acornes eat:
'Twere simple fury, still, thy selfe to waste
On such as have no taste!
To offer them a surfeit of pure bread,
Whose appetites are dead!
No, give them graines their fill,
Huskes, draff to drink and swill.
If they love lees, and leave the lusty wine,
Envy them not, their palate 's with the swine.

No doubt some mouldy tale,
Like *Pericles*; and stale
As the Shrieve's crusts, and nasty as his fish—
Scraps out of every dish
Throwne forth, and rak't into the common tub,
May keepe up the *Play-club*:
There, sweepings doe as well
As the best order'd meale.
For, who the relish of these guests will fit,
Needs set them but the almes-basket of wit.

And much good do 't you then:
Brave plush and velvet-men;
Can feed on orts: and safe in your stage-clothes,
Dare quit, upon your oathes,
The stagers and the stage-wrights too (your peeres)
Of larding your large eares
With their foule *comic* socks,
Wrought upon twenty blocks:
Which if they are torne, and turn'd, and patch't enough,
The gamesters share your gilt, and you their stuffe.—

Leave things so prostitute,
And take the *Alcaick* lute;
Or thine own *Horace* or *Anacreons* lyre;
Warme thee by *Pindares* fire:
And though thy nerves be shrunke, and blood be cold,
Ere yeares have made thee old,
Strike that disdaineful heate
Throughout, to their defeate:
As curious fooles, and envious of thy straine,
May, blushing, sweare no palsy 's in thy braine.

But when they heare thee sing
The glories of thy *king*,
His zeale to *God*, and his just awe o'er men:
They may, blood-shaken, then,
Feele such a flesh-quake to possesse their powers
As they shall cry, 'Like ours,
In sound of peace or wars,
No Harp e'er hit the stars,
In tuning forth the acts of his sweet raigne:
And raising *Charles* his chariot 'bove his *Waine*.'

The New Inn, 1631

120 *(It was a beauty that I saw)*

IT was a beauty that I saw
So pure, so perfect, as the frame
Of all the universe was lame,
To that one figure, could I draw,
Or give least line of it a law!

A skeine of silke without a knot!
A faire march made without a halt!
A curious forme, without a fault!
A printed book without a blot.
All beauty and without a spot.

The New Inn, 1631

121 *Pans Anniversarie*

THUS, thus, begin the yearly rites
Are due to PAN on these bright nights;
His Morne now riseth, and invites
To sports, to dances, and delights:
All envious, and Prophane away,
This is the Shepherds Holy-day.

Strew, strew, the glad and smiling ground
With every flower, yet not confound
The Prime-rose drop, the Springs owne spouse,
Bright Dayes-eyes, and the lips of Cowes,
The Garden-star, the Queene of May,
The Rose, to crowne the Holy-day.

Drop, drop you Violets, change your hues,
Now red, now pale, as Lovers use,
And in your death goe out as well,
As when you liv'd unto the smell:
  That from your odour all may say,
  This is the Shepherds Holy-day.

Masques, 1641

THOMAS HEYWOOD

d. 1650?

122 *The Author to his Booke*

THE world's a Theater, the earth a Stage,
  Which God, and nature doth with Actors fill,
Kings have their entrance in due equipage,
And some there parts play well and others ill.
The best no better are (in this Theater,)
Where every humor 's fitted in his kinde;
This a true subject acts, and that a Traytor,
The first applauded, and the last confin'd;
This plaies an honest man, and that a knave,
A gentle person this, and he a clowne,
One man is ragged, and another brave;
All men have parts, and each man acts his owne.
She a chaste Lady acteth all her life,
A wanton Curtezan another playes.
This, covets marriage love, that, nuptial strife,
Both in continuall action spend their dayes.
Some Citizens, some Soldiers, borne to adventer,
Shepherds and Sea-men; then our play 's begun,
When we are born, and to the world first enter,
And all finde *Exits* when their parts are done.

If then the world a Theater present,
As by the roundnesse it appeares most fit,
Built with starre-galleries of hye ascent,
In which *Jehove* doth as spectator sit,
And chiefe determiner to applaud the best,
And their indevours crowne with more than merit,
But by their evill actions doomes the rest,
To end disgrac'd whilst others praise inherit,
He that denyes then Theaters should be,
He may as well deny a world to me.

An Apology for Actors, 1612

ANONYMOUS

123 *Verses of Mans Mortalitie, with an other of the hope of his resurrection* [1]

LIKE as the Damaske Rose you see,
Or like the blossome on the Tree,
Or like the dainty flowre of May,
Or like the morning to the day,
Or like the Sunne, or like the shade,
Or like the Gourd which *Jonas* had:
Even such is Man; whose thred is spun,
Drawne out, and cut, and so is done.
The Rose withers, the Blossom blasteth,
The Flower fades, the Morning hasteth:
The Sun sets, the shadow flyes;
The Gourd consumes, and Man he dyes.
Like to the grasse that 's newly sprung,
Or like a Tale that 's new begun:

[1] Cf. F. Quarles, who claimed lines 1–12; and the similar poem by H. King.

Or like the Bird that 's here to day,
Or like the pearled dew of May;
Or like an houre, or like a span,
Or like the singing of a Swan:
Even such is Man, who lives by breath;
Is here, now there: so life, and death.
The grasse withers, the tale is ended,
The Bird is flowne, the Dew 's ascended,
The Houre is short, the span not long;
The Swan's neere death: Mans life is done.
Like to the Bubble in the Brooke,
Or in a Glasse much like a looke,
Or like a shuttle in Weavers hand,
Or like a writing in the sand,
Or like a thought, or like a dreame,
Or like the gliding of the streame:
Even such is Man, who lives by breath;
Is here, now there: so life, and death.
The Bubble's cut, the look 's forgot,
The Shuttle's flung, the writing's blot,
The thought is past, the dream is gone;
The water glides; Mans life is done.
Like to an Arrow from the Bow,
Or like swift course of watery flow,
Or like the time 'twixt floud and ebbe,
Or like the Spiders tender webbe,
Or like a Race, or like a Goale,
Or like the dealing of a Dole:
Even such is Man, whose brittle state
Is alwayes subject unto Fate.
The arrow's shot, the flood soone spent,
The time no time, the web soone rent,

ANONYMOUS

The Race soone run, the Goale soone won,
The Dole soone dealt, Mans life first done.
Like to the lightning from the skie,
Or like a Post that quicke doth hie,
Or like a quaver in short song,
Or like a journey three dayes long,
Or like the snow when Summers come,
Or like the Peare, or like the Plum:
Even such is man who heapes up sorrow,
Lives but this daye, and dyes to morrow.
The lightning 's past, the Post must go,
The song is short, the journey's so,
The Peare doth rot, the Plum doth fall,
The Snow dissolves, and so must all.
Like to the seed put in Earths wombe,
Or like dead *Lazarus* in his tombe;
Or like *Tabitha* being asleepe,
Or *Jonas*-like within the deepe;
Or like the Night, or Stars by day,
Which seeme to vanish cleane away:
Even so this Death, Mans life bereaves,
But being dead, Man death deceaves.
The Seed it springeth, *Lazarus* standeth,
Tabitha wakes, and *Jonas* landeth;
The night is past, the Stars remaine,
So man that dyes shall live againe.

M. Sparkes, *Crumbs of Comfort*, 1628

ROBERT BURTON

1577–1640

124 *The Authors Abstract of Melancholy, Διαλογικῶς.*

WHEN I goe musing all alone,
Thinking of diverse things fore-known,
When I build Castles in the aire,
Voide of sorrow and voide of feare,
Pleasing my selfe with phantasms sweete,
Me thinkes the time runnes very fleete.
All my joyes to this are folly,
Naught so sweet as Melancholy.
When I lie waking all alone,
Recounting what I have ill done,
My thoughts on me then tyrannise,
Feare and sorrow me surprise,
Whether I tarry still or go,
Me thinkes the time goes very slow.
All my griefes to this are jolly,
Naught so sad as Melancholy.
When to my selfe I act and smile,
With pleasing thoughts the time beguile,
By a brook side or wood so greene,
Unheard, unsought for, or unseene,
A thousand pleasures doe me blesse,
And crowne my soule with happinesse.
All my joyes besides are folly,
None so sweete as Melancholy.
When I lie, sit, or walke alone,
I sigh, I grieve, making great moane,

ROBERT BURTON

In a darke grove, or irksome den,
With discontents and Furies then,
A thousand miseries at once,
Mine heavy heart and soule ensconce.
  All my griefes to this are jolly,
  None so soure as Melancholy.
Me thinkes I heare, me thinkes I see,
Sweete musicke, wondrous melodie,
Townes, palaces and Citties fine,
Here now, then there, the world is mine,
Rare Beauties, gallant Ladies shine,
What e'er is lovely or divine.
  All other joyes to this are folly,
  None so sweete as Melancholy.
Me thinkes I heare, me thinkes I see
Ghostes, goblins, fiendes, my phantasie
Presents a thousand ugly shapes,
Headlesse bears, blackmen and apes,
Dolefull outcries, and fearefull sightes,
My sad and dismall soule affrightes.
  All my griefes to this are jolly,
  None so damn'd as Melancholy.
Me thinkes I court, me thinkes I kisse,
Me thinkes I now embrace my Miss.
O blessed dayes, O sweete content,
In Paradise my time is spent.
Such thoughts may still my fancy move,
Let me not die, but live in love.
  All my joyes to this are folly,
  Naught so sweete as Melancholy.
When I recount loves many frightes,
My sighes and teares, my waking nightes,

My jealous fits; O mine hard fate,
I now repent, but 'tis too late.
No torment is so bad as love,
So bitter to my soule can prove.
  All my griefes to this are jolly,
  Naught so harsh as Melancholy.
Friends and Companions get you gone,
'Tis my desire to be alone,
Ne'er well but when my thoughts and I,
Doe domineer in privacie.
No Gem, no treasure like to this,
'Tis my delight, my Crowne, my blisse.
  All my joyes to this are folly,
  Naught so sweete as Melancholy.
'Tis my sole plague to be alone,
I am a beast, a monster growne,
I will no light nor company,
I finde it now my misery.
The scene is turn'd, my joyes are gone,
Feare, discontent and sorrowes come.
  All my griefes to this are jolly,
  Naught so fierce as Melancholy.
I'll not change life with any King,
I ravish't am: can the world bring
More joy, than still to laugh and smile,
In pleasant toyes times to beguile?
Doe not, O doe not trouble me,
So sweete content I feele and see.
  All my joyes to this are folly,
  None so divine as Melancholy.
I'll change my state with any wretch,
Thou canst from gaole or dunghill fetch:

ROBERT BURTON

My paines past cure, another Hell,
I may not in this torment dwell,
Now desperate I hate my life,
Lend me an halter or a knife.
  All my griefes to this are jolly,
  Naught so damn'd as Melancholy.

Anatomy of Melancholy, 1628

GEORGE SANDYS

1578–1644

125 *Psalme cxxxvii*

AS on Euphrates shady banks we lay,
  And there, O Sion, to thy Ashes pay
Our funerall teares: our silent Harps, unstrung,
And unregarded, on the Willowes hung.
Lo, they who had thy desolation wrought,
And captiv'd Judah unto Babel brought,
Deride the teares which from our Sorrowes spring;
And say in scorne, A Song of Sion sing.
Shall we prophane our Harps at their command?
Or holy Hymnes sing in a forraigne Land?
O Solyma! thou that art now become
A heape of stones, and to thy selfe a Tomb!
When I forget thee, my deare Mother, let
My fingers their melodious skill forget:
When I a joy disjoyn'd from thine, receive;
Then may my tongue unto my palate cleave.
Remember Edom, Lord; their cruell pride,
Who in the Sack of wretched Salem cry'd;
Downe with their Buildings, rase them to the ground,
Nor let one Stone be on another found.

Thou Babylon, whose Towers now touch the Skie,
That shortly shalt as low in ruines lie;
O happy! O thrice happy they, who shall
With equall cruelty revenge our fall!
That dash thy Childrens braines against the stones:
And without pity heare their dying grones.

Paraphrase on the Psalms, 1638

126 *Deo Opt. Max.*

O THOU who All-things hast of Nothing made,
Whose Hand the radiant Firmament display'd,
With such an undiscerned swiftnesse hurl'd
About the stedfast Centre of the World:
Against whose rapid course the restlesse Sun,
And wandring Flames in varied Motions run;
Which Heat, Light, Life infuse; Time, Night, and Day
Distinguish, in our Humane Bodies sway:
That hung'st the solid Earth in fleeting Aire,
Vein'd with cleare Springs, which ambient Seas repaire.
In Clouds the Mountaines wrap their hoary Heads;
Luxurious Vallies cloth'd with flowry Meads:
Her trees yield Fruit and Shade; with liberall Breasts
All creatures She (their common Mother) feasts.
Then Man thy Image mad'st; in Dignity,
In Knowledge, and in Beauty, like to Thee:
Plac'd in a Heaven on Earth: without his toil
The ever-flourishing and fruitful Soil
Unpurchas'd Food produc'd: all Creatures were
His Subjects, serving more for Love than Feare.
He knew no Lord, but Thee. But when he fell
From his Obedience, all at once rebell,

And in his Ruine exercise their Might:
Concurring Elements against him fight:
Troups of unknowne Diseases; Sorrow, Age,
And Death, assaile him with successive rage.
Hell let forth all her Furies: none so great,
As Man to Man. Ambition, Pride, Deceit,
Wrong arm'd with Power, Lust, Rapine, Slaughter reign'd:
And flatter'd Vice the name of Vertue gain'd.
Then Hills beneath the swelling Waters stood;
And all the Globe of Earth was but one Flood:
Yet could not cleanse their Guilt: the following Race
Worse than their Fathers, and their Sons more base.
Their God-like Beauty lost; Sins wretched Thrall:
No sparke of their Divine Originall
Left unextinguisht: All inveloped
With Darknesse; in their bold Transgressions dead.
When thou didst from the East a Light display,
Which rendred to the World a clearer Day:
Whose Precepts from Hells jawes our Steps withdraw;
And whose Example with a living Law:
Who purg'd us with his Blood; the Way prepar'd
To Heaven, and those long-chain'd-up Doores unbarr'd.
How infinite thy Mercy! which exceeds
The World thou mad'st, as well as our Misdeeds!
Which greater Reverence than thy Justice wins,
And still augments thy Honour by our Sins.
O who hath tasted of thy Clemency
In greater measure, or more oft than I!
My gratefull Verse thy Goodnesse shall display,
O Thou who went'st along in all my way;
To Where the Morning with perfumed Wings
From the high Mountaines of Panchæa springs:

To that New-found-out World, where sober Night
Takes from th' Antipodes her silent flight;
To those darke Seas where horrid Winter reignes,
And binds the stubborne Floods in Icie chaines:
To Lybian Wasts, whose Thirst no showres assuage;
And where swolne Nilus cooles the Lions rage.
Thy Wonders in the Deepe have I beheld;
Yet all by those on Judah's Hills excell'd:
There where the Virgins Son his Doctrine taught,
His Miracles, and our Redemption wrought:
Where I by Thee inspir'd his Praises sung;
And on his Sepulchre my Offering hung.
Which way so e'er I turne my Face, or Feet,
I see thy Glory, and thy Mercy meet.
Met on the Thracian Shores; when in the strife
Of frantick Simoans thou preserv'dst my Life.
So when Arabian Thieves belaid us round,
And when by all abandon'd, Thee I found.
That false Sidonian Wolfe, whose craft put on
A Sheepe soft Fleece, and me Bellerephon
To Ruine by his cruell Letter sent,
Thou didst by thy protecting Hand prevent.
Thou sav'dst me from the bloody Massacres
Of faithlesse Indians; from their treacherous Wars;
From raging Feavers, from the sultry breath
Of tainted Aire; which cloy'd the jawes of Death.
Preserv'd from swallowing Seas; when tow'ring Waves
Mixt with the Clouds, and opened their deep Graves.
From barbarous Pirates ransom'd: by those taught,
Successfully with Salian Moores we fought.
Then brought'st me Home in safety; that this Earth
Might bury me, which fed me from my Birth:

Blest with a healthfull Age; a quiet Mind,
Content with little; to this Worke design'd:
Which I at length have finisht by thy Aid:
And now my Vowes have at thy Altar paid.
Iam tetigi Portum,—Valete.

Paraphrase on the Psalms, 1638

JOHN FLETCHER

1579–1625

Songs from the Plays

127 *(i)*

ORPHEUS with his Lute made Trees,
And the Mountaine tops that freeze,
Bow themselves when he did sing.
To his Musicke, Plants and Flowers
Ever sprung; as Sunne and Showers,
There had made a lasting Spring.
Everything that heard him play,
Even the Billowes of the Sea,
Hung their heads, and then lay by.
In sweet Musicke is such Art,
Killing care, and griefe of heart,
Fall asleepe, or hearing die.

Henry VIII, Act III, Sc. i (text 1623)

128 *(ii)*

BEAUTY clear and fair,
Where the Air
Rather like a perfume dwells,
Where the Violet and the Rose
The blew Veins in blush disclose,
And come to honour nothing else.

Where to live near,
And planted there,
Is to live, and still live new;
Where to gain a favour is
More than light, perpetual bliss;
Make me live by serving you.

Dear again, back recall
To this light,
A stranger to himself and all;
Both the wonder and the story
Shall be yours, and eke the glory;
I am your servant and your thrall.

The Elder Brother, Act III, Sc. v (text 1679)

129 *(iii)*

LET the Bells ring, and let the Boys sing,
The young Lasses skip and play,
Let the Cups go round, till round goes the ground,
Our Learned old Vicar will stay.

Let the Pig turn merrily, merrily ah,
And let the fat Goose swim,
For verily, verily, verily ah,
Our Vicar this day shall be trim.

The stew'd Cock shall Crow, Cock-a-loodle-loo,
A loud Cock-a-loodle shall he Crow;
The Duck and the Drake, shall swim in a lake
Of Onions and Claret below.

Our Wives shall be neat, to bring in our meat;
To thee our most noble adviser,
Our pains shall be great, and Bottles shall sweat,
And we our selves will be wiser.

We'll labour and swink, we'll kiss and we'll drink,
 And Tithes shall come thicker and thicker;
We'll fall to our Plow, and get Children enough,
 And thou shalt be learned old Vicar.

The Spanish Curate, Act III, Sc. ii (text 1679)

130 (*iv*)

SING his praises that doth keep
 Our Flocks from harm,
Pan the Father of our Sheep,
 And arm in arm
Tread we softly in a round,
Whil'st the hollow neighbouring ground
Fills the Musick with her sound.

Pan, O great God *Pan*, to thee
 Thus do we sing:
Thou that keep'st us chaste and free
 As the young spring,
Ever be thy honour spoke,
From that place the morn is broke,
To that place Day doth unyoke.

The Faithful Shepherdess, Act I, Sc. i (text 1679)

131 (*v*) *The Priest's Chant*

SHEPHERDS all, and maidens fair,
 Fold your flocks up, for the Air
'Gins to thicken, and the sun
Already his great course hath run.
See the dew-drops how they kiss
Every little flower that is:

Hanging on their velvet heads,
Like a rope of crystal beads.
See the heavy clouds low falling,
And bright *Hesperus* down calling
The dead night from under ground,
At whose rising mists unsound,
Damps, and vapours fly apace,
Hovering o'er the wanton face
Of these pastures, where they come,
Striking dead both bud and bloom;
Therefore from such danger lock
Every one his loved flock,
And let your Dogs lye loose without,
Lest the Wolf come as a scout
From the mountain, and ere day
Bear a Lamb or kid away,
Or the crafty theevish Fox,
Break upon your simple flocks:
To secure your selves from these,
Be not too secure in ease;
Let one eye his watches keep
Whilst the t'other eye doth sleep;
So you shall good Shepherds prove,
And for ever hold the love
Of our great god. Sweetest slumbers
And soft silence fall in numbers
On your eye-lids: so farewell,
Thus I end my evenings knell.

The Faithful Shepherdess, Act II, Sc. i (text 1679)

132

(vi) *The Song*

DO not fear to put thy feet
Naked in the River sweet;
Think not Leach, or Newt or Toad
Will bite thy foot, when thou hast troad;
Nor let the water rising high,
As thou wad'st in, make thee crie
And sob, but ever live with me,
And not a wave shall trouble thee.

The Faithful Shepherdess, Act III, Sc. i (text 1679)

133

(vii) *Satyr's Song*

SEE the day begins to break,
And the light shoots like a streak
Of subtil fire, the wind blows cold,
Whilst the morning doth unfold;
Now the Birds begin to rouse,
And the Squirril from the boughs
Leaps to get him Nuts and fruit;
The early Lark that erst was mute,
Carrols to the rising day
Many a note and many a lay.

The Faithful Shepherdess, Act IV, Sc. i (text 1679)

134

(viii) *The Satyr's Farewell*

THOU divinest, fairest, brightest,
Thou most powerful maid, and whitest,
Thou most vertuous and most blessed,
Eyes of stars, and golden tressed

Like *Apollo*, tell me sweetest
What new service now is meetest
For the *Satyr*? shall I stray
In the middle air and stay
The sayling Rack, or nimbly take
Hold by the Moon, and gently make
Sute to the pale Queen of night
For a beam to give thee light?
Shall I dive into the Sea,
And bring thee Coral, making way
Through the rising waves that fall
In snowie fleeces; dearest, shall
I catch the wanton Fawns, or Flyes,
Whose woven wings the Summer dyes
Of many colours? get thee fruit?
Or steal from Heaven old *Orpheus* Lute?
All these I'll venture for, and more,
To do her service all these woods adore.
Holy Virgin, I will dance
Round about these woods as quick
As the breaking light, and prick
Down the lawns, and down the vails
Faster than the Wind-mill sails
So I take my leave, and pray
All the comforts of the day,
Such as *Phœbus* heat doth send
On the earth, may still befriend
Thee, and this arbour.

The Faithful Shepherdess, Act v, Sc. i (text 1679)

135 *(ix) Song*

CARE charming sleep, thou easer of all woes,
Brother to death, sweetly thy self dispose
On this afflicted Prince, fall like a Cloud
In gentle showrs, give nothing that is loud,
Or painfull to his slumbers; easie, sweet,
And as a purling stream, thou son of night,
Pass by his troubled senses; sing his pain
Like hollow murmuring wind, or silver Rain,
Into this Prince gently, Oh gently slide,
And kiss him into slumbers like a Bride.

The Tragedy of Valentinian, Act V, Sc. i (text 1679)

136 *(x) Merrythought's Song*

I WOULD not be a Servingman to carry the cloke-bag still.
Nor would I be a Fawlconer the greedy Hawkes to fill.
But I would be in a good house, and have a good Master too:
But I would eat and drink of the best, and no work would I do.

The Knight of the Burning Pestle, Act IV, Sc. i (text 1679)

137 *(xi) Another*

FOR *Jillian* of *Berry*, she dwells on a hill,
And she hath good Beer and Ale to sell,
And of good fellows she thinks no ill,
And thither will we go now, now, now,
And thither will we go now.
And when you have made a little stay,
You need not know what is to pay,
But kiss your Hostess and go your way.
And thither will we go now!

The Knight of the Burning Pestle, Act IV, Sc. i (text 1679)

138 *(xii) Song*

OH fair sweet face, oh eyes celestial bright,
Twin Stars in Heaven, that now adorn the night;
Oh fruitful Lips, where Cherries ever grow,
And Damask cheeks, where all sweet beauties blow;
Oh thou from head to foot divinely fair,
Cupid's most cunning Net 's made of that hair,
And as he weaves himself for curious eyes,
Oh me, Oh me, I am caught my self, he cries:
Sweet rest about thee, sweet and golden sleep,
Soft peaceful thoughts, your hourly watches keep,
Whilst I in wonder sing this sacrifice,
To beauty sacred, and those Angel-eyes.

Women Pleased, Act III, Sc. iv (text 1679)

139 *(xiii) Funeral Song*

URNS and Odours, bring away,
Vapors, sighs, darken the day;
Our dole more deadly looks, than dying
Balmes, and Gumms, and heavy cheers,

Sacred vials fill'd with tears,
And clamors, through the wild air flying:

Come all sad and solemn Shows,
That are quick-ey'd pleasures foes;
We convent nought else but woes.
We convent nought else but woes.

The Two Noble Kinsmen, Act I, Sc. v (text 1679)

JOHN FLETCHER

140 (*xiv*) *The Passionate Man's Song*

HENCE all you vain Delights,
As short as are the nights,
Wherein you spend your folly,
There's nought in this life sweet,
If man were wise to see't,
But only melancholly,
Oh sweetest melancholly.
Welcome folded Arms, and fixed Eyes,
A sigh that piercing mortifies,
A look that's fast'ned to the ground,
A tongue chain'd up without a sound.

Fountain heads, and pathless Groves,
Places which pale passion loves:
Moon-light walks, when all the Fowls
Are warmly hous'd, save Bats and Owls;
A mid-night Bell, a parting groan,
These are the sounds we feed upon;
Then stretch our bones in a still gloomy valley,
Nothing's so dainty sweet, as lovely melancholly.

The Nice Valour, Act III, Sc. i (text 1679)

TOBIAS HUME

d. 1645

141 (*Fain would I change that note*)

FAIN would I change that note
To which fond love hath charmd me,
Long, long to sing by rote,
Fancying that that harmd me.

Yet when this thought doth come,
Love is the perfect summe
Of all delight;
I have no other choice
Either for pen or voyce,
To sing or write.

O Love they wrong thee much
That say thy sweete is bitter.
When thy ripe fruit is such,
As nothing can be sweeter,
Faire house of joy and blisse,
Where truest pleasure is,
I doe adore thee:
I know thee what thou art,
I serve thee with my heart
And fall before thee.

Ayres, 1605

THOMAS FORD

d. 1648

142 (*There is a Lady sweet and kind*)

THERE is a Lady sweet and kind,
Was never face so pleas'd my mind;
I did but see her passing by,
And yet I love her till I die.

Her gesture, motion and her smiles,
Her wit, her voyce, my heart beguiles,
Beguiles my heart, I know not why,
And yet I love her till I die.

Her free behaviour, winning lookes,
Will make a Lawyer burne his bookes.
I touchd her not, alas, not I,
And yet I love her till I die.

Had I her fast betwixt mine armes,
Judge you that thinke such sports were harmes,
Wer't any harm? no, no, fie, fie!
For I will love her till I die.

Should I remaine confined there,
So long as Phebus in his sphere,
I to request, she to denie,
Yet would I love her till I die.

Cupid is winged and doth range,
Her countrie so my love doth change,
But change she earth, or change she skie,
Yet will I love her till I die.

Music of Sundrie Kindes, 1607

JOHN WEBSTER 1580?–1625?

143 *Cornelia's Song*

CALL for the Robin-Red-brest and the wren,
Since o'er shadie groves they hover,
And with leaves and flowres doe cover
The friendlesse bodies of unburied men.
Call unto his funerall Dole
The Ante, the field-mouse, and the mole
To reare him hillockes, that shall keepe him warme,
And (when gay tombes are robb'd) sustaine no harme,
But keepe the wolfe far thence, that's foe to men,
For with his nailes he'll dig them up agen.

The White Divel, 1612

144 *(Hearke, now every thing is still)*

HEARKE, now every thing is still—
The Screech-Owle, and the whistler shrill,
Call upon our Dame, aloud,
And bid her quickly don her shrowd:
Much you had of Land and rent,
Your length in clay 's now competent.
A long war disturb'd your minde,
Here your perfect peace is sign'd—
Of what is 't fooles make such vaine keeping?
Sin their conception, their birth, weeping:
Their life, a generall mist of error,
Their death, a hideous storme of terror—
Strew your haire, with powders sweete:
Don cleane linnen, bathe your feete,
And (the foule fiend more to checke)
A crucifixe let blesse your necke,
'Tis now full tide, 'tweene night, and day,
End your groane, and come away.

The Duchess of Malfi, 1623

145 *(All the Flowers of the Spring)*

ALL the Flowers of the Spring
Meet to perfume our burying:
These have but their growing prime,
And man does flourish but his time.
Survey our progresse from our birth,
We are set, we grow, we turne to earth.
Courts adieu, and all delights,
All bewitching appetites;

Sweetest Breath, and clearest eye,
Like perfumes goe out and dye;
And consequently this is done,
As shadowes wait upon the Sunne.
Vaine the ambition of Kings,
Who seeke by trophies and dead things,
To leave a living name behind,
And weave but nets to catch the wind.

The Devil's Law-Case, 1623

RICHARD CORBET

1582–1635

146 *On Mr. Francis Beaumont (then newly dead)*

HE that hath such acuteness, and such wit,
As would aske ten good heads to husband it;
He that can write so well that no man dare
Refuse it for the best, let him beware:
BEAUMONT is dead, by whose sole death appeares,
Wit 's a Disease consumes men in few yeares.

Beaumont and Fletcher, First Folio, 1647

147 *To his Son, Vincent Corbet, on his Birth-Day, November* 10, 1630, *being then Three Years old*

WHAT I shall leave thee none can tell,
But all shall say I wish thee well;
I wish thee, Vin, before all wealth,
Both bodily and ghostly health:
Nor too much wealth, nor wit, come to thee,
So much of either may undoe thee.

I wish thee learning, not for show,
Enough for to instruct, and know;
Not such as Gentlemen require,
To prate at Table, or at Fire.
I wish thee all thy mothers graces,
Thy fathers fortunes, and his places.
I wish thee friends, and one at Court,
Not to build on, but support;
To keep thee, not in doing many
Oppressions, but from suffering any.
I wish thee peace in all thy ways,
Nor lazy nor contentious days;
And when thy soul and body part,
As innocent as now thou art.

Poems, 1647

148 *A Proper New Ballad, intituled The Fairies Farewell; or, God-a-Mercy Will*

FAREWELL rewards and Fairies,
  Good housewives now may say,
For now foule sluts in Dairies
  Doe fare as well as they.
And though they sweepe their hearths no less
  Than maides were wont to doe,
Yet who of late for cleanliness,
  Finds Sixpence in her shoe?

Lament, lament, old Abbies,
  The Fairies lost command;
They did but change Priests babies,
  But some have chang'd your land:

And all your children stolne from thence
   Are now growne puritanes;
Who live as changelings ever since
   For love of your demaines.

At morning and at evening both
   You merry were and glad,
So little care of sleepe and sloth
   These prettie Ladies had;
When *Tom* came home from labour,
   Or *Cisse* to milking rose,
Then merrily merrily went their Tabor,
   And nimbly went their Toes.

Wittness those rings and roundelayes
   Of theirs, which yet remaine,
Were footed in Queene *Maries* dayes
   On many a grassy playne;
But since of late, *Elizabeth*,
   And later *James* came in,
They never daunc'd on any heath
   As when the time hath bin.

By which we note the Fairies
   Were of the old profession;
Their songs were Ave Maryes,
   Their daunces were procession:
But now, alas! they all are dead
   Or gone beyond the Seas,
Or farther for Religion fled,
   Or else they take their ease.

A tell-tale in their company
They never could endure,
And who so kept not secretly
Their mirth was punisht sure;
It was a just and Christian deed
To pinch such blacke and blew:
O how the Common-wealth doth need
Such Justices as you!

Now they have left our Quarters
A Register they have,
Who looketh to their Charters,
A Man both wise and grave;
An hundred of their merry pranks
By one that I could name
Are kept in store, con twenty thanks
To *William* for the same.

To *William Churne of Staffordshire*,
Give laud and prayses due;
Who every meale can mend your cheere,
With Tales both old and true:
To *William* all give audience,
And pray ye for his Noddle;
For all the Fairies evidence
Were lost, if it were addle.

Poems, 1647

con: offer.

PHINEAS FLETCHER

1582–1650

149 *An Hymne*

DROP, drop, slow tears,
and bathe those beauteous feet,
Which brought from heav'n
the news and Prince of peace:
Cease not, wet eyes,
his mercies to intreat;
To crie for vengeance
sinne doth never cease:
In your deep floods
drown all my faults and fears;
Nor let his eye
see sinne, but through my tears.

Poetical Miscellanies, 1633

150 *Sin, Despair, and Lucifer*

THE Porter to th' infernall gate is Sin,
A shapeless shape, a foule deformed thing,
Nor nothing, nor a substance: as those thin
And empty formes, which through the ayer fling
Their wandring shapes, at length they're fastned in
The Chrystall sight. It serves, yet reignes as King:
It lives, yet 's death: it pleases, full of paine:
Monster! ah who, who can thy being feigne?
Thou shapeless shape, live death, paine pleasing, servile raigne.

Of that first woman, and th' old serpent bred,
By lust and custome nurst; whom when her mother
Saw so deform'd, how faine would she have fled
Her birth, and selfe! But she her dam would smother,

And all her brood, had not He rescued
Who was his mothers sire, his childrens brother;
  Eternitie, who yet was borne and died:
  His owne Creatour, earths scorne, heavens pride,
Who th' Deitie inflesht, and mans flesh deified.

Her former parts her mother seemes resemble,
Yet onely seemes to flesh and weaker sight;
For she with art and paint could fine dissemble
Her loathsome face: her back parts (blacke as night)
Like to her horrid Sire would force to tremble
The boldest heart; to th' eye that meetes her right
  She seemes a lovely sweet, of beauty rare;
  But at the parting, he that shall compare,
Hell will more lovely deem, the divel's selfe more faire.

. . . . . .

Close by her sat Despaire, sad ghastly Spright,
With staring lookes, unmoov'd, fast nayl'd to Sinne;
Her body all of earth, her soule of fright,
About her thousand deaths, but more within:
Pale, pined cheeks, black hayre, torne, rudely dight;
Short breath, long nayles, dull eyes, sharp-pointed chin:
  Light, life, heaven, earth, her selfe, and all shee fled.
  Fayne would she die, but could not: yet halfe dead,
A breathing corse she seem'd, wrap't up in living lead.

. . . . . .

The mid'st, but lowest (in hells heraldry
The deepest is the highest roome) in state
Sat Lordly Lucifer: his fiery eye,
Much swol'ne with pride, but more with rage, and hate,
As Censour, muster'd all his company;

Who round about with awefull silence sate.
  This doe, this let rebellious Spirits gaine,
  Change God for Satan, heaven's for hells Sov'raigne:
O let him serve in hell, who scornes in heaven to raigne!

Ah wretch, who with ambitious cares opprest,
Long'st still for future, feel'st no present good:
Despising to be better, would'st be best,
Good never; who wilt serve thy lusting mood,
Yet all command: not he, who rais'd his crest,
But pull'd it downe, hath high and firmely stood.
  Foole, serve thy towring lusts, grow still, still crave,
  Rule, raigne, this comfort from thy greatness have,
Now at thy top, Thou art a great commanding slave.

Thus fell this Prince of darkness, once a bright
And glorious starre: he wilfull turn'd away
His borrowed globe from that eternall light:
Himselfe he sought, so lost himselfe: his ray
Vanish't to smoke, his morning sunk in night,
And never more shall see the springing day:
  To be in heaven the second he disdaines:
  So now the first in hell, and flames he raignes,
Crown'd once with joy, and light: crown'd now with fire and
    paines.

The Locusts, 1627 (Canto 1, stanzas 10–12, 15, 18–20)

151 *Desiderium*

HAPPY, thrice happy times in silver age!
  When generous plants advanc't their lofty crest;
When honour stoopt to be learn'd wisdomes page;
When baser weeds starv'd in their frozen nest;

When th' highest flying Muse still highest climbes;
And vertues rise keeps down all rising crimes.
Happy, thrice happy age! happy, thrice happy times!

But wretched we, to whom these iron daies
(Hard daies) afford nor matter, nor reward!
Sings *Maro*? men deride high *Maro's* layes;
Their hearts with lead, with steel their sense is barr'd:
Sing *Linus*, or his father, as he uses,
Our *Midas* eares their well tun'd verse refuses.
What cares an asse for arts? he brayes at sacred Muses.

But if fond *Bavius* vent his clouted song,
Or *Maevius* chaunt his thoughts in brothell charm;
The witlesse vulgar, in a numerous throng,
Like summer flies about their dunghills swarm:
They sneer, they grinne. *Like to his like will move.*
Yet never let them greater mischief prove
Than this, *Who hates not one, may he the other love.*

Witnesse our *Colin*; whom though all the Graces,
And all the Muses nurst; whose well taught song
Parnassus self, and *Glorian* embraces,
And all the learn'd, and all the shepherds throng;
Yet all his hopes were crost, all suits deni'd;
Discourag'd, scorn'd, his writing vilifi'd:
Poorly (poore man) he liv'd; poorly (poore man) he di'd.

And had not that great *Heart* (whose honour'd head
Ah! lies full low) piti'd thy wofull plight;
There hadst thou lien unwept, unburied,
Unblest, nor grac't with any common rite:

Colin: Spenser.

Yet shalt thou live, when thy great foe shall sink
Beneath his mountain tombe, whose fame shall stink;
And time his blacker name shall blurre with blackest ink.

O let th' Iambick Muse revenge that wrong,
Which cannot slumber in thy sheets of lead:
Let thy abused honour crie as long
As there be quills to write, or eyes to reade:
On his rank name let thine own votes be turn'd,
Oh may that man that hath the Muses scorn'd,
Alive, nor dead, be ever of a Muse adorn'd!

Oft therefore have I chid my tender Muse;
Oft my chill breast beats off her fluttering wing:
Yet when new spring her gentle rayes infuse,
All storms are laid, I 'gin to chirp and sing:
At length soft fires disperst in every vein,
Yeeld open passage to the thronging train,
And swelling numbers tide rolls like the surging main.

So where fair *Thames*, and crooked *Isis* sonne
Payes tribute to his King, the mantling stream
Encounter'd by the tides (now rushing on
With equall force) of's way doth doubtfull seem:
At length the full-grown sea, and waters King
Chide the bold waves with hollow murmuring:
Back flie the streams to shroud them in their mother spring.

Yet thou sweet numerous Muse, why should'st thou droop
That every vulgar eare thy musick scorns?
Nor can they rise, nor thou so low canst stoop;
No seed of heav'n takes root in mud or thorns.
When owls or crows, imping their flaggy wing
With thy stoln plumes, their notes through th'ayer fling;
Oh shame! They howl and croak, while fond they strain to sing.

Enough for thee in heav'n to build thy nest;
(Farre be dull thoughts of winning dunghill praise)
Enough, if Kings enthrone thee in their breast,
And crown their golden crowns with higher baies:
  Enough that those who weare the crown of Kings
  (Great *Israels* Princes) strike thy sweetest strings:
Heav'ns Dove when high'st he flies, flies with thy heav'nly
    wings.

Let others trust the seas, dare death and hell,
Search either *Inde*, vaunt of their scarres and wounds;
Let others their deare breath (nay silence) sell
To fools, and (swoln, not rich) stretch out their bounds
  By spoiling those that live, and wronging dead;
  That they may drink in pearl, and couch their head
In soft, but sleeplesse down; in rich, but restlesse bed.

Oh let them in their gold quaffe dropsies down;
Oh let them surfets feast in silver bright:
While sugar hires the taste the brain to drown,
And bribes of sauce corrupt false appetite,
  His masters rest, health, heart, life, soul to sell.
  Thus plentie, fulnesse, sicknesse, ring their knell:
Death weds and beds them; first in grave, and then in hell.

But (ah!) let me under some *Kentish* hill
Neare rolling *Medway* 'mong my shepherd peers,
With fearelesse merrie-make, and piping still,
Securely passe my few and slow-pac'd yeares:
  While yet the great *Augustus* of our nation
  Shuts up old *Janus* in this long cessation,
Strength'ning our pleasing ease, and gives us sure vacation.

There may I, master of a little flock,
Feed my poore lambes, and often change their fare:
My lovely mate shall tend my sparing stock,
And nurse my little ones with pleasing care;
    Whose love and look shall speak their father plain.
    Health be my feast, heav'n hope, content my gain:
So in my little house my lesser heart shall reigne.

The beech shall yield a cool safe canopie,
While down I sit, and chaunt to th' echoing wood:
Ah singing might I live, and singing die!
So by fair Thames, or silver Medwayes floud,
    The dying swan, when yeares her temples pierce,
    In musick strains breathes out her life and verse;
And chaunting her own dirge tides on her wat'ry hearse.

What shall I then need seek a patron out,
Or begge a favour from a mistress' eyes,
To fence my song against the vulgar rout,
Or shine upon me with her Geminies?
    What care I, if they praise my slender song?
    Or reck I, if they do me right, or wrong?
A shepherds blisse nor stands nor falls to ev'ry tongue.

Great prince of shepherds, than thy heav'ns more high,
Low as our earth, here serving, ruling there;
Who taught'st our death to live, thy life to die;
Who when we broke thy bonds, our bonds would'st bear;
    Who reignedst in thy heav'n, yet felt'st our hell;
    Who (God) bought'st man, whom man (though God) did
        sell;
Who in our flesh, our graves, (and worse) our hearts would'st
        dwell:

Great Prince of shepherds, thou who late didst deigne
To lodge thy self within this wretched breast,
(Most wretched breast such guest to entertain,
Yet oh, most happy lodge in such a guest!)
  Thou first and last, inspire thy sacred skill;
  Guide thou my hand, grace thou my artlesse quill:
So shall I first begin, so last shall end thy will.

The Purple Island, 1633 (Canto 1, stanzas 16–33)

152 *The Overthrow of Lucifer*

WITH that a thundring noise seem'd shake the skie,
As when with iron wheels through stonie plain
A thousand chariots to the battell flie;
Or when with boistrous rage the swelling main,
  Puft up with mighty windes, does hoarsly roar;
  And beating with his waves the trembling shore,
His sandie girdle scorns, and breaks earths ramperd doore.

And straight an Angel full of heav'nly might,
(Three severall crowns circled his royall head)
From Northern coast heaving his blazing light,
Through all the earth his glorious beams dispread,
  And open laies the Beasts and Dragons shame:
  For to this end th' Almighty did him frame,
And therefore from supplanting gave his ominous name.

A silver trumpet oft he loudly blew,
Frighting the guiltie earth with thundring knell;
And oft proclaim'd, as through the world he flew,
Babel, great *Babel* lies as low as hell:

Angel: James I 'in his remonstrance and comment on the Apocalypse'.

Let every Angel loud his trumpet sound,
Her heav'n-exalted towers in dust are drown'd:
Babel, proud *Babel's* fall'n, and lies as low as ground.

The broken heav'ns dispart with fearfull noise,
And from the breach out shoots a suddain light;
Straight shrilling trumpets with loud sounding voice
Give echoing summons to new bloudy fight:
Well knew the Dragon that all-quelling blast,
And soon perceiv'd that day must be his last;
Which strook his frighted heart, and all his troops aghast.

Yet full of malice and of stubborn pride,
Though oft had strove, and had been foild as oft,
Boldly his death and certain fate defi'd:
And mounted on his flaggie sails aloft,
With boundlesse spite he long'd to try again
A second losse, and new death; glad and fain
To shew his pois'nous hate, though ever shew'd in vain.

So up he rose upon his stretched sails,
Fearlesse expecting his approaching death:
So up he rose, that th' ayer starts, and fails,
And over-pressed sinks his load beneath:
So up he rose, as does a thunder-cloud,
Which all the earth with shadows black does shroud:
So up he rose, and through the weary ayer row'd.

Now his Almighty foe farre off he spies;
Whose Sun-like arms daz'd the eclipsed day,
Confounding with their beams lesse-glitt'ring skies,
Firing the aire with more than heav'nly ray;
Like thousand Sunnes in one: such is their light;
A subject onely for immortall sprite,
Which never can be seen, but by immortall sight.

His threatning eyes shine like that dreadfull flame,
With which the Thunderer arms his angry hand:
Himself had fairly wrote his wondrous name,
Which neither earth nor heav'n could understand:
  A hundred crowns, like towers, beset around
  His conqu'ring head: well may they there abound,
When all his limbes and troops with gold are richly crown'd.

His armour all was dy'd in purple blood;
(In purple bloud of thousand rebell Kings)
In vain their stubborn powers his arm withstood:
Their proud necks chain'd he now in triumph brings,
  And breaks their spears, and cracks their traitour swords
  Upon whose arms and thigh, in golden words
Was fairly writ, *The* KING *of Kings, and* LORD *of Lords.*

His snow-white steed was born of heav'nly kinde,
Begot by *Boreas* on the *Thracian* hills;
More strong and speedy than his parent Winde:
And (which his foes with fear and horrour fills)
  Out from his mouth a two-edg'd sword he darts;
  Whose sharpest steel the bone and marrow parts,
And with his keenest point unbreasts the naked hearts.

The Dragon, wounded with this flaming brand,
They take, and in strong bonds and fetters tie:
Short was the fight, nor could he long withstand
Him, whose appearance is his victorie.
  So now he's bound in adamantine chain;
  He storms, he roars, he yells for high disdain:
His net is broke, the fowl go free, the fowler ta'en.

The Purple Island, 1633 (Canto 12, stanzas 54–64)

SIR JOHN BEAUMONT

1583–1627

153

Of true Liberty

HE that from dust of worldly tumults flies,
May boldly open his undazled eyes,
To reade wise Natures booke, and with delight
Surveyes the Plants by day, and starres by night.
We need not travel, seeking wayes to blisse:
He that desires contentment, cannot misse:
No garden walles this precious flowre imbrace:
It common growes in ev'ry desart place.
Large scope of pleasure drownes us like a flood,
To rest in little, is our greatest good.
Learne ye that climb the top of Fortunes wheele,
That dang'rous state which ye disdaine to feele:
Your highnesse puts your happinesse to flight,
Your inward comforts fade with outward light,
Unlesse it be a blessing not to know
This certaine truth, lest ye should pine for woe,
To see inferiours so divinely blest
With freedome, and your selves with fetters prest,
Ye sit like pris'ners barr'd with doores and chaines,
And yet no care perpetuall care restraines.
Ye strive to mixe your sad conceits with joyes,
By curious pictures, and by glitt'ring toyes,
While others are not hind'red from their ends,
Delighting to converse with bookes or friends,
And living thus retir'd, obtaine the pow'r
To reigne as Kings, of every sliding houre:
They walke by *Cynthia's* light, and lift their eyes
To view the ord'red armies in the skies.

The heav'ns they measure with imagin'd lines,
And when the Northerne Hemisphere declines,
New constellations in the South they find,
Whose rising may refresh the studious mind.
In these delights, though freedome shew more high:
Few can to things above their thoughts apply.
But who is he that cannot cast his looke
On earth, and reade the beauty of that booke?
A bed of smiling flow'rs, a trickling Spring,
A swelling River, more contentment bring,
Than can be shadow'd by the best of Art:
Thus still the poore man hath the better part.

Bosworth-field, 1629

154 *Of my deare Sonne, Gervase Beaumont*

CAN I, who have for others oft compil'd
The Songs of Death, forget my sweetest child,
Which like a flow'r crusht, with a blast is dead,
And ere full time hangs downe his smiling head,
Expecting with cleare hope to live anew,
Among the Angels fed with heav'nly dew?
We have this signe of Joy, that many dayes,
While on the earth his struggling spirit stayes,
The name of *Jesus* in his mouth containes,
His only food, his sleepe, his ease from paines.
O may that sound be rooted in my mind,
Of which in him such strong effect I find.
Deare Lord, receive my Sonne, whose winning love
To me was like a friendship, farre above
The course of nature, or his tender age,
Whose lookes could all my bitter griefes assuage;

Let his pure soule ordain'd sev'n yeares to be
In that fraile body, which was part of me,
Remaine my pledge in heav'n, as sent to shew,
How to this Port at ev'ry step I goe.

Bosworth-Field, 1629

155 *To his late Majesty, concerning the true forme of English Poetry*

GREAT King, the Sov'raigne Ruler of this Land,
By whose grave care, our hopes securely stand:
Since you descending from that spacious reach,
Vouchsafe to be our Master, and to teach
Your English Poets to direct their lines,
To mixe their colours, and expresse their signes.
Forgive my boldnesse, that I here present
The life of Muses yeelding true content
In ponder'd numbers, which with ease I try'd,
When your judicious rules have been my guide.

. . . .

In ev'ry Language now in Europe spoke
By Nations which the Roman Empire broke,
The relish of the Muse consists in rime,
One verse must meete another like a chime.
Our Saxon shortnesse hath peculiar grace
In choice of words, fit for the ending place,
Which leave impression in the mind as well
As closing sounds, of some delightfull bell:
These must not be with disproportion lame,
Nor should an Eccho still repeate the same.
In many changes these may be exprest:
But those that joyne most simply, run the best:

Their forme surpassing farre the fetter'd staves,
Vaine care, and needlesse repetition saves.
These outward ashes keepe those inward fires,
Whose heate the Greeke and Roman works inspires:
Pure phrase, fit Epithets, a sober care
Of Metaphors, descriptions cleare, yet rare,
Similitudes contracted smooth and round,
Not vext by learning, but with Nature crown'd:
Strong figures drawne from deepe inventions springs,
Consisting lesse in words, and more in things:
A language not affecting ancient times,
Nor Latine shreds, by which the Pedant climes:
A noble subject which the mind may lift
To easie use of that peculiar gift,
Which Poets in their raptures hold most deare,
When actions by the lively sound appeare.
Give me such helpes, I never will despaire,
But that our heads which sucke the freezing aire,
As well as hotter braines, may verse adorne,
And be their wonder, as we were their scorne.

Bosworth-Field, 1629

PHILIP MASSINGER

1583–1640

156 *A Sad Song*

WHY art thou slow, thou rest of trouble, Death,
To stop a wretches breath,
That calls on thee, and offers her sad heart
A prey unto thy dart?
I am not young, nor faire, be therefore bold,
Sorrow hath made me old,

Deform'd, and wrinkl'd, all that I can crave,
    Is quiet in my grave.
Such as live happy, hold long life a Jewell,
    But to me thou art cruell:
If thou end not my tedious miserie,
    And I soone cease to be.
Strike, and strike home then, pitty unto me
In one short hours delay is tyrannie.

The Emperor of the East, 1632, Act v, Sc. iii

AURELIAN TOWNSHEND

c. 1583–1643

157 *A Dialogue betwixt Time and a Pilgrime*

Pilgr. Aged man, that mowes these fields.
Time. Pilgrime speak, what is thy will?
Pilgr. Whose soile is this that such sweet Pasture yields?
    Or who art thou whose Foot stand never still?
        Or where am I? *Time.* In love.
Pilgr. His Lordship lies above.
Time. Yes and below, and round about
    Where in all sorts of flow'rs are growing
Which as the early Spring puts out,
        Time falls as fast a mowing.
Pilgr. If thou art Time, these Flow'rs have Lives,
    And then I fear,
Under some Lilly she I love
    May now be growing there.
Time. And in some Thistle or some spire of grasse,
My scythe thy stalk before hers come may passe.

Pilgr. Wilt thou provide it may? *Time.* No.
Pilgr. Allege the cause.
Time. Because Time cannot alter but obey Fates laws.
Cho. Then happy those whom Fate, that is the stronger,
Together twists their threads, and yet draws hers the longer.

H. Lawes, *Ayres and Dialogues*, Bk. I, 1653

158 *To the Countesse of Salisbury*[1]

VICTORIOUS beauty, though your eyes
Are able to subdue an host,
And therefore are unlike to boast
The taking of a little prize,
Do not a single heart dispise.

It came alone, but yet so arm'd
With former love, I durst have sworne
That where a privy coat was worne,
With characters of beauty charm'd,
Thereby it might have scap'd unharm'd.

But neither steele nor stony breast
Are proofe against those lookes of thine,
Nor can a Beauty lesse divine
Of any heart be long possest,
Where thou pretend'st an interest.

Thy Conquest in regard of me
Alasse is small, but in respect
Of her that did my Love protect,
Were it divulged, deserv'd to be
Recorded for a Victory.

[1] Ascribed sometimes to Pembroke.

And such a one, as some that view
Her lovely face perhaps may say,
Though you have stolen my heart away,
If all your servants prove not true,
May steale a heart or two from you.

Playford, *Select Ayres*, 1652

159 *Upon Kinde and True Love*

'TIS not how witty, nor how free,
Nor yet how beautifull she be,
But how much kinde and true to me.
Freedom and Wit none can confine,
And Beauty like the Sun doth shine,
But kinde and true are only mine.

Let others with attention sit,
To listen, and admire her wit,
That is a rock where I'll not split.
Let others dote upon her eyes,
And burn their hearts for sacrifice,
Beauty 's a calm where danger lyes.

But Kinde and True have been long tried
A harbour where we may confide,
And safely there at anchor ride.
From change of winds there we are free,
And need not feare Storme's tyrannie,
Nor Pirate, though a Prince he be.

Choice Drollery, 1656

LORD HERBERT OF CHERBURY

1583–1648

160 *Ditty in imitation of the Spanish*
Entre tanto que L'Avril

NOW that the *April* of your youth adorns
The Garden of your face,
Now that for you each knowing Lover mourns,
And all seek to your Grace:
Do not repay affection with Scorns.

What though you may a matchless Beauty vaunt,
And that all Hearts can move,
By such a power, as seemeth to inchant?
Yet without help of Love
Beauty no pleasure to it self can grant.

Then think each minute that you lose, a day;
The longest Youth is short,
The shortest Age is long; time flies away,
And makes us but his sport;
And that which is not Youth's is Age's prey.

See but the bravest Horse, that prideth most,
Though he escape the War,
Either from master to the man is lost,
Or turn'd unto the Car,
Or else must die with being ridden Post.

Then lose not beauty, Lovers, time, and all,
Too late your fault you see,
When that in vain you would these dayes recall;
Nor can you vertuous be,
When without these you have not wherewithall.

Poems, 1665

161 *Tears, flow no more*

TEARS, flow no more, or if you needs must flow,
Fall yet more slow,
Do not the world invade,
From smaller springs than yours rivers have grown,
And they again a Sea have made,
Brackish like you, and which like you hath flown.

Ebb to my heart, and on the burning fires
Of my desires,
O let your torrents fall,
From smaller heate than theirs such sparks arise
As into flame converting all,
This world might be but my love's sacrifice.

Yet if the tempests of my sighs so blow
You both must flow,
And my desires still burn,
Since that in vain all help my love requires,
Why may not yet their rages turn
To dry those tears, and to blow out those fires?

Poems, 1665

162 *Elegy over a Tomb*

MUST I then see, alas! eternal night
Sitting upon those fairest eyes,
And closing all those beams, which once did rise
So radiant and bright,
That light and heat in them to us did prove
Knowledge and Love?

Oh, if you did delight no more to stay
    Upon this low and earthly stage,
But rather chose an endless heritage,
    Tell us at least, we pray,
Where all the beauties that those ashes ow'd
    Are now bestow'd?

Doth the Sun now his light with yours renew?
    Have Waves the curling of your hair?
Did you restore unto the Sky and Air,
    The red, and white, and blew?
Have you vouchsaf'd to flowers since your death
    That sweetest breath?

Had not Heav'ns Lights else in their houses slept,
    Or to some private life retir'd?
Must not the Sky and Air have else conspir'd,
    And in their Regions wept?
Must not each flower else the earth could breed
    Have been a weed?

But thus enrich'd may we not yield some cause
    Why they themselves lament no more?
That must have chang'd the course they held before,
    And broke their proper Laws,
Had not your beauties giv'n this second birth
    To Heaven and Earth?

Tell us, for Oracles must still ascend,
    For those that crave them at your tomb:
Tell us, where are those beauties now become,
    And what they now intend:
Tell us, alas, that cannot tell our grief,
    Or hope relief.

Poems, 1665

163 *To her Eyes*

BLACK eyes if you seem dark,
It is because your beams are deep,
And with your soul united keep:
Who could discern
Enough into them, there might learn,
Whence they derive that mark;
And how their power is such,
That all the wonders which proceed from thence,
Affecting more the mind than sense,
Are not so much
The works of light, as influence.

As you then joined are
Unto the Soul, so it again
By its connexion doth pertain
To that first cause,
Who giving all their proper Laws,
By you doth best declare
How he at first being hid
Within the veil of an eternal night,
Did frame for us a second light,
And after bid
It serve for ordinary sight.

His image then you are.
If there be any yet who doubt
What power it is that doth look out
Through that your black,
He will not an example lack,
If he suppose that there
Were grey, or hazel Glass,

And that through them, though sight or soul might shine,
He must yet at the last define,
That beams which pass
Through black, cannot but be divine.

Poems, 1665

164 *To a Lady who did sing excellently*

WHEN our rude and unfashion'd words, that long
A being in their elements enjoy'd,
Senseless and void,
Come at last to be formed by thy tongue,
And from thy breath receive that life and place,
And perfect grace,
That now thy power diffus'd through all their parts
Are able to remove
All the obstructions of the hardest hearts,
And teach the most unwilling how to love;

When they again, exalted by thy voice,
Tun'd by thy soul, dismiss'd into the air,
To us repair,
A living, moving, and harmonious noise,
Able to give the love they do create
A second state,
And charm not only all his griefs away,
And his defects restore,
But make him perfect, who, the Poets say,
Made all was ever yet made heretofore;

When again all these rare perfections meet,
Composed in the circle of thy face,
As in their place,
So to make up of all one perfect sweet,

Who is not then so ravish'd with delight
Ev'n of thy sight,
That he can be assur'd his sense is true,
Or that he die, or live,
Or that he do enjoy himself, or you,
Or only the delights, which you did give?

Poems, 1665

165 *An Ode upon a Question moved, Whether Love should continue for ever?*

HAVING interr'd her Infant-birth,
The watry ground that late did mourn,
Was strew'd with flow'rs for the return
Of the wish'd Bridegroom of the earth.

The well accorded Birds did sing
Their hymns unto the pleasant time,
And in a sweet consorted chime
Did welcom in the chearful Spring.

To which, soft whistles of the Wind,
And warbling murmurs of a Brook,
And vari'd notes of leaves that shook,
An harmony of parts did bind.

While doubling joy unto each other,
All in so rare concent was shown,
No happiness that came alone,
Nor pleasure that was not another.

When with a love none can express,
That mutually happy pair,
Melander and *Celinda* fair,
The season with their loves did bless.

Walking thus towards a pleasant Grove,
  Which did, it seem'd, in new delight
  The pleasures of the time unite,
To give a triumph to their love,

They stay'd at last, and on the Grass
  Reposed so, as o'er his breast
  She bow'd her gracious head to rest,
Such a weight as no burden was.

While over eithers compass'd waist
  Their folded arms were so compos'd,
  As if in straitest bonds inclos'd,
They suffer'd for joys they did taste.

Long their fixt eyes to Heaven bent,
  Unchanged, they did never move,
  As if so great and pure a love
No Glass but it could represent.

When with a sweet, though troubled look,
  She first brake silence, saying, Dear friend,
  O that our love might take no end,
Or never had beginning took!

I speak not this with a false heart,
  (Wherewith his hand she gently strain'd)
  Or that would change a love maintain'd
With so much faith on either part.

Nay, I protest, though Death with his
  Worst Counsel should divide us here,
  His terrors could not make me fear,
To come where your lov'd presence is.

Only if loves fire with the breath
  Of life be kindled, I doubt,
  With our last air 'twill be breath'd out,
And quenched with the cold of death.

That if affection be a line,
  That is clos'd up in our last hour;
  Oh how 'twould grieve me, any pow'r
Could force so dear a love as mine!

She scarce had done, when his shut eyes
  An inward joy did represent,
  To hear *Celinda* thus intent
To a love he so much did prize.

Then with a look, it seem'd, deny'd
  All earthly pow'r but hers, yet so,
  As if to her breath he did owe
This borrow'd life, he thus repli'd;

O you, wherein, they say, Souls rest,
  Till they descend pure heavenly fires,
  Shall lustful and corrupt desires
With your immortal seed be blest?

And shall our Love, so far beyond
  That low and dying appetite,
  And which so chast desires unite,
Not hold in an eternal bond?

Is it, because we should decline,
  And wholly from our thoughts exclude
  Objects that may the sense delude,
And study only the Divine?

No sure, for if none can ascend
   Ev'n to the visible degree
   Of things created, how should we
The invisible comprehend?

Or rather since that Pow'r exprest
   His greatness in his works alone,
   B'ing here best in his Creatures known,
Why is he not lov'd in them best?

But is't not true, which you pretend,
   That since our love and knowledge here,
   Only as parts of life appear,
So they with it should take their end.

O no, Belov'd, I am most sure,
   Those vertuous habits we acquire,
   As being with the Soul intire,
Must with it evermore endure.

For if where sins and vice reside,
   We find so foul a guilt remain,
   As never dying in his stain,
Still punish'd in the Soul doth bide,

Much more that true and real joy,
   Which in a vertuous love is found,
   Must be more solid in its ground,
Than Fate or Death can e'er destroy.

Else should our Souls in vain elect,
   And vainer yet were Heavens laws,
   When to an everlasting Cause
They gave a perishing Effect.

Nor here on earth then, nor above,
  Our good affection can impair,
  For where God doth admit the fair,
Think you that he excludeth Love?

These eyes again, then, eyes shall see,
  And hands again these hands enfold,
  And all chast pleasures can be told
Shall with us everlasting be.

For if no use of sense remain
  When bodies once this life forsake,
  Or they could no delight partake,
Why should they ever rise again?

And if every imperfect mind
  Make love the end of knowledge here,
  How perfect will our love be, where
All imperfection is refin'd?

Let then no doubt, *Celinda*, touch,
  Much less your fairest mind invade,
  Were not our souls immortal made,
Our equal loves can make them such.

So when one wing can make no way,
  Two joyned can themselves dilate,
  So can two persons propagate,
When singly either would decay.

So when from hence we shall be gone,
  And be no more, nor you, nor I,
  As one anothers mystery,
Each shall be both, yet both but one.

This said, in her up-lifted face,
  Her eyes which did that beauty crown,
  Were like two stars, that having faln down,
Look up again to find their place:

While such a moveless silent peace
  Did seize on their becalmed sense,
  One would have thought some Influence
Their ravish'd spirits did possess.

Poems, 1665

166 *Platonick Love*

DISCONSOLATE and sad,
  So little hope of remedy I find,
That when my matchless Mistress were inclin'd
  To pity me, 'twould scarcely make me glad,
The discomposing of so fair a Mind
  Being that which would to my Afflictions add.

For when she should repent,
This Act of Charity had made her part
With such a precious Jewel as her Heart,
  Might she not grieve that e'er she did relent?
And then were it (not) fit I felt the smart
  Untill I grew the greater Penitent?

Nor were't a good excuse,
When she pleas'd to call for her Heart again,
To tell her of my suffering and pain,
  Since that I should her Clemency abuse,
While she did see what wrong she did sustain,
  In giving what she justly might refuse.

Vex'd thus with me at last,
When from her kind restraint she now were gone,
And I left to the Manacles alone,
Should I not on another Rock be cast?
Since they who have not yet content, do moan
Far less than they whose hope thereof is past.

Besides I would deserve,
And not live poorly on the alms of Love,
Or claim a favour did not singly move
From my regard: If she her joys reserve
Unto some other, she at length should prove,
Rather than beg her pity I would sterve.

Let her then be serene,
Alike exempt from pity and from hate:
Let her still keep her dignity and state;
Yet from her glories something I shall glean,
For when she doth them every where dilate,
A beam or two to me must intervene.

And this shall me sustain,
For though due merit I cannot express,
Yet she shall know none ever lov'd for less,
Or easier reward: Let her remain
Still Great and Good, and from her happiness
My chief contentment I will entertain.

Poems, 1665

WILLIAM BASSE

fl. 1602

167 *Elegy on Shakespeare*

RENOWNED Spencer lye a thought more nye
To learned Chaucer, and rare Beaumont lye
A little neerer Spenser, to make roome
For Shakespeare in your threefold, fowerfold Tombe.
To lodge all foure in one bed make a shift
Untill Doomesdaye, for hardly will a fift
Betwixt this day and that by Fate be slayne,
For whom your Curtaines may be drawn againe.
If your precedency in death doth barre
A fourth place in your sacred sepulcher,
Under this carved marble of thine owne,
Sleepe, rare Tragædian, Shakespeare, sleep alone;
Thy unmolested peace, unshared Cave,
Possesse as Lord, not Tenant, of thy Grave,
That unto us and others it may be
Honor hereafter to be layde by thee.

Lansdowne, 777 Plut. lxxvi A

168 *The Anglers Song*

AS inward love breeds outward talk,
The *Hound* some praise, and some the *Hawk*,
Some better pleas'd with private sport
Use *Tennis*; some a *Mistris* court:
But these delights I neither wish,
Nor envy, while I freely fish.

WILLIAM BASSE

Who *hunts*, doth oft in danger ride;
Who *hawks*, lures oft both far and wide;
Who uses *games*, may often prove
A loser; but who falls in love,
  Is fettered in fond *Cupids* snare:
  My Angle breeds me no such care.

Of Recreation there is none
So free as fishing is alone;
All other pastimes do no less
Than mind and body both possess;
  My hand alone my work can do,
  So I can fish and study too.

I care not, I, to fish in seas,
Fresh rivers best my mind do please,
Whose sweet calm course I contemplate,
And seek in life to imitate;
  In civil bounds I fain would keep,
  And for my past offences weep.

And when the timorous Trout I wait
To take, and he devours my bait,
How poor a thing, sometimes I find,
Will captivate a greedy mind;
  And when none bite, I praise the wise,
  Whom vain allurements ne'er surprise.

But yet though while I fish I fast,
I make good fortune my repast,
And thereunto my friend invite,
In whom I more than that delight:
  Who is more welcome to my dish,
  Than to my Angle is my fish.

As well content no prize to take
As use of taken prize to make;
For so our Lord was pleased when
He Fishers made Fishers of men;
  Where (which is in no other game)
  A man may fish and praise his name.

The first men that our Saviour dear
Did chuse to wait upon him here,
Blest Fishers were; and fish the last
Food was, that he on earth did taste:
  I therefore strive to follow those
  Whom he to follow him hath chose.

I. Walton, *The Compleat Angler*, 1653

ANONYMOUS (? W. BASSE)

169 *A Memento for Mortalitie*

MORTALITIE behold and feare,
What a change of flesh is here?
Thinke how many royall bones,
Sleepe within this heape of stones,
Hence remov'd from beds of ease,
Daintie fare, and what might please,
Fretted roofes, and costlie showes,
To a roofe that flats the nose:
Which proclaimes all flesh is grasse,
How the worlds faire Glories passe:
That there is no trust in Health,
In youth, in age, in Greatnesse, wealth:

For if such could have repriv'd,
Those had beene immortall liv'd.
Know from this the world's a snare,
How that greatnesse is but care,
How all pleasures are but paine,
And how short they do remaine:
For here they lye had Realmes and Lands,
That now want strength to stirre their hands;
Where from their pulpits seel'd with dust
They preach: *In Greatnesse is no trust.*
Here's an Acre sowne indeed,
With the richest royall seed,
That the earth did e'er sucke in,
Since the first man dy'd for sin,
Here the bones of birth have cry'd,
Though Gods they were, as men have dy'd.
Here are sands (ignoble things)
Dropt from the ruin'd sides of Kings;
With whom the poore mans earth being showne,
The difference is not easily knowne.
Here's a world of pompe and state,
Forgotten, dead, disconsolate;
Think then this Sithe that mowes downe kings,
Exempts no meaner mortall things.
Then bid the wanton Lady tread,
Amid these mazes of the dead.
And these truly understood,
More shall coole and quench the blood,
Than her many sports a day,
And her nightly wanton play.

seel'd: i.e. closed as a hawk's eyes when being tamed.
Sithe: scythe.

Bid her paint till day of doome,
To this favour she must come.
Bid the Merchant gather wealth,
The usurer exact by stealth,
The proud man beate it from his thought,
Yet to this shape all must be brought.

J. Weever, *Funerall Monuments*, 1631.

ANONYMOUS (? ROBERT WISDOM [1])

170 *A religious Use of taking Tobacco*

THE Indian Weed withered quite
Greene at Morne cut downe at night
Shewes thy decay all flesh is hay;
Thus thinke, then drinke Tobacco.

And when the smoke ascends on high
Thinke thou behouldst the Vanitie
Of worldly stuffe, gone with a puffe;
Thus thinke, then drinke Tobacco.

But when the Pipe growes foule within
Thinke of thy soule defil'd with sinne
And that the fire doth it require;
Thus thinke, then drinke Tobacco.

The Ashes that are left behind
May serve to put thee still in mind
That into dust returne thou must;
Thus thinke, then drinke Tobacco.

Trinity College, Dublin, MS. G. 2. 21.

[1] Not the Wisdome who wrote psalms.

FRANCIS BEAUMONT

1584–1616

171 *Mr. Francis Beaumonts Letter to Ben Johnson, written before he and Mr. Fletcher came to London, with two of the precedent Comedies then not finisht, which deferrd their merry meetings at the Mermaid*

THE Sun which doth the greatest comfort bring
To absent friends, because the self-same thing
They know they see however absent, is
Here our best Hay-maker (forgive me this,
It is our Countreys style). In this warme shine,
I lie and dreame of your full Mermaid wine.
Oh we have water mixt with Claret Lees,
Drinke apt to bring in dryer heresies
Than beere, good only for the Sonnets strain,
With fustian metaphors to stuffe the brain,
So mixt, that given to the thirstiest one,
'Twill not prove almes, unlesse he have the stone:
I thinke with one draught mans invention fades,
Two Cups had quite spoil'd *Homers Illiads*;
'Tis Liquor that will find out *Sutcliffs* wit,
Lie where he will, and make him write worse yet;
Fill'd with such moisture in most grievous qualmes,
Did *Robert Wisdome* write his singing Psalmes;
And so must I doe this, and yet I thinke
It is a potion sent us down to drink
By special Providence, keeps us from fights,
Makes us not laugh, when we make legs to Knights.
'Tis this that keeps our minds fit for our States,
A Medicine to obey our Magistrates:

For we do live more free than you, no hate,
No envy at one anothers *happy* State
Moves us, we are all equal every whit:
Of Land that God gives men here is their wit,
If we consider fully: for our best
And gravest man will, with his main house jest,
Scarce please you; we want subtilty to do
The Citie tricks, lie, hate, and flatter too:
Here are none that can bear a painted show,
Strike when you winch, and then lament the blow:
Who like Mills set the right way for to grind,
Can make their gaines alike with every wind:
Only some fellows with the subtil'st pate
Amongst us, may perchance æquivocate
At selling of a Horse, and that 's the most.
Methinks the little wit I had is lost
Since I saw you, for wit is like a rest
Held up at Tennis, which men doe the best,
With the best gamesters: What things have we seen,
Done at the Mermaid! heard words that have been
So nimble, and so full of subtill flame,
As if that every one from whence they came,
Had meant to put his whole wit in a jest,
And had resolv'd to live a foole, the rest
Of his dull life; then when there hath been throwne
Wit able enough to justifie the Towne
For three dayes past, wit that might warrant be
For the whole City to talk foolishly
Till that were cancel'd, and when that was gone,
We left an aire behind us, which alone,
Was able to make the two next companies
Right witty; though but downright fools, more wise.

When I remember this, and see that now
The Country gentlemen begin to allow
My wit for dry bobs, then I needs must cry,
I see my days of ballating grow nigh;
I can already riddle, and can sing
Catches, sell bargains, and I feare shall bring
My self to speak the hardest words I find,
Over as oft as any, with one wind,
That takes no medicines: But one thought of thee
Makes me remember all these things to be
The wit of our young men, fellows that show
No part of good, yet utter all they know:
Who like trees of the Guard, have growing soules.
Only strong destiny, which all controules,
I hope hath left a better fate in store,
For me thy friend, than to live ever poor,
Banisht unto this home; fate once againe
Bring me to thee, who canst make smooth and plain
The way of Knowledge for me, and then I,
Who have no good but in thy company,
Protest it will my greatest comfort be
To acknowledge all I have to flow from thee.
Ben, when these Scænes are perfect, we'll taste wine;
I'll drink thy Muses health, thou shalt quaff mine.

Comedies and Tragedies, 1679

ballating: writing catchpenny ballads.

172 *Songs from The Masque of the Gentlemen of Gray's-Inne and the Inner-Temple*

(*i*)

SHAKE off your heavy trance,
  and leap into a dance,
Such as no mortals use to tread,
  fit only for *Apollo*
To play to, for the Moon to lead,
  And all the Stars to follow.

(*ii*)

On blessed youths, for *Jove* doth pause,
Laying aside his graver Laws
  For this device:
And at the wedding such a pair,
Each dance is taken for a prayer,
  Each Song a Sacrifice.

(*iii*)

Single.

More pleasing were these sweet delights,
If Ladies mov'd as well as Knights;
Run every one of you and catch
A Nymph, in honor of this match;
And whisper boldly in her ear,
Jove will but laugh, if you forswear.

All.

And this days sins he doth resolve,
That we his Priests should all absolve.

(*iv*)

You should stay longer if we durst.
Away, alas! that he that first
Gave time wild wings to fly away,
Has now no power to make him stay.
But though these games must needs be plaid,
I would this pair, when they are laid,
  And not a creature nigh 'em,
Could catch his sithe, as he doth passe,
And cut his wings, and break his glasse,
  And keep him ever by 'em.

(*v*)

Peace and silence be the guide
To the man, and to the Bride:
If there be a joy yet new
In marriage, let it fall on you,
  That all the World may wonder:
If we should stay, we should do worse,
And turn our blessings to a curse,
  By keeping you asunder.

Comedies and Tragedies, 1647

173 *Aspatia's Song*

LAY a Garland on my Hearse of the dismal yew;
  Maidens, Willow branches bear; say I died true:
My Love was false, but I was firm from my hour of birth;
Upon my buried body lay lightly gentle earth.

The Maid's Tragedy, Act II, Sc. ii (text from *Plays*, 1679)

(T. BONHAM ?)

d. 1629?

174 *In Praise of Ale*

WHENAS the Chill Sirocco blowes,
And Winter tells a heavy tale;
When Pyes and Dawes and Rookes and Crows,
Sit cursing of the frosts and snowes;
Then give me Ale.

Ale in a Saxon Rumkin then,
Such as will make grim *Malkin* prate;
Rouseth up valour in all men,
Quickens the Poets wit and pen,
Despiseth Fate.

Ale that the absent battle fights,
And scorns the march of Swedish drums;
Disputes the Prince's Lawes and rights,
And what is past and what 's to come,
Tells mortal wights.

Ale that the Plowmans heart upkeeps,
And equals it to Tyrants thrones;
That wipes the eye that over weepes,
And lulls in dainty and secure sleepes,
His wearied bones.

Grandchild of *Ceres*, *Barley's* Daughter,
Wines Emulous neighbour, if but stale;
Ennobling all the Nimphs of water,
And filling each mans heart with laughter;
Ha, ha, give me ale.

Wit and Drollery, 1656

WILLIAM DRUMMOND

1585–1649

175 *Sonnet vii*

THAT learned *Græcian* (who did so excell
In Knowledge passing Sense, that hee is nam'd
Of all the after-Worlds *Divine*) doth tell,
That at the Time when first our Soules are fram'd,
Ere in these Mansions blinde they come to dwell,
They live bright Rayes of that *Eternall Light*,
And others see, know, love, in Heavens great Hight,
Not toylde with ought to *Reason* doth rebell;
Most true it is, for straight at the first Sight
My Minde mee told, that in some other Place
It elsewhere saw the *Idea* of that Face,
And lov'd a Love of heavenly pure Delight.
No Wonder now I feele so faire a Flame,
Sith I Her lov'd ere on this *Earth* shee came.

Poems, 1616, Part I

176 *Sonnet ix*

SLEEPE, *Silence* Child, sweet Father of soft Rest,
Prince whose Approach Peace to all Mortalls brings,
Indifferent Host to Shepheards and to Kings,
Sole Comforter of Minds with Griefe opprest.
Lo, by thy charming Rod all breathing things
Lie slumbring, with forgetfulnesse possest,
And yet o'er me to spred thy drowsie Wings
Thou spares (alas) who cannot be thy Guest.
Since I am thine, O come, but with that Face
To inward Light which thou art wont to show,
With fained Solace ease a true felt Woe,
Or if *deafe God* thou doe denie that Grace,
Come as thou wilt, and what thou wilt bequeath,
I long to kisse the *Image of my Death*.

Poems, 1616, Part I

177

Madrigal iii

LIKE the Idalian Queene
Her Haire about her Eyne,
With Necke and Brests ripe Apples to be seene,
At first Glance of the Morne
In Cyprus Gardens gathering those faire Flowrs
Which of her Blood were borne,
I saw, but fainting saw, my Paramours.
The Graces naked danc'd about the Place,
The Winds and Trees amaz'd
With Silence on Her gaz'd,
The Flowrs did smile, like those upon her Face,
And as their Aspen Stalkes those Fingers band
(That Shee might read my Case)
A Hyacinth I wisht mee in her Hand. *Poems*, 1616, Part I

178

Sonnet xxiv

IN Minds pure Glasse when I my selfe behold,
And vively see how my best Dayes are spent,
What Clouds of Care above my Head are roll'd,
What coming Harmes, which I can not prevent:
My begunne Course I (wearied) doe repent,
And would embrace what *Reason* oft hath told,
But scarce thus thinke I, when Love hath controld
All the best Reasons *Reason* could invent.
Though sure I know my Labours End is Griefe,
The more I strive that I the more shall pine,
That only Death can be my last Reliefe:
Yet when I thinke upon that Face divine,
Like one with Arrow shot in Laughters Place,
Maulgre my Heart I joye in my Disgrace.

Poems, 1616, Part I

vively: clearly.

179

Song ii

PHŒBUS arise,
And paint the sable Skies
With azure, white, and Red:
Rouse *Memnons* Mother from her *Tythons* Bed,
That Shee thy Cariere may with Roses spred,
The Nightingalles thy Coming each where sing,
Make an eternall Spring,
Give Life to this darke World which lieth dead.
Spreade forth thy golden Haire
In larger Lockes than thou wast wont before,
And Emperour-like decore
With Diademe of Pearle thy Temples faire:
Chase hence the uglie *Night*
Which serves but to make deare thy glorious Light.
This is that happie Morne,
That Day long wished Day,
Of all my Life so darke,
(If cruell Starres have not my Ruine sworne,
And *Fates* not Hope betray)
Which (only white) deserves
A *Diamond* for ever should it marke:
This is the Morne should bring unto this Grove
My Love, to heare, and recompense my love.
Faire King who all preserves,
But show thy blushing Beames,
And thou two sweeter *Eyes*
Shalt see than those which by *Peneus* Streames
Did once thy Heart surprise:
Nay, *Sunnes*, which shine as cleare
As thou when two thou did to *Rome* appeare.
Now *Flora* decke thy selfe in fairest Guise,

Cariere: career, course.

If that yee, *Winds*, would heare
A Voyce surpassing farre *Amphions* Lyre,
Your stormie chiding stay,
Let *Zephyre* only breath,
And with her Tresses play,
Kissing sometimes these purple Ports of Death.
The *Windes* all silent are,
And *Phœbus* in his Chaire
Ensaffroning Sea and Aire,
Makes vanish every Starre:
Night like a Drunkard reeles
Beyond the Hills to shunne his flaming Wheeles.
The Fields with Flowrs are deckt in every Hue,
The Clouds bespangle with bright Gold their Blew:
Here is the pleasant Place
And ev'ry thing, save *Her*, who all should grace.

Poems, 1616, Part I

180 *Sonnet xlvi*

ALEXIS, here *shee* stay'd among these Pines
(*Sweet Hermitresse*) *shee* did alone repaire,
Here did *shee* spreade the Treasure of her Haire,
More rich than that brought from the *Colchian* Mines.
Shee set Her by these musket Eglantines,
The happie Place the Print seemes yet to beare,
Her Voyce did sweeten here thy sugred Lines,
To which Winds, Trees, Beasts, Birds did lend their Eare.
Mee here *shee* first perceiv'd, and here a Morne
Of bright *Carnations* did o'erspreade her Face,
Here did shee sigh, here first my Hopes were borne,
And I first got a Pledge of promis'd Grace:
But *ah!* what serv'd it to bee happie so?
Sith passed Pleasures double but new Woe.

Poems, 1616, Part I

181 *Madrigal vii*

UNHAPPIE Light,
Doe not approach to bring the wofull Day,
When I must bid for ay
Farewell to Her, and live in endlesse Plight.
Faire *Moone*, with gentle Beames
The Sight who never marres,
Long cleare Heavens sable Vault, and you bright Starres
Your golden Lockes long glasse in Earths pure Streames,
Let *Phœbus* never rise
To dimme your watchfull Eyes:
Prolong (alas) prolong my short Delight,
And if yee can, make an eternall Night.

Poems, 1616, Part 1

182 *Madrigal i*

THIS life which seemes so faire,
Is like a Bubble blowen up in the Aire,
By sporting Childrens Breath,
Who chase it every where,
And strive who can most Motion it bequeath:
And though it sometime seeme of its owne Might
(Like to an Eye of gold) to be fix'd there,
And firme to hover in that emptie Hight,
That only is *because it is so light*,
But in that Pompe it doth not long appeare;
For even when most admir'd, it in a Thought
As swell'd from nothing, doth dissolve in nought.

Poems, 1616, Part 2

183 *Sonnet viii*

MY Lute be as thou wast when thou didst grow
With thy green Mother in some shady Grove,
When immelodious *Windes* but made thee move,
And *Birds* on thee their Ramage did bestow.
Sith that deare Voyce which did thy Sounds approve,
Which us'd in such harmonious Straines to flow,
Is reft from Earth *to tune those Spheares above*,
What art thou but a Harbenger of Woe?
Thy pleasing Notes be pleasing Notes no more,
But Orphan wailings to the fainting Eare;
Each Stop a Sigh, each Sound drawes forth a Teare,
Be therefore silent as in Woods before,
Or if that any Hand to touch thee daigne,
Like widow'd Turtle, still her Loss complaine.

Poems, 1616, Part 2

184 *Sonnet xii*

AS in a duskie and tempestuous Night,
A Starre is wont to spreade her Lockes of Gold,
And while her pleasant Rayes abroad are roll'd,
Some spiteful Cloude doth robbe us of her Sight:
(Faire Soule) in this black Age so shin'd thou bright,
And made all Eyes with Wonder thee beholde,
Till uglie *Death* depriving us of Light,
In his grimme mistie Armes thee did enfolde.
Who more shall vaunt true Beautie heere to see?
What Hope doth more in any Heart remaine,
That such Perfections shall his *Reason* raine?
If Beautie with thee born too died with thee?
World, plaine no more of *Love*, nor count his Harmes,
With his pale Trophees *Death* hath hung his Armes.

Poems, 1616, Part 2

185 *Madrigal v*

MY Thoughts hold mortall Strife,
I doe detest my Life,
And with lamenting Cries
(Peace to my Soule to bring)
Oft calles that Prince which here doth Monarchise,
But Hee grimme-grinning King,
Who Catives scornes, and doth the Blest surprise,
Late having deckt with *Beauties* Rose his Tombe,
Disdaines to croppe a Weede, and will not come.

Poems, 1616, Part 2

186 *Song ii*

IT *Autumne* was, and on our Hemispheare
Faire *Ericyne* began bright to appeare,
Night West-ward did her gemmie World decline,
And hide her Lights, that greater Light might shine:
The crested Bird had given Alarum twice
To lazie Mortalls, to unlocke their Eyes,
The Owle had left to plaine, and from each Thorne
The wing'd Musicians did salute the *Morne*,
Who (while shee glass'd her Lockes in *Ganges* Streames)
Set open wide the christall Port of Dreames:
When I, whose Eyes no drowsie Night could close,
In *Sleepes* soft Armes did quietly repose,
And, for that Heavens to die mee did denie,
Deaths Image kissed, and as dead did lie.
I lay as dead, but scarce charm'd were my Cares,
And slaked scarce my Sighes, scarce dried my Teares,

Catives: caitiffs, wretches. Ericyne: Venus.

Sleepe scarce the uglie Figures of the Day
Had with his sable Pincell put away,
And left mee in a still and calmie Mood,
When by my Bed (me thought) a Virgine stood,
A Virgine in the blooming of her Prime,
If such rare Beautie measur'd bee by Time?
Her Head a Garland ware of Opalls bright,
About her flow'd a Gowne as pure as Light,
Deare amber Lockes gave Umbrage to her Face,
Where *Modestie* high *Majestie* did grace,
Her Eyes such Beames sent forth, that but with Paine
Here weaker Sights their sparkling could sustaine:
No Deitie faign'd which haunts the silent Woods
Is like to Her, nor *Syrene* of the Floods:
Such is the golden Planet of the Yeare,
When blushing in the East hee doth appeare.
Her Grace did Beautie, Voyce yet Grace did passe,
Which thus through Pearles and Rubies broken was.
  How long wilt thou (said shee) estrang'd from Joy,
Paint Shadowes to thy selfe of false Annoy?
How long thy Minde with horride Shapes affrighte,
And in imaginarie Evills delighte?
Esteeme that Losse which (well when view'd) is Gaine,
Or if a Losse, yet not a Losse to plaine?
O Leave thy tired Soule more to molest,
And thinke that Woe when shortest then is best.
If shee for whom thou deafnest thus the Skie
Bee dead? what then? was shee not borne to die?
Was shee not mortall borne? if thou dost grieve
That Times should bee, in which shee should not live,
Ere e'er shee was, weepe that Dayes Wheele was roll'd,

Pincell: Pencil.

Weepe that shee liv'd not in the Age of Gold:
For that shee was not then, thou may'st deplore
As duely as that now shee is no more.
If onely shee had died, thou sure hadst Cause
To blame the *Destines* and Heavens iron Lawes:
But looke how many Millions Her advance,
What numbers with Her enter in this Dance,
With those which are to come: shall Heavens them stay,
And *Alls* faire Order breake, thee to obay?
Even as thy Birth, Death which thee doth appall,
A Piece is of the Life of this great *All*.
Strong Cities die, die doe high palmie Raignes,
And (weakling) thou thus to bee handled plaines.
  If she bee dead? then shee of lothsome Dayes
Hath past the Line, whose Length but Losse bewrayes;
Then shee hath left this filthie Stage of Care,
Where Pleasure seldome, Woe doth still repaire:
For all the Pleasures which it doth containe,
Not contervaile the smallest Minutes Paine.
And tell mee, Thou who dost so much admire
This little Vapour, Smoake, this Sparke, or Fire,
Which *Life* is call'd, what doth it thee bequeath,
But some few Yeeres which Birth drawes out to Death?
Which if thou paragone, with Lusters runne,
And them whose Carriere is but now begunne,
In Dayes great Vaste they shall farre lesse appeare,
Than with the Sea when matched is a Teare.
But why wouldst thou Here longer wish to bee?
One Yeere doth serve all *Natures* Pompe to see,
Nay, even one Day, and Night: This Moone, that Sunne,
Those lesser Fires about this Round which runne,
Bee but the same which under *Saturnes* Raigne

Did the serpenting *Seasons* enterchaine.
How oft doth Life grow lesse by living long?
And what excelleth but what dieth yong?
For Age which all abhorre (yet would embrace)
Whiles makes the Minde as wrinkled as the Face:
And when that *Destinies* conspire with Worth,
That Yeeres not glorie Wrong, Life soone goes forth.
Leave then Laments, and thinke thou didst not live,
Lawes to that first eternall Cause to give,
But to obey those Lawes which hee hath given,
And bow unto the just Decrees of Heaven,
Which can not erre, what ever foggie Mists
Doe blinde Men in these sublunarie Lists.
  But what if shee for whom thou spend'st those Grones,
And wastest Lifes deare Torch in ruthfull Mones,
Shee for whose sake thou hat'st the joyfull Light,
Court'st solitarie Shades, and irksome Night,
Doth live? O! (if thou canst) through Teares a Space
Lift thy dimm'd Lights, and looke upon this Face,
Looke if those Eyes which (foole) thou didst adore,
Shine not more bright than they were wont before?
Looke if those Roses *Death* could aught impaire,
Those Roses to thee once which seem'd so faire?
And if these Lockes have lost aught of that Gold,
Which erst they had when thou them didst behold?
I live, and happie live, but thou art dead,
And still shalt bee, till thou be like mee made.
Alas! whilst wee are wrapt in Gownes of Earth,
And blinde, heere sucke the Aire of Woe beneath,
Each thing in Senses Ballances wee wie,
And but with Toyle, and Paine the Trueth descrie.

wie: Scots 'weigh'.

Above this vaste and admirable Frame,
This Temple visible, which *World* wee name,
Within whose Walles so many Lamps doe burne,
So many Arches opposite doe turne,
Where Elementall Brethren nurse their Strife,
And by intestine Warres maintaine their Life,
There is a World, a World of perfect Blisse,
Pure, immateriall, bright, more farre from this,
Than that high Circle which the rest enspheares
Is from this dull ignoble Vale of Teares,
A World, where all is found, that heere is found,
But further discrepant than Heaven and Ground:
It hath an Earth, as hath this World of yours,
With Creatures peopled, stor'd with Trees, and Flowrs,
It hath a Sea, like Saphire Girdle cast,
Which decketh of harmonious Shores the Waste,
It hath pure Fire, it hath delicious Aire,
Moone, Sunne, and Starres, Heavens wonderfully faire:
But there Flowres doe not fade, Trees grow not olde,
The Creatures doe not die through Heat nor Colde,
Sea there not tossed is, nor Aire made blacke,
Fire doth not nurse it selfe on others Wracke;
There Heavens bee not constrain'd about to range,
For this World hath no neede of any Change,
The Minutes grow not Houres, Houres rise not Dayes,
Dayes make no Months, but ever-blooming Mayes.
Heere I remaine, and hitherward doe tend
All who their Spanne of Dayes in Vertue spend:
What ever Pleasure this low Place containes,
It is a Glance but of what high remaines.
Those who (perchance) thinke there can nothing bee
Without this wide Expansion which they see,

And that nought else mounts Starres Circumference,
For that nought else is subject to their Sense,
Feele such a Case, as one whom some Abisme
Of the Deepe *Ocean* kept had all his Time:
Who borne and nourish'd there, can scarcely dreame
That ought can live without that brinie Streame,
Can not beleeve that there be Temples, Towres,
Which goe beyond his Caves and dampish Bowres,
Or there bee other People, Manners, Lawes,
Than them hee finds within the roaring Waves,
That sweeter Flowrs doe spring than grow on Rockes,
Or Beasts bee which excell the scalie Flockes,
That other Elements be to be found,
Than is the Water, and this Ball of Ground.
But thinke that Man from those Abismes were brought,
And saw what curious *Nature* here hath wrought,
Did see the Meads, the tall and shadie Woods,
The Hilles did see, the cleare and ambling Floods,
The diverse Shapes of Beasts which Kinds forth bring,
The feathred Troupes, that flie and sweetly sing:
Did see the Palaces, the Cities faire,
The Forme of humane Life, the Fire, the Aire,
The brightnesse of the Sunne that dimmes his Sight,
The Moone, the ghastly Splendors of the Night:
What uncouth Rapture would his Minde surprise?
How would hee his (late-deare) Resort despise?
How would hee muse how foolish hee had beene
To thinke nought bee, but what hee there had seene?
Why did wee get this high and vaste Desire,
Unto immortall things still to aspire?
Why doth our Minde extend it beyond *Time*,
And to that *highest Happinesse* even clime?

If wee be nought but what to Sense wee seeme,
And Dust, as most of Worldlings us esteeme?
Wee bee not made for Earth, though here wee come,
More than the *Embryon* for the Mothers Wombe:
It weepes to bee made free, and wee complaine
To leave this loathsome Jayle of Care and Paine.
  But thou who vulgare Foot-steps dost not trace,
Learne to raise up thy Minde unto this Place,
And what Earth-creeping Mortalles most affect,
If not at all to scorne, yet to neglect:
O chase not Shadowes vaine, which when obtain'd,
Were better lost, than with such Travell gain'd.
Thinke that, on Earth which Humanes *Greatnesse* call,
Is but a glorious Title to live thrall:
That Scepters, Diadems, and Chaires of State,
Not in themselves, but to small Mindes are great:
How those who loftiest mount, doe hardest light,
And deepest Falls bee from the highest Hight;
How *Fame* an *Eccho* is, how all Renowne
Like to a blasted Rose, ere Night falles downe:
And though it something were, thinke how this Round
Is but a little Point, which doth it bound.
O leave that Love which reacheth but to Dust,
And in that *Love eternall* only trust,
And *Beautie*, which when once it is possest,
Can only fill the Soule, and make it blest.
Pale Envie, jealous Emulations, Feares,
Sighs, Plaints, Remorse, here have no Place, nor Teares,
False Joyes, vaine Hopes, here bee not, Hate nor Wrath,
What ends all Love, here most augments it, *Death*.
If such Force had the dimme Glance of an Eye,
Which some few Dayes thereafter was to die,

That it could make thee leave all other things,
And like the Taper-flie there burne thy Wings?
And if a Voyce, of late which could but waile,
Such Power had, as through Eares thy Soule to steale?
If once thou on that *only Faire* couldst gaze,
What Flames of Love would hee within thee raise?
In what a mazing Maze would it thee bring,
To heare but once that Quire celestiall sing?
The fairest Shapes on which thy Love did sease,
Which erst did breede Delight, then would displease,
Then Discords hoarse were Earth's enticing Sounds,
All Musicke but a Noyse which Sense confounds.
This great and burning Glasse that cleares all Eyes,
And musters with such Glorie in the Skies,
That silver Starre which with its sober Light,
Makes Day oft envie the eye-pleasing Night,
Those golden Letters which so brightly shine
In Heavens great Volume gorgeously divine,
The Wonders all in Sea, in Earth, in Aire,
Bee but darke Pictures of that *Soveraigne Faire*,
Bee Tongues, which still thus crie into your Eare,
(Could yee amidst Worlds *Cataracts* them heare)
From fading things (fond Wights) lift your Desire,
And in our Beautie, his us made admire,
If wee seeme faire? O thinke how faire is Hee,
Of whose faire Fairnesse, Shadowes, Steps, we bee.
No Shadow can compare it with the Face,
No Step with that deare Foot which did it trace;
Your Soules immortall are, then place them hence,
And doe not drowne them in the Must of Sense:
Doe not, O doe not by false Pleasures Might

sease: seize.

Deprive them of that true, and sole Delight.
That Happinesse yee seeke is not below,
Earths sweetest Joy is but disguised Woe.
  Heere did shee pause, and with a milde Aspect
Did towards mee those lamping Twinnes direct:
The wonted Rayes I knew, and thrice essay'd
To answere make, thrice faultring Tongue it stay'd.
And while upon that Face I fed my Sight,
Mee thought shee vanish'd up in *Titans* Light,
Who gilding with his Rayes each Hill and Plaine,
Seem'd to have brought the Gold-smiths World againe.

Poems, 1616, Part 2

187 *The World*

OF this faire Volume which wee World doe name
  If we the sheetes and leaves could turne with care,
Of Him who it corrects and did it frame
Wee cleare might read the Art and Wisdom rare!
Find out his Power which wildest Pow'rs doth tame,
His Providence extending everywhere,
His Justice which proud Rebels doth not spare,
In every Page, no Period of the same:
But silly wee (like foolish Children) rest
Well pleased with colour'd Vellum, Leaves of Gold,
Fair dangling Ribbons, leaving what is best,
On the great Writers sense ne'er taking hold;
  Or if by chance our minds doe muse on ought,
  It is some Picture on the Margin wrought.

Flowres of Sion, 1630

188 *The Nativitie*

RUNNE (Sheepheards) run where *Bethleme* blest appeares,
Wee bring the best of newes, be not dismay'd,
A Saviour there is born, more old than yeares,
Amidst Heav'ns rolling heights this Earth who stay'd;
In a poore Cottage Inn'd, a *Virgine* Maide
A weakling did him beare, who all upbeares,
This is hee poorly swadl'd, in Manger laid,
To whom too narrow Swadlings are our Spheares:
Runne (Shepheards) runne, and solemnise his Birth,
This is that Night, no, Day grown great with Blisse,
In which the power of *Sathan* broken is,
In Heaven be glorie, Peace unto the Earth.
Thus singing through the Aire the Angels swame,
And Cope of Starres re-echoed the same.

Flowres of Sion, 1630

189 *For the Baptiste*

THE last and greatest Herald of Heavens King,
Girt with rough Skinnes, hies to the Desarts wilde,
Among that savage brood the Woods forth bring,
Which hee than Man more harmlesse found and milde:
His food was Blossomes, and what yong doth spring,
With Honey that from virgine Hives distil'd;
Parcht Bodie, hollow Eyes, some uncouth thing
Made him appeare, long since from Earth exilde.
There burst hee forth; All yee, whose Hopes relye
On GOD, with mee amidst these Desarts mourne,
Repent, repent, and from olde errours turne.
Who listned to his voyce, obey'd his crye?
Onelie the Ecchoes which hee made relent,
Rung from their Marble Caves, repent, repent.

Flowres of Sion, 1630

190 *An Hymne of the Ascension*

BRIGHT Portalles of the Skie,
Emboss'd with sparkling Starres,
Doores of Eternitie,
With diamantine barres,
Your Arras rich up-hold,
Loose all your bolts and Springs,
Ope wide your Leaves of gold;
That in your Roofes may come the King of
kings.
Scarf'd in a rosie Cloud,
Hee doth ascend the Aire,
Straight doth the Moone him shrowd
With her resplendant Haire;
The next enchristall'd Light
Submits to him its Beames,
And hee doth trace the hight
Of that faire Lamp which flames of beautie
streames.
Hee towers those golden Bounds
Hee did to Sunne bequeath,
The higher wandring Rounds
Are found his Feete beneath;
The milkie-way comes neare,
Heavens Axell seemes to bend,
Above each turning Spheare
That rob'd in Glorie Heavens King may ascend.
O Well-spring of this All,
Thy Fathers Image vive,
Word, that from nought did call
What is, doth reason, live;

The Soules eternall Food,
Earths Joy, Delight of Heaven;
All Truth, Love, Beautie, Good,
To Thee, to Thee bee praises ever given.
What was dismarshall'd late
In this thy noble Frame,
And lost the prime estate,
Hath re-obtain'd the same,
Is now most perfect seene;
Streames which diverted were
(And troubled strayed uncleene)
From their first Source, by Thee home turned are.
By Thee that blemish old,
Of *Edens* leprous Prince,
Which on his Race tooke hold,
And him exil'd from thence,
Now put away is farre;
With Sword, in irefull guise,
No Cherub more shall barre
Poore man the Entries into Paradise.
By Thee those Spirits pure,
First Children of the Light,
Now fixed stand and sure,
In their eternall Right;
Now humane Companies
Renew their ruin'd Wall,
Fall'n man as thou makst rise,
Thou giv'st to Angels that they shall not fall.
By Thee that Prince of Sinne,
That doth with mischiefe swell,

Hath lost what hee did winne,
And shall endungeon'd dwell;
His spoyles are made thy prey,
His Fanes are sackt and torne,
His Altars raz'd away,
And what ador'd was late, now lyes a Scorne.
These Mansions pure and cleare,
Which are not made by hands,
Which once by him joy'd were,
And his (then not stain'd) Bands
(Now forfeit'd, dispossest,
And head-long from them throwne)
Shall Adams Heires make blest,
By Thee their great Redeemer made their owne.
O Well-spring of this All,
Thy Fathers Image vive,
Word, that from nought did call,
What is, doth Reason, live;
Whose worke is, but to will,
Gods coeternall Sonne,
Great Banisher of ill,
By none but Thee could these great Deedes bee
done.
Now each etheriall Gate,
To him hath opened bin;
And glories King in state,
His Pallace enters in;
Now come is this high Priest,
In the most holie Place,
Not without Blood addrest,
With Glorie Heaven the Earth to crowne with
Grace.

Starres which all Eyes were late,
And did with wonder burne,
His Name to celebrate,
In flaming Tongues them turne;
Their orby Chrystales move
More active than before,
And entheate from above,
Their soveraigne Prince laude, glorifie, adore.
The Quires of happie Soules,
Wakt with that Musicke sweete,
Whose Descant Care controules,
Their Lord in Triumph meete;
The spotlesse Sprightes of light,
His Trophees doe extole,
And archt in Squadrons bright,
Greet their great victor in his Capitole.
O Glorie of the Heaven,
O sole Delight of Earth,
To thee all power bee given,
Gods uncreated Birth;
Of Man-kind lover true,
Indeerer of his wrong,
Who dost the world renew,
Still bee thou our Salvation and our Song.
From Top of *Olivet* such notes did rise,
When mans Redeemer did transcend the Skies.

Flowres of Sion, 1630

entheate: inspired (ad. L. entheātus).
Indeerer: conciliator, atoner.

191 *The World a Hunt*

THE World a Hunting is,
The prey, poore Man, the *Nimrod* fierce is Death,
His speedy Grey-hounds are
Lust, Sicknesse, Enuie, Care,
Strife that ne'er falls amisse,
With all those ills which haunt us while we breathe.
Now if (by chance) wee flie
Of these the eager Chase,
Old Age with stealing Pace
Casts up his Nets, and there wee panting die.

Flowres of Sion, 1630

192 *A Solitary Life*

THRICE happie hee who by some shadie Grove,
Farre from the clamorous World did live his owne,
Though solitary, who is not alone,
But doth converse with that Eternal Love:
O how more sweet is birds harmonious Moane,
Or the hoarse Sobbings of the widow'd Dove,
Than those smooth whisperings neere a Princes Throne,
Which Good make doubtfull, doe the Evill approve!
O how more sweet is Zephyrs wholesome Breath,
And Sighes embalm'd, which new-born Flowrs unfold,
Than that applause vaine Honour doth bequeath!
How sweet are Streames to poison drunk in Gold!
The World is full of Horrours, Troubles, Slights,
Woods harmlesse Shades have only true Delights.

Flowres of Sion, 1630

193 *To a Nightingale*

SWEET Bird, that sing'st away the early Howres,
Of Winters past or coming void of Care,
Well pleased with Delights which Present are,
Faire Seasones, budding Sprayes, sweet-smelling Flowers:
To Rocks, to Springs, to Rills, from leavy Bowres
Thou thy Creators Goodnesse dost declare,
And what deare Gifts on thee hee did not spare,
A Staine to humane sense in sinne that lowres.
What Soule can be so sicke, which by thy Songs
(Attir'd in sweetnesse) sweetly is not driven
Quite to forget Earths turmoiles, spights, and wrongs,
And lift a reverend Eye and Thought to Heaven?
Sweet Artlesse Songstarre, thou my Minde dost raise
To Ayres of Spheares, yes, and to Angels Layes.

Flowres of Sion, 1630

194 *To Sir William Alexander*

THOUGH I have twice been at the Doores of *Death*,
And twice found shut those gates which ever mourne,
This but a lightning is, Truce ta'en to Breath,
For late-born Sorrows augure fleete returne.
Amidst thy sacred Cares, and Courtlie Toyles,
Alexis, when thou shalt heare wandring Fame
Tell *Death* hath triumph'd o'er my mortall Spoyles,
And that on Earth I am but a sad Name;
If thou e'er held me deare, by all our Love,
By all that Blisse, those Joyes Heav'n here us gave,
I conjure thee, and by that Maide of *Jove*,
To grave this short Remembrance on my Grave.

Here *Damon* lies, whose Songes did some-time grace
The murmuring Esk; may Roses shade the place.

Flowres of Sion, 1630

JOHN FORD

fl. 1629–1638

195

A Song

OH no more, no more, too late
  Sighes are spent; the burning Tapers
Of a life as chaste as Fate,
  Pure as are unwritten papers,
  Are burnt out: no heat, no light
  Now remaines; 'tis ever night.
Love is dead; let lovers eyes,
  Lock'd in endless dreames,
  Th' extremes of all extremes,
Ope no more, for now Love dyes.
  Now Love dyes, implying
Love's Martyrs must be ever, ever dying.

The Broken Heart, 1633, Act IV, Sc. iii

196

A Song

All. GLORIES, pleasures, pomps, delights, and ease,
    Can but please
  The outward senses, when the mind
  Is [or][1] untroubled, or by peace refin'd.
First Voice. Crownes may flourish and decay,
  Beauties shine, but fade away.
Second. Youth may revell, yet it must
  Lye down in a bed of dust:
Third. Earthly honours flow and waste,
  Time alone doth change and last.

1 'not' 1633.

Cho. Sorrowes mingled with contents, prepare
Rest for care;
Love only reignes in death; though Art
Can find no comfort for a Broken Heart.

The Broken Heart, 1633, Act v, Sc. iii

NATHANIEL FIELD

1587–1633

197 *Song*

RISE Lady Mistresse, rise:
The night hath tedious beene,
No sleepe hath fallen into my eyes,
Nor slumbers made me sinne.
Is not she a Saint then say,
Thought of whom keepes sinne away?
Rise Madam, rise and give me light,
Whom darknesse still will cover,
And ignorance darker than night,
Till thou smile on thy lover;
All want day till thy beauty rise,
For the gray morne breakes from thine eyes.

Amends for Ladies, 1611

SIR FRANCIS KYNASTON

1587–1642

198 *To Cynthia. On concealment of her beauty*

DO not conceale thy radiant eyes,
The starre-light of serenest skies,
Lest wanting of their heavenly light,
They turne to *Chaos* endlesse night.

SIR FRANCIS KYNASTON

Do not conceale those tresses faire,
The silken snares of thy curl'd haire,
Lest finding neither gold, nor Ore,
The curious Silke-worme worke no more.

Do not conceale those breasts of thine,
More snowe white than the Apenine,
Lest if there be like cold or frost,
The Lilly be for ever lost.

Do not conceale that fragrant scent,
Thy breath, which to all flowers hath lent
Perfumes, lest it being supprest,
No spices growe in all the East.

Do not conceale thy heavenly voice,
Which makes the hearts of gods rejoyce,
Lest Musicke hearing no such thing,
The Nightingale forget to sing.

Do not conceale, not yet eclipse
Thy pearly teeth with Corrall lips,
Lest that the Seas cease to bring forth
Gems, which from thee have all their worth.

Do not conceale no beauty, grace,
That's either in thy minde or face,
Lest vertue overcome by vice,
Make men beleeve no Paradise.

Cynthiades, in *Leoline and Sydanis*, 1642

THOMAS BEEDOME

d. 1641?

199 *The broken heart*

COUNT the sighs, and count the teares,
Which have in part my budding yeares:
Comment on my wofull looke,
Which is now blacke sorrows booke.
Read how love is overcome,
Weepe and sigh, and then be dumbe.
Say it was your charity
To helpe him whose eyes are dry.
Here paint my Cleora's name,
Then a heart, and then a flame,
Then marke how the heart doth fry
When Cleora is so nigh.
Though the flame did do its part,
'Twas the name that broke the heart.
Peace, no more, no more you need
My sad history to read.
Fold the paper up agen,
And report to other men
These complaints can justly prove
Hearts may breake, that be in love.

Poems, 1641

ANONYMOUS

200 *Epigram: Fatum Supremum*

ALL buildings are but monuments of death,
All clothes, but winding sheets for our last knell,
All dainty, fattings for the worms beneath,
All curious musique, but our passing bell;
Thus death is nobly waited on, for why?
All that we have is but deaths livery.

Wits Recreations, 1640

201 *Epigram: On Sir Francis Drake*

SIR *Drake*, whom well the worlds end knew,
Which thou didst compasse round,
And whom both Poles of Heaven once saw,
Which North and South do bound,
The Stars above would make thee known,
If men here silent were;
The Sun himselfe cannot forget
His fellow Traveller.

Wits Recreations, 1640

202 *Epitaph: On Sir Walter Rawleigh at his Execution*

GREAT heart, who taught thee so to dye?
Death yielding thee the victory?
Where took'st thou leave of life? if there,
How couldst thou be so freed from feare?
But sure thou dy'st and quit'st the state
Of flesh and blood before thy fate.
Else what a miracle were wrought,
To triumph both in flesh and thought?
I saw in every stander by,
Pale death, life onely in thine eye:
Th' example that thou left'st was then,
We look for when thou dy'st agen.
Farewell, truth shall thy story say,
We dy'd, thou onely liv'dst that day.

Wits Recreations, 1640

GILES FLETCHER

1588?–1623

203 *The Celestial City*

HERE let my Lord hang up his conquering lance,
And bloody armour with late slaughter warme,
And looking downe on his weake Militants,
Behold his Saints, 'midst of their hot alarme,
Hang all their golden hopes upon his arme.
  And in this lower field dispacing wide,
  Through windie thoughts, that would thei[r] sayles mis-
    guide,
Anchor their fleshly ships fast in his wounded side.

Here may the Band, that now in tryumph shines,
And that (before they were invested thus)
In earthly bodies carried heavenly mindes,
Pitcht round about in order glorious,
Their sunny Tents, and houses luminous,
  All their eternall day in songs employing,
  Joying their ends, without ende of their joying,
While their almightie Prince Destruction is destroying.

Full, yet without satietie, of that
Which whets and quiets greedy Appetite,
Where never Sunne did rise, nor ever sat,
But one eternall day, and endless light
Gives time to those, whose time is infinite,
  Speaking with thought, obtaining without fee,
  Beholding him, whom never eye could see,
And magnifying him, that cannot greater be.

How can such joy as this want words to speake?
And yet what words can speake such joy as this?
Far from the world, that might their quiet breake,
Here the glad Soules the face of beauty kisse,
Pour'd out in pleasure, on their beds of blisse.
  And drunke with nectar torrents, ever hold
  Their eyes on him, whose graces manifold,
The more they doe behold, the more they would behold.

Their sight drinkes lovely fires in at their eyes,
Their braine sweete incense with fine breath accloyes,
That on Gods sweating altar burning lies,
Their hungrie cares feede on their heav'nly noyse,
That Angels sing, to tell their untold joyes;
  Their understanding naked Truth, their wills
  The all, and selfe-sufficient Goodnesse fills,
That nothing here is wanting, but the want of ills.

No Sorrowe now hangs clouding on their browe,
No bloodless Maladie empales their face,
No Age drops on their hairs his silver snowe,
No Nakednesse their bodies doth embase,
No Povertie themselves, and theirs disgrace,
  No feare of death the joy of life devours,
  No unchast sleepe their precious time deflowrs,
No losse, no griefe, no change waite on their winged hours.

But now their naked bodies scorne the cold,
And from their eyes joy lookes, and laughs at paine,
The Infant wonders how he came so old,
And old man how he came so young againe;

Still resting, though from sleepe they still refraine,
  Where all are rich, and yet no gold they owe,
  And all are Kings, and yet no Subjects knowe,
All full, and yet no time on foode they doe bestowe.

For things that passe are past, and in this field,
The indeficient Spring no Winter feares,
The Trees together fruit, and blossome yield,
Th' unfading Lilly leaves of silver beares,
And crimson rose a scarlet garment weares:
  And all of these on the Saints bodies growe,
  Not, as they wont, on baser earth belowe;
Three rivers here of milke, and wine, and honie flowe.

About the holy Cittie rolls a flood
Of molten chrystall, like a sea of glasse,
On which weake stream a strong foundation stood;
Of living Diamounds the building was,
That all things else, besides itselfe, did passe.
  Her streetes, in stead of stones, the starres did pave,
  And little pearles, for dust, it seem'd to have,
On which soft-streaming Manna, like pure snowe, did wave.

In 'midst of this Citie cœlestiall,
Where the eternall Temple should have rose,
Light'ned th' Idea Beatificall:
End, and beginning of each thing that growes,
Whose selfe no end, nor yet beginning knowes,
  That hath no eyes to see, nor ears to heare,
  Yet sees, and heares, and is all-eye, all-eare,
That no where is contain'd, and yet is every where.

Changer of all things, yet immutable,
Before, and after all, the first, and last,
That moving all, is yet immoveable,
Great without quantitie, in whose forecast,
Things past are present, things to come are past,
  Swift without motion, to whose open eye
  The hearts of wicked men unbrested lie,
At once absent, and present to them, farre, and nigh.

It is no flaming lustre, made of light,
No sweet concent, or well-tim'd harmonie,
Ambrosia, for to feast the Appetite,
Or flowrie odour, mixt with spicerie.
No soft embrace, or pleasure bodily,
  And yet it is a kinde of inward feast,
  A harmony, that sounds within the brest,
An odour, light, embrace, in which the soule doth rest.

A heav'nly feast, no hunger can consume,
A light unseene, yet shines in every place,
A sound, no time can steale, a sweet perfume,
No windes can scatter, an intire embrace,
That no satietie can e'er unlace,
  Ingrac'd into so high a favour, there
  The Saints, with their Beau-peers, whole worlds outwear,
And things unseene doe see, and things unheard doe hear.

Ye blessed soules, growne richer by your spoile,
Whose losse, though great, is cause of greater gaines,
Here may your weary Spirits rest from toyle,
Spending your endlesse ev'ning, that remaines,

Among those white flocks, and celestiall traines,
  That feed upon their Sheapheards eyes, and frame
  That heav'nly musique of so wondrous fame,
Psalming aloude the holy honours of his name.

Had I a voice of steel to tune my song,
Were every verse as smoothly fil'd as glasse,
And every member turned to a tongue,
And every tongue were made of sounding brasse,
Yet all that skill, and all this strength, alas,
  Should it presume to gild, were misadvis'd,
  The place, where David hath new songs devis'd,
As in his burning throne he sits emparadis'd.

Christs Triumph after Death, 1610 (stanzas 30–43)

GEORGE WITHER

1588–1677

204 *Philarete praises Poetry*

SEE'ST thou not in clearest dayes,
Oft thicke fogs cloud Heav'ns rayes.
And that vapours which doe breathe
From the earths grosse wombe beneath,
Seeme not to us with black steames,
To pollute the Sunnes bright beames,
And yet vanish into ayre,
Leaving it (unblemisht) faire?
So (my *Willy*) shall it bee

With *Detractions* breath on thee.
It shall never rise so hie,
As to staine thy Poesie.
As that Sunne doth oft exhale
Vapours from each rotten Vale:
Poesie so sometime draines,
Grosse conceits from muddy braines;
Mists of Envy, fogs of spight,
Twixt mens judgements and her light:
But so much her power may do,
That shee can dissolve them too.
If thy Verse doe bravely tower,
As shee makes wing, she gets power:
Yet the higher she doth soare,
Shee's affronted still the more:
Till shee to the high'st hath past,
Then she rests with Fame at last,
Let nought therefore, thee affright:
But make forward in thy flight:
For if I could match thy Rime,
To the very Starres I'd climb.
There begin again, and flye,
Till I reach'd Æternity.
But (alasse) my Muse is slow:
For thy place shee flags too low:
Yea, the more's her haplesse fate,
Her short wings were clipt of late.
And poore I, her fortune ruing,
Am my selfe put up a mewing.
But if I my Cage can rid,
I'll flye where I never did.
And though for her sake I'm crost,

Though my best hopes I have lost,
And knew she would make my trouble
Ten times more than ten times double:
I should love and keepe her to,
Spight of all the world could do.
For though banish't from my flockes,
And confin'd within these rockes,
Here I waste away the light,
And consume the sullen Night,
She doth for my comfort stay,
And keepes many cares away.
Though I misse the flowry Fields,
With those sweets the Spring-tide yeelds,
Though I may not see those Groves,
Where the Shepheards chant their Loves,
(And the Lasses more excell,
Than the sweet voic'd *Philomel*)
Though of all those pleasures past,
Nothing now remaines at last,
But *Remembrance* (poore reliefe)
That more makes, than mends my griefe:
Shee 's my mindes companion still,
Maugre Envies evil will.
(Whence she should be driven too,
Wer't in mortals power to do.)
She doth tell me where to borrow
Comfort in the midst of sorrow;
Makes the desolatest place
To her presence be a grace;
And the blackest discontents
To be pleasing ornaments.
In my former dayes of blisse,

Her divine skill taught me this,
That from every thing I saw,
I could some invention draw:
And raise pleasure to her height,
Through the meanest objects sight.
By the murmur of a spring,
Or the least boughes rusteling.
By a Dazie whose leaves spred,
Shut when *Titan* goes to bed;
Or a shady bush or tree,
She could more infuse in mee,
Than all Natures beauties can,
In some other wiser man.
By her helpe I also now,
Make this churlish place allow
Some things that may sweeten gladness,
In the very gall of sadness,
The dull loneness, the blacke shade,
That these hanging vaults have made,
The strange Musicke of the waves,
Beating on these hollow Caves,
This blacke Den which Rocks embosse
Over-growne with eldest Mosse.
The rude Portals that give light,
More to *Terror* than *Delight*.
This my Chamber of *Neglect*,
Wall'd about with *Disrespect*,
From all these and this dull aire,
A fit object for *Despaire*,
She hath taught me by her might
To draw comfort and delight.

Her divine: 1620 His divine.

Therefore *thou best earthly blisse*,
I will clerish thee for this.
Poesie; thou sweetest content
That e'er Heav'n to mortal lent,
Though they as a trifle leave thee
Whose dull thoughts cannot conceive thee,
Though thou be to them a scorne,
That to nought but earth are borne:
Let my life no longer be
Than I am in love with thee.

The Shepherds Hunting, 1615; Eclog. 4 (text 1620)

205 *Shall I wasting in Dispaire*

SHALL I wasting in Dispaire,
Dye because a *Womans* faire?
Or make pale my cheekes with care,
Cause anothers Rosie are?
Be shee fairer than the Day,
Or the Flowry Meads in May;
If She be not so to me,
What care I how faire shee be.

Should my heart be grievd or pin'd,
Cause I see a *Woman* kind?
Or a well disposed Nature,
Joyned with a lovely Feature?
Be shee meeker, kinder, than
Turtle-Dove, or *Pelican*:
If shee be not so to me,
What care I, how kind she be.

GEORGE WITHER

Shall a *Womans* Virtues move,
Me, to perish for her love?
Or, her well-deserving knowne,
Make me quite forget mine owne?
Be shee with that Goodnesse blest,
Which may gaine her, name of *Best*:
  If she be not such to me,
  What care I, how good she be.

Cause her Fortune seemes too high,
Shall I play the foole, and dye?
Those that beare a Noble minde,
Where they want of Riches find,
Thinke, what with them, they would doe,
That without them, dare to wooe.
  And, unlesse that mind I see,
  What care I, though Great she be.

Great, or *Good*, or *Kind*, or *Faire*,
I will ne'er the more dispaire,
If She love me, this beleeve;
I will die, ere she shall grieve.
If she slight me, when I wooe;
I can scorne, and let her goe.
  For, if shee be not for me,
  What care I, for whom she be.

Faire-Virtue, 1622

206 (*Ah me! Am I the Swaine*)

Ah me!
Am I the Swaine,
That late from sorrow free,
Did all the cares on earth disdaine?
And still untoucht, as at some safer Games,
Play'd with the burning coals of Love, & Beauties flames?
Was't I, could dive, & sound each passions secret depth at will;
And, from those huge overwhelmings, rise, by help of Reason still?
And am I now, oh heavens! for trying this in vaine,
So sunke, that I shall never rise againe?
Then let Dispaire, set Sorrows string,
For *Strains* that dolefulst be,
And I will sing,
Ah me.

But why,
Oh fatall *Time*!
Dost thou constraine that I,
Should perish, in my youths sweet prime?
I, but a while ago (you cruell Powers)
In spight of Fortune, cropt contentments sweetest flowers.
And yet, unscorned, serve a gentle *Nymph*, the fairest *Shee*,
That ever was belov'd of Man, or Eyes did ever see.
Yea, one, whose tender heart, would rue for my distresse;
Yet I, poore I, must perish nay-the-lesse.
And (which much more augments my care)
Unmoaned I must dye:
And, no man e'er,
Know why.

Thy leave,
My dying *Song*,
Yet take, ere griefe bereave,
The breath which I enjoy too long.
Tell thou that *Fair-one* this; my soul prefers,
Her love above my life, and that I died hers:
And let *Him* be, for evermore, to her remembrance deare,
Who lov'd the very thought of *Her*, whilst he remained here.
And now, farewell thou Place of my unhappy birth;
Where once I breathd the sweetest aire on earth.
Since me, my wonted joyes forsake;
And all my trust deceive:
Of all, I take
My leave.

Farewell,
Sweet Groves to you:
You Hills, that highest dwell;
And all you humble Vales, adieu.
You wanton Brookes, and solitary Rockes,
My deare companions all, and you, my tender flockes.
Farewell my *Pipe*, and all those pleasing *Songs*, whose moving straines
Delighted once the fairest *Nymphes*, that daunce upon the Plaines.
You *Discontents* (whose deep, & over-deadly smart,
Have, without pitie, broke the truest heart)
Sighs, *Teares*, and every sad annoy,
That erst did with me dwell,
And all others Joy,
Farewell.

Adieu,
Faire *Shepherdesses*:
Let Garlands of sad Yewe,
Adorne your daintie golden Tresses.
I, that lovd you; and often with my Quill,
Made musick that delighted Fountain, Grove, & Hill:
I, whom you loved so; and with a sweet and chast embrace,
(Yea, with a thousand rarer favors) would vouchsafe to grace.
I, now must leave you all alone, of *Love* to plaine:
And never Pipe, nor never Sing againe.
I must, for evermore, bee gone;
And therefore, bid I you,
And every one,
Adieu.

Faire-Virtue, 1622

207 *A Christmas Carroll*

SO, now is come our joyfulst *Feast*;
Let ever man be jolly.
Each Roome, with Ivie leaves is drest,
And every Post, with Holly.
Though some Churles at our mirth repine,
Round your foreheads Garlands twine,
Drowne sorrow in a Cup of Wine.
And let us all be merry.

Now, all our Neighbours Chimneys smoke,
And *Christmas* blocks are burning;
Their Ovens, they with bakt-meats choke,
And all their Spits are turning.

Without the doore, let sorrow lie:
And, if for cold, it hap to die,
We'll bury 't in a *Christmas* Pie.
And evermore be merry.

Now, every *Lad* is wondrous trim,
And no man minds his Labour.
Our Lasses have provided them,
A Bag-pipe, and a Tabor.
Young men, and Mayds, and Girles & Boyes,
Give life, to one anothers Joyes:
And, you anon shall by their noyse,
Perceive that they are merry.

Ranke Misers now, doe sparing shun:
Their Hall of Musicke soundeth:
And, Dogs, thence with whole shoulders run,
So, all things there aboundeth.
The Countrey-folke, themselves advance;
For *Crowdy-Mutton's* come out of *France*:
And *Jack* shall pipe, and *Jill* shall dance,
And all the Towne be merry.

Ned Swash hath fetcht his Bands from pawne,
And all his best Apparell.
Brisk *Nell* hath brought a Ruffe of Lawne,
With droppings of the Barrell.
And those that hardly all the yeare
Had Bread to eat, or Raggs to weare,
Will have both Clothes, and daintie fare:
And all the day be merry.

Now poore men to the *Justices*,
With Capons make their arrants,
And if they hap to faile of these,
They plague them with their Warrants.
  But now they feed them with good cheere,
  And what they want, they take in Beere:
  For, Christmas *comes but once a yeare*:
And then they shall be merry.

Good *Farmers*, in the Country, nurse
The poore, that else were undone.
Some *Land*-lords, spend their money worse
On Lust, and Pride at *London*.
  There, the Roysters they doe play;
  Drabb and Dice their Lands away,
  Which may be ours, another day:
And therefore let 's be merry.

The Client now his suit forbeares,
The Prisoners heart is eased,
The Debtor drinks away his cares,
And, for the time is pleased.
  Though others purses be more fat,
  Why should we pine or grieve at that?
  Hang sorrow, care will kill a Cat.
And therefore let 's be merry.

Harke, how the *Wagges*, abroad doe call
Each other foorth to rambling.
Anon, you'll see them in the Hall,
For Nuts, and Apples scambling.

Harke, how the Roofes with laughters sound
Anon they'll thinke the house goes round:
For, they the Cellars depth have found.
And there they will be merry.

The *Wenches* with their *Wassell-Bowles,*
About the Streets are singing:
The *Boyes* are come to catch the *Owles,*
The *Wild-mare,* in is bringing.
Our *Kitchin-Boy* hath broke his Boxe,
And, to the dealing of the Oxe,
Our honest neighbours come by flocks,
And here they will be merry.

Now *Kings* and *Queenes,* poore Sheep-cotes have,
And mate with every body:
The honest, now, may play the *knave,*
And wise men play at *Noddy.*
Some Youths will now a *Mumming* goe;
Some others play at *Rowland-hoe,*
And, twenty other Gameboyes moe:
Because they will be merry.

Then wherefore in these merry daies,
Should we I pray, be duller?
No; let us sing some *Roundelayes,*
To make our mirth the fuller.
And, whilest thus inspir'd we sing,
Let all the Streets with ecchoes ring:
Woods, and Hills, and every thing,
Beare witnesse we are merry.

Faire-Virtue, 1622 (*A Miscellany of Epigrams*)

208

A Love Sonnet

I LOVED a lass, a fair one,
  As fair as e'er was seen;
She was indeed a rare one,
  Another Sheba queen.
But fool as then I was,
  I thought she loved me too,
But now alas she's left me,
  Falero, lero, loo.

Her hair like gold did glister,
  Each eye was like a starre;
She did surpass her sister,
  Which passed all others farre.
She would me honie call,
  She'd, O she'd kiss me too;
But now alas she's left me,
  Falero, lero, loo.

In summer time to *Medley*
  My love and I would goe;
The boatmen there stood ready,
  My love and I to rowe.
For Cream there would we call,
  For Cakes, and for Prunes too,
But now alas she's left me,
  Falero, lero, loo.

Many a merry meeting
  My love and I have had;
She was my only sweeting,
  She made my heart full glad,

The tears stood in her eies,
  Like to the morning dew,
But now alas she's left me,
  Falero, lero, loo.

And as abroad we walked,
  As Lovers' fashion is,
Oft [as] we sweetly talked
  The Sun should steal a kisse:
The winde upon her lips
  Likewise most sweetly blew;
But now alas she's left me,
  Falero, lero, loo.

Her cheeks were like the Cherrie,
  Her skin as white as snow,
When she was blithe and merrie,
  She Angel-like did show.
Her waist exceeding small,
  The fives did fit her shoe;
But now alas she's left me,
  Falero, lero, loo.

In Summer time or winter
  She had her heart's desire;
I still did scorne to stint her
  From sugar, sacke, or fire:
The world went round about,
  No cares we ever knew,
But now alas she's left me,
  Falero, lero, loo.

GEORGE WITHER

As we walked home together
  At midnight through the towne,
To keep away the weather
  O'er her I'd cast my gowne.
No cold my Love should feel,
  Whate'er the heavens could do;
But now alas she's left me,
  Falero, lero, loo.

Like Doves we would be billing,
  And clip and kiss so fast;
Yet she would be unwilling
  That I should kiss the last;
They're *Judas* kisses now,
  Since that they prov'd untrue.
For now alas she's left me,
  Falero, lero, loo.

To Maidens vows and swearing
  Henceforth no credit give,
You may give them the hearing,
  But never them beleeve.
They are as false as faire,
  Unconstant, fraile, untrue;
For mine alas has left me,
  Falero, lero, loo.

'Twas I that paid for all things,
  'Twas others dranke the wine,
I cannot now recall things,
  Live but a foole to pine.

'Twas I that beat the bush,
The bird to others flew,
For she alas hath left me,
Falero, lero, loo.

If ever that Dame Nature,
For this false lover's sake,
Another pleasing creature
Like unto her would make,
Let her remember this,
To make the other true;
For this alas hath left me,
Falero, lero, loo.

No riches now can raise me,
No want make me despair,
No misery amaze me,
Nor yet for want I care:
I have lost a world it selfe,
My earthly heaven, adieu,
Since she alas hath left me,
Falero, lero, loo.

A Description of Love, 1620

209 *The Marigold*

Whil'st I, the Sunne's *bright Face may view,*
I will no meaner Light *pursue.*

WHEN, with a serious musing, I behold
The gratefull, and obsequious *Marigold*,
How duely, ev'ry morning, she displayes
Her open breast, when *Titan* spreads his Rayes;

How she observes him in his daily walke,
Still bending towards him, her tender stalke;
How, when he downe declines, she droopes and mournes,
Bedew'd (as 'twere) with teares, till he returnes;
And, how she vailes her *Flow'rs*, when he is gone,
As if she scorned to be looked on
By an inferiour *Eye*; or, did contemne
To wayt upon a meaner *Light*, than *Him*.
When this I meditate, me-thinkes, the *Flowers*
Have *spirits*, farre more generous, than ours;
And, give us faire Examples, to despise
The servile Fawnings, and Idolatries,
Wherewith we court these earthly things below,
Which merit not the service we bestow.
  But, oh my God! though groveling I appeare
Upon the Ground, (and have a rooting here,
Which hales me downwards) yet in my desire,
To that, which is above mee, I aspire:
And, all my best *Affections* I professe
To *Him*, that is the *Sunne of Righteousnesse*.
Oh! keepe the *Morning* of his *Incarnation*,
The burning *Noone tide* of his bitter *Passion*,
The *Night* of his *Descending*, and the *Height*
Of his *Ascension*, ever in my sight:
  That imitating him, in what I may,
  I never follow an inferiour *Way*.

Emblemes, 1635

210 *For a Musician*

Many Musicians *are more out of order than their Instruments: such as are so, may by singing this Ode, become reprovers of their own untuneable affections. They who are better tempered are hereby remembered what Musick is most acceptable to* G O D, *and most profitable to themselves.*

1. WHAT helps it those,
      Who skill in *Song* have found;
Well to compose
      (Of disagreeing notes)
By artfull choice
      A sweetly pleasing sound;
To fit their Voice,
      And their melodious throats?
What helps it them,
      That they this cunning know;
If most condemn
      The way in which they go?

2. What will he gain
      By touching well his *Lute*,
Who shall disdain
      A grave advise to hear?
What from the sounds,
      Of Organ, Fife, or Lute,
To him redounds,
      Who doth no sin forbear?
A mean respect,
      By tuning strings, he hath,
Who doth neglect
      A *rectified-path*.

3. Therefore, oh Lord,
So tuned, let me be
Unto thy word,
And thy *ten-stringed-law*,
That in each part,
I may thereto agree;
And feel my heart
Inspir'd with loving awe:
He sings and plaies,
The Songs which best thou lovest,
Who does and sayes,
The things which thou approvest.

4. Teach me the *skill*,
Of him, whose Harp asswag'd
Those passions ill,
Which oft afflicted Saul.
Teach me the strain
Which calmeth mindes enrag'd;
And which from vain
Affections doth recall.
So, to the Quire,
Where *Angels* musicke make,
I may aspire,
When I this life forsake.

Hallelujah, 1641 (Pt. 3, Hymn xxxviii)

ROBERT HERRICK

1591–1674

211 *The Argument of his Book*

I SING of *Brooks*, of *Blossomes*, *Birds*, and *Bowers*:
Of *April*, *May*, of *June*, and *July*-Flowers.
I sing of *May-poles*, *Hock-carts*, *Wassails*, *Wakes*,
Of *Bride-grooms*, *Brides*, and of their *Bridall-cakes*.
I write of *Youth*, of *Love*, and have Accesse
By these, to sing of cleanly-*Wantonnesse*.
I sing of *Dewes*, of *Raines*, and piece by piece
Of *Balme*, of *Oyle*, of *Spice*, and *Amber-gris*.
I sing of *Times trans-shifting*; and I write
How *Roses* first came *Red*, and *Lillies White*.
I write of *Groves*, of *Twilights*, and I sing
The Court of *Mab*, and of the *Fairie-King*.
I write of *Hell*; I sing (and ever shall)
Of *Heaven*, and hope to have it after all.

Hesperides, 1648

212 *When he would have his verses read*

IN sober mornings, doe not thou reherse
The holy incantation of a verse;
But when that men have both well drunke, and fed,
Let my Enchantments then be sung, or read.
When Laurell spirts i'th fire, and when the Hearth
Smiles to it selfe, and gilds the roofe with mirth;
When up the *Thyrse* is rais'd, and when the sound
Of sacred *Orgies* flyes, A round, A round.
When the *Rose* raignes, and locks with ointments shine,
Let rigid *Cato* read these Lines of mine.

Hesperides, 1648

213 *To Perilla*

AH my *Perilla*! do'st thou grieve to see
Me, day by day, to steale away from thee?
Age calls me hence, and my gray haires bid come,
And haste away to mine eternal home;
'Twill not be long (*Perilla*) after this,
That I must give thee the *supremest* kisse;
Dead when I am, first cast in salt, and bring
Part of the creame from that *Religious Spring*;
With which (*Perilla*) wash my hands and feet;
That done, then wind me in that very sheet
Which wrapt thy smooth limbs (when thou didst implore
The Gods protection, but the night before),
Follow me weeping to my Turfe, and there
Let fall a *Primrose*, and with it a teare:
Then lastly, let some weekly-strewings be
Devoted to the memory of me:
Then shall my *Ghost* not walk about, but keep
Still in the coole, and silent shades of sleep.

Hesperides, 1648

214 *To Anthea*

IF deare *Anthea*, my hard fate it be
To live some few-sad-howers after thee:
Thy *sacred Corse* with *Odours* I will burne;
And with my *Lawrell* crown thy *Golden Urne*.
Then holding up (there) such religious Things,
As were (time past) thy holy *Filletings:*
Near to thy *Reverend Pitcher* I will fall
Down dead for grief, and end my woes withall:
So three in one small plat of ground shall ly,
Anthea, *Herrick*, and his *Poetry*.

Hesperides, 1648

215 *To Robin Red-breast*

LAID out for dead, let thy last kindnesse be
With leaves and mosse-work for to cover me:
And while the Wood-nimphs my cold corps inter,
Sing thou my Dirge, sweet-warbling Chorister!
For Epitaph, in Foliage, next write this,
Here, here the Tomb of Robin Herrick is.

Hesperides, 1648

216 *To Anthea*

NOW is the time, when all the lights wax dim;
And thou (*Anthea*) must withdraw from him
Who was thy servant. Dearest, bury me
Under that *Holy-oke*, or *Gospel-tree*:
Where (though thou see'st not) thou may'st think upon
Me, when thou yeerly go'st Procession:
Or for mine honour, lay me in that Tombe
In which thy sacred Reliques shall have roome:
For my Embalming (Sweetest) there will be
No Spices wanting, when I'm laid by thee.

Hesperides, 1648

217 *His request to Julia*

JULIA, if I chance to die
Ere I print my Poetry;
I most humbly thee desire
To commit it to the fire:
Better 'twere my Book were dead,
Than to live not perfected.

Hesperides, 1648

218 *To the reverend shade of his religious Father*

THAT for seven *Lusters* I did never come
To doe the *Rites* to thy Religious Tombe:
That neither haire was cut, or true teares shed
By me, o'er thee, (*as justments to the dead*)
Forgive, forgive me; since I did not know
Whether thy bones had here their Rest, or no.
But now 'tis known, Behold; behold, I bring
Unto thy Ghost, th' Effused Offering:
And look, what Smallage, Night-shade, Cypresse, Yew,
Unto the shades have been, or now are due,
Here I devote; And something more than so;
I come to pay a Debt of Birth I owe.
Thou gav'st me life, (but Mortall;) For that one
Favour, I'll make full satisfaction;
For my life mortall, Rise from out thy Herse,
And take a life immortall from my Verse.

Hesperides, 1648

219 *Delight in Disorder*

A SWEET disorder in the dresse
Kindles in cloathes a wantonnesse:
A Lawne about the shoulders thrown
Into a fine distraction:
An erring Lace, which here and there
Enthralls the Crimson Stomacher:
A Cuffe neglectfull, and thereby
Ribbands to flow confusedly:
A winning wave (deserving Note)
In the tempestuous petticote:

Smallage: wild celery, water parsley.

A carelesse shoe-string, in whose tye
I see a wilde civility:
Doe more bewitch me, than when Art
Is too precise in every part. *Hesperides*, 1648

220 *Divination by a Daffadill*

WHEN a Daffadill I see,
Hanging down his head t'wards me;
Guesse I may, what I must be:
First, I shall decline my head;
Secondly, I shall be dead;
Lastly, safely buryed. *Hesperides*, 1648

221 *To Dianeme*

SWEET, be not proud of those two eyes,
Which Star-like sparkle in their skies:
Nor be you proud, that you can see
All hearts your captives; yours, yet free:
Be you not proud of that rich haire,
Which wantons with the Love-sick aire:
When as that *Rubie*, which you weare,
Sunk from the tip of your soft eare,
Will last to be a precious Stone,
When all your world of Beautie 's gone.
Hesperides, 1648

222 *Corinna's going a Maying*

GET up, get up for shame, the Blooming Morne
Upon her wings presents the god unshorne.
See how *Aurora* throwes her faire
Fresh-quilted colours through the aire:

Get up, sweet-Slug-a-bed, and see
The Dew bespangling Herbe and Tree.
Each Flower has wept, and bow'd toward the East,
Above an houre since; yet you not drest,
Nay! not so much as out of bed?
When all the Birds have Mattens said,
And sung their thankfull Hymnes: 'tis sin,
Nay, profanation to keep in,
When as a thousand Virgins on this day,
Spring, sooner than the Lark, to fetch in May.

Rise; and put on your Foliage, and be seene
To come forth, like the Spring-time, fresh and greene;
And sweet as *Flora*. Take no care
For Jewels for your Gowne, or Haire:
Feare not; the leaves will strew
Gems in abundance upon you:
Besides, the childhood of the Day has kept,
Against you come, some *Orient Pearls* unwept:
Come, and receive them while the light
Hangs on the Dew-locks of the night:
And *Titan* on the Eastern hill
Retires himselfe, or else stands still
Till you come forth. Wash, dresse, be briefe in praying:
Few Beads are best, when once we goe a Maying.

Come, my *Corinna*, come; and coming, marke
How each field turns a street; each street a Parke
Made green, and trimm'd with trees: see how
Devotion gives each House a Bough,
Or Branch: Each Porch, each doore, ere this,
An Arke a Tabernacle is

Made up of white-thorn neatly enterwove;
As if here were those cooler shades of love.
Can such delights be in the street,
And open fields, and we not see't?
Come, we'll abroad; and let's obay
The Proclamation made for May:
And sin no more, as we have done, by staying;
But my *Corinna*, come, let's goe a Maying.

There's not a budding Boy, or Girle, this day,
But is got up, and gone to bring in May.
A deale of Youth, ere this, is come
Back, and with *White-thorn* laden home.
Some have dispatcht their Cakes and Creame,
Before that we have left to dreame:
And some have wept, and woo'd, and plighted Troth,
And chose their Priest, ere we can cast off sloth:
Many a green-gown has been given;
Many a kisse, both odde and even:
Many a glance too has been sent
From out the eye, Loves Firmament:
Many a jest told of the Keyes betraying
This night, and Locks pickt, yet w'are not a Maying.

Come, let us goe, while we are in our prime;
And take the harmlesse follie of the time.
We shall grow old apace, and die
Before we know our liberty.
Our life is short; and our dayes run
As fast away as do's the Sunne:
And as a vapour, or a drop of raine
Once lost, can ne'er be found againe:

So when or you or I are made
A fable, song, or fleeting shade;
All love, all liking, all delight
Lies drown'd with us in endlesse night.
Then while time serves, and we are but decaying;
Come, my *Corinna*, come, let 's goe a Maying.

Hesperides, 1648

223 *To live merrily, and to trust to Good Verses*

NOW is the time for mirth,
Nor cheek, or tongue be dumbe:
For with the flowrie earth,
The golden pomp is come.

The golden Pomp is come;
For now each tree does weare
(Made of her Pap and Gum)
Rich beads of *Amber* here.

Now raignes the *Rose*, and now
Th' *Arabian* Dew besmears
My uncontrolled brow,
And my retorted haires.

Homer, this Health to thee,
In Sack of such a kind,
That it would make thee see,
Though thou wert ne'er so blind.

Next, Virgil, I'll call forth,
To pledge this second Health
In Wine, whose each cup 's worth
An Indian Common-wealth.

A Goblet next I'll drink
   To *Ovid*; and suppose,
Made he the pledge, he'd think
   The world had all *one Nose*.

Then this immensive cup
   Of *Aromatike* wine,
Catullus, I quaffe up
   To that terse Muse of thine.

Wild I am now with heat;
   O *Bacchus*! coole thy Rayes!
Or frantick I shall eate
   Thy *Thyrse*, and bite the *Bayes*.

Round, round, the roof does run;
   And being ravisht thus,
Come, I will drink a Tun
   To my *Propertius*.

Now, to *Tibullus*, next,
   This flood I drink to thee:
But stay; I see a Text,
   That this presents to me.

Behold, *Tibullus* lies
   Here burnt, whose small return
Of ashes, scarce suffice
   To fill a little Urne.

Trust to good Verses then;
   They onely will aspire,
When Pyramids, as men,
   Are lost, i'th'funerall fire.

And when all Bodies meet
  In *Lethe* to be drown'd;
Then onely Numbers sweet,
  With endlesse life are crown'd.

Hesperides, 1648

224 *To Violet*

WELCOME Maids of Honour,
    You doe bring
    In the Spring;
And wait upon her.

She has Virgins many,
    Fresh and faire;
    Yet you are
More sweet than any.

Y'are the Maiden Posies,
    And so grac't,
    To be plac't,
'Fore Damask Roses.

Yet though thus respected,
    By and by
    Ye doe lie,
Poore Girles, neglected.

Hesperides, 1648

225 *To the Virgins, to make much of Time*

GATHER ye Rose-buds while ye may,
  Old Time is still a flying:
And this same flower that smiles to day,
  To morrow will be dying.

The glorious Lamp of Heaven, the Sun,
The higher he 's a getting;
The sooner will his Race be run,
And neerer he 's to Setting.

That Age is best, which is the first,
When Youth and Blood are warmer;
But being spent, the worse, and worst
Times, still succeed the former.

Then be not coy, but use your time;
And while ye may, goe marry:
For having lost but once your prime,
You may for ever tarry. *Hesperides*, 1648

226 *His Poetrie his Pillar*

ONELY a little more
I have to write,
Then I'll give o'er,
And bid the world Good-night.

'Tis but a flying minute,
That I must stay,
Or linger in it;
And then I must away.

O time that cut'st down all!
And scarce leav'st here
Memoriall
Of any men that were.

How many lye forgot
In Vaults beneath?
And piece-meale rot
Without a fame in death?

Behold this living stone,
I reare for me,
Ne'er to be thrown
Downe, envious Time by thee.

Pillars let some set up,
(If so they please)
Here is my hope,
And my *Pyramides*.

Hesperides, 1648

227 *A Meditation for his Mistresse*

YOU are a *Tulip* seen to day,
But (Dearest) of so short a stay;
That where you grew, scarce man can say.

You are a lovely *July-flower*,
Yet one rude wind, or ruffling shower,
Will force you hence, (and in an houre.)

You are a sparkling *Rose* i'th'bud,
Yet lost, ere that chast flesh and blood
Can shew where you or grew, or stood.

You are a full-spread faire-set Vine,
And can with Tendrills love intwine,
Yet dry'd, ere you distill your Wine.

You are like Balme inclosed (well)
In *Amber*, or some *Chrystall* shell,
Yet lost ere you transfuse your smell.

You are a dainty *Violet*,
Yet wither'd, ere you can be set
Within the Virgins Coronet.

Pyramides: monumental pyramid.

You are the *Queen* all flowers among,
But die you must (faire Maid) ere long,
As He, the maker of this Song.

Hesperides, 1648

228 *Lyrick for Legacies*

GOLD I've none, for use or show,
Neither Silver to bestow
At my death; but thus much know,
That each Lyrick here shall be
Of my love a Legacie,
Left to all posterity.
Gentle friends, then doe but please,
To accept such coynes as these;
As my last Remembrances.

Hesperides, 1648

229 *To Musique, to becalme his Fever*

CHARM me asleep, and melt me so
With thy Delicious Numbers;
That being ravisht, hence I goe
  Away in easie slumbers.
    Ease my sick head,
    And make my bed,
Thou Power that canst sever
    From me this ill:
    And quickly still:
    Though thou not kill
      My Fever.

Thou sweetly canst convert the same
From a consuming fire,
Into a gentle-licking flame,
And make it thus expire.
Then make me weep
My paines asleep;
And give me such reposes,
That I, poore I,
May think, thereby,
I live and die
'Mongst Roses.

Fall on me like a silent dew,
Or like those Maiden showrs,
Which, by the peepe of day, doe strew
A Baptime o'er the flowers.
Melt, melt my paines,
With thy soft straines;
That having ease me given,
With full delight,
I leave this light;
And take my flight
For Heaven.

Hesperides, 1648

230 *To the Rose. Song*

GOE happy Rose, and enterwove
With other Flowers, bind my Love.
Tell her too, she must not be,
Longer flowing, longer free,
That so oft has fetter'd me.

Baptime: baptism, blessing.

Say (if she 's fretfull) I have bands
Of Pearle, and Gold, to bind her hands:
Tell her, if she struggle still,
I have Mirtle rods, (at will)
For to tame, though not to kill.

Take thou my blessing, thus, and goe,
And tell her this—but doe not so,
Lest a handsome anger flye,
Like a Lightning, from her eye,
And burn thee up, as well as I.

Hesperides, 1648

231 *The Hock-Cart, or Harvest Home: To the Right Honourable Mildmay, Earle of Westmorland*

COME Sons of Summer, by whose toile,
We are the Lords of Wine and Oile:
By whose tough labours, and rough hands,
We rip up first, then reap our lands.
Crown'd with the eares of corne, now come,
And, to the Pipe, sing Harvest home.
Come forth, my Lord, and see the Cart
Drest up with all the Country Art.
See, here a *Maukin*, there a sheet,
As spotlesse pure, as it is sweet:
The Horses, Mares, and frisking Fillies,
(Clad, all, in Linnen, white as Lillies.)
The Harvest Swaines, and Wenches bound
For joy, to see the *Hock-cart* crown'd.
About the Cart, heare, how the Rout
Of Rurall Younglings raise the shout;

Pressing before, some coming after,
Those with a shout, and these with laughter.
Some blesse the Cart; some kisse the sheaves;
Some prank them up with Oaken leaves:
Some crosse the Fill-horse; some with great
Devotion, stroke the home-borne wheat:
While other rusticks, lesse attent
To Prayers, than to Merryment,
Run after with their breeches rent.
Well, on, brave boyes, to your Lords Hearth,
Glitt'ring with fire; where, for your mirth,
Ye shall see first the large and cheefe
Foundation of your Feast, Fat Beefe:
With Upper Stories, Mutton, Veale
And Bacon, (which makes full the meale)
With sev'rall dishes standing by,
As here a Custard, there a Pie,
And here all tempting Frumentie.
And for to make the merry cheere,
If smirking Wine be wanting here,
There's that, which drowns all care, stout Beere;
Which freely drink to your Lords health,
Then to the Plough, (the Common-wealth)
Next to your Flailes, your Fanes, your Fats;
Then to the Maids with Wheaten Hats:
To the rough Sickle, and crookt Scythe,
Drink frollick boyes, till all be blythe.
Feed, and grow fat; and as ye eat,
Be mindfull, that the lab'ring Neat
(As you) may have their fill of meat.
And know, besides, ye must revoke

Fill-horse: shaft-horse.

The patient Oxe unto the Yoke
And all goe back unto the Plough
And Harrow, (though they're hang'd up now.)
And, you must know, your Lords word 's true,
Feed him ye must, whose food fills you.
And that this pleasure is like raine,
Not sent ye for to drowne your paine,
But for to make it spring againe.

Hesperides, 1648

232 *To Primroses fill'd with morning-dew*

WHY doe ye weep, sweet Babes? can Tears
Speake griefe in you,
Who were but borne
Just as the modest Morne
Teem'd her refreshing dew?
Alas you have not known that shower,
That marres a flower;
Nor felt th'unkind
Breath of a blasting wind;
Nor are ye worne with yeares;
Or warpt, as we,
Who think it strange to see,
Such pretty flowers, (like to Orphans young)
To speak by Teares, before ye have a Tongue.

Speak, whimp'ring Younglings, and make known
The reason, why
Ye droop, and weep;
Is it for want of sleep?
Or childish Lullabie?
Or that ye have not seen as yet
The *Violet*?

Or brought a kisse
From that Sweet-heart, to this?
No, no, this sorrow shown
By your teares shed,
Would have this Lecture read,
That things of greatest, so of meanest worth,
Conceiv'd with grief are, and with teares brought forth.

Hesperides, 1648

233 *To Anthea, who may command him any thing*

BID me to live, and I will live
Thy Protestant to be:
Or bid me love, and I will give
A loving heart to thee.

A heart as soft, a heart as kind,
A heart as sound and free,
As in the whole world thou canst find,
That heart I'll give to thee.

Bid that heart stay, and it will stay,
To honour thy Decree:
Or bid it languish quite away,
And't shall doe so for thee.

Bid me to weep, and I will weep,
While I have eyes to see:
And having none, yet I will keep:
A heart to weep for thee.

Bid me despaire, and I'll despaire,
Under that *Cypresse* tree:
Or bid me die, and I will dare
E'en Death, to die for thee.

Thou art my life, my love, my heart,
  The very eyes of me:
And hast command of every part,
  To live and die for thee.

Hesperides, 1648

234 *To Meddowes*

YE have been fresh and green,
  Ye have been fill'd with flowers:
And ye the Walks have been
  Where Maids have spent their houres.

You have beheld, how they
  With *Wicker Arks* did come
To kisse, and beare away
  The richer Cowslips home.

Y'ave heard them sweetly sing,
  And seen them in a Round:
Each Virgin, like a Spring,
  With Hony-suckles crown'd.

But now, we see, none here,
  Whose silv'rie feet did tread,
And with dishevell'd Haire,
  Adorn'd this smoother Mead.

Like Unthrifts, having spent,
  Your stock, and needy grown,
Y'are left here to lament
  Your poore estates, alone.

Hesperides, 1648

235 *To Daffadills*

FAIRE Daffadills, we weep to see
You haste away so soone:
As yet the early-rising Sun
Has not attain'd his Noone.
Stay, stay,
Untill the hasting day
Has run
But to the Even-song;
And, having pray'd together, wee
Will goe with you along.

We have short time to stay, as you,
We have as short a Spring;
As quick a growth to meet Decay,
As you, or any thing.
We die,
As your hours doe, and drie
Away,
Like to the Summers raine;
Or as the pearles of Mornings dew
Ne'er to be found againe. *Hesperides*, 1648

236 *To his Maid Prew*

THESE *Summer-Birds* did with thy Master stay
The times of warmth; but then they flew away;
Leaving their Poet (being now grown old)
Expos'd to all the coming Winters cold.
But thou *kind Prew* did'st with my Fates abide,
As well the Winters, as the Summers Tide:
For which thy Love, live with thy Master here,
Not two, but all the seasons of the yeare. *Hesperides*, 1648

237

To Daisies, not to shut so soone

SHUT not so soon; the dull-ey'd night
Has not as yet begunne
To make a seizure on the light,
Or to seale up the Sun.

No Marigolds yet closed are;
No shadowes great appeare;
Nor doth the early Shepheards Starre
Shine like a spangle here.

Stay but till my *Julia* close
Her life-begetting eye;
And let the whole world then dispose
It selfe to live or dye.

Hesperides, 1648

238

To Blossoms

FAIRE pledges of a fruitfull Tree,
Why do yee fall so fast?
Your date is not so past;
But you may stay yet here a while,
To blush and gently smile;
And go at last.

What, were yee borne to be
An houre or half's delight;
And so to bid goodnight?
'Twas pitie Nature brought yee forth
Merely to shew your worth,
And lose you quite.

But you are lovely Leaves, where we
May read how soon things have
Their end, though ne'er so brave:
And after they have shown their pride,
Like you a while: They glide
Into the Grave. *Hesperides*, 1648

239 *The Fairies*

IF ye will with *Mab* find grace,
Set each Platter in his place:
Rake the Fire up, and get
Water in, ere Sun be set.
Wash your Pailes, and clense your Dairies;
Sluts are loathsome to the Fairies:
Sweep your house: Who doth not so,
Mab will pinch her by the toe. *Hesperides*, 1648

240 *His Prayer to Ben. Johnson*

WHEN I a Verse shall make,
Know I have pray'd thee,
For old *Religions* sake,
Saint *Ben* to aide me.

Make the way smooth for me,
When I, thy *Herrick*,
Honouring thee, on my knee
Offer my *Lyrick*.

Candles I'll give to thee,
And a new Altar;
And thou Saint *Ben*, shalt be
Writ in my *Psalter*. *Hesperides*, 1648

241 *The Night-piece to Julia*

HER Eyes the Glow-worme lend thee,
The Shooting Starres attend thee;
And the Elves also,
Whose little eyes glow,
Like the sparks of fire, befriend thee.

No *Will-o'th'-Wispe* mis-light thee;
Nor Snake, or Slow-worme bite thee:
But on, on thy way
Not making a stay,
Since Ghost there's none to affright thee.

Let not the darke thee cumber;
What though the Moon does slumber?
The Starres of the night
Will lend thee their light,
Like Tapers cleare without number.

Then *Julia* let me wooe thee,
Thus, thus to come unto me:
And when I shall meet
Thy silv'ry feet,
My soule I'll poure into thee.

Hesperides, 1648

242 *Upon a Child*

HERE a pretty Baby lies
Sung asleep with Lullabies:
Pray be silent, and not stirre
Th' easie earth that covers her.

Hesperides, 1648

243 *To Electra*

I DARE not ask a kisse;
I dare not beg a smile;
Lest having that, or this,
I might grow proud the while.

No, no, the utmost share
Of my desire, shall be
Onely to kisse that Aire,
That lately kissed thee.

Hesperides, 1648

244 *Upon Julia's Clothes*

WHEN as in silks my *Julia* goes,
Then, then (me thinks) how sweetly flowes
That liquefaction of her clothes.

Next, when I cast mine eyes and see
That brave Vibration each way free;
O how that glittering taketh me!

Hesperides, 1648

245 *Ceremonies for Candlemasse Eve*

DOWN with the Rosemary and Bayes,
Down with the Misletoe;
Instead of Holly, now up-raise
The greener Box (for show.)

The Holly hitherto did sway;
Let Box now domineere;
Untill the dancing Easter-day,
Or Easters Eve appeare.

Then youthfull Box which now hath grace,
Your houses to renew;
Grown old, surrender must his place,
Unto the crisped Yew.

When Yew is out, then Birch comes in,
And many Flowers beside;
Both of a fresh, and fragrant kinne
To honour Whitsontide.

Green Rushes then, and sweetest Bents,
With cooler Oken boughs;
Come in for comely ornaments,
To re-adorn the house.
Thus times do shift; each thing his turne does hold;
New things succeed, as former things grow old.

Hesperides, 1648

246 *Upon Ben. Johnson*

HERE lyes *Johnson* with the rest
Of the Poets; but the Best.
Reader, wouldst thou more have known?
Aske his Story, not this Stone.
That will speake what this can't tell
Of his glory. *So farewell.*

Hesperides, 1648

247 *An Ode for him*

AH *Ben*!
Say how, or when
Shall we thy Guests
Meet at those *Lyrick* Feasts,

Made at the *Sun*,
The *Dog*, the triple *Tunne*?
Where we such clusters had,
As made us nobly wild, not mad;
And yet each Verse of thine
Out-did the meate, out-did the frolick wine.

My *Ben*
Or come agen:
Or send to us,
Thy wits great over-plus;
But teach us yet
Wisely to husband it;
Lest we that Talent spend:
And having once brought to an end
That precious stock; the store
Of such a wit the world should have no more.

Hesperides, 1648

248 *Upon Time*

TIME was upon
The wing, to flie away;
And I call'd on
Him but a while to stay;
But he'd be gone,
For ought that I could say.

He held out then,
A Writing, as he went;
And askt me, when
False man would be content
To pay agen,
What God and Nature lent.

An houre-glasse,
In which were sands but few,
As he did passe,
He shew'd, and told me too,
Mine end near was,
And so away he flew.

His Noble Numbers, 1647

249 *His Letanie, to the Holy Spirit*

In the houre of my distresse,
When temptations me oppresse,
And when I my sins confesse,
Sweet Spirit comfort me!

When I lie within my bed,
Sick in heart, and sick in head,
And with doubts discomforted,
Sweet Spirit comfort me!

When the house doth sigh and weep,
And the world is drown'd in sleep,
Yet mine eyes the watch do keep;
Sweet Spirit comfort me!

When the artlesse Doctor sees
No one hope, but of his Fees,
And his skill runs on the lees;
Sweet Spirit comfort me!

When his Potion and his Pill,
Has, or none, or little skill,
Meet for nothing, but to kill;
Sweet Spirit comfort me!

When the passing-bell doth toll,
And the Furies in a shoal
Come to fright a parting soule;
Sweet Spirit comfort me!

When the tapers now burne blew,
And the comforters are few,
And that number more than true;
Sweet Spirit comfort me!

When the Priest his last hath pray'd,
And I nod to what is said,
'Cause my speech is now decay'd;
Sweet Spirit comfort me!

When (God knowes) I'm tost about,
Either with despaire, or doubt;
Yet before the glasse be out,
Sweet Spirit comfort me!

When the Tempter me pursu'th
With the sins of all my youth,
And halfe damns me with untruth;
Sweet Spirit comfort me!

When the flames and hellish cries
Fright mine eares, and fright mine eyes,
And all terrors me surprize;
Sweet Spirit comfort me!

When the Judgment is reveal'd,
And that open'd which was seal'd,
When to Thee I have appeal'd;
Sweet Spirit comfort me!

His Noble Numbers, 1647

250 *A Thanksgiving to God, for his House*

LORD, Thou hast given me a cell
Wherein to dwell,
A little house, whose humble Roof
Is weather-proof;
Under the sparres of which I lie
Both soft, and drie;
Where Thou my chamber for to ward
Hast set a Guard
Of harmlesse thoughts, to watch and keep
Me, while I sleep.
Low is my porch, as is my Fate,
Both void of state;
And yet the threshold of my doore
Is worn by th' poore,
Who thither come, and freely get
Good words, or meat:
Like as my Parlour, so my Hall
And Kitchin 's small:
A little Butterie, and therein
A little Bin,
Which keeps my little loafe of Bread
Unchipt, unflead:
Some brittle sticks of Thorne or Briar
Make me a fire,
Close by whose living coale I sit,
And glow like it.
Lord, I confesse too, when I dine,
The Pulse is Thine,

unflead: unflayed, whole.

And all those other Bits, that bee
    There plac'd by Thee;
The Worts, the Purslain, and the Messe
    Of Water-cresse,
Which of Thy kindnesse Thou hast sent;
    And my content
Makes those, and my beloved Beet,
    To be more sweet.
'Tis Thou that crown'st my glittering Hearth
    With guiltlesse mirth;
And giv'st me Wassaile Bowles to drink,
    Spic'd to the brink.
Lord, 'tis thy plenty-dropping hand,
    That soiles my land;
And giv'st me, for my Bushell sown,
    Twice ten for one:
Thou mak'st my teeming Hen to lay
    Her egg each day:
Besides my healthfull Ewes to beare
    Me twins each yeare:
The while the conduits of my Kine
    Run Creame, (for Wine.)
All these, and better Thou dost send
    Me, to this end,
That I should render, for my part,
    A thankfull heart;
Which, fir'd with incense, I resigne,
    As wholly Thine;
But the acceptance, that must be,
    My Christ, by Thee.

His Noble Numbers, 1647

251 *Another Grace for a Child*

HERE a little child I stand,
Heaving up my either hand;
Cold as Paddocks though they be,
Here I lift them up to Thee,
For a Benizon to fall
On our meat, and on us all. *Amen.*

His Noble Numbers, 1647

252 *The Bell-man*

ALONG the dark, and silent night,
With my Lantern, and my Light,
And the tinkling of my Bell,
Thus I walk, and this I tell:
Death and dreadfulnesse call on,
To the gen'rall Session;
To whose dismall Barre, we there
All accompts must come to cleere:
Scores of sins w'ave made here many,
Wip't out few, (God knowes) if any.
Rise ye Debters then, and fall
To make payment, while I call.
Ponder this, when I am gone;
By the clock 'tis almost *One*.

His Noble Numbers, 1647

253 *The white Island: or place of the Blest*

IN this world (the *Isle of Dreames*)
While we sit by sorrowes streames,
Teares and terrors are our theames
Reciting:

But when once from hence we flie,
More and more approaching nigh
Unto young Eternitie
Uniting:

In that *whiter Island*, where
Things are evermore sincere;
Candor here, and lustre there
Delighting:

There no monstrous fancies shall
Out of hell an horrour call,
To create (or cause at all)
Affrighting.

There in calm and cooling sleep
We our eyes shall never steep;
But eternall watch shall keep,
Attending

Pleasures, such as shall pursue
Me immortaliz'd, and you;
And fresh joyes, as never too
Have ending.

His Noble Numbers, 1647

254 *Upon Master Fletchers Incomparable Playes*

APOLLO sings, his harpe resounds; give roome,
For now behold the golden Pompe is come,
The Pompe of Playes which thousands come to see,
With admiration both of them and thee.
O Volume worthy leafe, by leafe and cover
To be with juice of Cedar washt all over;

Here words with lines, and lines with Scenes consent,
To raise an Act to full astonishment;
Here melting numbers, words of power to move
Young men to swoone, and Maides to dye for love.
Love lyes a bleeding here, *Evadne* there
Swells with brave rage, yet comely every where,
Here's a mad lover, there that high designe
Of *King and no King* (and the rare Plot thine):
So that where'er we circumvolve our Eyes,
Such rich, such fresh, such sweet varietyes,
Ravish our spirits, that entranc't we see
None writes love's passion in the world, like Thee.

Beaumont and Fletcher, *Plays*, 1647

WILLIAM BROWNE

1592–1643?

255 *From 'Britannias Pastorals'*
Praise of Poets

(*i*)

At *Thames* faire port
The *Nymphes* and *Shepherds* of the *Isle* resort.
And thence did put to Sea with mirthfull rounds,
Whereat the billowes dance above their bounds,
And bearded Goats, that on the clouded head
Of any sea-survaying Mountaine fed,
Leaving to crop the Ivy, listning stood
At those sweet ayres which did intrance the flood.
In jocund sort the *Goddesse* thus they met,
And after rev'rence done, all being set
Upon their finny Coursers, round her throne,
And she prepar'd to cut the watry Zone

Ingirting *Albion*; all their pipes were still,
And *Colin Clout* began to tune his quill
With such deepe Art, that every one was given
To thinke *Apollo* (newly slid from heav'n)
Had ta'en a humane shape to win his love,
Or with the *Westerne Swaines* for glory strove.
He sung th' heroicke Knights of *Fairy* land
In lines so elegant, of such command,
That had the *Thracian* play'd but halfe so well,
He had not left *Eurydice* in hell.
But ere he ended his melodious song
An host of *Angels* flew the clouds among,
And rapt this Swan from his attentive mates,
To make him one of their associates
In heavens faire Quire: where now he sings the praise
Of him that is the *first and last of dayes.*
Divinest *Spenser* heav'n-bred, happy Muse!
Would any power into my braine infuse
Thy worth, or all that *Poets* had before,
I could not praise till thou deserv'st no more.

Book 2, Song 1

(*ii*)

As I have seene when on the breast of *Thames*
A heavenly *beauty* of sweet *English Dames*,
In some calme Ev'ning of delightfull *May*,
With *Musick* give a farewell to the *day*,
Or as they would (with an admired tone)
Greet *Nights* ascension to her *Eben Throne*,
Rapt with their melodie, a thousand more
Run to be wafted from the bounding shore:

Colin Clout: Spenser. *Thracian*: Orpheus.

So ran the Shepherds, and with hasty feet
Strove which should first increase that happy fleet.
The true presagers of a coming storme,
Teaching their fins to steere them to the forme
Of *Thetis* will, like Boats at Anchor stood,
As ready to convay the *Muses* brood
Into the brackish *Lake*, that seem'd to swell,
As proud so rich a burden on it fell.
Ere their arrival *Astrophel* had done
His shepherds *lay*, yet equaliz'd of none.
Th' admired mirrour, glory of our *Isle*,
Thou far-far-more than mortall man, whose style
Strucke more men dumbe to hearken to thy song,
Than *Orpheus* Harpe, or *Tully's* golden tongue.
To him (as right) for wits deepe quintessence,
For honour, valour, vertue, excellence,
Be all the Garlands, crowne his tombe with Bay,
Who spake as much as e'er our tongue can say.

. . . .

He sweetly touched, what I harshly hit,
Yet thus I glory in what I have writ;
Sidney began (and if a wit so meane
May taste with him the dewes of *Hippocrene*)
I sung the *Past'rall* next; his *Muse*, my mover:
And on the Plaines full many a pensive lover
Shall sing us to their loves, and praising be
My humble lines: the more, for praising thee.
Thus we shall live with them, by Rocks, by Springs,
As well as *Homer* by the death of Kings.
Then in a straine beyond an Oaten Quill
The learned Shepherd of faire *Hitching* hill

presagers: Dolphins. *Astrophel*: Sidney. Shepherd: Chapman.

Sung the heroicke deeds of *Greece* and *Troy*,
In lines so worthy life, that I imploy
My Reed in vaine to overtake his fame.
All praisefull tongues doe wait upon that name.
  Our second *Ovid*, the most pleasing Muse
That heav'n did e'er in mortals braine infuse,
All-loved *Drayton*, in soule-raping straines,
A genuine note, of all the *Nymphish* traines
Began to tune; on it all eares were hung
As sometime *Dido's* on *Æneas* tongue.
  Jonson whose full of merit to reherse
Too copious is to be confinde in verse;
Yet therein onely fittest to be knowne,
Could any write a line which he might owne.
One, so judicious; so well knowing; and
A man whose least worth is to understand;
One so exact in all he doth prefer
To able censure; for the *Theater*
Not *Seneca* transcends his worth of praise;
Who writes him well shall well deserve the *Bayes*.

Book 2, Song 2
Britannia's Pastorals, 1616 (text 1625)

256 *Celadyne's Song*

MARINA'S gone, and now sit I,
  As *Philomela* (on a thorne,
Turn'd out of nature's livery),
  Mirthless, alone, and all forlorne:
Onely she sings not, while my sorrowes can
Breathe forth such notes as fit a dying swan.

Soe shuts the marigold her leaves
At the departure of the sun;
Soe from the hony-suckle sheaves
The bee goes when the day is done;
So sits the turtle when she is but one,
And soe all woe, as I, since she is gone.

To some fewe birds, kinde Nature hath
Made all the summer as one daye;
Which once enjoy'd, colde winter's wrath,
As night, they sleeping passe away.
Those happy creatures are, that knowe not yet
The payne to be depriv'd or to forget.

I oft have heard men saye there be
Some, that with confidence professe
The helpfull Art of Memorie;
But could they teach forgetfulnesse,
I'd learne, and try what further art could doe,
To make me love her and forget her too.

Sad melancholy, that persuades
Men from themselves, to thinke they be
Headlesse, or other bodyes shades,
Hath long and bootless dwelt with me;
For coulde I thinke she some idea were,
I still might love, forget, and have her here.

But such she is not: nor would I,
For twice as many torments more,
As her bereaved company
Hath brought to those I felt before,
For then no future tyme might hap to knowe
That she deserv'd, or I did love her soe.

Yee houres, then, but as minutes be!
(Though soe I shall be sooner olde)
Till I those lovely graces see,
Which, but in her, can none beholde;
Then be an age! That we maye never try
More griefe in parting, but growe olde and dye.

Britannia's Pastorals, Book 3, Song 1

257 *Song of the Syrens*

STEERE hither, steere, your winged pines,
All beaten mariners,
Here lye Loves undiscov'red mynes,
A prey to passengers;
Perfumes farre sweeter than the best
Which make the Phoenix urne and nest.
Fear not your ships,
Nor any to oppose you save our lips,
But come on shore,
Where no joy dyes till love hath gotten more.

For swellinge waves, our panting brestes
Where never stormes arise,
Exchange; and be awhile our guestes:
For starres gaze on our eyes.
The compasse love shall hourely sing,
And as he goes about the ring,
We will not misse
To tell each pointe he nameth with a kisse.

The Inner Temple Masque (Emman. Coll. MS.)

WILLIAM BROWNE

258

An Ode

AWAKE, faire Muse; for I intend
These everlasting lines to thee,
And, honor'd *Drayton*, come and lend
An eare to this sweet melodye:
For on my harpes most high and silver string,
To those Nine Sisters whom I love, I sing.

This man through death and horror seekes
Honor, by the Victorious Steele;
Another in unmapped creekes
For Jewells moores his winged keele.
The clam'rous Barre wins some, and others bite
At lookes throwne from a mushroom Favorite.

But I, that serve the lovely Graces,
Spurne at that drosse, which most adore;
And titles hate, like paynted faces,
And heart-fed Care for evermore.
Those pleasures I disdaine, which are pursude
With praise and wishes by the multitude.

The Bayes, which deathless Learning crownes,
Me of Apollo's troope installs:
The Satyres following o'er the downes
Fair Nymphs to rusticke festivalls,
Make me affect (where men no traffique have)
The holy horror of a Savage Cave.

Through the faire skyes I thence intend,
With an unus'd and powerfull wing,
To beare me to my Journeyes end:
And those that taste the Muses spring,
Too much celestiall fire have at their birth,
To live long time like common soules in Earth.

From faire Aurora will I reare
My selfe unto the source of floods;
And from the Ethiopian Beare,
To him as white as snowy woods;
Nor shall I feare (for this daye taking flight)
To be wounde up in any veil of night.

Of Death I may not feare the dart,
As is the use of Human State;
For well I knowe my better part
Dreads not the hand of Time or Fate.
Tremble at Death, Envye, and Fortune who
Have but one life: Heaven gives a Poet two.

All costly obsequies inveigh,
Marble and painting too, as vayne;
My ashes shall not meet with Clay,
As those doe of the vulgar trayne.
And if my Muse to Spensers glory come
No King shall owne my verses for his Tombe.

Lansdowne MS. 777

259 *Epitaph*

In Obitum M.S. x° Maij, 1614.

MAY! Be thou never grac'd with birds that sing,
Nor Flora's pride!
In thee all flowers and Roses spring.
Mine only died.

WILLIAM BROWNE

260 *Epitaph on the Countesse Dowager of Pembroke*

UNDERNEATH this sable Herse
Lyes the subject of all verse:
Sydney's sister, Pembroke's Mother:
Death, ere thou hast slaine another,
Faire, and Learn'd, and good as she,
Time shall throw a dart at thee.

Lansdowne MS. 777

FRANCIS QUARLES

1592–1644

261 *Hos ego versiculos*

LIKE to the damaske rose you see,
Or like the blossome on the tree,
Or like the daintie flower of May,
Or like the Morning to the day,
Or like the Sunne, or like the shade,
Or like the Gourd which Jonas had;
Even such is man whose thred is spun,
Drawne out and cut, and so is done.

The Rose withers, the blossome blasteth,
The flowre fades, the morning hasteth:
The Sunne sets, the shadow flies,
The Gourd consumes, and man he dies.

Like to the blaze of fond delight;
Or like a morning cleare and bright;
Or like a frost, or like a showre;
Or like the pride of Babel's Tower;

Or like the houre that guides the time;
Or like to beauty in her prime;
  Even such is man, whose glory lends
  His life a blaze or two, and ends.

Delights vanish; the morne o'ercasteth,
The frost breaks, the shower hasteth;
The Tower falls, the hower spends;
The beauty fades, and man's life ends.

Finis. Fr. Qu.

Argalus and Parthenia, 1629

262 *The Authour's Dreame*

MY sinnes are like the haires upon my head,
  And raise their Audit to as high a score:
In this they differ: these doe dayly shed;
But ah! my sinnes grow dayly more and more.
  If by my haires thou number out my sinnes;
  Heaven make me bald before the day begins.

My sinnes are like the sands upon the shore;
Which every ebbe layes open to the eye:
In this they differ: These are cover'd o'er
With every tide, My sinnes still open lye.
  If thou wilt make my head a sea of teares,
  O they will hide the sinnes of all my yeares.

My sinnes are like the Starres within the skies,
In view, in number, even as bright as great:
In this they differ: these doe set and rise;
But ah! my sinnes doe rise, but never set.
  Shine Son of glory, and my sinnes are gone
  Like twinkling Starres before the rising Sunne.

Argalus and Parthenia, 1629, and *Divine Fancies*, 1632

the day: that day *D.F.*   Son: *D.F.* 1629 Sunne.

263 *On the Infancy of our Saviour*

HAIL blessed *Virgin*, full of heavenly *Grace*,
Blest above all that sprang from humane race;
Whose Heav'n-saluted *Womb* brought forth in *One*,
A blessed *Saviour*, and a blessed *Son*:
O! What a ravishment 't had been, to see
Thy little *Saviour* perking on thy *Knee!*
To see him nuzzle in thy Virgin-Breast:
His milk-white body all unclad, undrest!
To see thy busie fingers cloathe and wrap
His spreading limbs in thy indulgent Lap!
To see his desp'rate *Eyes*, with Childish grace,
Smiling upon his smiling Mothers face!
And when his forward strength began to bloom,
To see him *diddle* up and down the Room!
O, who would think so sweet a *Babe* as this,
Should e'er be slain by a false-hearted kisse!
Had I a *Ragge*, if sure thy Body wore it,
Pardon, sweet *Babe*, I think I should adore it:
Till then, O grant this Boon, (a boon or dearer)
The *Weed* not being, I may adore the *Wearer*.

Divine Fancies, 1632

264 *On the Needle of a Sun-Dial*

BEHOLD this needle; when the *Artick* stone
Had touch'd it, how it trembles up and down;
Hunts for the *Pole*; and cannot be possest
Of peace, until it find that point, that rest:

Such is the *heart* of Man: which when it hath
Attain'd the virtue of a lively Faith,
It finds no rest on earth, makes no abode,
In any Object, but his *heav'n*, his *God*.

Divine Fancies, 1632

265 *On Those that Deserve it*

O WHEN our Clergie, at the dreadful *Day*,
Shall make their Audit; when the *judge* shall say,
Give your accompts: What, have my Lambs been fed?
Say, do they all stand sound? Is there none dead
By your defaults? Come Shephards bring them forth
That I may crowne your labours in their worth.
O what an answer will be given by some!
We have been silenc'd: Canons struck us dumb;
The Great ones would not let us feed thy flock,
Unless we play'd the fools, and wore a Frock:
We were forbid unless we'd yeeld to signe
And cross their browes, they say, *a mark of thine*.
To say the truth, great Judge, they were not fed;
Lord, here they be; but Lord, they be all dead.
Ah cruel Shephards! Could your conscience serve
Not to be fooles, and yet to let them sterve?
What if your Fiery spirits had been bound
To Antick Habits; or your heads been crown'd
With *Peacocks* Plumes; had ye been forc'd to feed
Your Saviour's dear-bought Flock in a fools weed;
He that was scorn'd, revil'd, endur'd the *Curse*
Of a base death, in your behalfs; nay worse,
Swallow'd the cup of wrath charg'd up to th' *brim*;
Durst ye not stoop to play the fooles for him?

Divine Fancies, 1632

266 *On Zacheus*

ME thinks, I see, with what a busie haste,
Zacheus climb'd the Tree: But O, how fast,
How full of speed, canst thou imagine (when
Our *Saviour* call'd) he powder'd down agen!
He ne'er made tryal, if the boughs were sound,
Or rotten; nor how far 'twas to the ground:
There was no danger fear'd; at such a Call,
He'll venture nothing, that dare feare a fall;
Needs must he downe, by such a *Spirit* driven,
Nor could he fall unless he fell to *Heaven*.
Downe came *Zacheus*, ravisht from the tree;
Bird that was shot ne'er dropt so quicke as he.

Divine Fancies, 1632

267 *On the Plough-man*

I HEARE the whistling Plough-man all day long,
Sweetning his labour with a chearful song;
His Bed 's a Pad of *Straw*; his dyet, coarse;
In both, he fares not better than his *Horse*;
He seldom slakes his thirst, but from the *Pump*;
And yet his heart is blithe, his visage, plump;
His thoughts are ne'er acquainted with such things,
As Griefs or Fears; he only sweats and sings:
When as the landed *Lord*, that cannot dine
Without a Qualm, if not refresht with *Wine*;
That cannot judge that controverted case,
'Twixt meat and mouth, without the *Bribe* of Sauce;
That claims the service of the purest linnen,
To pamper and to shroud his dainty skin in;
Groans out his days, in lab'ring to appease
The rage of either *Business* or *Disease*:

Alas, his silken *Robes*, his costly *Diet*,
Can lend a little pleasure, but no *Quiet*:
The untold sums of his descended wealth
Can give his Body plenty, but not *Health*:
The one, in Pains, and want, possesses all;
T'other, in Plenty, finds no peace at all;
'Tis strange! And yet the cause is easly showne;
T' one's at God's finding; t'other at his owne.

Divine Fancies, 1632

268 *A Good-night*

CLOSE now thine eyes, and rest secure;
Thy *Soule* is safe enough; thy *Body* sure;
He that loves thee, he that keepes
And guards thee, never slumbers, never sleepes.
The smiling Conscience in a sleeping breast
Has only peace, has only rest:
The musicke and the mirth of Kings,
Are all but very *Discords*, when she sings:
Then close thine Eyes and rest secure;
No Sleepe so sweet as thine, no rest so sure.

Divine Fancies, 1632

269 *Wilt thou set thine eyes upon that which is not? for riches make them selves wings, they flie away as an Eagle*

(Proverbs xxiii. 5)

FALSE world, thou ly'st: Thou canst not lend
The least delight:
Thy favours cannot gain a Friend,
They are so slight:

Thy morning pleasures make an end
    To please at night:
Poore are the wants that thou supply'st:
And yet thou vaunt'st, and yet thou vy'st
With heav'n; Fond earth, thou boasts; false world, thou ly'st.

Thy babbling tongue tells golden tales
    Of endless treasure;
Thy bountie offers easie sales
    Of lasting pleasure;
Thou ask'st the Conscience what she ails,
    And swear'st to ease her;
There 's none can want where thou supply'st:
There 's none can give where thou deny'st.
Alas, fond world, thou boasts; false world, thou ly'st.

What well-advised ear regards
    What earth can say?
Thy words are gold, but thy rewards
    Are painted clay;
Thy cunning can but pack the cards;
    Thou canst not play:
Thy game at weakest, still thou vy'st;
If seen, and then revy'd, deny'st;
Thou art not what thou seem'st: false world, thou ly'st.

Thy tinsel bosome seems a mint
    Of new-coin'd treasure,
A Paradise, that has no stint,
    No change, no measure;
A painted cask, but nothing in't,
    Nor wealth, nor pleasure:

revy'd: challenged.

Vain earth! that falsly thus comply'st
With man: Vain man! that thus rely'st
On earth: Vain man, thou dot'st: Vain earth, thou ly'st.

What mean dull souls, in this high measure
    To haberdash
In earth's base wares; whose greatest treasure
    Is dross and trash?
The height of whose inchanting pleasure
    Is but a flash?
Are these the goods that thou supply'st
Us mortalls with? Are these the high'st?
Can these bring cordial peace? False world, thou ly'st.

Emblemes, Book 2, v, 1635 (text, 1643)

270 *Wherefore hidest thou thy face, and holdest me for thine enemy?*

(Job xiii. 24)

WHY dost thou shade thy lovely face? O why
Doth that eclipsing hand so long deny
The Sun-shine of thy soul-enliv'ning eye?

Without that *Light*, what light remaines in me?
Thou art my *Life*, my *Way*, my *Light*; in thee
I live, I move, and by thy beams I see.

Thou art my *Life*; if thou but turn away,
My life 's a thousand deaths: thou art my *Way*:
Without thee, Lord, I travel not, but stray.

My *Light* thou art; without thy glorious sight,
Mine eyes are darkned with perpetuall night.
My God, thou art my *Way*, my *Life*, my *Light*.

Thou art my *Way*; I wander, if thou fly:
Thou art my *Light*; If hid, how blind am I!
Thou art my *Life*; If thou withdraw, I die.

Mine eyes are blind and dark; I cannot see;
To whom, or whither should my darkness flee,
But to the *Light*? And who's that *Light* but thee?

My path is lost; my wandring steps do stray;
I cannot safely go, nor safely stay;
Whom should I seek but thee, my *Path*, my *Way*?

O, I am dead: to whom shall I, poor I,
Repair? to whom shall my sad ashes fly
But *Life*? And where is *Life* but in thine eye?

And yet thou turn'st away thy face, and fly'st me;
And yet I sue for grace, and thou deny'st me;
Speak, art thou angry, Lord, or only try'st me?

Unscreen those Heav'nly lamps, or tell me why
Thou shad'st thy face; perhaps thou thinkst, no eye
Can view those flames, and not drop down and die.

If that be all, shine forth, and draw thee nigher;
Let me behold and die, for my desire
Is *Phoenix*-like to perish in that fire.

Death-conquer'd *Laz'rus* was redeem'd by thee;
If I am dead, Lord, set death's prisoner free;
Am I more spent, or stink I worse than he?

If my puff'd light be out, give leave to tine
My flameless snuff at that bright *Lamp* of thine;
O what's thy *Light* the lesse for lightning mine?

tine: tind, kindle.

If I have lost my *Path*, great Shepherd, say,
Shall I still wander in a doubtfull way?
Lord, shall a Lamb of *Israel's* sheepfold stray?

Thou art the Pilgrim's *Path*; the blind man's *Eye*;
The dead man's *Life*; on thee my hopes rely;
If thou remove, I erre; I grope; I die.

Disclose thy Sun beams; close thy wings, and stay;
See, see how I am blind, and dead, and stray,
O thou, that art my *Light*, my *Life*, my *Way*.

Emblemes, Book 3, vii, 1635 (text 1643)

271 *My beloved is mine, and I am his; He feedeth among the lillies*

(Canticles ii. 16)

EV'N like two little bank-dividing brooks,
That wash the pebbles with their wanton streams,
And having rang'd and search'd a thousand nooks,
Meet both at length in silver-breasted Thames,
Where in a greater current they conjoyn:
So I my best-beloved's am; so he is mine.

Ev'n so we met; and after long pursuit,
Ev'n so we joyn'd; we both became entire;
No need for either to renew a suit,
For I was flax and he was flames of fire:
Our firm-united souls did more than twine;
So I my best-beloved's am; so he is mine.

FRANCIS QUARLES

If all those glitt'ring Monarchs that command
  The servile quarters of this earthly ball,
Should tender, in exchange, their shares of land,
  I would not change my fortunes for them all:
    Their wealth is but a counter to my coin:
The world 's but theirs; but my beloved 's mine.

Nay more; If the fair Thespian Ladies all
  Should heap together their diviner treasure:
That treasure should be deem'd a price too small
  To buy a minutes lease of half my pleasure.
    'Tis not the sacred wealth of all the nine
Can buy my heart from him, or his, from being mine.

Nor Time, nor Place, nor Chance, nor Death can bow
  My least desires unto the least remove;
He 's firmly mine by oath; I his by vow;
  He's mine by faith; and I am his by love;
    He 's mine by water; I am his by wine;
Thus I my best-beloved's am; thus he is mine

He is my Altar; I, his Holy Place;
  I am his guest; and he, my living food;
I'm his by penitence; he mine by grace;
  I'm his by purchase; he is mine, by blood;
    He 's my supporting elm; and I his vine:
Thus I my best-beloved's am; thus he is mine.

He gives me wealth, I give him all my vows:
  I give him songs; he gives me length of dayes:
With wreaths of grace he crowns my conqu'ring brows:
  And I his Temples with a crown of Praise,
    Which he accepts as an ev'rlasting signe,
That I my best-beloved's am; that he is mine.

Emblemes, Book 5, iii, 1635 (text, 1643)

272 *I am my Beloved's, and his desire is towards me*

(Canticles, vii. 10)

LIKE to the Artick needle, that doth guide
The wand'ring shade by his magnetick pow'r,
And leaves his silken Gnomon to decide
The question of the controverted houre;
First franticks up and down, from side to side,
And restlesse beats his crystall'd Iv'ry case
With vain impatience; jets from place to place,
And seeks the bosome of his frozen bride;
At length he slacks his motion, and doth rest
His trembling point at his bright Poles beloved brest.

Ev'n so my soul, being hurried here and there,
By ev'ry object that presents delight,
Fain would be settled, but she knowes not where;
She likes at morning what she loaths at night;
She bowes to honour; then she lends an eare
To that sweet swan like voice of dying pleasure,
Then tumbles in the scatter'd heaps of treasure;
Now flatter'd with false hope; now foyl'd with fear:
Thus finding all the worlds delights to be
But empty toyes, good God, she points alone to thee.

But hath the virtued steel a power to move?
Or can the untouch'd needle point aright?
Or can my wandring thoughts forbear to rove,
Unguided by the virtue of thy spirit?
O hath my leaden soul the art t' improve
Her wasted talent, and unrais'd, aspire
In this sad moulting time of her desire?

Not first belov'd have I the pow'r to love?
 I cannot stirre, but as thou please to move me,
Nor can my heart return thee love, untill thou love me.

The still Commandresse of the silent night
 Borrows her beams from her bright brother's eye;
His fair aspect filles her sharp horns with light;
 If he withdraw, her flames are quench'd and die:
Even so the beams of thy enlightning sp'rite
 Infus'd and shot into my dark desire,
 Inflame my thoughts, and fill my soul with fire,
That I am ravisht with a new delight;
 But if thou shroud thy face, my glory fades,
And I remain a *Nothing*, all compos'd of shades.

Eternall God, O thou that onely art
 The sacred Fountain of eternall light,
And blessed Loadstone of my better part;
 O thou my heart's desire, my soul's delight,
Reflect upon my soul, and touch my heart,
 And then my heart shall prize no good above thee;
 And then my soul shall know thee; knowing, love thee;
And then my trembling thoughts shall never start
 From thy commands, or swerve the least degree,
Or once presume to move, but as they move in thee.

Emblemes, Book 5, iv, 1635 (text, 1643)

sp'rite: 1635. 1643 spirit.

HENRY KING

1592–1669

273 *From An Elegy upon the most Incomparable King Charles the First*

THOU from th' enthroned Martyrs Blood-stain'd Line,
Dost in thy Virtues bright Example shine.
And when thy Darted Beam from the moist Sky
Nightly salutes thy grieving Peoples Eye,
Thou like some Warning Light rais'd by our fears,
Shalt both provoke and still supply our Tears,
Till the *Great Prophet* wak'd from his long Sleep,
Again bids *Sion* for *Josiah* weep:
That all Successions by a *firm Decree*
May teach their Children to Lament for Thee.
  Beyond these Mournfull Rites there is no Art
Or Cost can *Thee* preserve. Thy better Part
Lives in despight of Death, and will endure
Kept safe in thy Unpattern'd *Portraiture*:
Which though in Paper drawn by thine own Hand,
Shall longer than *Corinthian-Marble* stand,
Or Iron Sculptures: There thy matchless Pen
Speaks Thee the *Best of Kings* as *Best of Men*:
Be this Thy *Epitaph*; for This alone
Deserves to carry Thy Inscription.
And 'tis but modest Truth: (so may I thrive
As not to please the Best of thine Alive,
Or flatter my *Dead Master*, here would I
Pay my last Duty in a Glorious Lie)
In that *Admired Piece* the World may read
Thy Virtues and Misfortunes Storied;
Which bear such curious Mixture, Men must doubt
Whether Thou *Wiser* wert or *more Devout*.

There live Blest Relick of a Saint-like mind,
With Honours endless as Thy Peace, Enshrin'd;
Whilst we, divided by that Bloody Cloud,
Whose purple Mists Thy Murther'd Body shroud,
Here stay behind at gaze: Apt for Thy sake
Unruly murmurs now 'gainst Heav'n to make,
Which binds us to Live well, yet gives no Fence
To Guard her dearest Sons from Violence.
But He whose Trump proclaims, *Revenge is mine*,
Bids us our Sorrow by our Hope confine,
And reconcile our *Reason* to our *Faith*,
Which in thy Ruine such Concussions hath;
It dares Conclude, God does not keep His Word
If *Zimri dye in Peace that slew his Lord*.

An Elegy, 1649

274 *The Vow-breaker*

WHEN first the Magick of thine eye
Usurpt upon my liberty,
Triumphing in my hearts spoyle, thou
Didst lock up thine in such a vow:
When I prove false, may the bright day
Be govern'd by the Moones pale ray,
(As I too well remember) this
Thou saidst, and seal'dst it with a kisse.

Oh heavens! and could so soon that tie
Relent in sad apostacy?
Could all thy Oaths and mortgag'd trust,
Vanish like Letters form'd in dust,

Concussions: MS. correction in 1649. Conclusions, 1664.

Which the next wind scatters? take heed,
Take heed Revolter; know this deed
Hath wrong'd the world, which will fare worse
By thy example, than thy curse.

Hide that false brow in mists; thy shame
Ne'er see light more, but the dimme flame
Of Funerall-lamps; thus sit and moane,
And learn to keep thy guilt at home;
Give it no vent, for if agen
Thy love or vowes betray more men,
At length I feare thy perjur'd breath
Will blow out day, and waken death.

Choyce Drollery, 1656

275

Sonnet

TELL me no more how fair she is,
  I have no minde to hear
The story of that distant bliss
  I never shall come near:
By sad experience I have found
That her perfection is my wound.

And tell me not how fond I am
  To tempt a daring Fate,
From whence no triumph ever came,
  But to repent too late:
There is some hope ere long I may
In silence dote my self away.

I ask no pity (Love) from thee,
  Nor will thy justice blame,
So that thou wilt not envy mee
  The glory of my flame:
Which crowns my heart when ere it dyes,
In that it falls her sacrifice.

Poems, 1657

276 *The Exequy*

ACCEPT thou Shrine of my dead Saint,
Instead of Dirges this complaint;
And for sweet flowres to crown thy hearse,
Receive a strew of weeping verse
From thy griev'd friend, whom thou might'st see
Quite melted into tears for thee.

Dear loss! since thy untimely fate
My task hath been to meditate
On thee, on thee: thou art the book,
The library whereon I look
Though almost blind. For thee (lov'd clay)
I languish out, not live the day,
Using no other exercise
But what I practise with mine eyes:
By which wet glasses I find out
How lazily time creeps about
To one that mourns: this, onely this
My exercise and bus'ness is:
So I compute the weary houres
With sighs dissolved into showres.

Nor wonder if my time go thus
Backward and most preposterous;

Thou hast benighted me, thy set
This Eve of blackness did beget,
Who wast my day, (though overcast
Before thou had'st thy Noon-tide past)
And I remember must in tears,
Thou scarce had'st seen so many years
As Day tells houres. By thy cleer Sun
My love and fortune first did run;
But thou wilt never more appear
Folded within my Hemisphear,
Since both thy light and motion
Like a fled Star is fall'n and gon,
And twixt me and my soules dear wish
The earth now interposed is,
Which such a strange eclipse doth make
As ne'er was read in Almanake.

I could allow thee for a time
To darken me and my sad Clime,
Were it a month, a year, or ten,
I would thy exile live till then;
And all that space my mirth adjourn,
So thou wouldst promise to return;
And putting off thy ashy shrowd
At length disperse this sorrows cloud.

But woe is me! the longest date
Too narrow is to calculate
These empty hopes: never shall I
Be so much blest as to descry
A glimpse of thee, till that day come
Which shall the earth to cinders doome,
And a fierce Feaver must calcine

The body of this world like thine,
(My Little World!); that fit of fire
Once off, our bodies shall aspire
To our soules bliss: then we shall rise,
And view our selves with cleerer eyes
In that calm Region, where no night
Can hide us from each others sight.

Mean time, thou hast her, earth: much good
May my harm do thee. Since it stood
With Heavens will I might not call
Her longer mine, I give thee all
My short-liv'd right and interest
In her, whom living I lov'd best:
With a most free and bounteous grief,
I give thee what I could not keep.
Be kind to her, and prethee look
Thou write into thy Dooms-day book
Each parcell of this Rarity
Which in thy Casket shrin'd doth ly:
See that thou make thy reck'ning streight,
And yield her back again by weight;
For thou must audit on thy trust
Each graine and atome of this dust,
As thou wilt answer *Him* that lent,
Not gave thee, my dear Monument.

So close the ground, and 'bout her shade
Black curtains draw, my *Bride* is laid.

Sleep on my *Love* in thy cold bed
Never to be disquieted!
My last good night! Thou wilt not wake
Till I thy fate shall overtake:

Till age, or grief, or sickness must
Marry my body to that dust
It so much loves; and fill the room
My heart keeps empty in thy Tomb.
Stay for me there; I will not faile
To meet thee in that hollow Vale.
And think not much of my delay;
I am already on the way,
And follow thee with all the speed
Desire can make, or sorrows breed.
Each minute is a short degree,
And ev'ry houre a step towards thee.
At night when I betake to rest,
Next morn I rise neerer my West
Of life, almost by eight houres saile,
Than when sleep breath'd his drowsie gale.

Thus from the Sun my Bottom stears,
And my dayes Compass downward bears:
Nor labour I to stemme the tide
Through which to *Thee* I swiftly glide.

'Tis true, with shame and grief I yield,
Thou like the *Van* first took'st the field,
And gotten hast the victory
In thus adventuring to dy
Before me, whose more years might crave
A just precedence in the grave.
But heark! My Pulse like a soft Drum
Beats my approach, tells *Thee* I come;
And slow howe'er my marches be,
I shall at last sit down by *Thee*.

The thought of this bids me go on,
And wait my dissolution
With hope and comfort. *Dear* (forgive
The crime) I am content to live
Divided, with but half a heart,
Till we shall meet and never part.

Poems, 1657

277 *Sic Vita*

LIKE to the falling of a Starre;
Or as the flights of Eagles are;
Or like the fresh springs gawdy hew;
Or silver drops of morning dew;
Or like a wind that chafes the flood;
Or bubbles which on water stood;
Even such is man, whose borrow'd light
Is straight call'd in, and paid to night.

The Wind blowes out; the Bubble dies;
The Spring entomb'd in Autumn lies;
The Dew dries up; the Starre is shot;
The Flight is past; and Man forgot.

Poems, 1657

278 *My Midnight Meditation*

ILL busi'd man! why should'st thou take such care
To lengthen out thy lifes short Kalendar?
When ev'ry spectacle thou lookst upon
Presents and acts thy execution.
Each drooping season and each flower doth cry,
Fool! as I fade and wither, thou must dy.

The beating of thy pulse (when thou art well)
Is just the tolling of thy Passing Bell:
Night is thy Hearse, whose sable Canopie
Covers alike deceased day and thee.
And all those weeping dewes which nightly fall,
Are but the tears shed for thy funerall.

Poems, 1657

279 *A Contemplation upon flowers*

BRAVE flowers, that I could gallant it like you
And be as little vaine,
You come abroad, and make a harmelesse shew,
And to your beds of Earthe againe;
You are not proud, you know your birth
For your Embroiderd garments are from Earth:

You doe obey your months, and times, but I
Would have it ever spring,
My fate would know no winter, never die
Nor thinke of such a thing;
Oh that I could my bed of Earth but view
And Smile, and looke as Chearefully as you:

Oh teach me to see Death, and not to fear
But rather to take truce;
How often have I seene you at a Bier,
And there look fresh and spruce;
You fragrant flowers, then teach me that my breath
Like yours may sweeten, and perfume my Death.

(Ascribed to King in Harl. MS. 6917)

GEORGE HERBERT

1593–1633

280 *Redemption*

HAVING been tenant long to a rich Lord,
Not thriving, I resolved to be bold,
And make a suit unto him, to afford
A new small-rented lease, and cancell th' old.

In heaven at his manor I him sought:
They told me there, that he was lately gone
About some land, which he had dearly bought
Long since on earth, to take possession.

I straight return'd, and knowing his great birth,
Sought him accordingly in great resorts;
In cities, theatres, gardens, parks, and courts:
At length I heard a ragged noise and mirth

Of theeves and murderers: there I him espied,
Who straight, *Your suit is granted*, said, & died.

The Temple, 1633

281 *Easter*

I GOT me flowers to straw thy way,
I got me boughs off many a tree,
But thou wast up by break of day,
And brought'st thy sweets along with thee.

The Sunne arising in the East,
Though he give light, and th' East perfume,
If they should offer to contest
With thy arising, they presume.

Can there be any day but this,
Though many sunnes to shine endeavour?
We count three hundred, but we misse;
There is but one, and that one ever.

The Temple, 1633

282 *Easter Wings*

LORD, who createdst man in wealth and store,
Though foolishly he lost the same,
Decaying more and more,
Till he became
Most poore:
With thee
O let me rise
As larks, harmoniously,
And sing this day thy victories:
Then shall the fall further the flight in me.

My tender age in sorrow did beginne:
And still with sicknesses and shame
Thou didst so punish sinne,
That I became
Most thinne.
With thee
Let me combine,
And feel this day thy victorie:
For, if I imp my wing on thine,
Affliction shall advance the flight in me.

The Temple, 1633

imp: strengthen by grafting.

283 *Affliction*

WHEN first thou didst entice to thee my heart,
I thought the service brave:
So many joyes I writ down for my part,
Besides what I might have
Out of my stock of naturall delights,
Augmented with thy gracious benefits.

I looked on thy furniture so fine,
And made it fine to me:
Thy glorious household-stuffe did me entwine,
And 'tice me unto thee;
Such starres I counted mine: both heav'n and earth
Payd me my wages in a world of mirth.

What pleasures could I want, whose King I served?
Where joyes my fellows were.
Thus argu'd into hopes, my thoughts reserved
No place for grief or fear.
Therefore my sudden soul caught at the place,
And made her youth and fiercenesse seek thy face.

At first thou gav'st me milk and sweetnesses;
I had my wish and way:
My dayes were straw'd with flow'rs and happinesse;
There was no month but May.
But with my yeares sorrow did twist and grow,
And made a partie unawares for wo.

My flesh began unto my soul in pain,
Sicknesses cleave my bones;
Consuming agues dwell in ev'ry vein,
And tune my breath to grones.
Sorrow was all my soul; I scarce beleeved,
Till grief did tell me roundly, that I lived.

When I got health, thou took'st away my life,
And more; for my friends die:
My mirth and edge was lost; a blunted knife
Was of more use than I.
Thus thinne and lean without a fence or friend,
I was blown through with ev'ry storm and winde.

Whereas my birth and spirit rather took
The way that takes the town;
Thou didst betray me to a lingring book,
And wrap me in a gown.
I was entangled in the world of strife,
Before I had the power to change my life.

Yet, for I threatned oft the siege to raise,
Not simpring all mine age,
Thou often didst with Academick praise
Melt and dissolve my rage.
I took thy sweetned pill, till I came neare;
I could not go away, nor persevere.

Yet lest perchance I should too happie be
In my unhappinesse,
Turning my purge to food, thou throwest me
Into more sicknesses.
Thus doth thy power crosse-bias me, not making
Thine own gift good, yet me from my wayes taking.

Now I am here, what thou wilt do with me
None of my books will show:
I reade, and sigh, and wish I were a tree;
For sure then I should grow
To fruit or shade: at least some bird would trust
Her household to me, and I should be just.

crosse-bias: divert, turn aside.

Yet, though thou troublest me, I must be meek;
        In weaknesse must be stout.
Well, I will change the service, and go seek
        Some other master out.
Ah my deare God! though I am clean forgot,
Let me not love thee, if I love thee not.

The Temple, 1633

284 *Prayer*

PRAYER the Churches banquet, Angels age,
    Gods breath in man returning to his birth,
The soul in paraphrase, heart in pilgrimage,
    The Christian plummet sounding heav'n and earth;

Engine against th' Almightie, sinners towre,
    Reversed thunder, Christ-side-piercing spear,
The six-daies-world-transposing in an houre,
    A kinde of tune, which all things heare and fear;

Softnesse, and peace, and joy, and love, and blisse,
    Exalted Manna, gladnesse of the best,
    Heaven in ordinarie, man well drest,
The milkie way, the bird of Paradise,

    Church-bells beyond the starres heard, the souls blood,
    The land of spices, something understood.

The Temple, 1633

285 *The Temper*

HOW should I praise thee, Lord! how should my rhymes
    Gladly engrave thy love in steel,
If what my soul doth feel sometimes,
    My soul might ever feel!

Although there were some fourtie heav'ns, or more,
Sometimes I peere above them all;
Sometimes I hardly reach a score,
Sometimes to hell I fall.

O rack me not to such a vast extent;
Those distances belong to thee:
The world's too little for thy tent,
A grave too big for me.

Wilt thou meet arms with man, that thou dost stretch
A crumme of dust from heav'n to hell?
Will great God measure with a wretch?
Shall he thy stature spell?

O let me, when thy roof my soul hath hid,
O let me roost and nestle there:
Then of a sinner thou art rid,
And I of hope and fear.

Yet take thy way; for sure thy way is best:
Stretch or contract me thy poore debter:
This is but tuning of my breast,
To make the musick better.

Whether I flie with angels, fall with dust,
Thy hands made both, and I am there:
Thy power and love, my love and trust
Make one place ev'rywhere.

The Temple, 1633

286 *Jordan*

WHO sayes that fictions onely and false hair
Become a verse? Is there in truth no beautie?
Is all good structure in a winding stair?
May no lines passe, except they do their dutie
Not to a true, but painted chair?

Is it no verse, except enchanted groves
And sudden arbours shadow course-spunne lines?
Must purling streams refresh a lovers loves?
Must all be vail'd, while he that reades, divines,
Catching the sense at two removes?

Shepherds are honest people; let them sing:
Riddle who list, for me, and pull for Prime:
I envie no mans nightingale or spring;
Nor let them punish me with losse of ryme,
Who plainly say, *My God, My King.*

The Temple, 1633

287 *The Church-Floore*

MARK you the floore? that square & speckled stone,
Which looks so firm and strong,
Is *Patience*:

And th' other black and grave, wherewith each one
Is checker'd all along,
Humilitie:

The gentle rising, which on either hand
Leads to the Quire above,
Is *Confidence*:

But the sweet cement, which in one sure band
Ties the whole frame, is *Love*
And *Charitie.*

Hither sometimes Sinne steals, and stains
The marbles neat and curious veins:
But all is cleansed when the marble weeps.
Sometimes Death, puffing at the doore,
Blows all the dust about the floore:
But while he thinks to spoil the room, he sweeps.
Blest be the *Architect*, whose art
Could build so strong in a weak heart.

The Temple, 1633

288 *The Church Windows*

LORD, how can man preach thy eternall word?
He is a brittle crazie glasse:
Yet in thy temple thou dost him afford
This glorious and transcendent place,
To be a window, through thy grace.

But when thou dost anneal in glasse thy storie,
Making thy life to shine within
The holy Preachers; then the light and glorie
More rev'rend grows, & more doth win;
Which else shows watrish, bleak, & thin.

Doctrine and life, colours and light, in one
When they combine and mingle, bring
A strong regard and aw: but speech alone
Doth vanish like a flaring thing,
And in the eare, not conscience ring.

The Temple, 1633

289

Sunday

O DAY most calm, most bright,
The fruit of this, the next world's bud,
Th' indorsement of supreme delight,
Writ by a friend, and with his bloud;
The couch of time, care's balm and bay,
The week were dark but for thy light:
Thy torch doth show the way.

The other dayes and thou
Make up one man, whose face thou art,
Knocking at heaven with thy brow.
The worky-daies are the back-part;
The burden of the week lies there
Making the whole to stoop and bow
Till thy release appeare.

Man had straight forward gone
To endlesse death; but thou dost pull
And turn us round to look on one
Whom, if we were not very dull,
We could not choose but look on still;
Since there is no place so alone
The which he doth not fill.

Sundays the pillars are
On which heav'ns palace arched lies:
The other dayes fill up the spare
And hollow room with vanities.
They are the fruitfull beds and borders
In God's rich garden; that is bare
Which parts their ranks and orders.

The Sundays of man's life,
Thredded together on time's string,
Make bracelets to adorn the wife
Of the eternall glorious King.
On Sunday heaven's gate stands ope,
Blessings are plentifull and rife,
More plentifull than hope.

This day my Saviour rose,
And did inclose this light for his;
That, as each beast his manger knows,
Man might not of his fodder misse.
Christ hath took in this piece of ground,
And made a garden there for those
Who want herbs for their wound.

The rest of our Creation
Our great Redeemer did remove
With the same shake which at his passion
Did th' earth and all things with it move.
As Samson bore the doores away,
Christ's hands, though nail'd, wrought our salvation
And did unhinge that day.

The brightnesse of that day
We sullied by our foul offence;
Wherefore that robe we cast away,
Having a new at his expence
Whose drops of bloud paid the full price
That was requir'd to make us gay,
And fit for Paradise.

Thou art a day of mirth;
And where the week-dayes trail on ground,
Thy flight is higher, as thy birth.
O let me take thee at the bound,
Leaping with thee from sev'n to sev'n,
Till that we both, being toss'd from earth,
Flie hand in hand to heav'n.

The Temple, 1633

290 *Employment*

HE that is weary, let him sit.
My soul would stirre
And trade in courtesies and wit,
Quitting the furre
To cold complexions needing it.

Man is no starre, but a quick coal
Of mortall fire:
Who blows it not, nor doth controll
A faint desire,
Lets his own ashes choke his soul.

When th' elements did for place contest
With him, whose will
Ordain'd the highest to be best,
The earth sat still,
And by the others is opprest.

Life is a businesse, not good cheer;
Ever in warres.
The sunne still shineth there or here,
Whereas the starres
Watch an advantage to appeare.

Oh that I were an Orange-tree,
        That busie plant!
Then should I ever laden be,
        And never want
Some fruit for him that dressed me.

But we are still too young or old;
        The man is gone,
Before we do our wares unfold:
        So we freeze on,
Untill the grave increase our cold.

The Temple, 1633

291 *The World*

LOVE built a stately house; where *Fortune* came,
    And spinning phansies, she was heard to say,
That her fine cobwebs did support the frame,
Whereas they were supported by the same:
But *Wisdome* quickly swept them all away.

Then *Pleasure* came, who liking not the fashion,
Began to make *Balcones*, *Terraces*,
Till she had weakened all by alteration:
But rev'rend *laws*, and many a *proclamation*
Reformed all at length with menaces.

Then enter'd *Sinne*, and with that Sycomore,
Whose leaves first sheltred man from drought and dew,
Working and winding slily evermore,
The inward walls and Sommers cleft and tore:
But *Grace* shor'd these, and cut that as it grew.

Balcones: stress was normally on the second syllable.
Sommers: summers, main beams.

Then *Sinne* combin'd with *Death* in a firm band
To raze the building to the very floore:
Which they effected, none could them withstand,
But *Love* and *Grace* took *Glorie* by the hand,
And built a braver *Palace* than before.

The Temple, 1633

292 *Vertue*

SWEET day, so cool, so calm, so bright,
The bridall of the earth and skie:
The dew shall weep thy fall to night;
For thou must die.

Sweet rose, whose hue angrie and brave
Bids the rash gazer wipe his eye:
Thy root is ever in its grave,
And thou must die.

Sweet spring, full of sweet dayes and roses,
A box where sweets compacted lie;
My musick shows ye have your closes,
And all must die.

Onely a sweet and vertuous soul,
Like season'd timber, never gives;
But though the whole world turn to coal,
Then chiefly lives.

The Temple, 1633

293 *Life*

I MADE a posie, while the day ran by:
Here will I smell my remnant out, and tie
My life within this band.
But time did beckon to the flowers, and they
By noon most cunningly did steal away,
And wither'd in my hand.

My hand was next to them, and then my heart:
I took, without more thinking, in good part
Times gentle admonition:
Who did so sweetly deaths sad taste convey,
Making my minde to smell my fatall day;
Yet sugring the suspicion.

Farewell deare flowers, sweetly your time ye spent,
Fit, while ye liv'd, for smell or ornament,
And after death for cures.
I follow straight without complaints or grief,
Since if my scent be good, I care not, if
It be as short as yours.

The Temple, 1633

294 *Jordan*

WHEN first my lines of heav'nly joyes made mention,
Such was their lustre, they did so excell,
That I sought out quaint words, and trim invention;
My thoughts began to burnish, sprout, and swell,
Curling with metaphors a plain intention,
Decking the sense, as if it were to sell.

Thousands of notions in my brain did runne,
Off'ring their service, if I were not sped:
I often blotted what I had begunne;

This was not quick enough, and that was dead.
Nothing could seem too rich to clothe the sunne,
Much lesse those joyes which trample on his head.

As flames do work and winde, when they ascend,
So did I weave my self into the sense.
But while I bustled, I might heare a friend
Whisper, *How wide is all this long pretence!*
There is in love a sweetnesse readie penn'd:
Copie out onely that, and save expense.

The Temple, 1633

295 *The Quip*

THE merrie world did on a day
With his train-bands and mates agree
To meet together where I lay,
And all in sport to jeer at me.

First, Beautie crept into a rose;
Which when I pluckt not, Sir, said she,
Tell me, I pray, whose hands are those?
But thou shalt answer, Lord, for me.

Then Money came, and chinking still,
What tune is this, poore man? said he,
I heard in Musick you had skill.
But thou shalt answer, Lord, for me.

Then came brave Glorie puffing by
In silks that whistled, who but he?
He scarce allow'd me half an eye.
But thou shalt answer, Lord, for me.

Then came quick Wit and Conversation,
  And he would needs a comfort be,
And, to be short, make an oration.
  But thou shalt answer, Lord, for me.

Yet when the houre of thy designe
  To answer these fine things shall come,
Speak not at large, say, I am thine;
  And then they have their answer home.

The Temple, 1633

296 *Iesu*

IESU is in my heart, his sacred name
  Is deeply carved there. But th' other week
A great affliction broke the little frame,
  Ev'n all to pieces; which I went to seek.
And first I found the corner where was *I*,
  After where *ES*, and next where *U* was graved.
When I had got these parcels, instantly
  I sat me down to spell them; and perceived
That to my broken heart he was *I ease you*,
  And to my whole is *IESU*.

The Temple, 1633

297 *Dialogue*

SWEETEST Saviour, if my soul
  Were but worth the having,
Quickly should I then controll
  Any thought of waving.
But when all my care and pains
Cannot give the name of gains
To thy wretch so full of stains,
What delight or hope remains?

What (childe) is the ballance thine,
Thine the poise and measure?
If I say, Thou shalt be mine,
Finger not my treasure.
What the gains in having thee
Do amount to, onely he
Who for man was sold can see,
That transferr'd th' accounts to me.

But as I can see no merit
Leading to this favour,
So the way to fit me for it
Is beyond my savour.
As the reason then is thine,
So the way is none of mine.
I disclaim the whole designe,
Sinne disclaims, and I resigne.

That is all, if that I could
Get without repining;
And my clay, my creature, would
Follow my resigning.
That as I did freely part
With my glorie and desert,
Left all joyes to feel all smart—
Ah, no more! Thou break'st my heart.

The Temple, 1633

298 *The Collar*

I STRUCK the board, and cry'd, No more.
I will abroad.
What? shall I ever sigh and pine?
My lines and life are free; free as the road,
Loose as the winde, as large as store.

Shall I be still in suit?
Have I no harvest but a thorn
To let me blood, and not restore
What I have lost with cordiall fruit?
Sure there was wine
Before my sighs did drie it: there was corn
Before my tears did drown it.
Is the yeare onely lost to me?
Have I no bayes to crown it?
No flowers, no garlands gay? all blasted?
All wasted?
Not so, my heart: but there is fruit,
And thou hast hands.
Recover all thy sigh-blown age
On double pleasures: leave thy cold dispute
Of what is fit, and not; forsake thy cage,
Thy rope of sands,
Which pettie thoughts have made, and made to thee
Good cable, to enforce and draw,
And be thy law,
While thou didst wink and wouldst not see.
Away; take heed:
I will abroad.
Call in thy deaths head there: tie up thy fears.
He that forbears
To suit and serve his need,
Deserves his load.
But as I rav'd and grew more fierce and wilde
At every word,
Me thought I heard one calling, *Childe*:
And I reply'd, *My Lord*.

The Temple, 1633

299 *The Pulley*

WHEN God at first made man,
Having a glasse of blessings standing by,
Let us (said he) poure on him all we can.
Let the world's riches, which dispersed lie,
Contract into a span.

So strength first made a way,
Then beautie flow'd, then wisdome, honour, pleasure.
When almost all was out, God made a stay,
Perceiving that alone of all his treasure
Rest in the bottome lay.

For if I should (said he)
Bestow this jewell also on my creature,
He would adore my gifts instead of me,
And rest in Nature, not the God of Nature.
So both should losers be.

Yet let him keep the rest,
But keep them with repining restlessnesse.
Let him be rich and wearie, that at least,
If goodnesse leade him not, yet wearinesse
May tosse him to my breast.

The Temple, 1633

300 *The Flower*

HOW fresh, O Lord, how sweet and clean
Are thy returns! Ev'n as the flowers in spring,
To which, besides their own demean,
The late-past frosts tributes of pleasure bring.
Grief melts away
Like snow in May,
As if there were no such cold thing.

demean: demesne.

Who would have thought my shrivel'd heart
Could have recover'd greennesse? It was gone
Quite under ground, as flowers depart
To see their mother-root when they have blown;
Where they together
All the hard weather,
Dead to the world, keep house unknown.

These are thy wonders, Lord of power,
Killing and quickning, bringing down to hell
And up to heaven in an houre;
Making a chiming of a passing-bell.
We say amisse,
This or that is;
Thy word is all, if we could spell.

O that I once past changing were,
Fast in thy Paradise, where no flower can wither!
Many a spring I shoot up fair,
Off'ring at heav'n, growing and groaning thither;
Nor doth my flower
Want a spring-showre,
My sinnes and I joining together.

But while I grow in a straight line,
Still upwards bent, as if heav'n were mine own,
Thy anger comes, and I decline.
What frost to that? What pole is not the zone
Where all things burn,
When thou dost turn,
And the least frown of thine is shown?

And now in age I bud again,
After so many deaths I live and write;
I once more smell the dew and rain,
And relish versing. O my onely light,
It cannot be
That I am he
On whom thy tempests fell all night.

These are thy wonders, Lord of love,
To make us see we are but flowers that glide.
Which when we once can finde and prove,
Thou hast a garden for us where to bide.
Who would be more,
Swelling through store,
Forfeit their Paradise by their pride.

The Temple, 1633

301 *Aaron*

HOLINESSE on the head,
Light and perfections on the breast,
Harmonious bells below, raising the dead
To leade them unto life and rest.
Thus are true Aarons drest.

Profanenesse in my head,
Defects and darknesse in my breast,
A noise of passions ringing me for dead
Unto a place where is no rest.
Poore priest thus am I drest.

Onely another head
I have, another heart and breast,
Another musick, making live not dead,
Without whom I could have no rest:
In him I am well drest.

Christ is my onely head,
My alone onely heart and breast,
My onely musick, striking me ev'n dead;
That to the old man I may rest,
And be in him new drest.

So holy in my head,
Perfect and light in my deare breast,
My doctrine tun'd by Christ, (who is not dead,
But lives in me while I do rest)
Come people; Aaron's drest.

The Temple, 1633

302 *The Odour*

(2 Cor. ii. 15)

HOW sweetly doth *My Master* sound! *My Master!*
As Amber-gris leaves a rich scent
Unto the taster,
So do these words a sweet content,
An orientall fragrancie, *My Master*.

With these all day I do perfume my minde,
My minde ev'n thrust into them both,
That I might finde
What cordials make this curious broth,
This broth of smells, that feeds and fats my minde.

My Master, shall I speak? O that to thee
My servant were a little so,
As flesh may be,
That these two words might creep and grow
To some degree of spicinesse to thee!

Then should the Pomander, which was before
A speaking sweet, mend by reflection
And tell me more;
For pardon of my imperfection
Would warm and work it sweeter than before.

For when *My Master*, which alone is sweet,
And ev'n in my unworthinesse pleasing,
Shall call and meet
My servant, as thee not displeasing,
That call is but the breathing of the sweet.

This breathing would with gains by sweetning me
(As sweet things traffick when they meet)
Return to thee;
And so this new commerce and sweet
Should all my life employ and busie me.

The Temple, 1633

303 *Discipline*

THROW away thy rod,
Throw away thy wrath:
O my God,
Take the gentle path.

For my hearts desire
Unto thine is bent:
I aspire
To a full consent.

Not a word or look
I affect to own,
But by book,
And thy book alone.

Though I fail, I weep:
Though I halt in pace,
Yet I creep
To the throne of grace.

Then let wrath remove;
Love will do the deed:
For with love
Stonie hearts will bleed.

Love is swift of foot;
Love 's a man of warre,
And can shoot,
And can hit from farre.

Who can scape his bow?
That which wrought on thee,
Brought thee low,
Needs must work on me.

Throw away thy rod;
Though man frailties hath,
Thou art God:
Throw away thy wrath.

The Temple, 1633

304 *Song*

Probably by the Earl of Pembroke

SOULES joy, now I am gone,
And you alone,
(Which cannot be,
Since I must leave my selfe with thee,
And carry thee with me)
Yet when unto our eyes
Absence denyes

Each others sight,
And makes to us a constant night,
When others change to light;
O give no way to griefe,
But let beliefe
Of mutuall love
This wonder to the vulgar prove,
Our bodyes, not wee move.

Let not thy wit beweepe
Wounds but sense-deepe,
For when we misse
By distance our lip-joying blisse,
Even then our soules shall kisse,
Fooles have no meanes to meet,
But by their feet.
Why should our clay,
Over our spirits so much sway,
To tie us to that way?
O give no way to griefe,
But let beliefe
Of mutuall love
This wonder to the vulgar prove,
Our bodyes, not wee move.

Poems by J.D., 1635

305 *A Parodie*

SOUL'S joy, when thou art gone,
And I alone—
Which cannot be,
Because thou dost abide with me
And I depend on thee—

Yet when thou dost suppresse
The cheerfulnesse
Of thy abode,
And in my powers not stirre abroad,
But leave me to my load;

O what a damp and shade
Doth me invade!
No stormie night
Can so afflict or so affright
As thy eclipsed light.

Ah Lord! Do not withdraw,
Lest want of awe
Make Sinne appeare,
And when thou dost but shine lesse cleare,
Say that thou art not here.

And then what life I have,
While Sinne doth rave,
And falsly boast
That I may seek but thou art lost,
Thou, and alone thou, know'st.

O what a deadly cold
Doth me infold!
I half beleeve
That Sinne sayes true. But while I grieve,
Thou com'st and dost relieve.

The Temple, 1633

306 *Death*

DEATH, thou wast once an uncouth hideous thing,
Nothing but bones,
The sad effect of sadder grones;
The mouth was open but thou couldst not sing.

For we consider'd thee as at some six
Or ten yeares hence,
After the losse of life and sense,
Flesh being turn'd to dust, and bones to sticks.

We lookt on this side of thee, shooting short;
Where we did finde
The shells of fledge souls left behinde,
Dry dust, which sheds no tears but may extort.

But since our Saviour's death did put some blood
Into thy face,
Thou art grown fair and full of grace,
Much in request, much sought for as a good.

For we do now behold thee gay and glad,
As at dooms-day;
When souls shall wear their new array,
And all thy bones with beautie shall be clad.

Therefore we can go die as sleep, and trust
Half that we have
Untc an honest faithfull grave,
Making our pillows either down or dust.

The Temple, 1633

307 *Love*

LOVE bade me welcome: yet my soul drew back,
Guiltie of dust and sinne.
But quick-ey'd Love, observing me grow slack
From my first entrance in,
Drew nearer to me, sweetly questioning,
If I lack'd any thing.

A guest, I answer'd, worthy to be here:
Love said, you shall be he.
I the unkinde, ungratefull? Ah my deare,
I cannot look on thee.
Love took my hand, and smiling did reply,
Who made the eyes but I?

Truth Lord, but I have marr'd them: let my shame
Go where it doth deserve.
And know you not, sayes Love, who bore the blame?
My deare, then I will serve.
You must sit down, sayes Love, and taste my meat:
So I did sit and eat.

The Temple, 1633

ANONYMOUS

308 *The Guest*

YET if his majesty, our Soveraign lord,
Should of his owne accord
Friendly himselfe invite,
And say I'll be your guest tomorrowe night,
How should we stir ourselves, call and command
All hands to worke! 'Let no man idle stand.
Set me fine Spanish tables in the hall,
See they be fitted all;
Let there be roome to eate,
And order taken that there want no meate.
See every sconce and candlestick made bright,
That without tapers they may give a light.
Looke to the presence: are the carpets spred,
The dazie o'er the head,

dazie: daïs, canopy.

The cushions in the chayre,
And all the candles lighted on the staire?
Perfume the chambers, and in any case
Let each man give attendance in his place.'
Thus if the king were coming would we do;
And 'twere good reason too;
For 'tis a duteous thing
To show all honor to an earthly king;
And, after all our travayle and our cost,
So he be pleas'd, to think no labour lost.
But at the coming of the King of heaven
All 's set at six and seven:
We wallow in our sin;
Christ cannot finde a chamber in the inn.
We entertaine him alwayes like a stranger,
And, as at first, still lodge him in the manger.

Oxford, Christ Church MS. 736–8

309 *The Thief*

'SAY bold but blessed theefe,
That in a trice
Slipt into paradise,
And in playne daye
Stol'st heaven awaye,
What trick couldst thou invent
To compass thy intent?
What armes?
What charmes?'
'Love and beleife.'
'Say bold but blessed theefe,
How couldst thou read
A crowne upon that head?

What text, what gloss,
A kingdome on a cross?
How couldst thou come to spy
God in a man to die?
What light?
What sight?'
'The sight of greife—

'I sight to God his paine;
And by that sight
I saw the light;
Thus did my greife
Beget releife.
And take this rule from me,
Pity thou him, he'll pity thee.
Use this,
Ne'er miss,
Heaven may be stolne againe.'

Oxford, Christ Church MS. 736–8

THOMAS CAREW

1595?–1639?

310 *A Beautifull Mistress*

IF when the sun at noone displayes
His brighter rayes,
Thou but appear,
He then all pale with shame and fear,
Quencheth his light,
Hides his dark brow, flyes from thy sight,
And growes more dim

I sight: word play on 'sight': examine, and 'sigh'd'.

Compar'd to thee, than stars to him.
If thou but shew thy face again,
When darkenesse doth at midnight raign,
The darkenesse flyes, and light is hurl'd
Round about the silent world:
So as alike thou driv'st away
Both light and darkenesse, night and day.

Poems, 1640 (text 1651)

311 *Good Counsell to a Young Maid*

GAZE not on thy beauties pride,
Tender Maid, in the false tide
That from Lovers eyes doth slide.

Let thy faithful Chrystall show,
How thy colours come, and goe,
Beautie takes a foyle from woe.

Love, that in those smooth streames lyes,
Under pities faire disguise,
Will thy melting heart surprize.

Nets, of passions finest thred,
Snaring Poems, will be spred,
All, to catch thy maiden-head.

Then beware, for those that cure
Loves disease, themselves endure
For reward a Calenture.

Rather let the Lover pine,
Than his pale cheek should assigne
A perpetuall blush to thine.

Poems, 1640 (text 1651)

312 *To my inconstant Mistris*

WHEN thou, poore excommunicate
  From all the joyes of love, shalt see
The full reward, and glorious fate,
  Which my strong faith shall purchase me,
Then curse thine owne inconstancy.

A fayrer hand than thine, shall cure
  That heart, which thy false oathes did wound;
And to my soul, a soul more pure
  Than thine, shall by Loves hand be bound,
And both with equall glory crown'd.

Then shalt thou weepe, entreat, complain
  To Love, as I did once to thee;
When all thy teares shall be as vain
  As mine were then, for thou shalt bee
Damn'd for thy false Apostasie.

Poems, 1640 (text 1651)

313 *A deposition from Love*

I WAS foretold, your rebell sex,
  Nor love, nor pitty knew;
And with what scorn you use to vex
  Poor hearts that humbly sue;
Yet I believ'd, to crown our pain,
  Could we the fortress win,
The happy Lover sure should gain
  A Paradise within:
I thought Loves plagues, like Dragons sate,
Only to fright us at the gate.

But I did enter, and enjoy
  What happy Lovers prove;
For I could kiss, and sport, and toy,
  And taste those sweets of love;
Which had they but a lasting state,
  Or if in *Celia's* brest
The force of love might not abate,
  Jove were too mean a guest.
But now her breach of faith, farre more
Afflicts, than did her scorn before.

Hard fate! to have been once possest,
  As victor, of a heart
Achiev'd with labour, and unrest,
  And then forc'd to depart.
If the stout Foe will not resigne
  When I besiege a Town,
I lose, but what was never mine;
  But he that is cast down
From enjoy'd beauty, feels a woe
Only deposed Kings can know.

Poems, 1640 (text 1651)

314 *Ingratefull beauty threatned*

KNOW *Celia*, (since thou art so proud,)
'Twas I that gave thee thy renown:
Thou hadst, in the forgotten crowd
  Of common beauties, liv'd unknown,
Had not my verse exhal'd thy name,
And with it impt the wings of fame.

That killing power is none of thine,
  I gave it to thy voyce, and eyes:
Thy sweets, thy graces, all are mine;
  Thou art my star, shin'st in my skies;
Then dart not from thy borrowed sphere
Lightning on him that fixt thee there.

Tempt me with such affrights no more,
  Lest what I made, I uncreate:
Let fools thy mystique forms adore,
  I'll know thee in thy mortall state;
Wise Poets that wrapp'd Truth in tales,
Knew her themselves through all her vailes.

Poems, 1640 (text 1651)

315 *Disdain returned*

HE that loves a Rosie cheek,
  Or a Corall lip admires,
Or from Star-like eyes doth seek
  Fuell to maintain his fires;
As old Time makes these decay,
So his flames must waste away.

But a smooth and stedfast mind,
  Gentle thoughts, and calme desires,
Hearts with equall love combind,
  Kindle never dying fires.
Where these are not, I despise
Lovely cheeks, or lips, or eyes.

No teares, *Celia*, now shall win,
  My resolv'd heart, to return;
I have search'd thy soul within,
  And find nought, but pride, and scorn;

I have learn'd thy arts, and now
Can disdain as much as thou.
Some power, in my revenge convey
That love to her, I cast away.

Poems, 1640 (text 1651)

316 *Eternity of Love protested*

HOW ill doth he deserve a Lovers name,
Whose pale weak flame
Cannot retain
His heat in spight of absence or disdain;
But doth at once, like paper set on fire,
Burn and expire;
True love can never change his seat,
Nor did he ever love, that could retreat.

That noble flame, which my brest keeps alive,
Shall still survive,
When my soule 's fled;
Nor shall my love dye, when my bodye 's dead,
That shall wait on me to the lower shade,
And never fade:
My very ashes in their urn,
Shall, like a hallowed Lamp, for ever burn.

Poems, 1640 (text 1651)

317 *To Saxham*

THOUGH frost, and snow, lock'd from mine eyes
That beauty which without door lyes,
Thy gardens, orchards, walks, that so
I might not all thy pleasures know;
Yet (*Saxham*) thou within thy gate,
Art of thy selfe so delicate,

So full of native sweets, that bless
Thy roof with inward happiness;
As neither from, nor to thy store,
Winter takes ought, or Spring adds more.
The cold and frozen ayr had sterv'd
Much poore, if not by thee preserv'd;
Whose prayers have made thy Table blest
With plenty, far above the rest.
The season hardly did afford
Coarse cates unto thy neighbours board,
Yet thou hadst dainties, as the sky
Had only been thy Volarie;
Or else the birds, fearing the snow
Might to another deluge grow,
The Pheasant, Partridge, and the Lark,
Flew to thy house, as to the Ark.
The willing Oxe, of himselfe came
Home to the slaughter, with the Lamb,
And every beast did thither bring
Himselfe, to be an offering.
The scalie herd, more pleasure took
Bath'd in the dish, than in the brook.
Water, Earth, Ayre, did all conspire,
To pay their tributes to thy fire,
Whose cherishing flames themselves divide
Through every room, where they deride
The night, and cold abroad; whilst they
Like Suns within, keep endlesse day.
Those chearfull beams send forth their light,
To all that wander in the night,
And seem to beckon from aloof,

Volarie: aviary.

The weary Pilgrim to thy roof;
Where, if refresh't he will away,
He's fairly welcome, or if stay
Far more, which he shall hearty find,
Both from the master, and the Hind.
The stranger's welcome, each man there
Stamp'd on his chearfull brow doth wear;
Nor doth this welcome, or his cheer
Grow lesse, cause he stayes longer here.
There's none observes (much less repines)
How often this man sups or dines.
Thou hast no Porter at the door
T' examin, or keep back the poor;
Nor locks, nor bolts; thy gates have been
Made only to let strangers in;
Untaught to shut, they doe not fear
To stand wide open all the year;
Careless who enters, for they know,
Thou never didst deserve a foe;
And as for theeves, thy bounty's such,
They cannot steal, thou giv'st so much.

Poems, 1640 (text 1651)

318 The Inscription on the Tombe of the Lady Mary Wentworth

MARIA WENTWORTH, *Thomae Comitis Cleveland, filia praemortua prima virginiam animam exhaluit. An. Dom. 1632 Æt. suae 18.*

AND here the precious dust is laid;
Whose purely-tempered Clay was made
So fine, that it the guest betray'd.

Else the soul grew so fast within,
It broke the outward shell of sin,
And so was hatch'd a Cherubin.

In height, it soar'd to God above;
In depth, it did to knowledge move,
And spread in breadth to general love.

Before, a pious duty shin'd
To Parents, courtesie behind,
On either side an equall mind.

Good to the Poor, to kindred dear,
To servants kind, to friendship clear,
To nothing but her self severe.

So though a Virgin, yet a Bride
To every Grace, she justifi'd
A chaste Poligamie, and dy'd.

Learn from hence (Reader) what small trust
We ow this world, where vertue must
Frail as our flesh crumble to dust.

Poems, 1640 (text 1651)

319 *An Elegie upon the Death of the Deane of Pauls, Dr. John Donne*

CAN we not force from widdowed Poetry,
Now thou art dead (Great DONNE), one Elegie
To crowne thy Hearse? Why yet dare we not trust
Though with unkneaded dowe-bak't prose thy dust,
Such as the uncisor'd Churchman from the flower
Of fading Rhetorique, short liv'd as his houre,

uncisor'd: carelessly barbered.

Dry as the sand that measures it, should lay
Upon thy Ashes, on the funerall day?
Have we no voice, no tune? Did'st thou dispense
Through all our language, both the words and sense?
'Tis a sad truth; The Pulpit may her plaine,
And sober Christian precepts still retaine,
Doctrines it may, and wholesome Uses frame,
Grave Homilies, and Lectures, But the flame
Of thy brave Soule, that shot such heat and light,
As burnt our earth, and made our darknesse bright,
Committed holy Rapes upon our Will,
Did through the eye the melting heart distill;
And the deepe knowledge of darke truths so teach,
As sense might judge, what phansie could not reach,
Must be desir'd for ever. So the fire,
That fills with spirit and heat the Delphique quire,
Which kindled first by thy Promethean breath,
Glow'd here a while, lies quench't now in thy death;
The Muses garden with Pedantique weedes
O'erspread, was purg'd by thee; The lazie seeds
Of servile imitation throwne away,
And fresh invention planted, Thou didst pay
The debts of our penurious bankrupt age;
Licentious thefts, that make poëtique rage
A Mimique fury, when our soules must bee
Possest, or with Anacreons Extasie,
Or Pindars, not their owne; The subtle cheat
Of slie Exchanges, and the jugling feat
Of two-edg'd words, or whatsoever wrong
By ours was done the Greeke, or Latine tongue,
Thou hast redeem'd, and open'd Us a Mine
Of rich and pregnant phansie, drawne a line

Of masculine expression, which had good
Old Orpheus seene, or all the ancient Brood
Our superstitious fooles admire, and hold
Their lead more precious than thy burnish't Gold,
Thou hadst beene their Exchequer, and no more
They each in others dust had rak'd for Ore.
Thou shalt yield no precedence, but of time,
And the blinde fate of language, whose tun'd chime
More charmes the outward sense; Yet thou maist claime
From so great disadvantage greater fame,
Since to the awe of thy imperious wit
Our stubborne language bends, made only fit
With her tough-thick-rib'd hoopes to gird about
Thy Giant phansie, which had prov'd too stout
For their soft melting Phrases. As in time
They had the start, so did they cull the prime
Buds of invention many a hundred yeare,
And left the rifled fields, besides the feare
To touch their Harvest, yet from those bare lands
Of what is purely thine, thy only hands
(And that thy smallest worke) have gleaned more
Than all those times, and tongues could reape before;
But thou art gone, and thy strict lawes will be
Too hard for Libertines in Poetrie.
They will repeale the goodly exil'd traine
Of gods and goddesses, which in thy just raigne
Were banish'd nobler Poems, now, with these
The silenc'd tales o'th'Metamorphoses
Shall stuffe their lines, and swell the windy Page,
Till Verse refin'd by thee, in this last Age
Turne ballad rime, or those old Idolls bee
Ador'd againe, with new apostasie;

Oh, pardon mee, that breake with untun'd verse
The reverend silence that attends thy herse,
Whose awfull solemne murmures were to thee
More than these faint lines, a loud Elegie,
That did proclaime in a dumbe eloquence
The death of all the Arts, whose influence
Growne feeble, in these panting numbers lies
Gasping short winded Accents, and so dies:
So doth the swiftly turning wheele not stand
In th'instant we withdraw the moving hand,
But some small time maintaine a faint weake course
By vertue of the first impulsive force:
And so whil'st I cast on thy funerall pile
Thy crowne of Bayes, Oh, let it crack a while,
And spit disdaine, till the devouring flashes
Suck all the moysture up, then turne to ashes.
I will not draw thee envy to engrosse
All thy perfections, or weepe all our losse;
Those are too numerous for an Elegie,
And this too great, to be express'd by mee,
Though every pen should share a distinct part.
Yet art thou Theme enough to tire all Art;
Let others carve the rest, it shall suffice
I on thy Tombe this Epitaph incise.

Here lies a King, that rul'd as hee thought fit
The universall Monarchy of wit;
Here lie two Flamens, and both those the best,
Apollo's first, at last, the true Gods Priest.

Donne's *Poems*, 1633

320 *To a Lady that desired I would love her*

NOW you have freely given me leave to love,
What will you do?
Shall I your mirth, or passion move,
When I begin to woo;
Will you torment, or scorn, or love me too?

Each petty beauty can disdain, and I
Spight of your hate
Without your leave can see, and die;
Dispence a nobler Fate!
Tis easie to destroy, you may create.

Then give me leave to love, & love me too
Not with designe
To raise, as Loves curst Rebels doe,
When puling Poets whine,
Fame to their beauty, from their blubbr'd eyn.

Grief is a puddle, and reflects not clear
Your beauties rayes;
Joyes are pure streames, your eyes appear
Sullen in sadder layes;
In cheerfull numbers they shine bright with prayse,

Which shall not mention to express you fayr,
Wounds, flames, and darts,
Storms in your brow, nets in your hair,
Suborning all your parts,
Or to betray, or torture captive hearts.

I'll make your eyes like morning Suns appear,
As mild, and fair;
Your brow as Crystall smooth, and clear,
And your dishevell'd hair
Shall flow like a calm Region of the Air.

Rich Nature's store, (which is the Poet's Treasure)
I'll spend, to dress
Your beauties, if your mine of Pleasure
In equall thankfulness
You but unlock, so we each other bless.

Poems, 1640 (text 1651)

321 *To my worthy friend Mr. George Sandys*

I PRESSE not to the Quire, nor dare I greet
The holy Place with my unhallow'd feet:
My unwasht Muse pollutes not things Divine,
Nor mingles her prophaner notes with thine;
Here, humbly at the Porch, she listning stayes,
And with glad eares sucks in thy Sacred Layes.
So, devout Penitents of old were wont,
Some without doore, and some beneath the Font,
To stand and heare the Churches Liturgies,
Yet not assist the solemne Exercise.
Sufficeth her, that she a Lay-place gaine,
To trim thy Vestments, or but beare thy traine:
Though nor in Tune, nor Wing, She reach thy Larke,
Her Lyricke feet may dance before the Arke.
Who knowes, but that Her wandring eyes, that run
Now hunting Glow-wormes, may adore the Sun.
A pure Flame may, shot by Almighty Power
Into my breast, the earthy flame devoure:

My Eyes, in Penitentiall dew may steepe
That brine, which they for sensuall love did weepe:
So (though 'gainst Natures course) fire may be quencht
With fire, and water be with water drencht.
Perhaps, my restlesse Soule, tir'd with pursuit
Of mortall beautie, seeking without fruit
Contentment there; which hath not, when enjoy'd,
Quencht all her thirst, nor satisfi'd, though cloy'd;
Weary of her vaine search below, above
In the first Faire may find th' immortall Love.
Prompted by thy Example then, no more
In moulds of Clay will I my God adore;
But teare those Idols from my Heart, and Write
What his blest Sp'rit, not fond Love, shall endite.
Then, I no more shall court the Verdant Bay,
But the dry leavelesse Trunk on Golgotha:
And rather strive to gaine from thence one Thorne,
Than all the flourishing Wreathes by Laureats worne.

G. Sandys, *A Paraphrase upon the Divine Poems*, 1638

322 *A Song*

ASK me no more where *Jove* bestowes,
When *June* is past, the fading rose:
For in your beauties orient deep,
These Flowers as in their causes sleep.

Ask me no more whither doe stray
The golden Atomes of the day:
For in pure love heaven did prepare
Those powders to inrich your hair.

Ask me no more whither doth hast
The Nightingale, when *May* is past:
For in your sweet dividing throat
She winters, and keeps warm her note.

Ask me no more where those starres light,
That downwards fall in dead of night:
For in your eyes they sit, and there,
Fixed, become as in their sphere.

Ask me no more if East or West,
The Phenix builds her spicy nest:
For unto you at last she flyes,
And in your fragrant bosome dies.

Poems, 1640 (text 1651)

ROBERT SEMPILL

1595?–1665?

323 *The Life and Death of the Piper of Kilbarchan*

or,

The Epitaph of Habbie Simson,
Who on his drone bore bonny flags;
He made his Cheeks as red as Crimson,
And babbed when he blew the Bags.

K*ILBARCHAN* now may say, alas!
For she hath lost her Game and Grace,
Both Trixie, and the Maiden Trace:
but what remead?
For no man can supply his place,
Hab Simson's dead.

dividing: warbling.

Now who shall play, the day it daws?
Or hunt up, when the Cock he craws?
Or who can for our Kirk-town-cause,
  stand us in stead?
On Bagpipes (now) no Body blaws,
  sen *Habbie*'s dead.

Or wha will cause our Shearers shear?
Wha will bend up the Brags of Weir,
Bring in the Bells, or good play meir,
  in time of need?
Hab Simson cou'd, what needs you speer?
  but (now) he's dead.

So kindly to his Neighbours neast,
At *Beltan* and Saint *Barchan*'s feast,
He blew, and then held up his Breast,
  as he were weid;
But now we need not him arrest,
  for *Habbie*'s dead.

At Fairs he play'd before the Spear-men,
All gaily graithed in their Gear, Men.
Steel Bonnets, Jacks, and Swords so clear then
  like any Bead.
Now wha shall play before such Weir-men,
  sen *Habbie*'s dead?

At Clark-plays when he wont to come;
His Pipe play'd trimly to the Drum,
Like Bikes of Bees he gart it Bum,
  and tun'd his Reed.
Now all our Pipers may sing dumb,
  sen *Habbie*'s dead.

And at Horse Races many a day,
Before the Black, the Brown, the Gray,
He gart his Pipe when he did play,
    baith Skirl and Skreed,
Now all such Pastimes quite away,
    sen *Habbie*'s dead.

He counted was a weil'd Wight-man,
And fiercely at Foot-ball he ran:
At every Game the Gree he wan,
    for Pith and Speed.
The like of *Habbie* was na than,
    but now he's dead.

And than, besides his valiant Acts,
At Bridals he wan many Placks,
He bobbed ay behind Fo'ks Backs,
    and shook his Head.
Now we want many merry Cracks,
    sen *Habbie*'s dead.

He was Convoyer of the Bride
With Kittock hinging at his side:
About the Kirk he thought a Pride
    the Ring to lead.
But now we may gae but a Guide
    for *Habbie*'s dead.

So well's he keeped his *Decorum*,
And all the Stots of *Whip-meg-morum*,
He slew a Man, and wae's me for him,
    and bure the Fead!
But yet the Man wan hame before him,
    and was not dead!

Ay whan he play'd, the Lasses Leugh,
To see him Teethless, Auld and teugh.
He wan his Pipes beside *Barcleugh*,
withoutten dread:
Which after wan him Gear eneugh,
but now he's dead.

Ay whan he play'd, the Gaitlings gedder'd,
And whan he spake, the Carl bledder'd:
On Sabbath days his Cap was fedder'd,
a seemly Weid.
In the Kirk-yeard, his Mare stood tedder'd,
where he lies dead.

Alas! for him my Heart is sair,
For of his Springs I gat a skair,
At every Play, Race, Feast and Fair,
but Guile or Greed.
We need not look for Pyping mair,
sen *Habbie*'s dead.

Watson, *Choice Collection of Scots Poems*, 1711

JAMES SHIRLEY

1596–1666

324 *To his Mistris confined*

THINK not my *Phebe*, cause a cloud
Doth now thy heavenly beauty shroud,
My wandring eye
Can stoop to common beauties of the sky,
Be thou but kind, and this Eclipse
Shall neither hinder eyes, nor lips;
For we will meet
Within our hearts, and kisse, when none shall see 't.

Nor canst thou in thy Prison be,
Without some loving signs of me,
When thou dost spy
A sun-beam peep into thy room, 'tis I,
For I am hid within that flame,
And thus unto thy chamber came,
To let thee see,
In what a Martyrdom I burn for thee.
There's no sad picture that doth dwell
Upon thy Arras wall, but well
Resembles me.
No matter though our years do not agree,
Love can make old, as well as time,
And he that doth but twenty clime,
If he will prove
As true as I, shews fourscore years in love.

Poems, 1646

325 *Io*

YOU Virgins that did late despair
To keep your wealth from cruel men,
Tye up in silk your careless hair,
Soft peace is come agen.

Now Lovers eyes may gently shoot
A flame that wo' not kill:
The Drum was angry, but the Lute
Shall whisper what you will.

Sing *Io*, *Io*, for his sake,
Who hath restor'd your drooping heads.
With choice of sweetest flowers make
A garden where he treads.

Whilst we whole groves of Laurel bring,
  A petty triumph to his brow,
Who is the Master of our Spring,
  And all the bloom we owe.

Poems, 1646

326 *The Garden*

THIS Garden does not take my eyes,
  Though here you shew how art of men
Can purchase Nature at a price
Would stock old Paradise agen.

These glories while you dote upon,
I envie not your Spring nor pride,
Nay boast the Summer all your own,
My thoughts with lesse are satisfied.

Give me a little plot of ground,
Where might I with the Sun agree,
Though every day he walk the Round,
My Garden he should seldom see.

Those Tulips that such wealth display,
To court my eye, shall lose their name,
Though now they listen, as if they
Expected I should praise their flame.

But I would see my self appear
Within the Violets drooping head,
On which a melancholy tear
The discontented Morne hath shed.

Within their buds let Roses sleep,
And virgin Lillies on their stemme,
Till sighes from Lovers glide, and creep
Into their leaves to open them.

I' th' Center of my ground compose
Of Bayes and Ewe my Summer room,
Which may so oft as I repose,
Present my Arbour, and my Tombe.

No woman here shall find me out,
Or if a chance do bring one hither,
I'll be secure, for round about
I'll moat it with my eyes foul weather.

No Bird shall live within my pale,
To charme me with their shames of Art,
Unlesse some wandring Nightingale
Come here to sing, and break her heart.

Upon whose death I'll try to write
An Epitaph in some funeral stone,
So sad, and true, it may invite
My self to die, and prove mine owne.

Poems, 1646

327 (*Victorious men of Earth*)

VICTORIOUS men of Earth, no more
Proclaime how wide your Empires are;
Though you bind in every shore,
And your triumphs reach as far
As Night or Day,
Yet you proud Monarchs must obey,
And mingle with forgotten ashes, when
Death calls ye to the crowd of common men.

Devouring Famine, Plague, and War,
Each able to undo Man-kind,
Death's servile Emissaries are,
Nor to these alone confin'd,

He hath at will
More quaint and subtle waies to kill.
A smile or kiss, as he will use the art,
Shall have the cunning skill to break a heart.

Cupid and Death, 1650

328 *(O fly my soul)*

O FLY my soul, what hangs upon
thy drooping wings,
and weighes them down,
With love of gaudy mortall things?
The Sun is now i' th' East, each shade
as he doth rise,
is shorter made,
That Earth may lessen to our eyes:
Oh be not careless then, and play
until the Star of peace
Hide all his beames in dark recess;
Poor Pilgrims needs must lose their way,
When all the shadowes do encrease.

The Imposture, 1652

329 *(The glories of our blood and state)*

THE glories of our blood and state,
Are shadows, not substantial things,
There is no armour against fate,
Death lays his icy hand on Kings,
Scepter and Crown,
Must tumble down,
And in the dust be equal made,
With the poor crooked sithe and spade.

Some men with swords may reap the field,
  And plant fresh laurels where they kill,
But their strong nerves at last must yield,
  They tame but one another still;
      Early or late,
      They stoop to fate,
And must give up the murmuring breath,
When they pale Captives creep to death.

The Garlands wither on your brow,
  Then boast no more your mighty deeds,
Upon Deaths purple Altar now,
  See where the Victor-victim bleeds,
      Your heads must come,
      To the cold Tomb;
Onely the actions of the just
Smell sweet, and blossom in their dust.

Ajax and Ulysses, 1659

THOMAS CARY

1597–1634

330 *On his Mistresse going to Sea*

FAREWELL fair Saint, may not the Seas and wind
  Swell like the heart and eyes you leave behind,
But calme and gentle (like the looks they bear)
Smile on your face and whisper in your eare:
Let no foule billow offer to arise
That it may nearer look upon your eyes,
Lest wind and waves enamoured with such form
Should throng and crowd themselves into a storm;
But if it be your fate (vast Seas) to love,
Of my becalmed heart learn how to move:

Move then, but in a gentle lovers pace,
No wrinkles nor no furrows in your face;
And ye fierce winds see that you tell your tale
In such a breath as may but fill her sail:
So whilst you court her each his severall way
You will her safely to her port convay;
And loose her in a noble way of wooing,
Whilst both contribute to your own undoing.

Fanshawe's *Il Pastor Fido*, 1648 (text from *Parnassus Biceps*, 1656)

WILLIAM STRODE

1602–1645

331 *On a Gentlewoman walking in the Snowe*

I SAW faire Cloris walke alone
Where feather'd raine came softly downe,
And Jove descended from his tower
To court her in a silver shower;
The wanton snowe flewe to her breast
Like little birds into their nest,
And overcome with whiteness there
For greife it thaw'd into a teare,
Thence falling on her garment's hem
For greife it freez'd into a gem.

First printed in W. Porter's *Madrigals and Airs*, 1632

OWEN FELLTHAM

1602?–1668

332 *This ensuing Copy the late Printer hath been pleased to honour, by mistaking it among those of the most ingenious and too early lost, Sir John Suckling*

WHEN, Dearest, I but think on thee,
Methinks all things that lovely be
Are present, and my soul delighted:
For beauties that from worth arise,
Are like the grace of Deities,
Still present with us, though unsighted.

Thus while I sit and sigh the day,
With all his spreading lights away,
Till nights black wings do overtake me:
Thinking on thee, thy beauties then,
As sudden lights do sleeping men,
So they by their bright rayes awake me.

Thus absence dies, and dying proves
No absence can consist with Loves,
That do partake of fair perfection:
Since in the darkest night they may
By their quick motion find a way
To see each other by reflection.

The waving Sea can with such flood,
Bath some high Palace that hath stood
Far from the Main up in the River:
Oh think not then but love can do
As much, for that 's an Ocean too,
That flows not every day, but ever.

Lusoria, 1661

JASPER MAYNE

1604–1672

333 *From To the Memory of Ben Johnson*

SCORNE then their censure, who gave out thy wit
As long about a Comedy did sit,
As Elephants bring forth; and that thy blots
And mendings took more time than *Fortune* plots:
That such thy drought was, and so great thy thirst,
That all thy Plays were drawn at the *Mermaid* first.
That the Kings yearly Butt wrote, and his wine
Had more right than thou to thy *Catiline*.

. . . . . .

He that writes well, writes quick, since the rules true,
Nothing is slowly done, that 's always new.
So when thy *Fox* had ten times Acted been,
Each day was first, but that twas cheaper seen.
And so thy *Alchymist* Played o'er and o'er,
Was new o' th' stage, when twas not at the door.
We, like the Actors, did repeat, the pit
The first time saw, the next conceived thy wit:
Which was cast in those forms, such rules, such arts,
That but to some not halfe thy Acts were parts:
Since of some silken judgements we may say
They fill'd a box two houres, but saw no Play.
So that the unlearned lost their money, and
Scholars saved onely, that could understand.
Thy Scene was free from monsters, no hard plot
Call'd down a God t' untie the unlikely knot.
The stage was still a stage, two entrances
Were not two parts of the world disjoyn'd by Seas.
Thine were land Tragedies, no Prince was found

To swim a whole Scene out, then o' th' stage drown'd,
Pitcht fields, and *Red-Bull* wars, still felt thy doom,
Thou laidst no sieges to the Musick Room;
Nor wouldst allow to thy best Comedies
Humors that should above the people rise:
Yet was thy language and thy stile so high
Thy Sock to the ankle, Buskin reachd to th' thigh:
And both so chast, so 'bove dramatick clean,
That we both safely saw and lived thy Scene.

Parnassus Biceps, 1656

THOMAS RANDOLPH

1605–1635

334 *A gratulatory to Mr. Ben. Johnson for his adopting of him to be his Son*

I WAS not born to *Helicon*, nor dare
Presume to thinke my selfe a *Muses* heire.
I have no title to *Parnassus* hill,
Nor any acre of it by the will
Of a dead Ancestor, nor could I bee
Ought but a tenant unto Poetrie,
But thy Adoption quits me of all feare,
And makes me challenge a childs portion there.
I am a kinne to Heroes being thine,
And part of my alliance is divine.
Orpheus, *Musaeus*, *Homer* too; beside
Thy Brothers by the *Roman* Mothers side;
As *Ovid*, *Virgil*, and the *Latin Lyre*,
That is so like thy *Horace*; the whole quire
Of Poets are by thy Adoption, all
My uncles; thou hast given me pow'r to call

Phœbus himselfe my grandsire, by this graunt
Each sister of the nine is made my Aunt.
Go you that reckon from a large descent
Your lineal Honours, and are well content
To glory in the age of your great name,
Though on a Heralds faith you build the same:
I do not envy you, nor thinke you blest
Though you may beare a Gorgon on your Crest
By direct line from *Perseus*; I will boast
No farther than my Father; that 's the most
I can, or should be proud of; and I were
Unworthy his adoption, if that here
I should be dully modest; boast I must
Being sonne of his Adoption, not his lust.
And to say truth, that which is best in mee
May call you father, 'twas begot by thee.
Have I a sparke of that cælestiall flame
Within me, I confesse I stole the same
Prometheus like, from thee; and may I feed
His vulture, when I dare deny the deed.
Many more moons thou hast, that shine by night,
All Bankrupts, wer 't not for a borrow'd light;
Yet can forsweare it; I the debt confesse,
And thinke my reputation ne'er the lesse.
For Father let me be resolv'd by you;
Is 't a disparagement from rich *Peru*
To ravish gold; or theft, for wealthy Ore
To ransack *Tagus*, or *Pactolus* shore?
Or does he wrong *Alcinous*, that for want
Doth take from him a sprig or two, to plant
A lesser Orchard? sure it cannot be:
Nor is it theft to steale some flames from thee.

Grant this, and I'll cry guilty, as I am,
And pay a filial reverence to thy name.
For when my Muse upon obedient knees,
Askes not a Fathers blessing, let her leese
The fame of this Adoption; 'tis a curse
I wish her 'cause I cannot thinke a worse.
And here, as Piety bids me, I intreat
Phœbus to lend thee some of his own heat,
To cure thy Palsie; else I will complaine
He has no skill in herbs; Poets in vaine
Make him the God of Physick; 'twere his praise
To make thee as immortall as thy Baies;
As his owne *Daphne*; 'twere a shame to see
The God not love his Priest, more than his Tree.
But if heaven take thee, envying us thy Lyre,
'Tis to pen Anthems for an Angels quire.

Poems, 1638

335 *An Ode to Mr. Anthony Stafford to hasten him into the Country*

COME spurre away,
I have no patience for a longer stay;
But must go downe,
And leave the chargeable noise of this great Towne.
I will the country see,
Where old simplicity,
Though hid in gray
Doth looke more gay
Than foppery in plush and scarlet clad.
Farewell you City-wits that are
Almost at Civil war;
Tis time that I grow wise, when all the world grows mad.

More of my dayes
I will not spend to gaine an Idiots praise;
Or to make sport
For some slight Punie of the Innes of Court.
Then worthy *Stafford* say
How shall we spend the day,
With what delights,
Shorten the nights?
When from this tumult we are got secure;
Where mirth with all her freedome goes,
Yet shall no finger loose;
Where every word is thought, and every thought is pure.

There from the tree
We'll cherries plucke, and pick the strawbery.
And every day
Go see the wholesome Country Girles make hay,
Whose browne hath lovelier grace,
Than any painted face,
That I doe know
Hyde-Parke can show.
Where I had rather gaine a kisse than meet
(Though some of them in greater state
Might court my love with plate,)
The beauties of the *Cheape*, and wives of *Lumbardstreet*.

But thinke upon
Some other pleasures, these to me are none;
Why doe I prate
Of women, that are things against my fate?
I never meane to wed,
That torture to my bed;

My Muse is shee
My Love shall bee.
Let Clownes get wealth, and heires; when I am gone,
And the great Bugbear grisly death
Shall take this idle breath,
If I a Poem leave, that Poem is my Sonne.

Of this no more;
We'll rather taste the bright Pomona's store.
No fruit shall scape
Our palates, from the damson, to the grape;
Then full we'll seek a shade,
And heare what musique 's made;
How Philomell
Her tale doth tell:
And how the other Birds doe fill the quire;
The Thrush and Blackbird lend their throats
Warbling melodious notes;
We will all sports enjoy, which others but desire.

Ours is the skie,
Where at what fowle we please our Hawke shall fly;
Nor will we spare
To hunt the crafty foxe, or timorous hare,
But let our hounds runne loose
In any ground they'll choose;
The buck shall fall,
The stag and all:
Our pleasures must from their owne warrants bee,
For to my *Muse*, if not to mee,
I'm sure all game is free;
Heaven, Earth, are all but parts of her great Royalty.

And when we meane
To taste of *Bacchus* blessings now and then,
And drinke by stealth
A cup or two to noble *Barkleys* health,
I'll take my pipe and try
The *Phrygian* melody;
Which he that heares
Lets through his eares
A madnesse to distemper all the braine.
Then I another pipe will take
And *Dorique* musique make,
To Civilize with graver notes our wits again.

Poems, 1638

336 *Poetry and Philosophy*

Damon. THE Reapers that with whetted sickles stand,
Gathering the falling ears i' th' other hand;
Though they endure the scorching summers heat,
Have yet some wages to allay their sweat:
The Lopper that doth fell the sturdy Oak
Labours, yet has good pay for every stroke.
The Plowman is rewarded: only we
That sing, are paid with our own melody.
Rich churls have learn't to praise us, and admire,
But have not learn't to think us worth the hire.
So toyling Ants perchance delight to hear
The summer musique of the Grasshopper,
But after rather let him starve with pain,
Than spare him from their store one single grain.
As when great *Junos* beauteous Bird displaies
Her starry tail, the boyes doe run and gaze
At her proud train; so look they now adaies
On Poets; and doe think if they but praise,

Or pardon what we sing, enough they doe:
Aye, and 'tis well if they doe so much too.
My rage is swell'd so high I cannot speak it,
Had I *Pan's* pipe, or thine I now should break it!
Tityrus. Let moles delight in Earth; Swine dunghills rake;
Crows prey on Carrion; Frogs a pleasure take
In slimy pools; And Niggards wealth admire;
But we, whose souls are made of purer fire,
Have other aimes: Who songs for gain hath made,
Has of a liberall Science fram'd a Trade.
Hark how the Nightingale in yonder tree,
Hid in the boughes, warbles melodiously
Her various musique forth, while the whole Quire
Of other birds flock round, and all admire!
But who rewards her? will the ravenous Kite
Part with her prey, to pay for her delight?
Or will the foolish, painted, prattling Jay
Now turn'd a hearer, to requite her play
Lend her a straw? or any of the rest
Fetch her a feather when she builds her nest?
Yet sings she ne'er the lesse, till every den
Doe catch at her last notes: And shall I then
His fortunes *Damon*, 'bove my own commend,
Who can more cheese into the market send?
Clowns for posterity may cark and care,
That cannot out-live death but in an Heire:
By more than wealth we propagate our Names,
That trust not to successions, but our Fames.
Let hide-bound churls yoak the laborious Oxe,
Milk hundred goats, and shear a thousand flocks;
Plant gainfull Orchards, and in silver shine;
Thou of all fruits should'st only prune the Vine:

Whose fruit being tasted, might erect thy brain
To reach some ravishing, high, and lofty strain,
The double birth of *Bacchus* to expresse,
First in the grape, the second in the presse.
And therefore tell me boy, what is 't can move
Thy mind, once fixed on the *Muses* Love?
Damon. When I contented liv'd by *Cam's* fair streams,
Without desire to see the prouder *Thames*,
I had no flock to care for, but could sit
Under a willow covert, and repeat
Those deep and learned layes, on every part
Grounded on judgment, subtilty, and Art,
That the great Tutor to the greatest King,
The shepherd of *Stagira*, us'd to sing:
The shepherd of *Stagira*, that unfolds
All natures closet, shows what e'er it holds;
The matter, form, sense, motion, place, and measure
Of every thing contain'd in her vast treasure.
How Elements doe change; What is the cause
Of Generation; what the Rule, and Laws
The Orbs doe move by; Censures every starre,
Why this is fixt, and that irregular;
Knows all the Heavens, as if he had been there,
And help't each Angell turn about her spheare.
The thirsty pilgrim travelling by land,
When the fierce Dog-starre doth the day command,
Half chok't with dust, parch't with the sultry heat;
Tir'd with his journey, and o'ercome with sweat,
Finding a gentle spring, at her cool brink
Doth not with more delight sit down and drink,
Than I record his songs; we see a cloud,
And fearing to be wet, doe run and shroud

Under a bush; when he would sit and tell
The cause that made her misty wombe to swell;
Why it sometimes in drops of rain doth flow,
Sometimes dissolves her self in flakes of snow:
Nor gaz'd he at a Comet, but would frame
A reason why it wore a beard of flame.
Ah *Tityrus*, I would with all my heart,
Even with the best of my carv'd mazers part,
To hear him as he us'd divinely shew,
What 'tis that paints the divers-colour'd bow:
Whence Thunders are discharg'd, whence the winds stray,
What foot through heaven hath worn the milky way!

From *An Eclogue to Mr. Johnson. Poems*, 1638

337 *A parley with his empty Purse*

PURSE, who'll not know you have a Poet's been
When he shall look and find no gold herein?
What respect (think you) will there now be shown
To this foule nest, when all the birds are flowne?
Unnaturall *vacuum*, can your emptinesse
Answer to some slight questions, such as these?
How shall my debts be paid? or can my scores
Be clear'd with verses to my Creditors?
Hexameter's no sterling, and I feare
What the brain coins goes scarce for current there.
Can metre cancell bonds? is here a time
Ever to hope to wipe out chalk with rhyme?
Or if I now were hurrying to the jaile
Are the nine *Muses* held sufficient baile?

mazers: drinking bowls.

Would they to any composition come
If we should mortgage our *Elisium*,
Tempe, *Parnassus*, and the golden streames
Of *Tagus*, and *Pactolus*, those rich dreames
Of active fancy? Can our *Orpheus* move
Those rocks, and stones with his best straines of love?
Should I (like *Homer*) sing in lofty tones
To them *Achilles*, and his *Myrmidons*;
Hector, and *Ajax* are but Sergeants names,
They relish bay-salt, 'bove the Epigrams
Of the most season'd braine, nor will they be
Content with Ode, or paid with Elegy.
Muse, burne thy bays, and thy fond quill resigne,
One crosse of theirs is worth whole books of mine.
Of all the treasure which the Poets hold
There 's none at all they weigh, except our gold;
And mine 's return'd to th' *Indies*, and hath swore
Never to visit this cold climate more.
Then crack your strings good Purse, for you need none;
Gape on, as they doe to be paid, gape on.

Poems, 1638

WILLIAM HABINGTON

1605–1654

338 *Against them who lay unchastity to the sex of Women*

THEY meet but with unwholesome Springs,
And Summers which infectious are:
They heare but when the Mermaid sings,
And onely see the falling starre:
Who ever dare,
Affirme no woman chaste and faire.

Goe cure your fevers: and you'll say
The Dog-dayes scorch not all the yeare:
In Copper Mines no longer stay,
But travell to the West, and there
            The right ones see:
And grant all gold's not Alchimie.

What madman 'cause the glow-wormes flame
Is cold, sweares there's no warmth in fire?
'Cause some make forfeit of their name,
And slave themselves to man's desire,
            Shall the sex free
From guilt, damn'd to the bondage be?

Nor grieve *Castara,* though 'twere fraile,
Thy Vertue then would brighter shine,
When thy example should prevaile,
And every woman's faith be thine.
            And were there none;
'Tis Majesty to rule alone.

Castara, 1634

339 *Nox nocti indicat Scientiam.* (DAVID)

WHEN I survey the bright
    Cœlestiall spheare:
So rich with jewels hung, that night
Doth like an Æthiop bride appeare.

  My soule her wings doth spread
    And heaven-ward flies,
Th' Almighty's Mysteries to read
In the large volumes of the skies.

For the bright firmament
Shootes forth no flame
So silent, but is eloquent
In speaking the Creators name.

No unregarded star
Contracts its light
Into so small a Character,
Remov'd far from our humane sight:

But if we stedfast looke,
We shall discerne
In it as in some holy booke,
How man may heavenly knowledge learne.

It tells the Conqueror,
That farre-stretcht powre
Which his proud dangers traffique for,
Is but the triumph of an houre.

That from the farthest North,
Some Nation may
Yet undiscovered issue forth,
And o'er his new got conquest sway.

Some Nation yet shut in
With hills of ice
May be let out to scourge his sinne
'Till they shall equall him in vice.

And then they likewise shall
Their ruine have,
For as your selves your Empires fall,
And every Kingdome hath a grave.

Thus those Celestiall fires,
Though seeming mute,
The fallacie of our desires
And all the pride of life confute.

For they have watcht since first
The World had birth:
And found sinne in itselfe accurst,
And nothing permanent on earth.

Castara: The Third Part, 1640

340 *(Fine Young Folly)*

FINE young Folly, though you wear
That fair Beauty, I did swear,
Yet you ne'er could reach my heart,
For we courtiers learn at school
Only with your sex to fool,
You're not worth our serious part.

When I sigh and kiss your hand,
Crosse mine Armes, and wondring stand,
Holding fairly with your eye:
Then dilate on my desires,
Swear the Sun ne'er shot such fires,
All is but a handsome lye.

When I eye your Curles or Lace,
Gentle soul, you think your face
Straight some murder doth commit;
And your conscience doth begin
To be scrup'lous of my sin,
When I court to shew my wit.

Wherefore Madam, wear no cloud,
Nor to check my flames grow proud;
For in sooth I much do doubt,
'Tis the powder in your hair,
Not your breath perfumes the Air,
And your clothes that set you out.
Yet though truth hath this confest,
And I swear I love in jest,
Courteous soul, when next I court,
And protest an amorous flame,
You'll vow, I in earnest am;
Bedlam, this is pretty sport.

The Queene of Aragon, 1640

SIR THOMAS BROWNE

1605–1682

341 *A Colloquy with God*

THE night is come, like to the day;
Depart not thou, great God, away.
Let not my sins, black as the night,
Eclipse the lustre of thy light:
Keep still in my Horizon; for to me
The Sun makes not the day, but thee.
Thou, whose nature cannot sleep,
On my temples sentry keep;
Guard me 'gainst those watchful foes,
Whose eyes are open while mine close.
Let no dreams my head infest,
But such as Jacob's temples blest.
While I do rest, my Soul advance;
Make my sleep a holy trance;

That I may, my rest being wrought,
Awake into some holy thought;
And with as active vigour run
My course, as doth the nimble Sun.
Sleep is a death; O make me try,
By sleeping, what it is to die;
And as gently lay my head
On my grave, as now my bed.
Howe'er I rest, great God, let me
Awake again at last with thee;
And thus assur'd, behold I lie
Securely, or to awake or die.
These are my drowsie days; in vain
I do now wake to sleep again:
O come that hour, when I shall never
Sleep again, but wake for ever.

Religio Medici, 1643

SIR WILLIAM DAVENANT

1606–1668

342

From Gondibert

BY what bold passion am I rudely led,
Like Fame's too curious and officious Spie,
Where I these Rolls in her dark Closet read,
Where Worthies wrapp'd in Time's disguises lie?

Why should we now their shady Curtains draw,
Who by a wise retirement hence are freed,
And gone to Lands exempt from Nature's Law,
Where Love no more can mourn, nor valor bleed?

Why to this stormy world from their long rest,
  Are these recall'd to be again displeas'd,
Where during Nature's reign we are opprest,
  Till we by Death's high priviledge are eas'd?

Is it to boast that Verse has Chymick pow'r,
  And that its rage (which is productive heat)
Can these revive, as Chymists raise a Flow'r,
  Whose scatter'd parts their Glass presents compleat?

Though in these Worthies gone, valor and love
  Did chastly as in sacred Temples meet,
Such reviv'd Patterns us no more improve,
  Than Flow'rs so rais'd by Chymists make us sweet,

Yet when the souls disease we desp'rate finde,
  Poets the old renown'd Physitians are,
Who for the sickly habits of the mind,
  Examples as the ancient cure prepare.

And bravely then Physitians honor gain,
  When to the World diseases cureless seem,
And they (in Science valiant) ne'er refrain
  Art's war with Nature, till they life redeem.

But Poets their accustom'd task have long
  Forborn, (who for Examples did disperse
The *Heroes* vertues in Heroick Song)
  And now think vertue sick, past cure of verse.

Yet to this desp'rate cure I will proceed,
  Such patterns shew as shall not fail to move;
Shall teach the valiant patience when they bleed,
  And hapless Lovers constancy in Love.

Gondibert, 1650, Book i, Canto 3, St. 1–9 (text from *Works*, 1673)

343 *To the Queen, entertain'd at night by the Countess of Anglesey*

FAIRE as unshaded Light; or as the Day
In its first birth, when all the Year was *May*;
Sweet, as the Altars smoke, or as the new
Unfolded Bud, swell'd by the early dew;
Smooth, as the face of waters first appear'd,
Ere Tides began to strive, or Winds were heard:
Kind as the willing Saints, and calmer farre,
Than in their sleeps forgiven Hermits are:
You that are more, than our discreter feare
Dares praise, with such full Art, what make you here?
Here, where the Summer is so little seen,
That leaves (her cheapest wealth) scarce reach at green,
You come, as if the silver Planet were
Misled a while from her much injur'd Sphere,
And t' ease the travailes of her beames to night,
In this small Lanthorn would contract her light.

Madagascar, 1638 (text from *Works*, 1673)

344 *For the Lady Olivia Porter; a Present upon a New-years Day*

GOE! hunt the whiter Ermine! and present
His wealthy skin, as this dayes Tribute sent
To my *Endimion*'s Love; Though she be farre
More gently smooth, more soft than Ermines are!
Goe! climbe that Rock! and when thou there hast found
A Star, contracted in a Diamond,
Give it *Endimion*'s Love, whose glorious Eyes,
Darken the starry Jewels of the Skies!

Goe! dive into the Southern Sea! and when
Th'ast found (to trouble the nice sight of Men)
A swelling Pearle; and such whose single worth,
Boasts all the wonders which the Seas bring forth;
Give it *Endimion*'s Love! whose ev'ry Teare,
Would more enrich the skilful Jeweller.
How I command! how slowly they obey!
The churlish *Tartar*, will not hunt to-day:
Nor will that lazy, sallow *Indian* strive
To climbe the Rock, nor that dull *Negro* dive.
Thus Poets like to Kings (by trust deceiv'd)
Give oftner what is heard of, than receiv'd.

Madagascar (text 1673)

345 *Song*

THE Lark now leaves his watry Nest
And climbing, shakes his dewy Wings;
He takes this Window for the East;
And to implore your Light, he Sings,
Awake, awake, the Morn will never rise,
Till she can dress her Beauty at your Eyes.

The Merchant bowes unto the Seamans Star,
The Ploughman from the Sun his Season takes;
But still the Lover wonders what they are,
Who look for day before his Mistress wakes.
Awake, awake, break through your Vailes of Lawne!
Then draw your Curtains, and begin the Dawne.

Works, 1673

346 *Song*

Endimion Porter and Olivia

Olivia

BEFORE we shall again behold
In his diurnal race the Worlds great Eye,
We may as silent be and cold,
As are the shades where buried Lovers lie.

Endimion

Olivia 'tis no fault of Love
To lose our selves in death, but O, I fear,
When Life and Knowledge is above
Restor'd to us, I shall not know thee there.

Olivia

Call it not Heaven (my Love) where we
Our selves shall see, and yet each other miss:
So much of Heaven I find in thee
As, thou unknown, all else privation is.

Endimion

Why should we doubt, before we go
To find the Knowledge which shall ever last,
That we may there each other know?
Can future Knowledge quite destroy the past?

Olivia

When at the Bowers in the Elizian shade
I first arrive, I shall examine where
They dwell, who love the highest Vertue made?
For I am sure to find *Endimion* there.

Endimion

From this vext World when we shall both retire,
Where all are Lovers, and where all rejoyce;
I need not seek thee in the Heavenly Quire;
For I shall know *Olivia* by her Voice.

Works, 1673

347 *Life and Death*

FRAIL Life! in which, through mists of human breath
We grope for truth, and make our progress slow,
Because by passion blinded; till, by death
Our passions ending, we begin to know.

O reverend Death! whose looks can soon advise
E'en scornful youth, while priests their doctrine waste;
Yet mocks us too; for he does make us wise,
When by his coming our affairs are past.

O harmless Death! whom still the valiant brave,
The wise expect, the sorrowful invite,
And all the good embrace, who know the grave
A short dark passage to eternal light.

From *The Christians Reply to the Philosopher* (*Works*, 1673)

EDMUND WALLER

1606–1687

348 *The story of Phoebus and Daphne applyed, &c*

THIRSIS a youth of the inspired train,
Faire *Sacharissa* lov'd, but lov'd in vain;
Like *Phœbus* sung, the no less amorous boy;
Like *Daphne*, she as lovely and as coy;

With numbers, he the flying Nymph pursues,
With numbers, such as *Phœbus* selfe might use;
Such is the chase, when love and fancy leads
O'er craggy mountains, and through flowry meads,
Invok'd to testifie the lovers care,
Or forme some image of his cruell Faire:
Urg'd with his fury like a wounded Deer
O'er these he fled, and now approaching neer,
Had reach'd the Nymph with his harmonious lay,
Whom all his charmes could not incline to stay.
Yet what he sung in his immortall straine,
Though unsuccessfull, was not sung in vaine,
All but the Nymph that should redress his wrong,
Attend his passion, and approve his song.
  Like *Phœbus* thus acquiring unsought praise,
  He catch'd at love, and fill'd his arm with bayes.

Poems, 1645

349 *The selfe banished*

IT is not that I love you less,
Than when before your feet I lay,
But to prevent the sad increase
Of hopeless love, I keep away.

In vaine (alas!) for everything
Which I have knowne belong to you,
Your forme does to my fancy bring,
And make my old wounds bleed anew.

Who in the Spring from the new Sun
Already has a Fever got,
Too late begins these shafts to shun
Which Phœbus through his veines has shot.

Too late he would the paine assuage,
And to thick shadowes does retire;
About with him he beares the rage,
And in his tainted blood the fire.

But vow'd I have, and never must
Your banish'd servant trouble you;
For if I breake, you may mistrust
The vow I made to love you too.

Poems, 1645

350 *Song*

GOE lovely Rose,
Tell her that wastes her time and me,
That now she knowes,
When I resemble her to thee,
How sweet and fair she seems to be.

Tell her that 's young,
And shuns to have her graces spied,
That hadst thou sprung
In deserts where no men abide,
Thou must have uncommended died.

Small is the worth
Of beauty from the light retir'd:
Bid her come forth,
Suffer her selfe to be desir'd,
And not blush so to be admir'd.

Then die, that she
The common fate of all things rare
May read in thee,
How small a part of time they share,
That are so wondrous sweet and faire.

Poems, 1645

351 *On a Girdle*

THAT which her slender waist confin'd,
Shall now my joyfull temples bind;
No Monarch but would give his Crowne
His Armes might doe what this has done.

It is my Heavens extreamest Spheare,
The pale which held the lovely Deare,
My joy, my griefe, my hope, my Love,
Doe all within this Circle move.

A narrow compass, and yet there
Dwells all that 's good, and all that 's faire:
Give me but what this Ribbon ty'd,
Take all the sun goes round beside.

Poems, 1645

352 *A Panegyrick to my Lord Protector*

WHILE with a strong, and yet a gentle Hand
You bridle Faction, and our Hearts command;
Protect us from our Selves, and from the Foe;
Make us Unite, and make us Conquer too;
Let partial Spirits still aloud complain,
Think themselves injur'd that they cannot Raign,
And own no Liberty, but where they may
Without controule upon their Fellows prey.
Above the Waves as *Neptune* shew'd his Face
To chide the Winds, and save the *Trojan* Race;
So has your Highness rais'd above the rest
Storms of Ambition tossing us represt:
Your drooping Country torn with Civill Hate,
Restor'd by you, is made a glorious State;

The seat of Empire, where the *Irish* come,
And the unwilling *Scotch* to fetch their doome:
The Sea 's our own, and now all Nations greet
With bending Sayles each Vessel of our Fleet;
Your Power extends as far as Winds can blowe,
Or swelling Sayles upon the Globe may goe.
  Heav'n, that has plac'd this Island to give Lawe,
To balance *Europe*, and her States to awe,
In this Conjunction does on *Britain* smile,
The greatest Leader, and the greatest Ile;
Whether this portion of the World were rent
By the rude Ocean from the Continent,
Or thus Created, it was sure design'd
To be the Sacred Refuge of Mankind.
Hither th' oppressed shall henceforth resort,
Justice to crave, and Succour at your Court;
And then your Highness, not for ours alone,
But for the Worlds Protector shall be known:
Fame, swifter than your winged Navie, flyes
Through every Land that near the Ocean lyes,
Sounding your Name, and telling dreadfull newes
To all that Piracy and Rapine use:
With such a Chief the meanest Nation blest,
Might hope to lift her Head above the rest;
What may be thought impossible to doe
For us embraced by the Sea and You?
  Lords of the Worlds great Waste, the Ocean, we
Whole Forrests send to Raigne upon the Sea,
And ev'ry Coast may trouble or relieve,
But none can visit us without your leave;
Angels and we have this Prerogative,
That none can at our happy Seat arrive,

While we descend at pleasure to invade
The Bad with vengeance, or the Good to aide:
Our little World, the Image of the Great,
Like that amidst the boundless Ocean set,
Of her own Growth has all that Nature craves,
And all that 's Rare as Tribute from the Waves;
As *Egypt* does not on the Clouds rely,
But to her *Nile* owes more, than to the Sky;
So what our Earth, and what our Heav'n denies,
Our ever constant Friend, the Sea, supplies;
The taste of hot *Arabia's* Spice we know,
Free from the scorching Sun that makes it grow;
Without the Worm in *Persian* Silks we shine,
And without Planting Drink of every Vine;
  To dig for Wealth we weary not our Limbs,
Gold, though the heavy'st Metall, hither swims;
Ours is the Harvest where the *Indians* mowe,
We plough the Deep, and reap what others Sowe.
Things of the noblest kinde our own soyle breeds,
Stout are our men, and Warlike are our Steeds;
Rome, though her Eagle through the world had flown,
Could never make this Island all her own;
Here the third *Edward*, and the black Prince too,
France conqu'ring *Henry* flourisht, and now You
For whom we stay'd, as did the *Grecian* State,
Till *Alexander* came to urge their Fate:
  When for more Worlds the *Macedonian* cry'd,
He wist not *Thetis* in her Lap did hide
Another yet, a world reserv'd for you
To make more great, than that he did subdue:
He safely might old Troops to Battle leade
Against th' unwarlike *Persian*, and the *Mede*,

Whose hastie flight did, from a bloodless Field,
More Spoyle than Honor to the Victor yield;
  A Race unconquer'd, by their Clime made bold,
The *Calidonians* arm'd with want and cold,
Have, by a fate indulgent to your Fame,
Bin, from all Ages, kept, for you to tame,
Whom the old *Roman* wall so ill confin'd,
With a new chain of Garisons you bind,
Here forraign Gold no more shall make them come,
Our *English* Iron holds them fast at home;
They, that henceforth must be content to know,
No warmer Region than their Hills of Snow,
May blame the Sun, but must extoll your Grace,
Which in our Senate has allow'd them place;
Preferr'd by Conquest, happily o'erthrowne,
Falling they rise, to be with us made one;
So kinde Dictators made, when they came home,
Their vanquish'd Foes, free Citizens of *Rome*.
  Like favor find the *Irish*, with like Fate
Advanc'd to be a portion of our State;
While by your Valour, and your Courteous mind
Nations divided by the Sea are joyn'd.
  Holland, to gain your Friendship, is content
To be our Out-guard on the Continent;
She from her fellow-Provinces would goe,
Rather than hazard to have you her Foe:
In our late Fight when Cannons did diffuse
Preventing posts, the terror and the newes
Our neighbor-Princes trembled at their roar,
But our Conjunction makes them tremble more.
  Your never failing Sword made War to cease,
And now you heale us with the arts of Peace,

Our minds with bounty, and with awe engage,
Invite affection, and restrain our rage:
Less pleasure take, brave minds in battles won,
Than in restoring such as are undon,
Tygers have courage, and the rugged Bear,
But man alone can, whom he conquers, spare.
To pardon willing, and to punish loath,
You strike with one hand, but you heal with both,
Lifting up all that prostrate lie, you grieve
You cannot make the dead again to live:
When Fate, or Error had our Age mis-led,
And o'er these Nations such confusion spred,
The onely cure which could from Heav'n come down,
Was so much Power and Clemency in one.
  One, whose Extraction from an ancient Line,
Gives hope again that well-born Men may shine,
The meanest in your Nature milde and good,
The noble rest secured in your Blood:
Oft have we wonder'd how you hid in Peace
A minde proportion'd to such things as these?
How such a Ruling-spirit you could restrain?
And practice first over your self to raign?
Your private Life did a just pattern give
How Fathers, Husbands, pious Sons, should live,
Born to command, your Princely vertues slept
Like humble *David's*, while the Flock he kept;
But when your troubled Countrey call'd you forth,
Your flaming Courage, and your Matchless worth
Dazzling the eyes of all that did pretend
To fierce Contention, gave a prosp'rous end:
Still as you rise, the State exalted too,
Finds no distemper, while 'tis chang'd by you.

Chang'd like the Worlds great Scene, when without noise,
The rising Sun Nights vulgar Lights destroyes.
  Had you some Ages past, this Race of glory
Run, with amazement, we should read your story;
But living Virtue, all achievements past,
Meets Envy still to grapple with at last.
This *Cæsar* found, and that ungrateful Age
Which losing him, fell back to blood and rage:
Mistaken *Brutus* thought to break their yoke,
But cut the bond of Union with that stroke.
That Sun once set, a thousand meaner Stars,
Gave a dim light to Violence and Wars,
To such a Tempest, as now threatens all,
Did not your mighty Arm prevent the fall.
  If *Romes* great Senate could not wield that Sword,
Which of the Conquer'd world had made them Lord,
What hope had ours, while yet their power was new,
To rule victorious Armies but by you?
You that had taught them to subdue their Foes,
Could Order teach, and their high Spirits compose,
To every Duty could their Minds engage,
Provoke their Courage, and command their Rage.
So when a Lyon shakes his dreadfull Mane,
And angry growes, if he that first took pain
To tame his youth, approach the haughty Beast,
He bends to him, but frights away the rest.
As the vex'd World to finde repose at last
It self into *Augustus* arms did cast;
So *England* now does with like toyle opprest,
Her weary Head upon your Bosome rest.
  Then let the Muses with such Notes as these
Instruct us what belongs unto our peace;

Your Battles they hereafter shall indite,
And draw the Image of our *Mars* in fight:
Tell of Towns storm'd, of Armies over-run,
And mighty Kingdomes by your Conduct won;
How while you thunder'd, Clouds of Dust did choke
Contending Troops, and Seas lay hid in smoke:
Illustrious acts high Raptures doe infuse,
And every Conqueror creates a Muse.
  Here in low Strains your milder Deeds we sing,
But there (my Lord) we'll Bayes and Olive bring
To Crown your Head, while you in Triumph ride
O'er vanquish'd Nations, and the Sea beside;
While all your Neighbor Princes unto you
Like *Josephs's* Sheaves pay reverence and bow.

A Panegyrick, 1655

353 *To a very young Lady*

WHY came I so untimely forth
Into a world which wanting thee
Could entertain us with no worth
Or shadow of felicity?
  That time should me so far remove
  From that which I was born to love.

Yet fairest blossome do not slight
That age which you may know so soon;
The rosie Morn resignes her light,
And milder glory to the Noon:
  And then what wonder shall you do,
  Whose dawning beauty warns us so?

Hope waits upon the flowry prime,
And Summer though it be less gay,
Yet is not look't on as a time
Of declination and decay.
  For with a full hand that does bring
  All that was promis'd by the Spring.

Poems, 1664

354 *Of English Verse*

POETS may boast (as safely vain)
  Their work shall with the world remain
Both bound together, live, or dye,
The Verses and the Prophecy.
  But who can hope his lines should long
Last in a daily changing Tongue?
While they are new, envy prevails,
And as that dies, our language fails;
  When Architects have done their part
The Matter may betray their Art,
Time, if we use ill-chosen stone,
Soon brings a well-built Palace down.
  Poets that lasting Marble seek
Must carve in *Latine* or in *Greek*,
We write in Sand, our Language grows,
And like the Tide our work o'erflows.
  Chaucer his Sense can only boast,
The glory of his numbers lost,
Years have defac'd his matchless strain,
And yet he did not sing in vain;
  The Beauties which adorn'd that age
The shining Subjects of his rage,

Hoping they should immortal prove
Rewarded with success his love.
  This was the generous Poets scope
And all an *English* Pen can hope,
To make the fair approve his Flame
That can so far extend their Fame.
  Verse thus design'd has no ill fate
If it arrive but at the Date
Of fading Beauty, if it prove
But as long liv'd as present love.

Poems, 1668

355 *Of the last Verses in the Book*

WHEN we for Age could neither read nor write
The subject made us able to indite.
The Soul with nobler Resolutions deckt,
The Body stooping, does Herself erect:
No Mortal Parts are requisite to raise
Her, that Unbody'd can her Maker praise.

The Seas are quiet, when the Winds give o'er
So calm are we, when Passions are no more:
For then we know how vain it was to boast
Of fleeting Things, so certain to be lost.
Clouds of Affection from our younger Eyes
Conceal that emptiness, which Age descries.

The Soul's dark Cottage, batter'd and decay'd,
Lets in new Light thro' chinks that time has made.
Stronger by weakness, wiser Men become
As they draw near to their Eternal home:
Leaving the old, both Worlds at once they view,
That stand upon the threshold of the New.

Poems, 1686

SIR RICHARD FANSHAWE

1608–1666

356 *An Ode, upon occasion of His Majesties Proclamation in the Year 1630. Commanding the Gentry to reside upon their Estates in the Countrey.*

NOW War is all the World about,
And everywhere *Erynnis* raigns,
Or else the Torch so late put out,
The stench remains.

Holland for many years hath been
Of Christian Tragedies the Stage,
Yet seldom hath she play'd a Scene
Of bloodier rage.

And *France* that was not long compos'd
With civil Drums again resounds,
And ere the old are fully clos'd,
Receives new wounds.

The great *Gustavus* in the West,
Plucks the Imperial Eagles wing,
Than whom the earth did ne'er invest
A fiercer King;

Revenging lost *Bohemia*,
And the proud wrongs which *Tilly* dud,
And tempereth the *German* clay
With *Spanish* blood.

What should I tell of *Polish* Bands,
And the bloods boyling in the North?
'Gainst whom the furied *Russians*
Their Troops bring forth

Both confident: This in his purse,
And needy Valor set on work;
He in his Axe; which oft did worse
Th' invading *Turk*.

Who now sustains a *Persian* storm:
There Hell (that made it) suffers Schism:
This War (forsooth) was to reform
Mahumetism.

Only the Island which we sow,
(A World without the World) so far
From present wounds, it cannot show
An ancient scar.

White Peace (the beautifull'st of things)
Seems here her everlasting rest
To fix, and spreads her downy Wings
Over the Nest:

As when great *Jove*, usurping Reign,
From the plagu'd World did her exile,
And ty'd her with a golden Chain
To one blest Isle:

Which in a Sea of plenty swam
And Turtles sang on ev'ry Bough,
A safe retreat to all that came
As ours is now.

Yet we, as if some Foe were here,
Leave the despised Fields to Clowns,
And come to save ourselves as 'twere
In walled Towns.

Hither we bring Wives, Babes, rich Cloaths
And Gems; Till now my Soveraign
The growing evil doth oppose:
Counting in vain

His care preserves us from annoy
Of Enemies his Realms t'invade,
Unless he force us to enjoy
The peace he made.

To roll themselves in envy'd leisure,
He therefore sends the Landed Heirs,
Whilst he proclaims not his own pleasure
So much as theirs.

The sap and blood o'th' Land, which fled
Into the Root, and choakt the Heart,
Are bid their quickning pow'r to spread
Through ev'ry part.

O! 'Twas an Act, not for my Muse
To celebrate, nor the dull Age,
Until the Countrey Air infuse
A purer rage!

And if the Fields as thankful prove
For benefits receiv'd, as seed,
They will, to quite so great a love,
A *Virgil* breed.

A *Tytirus*, that shall not cease
Th' *Augustus* of our World to praise
In equal Verse, Author of Peace
And *Halcyon* days.

Nor let the Gentry grudge to go
Into those places whence they grew,
But think them blest they may do so.
Who would pursue

The smoky glory of the Town,
That may go till his native Earth,
And by the shining Fire sit down
Of his own hearth,

Free from the griping Scriveners Bands,
And the more biting Mercers Books;
Free from the bait of oyled hands
And painted looks?

The Countrey too ev'n chops for rain:
You that exhale it by your power,
Let the fat drops fall down again
In a full shower.

And you bright beauties of the time,
That waste your selves here in a blaze,
Fix to your Orb and proper Clime
Your wandring rays.

Let no dark corner of the Land
Be unimbellisht with one Gem;
And those which here too thick do stand
Sprinkle on them.

Believe me Ladies you will find
In that sweet life, more solid joyes,
More true contentment to the mind
Than all Town-toys.

Nor *Cupid* there less blood doth spill,
But heads his shafts with chaster love,
Not feathered with a Sparrows quill,
But of a Dove.

There shall you hear the Nightingale
(The harmless Syren of the Wood)
How prettily she tells a tale
Of Rape and Blood.

The Lyrick Lark, with all beside
Of Natures feathered quire: and all
The Commonwealth of Flowers in 'ts pride
Behold you shall.

The Lilly (Queen) the (Royal) Rose,
The Gilly-flower (Prince of the blood)
The (Courtier) Tulip (gay in Cloaths)
The (Regal) Bud

The Violet (purple Senator),
How they do mock the pomp of State,
And all that at the surly door
Of great ones wait.

Plant Trees you may, and see them shoot
Up with your Children, to be serv'd
To your clean Boards, and the fair'st Fruit
To be preserv'd:

And learn to use their several Gums;
'Tis innocence in the sweet blood
Of Cherry, Apricocks and Plums
To be imbru'd.

Il Pastor Fido, 1648 (text 1676)

357

Hope

TO hope is good, but with such wild applause
Each promise *Fabius* thou dost entertain;
As if decreed thee by fates certain Laws,
Or in possession *now* it did remain.

Wisdom is arm'd 'gainst all that can succeed,
Time's changes and his stratagems: for such
His nature is, that when his wings we need,
He will come creeping on his halting Crutch.

Do not, if wise, then to thy self assure
The future, nor on present goods rely,
Or think there's any time from time secure:
For then when patience sees her Harvest nigh,

That mocking Tyrant in an instant rears
A wall between the sickle and the ears.

Il Pastor Fido, 1648 (text 1676)

358

The Fall

THE bloody trunk of him who did possess
Above the rest a hapless happy state,
This little stone doth seal, but not depress,
And scarce can stop the rolling of his fate.

Brass Tombs which justice hath deny'd t' his fault,
The common pity to his virtues payes,
Adorning an imaginary Vault,
Which from our minds time strives in vain to raze.

'gainst: against 1676. *The Fall.* On the death of Charles I.

Ten years the world upon him falsly smil'd,
Sheathing in fawning looks the deadly Knife
Long aimed at his head; that so beguil'd
It more securely might bereave his life:

Then threw him to a Scaffold from a Throne,
Much Doctrine lies under this little Stone.

Il Pastor Fido, 1648 (text 1676)

359 *A Rose*

BLOWN in the morning, thou shalt fade ere noon:
What boots a life which in such haste forsakes thee?
Th' art wond'rous frolick being to die so soon:
And passing proud a little colour makes thee.

If thee thy brittle beauty so deceives,
Know then the thing that swells thee is thy bane;
For the same beauty doth in bloody Leaves
The sentence of thy early death contain.

Some clowns coarse lungs will poyson thy sweet flow'r
If by the careless Plow thou shalt be torn:
And many *Herods* lie in wait each hour
To murther thee as soon as thou art born:

Nay, force thy bud to blow; their tyrant breath
Anticipating life, to hasten Death.

Il Pastor Fido, 1648 (text 1676)

JOHN MILTON

1608–1674

360 *At a Vacation Exercise*

HAIL native Language, that by sinews weak
Didst move my first endeavouring tongue to speak,
And mad'st imperfect words with childish tripps,
Half unpronounc't, slide through my infant-lipps,
Driving dum silence from the portal dore,
Where he had mutely sate two years before:
Here I salute thee and thy pardon ask,
That now I use thee in my latter task:
Small loss it is that thence can come unto thee,
I know my tongue but little Grace can do thee:
Thou needst not be ambitious to be first,
Believe me I have thither packt the worst:
And, if it happen as I did forecast,
The daintest dishes shall be serv'd up last.
I pray thee then deny me not thy aide
For this same small neglect that I have made:
But haste thee strait to do me once a Pleasure,
And from thy wardrope bring thy chiefest treasure;
Not those new fangled toys, and trimming slight
Which takes our late fantasticks with delight,
But cull those richest Robes, and gay'st attire
Which deepest Spirits, and choicest Wits desire:
I have some naked thoughts that rove about
And loudly knock to have their passage out;
And wearie of their place do only stay
Till thou hast deck't them in thy best aray;
That so they may without suspect or fears
Fly swiftly to this fair Assembly's ears;

Yet I had rather if I were to chuse,
Thy service in some graver subject use,
Such as may make thee search thy coffers round,
Before thou cloath my fancy in fit sound:
Such where the deep transported mind may soare
Above the wheeling poles, and at Heav'ns dore
Look in, and see each blissful Deitie
How he before the thunderous throne doth lie,
Listening to what unshorn *Apollo* sings
To th' touch of golden wires, while *Hebe* brings
Immortal Nectar to her Kingly Sire:
Then passing through the Spheres[1] of watchful fire,
And mistie Regions of wide air next under,
And hills of Snow and lofts of piled Thunder,
May tell at length how green-ey'd *Neptune* raves,
In Heav'ns defiance mustering all his waves;
Then sing of secret things that came to pass
When Beldam Nature in her cradle was;
And last of Kings and Queens and *Heroes* old,
Such as the wise *Demodocus* once told
In solemn Songs at King *Alcinous* feast,
While sad *Ulisses* soul and all the rest
Are held with his melodious harmonie
In willing chains and sweet captivitie.

Poems, &c., upon Several Occasions, 1673

[1] Spherse 1645 and 1673.

361 *On the Morning of Christs Nativity*

THIS is the Month, and this the happy morn
Wherin the Son of Heav'ns eternal King,
Of wedded Maid, and Virgin Mother born,
Our great redemption from above did bring;
For so the holy sages once did sing,
That he our deadly forfeit should release,
And with his Father work us a perpetual peace.

That glorious Form, that Light unsufferable,
And that far-beaming blaze of Majesty,
Wherwith he wont at Heav'ns high Councel-Table,
To sit the midst of Trinal Unity,
He laid aside; and here with us to be,
Forsook the Courts of everlasting Day,
And chose with us a darksom House of mortal Clay.

Say Heav'nly Muse, shall not thy sacred vein
Afford a present to the Infant God?
Hast thou no verse, no hymn, or solemn strein,
To welcom him to this his new abode,
Now while the Heav'n by the Suns team untrod,
Hath took no print of the approching light,
And all the spangled host keep watch in squadrons bright?

See how from far upon the Eastern rode
The Star-led Wisards haste with odours sweet,
O run, prevent them with thy humble ode,
And lay it lowly at his blessed feet;
Have thou the honour first, thy Lord to greet,
And joyn thy voice unto the Angel Quire,
From out his secret Altar toucht with hallow'd fire.

The Hymn

It was the Winter wilde,
While the Heav'n-born-childe,
  All meanly wrapt in the rude manger lies;
Nature in aw to him
Had doff't her gawdy trim,
  With her great Master so to sympathize:
It was no season then for her
To wanton with the Sun her lusty Paramour.

Only with speeches fair
She woo's the gentle Air
  To hide her guilty front with innocent Snow,
And on her naked shame,
Pollute with sinfull blame,
  The Saintly Vail of Maiden white to throw,
Confounded, that her Makers eyes
Should look so neer upon her foul deformities.

But he her fears to cease,
Sent down the meek-eyd Peace,
  She crown'd with Olive green, came softly sliding
Down through the turning sphear
His ready Harbinger,
  With Turtle wing the amorous clouds dividing,
And waving wide her mirtle wand,
She strikes a universall Peace through Sea and Land.

JOHN MILTON

No War, or Battails sound
Was heard the World around,
  The idle spear and shield were high up hung;
The hooked Chariot stood
Unstain'd with hostile blood,
  The Trumpet spake not to the armed throng,
And Kings sate still with awfull eye,
As if they surely knew their sovran Lord was by.

But peacefull was the night
Wherin the Prince of light
  His raign of peace upon the earth began:
The Windes with wonder whist,
Smoothly the waters kist,
  Whispering new joyes to the milde Ocean,
Who now hath quite forgot to rave,
While Birds of Calm sit brooding on the charmed wave.

The Stars with deep amaze
Stand fixt in stedfast gaze,
  Bending one way their pretious influence,
And will not take their flight,
For all the morning light,
  Or *Lucifer* that often warn'd them thence;
But in their glimmering Orbs did glow,
Untill their Lord himself bespake, and bid them go.

And though the shady gloom
Had given day her room,
  The Sun himself with-held his wonted speed,
And hid his head for shame,
As his inferiour flame,
  The new enlightn'd world no more should need;
He saw a greater Sun appear
Than his bright Throne, or burning Axletree could bear.

The Shepherds on the Lawn,
Or ere the point of dawn,
  Sate simply chatting in a rustick row;
Full little thought they than,
That the mighty *Pan*
  Was kindly com to live with them below;
Perhaps their loves, or els their sheep,
Was all that did their silly thoughts so busie keep.

When such musick sweet
Their hearts and ears did greet,
  As never was by mortall finger strook,
Divinely-warbled voice
Answering the stringed noise,
  As all their souls in blisfull rapture took:
The Air such pleasure loth to lose,
With thousand echo's still prolongs each heav'nly close.

Nature that heard such sound
Beneath the hollow round
  Of *Cynthia's* seat, the Airy region thrilling,
Now was almost won
To think her part was don,
  And that her raign had here its last fulfilling;
She knew such harmony alone
Could hold all Heav'n and Earth in happier union.

At last surrounds their sight
A Globe of circular light,
  That with long beams the shame-fac't night array'd,
The helmed Cherubim
And sworded Seraphim,
  Are seen in glittering ranks with wings displaid,
Harping in loud and solemn quire,
With unexpressive notes to Heav'ns new-born Heir.

Such Musick (as 'tis said)
Before was never made,
  But when of old the sons of morning sung,
While the Creator Great
His constellations set,
  And the well-ballanc't world on hinges hung,
And cast the dark foundations deep,
And bid the weltring waves their oozy channel keep.

Ring out ye Crystall sphears,
Once bless our human ears,
  (If ye have power to touch our senses so)
And let your silver chime
Move in melodious time;
  And let the Base of Heav'ns deep Organ blow,
And with your ninefold harmony
Make up full consort to th' Angelike symphony.

For if such holy Song
Enwrap our fancy long,
  Time will run back, and fetch the age of gold,
And speckl'd vanity
Will sicken soon and die,
  And leprous sin will melt from earthly mould,
And Hell it self will pass away,
And leave her dolorous mansions to the peering day.

Yea Truth, and Justice then
Will down return to men,
  Th' enameld *Arras* of the Rain-bow wearing,
And Mercy set between,[1]
Thron'd in Celestiall sheen,
  With radiant feet the tissued clouds down stearing,
And Heav'n as at som festivall,
Will open wide the Gates of her high Palace Hall.

[1] Orb'd in a Rain-bow; and like glories wearing
Mercy will sit between   1673

But wisest Fate sayes no,
This must not yet be so,
  The Babe lies yet in smiling Infancy,
That on the bitter cross
Must redeem our loss;
  So both himself and us to glorifie:
Yet first to those ychain'd in sleep,
The wakefull trump of doom must thunder through the deep,

With such a horrid clang
As on mount *Sinai* rang
  While the red fire, and smouldring clouds out brake:
The aged Earth agast
With terrour of that blast,
  Shall from the surface to the center shake;
When at the worlds last session,
The dreadfull Judge in middle Air shall spread his throne.

And then at last our bliss
Full and perfect is,
  But now begins; for from this happy day
Th'old Dragon under ground
In straiter limits bound,
  Not half so far casts his usurped sway,
And wrath to see his Kingdom fail,
Swindges the scaly Horrour of his foulded tail.

The Oracles are dumm,
No voice or hideous humm
  Runs through the arched roof in words deceiving.
Apollo from his shrine
Can no more divine,
  With hollow shreik the steep of *Delphos* leaving.
No nightly trance, or breathed spell,
Inspire's the pale-ey'd Priest from the prophetic cell.

The lonely mountains o're,
And the resounding shore,
  A voice of weeping heard, and loud lament;
From haunted spring, and dale
Edg'd with poplar pale,
  The parting Genius is with sighing sent,
With flowre-inwov'n tresses torn
The Nimphs in twilight shade of tangled thickets mourn.

In consecrated Earth,
And on the holy Hearth,
  The *Lars*, and *Lemures* moan with midnight plaint,
In Urns, and Altars round,
A drear, and dying sound
  Affrights the *Flamins* at their service quaint;
And the chill Marble seems to sweat,
While each peculiar power forgoes his wonted seat.

Peor, and *Baalim*,
Forsake their Temples dim,
  With that twice-batter'd god of *Palestine*,
And mooned *Ashtaroth*,
Heav'ns Queen and Mother both,
  Now sits not girt with Tapers holy shine,
The Libyc *Hammon* shrinks his horn,
In vain the *Tyrian* Maids their wounded *Thamuz* mourn.

And sullen *Moloch* fled,
Hath left in shadows dred,
  His burning Idol all of blackest hue,
In vain with Cymbals ring,
They call the grisly king,
  In dismall dance about the furnace blue;
The brutish gods of *Nile* as fast,
Isis and *Orus*, and the Dog *Anubis* hast.

Nor is *Osiris* seen
In *Memphian* Grove, or Green,
  Trampling the unshowr'd Grasse with lowings loud:
Nor can he be at rest
Within his sacred chest,
  Naught but profoundest Hell can be his shroud,
In vain with Timbrel'd Anthems dark
The sable-stoled Sorcerers bear his worshipt Ark.

He feels from *Juda's* Land
The dredded Infants hand,
  The rayes of *Bethlehem* blind his dusky eyn;
Nor all the gods beside,
Longer dare abide,
  Not *Typhon* huge ending in snaky twine:
Our Babe to shew his Godhead true,
Can in his swadling bands controul the damned crew.

So when the Sun in bed,
Curtain'd with cloudy red,
  Pillows his chin upon an Orient wave,
The flocking shadows pale,
Troop to th' infernall jail,
  Each fetter'd Ghost slips to his severall grave,
And the yellow-skirted *Fayes*,
Fly after the Night-steeds, leaving their Moon-lov'd maze.

But see the Virgin blest,
Hath laid her Babe to rest.
  Time is our tedious Song should here have ending,
Heav'ns youngest teemed Star,
Hath fixt her polisht Car,
  Her sleeping Lord with Handmaid Lamp attending:
And all about the Courtly Stable,
Bright-harnest Angels sit in order serviceable.

Poems, 1645

362 *An Epitaph on the Marchioness of Winchester*

THIS rich Marble doth enter
The honour'd Wife of *Winchester*,
A Vicounts daughter, an Earls heir,
Besides what her vertues fair
Added to her noble birth,
More than she could own from Earth.
Summers three times eight save one
She had told, alas too soon,
After so short time of breath,
To house with darknes, and with death.
Yet had the number of her days
Bin as compleat as was her praise,
Nature and fate had had no strife
In giving limit to her life.
Her high birth, and her graces sweet,
Quickly found a lover meet;
The Virgin quire for her request
The God that sits at marriage feast;
He at their invoking came
But with a scarce-wel-lighted flame;
And in his Garland as he stood,
Ye might discern a Cypress bud.
Once had the early Matrons run
To greet her of a lovely son,
And now with second hope she goes,
And calls *Lucina* to her throws;
But whether by mischance or blame
Atropos for *Lucina* came;
And with remorsless cruelty,

enter: inter

Spoil'd at once both fruit and tree:
The hapless Babe before his birth
Had burial, yet not laid in earth,
And the languisht Mothers Womb
Was not long a living Tomb.
So have I seen som tender slip
Sav'd with care from Winters nip,
The pride of her carnation train,
Pluck't up by som unheedy swain,
Who onely thought to crop the flowr
New shot up from vernall showr;
But the fair blossom hangs the head
Side-ways as on a dying bed,
And those Pearls of dew she wears,
Prove to be presaging tears
Which the sad morn had let fall
On her hast'ning funerall.
Gentle Lady may thy grave
Peace and quiet ever have;
After this thy travail sore
Sweet rest sease thee evermore,
That to give the world encrease,
Shortned hast thy own lives lease;
Here besides the sorrowing
That thy noble House doth bring,
Here be tears of perfect moan
Weept for thee in *Helicon*,
And som Flowers, and som Bays,
For thy Hearse to strew the ways,
Sent thee from the banks of *Came*,
Devoted to thy vertuous name;
Whilst thou bright Saint high sit'st in glory,

Next her much like to thee in story,
That fair *Syrian* Shepherdess,
Who after yeers of barrenness,
The highly favour'd *Joseph* bore
To him that serv'd for her before,
And at her next birth much like thee,
Through pangs fled to felicity,
Far within the boosom bright
Of blazing Majesty and Light,
There with thee, new welcom Saint,
Like fortunes may her soul acquaint,
With thee there clad in radiant sheen,
No Marchioness, but now a Queen.

Poems, 1645

363 *On Time*

FLY envious *Time*, till thou run out thy race,
Call on the lazy leaden-stepping hours,
Whose speed is but the heavy Plummets pace;
And glut thy self with what thy womb devours,
Which is no more than what is false and vain,
And meerly mortal dross;
So little is our loss,
So little is thy gain.
For when as each thing bad thou hast entomb'd,
And last of all, thy greedy self consum'd,
Then long Eternity shall greet our bliss
With an individual kiss;
And Joy shall overtake us as a flood,
When every thing that is sincerely good
And perfectly divine,
With Truth, and Peace, and Love shall ever shine

About the supreme Throne
Of him, t' whose happy-making sight alone,
When once our heav'nly-guided soul shall clime,
Then all this Earthy grossness quit,
Attir'd with Stars, we shall for ever sit,
Triumphing over Death, and Chance, and thee O Time.

Poems, 1645

364 *At a Solemn Musick*

BLEST pair of *Sirens*, pledges of Heav'ns joy,
Sphear-born harmonious Sisters, Voice, and Verse,
Wed your divine sounds, and mixt power employ
Dead things with inbreath'd sense able to pierce,
And to our high-rais'd phantasie present,
That undisturbed Song of pure concent,
Ay sung before the saphire-colour'd throne
To him that sits theron
With Saintly shout, and solemn Jubily,
Where the bright Seraphim in burning row
Their loud up-lifted Angel trumpets blow,
And the Cherubick host in thousand quires
Touch their immortal Harps of golden wires,
With those just Spirits that wear victorious Palms,
Hymns devout and holy Psalms
Singing everlastingly;
That we on Earth with undiscording voice
May rightly answer that melodious noise;
As once we did, till disproportion'd sin
Jarr'd against natures chime, and with harsh din
Broke the fair musick that all creatures made
To their great Lord, whose love their motion sway'd

concent 1673; content 1645.

In perfect Diapason, whilst they stood
In first obedience, and their state of good.
O may we soon again renew that Song,
And keep in tune with Heav'n, till God ere long
To his celestial consort us unite,
To live with him, and sing in endless morn of light.

Poems, 1645

365 *L'Allegro*

HENCE loathed Melancholy
 Of *Cerberus*, and blackest midnight born,
In *Stygian* Cave forlorn
 'Mongst horrid shapes, and shreiks, and sights unholy,
Find out som uncouth cell,
 Where brooding darkness spreads his jealous wings,
And the night-Raven sings;
 There under *Ebon* shades, and low-brow'd Rocks,
As ragged as thy Locks,
 In dark *Cimmerian* desert ever dwell.
But com thou Goddes fair and free,
In Heav'n ycleap'd *Euphrosyne*,
And by men, heart-easing Mirth,
Whom lovely *Venus* at a birth
With two sister Graces more
To Ivy-crowned *Bacchus* bore;
Or whether (as som Sager sing)
The frolick Wind that breathes the Spring,
Zephir with *Aurora* playing,
As he met her once a Maying,
There on Beds of Violets blew,
And fresh-blown Roses washt in dew,

Fill'd her with thee a daughter fair,
So bucksom, blith, and debonair.
Haste thee nymph, and bring with thee
Jest and youthful Jollity,
Quips and Cranks, and wanton Wiles,
Nods, and Becks, and Wreathed Smiles,
Such as hang on *Hebe's* cheek,
And love to live in dimple sleek;
Sport that wrinkled Care derides,
And Laughter holding both his sides.
Com, and trip it as ye go
On the light fantastick toe,
And in thy right hand lead with thee,
The Mountain Nymph, sweet Liberty;
And if I give thee honour due,
Mirth, admit me of thy crue
To live with her, and live with thee,
In unreproved pleasures free;
To hear the Lark begin his flight,
And singing startle the dull night,
From his watch-towre in the skies,
Till the dappled dawn doth rise;
Then to com in spight of sorrow,
And at my window bid good morrow,
Through the Sweet-Briar, or the Vine,
Or the twisted Eglantine.
While the Cock with lively din,
Scatters the rear of darkness thin,
And to the stack, or the Barn dore,
Stoutly struts his Dames before,
Oft list'ning how the Hounds and horn
Chearly rouse the slumbring morn,

From the side of som Hoar Hill,
Through the high wood echoing shrill.
Som time walking not unseen
By Hedge-row Elms, on Hillocks green,
Right against the Eastern gate,
Wher the great Sun begins his state,
Rob'd in flames, and Amber light,
The clouds in thousand Liveries dight.
While the Plowman neer at hand,
Whistles o'er the Furrow'd Land,
And the Milkmaid singeth blithe,
And the Mower whets his sithe,
And every Shepherd tells his tale
Under the Hawthorn in the dale.
Strait mine eye hath caught new pleasures
Whilst the Lantskip round it measures,
Russet Lawns, and Fallows Gray,
Where the nibling flocks do stray,
Mountains on whose barren brest
The labouring clouds do often rest:
Meadows trim with Daisies pide,
Shallow Brooks, and Rivers wide.
Towers, and Battlements it sees
Boosom'd high in tufted Trees,
Where perhaps som beauty lies,
The Cynosure of neighbouring eyes.
Hard by, a Cottage chimney smokes,
From betwixt two aged Okes,
Where *Corydon* and *Thyrsis* met,
Are at their savory dinner set
Of Hearbs, and other Country Messes,
Which the neat-handed *Phillis* dresses;

And then in haste her Bowre she leaves,
With *Thestylis* to bind the Sheaves;
Or if the earlier season lead
To the tann'd Haycock in the Mead,
Som times with secure delight
The up-land Hamlets will invite,
When the merry Bells ring round,
And the jocond rebecks sound
To many a youth, and many a maid,
Dancing in the Chequer'd shade;
And young and old com forth to play
On a Sunshine Holyday,
Till the live-long day-light fail,
Then to the Spicy Nut-brown Ale,
With stories of many a feat,
How *Faery Mab* the junkets eat,
She was pincht, and pull'd she sed,
And he by Friars Lanthorn led;
Tells how the drudging *Goblin* swet,
To earn his Cream-bowle duly set,
When in one night, ere glimps of morn,
His shadowy Flale hath thresh'd the Corn
That ten day-labourers could not end,[1]
Then lies him down the Lubbar Fend.
And stretch'd out all the Chimney's length,
Basks at the fire his hairy strength;
And Crop-full out of dores he flings,
Ere the first Cock his Mattin rings.
Thus don the Tales, to bed they creep,
By whispering Windes soon lull'd asleep.
Towred Cities please us then,

[1] *Pronounced* eend.

And the busie hum of men,
Where throngs of Knights and Barons bold,
In weeds of Peace high triumphs hold,
With store of Ladies, whose bright eies
Rain influence, and judge the prise
Of Wit, or Arms, while both contend
To win her Grace, whom all commend.
There let *Hymen* oft appear
In Saffron robe, with Taper clear,
And pomp, and feast, and revelry,
With mask, and antique Pageantry,
Such sights as youthful Poets dream
On Summer eeves by haunted stream.
Then to the well-trod stage anon,
If *Jonsons* learned Sock be on,
Or sweetest *Shakespear* fancies childe,
Warble his native Wood-notes wilde.
And ever against eating Cares,
Lap me in soft *Lydian* Aires,
Married to immortal verse
Such as the meeting soul may pierce
In notes, with many a winding bout
Of linked sweetness long drawn out,
With wanton heed, and giddy cunning,
The melting voice through mazes running;
Untwisting all the chains that ty
The hidden soul of harmony.
That *Orpheus* self may heave his head
From golden slumber on a bed
Of heapt *Elysian* flowres, and hear
Such streins as would have won the ear
Of *Pluto*, to have quite set free

His half regain'd *Eurydice.*
These delights, if thou canst give,
Mirth with thee, I mean to live.

Poems, 1645

366 *Il Penseroso*

HENCE vain deluding joyes,
  The brood of folly without father bred,
How little you bested,
  Or fill the fixed mind with all your toyes;
Dwell in som idle brain,
  And fancies fond with gaudy shapes possess,
As thick and numberless
  As the gay motes that people the Sun Beams,
Or likest hovering dreams
  The fickle Pensioners of *Morpheus* train.
But hail thou Goddess, sage and holy,
Hail divinest Melancholy,
Whose Saintly visage is too bright
To hit the Sense of human sight;
And therfore to our weaker view,
O'er laid with black staid Wisdoms hue.
Black, but such as in esteem,
Prince *Memnons* sister might beseem,
Or that Starr'd *Ethiope* Queen that strove
To set her beauties praise above
The Sea Nymphs, and their powers offended.
Yet thou art higher far descended,
Thee bright-hair'd *Vesta* long of yore,
To solitary *Saturn* bore;
His daughter she (in *Saturns* raign,
Such mixture was not held a stain)

Oft in glimmering Bowres, and glades
He met her, and in secret shades
Of woody *Ida's* inmost grove,
While yet there was no fear of *Jove*.
Com pensive Nun, devout and pure,
Sober, stedfast, and demure,
All in a robe of darkest grain,
Flowing with majestick train,
And sable stole of *Cipres* Lawn,
Over thy decent shoulders drawn.
Com, but keep thy wonted state,
With eev'n step, and musing gate,
And looks commercing with the skies,
Thy rapt soul sitting in thine eyes:
There held in holy passion still,
Forget thy self to Marble, till
With a sad Leaden downward cast,
Thou fix them on the earth as fast.
And joyn with thee calm Peace, and Quiet,
Spare Fast, that oft with gods doth diet,
And hears the Muses in a ring,
Ay round about *Joves* Altar sing.
And adde to these retired Leasure,
That in trim Gardens takes his pleasure;
But first, and chiefest, with thee bring,
Him that yon soars on golden wing,
Guiding the fiery-wheeled throne,
The Cherub Contemplation,
And the mute Silence hist along,
'Less *Philomel* will daign a Song,
In her sweetest, saddest plight,
Smoothing the rugged brow of night,

While *Cynthia* checks her Dragon yoke,
Gently o'er th' accustom'd Oke;
Sweet Bird that shunn'st the noise of folly,
Most musicall, most melancholy!
Thee Chauntress oft the Woods among,
I woo to hear thy eeven-Song;
And missing thee, I walk unseen
On the dry smooth-shaven Green,
To behold the wandring Moon,
Riding neer her highest noon,
Like one that had bin led astray
Through the Heav'ns wide pathless way;
And oft, as if her head she bow'd,
Stooping through a fleecy cloud.
Oft on a Plat of rising ground,
I hear the far-off *Curfeu* sound,
Over som wide-water'd shoar,
Swinging slow with sullen roar;
Or if the Ayr will not permit,
Som still removed place will fit,
Where glowing Embers through the room
Teach light to counterfeit a gloom,
Far from all resort of mirth,
Save the Cricket on the hearth,
Or the Belmans drousie charm,
To bless the dores from nightly harm:
Or let my Lamp at midnight hour,
Be seen in som high lonely Towr,
Where I may oft out-watch the *Bear*,
With thrice great *Hermes*, or unsphear
The spirit of Plato to unfold
What Worlds, or what vast Regions hold

The immortal mind that hath forsook
Her mansion in this fleshly nook:
And of those *Dæmons* that are found
In fire, air, flood, or under ground,
Whose power hath a true consent
With Planet, or with Element.
Som time let Gorgeous Tragedy
In Scepter'd Pall com sweeping by,
Presenting *Thebs*, or *Pelops* line,
Or the tale of *Troy* divine.
Or what (though rare) of later age,
Ennobled hath the Buskind stage.
But, O sad Virgin, that thy power
Might raise *Musæus* from his bower,
Or bid the soul of *Orpheus* sing
Such notes as warbled to the string,
Drew Iron tears down *Pluto's* cheek,
And made Hell grant what Love did seek.
Or call up him that left half told
The story of *Cambuscan* bold,
Of *Camball*, and of *Algarsife*,
And who had *Canace* to wife,
That own'd the vertuous Ring and Glass,
And of the wondrous Horse of Brass,
On which the *Tartar* King did ride;
And if ought else, great *Bards* beside,
In sage and solemn tunes have sung,
Of Turneys and of Trophies hung;
Of Forests, and inchantments drear,
Where more is meant than meets the ear.
Thus night oft see me in thy pale career,
Till civil-suited Morn appeer,

Not trickt and frounc't as she was wont,
With the Attick Boy to hunt,
But Cherchef't in a comly Cloud,
While rocking Winds are Piping loud,
Or usher'd with a shower still,
When the gust hath blown his fill,
Ending on the russling Leaves,
With minute drops from off the Eaves.
And when the Sun begins to fling
His flaring beams, me Goddes bring
To arched walks of twilight groves,
And shadows brown that *Sylvan* loves
Of Pine, or monumental Oake,
Where the rude Ax with heaved stroke,
Was never heard the Nymphs to daunt,
Or fright them from their hallow'd haunt.
There in close covert by som Brook,
Where no profaner eye may look,
Hide me from Day's garish eie,
While the Bee with Honied thie,
That at her flowry work doth sing
And the Waters murmuring
With such consort as they keep,
Entice the dewy-feather'd Sleep;
And let som strange mysterious dream,
Wave at his Wings in Airy stream,
Of lively portrature display'd,
Softly on my eye-lids laid.
And as I wake, sweet musick breath
Above, about, or underneath,
Sent by som spirit to mortals good,

Cherchef't: kerchief'd. thie: thigh.

Or th' unseen Genius of the Wood.
But let my due feet never fail,
To walk the studious Cloysters pale,
And love the high embowed Roof,
With antick Pillars massy proof,
And storied Windows richly dight,
Casting a dim religious light.
There let the pealing Organ blow,
To the full voic'd Quire below,
In Service high, and Anthems cleer,
As may with sweetness, through mine ear,
Dissolve me into extasies,
And bring all Heav'n before mine eyes.
And may at last my weary age
Find out the peacefull hermitage,
The Hairy Gown and Mossy Cell,
Where I may sit and rightly spell
Of every Star that Heav'n doth shew,
And every Herb that sips the dew;
Till old experience do attain
To somthing like Prophetic strain.
These pleasures *Melancholy* give,
And I with thee will choose to live.

Poems, 1645

367 *The Invocation of Comus*

THE Star that bids the Shepherd fold,
Now the top of Heav'n doth hold,
And the gilded Car of Day,
His glowing Axle doth allay
In the steep *Atlantick* stream,
And the slope Sun his upward beam

Shoots against the dusky Pole,
Pacing toward the other gole
Of his Chamber in the East.
Mean while welcom Joy, and Feast,
Midnight shout, and revelry,
Tipsie dance, and Jollity.
Braid your Locks with rosie Twine
Dropping odours, dropping Wine.
Rigor now is gon to bed,
And Advice with scrupulous head,
Strict Age, and sowre Severity,
With their grave Saws in slumber ly.
We that are of purer fire
Imitate the Starry Quire,
Who in their nightly watchfull Sphears,
Lead in swift round the Months and Years.
The Sounds, and Seas with all their finny drove
Now to the Moon in wavering Morrice move,
And on the Tawny Sands and Shelves,
Trip the pert Fairies and the dapper Elves;
By dimpled Brook, and Fountain brim,
The Wood-Nymphs deckt with Daisies trim,
Their merry wakes and pastimes keep:
What hath night to do with sleep?
Night hath better sweets to prove,
Venus now wakes, and wak'ns Love.
Com let us our rights begin,
'Tis onely day-light that makes Sin
Which these dun shades will ne'er report.
Hail Goddesse of Nocturnal sport,
Dark vaild *Cotytto*, t' whom the secret flame

gole: goal. rights: rites.

Of mid-night Torches burns; mysterious Dame
That ne'er art call'd, but when the Dragon woom
Of Stygian darkness spets her thickest gloom,
And makes one blot of all the ayr,
Stay thy cloudy Ebon chair,
Wherin thou rid'st with *Hecat'*, and befriend
Us thy vow'd Priests, till utmost end
Of all thy dues be done, and none left out,
Ere the blabbing Eastern scout,
The nice Morn on th' *Indian* steep
From her cabin'd loop hole peep,
And to the tel-tale Sun discry
Our conceal'd Solemnity.
Com, knit hands, and beat the ground,
In a light fantastick round. *Comus*, lines 93–144

368

Echo

SWEET Echo, sweetest Nymph that liv'st unseen
Within thy airy shell
By slow *Meander's* margent green,
And in the violet imbroider'd vale
Where the love-lorn Nightingale
Nightly to thee her sad Song mourneth well.
Canst thou not tell me of a gentle Pair
That likest thy *Narcissus* are?
O if thou have
Hid them in som flowry Cave,
Tell me but where,
Sweet Queen of Parly, Daughter of the Sphear,
So maist thou be translated to the skies,
And give resounding grace to all Heav'ns Harmonies.
Comus, lines 230–43

woom: womb.

369 *Chastity*

A hidden strength
Which if Heav'n gave it, may be term'd her own:
'Tis chastity, my brother, chastity:
She that has that, is clad in compleat steel,
And like a quiver'd Nymph with Arrows keen
May trace huge Forests, and unharbour'd Heaths,
Infamous Hills, and sandy perilous wildes,
Where through the sacred rayes of Chastity,
No savage fierce, Bandite, or mountaneer
Will dare to soyl her Virgin purity,
Yea there, where very desolation dwels
By grots, and caverns shag'd with horrid shades,
She may pass on with unblench't majesty,
Be it not don in pride, or in presumption.
Som say no evil thing that walks by night
In fog, or fire, by lake, or moorish fen,
Blew meager Hag, or stubborn unlaid ghost,
That breaks his magick chains at *curfeu* time,
No goblin, or swart faëry of the mine,
Hath hurtfull power o'er true virginity.
Do ye beleeve me yet, or shall I call
Antiquity from the old Schools of Greece
To testifie the arms of Chastity?
Hence had the huntress *Dian* her dred bow
Fair silver-shafted Queen for ever chaste,
Wherwith she tam'd the brinded lioness
And spotted mountain pard, but set at nought
The frivolous bolt of *Cupid*, gods and men
Fear'd her stern frown, and she was queen o' th' Woods.
What was that snaky-headed *Gorgon* sheild

That wise *Minerva* wore, unconquer'd Virgin,
Wherwith she freez'd her foes to congeal'd stone?
But rigid looks of Chast austerity,
And noble grace that dash't brute violence
With sudden adoration, and blank aw.
So dear to Heav'n is Saintly chastity,
That when a soul is found sincerely so,
A thousand liveried Angels lacky her,
Driving far off each thing of sin and guilt,
And in cleer dream, and solemn vision
Tell her of things that no gross ear can hear,
Till oft convers with heav'nly habitants
Begin to cast a beam on th' outward shape,
The unpolluted temple of the mind,
And turns it by degrees to the souls essence,
Till all be made immortal: but when lust
By unchaste looks, loose gestures, and foul talk,
But most by lewd and lavish act of sin,
Lets in defilement to the inward parts,
The soul grows clotted by contagion,
Imbodies, and imbrutes, till she quite loose
The divine property of her first being.
Such are those thick and gloomy shadows damp
Oft seen in Charnell vaults, and Sepulchers
Lingering, and sitting by a new made grave,
As loath to leave the body that it lov'd,
And link't it self by carnal sensualty
To a degenerate and degraded state.

Comus, lines 418–75

370 *Temperance and Virginity*

I HAD not thought to have unlockt my lips
In this unhallow'd air, but that this Jugler
Would think to charm my judgement, as mine eyes,
Obtruding false rules pranckt in reasons garb.
I hate when vice can bolt her arguments,
And vertue has no tongue to check her pride:
Impostor do not charge most innocent nature,
As if she would her children should be riotous
With her abundance, she good cateress
Means her provision onely to the good
That live according to her sober laws,
And holy dictate of spare Temperance:
If every just man that now pines with want
Had but a moderate and beseeming share
Of that which lewdly-pamper'd Luxury
Now heaps upon som few with vast excess,
Natures full blessings would be well dispenc't
In unsuperfluous eeven proportion,
And she no whit encomber'd with her store,
And then the giver would be better thank't,
His praise due paid, for swinish gluttony
Ne'er looks to Heav'n amidst his gorgeous feast,
But with besotted base ingratitude
Crams, and blasphemes his feeder. Shall I go on?
Or have I said anough? To him that dares
Arm his profane tongue with contemptuous words
Against the Sun-clad power of Chastity,
Fain would I somthing say, yet to what end?
Thou hast nor Eare, nor Soul to apprehend

The sublime notion, and high mystery
That must be utter'd to unfold the sage
And serious doctrine of Virginity,
And thou art worthy that thou shouldst not know
More happiness than this thy present lot.
Enjoy your deer Wit, and gay Rhetorick
That hath so well been taught her dazling fence,
Thou art not fit to hear thy self convinc't;
Yet should I try, the uncontrouled worth
Of this pure cause would kindle my rapt spirits
To such a flame of sacred vehemence,
That dumb things would be mov'd to sympathize,
And the brute Earth would lend her nerves, and shake,
Till all thy magick structures rear'd so high,
Were shatter'd into heaps o'er thy false head.

Comus, lines 756–99

371 *Sabrina*

THERE is a gentle Nymph not far from hence,
That with moist curb sways the smooth Severn stream.
Sabrina is her name, a Virgin pure,
Whilom she was the daughter of *Locrine*,
That had the Scepter from his father *Brute*.
The guiltless damsel flying the mad pursuit
Of her enraged stepdam *Guendolen*,
Commended her fair innocence to the flood
That stay'd her flight with his cross-flowing course,
The water Nymphs that in the bottom plaid,
Held up their pearled wrists and took her in,
Bearing her straight to aged *Nereus* Hall,
Who piteous of her woes, rear'd her lank head,

And gave her to his daughters to imbathe
In nectar'd lavers strew'd with Asphodil,
And through the porch and inlet of each sense
Dropt in Ambrosial Oils till she reviv'd,
And underwent a quick immortal change
Made Goddess of the River; still she retains
Her maid'n gentleness, and oft at Eeve
Visits the herds along the twilight meadows,
Helping all urchin blasts, and ill luck signes
That the shrewd medling Elfe delights to make,
Which she with pretious vial'd liquors heals.
For which the Shepherds at their festivals
Carrol her goodness lowd in rustick layes,
And throw sweet garland wreaths into her stream
Of pansies, pinks, and gaudy Daffadils.
And, as the old Swain said, she can unlock
The clasping charm, and thaw the numbing spell,
If she be right invok't in warbled Song,
For maid'nhood she loves, and will be swift
To aid a Virgin, such as was her self
In hard besetting need, this will I try
And adde the power of som adjuring verse.

SONG

Sabrina fair,
Listen where thou art sitting
Under the glassie, cool, translucent wave,
In twisted braids of Lillies knitting
The loose train of thy amber-dropping hair,
Listen for dear honour's sake,
Goddess of the silver lake,
Listen and save.

JOHN MILTON

Listen and appear to us
In name of great *Oceanus*,
By the earth-shaking *Neptune's* mace,
And *Tethys* grave majestick pace,
By hoary *Nereus* wrinkled look,
And the *Carpathian* wisards hook,
By scaly *Tritons* winding shell,
And old sooth-saying *Glaucus* spell,
By *Leucothea's* lovely hands,
And her son that rules the strands,
By *Thetis* tinsel-slipper'd feet,
And the Songs of *Sirens* sweet,
By dead *Parthenope's* dear tomb,
And fair *Ligea's* golden comb,
Wherwith she sits on diamond rocks
Sleeking her soft alluring locks,
By all the *Nymphs* that nightly dance
Upon thy streams with wily glance,
Rise, rise, and heave thy rosie head
From thy coral-pav'n bed,
And bridle in thy headlong wave,
Till thou our summons answered have.
Listen and save.

Sabrina rises, attended by water-Nymphes, and sings.

By the rushy-fringed bank,
Where grows the Willow and the Osier dank,
My sliding Chariot stayes,
Thick set with Agat, and the azurn sheen
Of Turkis blew, and Emrauld green
That in the channell strayes,
Whilst from off the waters fleet

Thus I set my printless feet
O'er the Cowslips Velvet head,
That bends not as I tread,
Gentle swain at thy request
I am here.

Comus, lines 824–901

372

The dances ended, the spirit Epiloguizes.

TO the Ocean now I fly,
And those happy climes that ly
Where day never shuts his eye,
Up in the broad fields of the sky:
There I suck the liquid ayr
All amidst the Gardens fair
Of *Hesperus*, and his daughters three
That sing about the golden tree:
Along the crisped shades and bowres
Revels the spruce and jocond Spring,
The Graces, and the rosie-boosom'd Howres,
Thither all their bounties bring,
That there eternal Summer dwels,
And West winds, with musky wing
About the cedar'n alleys fling
Nard, and *Cassia's* balmy smels.
Iris there with humid bow,
Waters the odorous banks that blow
Flowers of more mingled hew
Than her purfl'd scarf can shew,
And drenches with *Elysian* dew
(List mortals, if your ears be true)

Beds of *Hyacinth*, and roses
Where young *Adonis* oft reposes,
Waxing well of his deep wound
In slumber soft, and on the ground
Sadly sits th' *Assyrian* Queen;
But far above in spangled sheen
Celestial *Cupid* her fam'd son advanc't,
Holds his dear *Psyche* sweet intranc't
After her wandring labours long,
Till free consent the gods among
Make her his eternal Bride,
And from her fair unspotted side
Two blissful twins are to be born,
Youth and Joy; so *Jove* hath sworn.
  But now my task is smoothly don,
I can fly, or I can run
Quickly to the green earths end,
Where the bow'd welkin slow doth bend,
And from thence can soar as soon
To the corners of the Moon.
  Mortals that would follow me,
Love vertue, she alone is free,
She can teach ye how to clime
Higher than the Spheary chime;
Or if Vertue feeble were,
Heav'n it self would stoop to her.

Comus, 1637. Lines 976–1023

373 *Lycidas*

In this Monody the Author bewails a learned Friend, unfortunatly drown'd in his Passage from *Chester* on the *Irish* Seas, 1637. And by occasion foretels the ruine of our corrupted Clergy then in their height.

YET once more, O ye Laurels, and once more
Ye Myrtles brown, with Ivy never-sear,
I com to pluck your Berries harsh and crude,
And with forc'd fingers rude,
Shatter your leaves before the mellowing year.
Bitter constraint, and sad occasion dear,
Compels me to disturb your season due:
For *Lycidas* is dead, dead ere his prime,
Young *Lycidas*, and hath not left his peer:
Who would not sing for *Lycidas*? he knew
Himself to sing, and build the lofty rhyme.
He must not flote upon his watry bear
Unwept, and welter to the parching wind,
Without the meed of som melodious tear.
Begin then, Sisters of the sacred well,
That from beneath the seat of *Jove* doth spring,
Begin, and somwhat loudly sweep the string.
Hence with denial vain, and coy excuse,
So may som gentle Muse
With lucky words favour my destin'd Urn,
And as he passes turn,
And bid fair peace be to my sable shrowd.
For we were nurst upon the self-same hill,
Fed the same flock, by fountain, shade, and rill.
Together both, ere the high Lawns appear'd
Under the opening eye-lids of the morn,
We drove a field, and both together heard

What time the Gray-fly winds her sultry horn,
Batt'ning our flocks with the fresh dews of night,
Oft till the Star that rose, at Ev'ning, bright
Toward Heav'ns descent had slop'd his westering wheel.
Mean while the Rural ditties were not mute,
Temper'd to th' Oaten Flute;
Rough *Satyrs* danc'd, and *Fauns* with clov'n heel,
From the glad sound would not be absent long,
And old *Damœtas* lov'd to hear our song.
  But O the heavy change, now thou art gon,
Now thou art gon, and never must return!
Thee Shepherd, thee the Woods, and desert Caves,
With wilde Thyme and the gadding Vine o'ergrown,
And all their echoes mourn.
The Willows, and the Hazle Copses green,
Shall now no more be seen,
Fanning their joyous Leaves to thy soft layes.
As killing as the Canker to the Rose,
Or Taint-worm to the weanling Herds that graze,
Or Frost to Flowers, that their gay wardrop wear,
When first the White thorn blows;
Such, *Lycidas*, thy loss to Shepherds ear.
  Where were ye Nymphs when the remorseless deep
Clos'd o'er the head of your lov'd *Lycidas*?
For neither were ye playing on the steep,
Where your old *Bards*, the famous *Druids* ly,
Nor on the shaggy top of *Mona* high,
Nor yet where *Deva* spreads her wisard stream:
Ay me, I fondly dream!
Had ye bin there—for what could that have don?
What could the Muse her self that *Orpheus* bore,
The Muse her self, for her inchanting son

Whom Universal nature did lament,
When by the rout that made the hideous roar,
His goary visage down the stream was sent,
Down the swift *Hebrus* to the *Lesbian* shore.
Alas! What boots it with uncessant care
To tend the homely slighted Shepherds trade,
And strictly meditate the thankless Muse,
Were it not better don as others use,
To sport with *Amaryllis* in the shade,
Or with the tangles of *Neæra's* hair?
Fame is the spur that the clear spirit doth raise
(That last infirmity of Noble mind)
To scorn delights, and live laborious dayes;
But the fair Guerdon when we hope to find,
And think to burst out into sudden blaze,
Comes the blind *Fury* with th' abhorred shears,
And slits the thin spun life. But not the praise,
Phœbus repli'd, and touch'd my trembling ears;
Fame is no plant that grows on mortal soil,
Nor in the glistering foil
Set off to th 'world, nor in broad rumour lies,
But lives and spreds aloft by those pure eyes,
And perfet witness of all judging *Jove*;
As he pronounces lastly on each deed,
Of so much fame in Heav'n expect thy meed.
O Fountain *Arethuse*, and thou honour'd floud,
Smooth-sliding *Mincius*, crown'd with vocall reeds,
That strain I heard was of a higher mood:
But now my Oate proceeds,
And listens to the Herald of the Sea
That came in *Neptune's* plea,
He ask'd the Waves, and ask'd the Felon winds,

What hard mishap hath doom'd this gentle swain?
And question'd every gust of rugged wings
That blows from off each beaked Promontory,
They knew not of his story,
And sage *Hippotades* their answer brings,
That not a blast was from his dungeon stray'd,
The Ayr was calm, and on the level brine,
Sleek *Panope* with all her sisters play'd.
It was that fatall and perfidious Bark
Built in th' eclipse, and rigg'd with curses dark,
That sunk so low that sacred head of thine.
  Next *Camus*, reverend Sire, went footing slow,
His Mantle hairy, and his Bonnet sedge,
Inwrought with figures dim, and on the edge
Like to that sanguine flower inscrib'd with woe.
Ah; Who hath reft (quoth he) my dearest pledge?
Last came, and last did go,
The Pilot of the *Galilean* lake,
Two massy Keyes he bore of metals twain,
(The Golden opes, the Iron shuts amain)
He shook his Miter'd locks, and stern bespake,
How well could I have spar'd for thee, young swain,
Anow of such as for their bellies sake,
Creep and intrude, and climb into the fold?
Of other care they little reck'ning make,
Than how to scramble at the shearers feast,
And shove away the worthy bidden guest.
Blind mouthes! that scarce themselves know how to hold
A Sheep-hook, or have learn'd ought else the least
That to the faithfull Herdmans art belongs!
What recks it them? What need they? They are sped;
And when they list, their lean and flashy songs

Grate on their scrannel Pipes of wretched straw,
The hungry Sheep look up, and are not fed,
But swoln with wind, and the rank mist they draw,
Rot inwardly, and foul contagion spread:
Besides what the grim Woolf with privy paw
Daily devours apace, and nothing sed,
But that two-handed engine at the door,
Stands ready to smite once, and smite no more.
   Return *Alpheus*, the dread voice is past,
That shrunk thy streams; Return *Sicilian* Muse,
And call the Vales, and bid them hither cast
Their Bells, and Flourets of a thousand hues.
Ye valleys low where the milde whispers use,
Of shades and wanton winds, and gushing brooks,
On whose fresh lap the swart Star sparely looks,
Throw hither all your quaint enameld eyes,
That on the green turf suck the honied showres,
And purple all the ground with vernal flowres.
Bring the rathe Primrose that forsaken dies,
The tufted Crow-toe, and pale Gessamine,
The white Pink, and the Pansie freakt with jeat,
The glowing Violet,
The Musk-rose, and the well attir'd Woodbine,
With Cowslips wan that hang the pensive hed,
And every flower that sad embroidery wears:
Bid *Amaranthus* all his beauty shed,
And Daffadillies fill their cups with tears,
To strew the Laureat Herse where *Lycid* lies.
For so to interpose a little ease,
Let our frail thoughts dally with false surmise.
Ay me! Whilst thee the shores, and sounding Seas
Wash far away, where e'er thy bones are hurld,

Whether beyond the stormy *Hebrides,*
Where thou perhaps under the whelming tide
Visit'st the bottom of the monstrous world;
Or whether thou to our moist vows deny'd,
Sleep'st by the fable of *Bellerus* old,
Where the great vision of the guarded Mount
Looks toward *Namancos* and *Bayona's* hold;
Look homeward Angel now, and melt with ruth.
And, O ye *Dolphins,* waft the hapless youth.
  Weep no more, woful Shepherds weep no more,
For *Lycidas* your sorrow is not dead,
Sunk though he be beneath the watry floor,
So sinks the day-star in the Ocean bed,
And yet anon repairs his drooping head,
And tricks his beams, and with new spangled Ore,
Flames in the forehead of the morning sky:
So *Lycidas* sunk low, but mounted high,
Through the dear might of him that walk'd the waves
Where other groves, and other streams along,
With *Nectar* pure his oozy Lock's he laves,
And hears the unexpressive nuptiall Song,
In the blest Kingdoms meek of joy and love.
There entertain him all the Saints above,
In solemn troops, and sweet Societies
That sing, and singing in their glory move,
And wipe the tears for ever from his eyes.
Now *Lycidas* the Shepherds weep no more;
Hence forth thou art the Genius of the shore,
In thy large recompense, and shalt be good
To all that wander in that perilous flood.
  Thus sang the uncouth Swain to th' Okes and rills,
While the still morn went out with Sandals gray,

He touch'd the tender stops of various Quills,
With eager thought warbling his *Dorick* lay:
And now the Sun had stretch'd out all the hills,
And now was dropt into the Western bay;
At last he rose, and twitch'd his Mantle blew:
To morrow to fresh Woods, and Pastures new.

Poems, 1645

374 *Sonnet i*

O NIGHTINGALE, that on yon bloomy Spray
Warbl'st at eeve, when all the Woods are still,
Thou with fresh hope the Lovers heart dost fill,
While the jolly hours lead on propitious *May*,
Thy liquid notes that close the eye of Day,
First heard before the shallow Cuccoo's bill
Portend success in love; O if *Jove's* will
Have linkt that amorous power to thy soft lay,
Now timely sing, ere the rude Bird of Hate
Foretell my hopeless doom in som Grove ny:
As thou from yeer to yeer hast sung too late
For my relief; yet hadst no reason why,
Whether the Muse, or Love call thee his mate,
Both them I serve, and of their train am I.

Poems, 1645

375 *Sonnet vii*

HOW soon hath Time the suttle theef of youth,
Stoln on his wing my three and twentith yeer!
My hasting dayes flie on with full career,
But my late spring no bud or blossom shew'th.
Perhaps my semblance might deceive the truth,
That I to manhood am arriv'd so near,
And inward ripeness doth much less appear,
That som more timely-happy spirits indu'th.
Yet be it less or more, or soon or slow,
It shall be still in strictest measure eev'n,
To that same lot, however mean, or high,
Toward which Time leads me, and the will of Heav'n;
All is, if I have grace to use it so,
As ever in my great task Masters eye. *Poems*, 1645

376 *Sonnet x*

DAUGHTER to that good Earl, once President
Of *Englands* Counsel, and her Treasury,
Who liv'd in both, unstain'd with gold or fee,
And left them both, more in himself content,
Till the sad breaking of that Parlament
Broke him, as that dishonest victory
At *Chæronéa*, fatal to liberty
Kil'd with report that Old man eloquent,
Though later born, than to have known the dayes
Wherin your Father flourisht, yet by you,
Madam, me thinks I see him living yet;
So well your words his noble vertues praise,
That all both judge you to relate them true,
And to possess them, Honour'd *Margaret*. *Poems*, 1645

377 *Sonnet xiii*

To Mr. H. Lawes, on his Aires

HARRY whose tuneful and well measur'd Song
First taught our English Musick how to span
Words with just note and accent, not to scan
With *Midas* Ears, committing short and long;
Thy worth and skill exempts thee from the throng,
With praise enough for Envy to look wan;
To after age thou shalt be writ the man,
That with smooth aire couldst humor best our tongue.
Thou honour'st Verse, and Verse must send her wing
To honour thee, the Priest of *Phœbus* Quire
That tun'st their happiest lines in Hymn, or Story.
Dante shall give Fame leave to set thee higher
Than his *Casella*, whom he woo'd to sing
Met in the milder shades of Purgatory. *Poems &c.*, 1673

378 *Sonnet xiv*

On the religious memorie of Mrs. Catherine Thomason my christian freind deceas'd Decem. 1646

WHEN Faith and Love which parted from thee never,
Had ripen'd thy just soul to dwell with God,
Meekly thou didst resign this earthy load
Of Death, call'd Life; which us from Life doth sever.
Thy Works and Alms and all thy good Endeavour
Staid not behind, nor in the grave were trod;
But as Faith pointed with her golden rod,
Follow'd thee up to joy and bliss for ever.
Love led them on, and Faith who knew them best
Thy hand-maids, clad them o'er with purple beams
And azure wings, that up they flew so drest,
And speak the truth of thee on glorious Theams
Before the Judge, who thenceforth bid thee rest
And drink thy fill of pure immortal streams. *Poems &c.*, 1673

379 *Sonnet xv*

On the late Massacre in Piemont

AVENGE O Lord thy slaughter'd Saints, whose bones
Lie scatter'd on the Alpine mountains cold,
Ev'n them who kept thy truth so pure of old
When all our Fathers worship't Stocks and Stones,
Forget not: in thy book record their groanes
Who were thy Sheep and in their antient Fold
Slayn by the bloody *Piemontese* that roll'd
Mother with Infant down the Rocks. Their moans
The Vales redoubl'd to the Hills, and they
To Heav'n. Their martyr'd blood and ashes sow
O'er all th' *Italian* fields where still doth sway
The triple Tyrant: that from these may grow
A hunder'd-fold, who having learnt thy way
Early may fly the *Babylonian* wo. *Poems &c.*, 1673

380 *Sonnet xvi*

WHEN I consider how my light is spent,
Ere half my days, in this dark world and wide,
And that one Talent which is death to hide,
Lodg'd with me useless, though my Soul more bent
To serve therewith my Maker, and present
My true account, lest he returning chide,
Doth God exact day-labour, light deny'd,
I fondly ask; But patience to prevent
That murmur, soon replies, God doth not need
Either man's work or his own gifts, who best
Bear his milde yoak, they serve him best, his State
Is Kingly. Thousands at his bidding speed
And post o'er Land and Ocean without rest:
They also serve who only stand and waite. *Poems &c.*, 1673

381

Sonnet xvii

L*AWRENCE* of vertuous Father vertuous Son,
Now that the Fields are dank, and ways are mire,
Where shall we sometimes meet, and by the fire
Help waste a sullen day; what may be won
From the hard Season gaining: time will run
On smoother, till *Favonius* re-inspire
The frozen earth; and cloth in fresh attire
The Lillie and Rose, that neither sow'd nor spun.
What neat repast shall feast us, light and choice,
Of Attick tast, with Wine, whence we may rise
To hear the Lute well toucht, or artfull voice
Warble immortal Notes and *Tuskan* Ayre?
He who of those delights can judge, and spare
To interpose them oft, is not unwise.

Poems &c., 1673

382

Sonnet xviii

C*YRIACK*, whose Grandsire on the Royal Bench
Of Brittish *Themis*, with no mean applause
Pronounc't and in his volumes taught our Lawes,
Which others at their Bar so often wrench:
To day deep thoughts resolve with me to drench
In mirth, that after no repenting drawes;
Let *Euclid* rest and *Archimedes* pause,
And what the *Swede* intend, and what the *French*.
To measure life, learn thou betimes, and know
Toward solid good what leads the nearest way;
For other things mild Heav'n a time ordains,
And disapproves that care, though wise in show,
That with superfluous burden loads the day,
And when God sends a cheerful hour, refrains.

Poems &c., 1673

383 *Sonnet xix*

METHOUGHT I saw my late espoused Saint
Brought to me like *Alcestis* from the grave,
Whom *Joves* great Son to her glad Husband gave,
Rescu'd from death by force though pale and faint.
Mine as whom washt from spot of child-bed taint,
Purification in the old Law did save,
And such, as yet once more I trust to have
Full sight of her in Heaven without restraint,
Came vested all in white, pure as her mind:
Her face was vail'd, yet to my fancied sight,
Love, sweetness, goodness, in her person shin'd
So clear, as in no face with more delight.
But O as to embrace me she enclin'd
I wak'd, she fled, and day brought back my night.

Poems &c., 1673

384 *On the Lord Gen. Fairfax at the siege of Colchester*

FAIRFAX, whose name in armes through Europe rings
Filling each mouth with envy, or with praise,
And all her jealous monarchs with amaze,
And rumors loud, that daunt remotest kings,
Thy firm unshak'n vertue ever brings
Victory home, though new rebellions raise
Thir Hydra heads, and the false North displaies
Her brok'n league, to impe their serpent wings,
O yet a nobler task awaites thy hand;
For what can War, but endless war still breed,
Till Truth, and Right from Violence be freed,
And Public Faith cleard from the shamefull brand
Of Public Fraud. In vain doth Valour bleed
While Avarice, and Rapine share the land. *Trin. Coll. MS.*

384. No. 15 in MS.

385 *To the Lord Generall Cromwell, May 1652*

On the proposalls of certaine ministers at the Committee for Propagation of the Gospell.

CROMWELL, our cheif of men, who through a cloud
Not of war onely, but detractions rude,
Guided by faith and matchless Fortitude
To peace and truth thy glorious way hast plough'd,
And on the neck of crowned Fortune proud
Hast reard Gods Trophies, and his work pursu'd,
While Darwen stream with blood of Scotts imbru'd,
And Dunbar feild resounds thy praises loud,
And Worsters laureat wreath; yet much remaines
To conquer still; peace hath her victories
No less renownd than war, new foes arise
Threatning to bind our soules with secular chaines:
Helpe us to save free Conscience from the paw
Of hireling wolves whose Gospell is their maw. *Ibid.*

386 *To Sr Henry Vane the younger*

VANE, young in yeares, but in sage counsell old,
Than whome a better Senatour ne'er held
The helme of Rome, when gownes not armes repelld
The feirce Epeirot and the African bold,
Whether to settle peace, or to unfold
The drift of hollow states, hard to be spelld,
Then to advise how war may best, upheld,
Move by her two maine nerves, Iron and Gold
In all her equipage; besides to know
Both spirituall powre and civill, what each meanes
What severs each thou 'hast learnt, which few have don.
The bounds of either sword to thee we ow.
Therfore on thy firme hand religion leanes
In peace, and reck'ns thee her eldest son. *Ibid.*

385. No. 16 in MS. arise: aries MS.

386. No. 17 in MS.

387 *To Mr. Cyriack Skinner upon his Blindness*

CYRIACK, this three years day these eys, though clear
To outward view, of blemish or of spot;
Bereft of light thir seeing have forgot,
Nor to thir idle orbs doth sight appear
Of Sun or Moon or Starre throughout the year,
Or man or woman. Yet I argue not
Against heavns hand or will, nor bate a jot
Of heart or hope; but still bear up and steer
Right onward. What supports me, dost thou ask?
The conscience, Friend, to have lost them overply'd
In libertyes defence, my noble task,
Of which all Europe talks from side to side.
This thought might lead me through the world's vain mask
Content though blind, had I no better guide.

Ibid.

388 *From 'Paradise Lost'*

(i) *Satan and the Fallen Angels*

HE scarce had ceas't when the superiour Fiend
Was moving toward the shore; his ponderous shield
Ethereal temper, massy, large and round,
Behind him cast; the broad circumference
Hung on his shoulders like the Moon, whose Orb
Through Optic Glass the *Tuscan* Artist views
At Ev'ning from the top of *Fesole*,
Or in *Valdarno*, to descry new Lands,
Rivers or Mountains in her spotty Globe.
His Spear, to equal which the tallest Pine

387. No. 22 in MS.

Hewn on *Norwegian* hills, to be the Mast
Of some great Ammiral, were but a wand,
He walkt with to support uneasie steps
Over the burning Marle, not like those steps
On Heavens Azure, and the torrid Clime
Smote on him sore besides, vaulted with Fire;
Nathless he so endur'd, till on the Beach
Of that inflamed Sea, he stood and call'd
His Legions, Angel Forms, who lay intrans't
Thick as Autumnal Leaves that strow the Brooks
In *Vallombrosa*, where th' *Etrurian* shades
High overarch't imbowr; or scatterd sedge
Afloat, when with fierce Winds *Orion* arm'd
Hath vext the Red-Sea Coast, whose waves o'erthrew
Busiris and his *Memphian* Chivalrie,
While with perfidious hatred they pursu'd
The Sojourners of *Goshen*, who beheld
From the safe shore their floating Carkases
And broken Chariot Wheels, so thick bestrown
Abject and lost lay these, covering the Flood,
Under amazement of their hideous change.

Book i, lines 283–313 (text 1674)

(ii) *Satan and his Host*

BUT he his wonted pride
Soon recollecting, with high words, that bore
Semblance of worth not substance, gently rais'd
Thir fainting courage, and dispel'd thir fears.
Then strait commands that at the warlike sound

Of Trumpets loud and Clarions be upreard
His mighty Standard; that proud honour claim'd
Azazel as his right, a Cherube tall:
Who forthwith from the glittering Staff unfurld
Th' Imperial Ensign, which full high advanc't
Shon like a Meteor streaming to the Wind
With Gems and Golden lustre rich imblaz'd,
Seraphic arms and Trophies: all the while
Sonorous mettal blowing Martial sounds:
At which the universal Host upsent
A shout that tore Hells Concave, and beyond
Frighted the Reign of *Chaos* and old Night.
All in a moment through the gloom were seen
Ten thousand Banners rise into the Air
With Orient Colours waving: with them rose
A Forrest huge of Spears: and thronging Helms
Appear'd, and serried Shields in thick array
Of depth immeasurable: Anon they move
In perfect *Phalanx* to the *Dorian* mood
Of Flutes and soft Recorders; such as rais'd
To hight of noblest temper Hero's old
Arming to Battel, and in stead of rage
Deliberate valour breath'd, firm and unmov'd
With dread of death to flight or foul retreat,
Nor wanting power to mitigate and swage
With solemn touches, troubl'd thoughts, and chase
Anguish and doubt and fear and sorrow and pain
From mortal or immortal minds. Thus they
Breathing united force with fixed thought
Mov'd on in silence to soft Pipes that charm'd
Thir painful steps o'er the burnt soyle; and now
Advanc't in view they stand, a horrid Front

Of dreadful length and dazling Arms, in guise
Of Warriers old with order'd Spear and Shield,
Awaiting what command thir mighty Chief
Had to impose: He through the armed Files
Darts his experienc't eye, and soon traverse
The whole Battalion views, thir order due,
Thir visages and stature as of Gods,
Thir number last he sums. And now his heart
Distends with pride, and hardning in his strength
Glories: For never since created man,
Met such imbodied force, as nam'd with these
Could merit more than that small infantry
Warr'd on by Cranes: though all the Giant brood
Of *Phlegra* with th' Heroic Race were joyn'd
That fought at *Theb's* and *Ilium*, on each side
Mixt with auxiliar Gods; and what resounds
In Fable or *Romance* of *Uthers* Son
Begirt with *British* and *Armoric* Knights;
And all who since, Baptiz'd or Infidel
Jousted in *Aspramont* or *Montalban*,
Damasco, or *Marocco*, or *Trebisond*,
Or whom *Biserta* sent from *Afric* shore
When *Charlemain* with all his Peerage fell
By *Fontarabbia*. Thus far these beyond
Compare of mortal prowess, yet observ'd
Thir dread commander: he above the rest
In shape and gesture proudly eminent
Stood like a Towr; his form had yet not lost
All her Original brightness, nor appear'd
Less than Arch Angel ruind, and th' excess
Of Glory obscur'd: As when the Sun new ris'n
Looks through the Horizontal misty Air

Shorn of his Beams, or from behind the Moon
In dim Eclips disastrous twilight sheds
On half the Nations, and with fear of change
Perplexes Monarchs. Dark'n'd, so, yet shon
Above them all th' Arch Angel: but his face
Deep scars of Thunder had intrencht, and care
Sat on his faded cheek, but under Browes
Of dauntless courage, and considerate Pride
Waiting revenge: cruel his eye, but cast
Signs of remorse and passion to behold
The fellows of his crime, the followers rather
(Far other once beheld in bliss) condemn'd
For ever now to have their lot in pain,
Millions of Spirits for his fault amerc't
Of Heav'n, and from Eternal Splendors flung
For his revolt, yet faithfull how they stood,
Thir Glory witherd. As when Heavens Fire
Hath scath'd the Forrest Oaks, or Mountain Pines,
With singed top their stately growth though bare
Stands on the blasted Heath. He now prepar'd
To speak; whereat their doubl'd Ranks they bend
From wing to wing, and half enclose him round
With all his Peers: attention held them mute.
Thrice he assayd, and thrice in spite of scorn,
Tears such as Angels weep, burst forth: at last
Words interwove with sighs found out their way.
  O Myriads of immortal Spirits, O Powers
Matchless, but with th' Almighty, and that strife
Was not inglorious, though th' event was dire,
As this place testifies, and this dire change
Hateful to utter: but what power of mind
Foreseeing or presaging, from the Depth

Of knowledge past or present, could have fear'd,
How such united force of Gods, how such
As stood like these, could ever know repulse?
For who can yet beleeve, though after loss,
That all these puissant Legions, whose exile
Hath emptied Heav'n, shall faile to re-ascend
Self-rais'd, and repossess their native seat?
For mee, be witness all the Host of Heav'n,
If counsels different, or danger shun'd
By me, have lost our hopes. But he who reigns
Monarch in Heav'n, till then as one secure
Sat on his Throne, upheld by old repute,
Consent or custome, and his Regal State
Put forth at full, but still his strength conceal'd,
Which tempted our attempt, and wrought our fall.
Henceforth his might we know, and know our own
So as not either to provoke, or dread
New war, provok't; our better part remains
To work in close design, by fraud or guile
What force effected not: that he no less
At length from us may find, who overcomes
By force, hath overcome but half his foe.
Space may produce new Worlds; whereof so rife
There went a fame in Heav'n that he ere long
Intended to create, and therein plant
A generation, whom his choice regard
Should favour equal to the Sons of Heaven:
Thither, if but to prie, shall be perhaps
Our first eruption, thither or elsewhere:
For this Infernal Pit shall never hold
Cælestial Spirits in Bondage, nor th' Abysse
Long under darkness cover. But these thoughts

Full Counsel must mature: Peace is despaird,
For who can think Submission! War then, War
Open or understood must be resolv'd.
He spake: and to confirm his words, out-flew
Millions of flaming swords, drawn from the thighs
Of mighty Cherubim; the sudden blaze
Far round illumin'd hell: highly they rag'd
Against the Highest, and fierce with grasped Arms
Clash'd on their sounding shields the din of war,
Hurling defiance toward the vault of Heav'n.

Book i, lines 527–669, 1674

(*iii*) *Hell*

AT once with him they rose;
Thir rising all at once was as the sound
Of Thunder heard remote. Towards him they bend
With awful reverence prone; and as a God
Extoll him equal to the highest in Heav'n:
Nor fail'd they to express how much they prais'd,
That for the general safety he despis'd
His own: for neither do the Spirits damn'd
Loose all thir vertue; lest bad men should boast
Thir specious deeds on earth, which glory excites,
Or close ambition varnisht o'er with zeal.
Thus they thir doubtful consultations dark
Ended rejoycing in thir matchless Chief:
As when from mountain tops the dusky clouds
Ascending, while the North wind sleeps, o'erspread
Heavn's chearful face, the lowring Element
Scowls o'er the dark'nd lantskip Snow, or showre;

lantskip: landscape.

If chance the radiant Sun with farewell sweet
Extend his ev'ning beam, the fields revive,
The birds thir notes renew, and bleating herds
Attest thir joy, that hill and valley rings.
O shame to men! Devil with Devil damn'd
Firm concord holds, men onely disagree
Of Creatures rational, though under hope
Of heavenly Grace; and God proclaiming peace,
Yet live in hatred, enmitie, and strife
Among themselves, and levie cruel warres,
Wasting the Earth, each other to destroy:
As if (which might induce us to accord)
Man had not hellish foes anow besides,
That day and night for his destruction waite.
  The *Stygian* Councel thus dissolv'd; and forth
In order came the grand infernal Peers,
Midst came thir mighty Paramount, and seemd
Alone th' Antagonist of Heav'n, nor less
Than Hells dread Emperour with pomp Supream,
And God-like imitated State; him round
A Globe of fierie Seraphim inclos'd
With bright imblazonrie, and horrent Arms.
Then of thir Session ended they bid cry
With Trumpets regal sound the great result:
Toward the four winds four speedy Cherubim
Put to thir mouths the sounding Alchymie
By Heralds voice explain'd: the hollow Abyss
Heard far and wide, and all the host of Hell
With deafning shout, return'd them loud acclaim.
Thence more at ease thir minds and somwhat rais'd
By false presumptuous hope, the ranged powers
Disband, and wandring, each his several way

Pursues, as inclination or sad choice
Leads him perplext, where he may likeliest find
Truce to his restless thoughts, and entertain
The irksome hours, till his great Chief return.
Part on the Plain, or in the Air sublime
Upon the wing, or in swift Race contend,
As at th' Olympian Games or *Pythian* fields;
Part curb thir fierie Steeds, or shun the Goal
With rapid wheels, or fronted Brigads form.
As when to warn proud Cities war appears
Wag'd in the troubl'd Skie, and Armies rush
To Battel in the Clouds, before each Van
Prick forth the Aerie Knights, and couch thir spears
Till thickest Legions close; with feats of Arms
From either end of Heav'n the welkin burns.
Others with vast *Typhœan* rage more fell
Rend up both Rocks and Hills, and ride the Air
In whirlwind; Hell scarce holds the wilde uproar.
As when *Alcides* from *Oechalia* Crown'd
With conquest, felt th' envenom'd robe, and tore
Through pain up by the roots *Thessalian* Pines,
And *Lichas* from the top of *Oeta* threw
Into th' *Euboic* Sea. Others more milde,
Retreated in a silent valley, sing
With notes Angelical to many a Harp
Thir own Heroic deeds and hapless fall
By doom of Battel; and complain that Fate
Free Vertue should enthrall to Force or Chance.
Thir song was partial, but the harmony
(What could it less when Spirits immortal sing?)
Suspended Hell, and took with ravishment
The thronging audience. In discourse more sweet

(For Eloquence the Soul, Song charms the Sense,)
Others apart sat on a Hill retir'd,
In thoughts more elevate, and reason'd high
Of Providence, Foreknowledge, Will, and Fate,
Fixt Fate, free will, foreknowledge absolute,
And found no end, in wandring mazes lost.
Of good and evil much they argu'd then,
Of happiness and final misery,
Passion and Apathie, and glory and shame,
Vain wisdom all, and false Philosophie:
Yet with a pleasing sorcerie could charm
Pain for a while or anguish, and excite
Fallacious hope, or arm th' obdured brest
With stubborn patience as with triple steel.
Another part in Squadrons and gross Bands
On bold adventure to discover wide
That dismal World, if any Clime perhaps
Might yeild them easier habitation, bend
Four ways thir flying March, along the Banks
Of four infernal Rivers that disgorge
Into the burning Lake thir baleful streams;
Abhorred *Styx* the flood of deadly hate,
Sad *Acheron* of Sorrow, black and deep;
Cocytus, nam'd of lamentation loud
Heard on the ruful stream; fierce *Phlegeton*
Whose waves of torrent fire inflame with rage.
Far off from these a slow and silent stream,
Lethe the River of Oblivion roules
Her watrie Labyrinth, whereof who drinks,
Forthwith his former state and being forgets,
Forgets both joy and grief, pleasure and pain.
Beyond this flood a frozen Continent

Lies dark and wilde, beat with perpetual storms
Of Whirlwind and dire Hail, which on firm land
Thaws not, but gathers heap, and ruin seems
Of ancient pile; all else deep snow and ice,
A gulf profound as that *Serbonian* Bog
Betwixt *Damiata* and mount *Casius* old,
Where Armies whole have sunk: the parching Air
Burns frore, and cold performs th' effect of Fire.
Thither by harpy-footed Furies hal'd,
At certain revolutions all the damn'd
Are brought: and feel by turns the bitter change
Of fierce extreams, extreams by change more fierce,
From Beds of raging Fire to starve in Ice
Thir soft Ethereal warmth, and there to pine
Immovable, infixt, and frozen round,
Periods of time, thence hurried back to fire.
They ferry over this *Lethean* Sound
Both to and fro, thir sorrow to augment,
And wish and struggle, as they pass, to reach
The tempting stream, with one small drop to loose
In sweet forgetfulness all pain and woe,
All in one moment, and so neer the brink;
But fate withstands, and to oppose th' attempt
Medusa with *Gorgonian* terror guards
The Ford, and of it self the water flies
All taste of living wight, as once it fled
The lip of *Tantalus*. Thus roving on
In confus'd march forlorn, th' adventrous Bands
With shuddring horror pale, and eyes agast
View'd first thir lamentable lot, and found
No rest: through many a dark and drearie Vale
They pass'd, and many a Region dolorous,

O'er many a Frozen, many a fierie Alpe,
Rocks, Caves, Lakes, Fens, Bogs, Dens, and shades of death,
A Universe of death, which God by curse
Created evil, for evil only good,
Where all life dies, death lives, and Nature breeds,
Perverse, all monstrous, all prodigious things,
Abominable, inutterable, and worse
Than Fables yet have feign'd, or fear conceiv'd,
Gorgons and *Hydra's*, and *Chimera's* dire.

Book ii, lines 475–628, 1674

(*iv*) *Light*

HAIL holy Light, ofspring of Heav'n first-born,
Or of th' Eternal Coeternal beam
May I express thee unblam'd? since God is light,
And never but in unapproached light
Dwelt from Eternitie, dwelt then in thee,
Bright effluence of bright essence increate.
Or hear'st thou rather pure Ethereal stream,
Whose Fountain who shall tell? before the Sun,
Before the Heavens thou wert, and at the voice
Of God, as with a Mantle didst invest
The rising world of waters dark and deep,
Won from the void and formless infinite.
Thee I re-visit now with bolder wing,
Escap't the *Stygian* Pool, though long detain'd
In that obscure sojourn, while in my flight
Through utter and through middle darkness borne
With other notes than to th' *Orphean* Lyre
I sung of *Chaos* and *Eternal Night*,
Taught by the heav'nly Muse to venture down

The dark descent, and up to reascend,
Though hard and rare: thee I revisit safe,
And feel thy sovran vital Lamp; but thou
Revisit'st not these eyes, that rowle in vain
To find thy piercing ray, and find no dawn;
So thick a drop serene hath quencht thir Orbs,
Or dim suffusion veild. Yet not the more
Cease I to wander where the Muses haunt
Cleer Spring, or shadie Grove, or Sunnie Hill,
Smit with the love of sacred song; but chief
Thee *Sion* and the flowrie Brooks beneath
That wash thy hallowd feet, and warbling flow,
Nightly I visit: nor somtimes forget
Those other two equal'd with me in Fate,
So were I equal'd with them in renown,
Blind *Thamyris* and blind *Mæonides*,
And *Tiresias* and *Phineus* Prophets old.
Then feed on thoughts, that voluntarie move
Harmonious numbers; as the wakeful Bird
Sings darkling, and in shadiest Covert hid
Tunes her nocturnal Note. Thus with the Year
Seasons return, but not to me returns
Day, or the sweet approach of Ev'n or Morn,
Or sight of vernal bloom, or Summers Rose,
Or flocks, or herds, or human face divine;
But cloud in stead, and ever-during dark
Surrounds me, from the chearful wayes of men
Cut off, and for the Book of knowledg fair
Presented with a Universal blank
Of Natures works to mee expung'd and ras'd,
And wisdome at one entrance quite shut out.

drop serene: from Latin *gutta serena*, amaurosis.

So much the rather thou Celestial light
Shine inward, and the mind through all her powers
Irradiate, there plant eyes, all mist from thence
Purge and disperse, that I may see and tell
Of things invisible to mortal sight.

Book iii, lines 1–55, 1674

(v) *The Atonement*

FATHER, thy word is past, man shall find grace;
And shall grace not find means, that finds her way,
The speediest of thy winged messengers,
To visit all thy creatures, and to all
Comes unprevented, unimplor'd, unsought,
Happie for man, so coming; he her aide
Can never seek, once dead in sins and lost;
Attonement for himself or offering meet,
Indebted and undon, hath none to bring:
Behold mee then, mee for him, life for life
I offer, on mee let thine anger fall;
Account mee man; I for his sake will leave
Thy bosom, and this glorie next to thee
Freely put off, and for him lastly die
Well pleas'd, on me let Death wreck all his rage;
Under his gloomie power I shall not long
Lie vanquisht; thou hast givn me to possess
Life in my self for ever, by thee I live,
Though now to Death I yeild, and am his due
All that of me can die, yet that debt paid,
Thou wilt not leave me in the loathsom grave
His prey, nor suffer my unspotted Soule
For ever with corruption there to dwell;
But I shall rise Victorious, and subdue

My Vanquisher, spoild of his vanted spoile;
Death his deaths wound shall then receive, & stoop
Inglorious, of his mortall sting disarm'd.
I through the ample Air in Triumph high
Shall lead Hell Captive maugre Hell, and show
The powers of darkness bound. Thou at the sight
Pleas'd, out of Heaven shalt look down and smile,
While by thee rais'd I ruin all my Foes,
Death last, and with his Carcass glut the Grave:
Then with the multitude of my redeemd
Shall enter Heaven long absent, and returne,
Father, to see thy face, wherein no cloud
Of anger shall remain, but peace assur'd,
And reconcilement; wrath shall be no more
Thenceforth, but in thy presence Joy entire.

Book iii, lines 227–65, 1674

(*vi*) *Heaven*

NO sooner had th' Almighty ceas't, but all
The multitude of Angels with a shout
Loud as from numbers without number, sweet
As from blest voices, uttering joy, Heav'n rung
With Jubilee, and loud Hosannas fill'd
Th' eternal Regions: lowly reverent
Towards either Throne they bow, & to the ground
With solemn adoration down they cast
Thir Crowns inwove with Amarant and Gold,
Immortal Amarant, a Flowr which once
In Paradise, fast by the Tree of Life
Began to bloom, but soon for mans offence
To Heav'n remov'd where first it grew, there grows,

And flours aloft shading the Fount of Life,
And where the river of Bliss through midst of Heavn
Rowls o'er *Elisian* Flowrs her Amber stream;
With these that never fade the Spirits Elect
Bind thir resplendent locks inwreath'd with beams,
Now in loose Garlands thick thrown off, the bright
Pavement that like a Sea of Jasper shon
Impurpl'd with Celestial Roses smil'd.
Then Crown'd again thir gold'n Harps they took,
Harps ever tun'd, that glittering by thir side
Like Quivers hung, and with Præamble sweet
Of charming symphonie they introduce
Thir sacred Song, and waken raptures high;
No voice exempt, no voice but well could joine
Melodious part, such concord is in Heav'n.

Book iii, lines 344–71, 1674

(*vii*) *New Worlds*

As when a Scout
Through dark and desart wayes with peril gone
All night; at last by break of chearful dawne
Obtains the brow of some high-climbing Hill,
Which to his eye discovers unaware
The goodly prospect of some forein land
First seen, or some renownd Metropolis
With glistering Spires and Pinnacles adornd,
Which now the Rising Sun gilds with his beams.
Such wonder seiz'd, though after Heaven seen,
The Spirit maligne, but much more envy seiz'd
At sight of all this World beheld so faire.
Round he surveys, and well might, where he stood

So high above the circling Canopie
Of Nights extended shade; from Eastern Point
Of *Libra* to the fleecie Star that bears
Andromeda far off *Atlantick* Seas
Beyond th' *Horizon*; then from Pole to Pole
He views in bredth, and without longer pause
Down right into the Worlds first Region throws
His flight precipitant, and windes with ease
Through the pure marble Air his oblique way
Amongst innumerable Stars, that shon
Stars distant, but nigh hand seemd other Worlds,
Or other Worlds they seemd, or happy Iles,
Like those *Hesperian* Gardens fam'd of old,
Fortunate Fields, and Groves and flowrie Vales,
Thrice happy Iles, but who dwelt happy there
He stayd not to enquire.

Book iii, lines 543–71, 1674

(*viii*) *Satan's Soliloquy*

O THOU that with surpassing Glory crownd,
Look'st from thy sole Dominion like the God
Of this new World; at whose sight all the Stars
Hide thir diminisht heads; to thee I call,
But with no friendly voice, and add thy name
O Sun, to tell thee how I hate thy beams
That bring to my remembrance from what state
I fell, how glorious once above thy Spheare;
Till Pride and worse Ambition threw me down
Warring in Heav'n against Heav'ns matchless King:
Ah wherefore! he deservd no such return
From me, whom he created what I was

In that bright eminence, and with his good
Upbraided none; nor was his service hard.
What could be less than to afford him praise,
The easiest recompence, and pay him thanks,
How due! yet all his good prov'd ill in me,
And wrought by malice; lifted up so high
I sdeind subjection, and thought one step higher
Would set me highest, and in a moment quit
The debt immense of endless gratitude,
So burthensome, still paying, still to ow;
Forgetful what from him I still receivd,
And understood not that a grateful mind
By owing owes not, but still pays, at once
Indebted and dischargd; what burden then?
O had his powerful Destiny ordaind
Me some inferiour Angel, I had stood
Then happie; no unbounded hope had rais'd
Ambition. Yet why not? som other Power
As great might have aspir'd, and me though mean
Drawn to his part; but other Powers as great
Fell not, but stand unshak'n, from within
Or from without, to all temptations arm'd.
Hadst thou the same free Will and Power to stand?
Thou hadst: whom hast thou then or what to accuse,
But Heav'ns free Love dealt equally to all?
Be then his Love accurst, since love or hate,
To me alike, it deals eternal woe.
Nay curs'd be thou; since against his thy will
Chose freely what it now so justly rues.
Me miserable! which way shall I flie
Infinite wrath, and infinite despaire?
Which way I flie is Hell; my self am Hell;

And in the lowest deep a lower deep
Still threatning to devour me opens wide,
To which the Hell I suffer seems a Heav'n.
O then at last relent: is there no place
Left for Repentance, none for Pardon left?
None left but by submission; and that word
Disdain forbids me, and my dread of shame
Among the spirits beneath, whom I seduc'd
With other promises and other vaunts
Than to submit, boasting I could subdue
Th' Omnipotent. Ay me, they little know
How dearly I abide that boast so vaine,
Under what torments inwardly I groane:
While they adore me on the Throne of Hell,
With Diadem and Scepter high advanc'd
The lower still I fall, onely Supream
In miserie; such joy Ambition findes.
But say I could repent and could obtaine
By Act of Grace my former state; how soon
Would highth recal high thoughts, how soon unsay
What feign'd submission swore: ease would recant
Vows made in pain, as violent and void.
For never can true reconcilement grow
Where wounds of deadly hate have peirc'd so deep:
Which would but lead me to a worse relapse,
And heavier fall: so should I purchase deare
Short intermission bought with double smart.
This knows my punisher; therefore as far
From granting hee, as I from begging peace:
All hope excluded thus, behold in stead
Of us out-cast, exil'd, his new delight,
Mankind created, and for him this World.

So farewell Hope, and with Hope farewell Fear,
Farewell Remorse: all Good to me is lost;
Evil be thou my Good; by thee at least
Divided Empire with Heav'ns King I hold
By thee, and more than half perhaps will reigne;
As Man ere long, and this new World shall know.

Book iv, lines 32–113, 1674

(*ix*) *Paradise*

ANOTHER side, umbrageous Grots and Caves
Of coole recess, o'er which the mantling Vine
Layes forth her purple Grape, and gently creeps
Luxuriant; mean while murmuring waters fall
Down the slope hills, disperst, or in a Lake,
That to the fringed Bank with Myrtle crownd,
Her chrystall mirror holds, unite thir streams.
The Birds thir quire apply; aires, vernal aires,
Breathing the smell of field and grove, attune
The trembling leaves, while Universal *Pan*
Knit with the *Graces* and the *Hours* in dance
Led on th' Eternal Spring. Not that faire field
Of *Enna*, where *Proserpin* gathring flours
Her self a fairer Flowre by gloomie *Dis*
Was gatherd, which cost *Ceres* all that pain
To seek her through the world; nor that sweet Grove
Of *Daphne* by *Orontes*, and th' inspir'd
Castalian Spring might with this Paradise
Of *Eden* strive; nor that *Nyseian* Ile
Girt with the River *Triton*, where old *Cham*,
Whom Gentiles *Ammon* call and *Libyan Jove*,
Hid *Amalthea* and her Florid Son

Young *Bacchus* from his Stepdame *Rhea's* eye;
Nor where *Abassin* Kings thir issue Guard,
Mount *Amara*, though this by som suppos'd
True Paradise under the *Ethiop* Line
By *Nilus* head, enclos'd with shining Rock,
A whole dayes journey high, but wide remote
From this *Assyrian* Garden, where the Fiend
Saw undelighted all delight, all kind
Of living Creatures new to sight and strange:
Two of far nobler shape erect and tall,
Godlike erect, with native Honour clad
In naked Majestie seemd Lords of all,
And worthie seemd, for in thir looks Divine
The image of thir glorious Maker shon,
Truth, Wisdome, Sanctitude severe and pure,
Severe, but in true filial freedom plac't.

Book iv, lines 257–94, 1674

(*x*) *Wedded Love*

HAILE wedded Love, mysterious Law, true source
Of human ofspring, sole proprietie,
In Paradise of all things common else.
By thee adulterous lust was driv'n from men
Among the bestial herds to raunge, by thee
Founded in Reason, Loyal, Just, and Pure,
Relations dear, and all the Charities
Of Father, Son, and Brother first were known.
Far be it, that I should write thee sin or blame,
Or think thee unbefitting holiest place,
Perpetual Fountain of Domestic sweets,
Whose Bed is undefil'd and chaste pronounc't,

Present, or past, as Saints and Patriarchs us'd.
Here Love his golden shafts imploies, here lights
His constant Lamp, and waves his purple wings,
Reigns here and revels; not in the bought smile
Of Harlots, loveless, joyless, unindeard,
Casual fruition, nor in Court Amours
Mixt Dance, or wanton Mask, or Midnight Ball,
Or Serenate, which the starv'd Lover sings
To his proud fair, best quitted with disdain.
These lulld by Nightingales imbraceing slept,
And on thir naked limbs the flowrie roof
Showrd Roses, which the Morn repair'd. Sleep on,
Blest pair; and O yet happiest if ye seek
No happier state, and know to know no more.

Book iv, lines 750–75, 1674

(*xi*) *Invocation to Urania*

DESCEND from Heav'n *Urania*, by that name
If rightly thou art call'd, whose Voice divine
Following, above th' *Olympian* Hill I soare,
Above the flight of *Pegasean* wing.
The meaning, not the Name I call: for thou
Nor of the Muses nine, nor on the top
Of old *Olympus* dwell'st, but Heav'nlie borne,
Before the Hills appeerd, or Fountain flow'd,
Thou with Eternal wisdom didst converse,
Wisdom thy Sister, and with her didst play
In presence of th' Almightie Father, pleas'd
With thy Celestial Song. Up led by thee
Into the Heav'n of Heav'ns I have presum'd,
An Earthlie Guest, and drawn Empyreal Aire,

Thy tempring; with like safetie guided down
Return me to my Native Element:
Lest from this flying Steed unrein'd, (as once
Bellerophon, though from a lower Clime)
Dismounted, on th' *Aleian* Field I fall
Erroneous, there to wander and forlorne.
Half yet remaines unsung, but narrower bound
Within the visible Diurnal Spheare;
Standing on Earth, not rapt above the Pole,
More safe I Sing with mortal voice, unchang'd
To hoarse or mute, though fall'n on evil dayes,
On evil dayes though fall'n, and evil tongues;
In darkness, and with dangers compast round,
And solitude; yet not alone, while thou
Visit'st my slumbers Nightly, or when Morn
Purples the East: still govern thou my Song,
Urania, and fit audience find, though few.
But drive far off the barbarous dissonance
Of *Bacchus* and his revellers, the Race
Of that wilde Rout that tore the *Thracian* Bard
In *Rhodope*, where Woods and Rocks had Eares
To rapture, till the savage clamor drownd
Both Harp and Voice; nor could the Muse defend
Her Son. So fail not thou, who thee implores:
For thou art Heav'nlie, shee an empty dreame.

Book vii, lines 1–39, 1674

(*xii*) *The Subject of Heroic Song*

NO more of talk where God or Angel Guest
With Man, as with his Friend, familiar us'd
To sit indulgent, and with him partake
Rural repast, permitting him the while

Venial discourse unblam'd: I now must change
Those Notes to Tragic; foul distrust, and breach
Disloyal on the part of Man, revolt,
And disobedience: On the part of Heav'n
Now alienated, distance and distaste,
Anger and just rebuke, and judgement giv'n,
That brought into this World a world of woe,
Sinne and her shadow Death, and Miserie
Deaths Harbinger: Sad task, yet argument
Not less but more Heroic than the wrath
Of stern *Achilles* on his Foe pursu'd
Thrice Fugitive about *Troy* Wall; or rage
Of *Turnus* for *Lavinia* disespous'd,
Or *Neptun*'s ire or *Juno*'s, that so long
Perplex'd the *Greek* and *Cytherea*'s Son;
If answerable style I can obtaine
Of my Celestial Patroness, who deignes
Her nightly visitation unimplor'd,
And dictates to me slumbring, or inspires
Easie my unpremeditated Verse:
Since first this Subject for Heroic Song
Pleas'd me long choosing, and beginning late;
Not sedulous by Nature to indite
Wars, hitherto the onely Argument
Heroic deem'd, chief maistrie to dissect
With long and tedious havoc fabl'd Knights
In Battels feign'd; the better fortitude
Of Patience and Heroic Martyrdom
Unsung; or to describe Races and Games,
Or tilting Furniture, emblazon'd Shields,
Impreses quaint, Caparisons and Steeds;

Impreses: emblems, devices.

Bases and tinsel Trappings, gorgious Knights
At Joust and Torneament; then marshal'd Feast
Serv'd up in Hall with Sewers, and Seneshals;
The skill of Artifice or Office mean,
Not that which justly gives Heroic name
To Person or to Poem. Mee of these
Nor skilld nor studious, higher Argument
Remaines, sufficient of it self to raise
That name, unless an age too late, or cold
Climat, or Years damp my intended wing
Deprest, and much they may, if all be mine,
Not Hers who brings it nightly to my Ear.

Book ix, lines 1–47, 1674

(*xiii*) *Eve*

IN Bowre and Field he sought, where any tuft
Of Grove or Garden-Plot more pleasant lay,
Thir tendance or Plantation for delight,
By Fountain or by shadie Rivulet.
He sought them both, but wish'd his hap might find
Eve separate, he wish'd, but not with hope
Of what so seldom chanc'd, when to his wish,
Beyond his hope, *Eve* separate he spies,
Veil'd in a Cloud of Fragrance, where she stood,
Half spi'd, so thick the Roses bushing round
About her glowd, oft stooping to support
Each Flowr of slender stalk, whose head though gay
Carnation, Purple, Azure, or spect with Gold,
Hung drooping unsustained, them she upstaies
Gently with Mirtle band, mindless the while,

Her self, though fairest unsupported Flowr,
From her best prop so far, and storm so nigh.
Neerer he drew, and many a walk travers'd
Of stateliest Covert, Cedar, Pine, or Palme,
Then voluble and bold, now hid, now seen
Among thick-wov'n Arborets and Flowrs
Imborderd on each Bank, the hand of *Eve*:
Spot more delicious than those Gardens feign'd
Or of reviv'd *Adonis*, or renownd
Alcinous, host of old *Laertes* Son,
Or that, not Mystic, where the Sapient King
Held dalliance with his faire *Egyptian* Spouse.
Much hee the Place admir'd, the Person more.
As one who long in populous City pent,
Where Houses thick and Sewers annoy the Aire,
Forth issuing on a Summers Morn to breathe
Among the pleasant Villages and Farmes
Adjoynd, from each thing met conceaves delight,
The smell of Grain, or tedded Grass, or Kine,
Or Dairie, each rural sight, each rural sound;
If chance with Nymphlike step fair Virgin pass,
What pleasing seemd, for her now pleases more,
She most, and in her looks sums all Delight.
Such Pleasure took the Serpent to behold
This Flowrie Plat, the sweet recess of *Eve*
Thus earlie, thus alone; her Heav'nly forme
Angelic, but more soft, and Feminine,
Her graceful Innocence, her every Aire
Of gesture or least action overawd
His Malice, and with rapine sweet bereav'd
His fierceness of the fierce intent it brought:
That space the Evil one abstracted stood

From his own evil, and for the time remaind
Stupidly good, of enmitie disarm'd,
Of guile, of hate, of envie, of revenge.

Book ix, lines 417–66, 1674

(*xiv*) *Eve Penitent*

FORSAKE me not thus, *Adam*, witness Heav'n
What love sincere, and reverence in my heart
I beare thee, and unweeting have offended,
Unhappilie deceav'd; thy suppliant
I beg, and clasp thy knees; bereave me not,
Whereon I live, thy gentle looks, thy aid,
Thy counsel in this uttermost distress,
My onely strength and stay: forlorn of thee,
Whither shall I betake me, where subsist?
While yet we live, scarse one short hour perhaps,
Between us two let there be peace, both joyning,
As joyn'd in injuries, one enmitie
Against a Foe by doom express assign'd us,
That cruel Serpent: On me exercise not
Thy hatred for this miserie befall'n,
On me already lost, mee, than thy self
More miserable; both have sin'd, but thou
Against God onely, I against God and thee,
And to the place of judgement will return,
There with my cries importune Heaven, that all
The sentence from thy head remov'd may light
On me, sole cause to thee of all this woe,
Mee mee onely just object of his ire.

She ended weeping, and her lowlie plight,
Immoveable till peace obtain'd from fault

Acknowledg'd and deplor'd, in *Adam* wrought
Commiseration; soon his heart relented
Towards her, his life so late and sole delight,
Now at his feet submissive in distress,
Creature so faire his reconcilement seeking,
His counsel whom she had displeas'd, his aide;
As one disarm'd, his anger all he lost,
And thus with peaceful words uprais'd her soon.

Book x, lines 914–46, 1674

(*xv*) *The Banishment*

SO spake our Mother *Eve*, and *Adam* heard
Well pleas'd, but answer'd not; for now too nigh
Th' Archangel stood, and from the other Hill
To thir fixt Station, all in bright array
The Cherubim descended; on the ground
Gliding meteorous, as Ev'ning Mist
Ris'n from a River o'er the marish glides,
And gathers ground fast at the Labourers heel
Homeward returning. High in Front advanc't,
The brandisht Sword of God before them blaz'd
Fierce as a Comet; which with torrid heat,
And vapour as the *Libyan* Air adust,
Began to parch that temperate Clime; whereat
In either hand the hastning Angel caught
Our lingring Parents, and to th' Eastern Gate
Led them direct, and down the Cliff as fast
To the subjected Plaine; then disappeer'd.
They looking back, all th' Eastern side beheld
Of Paradise, so late thir happie seat,
Wav'd over by that flaming Brand, the Gate

With dreadful Faces throng'd and fierie Armes:
Som natural tears they drop'd, but wip'd them soon;
The World was all before them, where to choose
Thir place of rest, and Providence thir guide:
They hand in hand with wandring steps and slow,
Through *Eden* took thir solitarie way.

Book xii, lines 624–49, 1674

389 *From 'Paradise Regained'*

(i) The Messiah

SO they in Heav'n their Odes and Vigils tun'd:
Mean while the Son of God, who yet some days
Lodg'd in *Bethabara* where *John* baptiz'd,
Musing and much revolving in his brest,
How best the mighty work he might begin
Of Saviour to mankind, and which way first
Publish his God-like office now mature,
One day forth walk'd alone, the Spirit leading;
And his deep thoughts, the better to converse
With solitude, till far from track of men,
Thought following thought, and step by step led on,
He entred now the bordering Desert wild,
And with dark shades and rocks environ'd round,
His holy Meditations thus persu'd.
O what a multitude of thoughts at once
Awakn'd in me swarm, while I consider
What from within I feel my self, and hear
What from without comes often to my ears,
Ill sorting with my present state compar'd.
When I was yet a child, no childish play

To me was pleasing, all my mind was set
Serious to learn and know, and thence to do
What might be publick good; my self I thought
Born to that end, born to promote all truth,
All righteous things: therefore above my years,
The Law of God I read, and found it sweet,
Made it my whole delight, and in it grew
To such perfection, that ere yet my age
Had measur'd twice six years, at our great Feast
I went into the Temple, there to hear
The Teachers of our Law, and to propose
What might improve my knowledge or their own;
And was admir'd by all, yet this not all
To which my Spirit aspir'd, victorious deeds
Flam'd in my heart, heroic acts, one while
To rescue *Israel* from the *Roman* yoke,
Thence to subdue and quell o'er all the earth
Brute violence and proud Tyrannick pow'r,
Till truth were freed, and equity restor'd:
Yet held it more humane, more heavenly first
By winning words to conquer willing hearts,
And make perswasion do the work of fear;
At least to try, and teach the erring Soul
Not wilfully mis-doing, but unware
Misled: the stubborn only to subdue.
These growing thoughts my Mother soon perceiving
By words at times cast forth inly rejoyc'd,
And said to me apart, high are thy thoughts
O Son, but nourish them and let them soar
To what highth sacred vertue and true worth
Can raise them, though above example high;
By matchless Deeds express thy matchless Sire.

For know, thou art no Son of mortal man,
Though men esteem thee low of Parentage,
Thy Father is the Eternal King, who rules
All Heaven and Earth, Angels and Sons of men.
A messenger from God fore-told thy birth
Conceiv'd in me a Virgin, he fore-told
Thou shouldst be great and sit on *David's* Throne,
And of thy Kingdom there should be no end.
At thy Nativity a glorious Quire
Of Angels in the fields of *Bethlehem* sung
To Shepherds watching at their folds by night,
And told them the Messiah now was born,
Where they might see him, and to thee they came;
Directed to the Manger where thou lais't,
For in the Inn was left no better room:
A Star, not seen before in Heaven appearing
Guided the Wise Men thither from the East,
To honour thee with Incense, Myrrh, and Gold,
By whose bright course led on they found the place,
Affirming it thy Star new grav'n in Heaven,
By which they knew thee King of *Israel* born.
Just *Simeon* and Prophetic *Anna*, warn'd
By Vision, found thee in the Temple, and spake
Before the Altar and the vested Priest,
Like things of thee to all that present stood.
This having heard, strait I again revolv'd
The Law and Prophets, searching what was writ
Concerning the Messiah, to our Scribes
Known partly, and soon found of whom they spake
I am; this chiefly, that my way must lie
Through many a hard assay even to the death,
Ere I the promis'd Kingdom can attain,

Or work Redemption for mankind, whose sins
Full weight must be transferr'd upon my head.
Yet neither thus disheartn'd or dismay'd,
The time prefixt I waited, when behold
The Baptist, (of whose birth I oft had heard,
Not knew by sight) now come, who was to come
Before Messiah and his way prepare.
I as all others to his Baptism came,
Which I believ'd was from above; but he
Strait knew me, and with loudest voice proclaim'd
Me him (for it was shew'n him so from Heaven)
Me him whose Harbinger he was; and first
Refus'd on me his Baptism to confer,
As much his greater, and was hardly won;
But as I rose out of the laving stream,
Heaven open'd her eternal doors, from whence
The Spirit descended on me like a Dove,
And last the sum of all, my Father's voice,
Audibly heard from Heav'n, pronounc'd me his,
Me his beloved Son, in whom alone
He was well pleas'd; by which I knew the time
Now full, that I no more should live obscure,
But openly begin, as best becomes
The Authority which I deriv'd from Heaven.
And now by some strong motion I am led
Into this wilderness, to what intent
I learn not yet, perhaps I need not know;
For what concerns my knowledge God reveals.

Book i, lines 182–293, 1671

JOHN MILTON

(ii) *Satan's Guile*

WHOM thus answer'd th' Arch Fiend now un-
disguis'd.
'Tis true, I am that Spirit unfortunate,
Who leagu'd with millions more in rash revolt
Kept not my happy Station, but was driv'n
With them from bliss to the bottomless deep,
Yet to that hideous place not so confin'd
By rigour unconniving, but that oft
Leaving my dolorous Prison I enjoy
Large liberty to round this Globe of Earth,
Or range in th' Air, nor from the Heav'n of Heav'ns
Hath he excluded my resort sometimes.
I came among the Sons of God, when he
Gave up into my hands *Uzzean Job*
To prove him, and illustrate his high worth;
And when to all his Angels he propos'd
To draw the proud King *Ahab* into fraud
That he might fall in *Ramoth*, they demurring,
I undertook that office, and the tongues
Of all his flattering Prophets glibb'd with lyes
To his destruction, as I had in charge.
For what he bids I do; though I have lost
Much lustre of my native brightness, lost
To be belov'd of God, I have not lost
To love, at least contemplate and admire
What I see excellent in good, or fair,
Or vertuous, I should so have lost all sense.
What can be then less in me than desire
To see thee and approach thee, whom I know
Declar'd the Son of God, to hear attent

Thy wisdom, and behold thy God-like deeds?
Men generally think me much a foe
To all mankind: why should I? they to me
Never did wrong or violence, by them
I lost not what I lost, rather by them
I gain'd what I have gain'd, and with them dwell
Copartner in these Regions of the World,
If not disposer; lend them oft my aid,
Oft my advice by presages and signs,
And answers, oracles, portents and dreams,
Whereby they may direct their future life.
Envy they say excites me, thus to gain
Companions of my misery and wo.
At first it may be; but long since with wo
Nearer acquainted, now I feel by proof,
That fellowship in pain divides not smart,
Nor lightens aught each mans peculiar load.
Small consolation then, were Man adjoyn'd:
This wounds me most (what can it less) that Man,
Man fall'n shall be restor'd, I never more.

Book i, lines 357–405, 1671

(iii) *True and False Glory*

TO whom our Saviour calmly thus reply'd.
Thou neither dost perswade me to seek wealth
For Empires sake, nor Empire to affect
For glories sake by all thy argument.
For what is glory but the blaze of fame,
The peoples praise, if always praise unmixt?
And what the people but a herd confus'd,
A miscellaneous rabble, who extol

Things vulgar, and well weigh'd, scarce worth the praise,
They praise and they admire they know not what;
And know not whom, but as one leads the other;
And what delight to be by such extoll'd,
To live upon thir tongues and be thir talk,
Of whom to be disprais'd were no small praise?
His lot who dares be singularly good.
Th' intelligent among them and the wise
Are few, and glory scarce of few is rais'd.
This is true glory and renown, when God
Looking on the Earth, with approbation marks
The just man, and divulges him through Heaven
To all his Angels, who with true applause
Recount his praises; thus he did to *Job*,
When to extend his fame through Heaven and Earth,
As thou to thy reproach mayst well remember,
He ask'd thee, hast thou seen my servant *Job*?
Famous he was in Heaven, on Earth less known;
Where glory is false glory, attributed
To things not glorious, men not worthy of fame.
They err who count it glorious to subdue
By Conquest far and wide, to over-run
Large Countries, and in field great Battels win,
Great Cities by assault: what do these Worthies,
But rob and spoil, burn, slaughter, and enslave
Peaceable Nations, neighbouring, or remote,
Made Captive, yet deserving freedom more
Than those thir Conquerours, who leave behind
Nothing but ruin wheresoe'er they rove,
And all the flourishing works of peace destroy,
Then swell with pride, and must be titl'd Gods,
Great Benefactors of mankind, Deliverers,

Worship't with Temple, Priest and Sacrifice;
One is the Son of *Jove*, of *Mars* the other,
Till Conquerour Death discover them scarce men,
Rolling in brutish vices, and deform'd,
Violent or shameful death thir due reward.
But if there be in glory aught of good,
It may by means far different be attain'd
Without ambition, war, or violence;
By deeds of peace, by wisdom eminent,
By patience, temperance; I mention still
Him whom thy wrongs with Saintly patience born,
Made famous in a Land and times obscure;
Who names not now with honour patient *Job*?
Poor *Socrates* (who next more memorable?)
By what he taught and suffer'd for so doing,
For truths sake suffering death unjust, lives now
Equal in fame to proudest Conquerours.
Yet if for fame and glory aught be done,
Aught suffer'd; if young *African* for fame
His wasted Country freed from *Punic* rage,
The deed becomes unprais'd, the man at least,
And loses, though but verbal, his reward.
Shall I seek glory then, as vain men seek
Oft not deserv'd? I seek not mine, but his
Who sent me, and thereby witness whence I am.

Book iii, lines 43–107, 1671

(*iv*) *The Parthians*

HE look't and saw what numbers numberless
The City gates out pour'd, light armed Troops
In coats of Mail and military pride;
In Mail thir horses clad, yet fleet and strong,

Prauncing their riders bore, the flower and choice
Of many Provinces from bound to bound;
From *Arachosia*, from *Candaor* East,
And *Margiana* to the *Hyrcanian* cliffs
Of *Caucasus*, and dark *Iberian* dales,
From *Atropatia* and the neighbouring plains
Of *Adiabene*, *Media*, and the South
Of *Susiana* to *Balsara's* hav'n.
He saw them in thir forms of battell rang'd,
How quick they wheel'd, and flying behind them shot
Sharp sleet of arrowie showers against the face
Of thir pursuers, and overcame by flight;
The field all iron cast a gleaming brown,
Nor wanted clouds of foot, nor on each horn,
Cuirassiers all in steel for standing fight;
Chariots or Elephants endorst with Towers
Of Archers, nor of labouring Pioners
A multitude with Spades and Axes arm'd
To lay hills plain, fell woods, or valleys fill,
Or where plain was raise hill, or over-lay
With bridges rivers proud, as with a yoke;
Mules after these, Camels and Dromedaries,
And Waggons fraught with Utensils of war.
Such forces met not, nor so wide a camp,
When *Agrican* with all his Northern powers
Besieg'd *Albracca*, as Romances tell;
The City of *Gallaphrone*, from thence to win
The fairest of her Sex *Angelica*
His daughter, sought by many Prowest Knights,
Both *Paynim*, and the Peers of *Charlemane*.

Book iii, lines 310–43, 1671

(*v*) *Rome*

THE City which thou seest no other deem
Than great and glorious *Rome*, Queen of the Earth
So far renown'd, and with the spoils enricht
Of Nations; there the Capitol thou seest
Above the rest lifting his stately head
On the *Tarpeian* rock, her Cittadel
Impregnable, and there Mount *Palatine*
The Imperial Palace, compass huge, and high
The Structure, skill of noblest Architects,
With gilded battlements, conspicuous far,
Turrets and Terrases, and glittering Spires.
Many a fair Edifice besides, more like
Houses of Gods (so well I have dispos'd
My Aerie Microscope) thou may'st behold
Outside and inside both, pillars and roofs
Carv'd work, the hand of fam'd Artificers
In Cedar, Marble, Ivory or Gold.
Thence to the gates cast round thine eye, and see
What conflux issuing forth, or entring in,
Pretors, Proconsuls to thir Provinces
Hasting or on return, in robes of State;
Lictors and rods the ensigns of thir power,
Legions and Cohorts, turmes of horse and wings:
Or Embassies from Regions far remote
In various habits on the *Appian* road,
Or on the *Æmilian*, some from farthest South,
Syene, and where the shadow both way falls,
Meroe, *Nilotic* Isle, and more to West,
The Realm of *Bocchus* to the Black-moor Sea;
From the *Asian* Kings and *Parthian* among these,

From *India* and the golden *Chersoness*,
And utmost *Indian* Isle *Taprobane*,
Dusk faces with white silken Turbants wreath'd:
From *Gallia*, *Gades*, and the *Brittish* West,
Germans and *Scythians*, and *Sarmatians* North
Beyond *Danubius* to the *Tauric* Pool.
All Nations now to *Rome* obedience pay,
To *Rome*'s great Emperour, whose wide domain
In ample Territory, wealth and power,
Civility of Manners, Arts, and Arms,
And long Renown thou justly may'st prefer
Before the *Parthian*; these two Thrones except,
The rest are barbarous, and scarce worth the sight,
Shar'd among petty Kings too far remov'd;
These having shewn thee, I have shewn thee all
The Kingdoms of the world, and all thir glory.
This Emperour hath no Son, and now is old,
Old, and lascivious, and from *Rome* retir'd
To *Capreæ* an Island small but strong
On the *Campanian* shore, with purpose there
His horrid lusts in private to enjoy,
Committing to a wicked Favourite
All publick cares, and yet of him suspicious,
Hated of all, and hating; with what ease
Indu'd with Regal Vertues as thou art,
Appearing, and beginning noble deeds,
Might'st thou expel this monster from his Throne
Now made a stye, and in his place ascending
A victor people free from servile yoke?
And with my help thou may'st; to me the power
Is given, and by that right I give it thee.
Aim therefore at no less than all the world,

Aim at the highest, without the highest attain'd
Will be for thee no sitting, or not long
On *David's* Throne, be propheci'd what will.

Book iv, lines 44–108, 1671

(*vi*) *Athens*

LOOK once more ere we leave this specular Mount
Westward, much nearer by Southwest, behold
Where on the *Ægean* shore a City stands
Built nobly, pure the air, and light the soil,
Athens the eye of *Greece*, Mother of Arts
And Eloquence, native to famous wits
Or hospitable, in her sweet recess,
City or Suburban, studious walks and shades;
See there the Olive Grove of *Academe*,
Plato's retirement, where the *Attic* Bird
Trills her thick-warbl'd notes the summer long,
There flowrie hill *Hymettus* with the sound
Of Bees industrious murmur oft invites
To studious musing; there *Ilissus* rolls
His whispering stream; within the walls then view
The schools of antient Sages; his who bred
Great *Alexander* to subdue the world,
Lyceum there, and painted *Stoa* next:
There thou shalt hear and learn the secret power
Of harmony in tones and numbers hit
By voice or hand, and various-measur'd verse,
Æolian charms and *Dorian Lyric* Odes,
And his who gave them breath, but higher sung,
Blind *Melesigenes* thence *Homer* call'd,
Whose Poem *Phœbus* challeng'd for his own.

Thence what the lofty grave Tragœdians taught
In *Chorus* or *Iambic*, teachers best
Of moral prudence, with delight receiv'd
In brief sententious precepts, while they treat
Of fate, and chance, and change in human life;
High actions, and high passions best describing:
Thence to the famous Orators repair,
Those antient, whose resistless eloquence
Wielded at will that fierce Democratie,
Shook the Arsenal and fulmin'd over *Greece*,
To *Macedon*, and *Artaxerxes* Throne;
To sage Philosophy next lend thine ear,
From Heaven descended to the low-rooft house
Of *Socrates*, see there his Tenement,
Whom well inspir'd the Oracle pronounc'd
Wisest of men; from whose mouth issu'd forth
Mellifluous streams that water'd all the schools
Of Academics old and new, with those
Sirnam'd *Peripatetics*, and the Sect
Epicurean, and the *Stoic* severe;
These here revolve, or, as thou lik'st, at home,
Till time mature thee to a Kingdom's waight;
These rules will render thee a King compleat
Within thy self, much more with Empire joyn'd.
  To whom our Saviour sagely thus repli'd.
Think not but that I know these things, or think
I know them not; not therefore am I short
Of knowing what I ought: he who receives
Light from above, from the fountain of light,
No other doctrine needs, though granted true;
But these are false, or little else but dreams,
Conjectures, fancies, built on nothing firm.

The first and wisest of them all profess'd
To know this only, that he nothing knew;
The next to fabling fell and smooth conceits,
A third sort doubted all things, though plain sense;
Others in vertue plac'd felicity,
But vertue joyn'd with riches and long life,
In corporal pleasure he, and careless ease,
The Stoic last in Philosophic pride,
By him call'd vertue; and his vertuous man,
Wise, perfect in himself, and all possessing
Equal to God, oft shames not to prefer,
As fearing God nor man, contemning all
Wealth, pleasure, pain or torment, death and life,
Which when he lists, he leaves, or boasts he can,
For all his tedious talk is but vain boast,
Or subtle shifts conviction to evade.
Alas what can they teach, and not mislead;
Ignorant of themselves, of God much more,
And how the world began, and how man fell
Degraded by himself, on grace depending?
Much of the Soul they talk, but all awrie,
And in themselves seek vertue, and to themselves
All glory arrogate, to God give none,
Rather accuse him under usual names,
Fortune and Fate, as one regardless quite
Of mortal things. Who therefore seeks in these
True wisdom, finds her not, or by delusion
Far worse, her false resemblance only meets,
An empty cloud. However many books
Wise men have said are wearisom; who reads
Incessantly, and to his reading brings not
A spirit and judgment equal or superior,

(And what he brings, what needs he elsewhere seek)
Uncertain and unsettl'd still remains,
Deep verst in books and shallow in himself,
Crude or intoxicate, collecting toys,
And trifles for choice matters, worth a spunge;
As Children gathering pebbles on the shore.
Or if I would delight my private hours
With Music or with Poem, where so soon
As in our native Language can I find
That solace? All our Law and Story strew'd
With Hymns, our Psalms with artful terms inscrib'd,
Our Hebrew Songs and Harps in *Babylon*,
That pleas'd so well our Victors ear, declare
That rather *Greece* from us these Arts deriv'd;
Ill imitated, while they loudest sing
The vices of thir Deities, and thir own
In Fable, Hymn, or Song, so personating
Thir Gods ridiculous, and themselves past shame.
Remove their swelling Epithetes thick laid
As varnish on a Harlots cheek, the rest,
Thin sown with aught of profit or delight,
Will far be found unworthy to compare
With *Sion*'s songs, to all true tasts excelling,
Where God is prais'd aright, and Godlike men,
The Holiest of Holies, and his Saints;
Such are from God inspir'd, not such from thee;
Unless where moral vertue is express't
By light of Nature not in all quite lost.
Thir Orators thou then extoll'st, as those
The top of Eloquence, Statists indeed,
And lovers of thir Country, as may seem;
But herein to our Prophets far beneath,

As men divinely taught, and better teaching
The solid rules of Civil Government
In thir majestic unaffected stile
Than all the Oratory of *Greece* and *Rome*.
In them is plainest taught, and easiest learnt,
What makes a Nation happy, and keeps it so,
What ruins Kingdoms, and lays Cities flat;
These only with our Law best form a King.

Book iv, lines 236–364, 1671

390 From '*Samson Agonistes*'

(*i*) *Samson Fallen*

THIS, this is he; softly a while,
Let us not break in upon him;
O change beyond report, thought, or belief!
See how he lies at random, carelessly diffus'd,
With languish't head unpropt,
As one past hope, abandon'd
And by himself given over;
In slavish habit, ill-fitted weeds
O'er worn and soild;
Or do my eyes misrepresent? Can this be hee,
That Heroic, that Renown'd,
Irresistible *Samson*? whom unarm'd
No strength of man, or fiercest wild beast could withstand;
Who tore the Lion, as the Lion tears the Kid,
Ran on embattelld Armies clad in Iron,
And weaponless himself,
Made Arms ridiculous, useless the forgery
Of brazen shield and spear, the hammer'd Cuirass,

Chalybean temper'd steel, and frock of mail
Adamantean Proof;
But safest he who stood aloof,
When insupportably his foot advanc't,
In scorn of thir proud arms and warlike tools,
Spurn'd them to death by Troops. The bold *Ascalonite*
Fled from his Lion ramp, old Warriors turn'd
Thir plated backs under his heel;
Or grovling soild thir crested helmets in the dust.
Then with what trivial weapon came to hand,
The Jaw of a dead Ass, his sword of bone,
A thousand fore-skins fell, the flower of *Palestin*
In *Ramath-lechi* famous to this day:
Then by main force pull'd up, and on his shoulders bore
The Gates of *Azza*, Post, and massie Bar
Up to the Hill by *Hebron*, seat of Giants old,
No journey of a Sabbath day, and loaded so;
Like whom the Gentiles feign to bear up Heav'n.
Which shall I first bewail,
Thy Bondage or lost Sight,
Prison within Prison
Inseparably dark?
Thou art become (O worst imprisonment!)
The Dungeon of thy self; thy Soul
(Which Men enjoying sight oft without cause complain)
Imprison'd now indeed,
In real darkness of the body dwells,
Shut up from outward light
To incorporate with gloomy night;
For inward light alas
Puts forth no visual beam.
O mirror of our fickle state,

Since man on earth unparallel'd!
The rarer thy example stands,
By how much from the top of wondrous glory,
Strongest of mortal men,
To lowest pitch of abject fortune thou art fall'n.
For him I reckon not in high estate
Whom long descent of birth
Or the sphear of fortune raises;
But thee whose strength, while vertue was her mate
Might have subdu'd the Earth,
Universally crown'd with highest praises.

Lines 115–75, 1671

(*ii*) *The Transcendence of God*

JUST are the ways of God,
  And justifiable to Men;
Unless there be who think not God at all,
If any be, they walk obscure;
For of such Doctrine never was there School,
But the heart of the Fool,
And no man therein Doctor but himself.
  Yet more there be who doubt his ways not just,
As to his own edicts, found contradicting,
Then give the rains to wandring thought,
Regardless of his glories diminution;
Till by thir own perplexities involv'd
They ravel more, still less resolv'd,
But never find self-satisfying solution.
  As if they would confine th' interminable,
And tie him to his own prescript,
Who made our Laws to bind us, not himself,
And hath full right to exempt

Whom so it pleases him by choice
From National obstriction, without taint
Of sin, or legal debt;
For with his own Laws he can best dispence.
  He would not else who never wanted means,
Nor in respect of the enemy just cause
To set his people free,
Have prompted this Heroic *Nazarite*,
Against his vow of strictest purity,
To seek in marriage that fallacious Bride,
Unclean, unchaste.
  Down Reason then, at least vain reasonings down,
Though Reason here aver
That moral verdit quits her of unclean:
Unchaste was subsequent, her stain not his.
  But see here comes thy reverend Sire
With careful step, Locks white as downe.
Old *Manoah*: advise
Forthwith how thou oughtst to receive him.

Lines 293–329, 1671

(iii) *The Ways of God to Men*

MANY are the sayings of the wise
  In antient and in modern books enroll'd;
Extolling Patience as the truest fortitude;
And to the bearing well of all calamities,
All chances incident to mans frail life
Consolatories writ
With studied argument, and much perswasion sought
Lenient of grief and anxious thought,
But with th' afflicted in his pangs thir sound
Little prevails, or rather seems a tune,

Harsh, and of dissonant mood from his complaint,
Unless he feel within
Some source of consolation from above;
Secret refreshings, that repair his strength,
And fainting spirits uphold.
  God of our Fathers, what is man!
That thou towards him with hand so various,
Or might I say contrarious,
Temperst thy providence through his short course,
Not evenly, as thou rul'st
The Angelic orders and inferiour creatures mute,
Irrational and brute.
Nor do I name of men the common rout,
That wandring loose about
Grow up and perish, as the summer flie,
Heads without name no more rememberd,
But such as thou hast solemnly elected,
With gifts and graces eminently adorn'd
To some great work, thy glory,
And peoples safety, which in part they effect:
Yet toward these thus dignifi'd, thou oft
Amidst thir highth of noon,
Changest thy countenance, and thy hand with no regard
Of highest favours past
From thee on them, or them to thee of service.
  Nor only dost degrade them, or remit
To life obscur'd, which were a fair dismission,
But throw'st them lower than thou didst exalt them high,
Unseemly falls in human eie,
Too grievous for the trespass or omission,
Oft leav'st them to the hostile sword
Of Heathen and prophane, thir carkasses

To dogs and fowls a prey, or else captiv'd:
Or to the unjust tribunals, under change of times,
And condemnation of the ingrateful multitude.
If these they scape, perhaps in poverty
With sickness and disease thou bow'st them down,
Painful diseases and deform'd,
In crude old age;
Though not disordinate, yet causless suffring
The punishment of dissolute days, in fine,
Just or unjust, alike seem miserable,
For oft alike, both come to evil end.
So deal not with this once thy glorious Champion,
The Image of thy strength, and mighty minister.
What do I beg? how hast thou dealt already?
Behold him in this state calamitous, and turn
His labours, for thou canst, to peaceful end.
But who is this, what thing of Sea or Land?
Female of sex it seems,
That so bedeckt, ornate, and gay,
Comes this way sailing
Like a stately Ship
Of *Tarsus*, bound for th' Isles
Of *Javan* or *Gadier*
With all her bravery on, and tackle trim,
Sails fill'd, and streamers waving,
Courted by all the winds that hold them play,
An Amber scent of odorous perfume
Her harbinger, a damsel train behind;
Some rich *Philistian* Matron she may seem,
And now at nearer view, no other certain
Than *Dalila* thy wife.

Lines 652–724, 1671

JOHN MILTON

(*iv*) *Woman*

IT is not vertue, wisdom, valour, wit,
Strength, comliness of shape, or amplest merit
That womans love can win or long inherit;
But what it is, hard is to say,
Harder to hit,
(Which way soever men refer it)
Much like thy riddle, *Samson*, in one day
Or seven, though one should musing sit;
If any of these or all, the *Timnian* bride
Had not so soon preferr'd
Thy Paranymph, worthless to thee compar'd,
Successour in thy bed,
Nor both so loosly disally'd
Thir nuptials, nor this last so trecherously
Had shorn the fatal harvest of thy head.
Is it for that such outward ornament
Was lavish't on thir Sex, that inward gifts
Were left for haste unfinish't, judgment scant,
Capacity not rais'd to apprehend
Or value what is best
In choice, but oftest to affect the wrong?
Or was too much of self-love mixt,
Of constancy no root infixt,
That either they love nothing, or not long?
What e'er it be, to wisest men and best
Seeming at first all heavenly under virgin veil,
Soft, modest, meek, demure,
Once join'd, the contrary she proves, a thorn
Intestin, far within defensive arms
A cleaving mischief, in his way to vertue

Adverse and turbulent, or by her charms
Draws him awry enslav'd
With dotage, and his sense deprav'd
To folly and shameful deeds which ruin ends.
What Pilot so expert but needs must wreck
Embarqu'd with such a Steers-mate at the Helm?
  Favour'd of Heav'n who finds
One vertuous rarely found,
That in domestic good combines:
Happy that house! his way to peace is smooth:
But vertue which breaks through all opposition,
And all temptation can remove,
Most shines and most is acceptable above.
  Therefore Gods universal Law
Gave to the man despotic power
Over his female in due awe,
Nor from that right to part an hour,
Smile she or lowre:
So shall he least confusion draw
On his whole life, not sway'd
By female usurpation, nor dismay'd.

Lines 1010–60, 1671

(v) *The Deliverer*

OH how comely it is and how reviving
  To the Spirits of just men long opprest!
When God into the hands of thir deliverer
Puts invincible might
To quell the mighty of the Earth, th' oppressour,
The brute and boist'rous force of violent men
Hardy and industrious to support
Tyrannic power, but raging to pursue

The righteous and all such as honour Truth;
He all thir Ammunition
And feats of War defeats
With plain Heroic magnitude of mind
And celestial vigour arm'd,
Thir Armories and Magazins contemns,
Renders them useless, while
With winged expedition
Swift as the lightning glance he executes
His errand on the wicked, who surpris'd
Lose thir defence distracted and amaz'd.
 But patience is more oft the exercise
Of Saints, the trial of thir fortitude,
Making them each his own Deliverer,
And Victor over all
That tyrannie or fortune can inflict,
Either of these is in thy lot,
Samson, with might endu'd
Above the Sons of men; but sight bereav'd
May chance to number thee with those
Whom Patience finally must crown.
This Idols day hath bin to thee no day of rest,
 Labouring thy mind
More than the working day thy hands,
And yet perhaps more trouble is behind.
For I descry this way
Some other tending, in his hand
A Scepter or quaint staff he bears,
Comes on amain, speed in his look.
By his habit I discern him now
A Public Officer, and now at hand.
His message will be short and voluble. Lines 1268–1307, 1671

JOHN MILTON

(*vi*) *Heroic Vengeance*

Chorus. O DEARLY-bought revenge, yet glorious!
Living or dying thou hast fulfill'd
The work for which thou wast foretold
To *Israel*, and now ly'st victorious
Among thy slain self-kill'd
Not willingly, but tangl'd in the fold
Of dire necessity, whose law in death conjoin'd
Thee with thy slaughter'd foes in number more
Than all thy life had slain before.
Semichor. While thir hearts were jocund and sublime,
Drunk with Idolatry, drunk with Wine,
And fat regorg'd of Bulls and Goats,
Chaunting thir Idol, and preferring
Before our living Dread who dwells
In *Silo* his bright Sanctuary:
Among them he a spirit of phrenzie sent,
Who hurt thir minds,
And urg'd them on with mad desire
To call in haste for thir destroyer;
They only set on sport and play
Unweetingly importun'd
Thir own destruction to come speedy upon them.
So fond are mortal men
Fall'n into wrath divine,
As thir own ruin on themselves to invite,
Insensate left, or to sense reprobate,
And with blindness internal struck.
Semichor. But he though blind of sight,
Despis'd and thought extinguish't quite,

With inward eyes illuminated
His fierie vertue rouz'd
From under ashes into sudden flame,
And as an ev'ning Dragon came,
Assailant on the perched roosts,
And nests in order rang'd
Of tame villatic Fowl; but as an Eagle
His cloudless thunder bolted on thir heads.
So vertue giv'n for lost,
Deprest, and overthrown, as seem'd,
Like that self-begott'n bird
In the *Arabian* woods embost,
That no second knows nor third,
And lay ere while a Holocaust,
From out her ashie womb now teem'd
Revives, reflourishes, then vigorous most
When most unactive deem'd,
And though her body die, her fame survives,
A secular bird ages of lives.

Lines 1660–1707, 1671

(*vii*)

ALL is best, though we oft doubt,
What th' unsearchable dispose
Of highest wisdom brings about,
And ever best found in the close.
Oft he seems to hide his face,
But unexpectedly returns
And to his faithful Champion hath in place
Bore witness gloriously; whence *Gaza* mourns
And all that band them to resist

His uncontroulable intent;
His servants he with new acquist
Of true experience from this great event
With peace and consolation hath dismist,
And calm of mind all passion spent.

Lines 1745–58, 1671

SIR ASTON COKAYNE

1608–1684

391 *Funeral Elegy on the Death of his very good Friend* Mr. *Michael Drayton*

PHŒBUS, art thou a God, and canst not give
A Priviledge unto thine own to live?
Thou canst: But if that Poets ne'er should dye,
In Heaven who should praise thy Deity?
Else still (my *Drayton*) thou hadst liv'd and writ;
Thy life had been immortal as thy wit.
But *Spenser* is grown hoarse, he that of late
Sung *Gloriana* in her *Elfin* state:
And so is *Sydney*, whom we yet admire
Lighting our little Torches at his fire.
These have so long before *Apollo's* Throne
Caroll'd Encomiums, that they now are growne
Weary and faint; and therefore thou didst dye,
Their sweet unfinish'd Ditty to supply,
So was the Iliad-writer rapt away
Before his lov'd *Achilles* fatall day,
And when his voice began to fail, the great
Unequall'd *Maro* did assume his seat:

Therefore we must not mourn, unless it be
'Cause none is left worthy to follow thee.
It is in vain to say thy lines are such
As neither time nor envies rage can touch:
For they must live, and will, whiles there 's an eye
To reade, or wit to judge of Poetrie.
You *Swans* of *Avon*, change your fates, and all
Sing, and then die at *Drayton's* Funeral:
Sure shortly there will not a drop be seen,
And the smooth-pebbled Bottom be turn'd green,
When the *Nymphes* (that inhabit in it) have
(As they did *Shakespeere*) wept thee to thy grave.
But I molest thy quiet; sleep, whilst we
That live, would leave our lives to die like thee.

A Chain of Golden Poems, 1658

SIR JOHN SUCKLING

1609–1642

392 ### (*Why so pale and wan*)

WHY so pale and wan fond lover?
Prethee why so pale?
Will, when looking well can't move her
Looking ill prevail?
Prethee why so pale?

Why so dull and mute young sinner?
Prethee why so mute?
Will, when speaking well can't win her?
Saying nothing do 't?
Prethee why so mute?

Quit, quit for shame, this will not move,
    This cannot take her;
If of her self she will not love,
    Nothing can make her:
    The divel take her.

Aglaura, 1638 (text from *Fragmenta Aurea*, 1646)

393

Song

NO, no, fair Heretick, it needs must be
    But an ill love in me,
  And worse for Thee;
For were it in my power,
To love thee now this hower
  More than I did the last;
I would then so fall
    I might not love at all;
Love that can flow, and can admit increase,
Admits as well an ebbe, and may grow lesse.

True Love is still the same; the Torrid Zones,
  And those more frigid ones
  It must not know:
For love grown cold or hot,
  Is lust, or friendship, not
  The thing we have.
For that's a flame would dye
Held down, or up too high:
Then think I love more than I can expresse,
And would love more could I but love thee lesse.

Aglaura, 1638 (text from *Fragmenta Aurea*, 1646)

394 *Loving and Beloved*

THERE never yet was honest man
    That ever drove the trade of love;
It is impossible, nor can
    Integrity our ends promove:
For Kings and Lovers are alike in this
That their chief art in reigne dissembling is.

Here we are lov'd, and there we love,
    Good nature now and passion strive
Which of the two should be above,
    And laws unto the other give.
So we false fire with art sometime discover,
And the true fire with the same art do cover.

What Rack can Fancy find so high?
    Here we must Court, and here ingage,
Though in the other place we die.
    O! 'tis torture all, and cozenage;
And which the harder is I cannot tell,
To hide true love, or make false love looke well.

Since it is thus, God of desire,
    Give me my honesty again,
And take thy brands back, and thy fire;
    I'm weary of the State I'm in:
Since (if the very best should now befal)
Loves Triumph, must be Honours Funeral.

Fragmenta Aurea, 1646

395

Sonnet ii

OF thee (kind boy) I ask no red and white
To make up my delight,
No odd becoming graces,
Black eyes, or little know-not-whats, in faces;
Make me but mad enough, give me good store
Of Love, for her I court,
I ask no more,
'Tis love in love that makes the sport.

There's no such thing as that we beauty call,
It is meer cosenage all;
For though some time ago
Like't certain colours mingled so and so,
That doth not tie me now from chusing new,
If I a fancy take
To black and blue,
That fancy doth it beauty make.

'Tis not the meat, but 'tis the appetite
Makes eating a delight,
And if I like one dish
More than another, that a Pheasant is;
What in our watches, that in us is found,
So to the height and nick
We up be wound,
No matter by what hand or trick.

Fragmenta Aurea, 1646

396

Sonnet iii

OH! for some honest Lovers ghost,
Some kind unbodied post
Sent from the shades below.
I strangely long to know
Whether the nobler Chaplets wear,
Those that their mistresse scorn did bear,
Or those that were us'd kindly.

For what-so-e'er they tell us here
To make those sufferings dear,
'Twill there I fear be found,
That to the being crown'd
T' have lov'd alone, will not suffice
Unlesse we also have been wise,
And have our Loves enjoy'd.

What posture can we think him in,
That here unlov'd agen
Departs and 's thither gone
Where each sits by his own?
Or how can that *Elizium* be
Where I my Mistresse still must see
Circled in others Armes?

For there the Judges all are just,
And *Sophonisba* must
Be his whom she held dear;
Not his who lov'd her here:
The sweet Philoclea since she died
Lies by her *Pirocles* his side,
Not by Amphialus.

Some Bayes (perchance) or Myrtle bough
    For difference crowns the brow
    Of those kind souls that were
    The noble Martyrs here;
And if that be the onely odds
(As who can tell) ye kinder Gods,
    Give me the Woman here.

Fragmenta Aurea, 1646

397 *A Ballad upon a Wedding*

I TELL thee *Dick* where I have been,
Where I the rarest things have seen;
        Oh things without compare!
Such sights again cannot be found
In any place on English ground,
        Be it at Wake, or Fair.

At *Charing-Crosse*, hard by the way
Where we (thou know'st) do sell our Hay,
        There is a house with stairs;
And there did I see coming down
Such folk as are not in our Town,
        Vorty at least, in Pairs.

Amongst the rest, one Pest'lent fine,
(His beard no bigger though than thine)
        Walkt on before the rest:
Our Landlord looks like nothing to him:
The King (God bless him) 'twould undo him,
        Should he go still so drest.

At Course-a-Park, without all doubt,
He should have just been taken out
By all the Maids i' th' Town:
Though lusty *Roger* there had been,
Or little *George* upon the Green,
Or *Vincent* of the Crown.

But wot you what? the youth was going
To make an end of all his wooing;
The Parson for him staid;
Yet by his leave (for all his haste)
He did not so much wish all past,
(Perchance) as did the maid.

The maid (and thereby hangs a tale)
For such a maid no Whitsun-ale
Could ever yet produce:
No Grape that 's kindly ripe, could be
So sound, so plump, so soft as she,
Nor half so full of Juice.

Her finger was so small, the Ring
Would not stay on, which they did bring,
It was too wide a Peck;
And to say truth (for out it must)
It lookt like a great Collar (just)
About our young Colts neck.

Her feet beneath her Petticoat,
Like little mice stole in and out,
As if they fear'd the light:
But oh! she dances such a way
No Sun upon an Easter day
Is half so fine a sight.

He would have kist her once or twice,
But she would not, she was so nice,
She would not do 't in sight,
And then she lookt as who should say
I will do what I list to day;
And you shall do 't at night.

Her Cheeks so rare a white was on,
No Dazy makes comparison,
(Who sees them is undone)
For streaks of red were mingled there,
Such as are on a Katherine Pear,
(The side that 's next the Sun.)

Her lips were red, and one was thin,
Compar'd to that was next her chin;
(Some Bee had stung it newly.)
But (*Dick*) her eyes so guard her face;
I durst no more upon them gaze,
Than on the Sun in *July*.

Her mouth so small when she does speak,
Thou 'dst swear her teeth her words did break,
That they might passage get,
But she so handled still the matter,
They came as good as ours, or better,
And are not spent a whit.

If wishing should be any sin,
The Parson himself had guilty bin;
(She lookt that day so purely,)
And did the youth so oft the feat
At night, as some did in conceit,
It would have spoil'd him, surely.

Katherine: Katherne *1646*.

Just in the nick the Cook knockt thrice,
And all the waiters in a trice
His summons did obey,
Each serving man with dish in hand,
Marcht boldly up, like our Train'd Band,
Presented, and away.

When all the meat was on the Table,
What man of knife, or teeth, was able
To stay to be intreated?
And this the very reason was,
Before the Parson could say Grace,
The Company was seated.

The bus'nesse of the Kitchin 's great,
For it is fit that men should eat;
Nor was it there deni'd:
Passion o' me! How I run on!
There 's that that would be thought upon,
(I trow) besides the Bride.

Now hats fly off, and youths carouse;
Healths first go round, and then the house,
The Bride's came thick and thick;
And when 'twas nam'd anothers health,
Perhaps he made it hers by stealth.
(And who could help it, *Dick*?)

O' th' sudden up they rise and dance;
Then sit again and sigh, and glance:
Then dance again and kisse:
Thus sev'ral waies the time did passe,
Till ev'ry Woman wisht her place,
And ev'ry Man wisht his.

By this time all were stoln aside
To counsel and undresse the Bride;
        But that he must not know:
But yet 'twas thought he guess'd her mind,
And did not mean to stay behind
        Above an hour or so.

When in he came (*Dick*) there she lay
Like new-faln snow melting away
        ('Twas time I trow to part)
Kisses were now the only stay,
Which soon she gave, as who would say,
        Good Boy! with all my heart.

But just as heav'ns would have to cross it,
In came the Bridemaids with the Posset:
        The Bridegroom eat in spight;
For had he left the Women to 't
It would have cost two hours to do 't,
        Which were too much that night.

At length the candles out and out,
All that they had not done, they do 't:
        What that is, who can tell?
But I believe it was no more
Than thou and I have done before
        With *Bridget*, and with *Nell*.

Fragmenta Aurea, 1646

398 *(Out upon it)*

OUT upon it, I have lov'd,
    Three whole days together;
And am like to love three more,
    If it prove fair weather.

Time shall moult away his wings
Ere he shall discover
In the whole wide world agen
Such a constant Lover.

But the spite on 't is, no praise
Is due at all to me:
Love with me had made no staies,
Had it any been but she.

Had it any been but she
And that very Face,
There had been at least ere this
A dozen dozen in her place.

Last Remains, 1659

SIDNEY GODOLPHIN

1610–1643

399 *(Quatrains)*

NOE more unto my thoughts appeare,
At least appeare lesse Fayre,
For crazy tempers justly Feare
The goodnesse of the ayre;

Whilst your pure Image hath a place
In my Impurer Minde,
Your very shaddow is the glasse
Where my defects I finde.

Shall I not Fly that brighter light
Which makes my Fyres looke Pale
And put that vertue out of sight
Which makes Mine none at all?

No, no, your picture doth impart
  Such value I not wish
The native worth to any heart
  That's unadorn'd with this.

Though poorer in desert I make
  My selfe whilst I admire,
The fuel which from hope I take
  I give to my desire.

If this flame lighted from your Eyes
  The subject doe calcine,
A Heart may be your sacrifice
  Too weake to be your shrine.

MS. Malone 13 (*Bodleian*)

400 *To the tune of, In fayth I cannot keepe my fathers sheepe*

CLORIS, it is not thy disdaine
  Can ever cover with dispaire,
  Or in cold ashes hide that care
Which I have fed with so long paine,
I may perhaps myne eyes refraine
And fruiteless wordes no more impart,
But yet still serve, still serve thee in my hearte;

What though I spend my haplesse dayes,
  In finding entertainements out
  Carelesse of what I go about,
Or seeke my peace in skillfull wayes
Applying to my Eyes new rays
Of Beauty, And another flame
Unto my Heart, my heart is still the same.

Tis true that I could love no face
  Inhabited by cold disdayne
  Taking delight in others paine;
Thy lookes are full of native grace.
Since then by chance scorne there hath place
Tis to be hop't I may remove
This scorne one day, one day by endless love.

MS. Malone 13 (*Bodleian*)

401 (*Lord when the wise men came from far*)

LORD when the wise men came from far
  Led to thy Cradle by A Star,
Then did the shepheards too rejoyce,
Instructed by thy Angells voyce,
Blest were the wisemen in their skill,
And shepheards in their harmelesse will.

Wisemen in tracing natures lawes
Ascend unto the highest cause,
Shepheards with humble fearefulnesse
Walke safely, though their light be lesse:
Though wisemen better know the way,
It seemes no honest heart can stray.

There is no merit in the wise
But love, (the shepheards sacrifice).
Wisemen, all wayes of knowledge past,
To th' shepheards wonder come at last;
To know, can only wonder breede,
And not to know, is wonders seede.

A wiseman at the Altar bowes
And offers up his studied vowes
And is received; may not the teares,
Which spring too from a shepheards feares,
And sighs upon his fraylty spent,
Though not distinct, be eloquent?

Tis true, the object sanctifies
All passions which within us rise,
But since no creature comprehends
The cause of causes, end of ends,
Hee who himselfe vouchsafes to know
Best pleases his creator so.

When then our sorrowes we applye
To our owne wantes and poverty,
When wee looke up in all distresse
And our owne misery confesse,
Sending both thankes and prayers above,
Then though wee do not know, we love.

MS. Malone 13 (*Bodleian*)

402 *Song*

OR love mee lesse, or love mee more
and play not with my liberty,
Either take all, or all restore,
bind mee at least, or set mee free,
Let mee some nobler torture finde
than of a doubtfull wavering mynd,
Take all my peace, but you betray
myne honour too this cruell way.

Tis true that I have nurst before
  that hope of which I now complaine,
And having little sought no more,
  fearing to meet with your disdaine:
The sparks of favour you did give,
  I gently blew to make them live:
And yet have gaind by all this care
  no rest in hope, nor in despaire.

I see you weare that pittying smile
  which you have still vouchsaf't my smart,
Content thus cheapely to beguile
  and entertaine an harmelesse heart:
But I no longer can give way
  to hope, which doeth so little pay,
And yet I dare no freedome owe
  whilst you are kind, though but in shew.

Then give me more, or give me lesse,
  do not disdaine a mutuall sense,
Or your unpittying beauties dresse
  in their owne free indifference;
But shew not a severer eye
  sooner to give mee liberty,
For I shall love the very scorne
  which for my sake you do put on.

MS. Malone 13 (*Bodleian*)

403 *Reply*

UNHAPPY East (not in that awe
  you pay your Lords, whose will is law)
but in your owne unmanly raigne
on the soft sex, and proud disdaine!

what state would bring the value downe
of treasure which is all their owne?
Their thoughts to worthlesse objects move
who thus suppresse the growth of Love,
Love that extends the high desire,
Love that improves the manly fire,
and makes the price of Beauty rise
and all our wishes multiplyes;
Such high content dwells not in sense,
nor can the captiv'd fayre dispense
such sweetes as these; no servile Dame
can with her Beauty feed this flame;
such joyes as these requires an heart
in which no other love hath part.
Ah! who would prize his Liberty
(this faint weake pleasure to be Free)
deare as the woundes, which love can give,
the bond in which such servaunts live?
who list in wandring loose desire
vary his love, disperse his fire,
aime at no more than to repeate
the thirst of sense, and quench that heate.
Let my collected passion rise
all and to one a sacrifice:
I fear not her discerning breast
should be with other love imprest,
be to the proud resign'd a prey,
or to the loud, or to the Gay.
why should distorted nature prove
more lovely than my humble love?
what taught the elder tymes successe
in love, but love, and humblenesse?

the Nimphes resign'd their virgin feares
to nothing but the Sheapheards teares.
Nature with wise distrust doth arme
and guard that tender sex from harme.
Long wayting love doth passage find
into the slow beleeving mynde.
Jove when he would with love comply
is sayd to lay his thunder by;
too rough he thinks the shape of Man;
now in the softnesse of a swan,
Now like another Nimph appeares,
and so beguiles Calistaes feares.
by force he could have soone comprest
that which contents the ruder East,
but he by this Diviner Art
makes conquest of the Heavenly part.

MS. Malone 13 (*Bodleian*) and *Tixall Poets*

WILLIAM CARTWRIGHT

1611–1643

404 *A Valediction*

BID me not go where neither Suns nor Show'rs
Do make or Cherish Flow'rs;
Where discontented things in sadness lie,
And Nature grieves as I;
When I am parted from those Eyes,
From which my better day doth rise,
Though some propitious Pow'r
Should plant me in a Bow'r,
Where amongst happy Lovers I might see
How Showers and Sun-Beams bring
One everlasting Spring,

Nor would those fall, nor these shine forth to me;
  Nature her Self to him is lost,
  Who loseth her he honours most.
Then Fairest to my parting view display
  Your Graces all in one full day;
Whose blessed Shapes I'll snatch and keep, till when
  I do return and view agen:
So by this Art Fancy shall Fortune cross;
And Lovers live by thinking on their loss.

Plays and Poems, 1651

405 *To Chloe who wish'd her self young enough for me*

CHLOE, why wish you that your years
  Would backwards run, till they meet mine,
That perfect Likeness, which endears
  Things unto things, might us Combine?
Our Ages so in date agree,
That Twins do differ more than we.

There are two Births, the one when Light
  First strikes the new awak'ned sense;
The Other when two Souls unite;
  And we must count our life from thence:
When you lov'd me, and I lov'd you,
Then both of us were born anew.

Love then to us did new Souls give,
  And in those Souls did plant new pow'rs;
Since when another life we live,
  The Breath we breathe is his, not ours;
Love makes those young, whom Age doth Chill,
And whom he finds young, keeps young still.

Love, like that Angell that shall call
  Our bodies from the silent Grave,
Unto one Age doth raise us all,
  None too much, none too little have;
Nay that the difference may be done,
He makes two not alike, but One.

And now since you and I are such,
  Tell me what 's yours, and what is mine?
Our Eyes, our Ears, our Taste, Smell, Touch,
  Do (like our Souls) in one Combine;
So by this, I as well may be
Too old for you, as you for me.

Plays and Poems, 1651

406 *Upon the Dramatick Poems of Mr. John Fletcher*

FLETCHER, though some call it thy fault, that wit
So overflow'd thy Scenes, that ere 'twas fit
To come upon the stage, *Beaumont* was fain
To bid thee be more dull, that 's write again,
And bate some of thy fire, which from thee came
In a clear, bright, full, but too large a flame;
And after all (finding thy Genius such)
That blunted, and allay'd, 'twas yet too much,
Added his sober spunge, and did contract
Thy plenty to less wit to make 't exact:
Yet we through his corrections could see
Much treasure in thy superfluity,
Which was so fil'd away, as when we do
Cut Jewels, that that 's lost is Jewell too;

Or as men use to wash Gold, which we know
By losing makes the Stream thence wealthy grow.
They who do on thy works severely sit,
And call thy Store the over-births of wit,
Say thy miscarriages were rare, and when
Thou wert superfluous, that thy fruitfull Pen
Had not fault but abundance, which did lay
Out in one Scene what might well serve a Play;
And hence do grant, that what they call excess
Was to be reckon'd as thy happiness,
From whom wit issued in a full Spring-Tide;
Much did inrich the Stage, much flow'd beside.
For that thou couldst thine own free fancy bind
In stricter numbers, and run so confin'd
As to observe the rules of Art, which sway
In the contrivance of a true-born Play,
These works proclame, which thou didst write retir'd
From *Beaumont*, by none but thy self inspir'd;
Where we see 'twas not chance that made them hit,
Nor were thy Playes the Lotteries of wit,
But like to *Durers* Pencill, which first knew
The Laws of Faces, and then Faces drew;
Thou knowst the Air, the Colour, and the place,
The Symmetry, which gives the Poem grace:
Parts are so fitted unto parts, as do
Shew thou hadst Wit, and Mathematicks too;
Knewst where by line to spare, where to dispence,
And didst beget just Comedies from thence;
Things unto which thou didst such life bequeath,
That they (their own Black-Friers) unacted breathe.
Johnson hath writ things lasting, and divine,
Yet his Love-Scenes, *Fletcher*, compar'd to thine,

Are cold and frosty, and exprest love so,
As heat with Ice, or warm fires mix'd with Snow;
Thou, as if struck with the same generous Darts,
Which burn, and reign in noble Lovers hearts,
Hast cloath'd Affections in such native tires,
And so describ'd them in their own true fires,
Such moving sighs, such undissembled tears,
Such charms of Language, such hopes mixt with fears,
Such grants after denials, such pursuits
After despair, such amorous recruits,
That some who sat Spectators have confest
Themselves transform'd to what they saw exprest,
And felt such shafts steal through their captiv'd sense,
As made them rise Parts, and go Lovers thence.
Nor was thy Stile wholly compos'd of Groves,
Or the soft strains of Shepheards and their Loves;
When thou wouldst Comick be, each smiling birth
In that kind, came into the world all mirth,
All point, all edge, all sharpness; we did sit
Sometimes five Acts out in pure sprightfull wit,
Which flow'd in such true salt, that we did doubt
In which Scene we laught most two shillings out.
Shakespeare to thee was dull, whose best Jest lies
I' th' Ladies questions, and the Fools replies,
Old fashion'd wit, which walk'd from Town to Town
In turn'd Hose, which our Fathers call'd the Clown;
Whose wit our nice times would obsceneness call,
And which made Bawdry pass for Comicall:
Nature was all his Art, thy vein was free
As his, but without his scurrility;
From whom mirth came unforc'd, no Jest perplex'd,

Parts: dramatis personæ.

But without labour clean, chaste and unvext.
Thou wert not like some, our small Poets, who
Could not be Poets, were not we Poets too;
Whose wit is pilfring, and whose vein and wealth
In Poetry lies meerly in their stealth;
Nor did'st thou feel their drought, their pangs, their qualms,
Their rack in writing, who do write for Alms,
Whose wretched Genius, and dependent fires,
But to their Benefactors dole aspires.
Nor hadst thou the sly trick, thy self to praise
Under thy friends names, or to purchase Bayes
Didst write stale commendations to thy Book,
Which we for *Beaumont's* or *Ben Johnson's* took:
That debt thou left'st to us, which none but he
Can truly pay, *Fletcher*, who writes like thee.

Plays and Poems, 1651

NATHANIEL WHITING

fl. 1629–63

407 *The Office of Poetry*

ME thinkes this draught such vertue does infuse,
As if in every sense there dwelt a Muse,
A spirit of valour, to un-god great warre,
Should he but send a ramme; but to the barre,
Who knowes not *Vaticinium* does imply
In equall measures verse and prophesie,
An inspiration, a celestiall touch?
Such is the Poets raptures, Prophets such:
Vates a Bard, and him that does presage,
Vaticinor possest with either rage.

Poema is a booke in numbers fram'd,
Fast cemented with sense, by working nam'd,
To which the choycest Oratour stands bare;
Poesis does in a sublimer aire,
Things humane and divine expose to view.
The first Philosophie that Fame e'er knew,
Was honourd with the name of Poetrie,
Enricht with rules of pure moralitie,
Reading instructions unto heathen men,
With more contentment than the Stoicks pen.
The ancient unto Poets onely gave
The Epithites of wise, divine and grave,
Because their meeters taught the world to know
To whom they did their holy worship owe.
The Greeke is free and kinder in her praise
Which she bestowes upon Poetick Layes;
She calles all that which takes not essence by
A matter pre-existent, Poesie.
So makes the world a Poem, and by this
The great creator a great Poet is.
Nay more, that language on the Nine bestowes;
(As ev'ry callent of that Idiom knowes)
In her etimologues an higher grace,
Calles them παιδεύτας, and whose measures trace
The steps of Nature, humane and divine,
The abstruse mysteries of both untwine,
Unlock the *exta* of each Science, Art,
By cunning search: againe, not as a part,
Nor a grand columne onely, but entreasures
The soule of learning in the Poets measures.
All other Arts (which use and learning gave)

callent: one who knows. *exta*: entrails.

NATHANIEL WHITING

Precepts and rules, as sure foundations, have,
When as the Poets pen alone's inspir'd
With high Enthusiasmes, by heaven fir'd,
Ennius them holy calles, and *Plato* sayes
Furies divine are in the Poets layes;
Nor wanted he himselfe the Poets wit,
He *Dithyrambos* and love passions writ.
The Regall Prophet was a true born Poet,
As to the life his well-tun'd meeters show it,
Compos'd to musicke by that holy man,
Ere *Hopkins* and *Sternhold* knew how to scan.

From *Il Insonio Insonnadado* in *Le Hore di recreatione*, 1637

MARTIN PARKER

d. 1656

408 *The King enjoys his own again*

WHAT *Booker* can Prognosticate?
Or speak of our Kingdom's present state?
I think my self to be as wise,
As he that most looks in the Skies:
My skill goes beyond the depths of a Pond,
Or Rivers, in the greatest Rain;
Whereby I can tell, all things will be well,
When the King enjoys his own again.

There 's neither Swallow, Dove, nor Dade,
Can soar more high or deeper wade;
Nor show a reason from the Stars,
What causeth peace, or Civil Wars:

Dade: *N.E.D.*, A waterbird.

The Man in the Moon, may wear out his shoon,
  By running after Charles-his-Wain,
But all 's to no end; for the times will not mend
  Till the King enjoys his own again.

Though for a time we see *White-Hall*,
With cobwebs hanging on the wall,
In stead of silk and silver brave,
Which formerly it used to have;
  With rich perfume in every room,
    Delightful to that Princely Train:
  Which again you shall see, when the time it shall be,
    That the King enjoys his own again.

Full fourty years the Royal Crown
Hath been his Father's and his own;
And is there anyone but he
That in the same should sharer be?
  For who better may the Scepter sway,
    Than he that hath such right to reign?—
  Then let 's hope for a Peace, for the wars will not cease,
    Till the King enjoys his own again.

Till then, upon *Ararat's-hill*,
My hope shall cast her Anchor still,
Until I see some peaceful dove,
Bring home the branch she dearly love;
  Then will I wait, till the waters abate,
    Which now disturb my troubled brain:
  Else never rejoice, till I hear the voice,
    That the King enjoys his own again.

Roxburghe Ballads

JAMES GRAHAM, MARQUIS OF MONTROSE

1612–1650

409 (*My dear and only Love*)

MY dear and only Love, I pray
  This noble World of thee,
Be govern'd by no other Sway
  But purest Monarchie.
For if Confusion have a Part,
  Which vertuous Souls abhor,
And hold a Synod in thy Heart,
  I'll never love thee more.

Like *Alexander* I will reign,
  And I will reign alone,
My Thoughts shall evermore disdain
  A Rival on my Throne.
He either fears his Fate too much,
  Or his Deserts are small,
That puts it not unto the Touch,
  To win or lose it all.

But I must rule and govern still,
  And always give the Law,
And have each Subject at my Will,
  And all to stand in awe.
But 'gainst my Battery if I find
  Thou shun'st the Prize so sore,
As that thou set'st me up a Blind,
  I'll never love thee more.

Or in the Empire of thy Heart,
Where I should solely be,
Another do pretend a Part,
And dares to Vie with me,
Or if Committees thou erect,
And goes on such a Score,
I'll sing and laugh at thy Neglect,
And never love thee more.

But if thou wilt be constant then,
And faithful of thy Word,
I'll make thee glorious by my Pen,
And famous by my Sword.
I'll serve thee in such noble Ways,
Was never heard before:
I'll crown and deck thee all with Bays,
And love thee evermore.

Watson, *Choice Collection*, 1711

410 *Epitaph on King Charles I*

GREAT, Good and Just, could I but rate
My Grief to Thy too Rigid Fate!
I'd weep the World in such a Strain,
As it would once deluge again:
But since Thy loud-tongu'd Blood demands Supplies,
More from *Briareus* Hands, than *Argus* Eyes,
I'll tune Thy Elegies to Trumpet-sounds,
And write Thy Epitaph in Blood and Wounds!

Watson, *Choice Collection*, 1711

411 *On Himself, upon hearing what was his Sentence*

LET them bestow on ev'ry Airth a Limb;
Open all my Veins, that I may swim
To Thee my Saviour, in that Crimson Lake;
Then place my purboil'd Head upon a Stake;
Scatter my Ashes, throw them in the Air:
Lord (since Thou know'st where all these Atoms are)
I'm hopeful, once Thou'lt recollect my Dust,
And confident Thou'lt raise me with the Just.

Watson, *Choice Collection*, 1711

SAMUEL BUTLER

1612–1680

412 *Presbyterian Knight and Independent Squire*

HE was in *Logick* a great Critick,
Profoundly skill'd in Analytick.
He could distinguish, and divide
A Hair 'twixt *South* and *South-West* side:
On either which he would dispute,
Confute, change hands, and still confute.
He'd undertake to prove by force
Of Argument, a Man 's no Horse.
He'd prove a Buzard is no Fowl,
And that a *Lord* may be an *Owl*,

Airth: Quarter of the compass.

A Calf an *Alderman*, a Goose a *Justice*,
And Rooks *Committee-men*, and *Trustees*;
He'd run in Debt by Disputation,
And pay with Ratiocination.
All this by Syllogism, true
In mood and Figure, he would do.

For *Rhetorick* he could not ope
His mouth, but out there flew a Trope:
And when he hapned to break off
I' th' middle of his speech, or cough,
H' had hard words, ready to shew why,
And tell what Rules he did it by.
Else when with greatest Art he spoke,
You'd think he talk'd like other folk,
For all a Rhetoricians Rules,
Teach nothing but to name his Tools,
His ordinary Rate of Speech
In loftiness of sound was rich,
A Babylonish dialect,
Which learned Pedants much affect.
It was a parti-colour'd dress
Of patch'd and pyball'd Languages:
'Twas English cut on *Greek* and *Latin*,
Like Fustian heretofore on Sattin.
It had an odd promiscuous Tone,
As if h' had talk'd three parts in one.
Which made some think when he did gabble,
Th' had heard three Labo'rers of *Babel*;
Or *Cerberus* himself pronounce
A Leash of Languages at once.
This he as volubly would vent

As if his stock would ne'er be spent.
And truly to support that charge
He had supplies as vast and large.
For he could coin or counterfeit
New words with little or no wit:
Words so debas'd and hard, no stone
Was hard enough to touch them on.
And when with hasty noise he spoke 'em,
The Ignorant for currant took 'em.
That had the Orator who once,
Did fill his Mouth with Pebble Stones
When he harangu'd, but known his Phrase,
He would have us'd no other ways.

. . . .

Beside he was a shrewd *Philosopher*,
And had read every Text and gloss over:
What e'er the crabbed'st Author hath
He understood b' implicit Faith,
What ever *Sceptick* could inquire for;
For every *why* he had a *wherefore*;
Knew more than forty of them do,
As far as words and terms could go.
All which he understood by Rote,
And as occasion serv'd, would quote;
No matter whether right or wrong:
They might be either said or sung.
His Notions fitted things so well,
That which was which he could not tell;
But oftentimes mistook th' one
For th' other, as great Clerks have done.
He could reduce all things to Acts,
And knew their Natures by Abstracts,

Where Entity and Quiddity
The Ghosts of defunct Bodies flie;
Where Truth in Person does appear,
Like words congeal'd in Northern Air.
He knew *what 's what*, and that 's as high
As *Metaphysick* Wit can fly,
In *School Divinity* as able
As he that hight *Irrefragable*;
Profound in all the Nominal
And real ways beyond them all;
And with as delicate a Hand,
Could twist as tough a Rope of Sand,
And weave fine Cobwebs, fit for Skull
That 's empty when the Moon is full;
Such as take Lodgings in a Head
That 's to be let unfurnished.
He could raise Scruples dark and nice,
And after solve 'em in a trice:
As if Divinity had catch'd
The Itch, of purpose to be scratch'd;
Or, like a Mountebank, did wound
And stab her self with doubts profound,
Only to shew with how small pain
The sores of faith are cur'd again;
Although by woful proof we find,
They always leave a Scar behind.
He knew the Seat of Paradise,
Could tell in what degree it lies:
And as he was dispos'd, could prove it,
Below the Moon, or else above it.
What *Adam* dreamt of when his Bride
Came from her Closet in his side:

Whether the Devil tempted her
By a *High Dutch* Interpreter:
If either of them had a Navel;
Who first made Musick malleable:
Whether the Serpent at the fall
Had cloven Feet, or none at all.
All this without a Gloss or Comment,
He would unriddle in a moment:
In proper terms, such as men smatter
When they throw out and miss the matter.
For his *Religion* it was fit
To match his Learning and his Wit:
'Twas *Presbyterian* true blew,
For he was of that stubborn Crew
Of Errant Saints, whom all men grant
To be the true Church *Militant:*
Such as do build their Faith upon
The holy Text of *Pike* and *Gun*;
Decide all Controversies by
Infallible *Artillery*;
And prove their Doctrine Orthodox
By Apostolick *Blows* and *Knocks*;
Call Fire and Sword and Desolation,
A *godly-thorough-Reformation*,
Which always must be carry'd on,
And still be doing, never done:
As if Religion were intended
For nothing else but to be mended.
A Sect, whose chief Devotion lies
In odd perverse Antipathies;
In falling out with that or this,
And finding somewhat still amiss:

More peevish, cross, and splenetick,
Than Dog distract, or Monky sick.
That with more care keep Holy-day
The wrong, than others the right way:
Compound for Sins, they are inclin'd to;
By damning those they have no mind to;
Still so perverse and opposite,
As if they worshipp'd God for spight,
The self-same thing they will abhor
One way, and long another for.
Free-will they one way disavow,
Another, nothing else allow.
All Piety consists therein
In them, in other Men all Sin.
Rather than fail, they will defie
That which they love most tenderly,
Quarrel with *minc'd Pies*, and disparage
Their best and dearest friend, *Plum-porridge;*
Fat *Pig* and *Goose* it self oppose,
And blaspheme *Custard* through the *Nose*.
Th' Apostles of this fierce Religion,
Like *Mahomet*'s, were Ass and Widgeon,
To whom our Knight, by fast instinct
Of Wit and Temper was so linkt,
As if Hipocrisie and Non-sence
Had got th' Advouson of his Conscience.

. . . . .

A Squire he had whose name was *Ralph*,
That in th' adventure went his half.
Though Writers (for more statelier tone)
Do call him *Ralpho*, 'tis all one:

And when we can with Meeter safe,
We'll call him so, if not plain *Ralph*,
For Rhime the Rudder is of Verses,
With which like Ships they steer their courses.
An equal stock of Wit and Valour
He had laid in, by birth a Taylor.
The mighty *Tyrian* Queen that gain'd
With subtle shreds a Tract of Land,
Did leave it with a Castle fair
To his great Ancestor, her Heir:
From him descended cross-leg'd Knights,
Fam'd for their Faith and Warlike Fights
Against the bloudy Caniball,
Whom they destroy'd both great and small.
This sturdy Squire had as well
As the bold *Trojan* Knight, seen hell,
Not with a counterfeited Pass
Of Golden Bough, but true Gold-lace.
His knowledge was not far behind
The Knights, but of another kind,
And he another way came by 't,
Some call it *Gift*, and some *New Light*;
A liberal Art, that cost no pains
Of Study, Industry, or Brains.
His Wits were sent him for a Token,
But in the Carriage crackt and broken
Like Commendation Nine-pence, crookt
With to and from my Love, it lookt,
He ne'er consider'd it, as loath
To look a Gift-horse in the Mouth;
And very wisely would lay forth
No more upon it than 'twas worth.

But as he got it freely, so
He spent it frank and freely too.
For Saints themselves will sometimes be,
Of Gifts that cost them nothing, free.
By means of this, with *hem* and *cough*,
Prolongers to enlightned Snuff,
He could deep Mysteries unriddle,
As easily as thread a Needle;
For as of Vagabonds we say,
That they are ne'er beside their way:
What e'er men speak by this *New Light*,
Still they are sure to be i' th' right.
'Tis a *Dark-Lanthorn* of the Spirit,
Which none see by but those that bear it.
A Light that falls down from on high,
For Spiritual Trades to couzen by:
An *Ignis Fatuus* that bewitches,
And leads Men into Pools and Ditches,
To make them *dip* themselves, and sound
For Christendom in dirty Pond;
To dive like Wild-fowl for Salvation,
And fish to catch Regeneration.
This Light inspires, and plays upon
The nose of Saint like Bag-pipe drone,
And speaks through hollow empty Soul,
As through a Trunk, or whisp'ring hole,
Such language as no mortal Ear
But spiritual Eve-droppers can hear.
So *Phœbus* or some friendly Muse
Into small Poets song infuse;
Which they at second-hand rehearse
Through Reed or Bag-pipe, Verse for Verse.

Thus *Ralph* became infallible,
As three or four-leg'd Oracle,
The ancient Cup, or modern Chair,
Spoke truth point-blank, though unaware:

For mystick Learning, wondrous able
In Magick *Talisman*, and *Cabal*,
Whose Primitive Tradition reaches
As far as *Adam's* first green Breeches:
Deep-sighted in Intelligences,
Ideas, Atoms, Influences;
And much of *Terra Incognita*,
Th' intelligible World could say;
A deep occult Philosopher,
As learn'd as the *Wild Irish* are,
Or Sir *Agrippa*, for profound
And solid Lying much renown'd:
He *Anthroposophus*, and *Floud*,
And *Jacob Behmen* understood;
Knew many an Amulet and Charm,
That would do neither good nor harm:
In *Rosy-Crucian* Lore as Learned,
As he that *Verè adeptus* earned.
He understood the speech of Birds
As well as they themselves do words:
Could tell what subtlest *Parrots* mean,
That speak and think contrary clean;
What *Member* 'tis of whom they talk
When they cry *Rope*, and *Walk Knave, walk.*
He'd extract numbers out of matter,
And keep them in a Glass, like water,
Of Sov'raign pow'r to make men wise;

For dropt in blere, thick-sighted Eyes,
They'd make them see in darkest night,
Like Owls, though pur-blind in the light.
By help of these (as he profest)
He had *First Matter* seen undrest:
He took her naked all alone,
Before one Rag of *Form* was on.
The *Chaos* too he had descry'd,
And seen quite through, or else he ly'd:
Not that of Past-board which men shew
For Groats at Fair of *Barthol'mew*;
But its great Gransire, first o' th' name,
Whence that and *Reformation* came:
Both Cousin-Germans, and right able
T' inveigle and draw in the Rabble.
But *Reformation* was, some say,
O' th' younger house to *Puppet-Play*.
He could foretell whats'ever was
By consequence to come to pass.
As Death of Great Men, Alterations,
Diseases, Battels, Inundations.
All this without th' Eclipse of Sun,
Or dreadful Comet, he hath done
By inward Light, a way as good,
And easie to be understood.
But with more lucky hit than those
That use to make the Stars depose,
Like Knights o' th' Post, and falsly charge
Upon themselves what others forge:
As if they were consenting to
All mischief in the World men do:
Or like the Dev'l, did tempt and sway 'em

To Rogueries, and then betray 'em.
They'll search a Planet's house, to know,
Who broke and robb'd a house below:
Examine *Venus*, and the *Moon*
Who stole a Thimble and a Spoon:
And though they nothing will confess,
Yet by their very looks can guess,
And tell what guilty Aspect bodes,
Who stole, and who receiv'd the Goods.
They'll question *Mars*, and by his look
Detect who 'twas that nimm'd a Cloke:
Make *Mercury* confess and peach
Those Thieves which he himself did teach.
They'll find i' th' Phisiognomies
O' th' Planets all mens destinies.
Like him that took the Doctor's Bill,
And swallow'd it instead o' th' Pill.
Cast the Nativity o' th' Question,
And from Positions to be guest on,
As sure as if they knew the Moment
Of Natives birth, tell what will come on't.
They'll feel the Pulses of the Stars,
To find out Agues, Coughs, Catarrhs;
And tell what *Crysis* does divine
The Rot in Sheep, or Mange in Swine:
In Men what gives or cures the Itch,
What make(s) them Cuckolds, poor or rich:
What gains or loses, hangs or saves;
What makes men great, what fools or knaves;
But not what wise, for only of those
The Stars (they say) cannot dispose,
No more than can the Astrologians.

There they say right, and like true *Trojans.*
This *Ralpho* knew, and therefore took
The other course, of which we spoke.

Thus was th' accomplish'd Squire endu'd
With Gifts and Knowledge, per'lous shrew'd.
Never did trusty Squire with Knight,
Or Knight with Squire jump more right.
Their Arms and Equipage did fit,
As well as Virtues, Parts, and Wit.
Their Valors too were of a Rate,
And out they sally'd at the Gate.

Hudibras, First Part, Canto I, 1663 (text 1678)

413 *Presbyterian Church Government*

SYNODS are whelps of th' *Inquisition,*
A mungrel breed of like pernicion,
And growing up became the Sires
Of *Scribes, Commissioners,* and *Triers;*
Whose bus'ness is, by cunning slight
To cast a figure for mens *Light;*
To find in lines of Beard and Face,
The Phisiognomy of *Grace;*
And by the sound and *twang of Nose,*
If all be sound within disclose,
Free from a crack or flaw of sinning,
As Men try *Pipkins* by the ringing.
By *Black Caps* underlaid with *White,*
Give certain guess at inward *Light;*
Which *Serjeants at the Gospel* wear,
To make the *Spiritual Calling clear.*

The *Hand[k]erchief* about the neck
(Canonical *Cravat* of *Smeck*,
From whom the Institution came
When Church and State they set on flame,
And worn by them as badges then
Of *Spiritual Warfaring Men*)
Judge rightly if *Regeneration*
Be of the *newest Cut* in fashion.
Sure 'tis an Orthodox opinion
That *Grace is founded in Dominion.*
Great *Piety* consists in *Pride*;
To *rule* is to be *sanctifi'd:*
To domineer and to controul
Both o'er the Body and the Soul,
Is the most perfect *discipline*
Of Church-rule, and by *right divine.*
Bell and the *Dragons* Chaplains were
More moderate than these by far:
For they (poor Knaves) were glad to cheat,
To get their Wives and Children Meat:
But these will not be fobb'd off so,
They must have Wealth and Power too,
Or else with blood and desolation,
They'll tear it out o' th' heart o' th' Nation,
Sure these themselves from Primitive
And Heathen Priesthood do derive,
When *Butchers* were the only *Clerks*,
Elders and *Presbyters* of *Kirks*,
Whose *Directory* was to *Kill*;
And some believe it is so still.
The onely diff'rence is, that then
They slaughter'd only Beasts, now Men.

For then to sacrifice a Bullock,
Or now and then a Child to *Moloch*,
They count a vile Abomination,
But not to slaughter a whole *Nation*.
Presbytery does but translate
The Papacy to a *Free State*,
A *Commonwealth of Popery*,
Where ev'ry Village is a *See*
As well as *Rome*, and must maintain
A *Tithe Pig Metropolitane:*
Where ev'ry *Presbyter* and *Deacon*
Commands the *Keys* for Cheese and Bacon;
And ev'ry Hamlet's governed
By's *Holiness*, the *Church*'s *Head*,
More haughty and severe in's place
Than *Gregory* and *Boniface*.
Such Church must (surely) be a Monster
With many heads: for if we conster
What in th' *Apocalypse* we find,
According to th' Apostles mind,
'Tis that the *Whore of Babylon*
With many heads did ride upon;
Which Heads denote the sinful Tribe
Of *Deacon*, *Priest*, *Lay-Elder*, *Scribe*.
Lay-Elder, *Simeon* to *Levi*,
Whose little finger is as heavy
As loins of Patriarchs, Prince-Prelate,
Archbishop-secular. This Zelot
Is of a mungrel, divers kind,
Clerick before, and *Lay* behind;
A Lawless *Linsy-woolsy Brother*,
Half of one Order, half another;

A Creature of amphibious nature,
On Land a Beast, a Fish in Water,
That always preys on Grace, or Sin;
A Sheep without, a Wolf within.
This fierce Inquisitor has chief
Dominion over Mens Belief
And Manners: Can pronounce a *Saint*
Idolatrous, or ignorant,
When superciliously he sifts,
Through coursest Boulter, others *gifts*.
For all Men live and judge amiss
Whose *Talents* jump not just with his.
He'll lay on *Gifts* with hands, and place
On dullest noddle *light* and *grace*,
The manufacture of the *Kirk*,
Whose Pastors are but th' Handiwork
Of his Mechanick Paws, instilling
Divinity in them by feeling.
From whence they start up *chosen Vessels*,
Made by Contact, as Men get *Meazles*.

Hudibras, First Part, Canto III, 1663 (text 1678)

414 ## *Godly Casuistry*

THE Sun had long since in the Lap
Of *Thetis*, taken out his *Nap*,
And like a *Lobster* boyl'd, the *Morn*
From *black* to *red* began to turn.
When *Hudibras*, whom thoughts and aching
'Twixt sleeping kept all night, and waking,
Began to rouse his drousie eyes,
And from his Couch prepar'd to rise;

Resolving to dispatch the Deed
He vow'd to do, with trusty speed.
But first, with knocking loud and bawling,
He rous'd the *Squire*, in *Truckle* lolling,
And, after many Circumstances,
Which vulgar *Authors* in *Romances*,
Do use to spend their *time* and *wits* on,
To make impertinent Description;
They got (with much ado) to *Horse*,
And to the *Castle* bent their Course,
In which he to the *Dame* before
To suffer *whipping* Duty swore:
Where now arriv'd, and half unharnest,
To carry on the work in earnest,
He stopp'd and paus'd upon the sudden,
And with a serious forehead plodding,
Sprung a new Scruple in his head,
Which first he scratch'd and after said;
Whether it be direct *infringing*
An *Oath*, if I should wave this *swinging*,
And what I've sworn to bear, forbear,
And so b' *Equivocation* swear;
Or whether 't be a lesser *Sin*,
To be forsworn, than act the thing,
Are deep and subtle *points*, which must,
T' inform my Conscience, be discust,
In which to *err* a little, may
To *errors* infinite make way:
And therefore I desire to know
Thy *Judgment*, ere we farther go.
  Quoth *Ralpho*, since you do injoin't
I shall enlarge upon the *Point*.

And for my own part do not doubt
Th' *Affirmative* may be made out.
But first to state the *Case* aright,
For best advantage of our light:
And thus 'tis: Whether 't be a *Sin*,
To *claw* and *curry* your own *skin*
Greater, or less, than to forbear,
And that you are forsworn, forswear.
But first, o' th' first: The *Inward Man*,
And *Outward*, like a *Clan* and *Clan*,
Have always been at Daggers-drawing,
And one another Clapper-clawing:
Not that they really cuff or fence,
But in a Spiritual *Mystique* sence,
Which to mistake, and make 'em squabble,
In literal fray, 's abhominable;
'Tis Heathenish, in frequent use,
With *Pagans*, and *Apostate Jews*,
To offer Sacrifice of *Bridewels*:
Like modern *Indians* to their *Idols*,
And mungrel *Christians* of our times,
That expiate less with greater *Crimes*,
And call the foul *Abhomination*,
Contrition, and *Mortification*.
Is 't not enough we're bruis'd and kicked,
With sinful members of the wicked;
Our Vessels, that are *sanctifi'd*,
Profan'd and *curri'd*, back and side;
But we must claw ourselves, with shameful,
And Heathen stripes, by their example?
Which (were there nothing to forbid it)
Is *impious* because they did it.

This therefore may be justly reckon'd
A *heinous* sin. Now to the second,
That *Saints* may claim a *Dispensation*
To *swear* and *forswear* on occasion;
I doubt not, but it will appear,
With pregnant light. The *point* is clear.
Oaths are but *words*, and *words* but *wind*,
Too feeble implements to *bind*;
And hold with *deeds* proportion, so
As *shadows* to a *substance* do.
Then when they strive for *place*, 'tis fit
The *weaker Vessel* should submit:
Although your *Church* be opposite
To ours, as *Black Friers* are to *White*,
In *Rule* and *Order*: Yet I grant
You are a *Reformado Saint*;
And what the *Saints* do claim as due,
You may pretend a Title to:
But *Saints*, whom *Oaths* or *Vows* oblige,
Know little of their *Priviledge*;
Farther (I mean) than carrying on
Some self-advantage of their own,
For if the *Dev'l*, to serve his turn,
Can tell *Truth*; why the *Saints* should scorn
When it serves theirs, to *swear*, and *lie*,
I think, there 's little reason why:
Else h' has a greater pow'r than they,
Which 'twere impiety to say.
W' are not commanded to forbear,
Indefinitely, at all to *swear*.
But to *swear* idly; and in vain,
Without self-interest or gain.

For, breaking of an *Oath*, and *Lying*,
Is but a kind of *Self-denying*,
A *Saint-like virtue*, and from hence,
Some have broke *Oaths* by *Providence*:
Some, to the *Glory of the Lord*,
Perjur'd themselves, and broke their word:
And this, the constant *Rule* and *Practise*
Of all our late *Apostles Acts* is,
Was not the *Cause* at first begun
With *Perjury*, and carry'd on?
Was there an *Oath* the *Godly* took,
But, in due time and place, they broke?
Did we not bring our *Oaths* in first,
Before our *Plate*, to have them burst,
And cast in fitter *models*, for
The present use of *Church* and *War*?
Did not our *Worthies* of the *House*,
Before they broke the *Peace*, break *Vows*?
For having freed us, first, from both
Th' *Allegiance* and *Supremacy Oath*;
Did they not, next, compel the *Nation*,
To take, and break the *Protestation*?
To *swear*, and after to *recant*
The *Solemn League and Covenant*?
To take th' *Engagement*, and disclaim it,
Enforc'd by those, who first did frame it?
Did they not swear at first, to *fight*
For the KING'S *Safety*, and His *Right*?
And after march'd to find him out,
And charg'd him home with *Horse* and *Foot*?
And yet still had the confidence,
To swear it was in his *defence*?

Did they not *swear* to *live* and *die*
With *Essex*, and streight laid him by?
If that were all, for some have *swore*
As false as they, if th' did no more.
Did they not *swear* to maintain *Law*,
In which that *swearing* made a *Flaw*?
For *Protestant Religion* Vow,
That did that *Vowing* disallow?
For *Priviledge* of *Parliament*,
In which that *swearing* made a *Rent*?
And, since, of all the *three*, not one
Is left in being, 'tis well known.
Did they not *swear*, in express words;
To prop and back the *House of Lords*?
And after turn'd out the whole *House-ful*
Of *Peers*, as dang'rous, and unuseful?
So *Cromwel* with deep *Oaths* and *Vows*,
Swore all the *Commons* out o' th' *House*,
Vow'd that the *Red-coats* would disband,
I marry would they at their Command.
And troul'd 'em on, and *swore*, and *swore*,
Till th' *Army* turn'd 'em out of *Door*;
This tells us plainly, what they thought,
That *Oaths* and *swearing* goes for nought.
And that by them th' were onely meant,
To serve for an *Expedient*.
What was the *Publick Faith* found out for,
But to slur men of what they fought for?
The *Publick Faith*, which ev'ry one
Is bound t' observe, yet kept by none;
And if that go for nothing, why
Should *Private Faith* have such a tye?

Oaths were not purpos'd more than *Law*,
To keep the *Good* and *Just* in aw,
But to confine the *Bad* and *Sinful*,
Like Moral Cattle in a *Pinfold*.
A *Saint*'s of th' heavenly Realm a *Peer*:
And as no *Peer* is bound to *swear*,
But on the *Gospel* of his *Honor*,
Of which he may dispose, as *Owner*;
It follows, though the thing be *forgery*,
And false, th' affirm, it is no *perjury*,
But a mere *Ceremony*, and a breach
Of nothing, but a form of speech,
And goes for no more when 'tis took,
Than mere *saluting* of the *Book*.
Suppose the *Scriptures* are of force,
They're but *Commissions* of Course,
And *Saints* have freedom to digress,
And vary from 'em as they please;
Or misinterpret them, by *private*
Instructions, to all *Aims* they drive at,
Then why should we our selves *abridge*
And *Curtail* our own *Priviledge*?
Quakers (that like to *Lanthorns*, bear
Their light within 'em) will not *swear*.
Their *Gospel* is an *Accidence*,
By which they construe *Conscience*,
And hold no *sin* so deeply *red*,
As that of breaking *Priscian's* head;
(The *Head* and *Founder* of their *Order*,
That stirring *Hats* held worse than murder)
These thinking th' are obliged to *Troth*
In *swearing*, will not take an *Oath*;

Like Mules, who if th' have not their will
To keep their own pace, stand stock still;
But they are weak, and little know
What Free-born *Consciences* may do,
'Tis the *temptation* of the Devil,
That makes all humane actions evil:
For *Saints* may do the same things by
The *Spirit*, in Sincerity,
Which other men are tempted to,
And at the Devils instance do;
And yet the Actions be contrary,
Just as the *Saints* and *Wicked* vary.
For as on land there is no *Beast*,
But in some *Fish* at Sea 's exprest;
So in the *Wicked* there 's no *Vice*,
Of which the *Saints* have not a spice;
And yet that thing that 's *pious* in
The one, in th' other is a *Sin*.
Is 't not *Ridiculous*, and *Nonsence*,
A *Saint* should be a slave to *Conscience*?
That ought to be above such Fancies,
As far, as above *Ordinances*,
She 's of the *Wicked*, as I guess,
B' her *looks*, her *language*, and her *dress*,
And though, like *Constables*, we search
For false Wares, one anothers *Church*:
Yet all of us hold this for true,
No Faith is to the wicked due;
For *Truth* is *Precious* and *Divine*,
Too rich a *Pearl* for *Carnal Swine*.

Hudibras, Second Part, Canto II, 1664 (text 1678)

THOMAS JORDAN?

1612?–1685

415

Pyms Anarchy

ASK me no more, why there appears
Dayly such troopes of Dragooners?
Since it is requisite, you know;
They rob *cum privilegio.*

Ask me no more, why th' Gaole confines
Our Hierarchy of best divines?
Since some in Parliament agree
'Tis for the Subjects Liberty.

Ask me no more, why from *Blackwall*
Great tumults come into *Whitehall*?
Since it 's allow'd, by free consent,
The Privilege of Parliament.

Ask me not, why to *London* comes
So many Musquets, Pikes and Drums?
Although you fear they'll never cease;
'Tis to protect the Kingdoms peace.

. . . . .

Ask me no more, why *Strafford's* dead,
And why they aim'd so at his head?
Faith, all the reason I can give,
'Tis thought he was too wise to live.

Ask me no more, where 's all the Plate,
Brought in at such an easie rate?
They will it back to th' Owners bring
In case it fall not to the King.

. . . . .

THOMAS JORDAN?

Ask me no more, by what strange sight
Londons Lord Mayor was made a Knight?
Since there 's a strength, not very far,
Hath as much power to make as mar.

Ask me no more, what in this Age
I sing so sharp without a Cage?
My answer is, I need not fear
Since *England* doth the burden bear.

Ask me no more, for I grow dull,
Why *Hotham* kept the Town of *Hull*?
This answer I in brief do sing,
All things were thus when *Pym* was *King*.

The Rump, 1662

JOHN CLEVELAND

1613–1658

416 *On the memory of Mr. Edward King, drown'd in the Irish Seas*

I LIKE not tears in tune, nor will I prize
His artificial grief that scans his eyes,
Mine weep down pious beads, but why should I
Confine them to the Muses Rosary?
I am no Poet here; my pen 's the spout,
Where the rain water of my eyes run out,
In pity of that name, whose fate wee see
Thus copied out in griefs Hydrography:
The Muses are not Mer-maids, though upon
His death the Ocean might turn *Helicon*.

The sea's too rough for verse; who rhimes upon't
With *Xerxes* strives to fetter th' *Hellespont.*
My tears will keep no channel, know no laws
To guide their streams; but like the waves their cause
Run with disturbance, till they swallow me
As a description of his misery.
But can his spacious virtue finde a grave
Within th' imposthum'd bubble of a wave?
Whose learning if we sound, we must confesse
The sea but shallow, and him bottomlesse.
Could not the winds to countermand thy death
With their whole card of lungs redeem thy breath?
Or some new Island in thy rescue peep
To heave thy resurrection from the deep?
That so the world might see thy safety wrought,
With no lesse miracle than thy self was thought.
The famous *Stagarite*, who in his life
Had nature as familiar as his wife,
Bequeath'd his widow to survive with thee,
Queen Dowager of all Philosophy:
An ominous legacy that did portend
Thy fate and Predecessors second end!
Some have affirm'd, that what on earth we find,
The Sea can parallel for shape and kind:
Books, arts and tongues were wanting, but in thee
Neptune hath got an University.
  We'll dive no more for pearl. The hope to see
Thy sacred reliques of mortality
Shall welcome storms, and make the sea-man prize
His shipwrack now, more than his merchandize.
He shall embrace the waves, and to thy tombe
(As to a Royaller Exchange) shall come.

What can we now expect? Water and Fire
Both elements our ruine do conspire:
And that dissolves us which doth us compound.
One *Vatican* was burnt, another drown'd.
We of the Gown our Libraries must tosse
To understand the greatnesse of our losse,
Be Pupils to our grief, and so much grow
In learning as our sorrows overflow.
When we have fill'd the rundlets of our eyes,
We'll issue't forth, and vent such elegies,
As that our tears shall seem the *Irish* Seas
We floating Islands, living *Hebrides.*

Juxta Edouardo King, 1638

417 *From The Rebell Scot*

COME keen *Iambicks* with your Badgers feet,
And Badger-like, bite till your teeth do meet.
Help ye tart Satyrists to imp my rage,
With all the Scorpions that should whip this age.
Scots are like Witches; do but whet your pen,
Scratch till the blood come, they'll not hurt you then.
Now as the Martyrs were inforc'd to take
The shapes of beasts, like hypocrites at stake,
I'll bait my *Scot* so, yet not cheat your eyes;
A *Scot* within a beast is no disguise.
No more let *Ireland* brag; her harmless Nation
Fosters no Venom, since the *Scots* Plantation:
Nor can ours feign'd antiquity maintain;
Since they came in, *England* hath Wolves again.
The *Scot* that kept the Tower, might have shown
(Within the grate of his own breast alone)

The Leopard and the Panther, and ingrost
What all those wilde Collegiates had cost
The honest high-shoes, in their termly fees,
First to the salvage Lawyer, next to these.
Nature her self doth Scotch-men beasts confess,
Making their Country such a wildernesse:
A Land that brings in question and suspence
Gods omni-presence, but that *Charles* came thence,
But that *Montrose* and *Crawfords* loyal band
Aton'd their sins, and christ'ned half the Land;
Nor is it all the Nation hath these spots;
There is a Church, as well as *Kirk* of *Scots*:
As in a Picture where the squinting paint
Shews fiend on this side, and on that side Saint.
He that saw Hell in 's melancholy dream,
And in the twilight of his fancy's theam
Scar'd from his sins repented in a fright,
Had he view'd *Scotland*, had turn'd Proselyte.
A Land, where one may pray with curst intent,
O may they never suffer banishment!
Had *Cain* been *Scot*, God would have chang'd his doom
Not forc't him wander, but confin'd him home.
Like Jews they spread, and as infection fly,
As if the Devil had ubiquity.
Hence 'tis they live at Rovers, and defie
This or that place; Rags of Geography.
They're Citizens o' th' world; they're all in all,
Scotland's a Nation Epidemicall.

Poems, 1647

at rovers: at random.

418 *Epitaph on the Earl of Strafford*

HERE lies wise and valiant dust,
Huddled up 'twixt fit and juste:
Strafford, who was hurried hence
'Twixt treason and convenience.
He spent his time here in a mist,
A *Papist*, yet a *Calvinist*;
His Prince's nearest joy and Grief:
He had, yet wanted, all relief:
The Prop and Ruine of the State,
The peoples violent love and hate.
One in extremes lov'd and abhorr'd.
Riddles lie here, or in a word,
Here lies blood, and let it lie
Speechlesse still, and never cry.

Poems, 1647

419 *An Elegy on Ben Jonson*

WHO first reform'd our *Stage* with justest *Laws*,
And was the first best *Judge* in his own *Cause*,
Who (when his *Actors* trembled for *Applause*)

Could (with a *noble Confidence*) prefer
His *own*, by right, to a noble *Theater*;
From *Principles*, which *he* knew could not *err*.

Who to *his Fable* did his Persons fit,
With all the *Properties* of *Art* and *Wit*,
And above all that could be *Acted, writ*.

Who publique Follies did to covert drive,
Which *he* again could cunningly *retrive*,
Leaving them no *ground* to rest on, and *thrive*.

Here JONSON lies, *whom* had I nam'd before,
In that one *word* alone I had paid more,
Than can be now, when *plentie* makes me *poore*.

Jonsonus Virbius, 1638

ANONYMOUS

420

A Song of Sack

COME let us drink away the time,
A *Pox* upon this pelting Rhyme,
When *Wine* runs high, Wit 's in the Prime:
Drink and stout Drinkers, are true Joys,
Odd *Sonnets* and such little Toys,
Are Exercises fit for Boys.

The whining Lover that doth place
His Fancy on a painted Face,
And wasts his Substance in the Chase
Would ne'er in Melancholy pine,
Had he Affections so Divine,
As once to fall in Love with *Wine*.

Then to our Liquor let us sit,
Wine makes the Soul for Action fit;
Who drinks most *Wine*, hath the most Wit:
The *Gods* themselves do Revels keep,
And in pure *Nectar* tipple deep,
When sloathful Mortals are asleep.

ANONYMOUS

They fuddled me for Recreation,
In Water, which by all Relation
Did cause *Deucalions* Inundation;
The *Spangle Globe* had it almost.
Their Cups were with Salt-Water dos'd,
The Sun-burnt Center was the Toast.

The Gods then let us imitate,
Secure from carping Care and Fate;
Wine, Wit, and Courage both create:
In Wine *Apollo* always chose
His darkest *Oracles* to disclose;
'Twas *Wine* gave him his Ruby-nose.

Who dares not drink 's a wretched Wight,
Nor do I think that Man dares fight
All Day, that dares not drink all Night:
Come fill my Cup untill it swim
With Foam, that overlooks the Brim.
Who drinks the deepest? *Here's to him.*

Cleveland's Poems, 1687

RICHARD CRASHAW

1613?–1649

421 *Musicks Duell*

NOW Westward *Sol* had spent the richest Beames
Of Noons high Glory, when hard by the streams
Of *Tiber*, on the sceane of a greene plat,
Under protection of an Oake; there sate

420. The concluding stanza is omitted.
Musicks Duell: a free translation from the Latin of F. Strada.

A sweet Lutes-master; in whose gentle aires
Hee lost the Dayes heat, and his owne hot cares.
  Close in the covert of the leaves there stood
A Nightingale, come from the neighbouring wood:
(The sweet inhabitant of each glad Tree,
Their Muse, their *Syren*, harmlesse *Syren* shee)
There stood she listning, and did entertaine
The Musicks soft report: and mould the same
In her owne murmures, that what ever mood
His curious fingers lent, her voyce made good:
The man perceiv'd his Rivall, and her Art;
Dispos'd to give the light-foot Lady sport,
Awakes his Lute, and 'gainst the fight to come
Informes it, in a sweet *Prœludium*
Of closer straines, and ere the warre begin,
Hee lightly skirmishes on every string
Charg'd with a flying touch: and straightway shee
Carves out her dainty voyce as readily,
Into a thousand sweet distinguish'd Tones,
And reckons up in soft divisions,
Quicke volumes of wild Notes; to let him know
By that shrill taste, shee could doe something too.
  His nimble hands instinct then taught each string
A cap'ring cheerefullnesse; and made them sing
To their owne dance; now negligently rash
Hee throwes his Arme, and with a long drawne dash
Blends all together; then distinctly trips
From this to that; then quicke returning skips
And snatches this againe, and pauses there.
Shee measures every measure, every where
Meets art with art; sometimes as if in doubt
Not perfect yet, and fearing to bee out

Trailes her plaine Ditty in one long-spun note,
Through the sleeke passage of her open throat:
A cleare unwrinkled song, then doth shee point it
With tender accents, and severely joynt it
By short diminutives, that being rear'd
In controverting warbles evenly shar'd,
With her sweet selfe shee wrangles; Hee amazed
That from so small a channell should be rais'd
The torrent of a voyce, whose melody
Could melt into such sweet variety
Straines higher yet; that tickled with rare art
The tattling strings (each breathing in his part)
Most kindly doe fall out; the grumbling Base
In surly groanes disdaines the Trebles Grace.
The high-perch't treble chirps at this, and chides,
Untill his finger (Moderatour) hides
And closes the sweet quarrell, rousing all
Hoarse, shrill, at once; as when the Trumpets call
Hot Mars to th' Harvest of Deaths field, and woo
Mens hearts into their hands; this lesson too
Shee gives him backe; her supple Brest thrills out
Sharpe Aires, and staggers in a warbling doubt
Of dallying sweetnesse, hovers o'er her skill,
And folds in wav'd notes with a trembling bill,
The plyant Series of her slippery song.
Then starts shee suddenly into a Throng
Of short thicke sobs, whose thundring volleys float,
And roll themselves over her lubricke throat
In panting murmurs, still'd out of her Breast
That ever-bubbling spring; the sugred Nest
Of her delicious soule, that there does lye
Bathing in streames of liquid Melodie;

Musicks best seed-plot, whence in ripen'd Aires
A Golden-headed Harvest fairely reares
His Honey-dropping tops, plow'd by her breath
Which there reciprocally laboureth
In that sweet soyle. It seemes a holy quire
Founded to th' Name of great *Apollo's* lyre.
Whose sylver-roofe rings with the sprightly notes
Of sweet-lipp'd Angell-Imps, that swill their throats
In creame of Morning *Helicon*, and then
Prefer soft Anthems to the Eares of men,
To woo them from their Beds, still murmuring
That men can sleepe while they their Mattens sing:
(Most divine service) whose so early lay,
Prevents the Eye-lidds of the blushing day.
There might you heare her kindle her soft voyce,
In the close murmur of a sparkling noyse.
And lay the ground-worke of her hopefull song,
Still keeping in the foreward streame, so long
Till a sweet whirle-wind (striving to get out)
Heaves her soft Bosome, wanders round about,
And makes a pretty Earthquake in her Breast,
Till the fledg'd Notes at length forsake their Nest;
Fluttering in wanton shoales, and to the Sky
Wing'd with their owne wild Eccho's prattling fly.
Shee opes the floodgate, and lets loose a Tide
Of streaming sweetnesse, which in state doth ride
On the wav'd backe of every swelling straine,
Rising and falling in a pompous traine.
And while shee thus discharges a shrill peale
Of flashing Aires; she qualifies their zeale
With the coole Epode of a graver Note,
Thus high, thus low, as if her silver throat

Would reach the brazen voyce of war's hoarse Bird;
Her little soule is ravisht: and so pour'd
Into loose extasies, that shee is plac't
Above her selfe, Musicks *Enthusiast*.
  Shame now and anger mixt a double staine
In the Musitians face; yet once againe
(Mistresse) I come; now reach a straine my Lute
Above her mocke, or bee for ever mute.
Or tune a song of victory to mee,
Or to thy selfe, sing thine owne Obsequie;
So said, his hands sprightly as fire hee flings,
And with a quavering coynesse tastes the strings.
The sweet-lip't sisters musically frighted,
Singing their feares are fearfully delighted.
Trembling as when *Apollo's* golden haires
Are fann'd and frizled, in the wanton ayres
Of his owne breath: which marryed to his lyre
Doth tune the *Sphæares*, and make Heavens selfe looke higher.
From this to that, from that to this hee flyes,
Feeles Musicks pulse in all her Arteryes;
Caught in a net which there *Apollo* spreads,
His fingers struggle with the vocall threads,
Following those little rills, hee sinkes into
A Sea of *Helicon*; his hand does goe
Those parts of sweetnesse which with *Nectar* drop,
Softer than that which pants in *Hebe's* cup.
The humourous strings expound his learned touch,
By various Glosses; now they seeme to grutch,
And murmurs in a buzzing din, then gingle
In shrill tongu'd accents: striving to bee single.
Every smooth turne, every delicious stroke
Gives life to some new Grace; thus doth h' invoke

Sweetnesse by all her Names; thus, bravely thus
(Fraught with a fury so harmonious)
The Lutes light *Genius* now does proudly rise,
Heav'd on the surges of swolne Rapsodyes.
Whose flourish (Meteor-like) doth curle the aire
With flash of high-borne fancyes: here and there
Dancing in lofty measures, and anon
Creeps on the soft touch of a tender tone:
Whose trembling murmurs melting in wild aires
Runs to and fro, complaining his sweet cares
Because those pretious mysteries that dwell
In musick's ravish't soule hee dare not tell,
But whisper to the world: thus doe they vary
Each string his Note, as if they meant to carry
Their Masters blest soule (snatcht out at his Eares
By a strong Extasy) through all the sphæares
Of Musicks heaven; and seat it there on high
In th' *Empyræum* of pure Harmony.
At length (after so long, so loud a strife
Of all the strings, still breathing the best life
Of blest variety attending on
His fingers fairest revolution
In many a sweet rise, many as sweet a fall)
A full-mouth *Diapason* swallowes all.
  This done, hee lists what shee would say to this,
And shee although her Breath's late exercise
Had dealt too roughly with her tender throate,
Yet summons all her sweet powers for a Note;
Alas! in vaine! for while (sweet soule) shee tryes
To measure all those wild diversities
Of chatt'ring stringes, by the small size of one
Poore simple voyce, rais'd in a Naturall Tone;

Shee failes, and failing grieves, and grieving dyes.
Shee dyes; and leaves her life the Victors prize,
Falling upon his Lute; O fit to have
(That liv'd so sweetly) dead, so sweet a Grave!

The Delights of the Muses, 1646

422 *Upon Bishop Andrewes his Picture before his Sermons*

THIS reverend shadow cast that setting Sun,
Whose glorious course through our Horizon run,
Left the dimme face of this dull Hemisphæare,
All one great eye, all drown'd in one great Teare.
Whose faire illustrious soule, led his free thought
Through Learnings Universe, and (vainely) sought
Roome for her spatious selfe, untill at length
Shee found the way home, with an holy strength
Snatch't her self hence, to Heaven: fill'd a bright place,
Mongst those immortall fires, and on the face
Of her great maker fixt her flaming eye,
There still to read true pure divinity.
And now that grave aspect hath deign'd to shrinke
Into this lesse appearance; If you thinke,
'Tis but a dead face, art doth here bequeath:
Looke on the following leaves, and see him breathe.

The Delights of the Muses, 1646

423 *An Epitaph Upon Husband and Wife, which died, and were buried together*

TO these, whom Death again did wed,
This grave 's the second Marriage-bed.
For though the hand of Fate could force
'Twixt Soul and Body a Divorce,
It could not sunder man and wife,
'Cause they both lived but one life.
Peace, good Reader. Doe not weep.
Peace, the Lovers are asleep.
They, sweet Turtles, folded lie
In the last knot Love could tie.
And though they lie as they were dead,
Their pillow stone, their sheetes of lead
(Pillow hard, and sheets not warm)
Love made the bed; they'll take no harm.
Let them sleep: let them sleep on,
Till this stormy night be gone,
Till the Æternal morrow dawn;
Then the curtaines will be drawn
And they wake into a light
Whose day shall never die in Night.

The Delights of the Muses, 1646

424 *Upon Ford's two Tragedies, 'Loves Sacrifice' and 'The Broken Heart'*

THOU cheat'st us Ford, mak'st one seem two by Art.
What is Loves Sacrifice but the Broken Heart.

The Delights of the Muses, 1646

425 *Loves Horoscope*

LOVE, brave Vertues younger Brother,
Erst hath made my Heart a Mother,
Shee consults the conscious Spheares,
To calculate her young sons yeares.
Shee askes if sad, or saving powers,
Gave Omen to his infant howers,
Shee askes each starre that then stood by,
If poore Love shall live or dy.

Ah my Heart, is that the way?
Are these the Beames that rule thy Day?
Thou know'st a Face in whose each looke,
Beauty layes ope Loves Fortune-booke;
On whose faire revolutions wait
The obsequious motions of Loves fate;
Ah my Heart, her eyes and shee,
Have taught thee new Astrologie.
How e'er Loves native houres were set,
What ever starry Synod met,
'Tis in the mercy of her eye,
If poore Love shall live or dye.

If those sharpe Rayes putting on
Points of Death bid Love be gon,
(Though the Heavens in counsell sate,
To crowne an uncontrouled Fate,
Though their best Aspects twin'd upon
The kindest Constellation,
Cast amorous glances on his Birth,
And whisper'd the confederate Earth

To pave his paths with all the good
That warms the Bed of youth and blood;)
Love has no plea gainst her eye,
Beauty frownes, and Love must dye.

But if her milder influence move,
And gild the hopes of humble Love:
(Though heavens inauspicious eye
Lay blacke on Loves Nativitie;
Though every Diamond in *Joves* crowne
Fixt his forehead to a frowne,)
Her Eye a strong appeale can give,
Beauty smiles and Love shall live.

O if Love shall live, O where,
But in her Eye, or in her Eare,
In her Brest, or in her Breath,
Shall I hide poore Love from Death?
For in the life ought else can give,
Love shall dye, although he live.

Or if Love shall dye, O where,
But in her Eye, or in her Eare,
In her Breath, or in her Breast,
Shall I Build his funerall Nest?
While Love shall thus entombed lye,
Love shall live, although he dye.

The Delights of the Muses, 1646

DY: We preserve the spelling Dy, dye, because of the frequent eye-rhymes.

426 *An Epitaph Upon Mr. Ashton a conformable Citizen*

THE modest front of this small floore
Beleeve mee, Reader, can say more
Than many a braver Marble can;
Here lyes a truly honest man.
One whose Conscience was a thing,
That troubled neither Church nor King.
One of those few that in this Towne,
Honour all Preachers; heare their owne.
Sermons he heard, yet not so many,
As left no time to practise any.
Hee heard them reverendly, and then
His practice preach'd them o'er agen.
His *Parlour-Sermons* rather were
Those to the Eye, than to the Eare.
His prayers tooke their price and strength
Not from the loudness, nor the length.
Hee was a Protestant at home,
Not onely in despight of *Rome*.
Hee lov'd his *Father*; yet his zeale
Tore not off his Mothers veile.
To th' Church hee did allow her Dresse,
True Beauty, to true *Holinesse*.
Peace, which hee lov'd in Life, did lend
Her hand to bring him to his end;
When Age and Death call'd for the score,
No surfets were to reckon for.
Death tore not (therefore) but sans strife
Gently untwin'd his thread of Life.

What remaines then, but that Thou
Write these lines, Reader, in thy Brow.
And by his faire Examples light,
Burne in thy Imitation bright.
So while these Lines can but bequeath
A Life perhaps unto his Death,
His better Epitaph shall bee,
His Life still kept alive in Thee.

The Delights of the Muses, 1646

427 *Wishes to his Supposed Mistresse*

WHO e'er she be,
That not impossible she
That shall command my heart and me;

Where e'er she lye,
Lock't up from mortall Eye,
In shady leaves of Destiny;

Till that ripe Birth
Of studied fate stand forth,
And teach her faire steps to our Earth;

Till that Divine
Idæa, take a shrine
Of Chrystall flesh, through which to shine;

Meet you her my wishes,
Bespeake her to my blisses,
And be ye call'd my absent kisses.

I wish her Beauty,
That owes not all his Duty
To gaudy Tire, or glistring shoo-ty.

Something more than
Taffata or Tissew can,
Or rampant feather, or rich fan.

More than the spoyle
Of shop, or silkewormes Toyle,
Or a bought blush, or a set smile.

A face that 's best
By its owne beauty drest,
And can alone command the rest.

A face made up,
Out of no other shop
Than what natures white hand sets ope.

A cheeke where Youth,
And Blood, with Pen of Truth
Write, what the Reader sweetly ru'th.

A Cheeke where growes
More than a Morning Rose:
Which to no Boxe his being owes.

Lips, where all Day
A lovers kisse may play,
Yet carry nothing thence away.

Lookes that oppresse
Their richest Tires, but dresse
And cloath their simplest Nakednesse.

Eyes, that displaces
The Neighbour Diamond, and out-faces
That Sunshine, by their own sweet Graces.

Tresses, that weare
Jewells, but to declare
How much themselves more pretious are.

Whose native Ray,
Can tame the wanton Day
Of Gems, that in their bright shades play.

Each Ruby there,
Or Pearle that dare appeare,
Be its own blush, be its own Teare.

A well tam'd Heart,
For whose more noble smart,
Love may be long chusing a Dart.

Eyes that bestow
Full quivers on loves Bow;
Yet pay lesse Arrowes than they owe.

Smiles, that can warme
The blood, yet teach a charme,
That Chastity shall take no harme.

Blushes, that bin
The burnish of no sin,
Nor flames of ought too hot within.

Joyes, that confesse,
Vertue their Mistresse,
And have no other head to dresse.

Feares, fond and slight,
As the coy Brides, when Night
First does the longing Lover right.

Teares, quickly fled,
And vaine, as those are shed
For a dying Maydenhead.

Dayes, that need borrow,
No part of their good Morrow,
From a fore spent night of sorrow.

Dayes, that in spight
Of Darkenesse, by the Light
Of a cleere mind are Day all Night.

Nights, sweet as they,
Made short by Lovers play,
Yet long by th' absence of the Day.

Life, that dares send
A challenge to his end,
And when it comes say *Welcome Friend*.

Sydnæan showers
Of sweet discourse, whose powers
Can Crown old Winters head with flowers.

Soft silken Hours,
Open sunnes, shady Bowers;
'Bove all, Nothing within that lowers.

What e'er Delight
Can make Dayes forehead bright,
Or give Downe to the Wings of Night.

In her whole frame,
Have Nature all the Name,
Art and ornament the shame.

Her flattery,
Picture and Poesy,
Her counsell her owne vertue be.

I wish, her store
Of worth may leave her poore
Of wishes; And I wish——No more.

Now if Time knowes
That her whose radiant Browes
Weave them a Garland of my vowes,

Her whose just Bayes,
My future hopes can raise,
A trophie to her present praise;

Her that dares be,
What these Lines wish to see:
I seeke no further, it is she.

'Tis she, and here
Lo I uncloath and cleare,
My wishes cloudy Character.

May she enjoy it,
Whose merit dare apply it,
But Modesty dares still deny it.

Such worth as this is
Shall fixe my flying wishes,
And determine them to kisses.

Let her full Glory,
My fancyes, fly before ye,
Be ye my fictions; but her story.

The Delights of the Muses, 1646

428 *Hymn of the Nativity*

Sung as by the Shepheards

Chorus.

COME we shepheards whose blest Sight
Hath met love's Noon in Nature's night;
Come lift we up our loftyer Song
And wake the SUN that lyes too long.

To all our world of well-stoln joy
He slept; and dream't of no such thing;
While we found out Heavn's fairer eye
And Kiss'd the Cradle of our KING.
Tell him He rises now too late
To show us ought worth looking at.

Tell him we now can show Him more
Then He e'er show'd to mortall Sight;
Then he Himselfe e'er saw before;
Which to be seen needes not His light.
Tell him, Tityrus, where th' hast been,
Tell him, Thyrsis, what th' hast seen.

Tityrus. Gloomy night embrac't the Place
Where The Noble Infant lay.
The BABE look't up and shew'd his Face;
In spite of Darkness, it was DAY.
It was THY day, SWEET! and did rise
Not from the EAST, but from thine EYES.
Chorus. It was THY day, SWEET, &c.

Thyrs. WINTER chidde aloud; and sent
The angry North to wage his warres.
The North forgot his fierce Intent;
And left perfumes in stead of scarres.

By those sweet eyes persuasive powrs
Where he mean't frost, he scatter'd flowrs.

Chorus. By those sweet eyes, &c.

Both. We saw thee in thy baulmy Nest,
Young dawn of our æternall Day!
We saw thine eyes break from their East
And chase the trembling shades away.
We saw thee; and we blest the sight,
We saw thee by thine own sweet light.

Tity. Poor World (said I) what wilt thou doe
To entertain this starry Stranger?
Is this the best thou canst bestow?
A cold, and not too cleanly, manger?
Contend ye powres of heav'n and earth
To fit a bed for this huge birthe.

Cho. Contend ye powers, &c.

Thyr. Proud world, said I; cease your contest,
And let the Mighty Babe alone.
The Phænix builds the Phænix' nest.
Love's architecture is his own.
The Babe whose birth embraves this morn,
Made his own bed ere he was born.

Cho. The Babe whose, &c.

Tit. I saw the curl'd drops, soft and slow,
Come hovering o'er the place's head;
Offring their whitest sheets of snow
To furnish the fair Infant's bed:
Forbear, said I; be not too bold.
Your fleece is white, But 'tis too cold.

Cho. Forbear, sayd I, &c.

Thyr. I saw the obsequious SERAPHINS
Their rosy fleece of fire bestow,
For well they now can spare their wings,
Since HEAVN it self lyes here below.
Well done, said I: but are you sure
Your down so warm, will passe for pure?
Cho. Well done sayd I, &c.

Tit. No no, your KING 's not yet to seeke
Where to repose his Royall HEAD,
See see, how soon his new-bloom'd CHEEK
Twixt 's mother's breasts is gone to bed.
Sweet choice, said we! no way but so
Not to lye cold, yet sleep in snow.
Cho. Sweet choise, said we, &c.

Both. We saw thee in thy balmy nest,
Bright dawn of our æternall Day!
We saw thine eyes break from their EAST
And chase the trembling shades away.
We saw thee: and we blest the sight.
We saw thee, by thine own sweet light.
Cho. We saw thee, &c.

Full Chorus.

Wellcome, all WONDERS in one sight!
Æternity shut in a span.
Sommer in Winter. Day in Night.
Heaven in earth, and GOD in MAN.
Great little one! whose all-embracing birth
Lifts earth to heaven, stoopes heav'n to earth.

WELLCOME. Though nor to gold nor silk,
To more than Cæsar's birth right is;
Two sister-seas of Virgin-Milk,
With many a rarely-temper'd kisse
That breathes at once both MAID and MOTHER,
Warmes in the one, cooles in the other.

WELLCOME, though not to those gay flyes
Gilded ith' Beames of earthly kings;
Slippery soules in smiling eyes;
But to poor Shepherds, home-spun things:
Whose Wealth 's their flock; whose wit, to be
Well read in their simplicity.

Yet when young April's husband showrs
Shall blesse the fruitfull Maia's bed,
We'll bring the First-born of her flowrs
To kisse thy FEET and crown thy HEAD.
To thee, dread Lamb! whose love must keep
The shepheards, more than they the sheep.

To THEE, meek Majesty! soft KING
Of simple GRACES and sweet LOVES.
Each of us his lamb will bring
Each his pair of sylver Doves;
Till burnt at last in fire of Thy fair eyes,
Our selves become our own best SACRIFICE.

Carmen deo Nostro, 1652

429 *Upon the Body of our Blessed Lord, Naked and Bloody*

THEY 'have left thee naked, Lord, O that they had!
This garment too I wish they had deny'd.
Thee with thy self they have too richly clad;
Opening the purple wardrobe in thy side.
O never could there be garment too good
For thee to wear, but this of thine own Blood.

Carmen Deo Nostro, 1652

430 *The Hymn of Saint Thomas in Adoration of the Blessed Sacrament*

Adoro Te

WITH all the powres my poor Heart hath
Of humble love and loyall Faith,
Thus low (my hidden life!) I bow to thee
Whom too much love hath bow'd more low for me.
Down down, proud sense! Discourses die.
Keep close, my soul's inquiring eye!
Nor touch nor taste must look for more
But each sit still in his own Door.

Your ports are all superfluous here,
Save That which lets in faith, the eare.
Faith is my skill. Faith can believe
As fast as love new lawes can give.
Faith is my force. Faith strength affords
To keep pace with those powrfull words.
And words more sure, more sweet, than they
Love could not think, truth could not say.

O let thy wretch find that reliefe
Thou didst afford the faithfull thiefe.
Plead for me, love! Allege and show
That faith has farther, here, to goe
And lesse to lean on. Because than
Though hid as God, wounds writ thee man,
Thomas might touch; None but might see
At least the suffring side of thee;
And that too was thy self which thee did cover,
But here ev'n That 's hid too which hides the other.

Sweet, consider then, that I
Though allow'd nor hand nor eye
To reach at thy lov'd Face; nor can
Taste thee God, or touch thee Man
Both yet believe; and wittnesse thee
My Lord too and my God, as loud as He.

Help lord, my Faith, my Hope increase;
And fill my portion in thy peace.
Give love for life; nor let my dayes
Grow, but in new powres to thy name and praise.

O dear memoriall of that Death
Which lives still, and allowes us breath!
Rich, Royall food! Bountyfull Bread!
Whose use denyes us to the dead;
Whose vitall gust alone can give
The same leave both to eat and live;
Live ever Bread of loves, and be
My life, my soul, my surer selfe to mee.

Line 5. than: then.

O soft self-wounding Pelican!
Whose breast weepes Balm for wounded man.
Ah this way bend thy benign flood
To 'a bleeding Heart that gasps for blood.
That blood, whose least drops soveraign be
To wash my worlds of sins from me.
Come love! Come LORD! and that long day
For which I languish, come away.
When this dry soul those eyes shall see,
And drink the unseal'd source of thee.
When Glory's sun faith's shades shall chase,
And for thy veil gave me thy FACE.

Carmen Deo Nostro, 1652

431 *On the Glorious Assumption of Our Blessed Lady*

The Hymn

HARK! she is call'd, the parting houre is come.
Take thy Farewell, poor world! heavn must goe home
A piece of heav'nly earth; Purer and brighter
Than the chaste starres, whose choice lamps come to light her
While through the crystall orbes, clearer than they
She climbes; and makes a far more milky way.
She 's call'd. Hark, how the dear immortall dove
Sighes to his silver mate, rise up, my love!
Rise up, my fair, my spotlesse one!
The winter's past, the rain is gone.

The spring is come, the flowrs appear
No sweets, but thou, are wanting here.
  Come away, my love!
  Come away, my dove! cast off delay,
  The court of heav'n is come
  To wait upon thee home; Come come away!
  The flowrs appear,
Or quickly would, wert thou once here.
The spring is come, or if it stay,
'Tis to keep time with thy delay.
The rain is gone, except so much as we
Detain in needful teares to weep the want of thee.
  The winter's past.
  Or if he make lesse haste,
His answer is, why, she does so.
If sommer come not, how can winter goe.
  Come away, come away.
The shrill winds chide, the waters weep thy stay;
The fountains murmur; and each loftiest tree
Bowes low'st his heavy top, to look for thee.
  Come away, my love.
  Come away, my dove, &c.
She 's call'd again. And will she goe?
When heavn bids come, who can say no?
Heavn calls her, and she must away.
Heavn will not, and she cannot stay.
GOE then; goe GLORIOUS.
  On the golden wings
Of the bright youth of heavn, that sings
Under so sweet a Burthen. Goe,
Since thy dread son will have it so.
And while thou goest, our song and we

Will, as we may, reach after thee.
HAIL, holy Queen of humble hearts!
We in thy prayse will have our parts.
    Thy pretious Name shall be
    Thy self to us; and we
    With holy care will keep it by us.
    We to the last
    Will hold it fast
    And no ASSUMPTION shall deny us.
    All the sweetest showres
    Of our fairest flowres
    Will we strow upon it.
    Though our sweets cannot make
    It sweeter, they can take
    Themselves new sweetness from it.
MARIA, men and Angels sing
MARIA, mother of our KING.
  LIVE, rosy princesse, LIVE. And may the bright
Crown of a most incomparable light
Embrace thy radiant browes. O may the best
Of everlasting joyes bath thy white brest.
LIVE, our chast love, the holy mirth
Of heavn; the humble pride of earth.
Live, crown of women; Queen of men.
Live mistresse of our song. And when
Our weak desires have done their best,
Sweet Angels come, and sing the rest.

Carmen Deo Nostro, 1652

432 *A Hymn to the Name and Honor of the Admirable Saint Teresa*

LOVE, thou art Absolute sole lord
Of Life and Death. To prove the word,
We'll now appeal to none of all
Those thy old Souldiers, Great and tall,
Ripe Men of Martyrdom, that could reach down
With strong armes, their triumphant crown;
Such as could with lusty breath
Speak loud into the face of death
Their Great Lord's glorious name, to none
Of those whose spacious Bosomes spread a throne
For Love at large to fill: spare blood and sweat;
And see him take a private seat
Making his mansion in the mild
And milky soul of a soft child.
  Scarce has she learn't to lisp the name
Of Martyr; yet she thinks it shame
Life should so long play with that breath
Which spent can buy so brave a death.
She never undertook to know
What death with love should have to doe;
Nor has she e'er yet understood
Why to show love, she should shed blood;
Yet though she cannot tell you why,
She can Love, and she can dy.
  Scarce has she Blood enough to make
A guilty sword blush for her sake;
Yet has she 'a Heart dares hope to prove
How much lesse strong is Death than Love.

Be love but there; let poor six yeares
Be pos'd with the maturest Feares
Man trembles at, you straight shall find
Love knowes no nonage, nor the Mind.
'Tis Love, not Yeares or Limbs that can
Make the Martyr, or the man.
Love touch't her Heart, and lo it beates
High, and burnes with such brave heates;
Such thirsts to dy, as dares drink up,
A thousand cold deaths in one cup.
Good reason. For she breathes All fire.
Her weake breast heaves with strong desire
Of what she may with fruitless wishes
Seek for amongst her Mother's kisses.
Since 'tis not to be had at home
She'll travel to a Martyrdom.
No home for hers confesses she
But where she may a Martyr be.
She'll to the Moores; And trade with them,
For this unvalued Diadem.
She'll offer them her dearest Breath,
With Christ's Name in't, in change for death.
She'll bargain with them; and will give
Them God; teach them how to live
In him: or, if they this deny,
For him she'll teach them how to dy.
So shall she leave amongst them sown
Her Lord's Blood; or at least her own.
Farewell then, all the world! Adieu.
Teresa is no more for you.
Farewell, all pleasures, sports, and joyes,
(Never till now esteemed toyes)

Farewell what ever deare may bee,
MOTHER's armes or FATHER's knee,
Farewell house, and farewell home!
SHE's for the MOORS, and MARTYRDOM.
  SWEET, not so fast! lo thy fair Spouse
Whom thou seekst with so swift vowes,
Calls thee back, and bids thee come
T'embrace a milder MARTYRDOM.
  Blest powres forbid, Thy tender life
Should bleed upon a barbarous knife;
Or some base hand have power to rase
Thy Breast's chaste cabinet, and uncase
A soul kept there so sweet, O no;
Wise heavn will never have it so.
THOU art love's victime; and must dy
A death more mysticall and high.
Into love's armes thou shalt let fall
A still-surviving funerall.
His is the DART must make the DEATH
Whose stroke shall taste thy hallow'd breath;
A Dart thrice dipt in that rich flame
Which writes thy spouse's radiant Name
Upon the roof of Heav'n; where ay
It shines, and with a soveraign ray
Beats bright upon the burning faces
Of soules which in that name's sweet graces
Find everlasting smiles. So rare,
So spirituall, pure, and fair
Must be th' immortall instrument
Upon whose choice point shall be sent
A life so lov'd; And that there be
Fit executioners for Thee,

The fair'st and first-born sons of fire
Blest Seraphim, shall leave their quire
And turn love's souldiers, upon Thee
To exercise their archerie.
   O how oft shalt thou complain
Of a sweet and subtle Pain.
Of intolerable Joyes;
Of a Death, in which who dyes
Loves his death, and dyes again.
And would for ever so be slain.
And lives, and dyes; and knowes not why
To live, But that he thus may never leave to dy.
   How kindly will thy gentle Heart
Kisse the sweetly-killing Dart!
And close in his embraces keep
Those delicious Wounds, that weep
Balsom to heal themselves with. Thus
When These thy Deaths, so numerous,
Shall all at last dy into one,
And melt thy Soul's sweet mansion;
Like a soft lump of incense, hasted
By too hot a fire, and wasted
Into perfuming clouds, so fast
Shalt thou exhale to Heavn at last
In a resolving Sigh, and then
O what? Ask not the Tongues of men.
Angels cannot tell, suffice,
Thy selfe shall feel thine own full joyes
And hold them fast for ever. There
So soon as thou shalt first appear,
The Moon of maiden stars, thy white
Mistresse, attended by such bright

Soules as thy shining self, shall come
And in her first rankes make thee room;
Where 'mongst her snowy family
Immortall welcomes wait for thee.
O what delight, when reveal'd LIFE shall stand
And teach thy lips heav'n with his hand;
On which thou now maist to thy wishes
Heap up thy consecrated kisses.
What joyes shall seize thy soul, when shee
Bending her blessed eyes on thee
(Those second Smiles of Heav'n) shall dart
Her mild rayes through thy melting heart!
Angels, thy old friends, there shall greet thee
Glad at their own home now to meet thee.
All thy good WORKES which went before
And waited for thee, at the door,
Shall own thee there; and all in one
Weave a constellation
Of CROWNS, with which the KING thy spouse
Shall build up thy triumphant browes.
All thy old woes shall now smile on thee
And thy paines sit bright upon thee,
All thy sorrows here shall shine,
All thy SUFFRINGS be divine.
TEARES shall take comfort, and turn gems,
And WRONGS repent to Diadems.
Ev'n thy DEATHS shall live; and new
Dresse the soul that erst they slew.
Thy wounds shall blush to such bright scarres
As keep account of the LAMB's warres.
Those rare WORKES where thou shalt leave writ,
Love's noble history, with wit

Taught thee by none but him, while here
They feed our soules, shall cloth THINE there.
Each heavnly word by whose hid flame
Our hard Hearts shall strike fire, the same
Shall flourish on thy browes, and be
Both fire to us and flame to thee;
Whose light shall live bright in thy FACE
By glory, in our hearts by grace.
  Thou shalt look round about, and see
Thousands of crown'd Soules throng to be
Themselves thy crown, Sons of thy vowes
The virgin-births with which thy soveraign spouse
Made fruitfull thy fair soul, goe now
And with them all about thee bow
To Him, put on (he'll say) put on
(My rosy love) that thy rich zone
Sparkling with the sacred flames
Of thousand soules, whose happy names
Heav'n keeps upon thy score. (Thy bright
Life brought them first to kisse the light
That kindled them to starrs.) and so
Thou with the LAMB, thy lord, shalt goe;
And wheresoe'er he sets his white
Steps, walk with HIM those wayes of light
Which who in death would live to see,
Must learn in life to dy like thee.

Carmen Deo Nostro, 1652

433 *From The Flaming Heart upon the Book and Picture of the Seraphicall Saint Teresa (as She is usually expressed with a Seraphim beside her)*

LIVE here, great HEART; and love and dy and kill;
And bleed and wound; and yeild and conquer still.
Let this immortall life where 'er it comes
Walk in a crowd of loves and MARTYRDOMES.
Let mystick DEATHS wait on't; and wise soules be
The love-slain witnesses of this life of thee.
O sweet incendiary! shew here thy art,
Upon this carcase of a hard, cold, heart;
Let all thy scatter'd shafts of light, that play
Among the leaves of thy large Books of day,
Combin'd against this BREAST at once break in
And take away from me my self and sin;
This gratious Robbery shall thy bounty be;
And my best fortunes such fair spoiles of me.
O thou undaunted daughter of desires!
By all thy dow'r of LIGHTS and FIRES;
By all the eagle in thee, all the dove;
By all thy lives and deaths of love;
By thy large draughts of intellectuall day,
And by thy thirsts of love more large than they;
By all thy brim-fill'd Bowles of fierce desire
By thy last Morning's draught of liquid fire;
By the full kingdome of that finall kisse
That seiz'd thy parting Soul, and seal'd thee his;
By all the heav'ns thou hast in him
(Fair sister of the SERAPHIM)

By all of HIM we have in THEE;
Leave nothing of my SELF in me.
Let me so read thy life, that I
Unto all life of mine may dy.

Carmen Deo Nostro, 1652

434 *To a Young Gentle-Woman, councel concerning her Choice*

DEAR, heavn-designing SOUL!
Amongst the rest
Of suitors that besiege your Maiden brest,
Why may not I
My fortune try
And venture to speak one good word
Not for my self alas, but for my dearer LORD?
You've seen already, in this lower sphear
Of froth & bubbles, what to look for here.
Say, gentle soul, what can you find
But painted shapes,
Peacocks & Apes,
Illustrious flyes,
Gilded dunghills, glorious LYES,
Goodly surmises
And deep disguises,
Oathes of water, words of wind?
TRUTH biddes me say, 'tis time you cease to trust
Your soul to any son of dust.
'Tis time you listen to a braver love,
Which from above
Calls you up higher
And biddes you come

And choose your roome
Among his own fair sonnes of fire,
Where you among
The golden throng
That watches at his palace doores
May passe along
And follow those fair starres of yours;
Starrs much too fair & pure to wait upon
The false smiles of a sublunary sun.
Sweet, let me prophesy that at last 'twill prove
Your wary love
Layes up his purer & more pretious vowes,
And meanes them for a farre more worthy SPOUSE
Than this world of Lyes can give ye,
Ev'n for Him with whom nor cost,
Nor love, nor labour can be lost;
Him who never will deceive ye.
Let not my lord, the Mighty lover
Of soules, disdain that I discover
The hidden art
Of his high stratagem to win your heart,
It was his heavnly art
Kindly to crosse you
In your mistaken love,
That, at the next remove
Thence he might tosse you
And strike your troubled heart
Home to himself; to hide it in his brest
The bright ambrosiall nest,
Of love, of life, & everlasting rest.
Happy Mistake!
That thus shall wake

Your wise soul, never to be won
Now with a love below the sun.
Your first choyce failes, O when you choose agen
May it not be amongst the sons of Men.

Carmen Deo Nostro, 1652

435 *M. Crashaws Answer for Hope*

DEAR hope! earth's dowry, and heavn's debt!
The entity of those that are not yet.
Subtlest, but surest beeing! Thou by whom
Our nothing has a definition!
Substantiall shade! whose sweet allay
Blends both the noones of night and day.
Fates cannot find out a capacity
Of hurting thee.
From Thee their lean dilemma, with blunt horn,
Shrinkes, as the sick moon from the wholesome morn.
Rich hope! love's legacy, under lock
Of faith! still spending, and still growing stock!
Our crown-land lyes above yet each meal brings
A seemly portion for the sonnes of kings.
Nor will the virgin joyes we wed
Come lesse unbroken to our bed,
Because that from the bridall cheek of blisse
Thou steal'st us down a distant kisse.
Hope's chast stealth harmes no more joye's maidenhead
Than spousall rites prejudge the marriage bed.
Fair hope! our earlyer heav'n by thee
Young time is taster to eternity

435. A reply to Cowley's *Against Hope*.

Thy generous wine with age growes strong, not sowre.
    Thy golden, growing, head never hangs down
    Till in the lappe of loves full noone
It falls; and dyes! O no, it melts away
    As does the dawn into the day.
As lumpes of sugar loose themselves; and twine
Their supple essence with the soul of wine.
  Fortune? alas, above the world's low warres
Hope walks; and kickes the curl'd heads of conspiring starres.
Her keel cuts not the waves where these winds stir
Fortune's whole lottery is one blank to her.
    Her shafts, and she fly farre above,
    And forage in the fields of light and love.
Sweet hope! kind cheat! fair fallacy by thee
We are not WHERE nor What we be,
But WHAT and WHERE we would be. Thus art thou
Our absent PRESENCE, and our future NOW.
  Faith's sister! nurse of fair desire!
Fear's antidote! a wise and well-stay'd fire!
Temper twixt chill despair, and torrid joy!
Queen Regent in young love's minority!
    Though the vext chymick vainly chases
    His fugitive gold though all her faces;
Though love's more fierce, more fruitlesse, fires assay
    One face more fugitive than all they;
True hope's a glorious hunter and her chase,
The GOD of nature in the fields of grace.

Carmen Deo Nostro, 1652

JEREMY TAYLOR

1613–1667

436 *The Penitent*

LORD, I have sinn'd, and the black Number swells,
To such a dismal Sum,
That should my Stony Heart and Eyes,
And this whole sinful Trunk a Flood become,
And melt to Tears, their drops could not suffice
To count my Score,
Much less to pay:
But Thou, my God, hast Blood in store,
Yet, since the Balsam of thy Blood,
Although it can, will do no Good,
Unless the Wound be cleans'd in Tears before;
Thou in whose sweet, but pensive Face,
Laughter could never steal a Place,
Teach but my Heart and Eyes
To melt away,
And then one Drop of Balsam will suffice.

Golden Grove, also Festival Hymns, 1655, 1657; text from *Miscellanea Sacra*, 1698

WILLIAM HAMMOND

b. 1614, fl. 1655

437 *To his Sister, Mrs. S.*

The Rose

AFTER the honey drops of pearly showers
Urania walk'd to gather flowers:
Sweet Rose (I heard her say) why are these fears?
Are these drops on thy cheek thy tears?
By those thy beauty fresher is, thy smell
Arabian spices doth excel.

This rain (the Rose replied) feeds and betrays
   My odours; adds and cuts off days:
Had I not spread my leaves to catch this dew,
   My scent had not invited you.
Urania sigh'd, and softly said, 'tis so,
   Showers blow the rose, and ripen woe;
For mine (alas) when washt in floods sweet clean,
   Heaven put his hand forth, and did glean.

Occasional Poems, 1655

438 *To the Same*

Man's Life

MAN'S life was once a span; now one of those
Atoms of which old Sophies did compose
The world; a thing so small, no emptiness
Nature can find at all by his decease;
Nor need she to attenuate the aire,
And spreading it, his vacancy repaire,
The swellings that in hearts and eyes arise
Repay with ample bulk deaths robberies.
   Why should we then weep for a thing so slight
Converting lifes short day to a long night?
For sorrowes make one Month seem many years;
Times multiplying glasse is made of tears.
Our life is but a painted perspective;
Grief the false light that doth the distance give;
Nor doth it with delight (as shaddowing)
Set off, but, as a staffe fixt in a spring
Seem crookt and larger; then dry up thy tears,
Since through a double mean nought right appears.

Occasional Poems, 1655

Sophies: Sophists.

HENRY MORE

1614–1687

439 *An hymne in honour of those two despised virtues, Charitie and Humilitie*

FARRE have I clambred in my mind
 But nought so great as love I find:
Deep-searching wit, mount-moving might
Are nought compar'd to that good spright.
Light of delight and soul of blisse!
Sure source of lasting happinesse!
Higher than Heaven! lower than hell!
What is thy tent? where maist thou dwell?
 My mansion hight humilitie,
Heavens vastest capabilitie.
The further it doth downward tend
The higher up it doth ascend;
If it go down to utmost nought
It shall return with that it sought.
Lord stretch thy tent in my strait breast,
Enlarge it downward, that sure rest
May there be pight; for that pure fire
Wherewith thou wontest to inspire
All self-dead souls. My life is gone,
Sad solitude's my irksome wonne.
Cut off from men and all this world
In Lethes lonesome ditch I am hurl'd.
Nor might nor sight doth ought me move,
Nor do I care to be above.
O feeble rayes of mentall light!
That best be seen in this dark night,

What are you? what is any strength
If it be not laid in one length
With pride or love? I nought desire
But a new life or quite t'expire.
Could I demolish with mine eye
Strong towers, stop the fleet Stars in skie,
Bring down to earth the pale-fac'd Moon,
Or turn black midnight to bright noon:
Though all things were put in my hand,
As parch'd as dry as th' Libyan sand
Would be my life if Charity
Were wanting. But Humility
Is more than my poore soul durst crave
That lies intomb'd in lowly grave.
But if 't were lawfull up to send
My voice to Heaven, this should it rend:
  Lord thrust me deeper into dust
That thou maist raise me with the just.

ΨΥΧΩΔΙΑ Platonica, 1642

SIR JOHN DENHAM

1615–1669

440 *The Thames from Cooper's Hill*

MY eye descending from the Hill surveys
  Where *Thames* amongst the wanton vallies strays.
Thames, the most lov'd of all the Oceans sons,
By his old Sire to his embraces runs,
Hasting to pay his tribute to the Sea
Like mortal life to meet Eternity.

Though with those streams he no resemblance hold,
Whose foam is Amber, and their Gravel Gold;
His genuine, and less guilty wealth t'explore,
Search not his bottom, but survey his shore;
O'er which he kindly spreads his spacious wing,
And hatches plenty for th' ensuing Spring.
Nor then destroys it with too fond a stay,
Like Mothers which their Infants overlay.
Nor with a sudden and impetuous wave,
Like profuse Kings, resumes the wealth he gave.
No unexpected inundations spoil
The mowers hopes, nor mock the plowmans toil:
But God-like his unwearied Bounty flows;
First loves to do, then loves the Good he does.
Nor are his Blessings to his banks confin'd,
But free, and common, as the Sea or Wind;
When he to boast, or to disperse his stores
Full of the tributes of his grateful shores,
Visits the world, and in his flying towers
Brings home to us, and makes both *Indies* ours;
Finds wealth where 'tis, bestows it where it wants,
Cities in deserts, woods in Cities plants.
So that to us no thing, no place is strange,
While his fair bosom is the worlds exchange.
O could I flow like thee, and make thy stream
My great example, as it is my theme!
Though deep, yet clear, though gentle, yet not dull,
Strong without rage, without o'er-flowing full.

Cooper's Hill, 1643 (text 1668)

441 *From On Mr. Abraham Cowley. His Death and Burial amongst the Ancient Poets*

OLD *Chaucer*, like the morning Star,
To us discovers day from far,
His light those Mists and Clouds dissolv'd,
Which our dark Nation long involv'd;
But he descending to the shades,
Darkness again the Age invades.
Next (like *Aurora*) *Spenser* rose,
Whose purple blush the day foreshows;
The other three, with his own fires,
Phœbus, the Poets God, inspires;
By *Shakespear's*, *Johnson's*, *Fletcher's* lines,
Our Stages lustre *Rome's* outshines:
These Poets neer our Princes sleep,
And in one Grave their Mansion keep;
They liv'd to see so many days,
Till time had blasted all their Bays:
But cursed be the fatal hour
That pluckt the fairest, sweetest flower
That in the Muses Garden grew,
And amongst wither'd Laurels threw.
Time, which made them their Fame outlive,
To *Cowley* scarce did ripeness give.
Old Mother Wit, and Nature gave
Shakespear and *Fletcher* all they have;
In *Spenser*, and in *Johnson*, Art,
Of slower Nature got the start;
But both in him so equal are,
None knows which bears the happy'st share;

To him no Author was unknown,
Yet what he wrote was all his own;
He melted not the ancient Gold,
Nor with *Ben Johnson* did make bold
To plunder all the *Roman* stores
Of Poets, and of Orators:
Horace his wit, and *Virgil's* state,
He did not steal, but emulate,
And when he would like them appear,
Their Garb, but not their Cloaths, did wear:
He not from *Rome* alone, but *Greece*,
Like *Jason* brought the Golden fleece;
To him that Language (though to none
Of th' others) as his own was known. . . .

Poems and Translations, 1668

GEORGE DANIEL

1616–1657

442 *The Robin*

POORE bird! I doe not envie thee;
  Pleas'd in the gentle Melodie
    Of thy owne Song.
Let crabbed winter Silence all
The winged Quire; he never shall
    Chaine up thy Tongue:
        Poore Innocent!
When I would please my selfe, I looke on thee;
And guess some sparkes of that Felicitie,
        That Selfe-Content.

GEORGE DANIEL

When the bleake Face of winter Spreads
The Earth, and violates the Meads
Of all their Pride;
When Sapless Trees and Flowers are fled,
Back to their Causes, and lye dead
To all beside:
I see thee Set,
Bidding defiance to the bitter Ayre,
Upon a wither'd Spray; by cold made bare,
And drooping yet.

There, full in notes, to ravish all
My Earth, I wonder what to call
My dullness; when
I heare thee, prettie Creature, bring
Thy better odes of Praise, and Sing,
To puzzle men:
Poore pious Elfe!
I am instructed by thy harmonie,
To sing the Time's uncertaintie,
Safe in my Selfe.

Poore Redbreast, caroll out thy Laye,
And teach us mortalls what to saye.
Here cease the Quire
Of ayerie Choristers; noe more
Mingle your notes; but catch a Store
From her Sweet Lire;
You are but weake,
Mere summer Chanters; you have neither wing
Nor voice, in winter. Prettie Redbreast, Sing,
What I would speake.

Ode xxiii (B.M. Add. MS. 19255)

JOSEPH BEAUMONT

1616–1699

443 *The Gnat*

ONE Night all tired with the weary Day,
And with my tedious selfe, I went to lay
My fruitlesse Cares
And needlesse feares
Asleep.
The Curtaines of the Bed, and of mine Eyes
Being drawne, I hop'd no trouble would surprise
That Rest which now
'Gan on my Brow
To creep.

When loe a little flie, lesse than its Name
(It was a Gnat) with angry Murmur came.
About She flew
And lowder grew
Whilst I
Faine would have scorn'd the silly Thing, and slept
Out all its Noise; I resolute silence kept,
And laboured so
To overthrow
The Flie.

But still with sharp Alarms vexatious She
Or challenged, or rather mocked Me.
Angry at last
About I cast
My Hand.

JOSEPH BEAUMONT

'Twas well Night would not let me blush, nor see
With whom I fought; And yet though feeble She
Nor Her nor my
Owne Wrath could I
Command.

Away She flies, and Her owne Triumph sings
I being left to fight with idler Things,
A feeble pair
My Selfe and Aire.
How true
A worme is Man, whom flies their sport can make!
Poor worme; true Rest in no Bed can he take,
But one of Earth
Whence He came forth
And grew.

For there None but his silent Sisters be,
Wormes of as true and genuine Earth as He,
Which from the same
Corruption came:
And there
Though on his Eyes they feed, though on his Heart,
They neither vex nor wake Him; every part
Rests in sound sleep,
And out doth keep
All feare.

Minor Poems, ed. E. Robinson

444 *House and Home*

WHAT is House, and what is Home,
Where with Freedome Thou hast roome,
And Mayst to all Tyrants say,
This you cannot take away?
'Tis No Thing with Doors and Walls,
Which at every earthquake falls:
No fair Towers, whose Princely fashion
Is but Plunders invitation:
No stout Marble Structure, where
Walls Eternitie doe dare:
No Brasse Gates, no Bars of Steel,
Though Times Teeth they scorne to feel:
Brasse is not so bold as Pride
If on Powers Wings it ride;
Marbles not so hard as Spight
Arm'd with lawlesse Strength to fight.
Right, and just Possession, be
Potent Names, when Laws stand free:
But if once that Rampart fall,
Stoutest Theeves inherit all:
To be rich and weak 's a Sure
And sufficient forfeiture.
Seek no more abroad say I
House and Home, but turne thine eye
Inward, and observe thy Breast;
There alone dwells solid Rest.
That's a close immured Tower
Which can mock all hostile Power.
To thy selfe a Tenant be,
And inhabit safe and free.

JOSEPH BEAUMONT

Say not that this House is small,
Girt up in a narrow wall;
In a cleanly sober Mind
Heavn it selfe full Room doth find.
The Infinite Creator can
Dwell in it, and may not Man?
Contented here make thy abode
With thy selfe, and with thy God
Here, in this sweet Privacie
Maist Thou with thy selfe agree,
And keep House in Peace, though all
The Universes Fabrick fall.
No disaster can distresse Thee:
Nor no furie dispossesse Thee:
Let all war and plunder come,
Still mayst Thou dwell safe at home.
Home is every where to Thee
Who canst thine owne dwelling be.
Yea though ruthlesse Death assaile Thee,
Still thy Lodging will not faile Thee:
Still thy Soule 's thine owne, and She
To an House remov'd shall be,
An eternall House above
Wall'd, and Roof'd and Pav'd with Love.
There shall these Mudwalls of thine
Gallantly repair'd outshine
Mortall Stars: No stars shall be
In that Heavn, but such as Thee.

First printed 1749, text from *Minor Poems,* ed. E. Robinson

445 *Love*

WHEN Love
Had strove
Us to subdue,
Whose Crime
With Time
Still bolder grew;
Though Ye
Said He
Will still
Rebell
Yet I
Reveng'd will bee,
Sufficientlie
Upon my Selfe for You, and die.

When Love
Was wove
And ty'd about
His Crosse
So close
That it forc'd out
A Flood
Of Blood;
I would
I could,
Sayes He
Forever bleed,
So They who need
This Blood, would fill their Cup from Me.

JOSEPH BEAUMONT

When Love
Above
Went up to sit
Upon
His Throne
He rain'd from it
Whole Streames
Of Flames
On Those
He Chose
To goe
To every Place
Under Heavens Face
And there Love's fierie businesse do.

When Love
Doth move
His sparkling Eye
This way
We may
In it descry
A light
More bright
Than Day's
Best rayes
Whereby
Our Hearts, although
Chill untill now,
Conceive an Holy Fervencie.

JOSEPH BEAUMONT

When Love
To prove
His noble Art
His Bow
Doth draw
Against an Heart;
Alwayes
He slayes
With Wound
Profound
But still
The Deaths they give
Doe make Us live
A sweeter Life, than that they spill.

When Love
A Grove
Had sought, wherein
He might
Delight
With Soules of Men,
No Trees
Could please
His Will
Untill
He spy'd
Faire *Paradise*,
And heere, He cryes,
My lovely Spouses shall abide.

Minor Poems, ed. E. Robinson

JOSEPH BEAUMONT

446 *Βιοθάνατος*

O VILE ingratefull Me,
That I should Live, and not in Thee!
Not to thy
Praise, from whom
All this my
Life doth come!
What Riddle 's this, that I should strive
Onely against my Life to Live!

Against Thee, gentle Love,
Life of my Life, long have I strove,
Still misusing
Thy sweet Grace,
Still refusing
To give place
To mine own bliss, which Thou with thy
Milde Yoke about my neck wouldst ty.

And thus, alas I have
All this wide World but for my grave;
Where the Stone
Which doth ly
Heavy on
Me and my
Earth-hamperd Thoughts, is onely this
Unhappy Hearts Obdurateness.

Minor Poems, ed. E. Robinson

447 *The Garden*

June 12.

THE Garden's quit with me: as yesterday
I walked in that, to day that walks in me;
Through all my memorie
It sweetly wanders, and has found a way
To make me honestly possess
What still Anothers is.

Yet this Gains dainty sense doth gall my Minde
With the remembrance of a bitter Loss.
Alas, how odd and cross
Are earths Delights, in which the Soule can finde
No Honey, but withall some Sting
To check the pleasing thing!

For now I'm haunted with the thought of that
Heavn-planted Garden, where felicitie
Flourishd on every Tree.
Lost, lost it is; for at the guarded gate
A flaming Sword forbiddeth Sin
(That 's I,) to enter in.

O Paradise! when I was turned out
Hadst thou but kept the Serpent still within,
My banishment had been
Less sad and dangerous: but round about
This wide world runneth rageing He
To banish me from me:

I feel that through my soule he death hath shot;
And thou, alas, hast locked up Lifes Tree.
O Miserable Me,
What help were left, had Jesus's Pity not
Shewd me another Tree, which can
Enliven dying Man.

That Tree, made Fertile by his own dear blood;
And by his Death with quickning virtue fraught.
I now dread not the thought
Of barracado'd Eden, since as good
A Paradise I planted see
On open Calvarie.

Minor Poems, ed. E. Robinson

SIR ROGER L'ESTRANGE

1616–1704

448 *Loyalty confin'd*

BEAT on proud Billowes, *Boreas* Blow,
Swell curled Waves, high as *Jove's* roof,
Your incivility doth shew,
That innocence is tempest proof,
Though surely *Nereus* frown, my thoughts are calm,
Then strike affliction, for thy wounds are balm.

That which the world miscalls a Gaole,
A private Closet is to me,
Whilst a good Conscience is my Baile,
And Innocence my Liberty:
Locks Barres and Solitude together met,
Make me no Prisoner but an Anchorit.

I whil'st I wish'd to be retir'd
Into this private room was turn'd,
As if their wisedomes had conspir'd,
The Salamander should be burn'd.
  Or like a Sophy yet would drown a fish,
  I am constrain'd to suffer what I wish.

The Cynick hugs his poverty,
The Pelican her wilderness,
And 'tis the *Indians* pride to be
Naken on frozen *Caucasus*.
  Contentment cannot smart, Stoicks we see
  Make torments easie to their Apathy.

These Manacles upon my Arm,
I as my Mistris's favours wear;
And for to keep my Ankles warm,
I have some Iron Shackles there.
  These walls are but my Garrison; this Cell
  Which men call Gaole, doth prove my Cittadel.

So he that strook at *Jasons* life,
Thinking he had his purpose sure:
By a malicious friendly Knife,
Did only wound him to a cure.
  Malice I see wants wit, for what is meant,
  Mischief oft-times, proves favour by th' event.

I'm in this Cabinet lockt up,
Like some high-prized *Margaret*,
Or like some great Mogul or Pope,
Are cloystered up from publick sight.
  Retirement is a piece of Majesty,
  And thus proud *Sultan*, I'm as great as thee.

SIR ROGER L'ESTRANGE

Here sin for want of food must starve,
Where tempting Objects are not seen;
And these strong Walls do only serve,
To keep Vice out, and keep me in.
  Malice of late 's grown charitable sure,
  I'm not committed, but I'm kept secure.

Whence once my Prince affliction hath,
Prosperity doth Treason seem;
And for to smooth so tough a Path,
I can learn Patience from him.
  Now not to suffer, shews no Loyal heart,
  When Kings want ease, Subjects must bear a part.

Have you not seen the Nightingale,
A Pilgrim coop'd into a Cage,
How doth she chant her wonted tale,
In that her narrow hermitage.
  Even then her charming melody doth prove,
  That all her Boughs are Trees, her Cage a Grove.

My soul is free as the ambient aire,
Although my baser part 's immur'd,
Whil'st Loyal thoughts do still repair,
T' accompany my Solitude.
  And though immur'd, yet I can chirp and sing,
  Disgrace to Rebels, glory to my King.

What though I cannot see my King,
Neither in his Person or his Coyne,
Yet contemplation is a thing,
That renders what I have not mine.
  My King from me, what Adamant can part,
  Whom I do wear engraven on my heart.

SIR ROGER L'ESTRANGE

I am that Bird whom they combine,
Thus to deprive of Liberty;
But though they do my Corps confine,
Yet maugre hate, my Soul is free.
  Although Rebellion do my Body bind,
  My King can only captivate my mind.

The Rump, 1656

FRANCIS SEMPILL

1616?–1682

449 *Maggie Lauder*

WHA wad na be in love
  Wi' bonnie Maggie Lauder?
A piper met her gaun to Fife,
  And speir'd what was 't they ca'd her;
Right scornfully she answer'd him,
  'Begone, you hallanshaker,
Jog on your gate, you bladderskate,
  My name is Maggie Lauder.'

'Maggie,' quoth he, 'and by my bags,
  I'm fidging fain to see thee;
Sit down by me, my bonnie bird,
  In troth I winna steir thee;
For I'm a piper to my trade,
  My name is Rob the Ranter;
The lasses loup as they were daft,
  When I blaw up my chanter.'

'Piper,' quoth Meg, 'Hae you your bags,
  Or is your drone in order?
If you be Rob, I've heard of you;
  Live you upo' the Border?

The lasses a', baith far and near,
Have heard of Rob the Ranter;
I'll shake my foot wi' right goodwill,
Gif you'll blaw up your chanter.'

Then to his bags he flew wi' speed,
About the drone he twisted;
Meg up and wallop'd o'er the green,
For brawly could she frisk it.
'Weel done,' quoth he: 'Play up,' quoth she:
'Weel bobb'd,' quoth Rob the Ranter;
''Tis worth my while to play indeed,
When I hae sic a dancer.'

'Weel hae you play'd your part,' quoth Meg,
'Your cheeks are like the crimson;
There's nane in Scotland plays sae weel,
Since we lost Habbie Simpson.
I've liv'd in Fife, baith maid and wife,
These ten years and a quarter;
Gin you should come to Anster Fair,
Speir ye for Maggie Lauder.'

Herd's Ancient and Modern Scottish Songs, 1769 (text from 1776)

ANONYMOUS

450 *Todlen butt, and todlen ben*

WHEN I've a saxpence under my thumb,
Then I'll get credit in ilka town,
But ay when I'm poor they bid me gang by;
O! poverty parts good company,
Todlen hame, todlen hame,
Cou'dna my love come todlen hame?

Todlen: i.e. toddling.

Fair fa' the goodwife, and send her good sale,
She gies us white bannocks to drink her ale;
Syne if that her tippenny chance to be sma',
We'll tak a good scour o't, and ca't awa'.
Todlen hame, todlen hame,
As round as a neep come todlen hame.

My kimmer and I lay down to sleep,
And twa pint-stoups at our bed's feet;
And ay when we waken'd, we drank them dry:
What think ye of my wee kimmer and I?
Todlen butt, and todlen ben,
Sae round as my love comes todlen hame.

Leez me on liquor, my todlen dow,
Ye're ay sae good-humour'd when weeting your mou';
When sober sae sour, ye'll fight with a flee,
That 'tis a blyth sight to the bairns and me,
When todlen hame, todlen hame,
When round as a neep ye come todlen hame.

Ramsay's *Tea-Table Miscellany*, 1724–7

451 *O, Waly, Waly*

O WALY, waly up the bank,
And waly, waly down the brae,
And waly, waly yon burn-side
Where I and my love wont to gae.
I lean'd my back unto an aik,
I thought it was a trusty tree;
But first it bow'd, and syne it brak:
Sae my true love did lightly me.

tippenny: beer. kimmer: wife.

O waly, waly but love be bonny,
  A little while when it is new;
But when it's auld, it waxes cauld
  And wears awa' like the morning dew.
O wherefore should I busk my head?
  Or wherefore should I kame my hair?
For my true love has me forsook,
  And says he'll never love me mair.

Now Arthur-seat shall be my bed,
  The sheets shall ne'er be fyl'd by me,
Saint Anton's well shall be my drink,
  Since my true love has forsaken me.
Martinmas wind, when wilt thou blaw,
  And shake the green leaves off the tree?
O gentle death, when wilt thou come?
  For of my life I am wearie.

'Tis not the frost that freezes fell,
  Nor blawing snaw's inclemency;
'Tis not sick cauld that makes me cry,
  But my love's heart grown cauld to me.
When we came in by Glasgow town,
  We were a comely sight to see;
My love was cled in the black velvet,
  And I mysel in cramasie.

But had I wist before I kiss'd
  That love had been sae ill to win,
I'd lock'd my heart in a case of gold,
  And pinn'd it with a silver pin.

Oh, oh! if my young babe were born,
And set upon the nurse's knee,
And I mysel were dead and gane;
For a maid again I'll never be.

Ramsay's *Tea-Table Miscellany*, 1724–7

452 *The Bonnie Earl of Murray*

YE Highlands and ye Lawlands.
Oh! where hae ye been?
They hae slain the Earl of Murray,
And hae laid him on the green.

Now wae be to thee, Huntly,
And wherefore did you sae?
I bade you bring him wi' you,
But forbade you him to slay.

He was a braw gallant,
And he rid at the ring;
And the bonnie Earl of Murray,
Oh! he might hae been a king.

He was a braw gallant,
And he play'd at the ba';
And the bonnie Earl of Murray
Was the flower amang them a'.

He was a braw gallant,
And he play'd at the glove;
And the bonnie Earl of Murray,
Oh! he was the Queen's luve.

Oh! lang will his lady
  Look owre the castle Down,
Ere she see the Earl of Murray
  Come sounding thro' the town.

Ramsay's *Tea-Table Miscellany*, 1724–7

453 *The Dowie Houms o' Yarrow*

LATE at e'en, drinking the wine,
  And ere they paid the lawing.
They set a combat them between,
  To fight it in the dawing.

'O stay at hame, my noble lord,
  O stay at hame, my marrow!
My cruel brother will you betray
  On the dowie houms o' Yarrow.'

'O fare ye weel, my ladye gay!
  O fare ye weel, my Sarah!
For I maun gae, though I ne'er return
  Frae the dowie banks o' Yarrow.'

She kissed his cheek, she kaim'd his hair,
  As oft she had done before, O;
She belted him with his noble brand,
  And he's away to Yarrow.

O, he's gane up yon high, high hill—
  I wat he gaed wi' sorrow—
An' in a den spied nine arm'd men,
  In the dowie houms o' Yarrow.

'O are you come to drink the wine,
  As ye hae done before, O?
Or are ye come to wield the brand,
  On the bonnie banks o' Yarrow?'

'I am no come to drink the wine,
  As I hae done before O;
But I am come to wield the brand,
  On the dowie houms o' Yarrow.

'If I see all, ye're nine to ane;
  And that's an unequal marrow;
Yet will I fight, while lasts my brand,
  On the bonnie banks of Yarrow.'

Four he hurt, an' five has slain,
  On the bloody braes o' Yarrow,
Till that stubborn knight came him behind,
  And ran his body thorough.

'Gae hame, gae hame, good-brother John,
  An' tell your sister Sarah,
To come and lift her noble lord,
  He's sleepin' sound on Yarrow.'

'Yestreen I dream'd a dolefu' dream;
  I ken'd there wad be sorrow!
I dreamed I pu'd the heather green,
  On the dowie banks o' Yarrow.'

She gaed up yon high, high hill—
  I wat she gaed wi' sorrow—
An' in the den spied ten slain men,
  On the dowie banks o' Yarrow.

She kiss'd his cheek, she kaim'd his hair,
  As oft she did before, O;
She drank the red blood frae him ran,
  On the dowie houms o' Yarrow.

'Now haud your tongue, my dochter dear!
  For a' this breeds but sorrow?
I'll wed ye to a better lord
  Than him ye lost on Yarrow.'

'O haud your tongue, my father dear!
  Ye mind me but of sorrow;
A fairer rose did never bloom
  Than now lies cropp'd on Yarrow.

The Minstrelsy of the Scottish Border: Text, *Scott's with some variants from Hogg*

454 *Here awa', there awa'*

HERE awa', there awa', here awa' Willie,
  Here awa', there awa', here awa' hame;
Long have I sought thee, dear have I bought thee,
Now have I gotten my Willie again.

Thro' the lang muir I have follow'd my Willie,
Thro' the lang muir I have follow'd him hame;
Whatever betide us, nought shall divide us;
Love now rewards all my sorrow and pain.

Here awa', there awa', here awa' Willie,
Here awa', there awa', here awa' hame;
Come Love, believe me, nothing can grieve me;
Ilka thing pleases while Willie 's at hame.

Herd's Ancient and Modern Scottish Songs, 1769 (text from 1776)

455

Old-Long-syne

SHOULD old Acquaintance be forgot,
And never thought upon,
The Flames of Love extinguished,
And freely past and gone?
Is thy kind Heart now grown so cold
In that Loving Breast of thine,
That thou canst never once reflect
On Old-long-syne?

Where are thy Protestations,
Thy Vows and Oaths, my Dear,
Thou made to me, and I to thee,
In Register yet clear?
Is Faith and Truth so violate
To the Immortal Gods Divine,
That thou canst never once reflect
On Old-long-syne?

Is 't *Cupid's* Fears, or frosty Cares,
That makes thy Sp'rits decay?
Or is 't some Object of more Worth,
That's stol'n thy Heart away?
Or some Desert, makes thee neglect
Him, so much once was thine,
That thou canst never once reflect
On Old-long-syne?

Is't Wordly Cares so desperate,
That makes thee to despair?
Is 't that makes thee exasperate,
And makes thee to forbear?

ANONYMOUS

If thou of that were free as I,
Thou surely should be Mine:
If this were true, we should renew
Kind Old-long-syne:

But since that nothing can prevail,
And all Hope is in vain,
From these rejected Eyes of mine
Still Showers of Tears shall rain:
And though thou hast me now forgot,
Yet I'll continue Thine,
And ne'er forget for to reflect
On Old-long-syne.

If e'er I have a House, my Dear,
That truly is call'd mine,
And can afford but Country Cheer,
Or ought that's good therein;
Tho' thou were Rebel to the King,
And beat with Wind and Rain,
Assure thy self of Welcome Love,
For Old-long-syne.

Watson, *Choice Collection of Scots Poems*, 1711

RICHARD LOVELACE

1618–1658

456 *To Lucasta going beyond the Seas*

IF to be absent were to be
Away from thee;
Or that when I am gone,
You or I were alone;
Then my *Lucasta* might I crave
Pity from blustring winde, or swallowing wave.

But I'll not sigh one blast or gale
        To swell my saile,
    Or pay a teare to swage
    The foaming blew-Gods rage;
For whether he will let me passe
Or no, I'm still as happy as I was.

Though Seas and Land be 'twixt us both,
        Our Faith and Troth,
    Like separated soules,
    All time and space controules:
Above the highest sphere wee meet
Unseene, unknowne, and greet as Angels greet.

So then we doe anticipate
        Our after-fate,
    And are alive i' th' skies
    If thus our lips and eyes
Can speake like spirits unconfin'd
In Heav'n, their earthy bodies left behind.

Lucasta, 1649

457 *Going to the Warres*

TELL me not (Sweet) I am unkinde,
    That from the Nunnerie
Of thy chaste breast, and quiet minde,
    To Warre and Armes I flie.

True; a new Mistresse now I chase,
    The first Foe in the Field;
And with a stronger Faith imbrace
    A Sword, a Horse, a Shield.

Yet this Inconstancy is such,
As you too shall adore;
I could not love thee (Deare) so much,
Lov'd I not Honour more.

Lucasta, 1649

458 *Gratiana dauncing and singing*

SEE! with what constant Motion
Even, and glorious, as the Sunne,
Gratiana steers that Noble Frame.
Soft as her breast, sweet as her voyce
That gave each winding Law and poyze,
And swifter than the wings of Fame,

She beat the happy Pavement
By such a Starre made Firmament,
Which now no more the Roofe envies;
But swells up high with *Atlas* ev'n,
Bearing the brighter, nobler Heav'n,
And in her, all the Deities.

Each step trod out a Lovers thought
And the Ambitious hopes he brought,
Chain'd to her brave feet with such arts;
Such sweet command, and gentle awe,
As when she ceas'd, we sighing saw
The floore lay pav'd with broken hearts.

Frame: Fame. Edns. altered by editors.

So did she move; so did she sing
Like the Harmonious spheres that bring
  Unto their Rounds their musick's ayd;
Which she performed such a way,
As all th' inamour'd world will say
  The *Graces* daunced, and *Apollo* play'd.

Lucasta, 1649

459 *The Scrutinie*

WHY should you sweare I am forsworn,
  Since thine I vow'd to be?
Lady it is already Morn,
  And 'twas last night I swore to thee
That fond impossibility.

Have I not lov'd thee much and long,
  A tedious twelve houres space?
I must all other Beauties wrong,
  And rob thee of a new imbrace;
Could I still dote upon thy Face.

Not, but all joy in thy browne haire,
  By others may be found;
But I must search the black and faire,
  Like skilfull Minerallists that sound
For Treasure in un-plow'd-up ground.

Then, if when I have lov'd my round,
  Thou prov'st the pleasant she;
With spoyles of meaner Beauties crown'd,
  I laden will returne to thee,
Ev'n sated with Varietie.

Lucasta, 1649

460

The Grasshopper

To my Noble Friend, Mr. Charles Cotton

OH thou that swing'st upon the waving eare
  Of some well-filled Oaten Beard,
Drunke ev'ry night with a Delicious teare
  Dropt thee from Heav'n, where now th'art reard.

The Joyes of Earth and Ayre are thine intire,
  That with thy feet and wings dost hop and flye;
And when thy Poppy workes thou dost retire
  To thy Carv'd Acron-bed to lye.

Up with the Day, the Sun thou welcomst then,
  Sport'st in the guilt-plats of his Beames,
And all these merry dayes mak'st merry men,
  Thy selfe, and Melancholy streames.

But ah the Sickle! Golden Eares are Cropt;
  Ceres and *Bacchus* bid goodnight;
Sharpe frosty fingers all your Flowr's have topt,
  And what scithes spar'd, Winds shave off quite.

Poore verdant foole! and now green Ice! thy Joys
  Large and as lasting as thy Perch of Grasse,
Bid us lay in 'gainst Winter Raine, and poize
  Their floods, with an o'erflowing glasse.

Thou best of *Men* and *Friends!* we will create
  A Genuine Summer in each others breast;
And spite of this cold Time and frozen Fate
  Thaw us a warme seate to our rest.

Acron: Acorn.   guilt-plats: gilded plates.

Our sacred hearths shall burne eternally
  As Vestall Flames; the North-wind, he
Shall strike his frost stretch'd Winges, dissolve and flye
  This *Ætna* in Epitome.

Dropping *December* shall come weeping in,
  Bewayle th' usurping of his Raigne;
But when in show'rs of old Greeke we beginne,
  Shall crie, he hath his Crowne againe!

Night as cleare *Hesper* shall our Tapers whip
  From the light Casements where we play,
And the darke Hagge from her black mantle strip,
  And sticke there everlasting Day.

Thus richer than untempted Kings are we,
  That asking nothing, nothing need:
Though Lord of all what Seas imbrace, yet he
  That wants himselfe, is poore indeed.

Lucasta, 1649

461 *Elinda's Glove*

THOU snowy Farme with thy five Tenements!
  Tell thy white Mistris here was one
  That call'd to pay his dayly Rents:
But she a gathering Flow'rs and Hearts is gone,
And thou left void to rude Possession.

But grieve not pretty *Ermin* Cabinet,
  Thy Alabaster Lady will come home;
  If not, what Tenant can there fit
The slender turnings of thy narrow Roome,
But must ejected be by his owne doome?

Then give me leave to leave my Rent with thee;
  Five kisses, one unto a place:
  For though the *Lute's* too high for me;
Yet Servants, knowing Minikin nor Base,
Are still allow'd to fiddle with the Case.

Lucasta, 1649

462 *To Fletcher reviv'd*

HOW have I bin Religious? what strange good
Has scap't me that I never understood?
Have I Hell-guarded *Heresie* o'erthrowne?
Heal'd wounded States? made Kings and Kingdoms one?
That *Fate* should be so merciful to me,
To let me live t' have said I have read thee.

  Fair Star ascend! the Joy! the Life! the Light
Of this tempestuous Age, this darke worlds sight!
Oh from thy Crowne of Glory dart one flame
May strike a sacred Reverence, whilst thy Name
(Like holy *Flamens* to their God of Day)
We bowing, sing; and whilst we praise, we pray.

  Bright Spirit! whose Æternal motion
Of Wit, like *Time*, still in it selfe did run,
Binding all others in it, and did give
Commission, how far this or that shall live;
Like *Destiny* of Poems, who, as she
Signes death to all, her selfe can never die.

Minikin nor Base: Treble nor Bass.

And now thy purple-robed *Tragedy*,
In her imbroider'd Buskins, calls mine eye,
Where brave *Aëtius* we see betray'd,
T' obey his Death, whom thousand lives obey'd;
Whilst that the *Mighty Foole* his Scepter breakes,
And through his *Gen'rals* wounds his own doome speakes,
Weaving thus richly *Valentinian*
The costliest Monarch with the cheapest man.

Souldiers may here to their old glories adde,
The *Lover* love, and be with reason *mad*:
Not as of old, *Alcides* furious,
Who wilder than his Bull did teare the house,
(Hurling his Language with the Canvas stone)
'Twas thought the Monster roar'd the sob'rer Tone.

But ah! when thou thy sorrow didst inspire
With Passions, Blacke as is her darke attire,
Virgins as *Sufferers* have wept to see
So white a Soule, so red a Crueltie;
That thou hast griev'd, and with unthought redresse,
Dri'd their wet eyes who now thy mercy blesse;
Yet loth to lose thy watry jewell, when
Joy wip't it off, Laughter straight sprung 't agen.

Now ruddy cheeked *Mirth* with Rosie wings,
Fans ev'ry brow with gladnesse, whilst she sings
Delight to all, and the whole Theatre
A Festivall in Heaven doth appeare:
Nothing but Pleasure, Love, and (like the Morne)
Each face a gen'ral smiling doth adorne.

Heare ye foul Speakers, that pronounce the Aire
Of Stewes and Shores, I will informe you where
And how to cloath aright your wanton wit,
Without her nasty Bawd attending it:
View here a loose thought said with such a grace,
Minerva might have spoke in *Venus* face;
So well disguis'd, that t'was conceiv'd by none
But *Cupid* had *Diana's* linnen on;

And all his naked parts so vail'd, they' expresse
The shape with clowding the uncomlinesse;
That if this *Reformation* which we
Receiv'd, had not been buried with thee,
The Stage (as this worke) might have liv'd and lov'd
Her Lines, the austere *Scarlet* had approv'd;
And th' *Actors* wisely been from that offence
As cleare, as they are now from *Audience*.

Thus with thy *Genius* did the *Scæne* expire,
Wanting thy Active and correcting fire,
That now (to spread a darknesse over all,)
Nothing remaines but *Poesie* to fall:
And though from these thy *Embers* we receive
Some warmth, so much as may be said, we live,
That we dare praise thee, blushlesse, in the head
Of the best piece *Hermes* to *Love* e'er read,
That we rejoyce and glory in thy Wit,
And feast each other with remembring it,
That we dare speak thy thought, thy Acts recite;
Yet all men henceforth be afraid to write.

Lucasta, 1649

463 *To Althea from Prison*

WHEN Love with unconfined wings
  Hovers within my Gates;
And my divine *Althea* brings
  To whisper at the Grates:
When I lye tangled in her haire,
  And fetter'd to her eye;
The *Birds*, that wanton in the Aire,
  Know no such Liberty.

When flowing Cups run swiftly round
  With no allaying *Thames*,
Our carelesse heads with Roses bound,
  Our hearts with Loyall Flames;
When thirsty griefe in Wine we steepe,
  When Healths and draughts go free,
Fishes that tipple in the Deepe,
  Know no such Libertie.

When (like committed Linnets) I
  With shriller throat shall sing
The sweetness, Mercy, Majesty,
  And glories of my KING;
When I shall voyce aloud, how Good
  He is, how Great should be;
Inlarged Winds that curle the Flood,
  Know no such Liberty.

Stone Walls doe not a Prison make,
  Nor Iron bars a Cage;
Mindes innocent and quiet take
  That for an Hermitage;

Birds: MS. later altered to *Gods*.

If I have freedome in my Love,
And in my soule am free;
Angels alone that soar above,
Injoy such Liberty.

Lucasta, 1649

464 *To Lucasta*

I LAUGH and sing, but cannot tell
Whether the folly on't sounds well;
But then I groan
Methinks in Tune,
Whilst Grief, Despair, and Fear, dance to the Air
Of my despised Prayer.

A pretty Antick Love does this,
Then strikes a Galliard with a Kiss;
As in the end
The Chords they rend;
So you but with a touch from your fair Hand,
Turn all to Saraband.

Lucasta (*Posthume Poems*), 1659–60

ABRAHAM COWLEY

1618-1667

465 *The Spring*

THOUGH you be absent here, I needs must say
The *Trees* as beauteous are, and *flowers* as gay,
As ever they were wont to be;
Nay the *Birds* rural musick too
Is as melodious and free,
As if they sung to pleasure you:
I saw a *Rose-Bud* ope this morn; I'll swear
The blushing *Morning* open'd not more fair.

How could it be so fair, and you away?
How could the *Trees* be beauteous, *Flowers* so gay?
    Could they remember but last year,
    How *you* did *Them*, *They you* delight,
    The sprouting leaves which saw you here,
    And call'd their *Fellows* to the sight,
Would, looking round for the same sight in vain,
Creep back into their silent *Barks* again.

Where e'er you walk'd trees were as reverend made,
As when of old *Gods* dwelt in every shade.
    Is't possible they should not know,
    What loss of honor they sustain,
    That thus they smile and flourish now,
    And still their former pride retain?
Dull *Creatures!* 'tis not without Cause that she,
Who fled the *God of wit*, was made a *Tree*.

In ancient times sure they much wiser were,
When they rejoyc'd the *Thracian* verse to hear;
    In vain did *Nature* bid them stay,
    When *Orpheus* had his song begun,
    They call'd their wondring *roots* away,
    And bade them silent to him run.
How would those learned trees have followed you?
You would have drawn *Them*, and their *Poet* too.

But who can blame them now? for, since you're gone,
They're here the *only Fair*, and *Shine alone*.
    You did their *Natural Rights* invade;
    Where ever you did walk or sit,
    The thickest Boughs could make no *shade*,
    Although the Sun had granted it:

The fairest *Flowers* could please no more, neer you,
Than *Painted Flowers*, set next to them, could do.

When e'er then you come hither, that shall be
The time, which this to others is, to *Me*.
 The little joys which here are now,
 The name of Punishments do bear;
 When by their sight they let us know
 How we depriv'd of greater are.
'Tis you the best of *Seasons* with you bring;
This is for *Beasts*, and that for *Men* the *Spring*.

The Mistress, 1647

466 *The Change*

LOVE in her Sunny Eyes does basking play;
 Love walks the pleasant Mazes of her Hair;
Love does on both her Lips for ever stray;
And *sows* and *reaps* a thousand *kisses* there.
In all her outward parts Love 's always seen;
 But, oh, He never went within.

Within *Love's* foes, his greatest foes abide,
 Malice, Inconstancy, and Pride.
So the Earths face, Trees, Herbs, and Flowers do dress,
 With other beauties numberless:
But at the *Center*, *Darkness* is, and *Hell*;
There wicked *Spirits*, and there the *Damned* dwell.

With me alas, quite contrary it fares;
Darkness and *Death* lies in my weeping eyes,
Despair and Paleness in my face appears,
And Grief, and Fear, Love's greatest Enemies;
But, like the Persian-Tyrant, Love within
 Keeps his proud Court, and ne'er is seen.

Oh take *my Heart*, and by that means you'll prove
  Within too stor'd enough of *Love*:
Give me but Yours, I'll by that change so thrive,
  That *Love* in all my parts shall live.
So powerful is this change, it render can,
My *outside Woman*, and your *inside Man*.

The Mistress, 1647

467

The Wish

WELL then; I now do plainly see,
  This busie world and I shall ne'er agree;
The very *Honey* of all earthly joy
  Does of all meats the soonest *cloy*,
  And they (methinks) deserve my pity,
Who for it can endure the stings,
The *Crowd*, and *Buz*, and *Murmurings*
  Of this great *Hive*, *the City*.

  Ah, yet, e'er I descend to th' Grave
May I a *small House*, and *large Garden* have!
And a *few Friends*, and *many Books*, both true,
  Both wise, and both delightful too!
  And since *Love* ne'er will from me flee,
A *Mistress* moderately fair,
And good as *Guardian-Angels* are,
  Only belov'd, and loving me!

  Oh, *Fountains*, when in you shall I
My self, eas'd of unpeaceful thoughts, espy?
Oh *Fields*! Oh *Woods*! when, when shall I be made
  The happy Tenant of your shade?

Here 's the Spring-head of *Pleasures* flood;
Where all the *Riches* lie, that she
Has coyn'd and stampt for good.

Pride and *Ambition* here,
Only in *far fetcht Metaphors* appear;
Here nought but *winds* can hurtful *Murmurs* scatter,
And nought but *Eccho flatter*.
The *Gods*, when they descended, hither
From Heav'en did always chuse their way;
And therefore we may boldly say,
That 'tis the *way* too *thither*.

How happy here should I,
And one dear *She* live, and embracing dy?
She who is all the world, and can exclude
In *desarts Solitude*.
I should have then this only fear,
Lest men, when they my pleasures see,
Should hither throng to live like me,
And so make a *City* here.

The Mistress, 1647

468 *Against Hope*

HOPE, whose weak *Being* ruin'd is,
Alike if it *succeed*, and if it *miss*;
Whom *Good* or *Ill* does equally confound,
And both the *Horns* of *Fates Dilemma* wound.
Vain *shadow*! which dost vanish quite,
Both at full *Noon*, and perfect *Night*!

468. Compare Crashaw's *Answer for Hope*.

The Stars have not a *possibility*
    Of blessing Thee;
If things then from their *End* we happy call,
'Tis *Hope* is the most *Hopeless* thing of all.

    Hope, thou bold *Taster* of Delight,
Who whilst thou shouldst but *tast*, *devour'st* it quite!
Thou bringst us an *Estate*, yet leav'st us *Poor*,
By clogging it with *Legacies* before!
    The *Joys* which we *entire* should wed,
    Come *deflowr'd Virgins* to our bed;
Good fortunes without gain imported be,
    Such mighty *Custom's* paid to Thee.
For *Joy*, like *Wine*, kept close does better tast;
If it take air before, its spirits wast.

    Hope, Fortunes cheating *Lottery*!
Where for one *prize* an hundred *blanks* there be;
Fond *Archer*, *Hope*, who tak'st thy aim so far,
That still or *short*, or *wide* thine arrows are!
    Thin, empty *Cloud*, which th' eye deceives
    With shapes that our own *Fancy* gives!
A *Cloud*, which gilt and painted now appears,
    But must drop presently in *tears*!
When thy false beams o'er *Reasons* light prevail,
By *Ignes fatui* for *North-Stars* we sail.

    Brother of *Fear*, more gaily clad!
The *merr'ier Fool* o' th' two, yet quite as *Mad*:
Sire of *Repentance*, *Child* of fond *Desire*!
That blow'st the *Chymicks*, and the *Lovers* fire!
    Leading them still insensibly'on
    By the strange *witchcraft* of *Anon*!

blow'st: blows 1647. strange: strong 1647.

By *Thee* the one does changing *Nature* through
Her endless *Labyrinths* pursue,
And th' other chases *Woman*, whilst She goes
More ways and turns than *hunted Nature* knows.

The Mistress, 1647

469 *Of Wit*

TELL me, O tell, what kind of thing is *Wit*,
Thou who *Master* art of it.
For the *First matter* loves *Variety* less;
Less *Women* love 't, either in *Love* or *Dress*.
A thousand different shapes it bears,
Comely in thousand shapes appears.
Yonder we saw it plain; and here 'tis now,
Like *Spirits* in *a Place*, we know not *How*.

London that vents of *false Ware* so much store,
In no *Ware* deceives us more.
For men led by the *Colour*, and the *Shape*,
Like *Zeuxes Birds* fly to the painted *Grape*;
Some things do through our Judgment pass
As through a *Multiplying Glass*.
And sometimes, if the *Object* be too far,
We take a *Falling Meteor* for a *Star*.

Hence 'tis a *Wit* that greatest *word* of *Fame*
Grows such a common Name.
And *Wits* by our *Creation* they become,
Just so, as *Tit'lar Bishops* made at *Rome*.
'Tis not a *Tale*, 'tis not a *Jest*
Admir'd with *Laughter* at a feast,
Nor florid *Talk* which can that *Title* gain;
The *Proofs* of *Wit* for ever must remain.

'Tis not to force some lifeless *Verses* meet
    With their five gouty feet.
All ev'ry where, like *Mans*, must be the *Soul*,
And *Reason* the *Inferior Powers* controul.
    Such were the *Numbers* which could call
    The *Stones* into the *Theban* wall.
Such *Miracles* are ceast; and now we see
No *Towns* or *Houses* rais'd by *Poetrie*.

Yet 'tis not to adorn, and gild each part;
    That shows more *Cost*, than *Art*.
Jewels at *Nose* and *Lips* but ill appear;
Rather than *all things Wit*, let *none* be there.
    Several *Lights* will not be seen,
    If there be nothing else between.
Men doubt, because they stand so thick i' th' skie,
If those be *Stars* which paint the *Galaxie*.

'Tis not when two like words make up one noise;
    Jests for *Dutch Men*, and *English Boys*.
In which who finds out *Wit*, the same may see
In *An'grams* and *Acrostiques Poetrie*.
    Much less can that have any place
    At which a *Virgin* hides her face,
Such *Dross* the *Fire* must purge away; 'tis just
The *Author Blush*, there where the *Reader* must.

'Tis not such *Lines* as almost crack the *Stage*
    When *Bajazet* begins to rage.
Nor a tall *Meta'phor* in the *Bombast way*,
Nor the dry chips of short lung'd *Seneca*.
    Nor upon all things to obtrude,
    And force some odd *Similitude*.

What is it then, which like the *Power Divine*
We only can by *Negatives* define?

In a true piece of *Wit* all things must be,
        Yet all things there *agree*.
As in the *Ark*, joyn'd without force or strife,
All *Creatures* dwelt; all *Creatures* that had *Life*.
        Or as the *Primitive Forms* of all
        (If we compare great things with small)
Which without *Discord* or *Confusion* lie,
In that strange *Mirror* of the *Deitie*.

But *Love* that moulds *One Man* up out of *Two*,
        Makes me forget and injure you.
I took *you* for *my self* sure when I thought
That you in any thing were to be *Taught*.
        Correct my error with thy Pen;
        And if any ask me then,
What thing right *Wit*, and height of *Genius* is,
I'll onely shew your *Lines*, and say, '*Tis This*.

Miscellanies, 1656

470 *On the Death of Mr. William Hervey*

Immodicis brevis est aetas, & rara Senectus. Mart.

IT was a dismal, and a fearful night,
  Scarce could the Morn drive on th' unwilling Light,
When *Sleep*, *Deaths Image*, left my troubled brest,
    By something *liker Death* possest.
My eyes with Tears did uncommanded flow,
    And on my Soul hung the dull weight
    Of some *Intolerable Fate*.
What Bell was that? Ah me! Too much I know.

My sweet *Companion*, and my gentle *Peere*,
Why hast thou left me thus unkindly here,
Thy *end* for ever, and my *Life* to moan;
    O thou hast left me all alone!
Thy *Soul* and *Body* when *Deaths Agonie*
    Besieg'd around thy noble heart,
    Did not with more reluctance part
Than I, my dearest *Friend*, do part from *Thee*.

. . . . . .

He was my *Friend*, the truest *Friend* on earth;
A strong and mighty *Influence* joyn'd our *Birth*.
Nor did we envy the most sounding *Name*
    By *Friendship* giv'n of old to *Fame*.
None but his *Brethren* he, and *Sisters* knew,
    Whom the kind youth preferr'd to Me;
    And ev'n in that we did agree,
For much above my self I lov'd them too.

Say, for you saw us, ye immortal *Lights*,
How oft unweari'd have we spent the Nights?
Till the *Ledaean Stars* so fam'd for *Love*,
    Wondred at us from above.
We spent them not in toys, in lusts, or wine;
    But search of deep *Philosophy*,
    Wit, *Eloquence*, and *Poetry*,
Arts which I lov'd, for they, my *Friend*, were *Thine*.

Ye fields of *Cambridge*, our dear *Cambridge*, say,
Have ye not seen us walking every day?
Was there a *Tree* about which did not know
    The *Love* betwixt us two?

Henceforth, ye gentle *Trees*, for ever fade;
    Or your sad branches thicker joyn,
    And into darksome shades combine,
Dark as the *Grave* wherein my *Friend* is laid.

Henceforth no learned *Youths* beneath you sing,
Till all the tuneful *Birds* to'your boughs they bring;
No tuneful *Birds* play with their wonted chear,
    And call the learned *Youths* to hear;
No whistling *Winds* through the glad branches fly,
    But all with sad solemnitie,
    Mute and unmoved be,
Mute as the *Grave* wherein my *Friend* does ly.

To him my *Muse* made haste with every strain
Whilst it was new, and *warm* yet from the *Brain*.
He lov'd my worthless *Rhimes*, and like a *Friend*
    Would find out something to *commend*.
Hence no, my *Muse*, thou canst not me delight;
    Be this my latest verse
    With which I now adorn his *Herse*,
And this my *Grief*, without *thy* help shall write.

. . . . . .

Large was his *Soul*; as large a *Soul* as e'er
Submitted to *inform* a *Body* here.
High as the Place, 'twas shortly' in *Heav'n* to have,
    But low, and humble as his *Grave*.
So *high* that all the *Virtues* there did come
    As to their chiefest seat
    Conspicuous, and great;
So *low* that for *Me* too it made a room.

He scorn'd this busie world below, and all
That we, *Mistaken Mortals*, Pleasure call;
Was fill'd with inn'ocent *Gallantry* and *Truth*,
    Triumphant o'er the sins of *Youth*.
He like the *Stars*, to which he now is gone,
    That shine with beams like *Flame*,
    Yet burn not with the same,
Had all the *Light* of *Youth*, of the *Fire* none.

Knowledge he only sought, and so soon caught,
As if for him *Knowledge* had rather *sought*.
Nor did more *Learning* ever crowded lie
    In such a short *Mortalitie*.
When e'er the skilful *Youth* discourst or writ,
    Still did the *Notions* throng
    About his eloquent Tongue,
Nor could his *Ink* flow faster than his *Wit*.

. . . . . .

His *Mirth* was the pure *Spirits* of various Wit,
Yet never did his *God* or *Friends* forget.
And when deep talk and wisdom came in view,
    Retir'd and gave to them their due.
For the rich help of *Books* he always took,
    Though his own searching mind before
    Was so with *Notions* written o'er
As if wise *Nature* had made that her *Book*.

So many *Virtues* joyn'd in him, as we
Can scarce pick here and there in *Historie*.
More than old *Writers Practice* e'er could reach,
    As much as they could ever *teach*.

These did *Religion*, *Queen* of Virtues sway,
And all their sacred *Motions* steare,
Just like the First and *Highest Sphere*
Which wheels about, and turns all *Heav'n* one way.

With as much Zeal, Devotion, Pietie,
He always *Liv'd*, as other Saints do *Die*.
Still with his soul severe account he kept,
Weeping all *Debts* out ere he slept.
Then down in peace and innocence he lay,
Like the *Suns* laborious light,
Which still in *Water* sets at Night,
Unsullied with his *Journey* of the *Day*.

. . . . . .

But happy Thou, ta'en from this frantick age,
Where *Igno'rance* and *Hypocrisie* does rage!
A fitter *time* for Heav'n no soul e'er chose,
The place now onely free from those.
There 'mong the *Blest* thou dost for ever shine,
And wheresoere thou cast'st thy view
Upon that white and radiant crew,
See'st not a *Soul* cloath'd with more *Light* than *Thine*.

And if the glorious *Saints* cease not to know
Their wretched Friends who *fight* with *Life* below;
Thy Flame to *Me* does still the same abide,
Onely more pure and rarifi'd.
There whilst immortal Hymns thou dost reherse,
Thou dost with holy pity see
Our dull and earthly *Poesie*,
Where *Grief* and *Mis'ery* can be join'd with *Verse*.

Miscellanies, 1656

cast'st: 1689. cast 1656.

471 *On the Death of Mr. Crashaw*

P*OET* and *Saint*! to thee alone are given
The two most sacred *Names* of *Earth* and *Heaven*.
The hard and rarest *Union* which can be
Next that of *Godhead* with *Humanitie*.
Long did the *Muses* banisht *Slaves* abide,
And built vain *Pyramids* to mortal pride;
Like *Moses* Thou (though Spells and Charms withstand)
Hast brought them nobly home back to their *Holy Land*.
Ah wretched *We*, *Poets* of *Earth*! but *Thou*
Wert *Living* the same *Poet* which thou'rt *Now*,
Whilst *Angels* sing to thee their ayres divine,
And joy in an applause so great as *thine*.
Equal society with them to hold,
Thou need'st not make *new Songs*, but say the *Old*.
And they (kind Spirits!) shall all rejoyce to see
How little less than *They*, *Exalted Man* may be.
Still the old *Heathen Gods* in *Numbers* dwell,
The *Heav'enliest* thing on Earth still keeps up *Hell*.
Nor have we yet quite purg'd the *Christian Land*;
Still *Idols* here, like *Calves* at *Bethel* stand.
And though *Pans Death* long since all *Oracles* breaks,
Yet still in Rhyme the *Fiend Apollo* speaks:
Nay with the worst of Heathen dotage We
(Vain men!) the *Monster Woman Deifie*;
Find *Stars*, and tie our *Fates* there in a *Face*,
And *Paradise* in them by whom we *lost* it, place.
What different faults corrupt our *Muses* thus?
Wanton as *Girles*, as *old Wives*, *Fabulous*!

breaks . . . speaks 1656: broke . . . spoke 1668.

Thy spotless *Muse*, like *Mary*, did contain
The boundless *Godhead*; she did well disdain
That her *eternal Verse* employ'd should be
On a less subject than *Eternitie*;
And for a sacred *Mistress* scorn'd to take,
But her whom *God* himself scorn'd not his *Spouse* to make.
It (in a kind) *her Miracle* did do;
A fruitful *Mother* was, and *Virgin* too.
How well (blest Swan) did Fate contrive thy death;
And made thee render up thy tuneful breath
In thy great *Mistress* Arms? thou most divine
And richest *Off'ering* of *Loretto's Shrine*!
Where like some holy *Sacrifice* t' expire,
A *Fever* burns thee, and *Love* lights the *Fire*.
Angels (they say) brought the fam'ed *Chappel* there,
And bore the sacred Load in Triumph through the air.
'Tis surer much they brought thee there, and *They*,
And *Thou*, their charge, went *singing* all the way.
Pardon, my *Mother Church*, if I consent
That *Angels* led him when from thee he went,
For even in *Error* sure no *Danger* is
When joyn'd with so much *Piety* as *His*.
Ah, mighty *God*, with shame I speak 't, and grief,
Ah that our greatest *Faults* were in *Belief*!
And our weak *Reason* were ev'en weaker yet,
Rather than thus our *Wills* too strong for it.
His *Faith* perhaps in some nice Tenents might
Be wrong; his *Life*, I'm sure, was *in the right*.
And I my self a *Catholick* will be,
So far at least, great *Saint*, to *Pray* to thee.
Hail, *Bard Triumphant*! and some care bestow
On *us*, the *Poets Militant* Below!

Oppos'ed by our old En'emy, adverse *Chance*,
Attack'ed by *Envy*, and by *Ignorance*,
Enchain'd by *Beauty*, tortur'd by *Desires*,
Expos'd by *Tyrant-Love* to savage *Beasts* and *Fires*.
Thou from low earth in nobler *Flames* didst rise,
And like *Elijah*, mount *Alive* the skies.
Elisha-like (but with a wish much less,
More fit thy *Greatness*, and my *Littleness*)
Lo here I beg (I whom thou once didst prove
So humble to *Esteem*, so Good to *Love*)
Not that thy *Spirit* might on me *Doubled* be,
I ask but *Half* thy mighty *Spirit* for Me.
And when my *Muse* soars with so strong a Wing,
'Twill learn of things *Divine*, and first of *Thee* to sing.

Miscellanies, 1656

472 *The Epicure*

FILL the *Bowl* with rosie Wine,
Around our temples *Roses* twine.
And let us chearfully awhile,
Like the *Wine* and *Roses* smile.
Crown'd with Roses we contemn
Gyges' wealthy *Diadem*.
To-day is *Ours*; what do we fear?
To-day is *Ours*; we have it here.
Let 's treat it kindly, that it may
Wish, at least, with us to stay.
Let 's banish *Business*, banish *Sorrow*;
To the *Gods* belongs *Tomorrow*.

Anacreontics, 1656

ABRAHAM COWLEY

473 From '*Davideis*'

(*i*) *The Power of Numbers*

TELL me, Oh *Muse* (for *Thou*, or none canst tell
The mystick pow'ers that in blest *Numbers* dwell,
Thou their great *Nature* know'st, nor is it fit
This noblest *Gem* of thine own *Crown* t' omit)
Tell me from whence these heav'nly charms arise;
Teach the dull world *t' admire* what they *despise*,
As first a various unform'd *Hint* we find
Rise in some god-like *Poets* fertile *Mind*,
Till all the parts and words their places take,
And with just marches *verse* and *musick* make;
Such was *Gods Poem*, this *Worlds* new *Essay*;
So wild and rude in its first draught it lay;
Th' ungovern'd parts no *Correspondence* knew,
An artless *war* from thwarting *Motions* grew;
Till they to *Number* and fixt *Rules* were brought
By the *eternal Minds Poetique Thought*.
Water and *Air* he for the *Tenor* chose,
Earth made the *Base*, the *Treble Flame* arose,
To th' active *Moon* a quick brisk stroke he gave,
To *Saturns* string a touch more soft and grave.
The *motions Strait*, and *Round*, and *Swift*, and *Slow*,
And *Short*, and *Long*, were mixt and woven so,
Did in such artful *Figures* smoothly fall,
As made this decent measur'd *Dance* of *All*.
And this is *Musick*; *Sounds* that charm our ears,
Are but one *Dressing* that rich *Science* wears.
Though no man hear 't, though no man it reherse,
Yet will there still be *Musick* in my *Verse*.

In this *Great World* so much of it we see;
The *Lesser*, *Man*, is all o'er *Harmonie*.
Storehouse of all *Proportions! single Quire!*
Which first *Gods Breath* did tunefully inspire!
From hence blest *Musicks* heav'enly charms arise,
From *sympathy* which *Them* and *Man* allies.
Thus they our *souls*, thus they our *Bodies* win,
Not by their *Force*, but *Party* that 's within.
Thus the strange *Cure* on our spilt *Blood* apply'd,
Sympathy to the distant *Wound* does guide.
Thus when two *Brethren strings* are set alike,
To *move* them *both*, but *one* of them we *strike*,
Thus *Davids Lyre* did *Sauls* wild rage controul.
And tun'd the harsh disorders of his *Soul*.

Davideis, Book I, 1656, lines 439–480

(ii) *The Creation*

They sung how *God spoke out* the worlds vast ball;
From *Nothing*, and from *No where* call'd forth *All*.
No *Nature* yet, or *place* for 't to possess,
But an unbottom'ed *Gulf* of *Emptiness*.
Full of *Himself*, th' *Almighty* sat, his own
Palace, and without *Solitude Alone*.
But he was *Goodness* whole, and all things will'd;
Which ere they *were*, his *active word* fulfill'd;
And their astonisht heads o' th' sudden rear'ed;
An unshap'ed kind of *Something* first appear'ed,
Confessing its new *Being*, and undrest
As if it stept in hast before the rest.
Yet buried in this *Matters* darksome womb,
Lay the rich *Seeds* of ev'ery thing to come.
From hence the chearful *Flame* leapt up so high;

Close at its heels the nimble *Air* did fly;
Dull *Earth* with his own weight did downwards pierce
To the fixt *Navel* of the *Universe*,
And was quite lost in *waters*: till God said
To the proud *Sea*, shrink in your ins'olent head,
See how the gaping *Earth* has made you place;
That durst not murmur, but shrunk in apace.
Since when his bounds are set, at which in vain
He foams, and rages, and turns back again.
With richer stuff he bad *Heav'ens* fabrick shine,
And from him a quick spring of *Light divine*
Swell'd up the *Sun*, from whence his cher'ishing flame
Fills the whole world, like *Him* from whom it came.
He smooth'd the rough-cast *Moons* imperfect mold,
And comb'ed her beamy locks with sacred gold;
Be thou (said he) *Queen* of the mournful night,
And as he spoke, she' arose clad o'er in *Light*,
With thousand *stars* attending on her train;
With her they rise, with her they set again.
Then *Herbs* peep'd forth, new *Trees* admiring stood,
And smelling *Flow'ers* painted the infant wood.
Then flocks of *Birds* through the glad ayr did flee,
Joyful, and safe before *Mans Luxurie*,
Teaching their *Maker* in their untaught lays:
Nay the *mute Fish* witness no less his praise.
For those he made, and cloath'd with silver scales;
From *Minnows* to those *living Islands, Whales*.
Beasts too were his command: what could he more?
Yes, *Man* he could, the *bond* of all before;
In him he all things with strange order hurl'd;
In him, that *full Abridgment* of the *World*.

Davideis, Book I, 1656, lines 780–826

474 *Hymn: to light*

FIRST born of *Chaos*, who so fair didst come
From the old *Negro's* darksome womb!
Which when it saw the lovely Child,
The melancholly Mass put on kind looks and smil'd,

Thou Tide of Glory which no Rest dost know,
But ever Ebb, and ever Flow!
Thou Golden shower of a true Jove!
Who does in thee descend, and Heav'n to Earth make Love!

Hail active Natures watchful Life and Health!
Her Joy, her Ornament, and Wealth!
Hail to thy Husband Heat, and Thee!
Thou the worlds beauteous Bride, and lusty Bridegroom He!

Say from what Golden Quivers of the Sky,
Do all thy winged Arrows fly?
Swiftness and Power by Birth are thine:
From thy Great Sire they came, thy Sire the word Divine.

'Tis, I believe, this Archery to show,
That so much cost in Colours thou,
And skill in Painting dost bestow,
Upon thy ancient Arms, the Gawdy Heav'nly Bow.

Swift as light Thoughts their empty Carriere run,
Thy Race is finisht, when begun,
Let a Post-Angel start with Thee,
And Thou the Goal of Earth shalt reach as soon as He:

Thou in the Moons bright Chariot proud and gay,
Dost thy bright wood of Stars survay;
And all the year dost with thee bring
Of thousand flowry Lights thine own Nocturnal Spring.

Thou *Scythian*-like dost round thy Lands above
The Suns gilt Tent for ever move,
And still as thou in pomp dost go
The shining Pageants of the World attend thy show.

Nor amidst all these Triumphs dost thou scorn
The humble Glow-worms to adorn,
And with those living spangles gild,
(O Greatness without Pride!) the Bushes of the Field.

Night, and her ugly Subjects thou dost fright,
And sleep, the lazy Owl of Night;
Asham'd and fearful to appear
They screen their horrid shapes with the black Hemisphere.

With 'em there hastes, and wildly takes the Alarm,
Of painted Dreams, a busie swarm,
At the first opening of thine eye,
The various Clusters break, the antick Atomes fly.

The guilty Serpents, and obscener Beasts
Creep conscious to their secret rests:
Nature to thee does reverence pay;
Ill Omens, and ill Sights removes out of thy way.

At thy appearance, Grief it self is said,
To shake his Wings, and rowse his Head.
And cloudy care has often took
A gentle beamy Smile reflected from thy Look.

At thy appearance, Fear it self grows bold;
Thy Sun-shine melts away his Cold.
Encourag'd at the sight of Thee,
To the cheek Colour comes, and firmness to the knee.

Even Lust the Master of a hardned Face,
    Blushes if thou beest in the place,
    To darkness' Curtains he retires,
In Sympathizing Night he rolls his smoaky Fires.

When, Goddess, thou liftst up thy wakened Head,
    Out of the Mornings purple bed,
    Thy Quire of Birds about thee play,
And all the joyful world salutes the rising day.

The Ghosts, and Monster Spirits, that did presume
    A Bodies Priv'lege to assume,
    Vanish again invisibly,
And Bodies gain agen their visibility.

All the Worlds bravery that delights our Eyes
    Is but thy sev'ral Liveries,
    Thou the Rich Dye on them bestowest,
Thy nimble Pencil Paints this Landskape as thou go'st.

A Crimson Garment in the Rose thou wear'st;
    A Crown of studded Gold thou bear'st,
    The Virgin Lillies in their White,
Are clad but with the Lawn of almost Naked Light.

The Violet, springs little Infant, stands,
    Girt in thy purple Swadling-bands:
    On the fair Tulip thou dost dote;
Thou cloath'st it in a gay and party-colour'd Coat.

With Flame condenst thou dost the Jewels fix,
    And solid Colours in it mix:
    Flora her self envyes to see
Flowers fairer than her own, and durable as she.

Ah, Goddess! would thou could'st thy hand withhold,
And be less Liberall to Gold;
Didst thou less value to it give,
Of how much care (alas) might'st thou poor Man relieve!

To me the Sun is more delightful far,
And all fair Dayes much fairer are.
But few, ah wondrous few there be,
Who do not Gold prefer, O Goddess, ev'n to Thee.

Through the soft wayes of Heaven, and Air, and Sea,
Which open all their Pores to Thee;
Like a cleer River thou dost glide,
And with thy Living Stream through the close Channels slide.

But where firm Bodies thy free course oppose,
Gently thy source the Land o'erflowes;
Takes there possession, and does make,
Of Colours mingled, Light, a thick and standing Lake.

But the vast Ocean of unbounded Day
In th' Empyraean Heaven does stay.
Thy Rivers, Lakes, and Springs below
From thence took first their Rise, thither at last must Flow.

Verses on Several Occasions, 1663

475 *Of Solitude*

HAIL, old *Patrician* Trees, so great and good!
Hail ye *Plebeian* under wood!
Where the Poetique Birds rejoyce,
And for their quiet Nests and plentious Food,
Pay with their grateful voice.

Hail, the poor Muses richest Manor Seat!
Ye Country Houses and Retreat,
Which all the happy Gods so Love,
That for you oft they quit their Bright and Great
Metropolis above.

Here Nature does a House for me erect,
Nature the wisest Architect,
Who those fond Artists does despise
That can the fair and living Trees neglect;
Yet the Dead Timber prize.

Here let me careless and unthoughtful lying,
Hear the soft winds above me flying,
With all their wanton Boughs dispute,
And the more tuneful Birds to both replying
Nor be my self too Mute.

A Silver stream shall roll his waters neer,
Gilt with the Sun-beams here and there
On whose enamel'd Bank I'll walk,
And see how prettily they Smile, and hear
How prettily they Talk.

Ah wretched, and too Solitary Hee
Who loves not his own Company!
He'll feel the weight of 't many a day
Unless he call in Sin or Vanity
To help to bear 't away.

Oh Solitude, first state of Human-kind!
Which blest remain'd till man did find
Even his own helpers Company.
As soon as two (alas!) together joyn'd,
The Serpent made up Three.

ABRAHAM COWLEY

Though God himself, through countless Ages Thee
His sole Companion chose to bee,
Thee, Sacred Solitude alone,
Before the Branchy head of Numbers Tree
Sprang from the Trunk of One.

Thou (though men think thine an unactive part)
Dost break and tame th' unruly heart,
Which else would know no settled pace,
Making it move, well manag'd by thy Art,
With Swiftness and with Grace.

Thou the faint beams of Reasons scatter'd Light,
Dost like a Burning-glass unite,
Dost multiply the feeble Heat,
And fortifie the strength, till thou dost bright
And noble Fires beget.

Whilst this hard Truth I teach, methinks, I see
The Monster *London* laugh at me,
I should at thee too, foolish City,
If it were fit to laugh at Misery,
But thy Estate I pity.

Let but thy wicked men from out thee go,
And all the Fools that crowd thee so,
Even thou who dost thy Millions boast,
A Village less than *Islington* wilt grow,
A Solitude almost.

Essays in Verse and Prose, 1668

476 *Of My self*

THIS only grant me, that my means may lye
Too low for Envy, for Contempt too high.
Some Honor I would have
Not from great deeds, but good alone.
The unknown are better than ill known.
Rumour can ope' the Grave,
Acquaintance I would have, but when 't depends
Not on the number, but the choice of Friends.

Books should, not business, entertain the Light,
And sleep, as undisturb'd as Death, the Night.
My House a Cottage, more
Than Palace, and should fitting be
For all my Use, no Luxury.
My Garden painted o'er
With Natures hand, not Arts; and pleasures yield,
Horace might envy in his Sabine field.

Thus would I double my Lifes fading space,
For he that runs it well, twice runs his race.
And in this true delight,
These unbought sports, this happy State,
I would not fear nor wish my fate,
But boldly say each night,
To-morrow let my Sun his beams display,
Or in clouds hide them; I have liv'd to-day.

Essays in Verse and Prose, 1668

476. This also appeared as part of a longer poem *A Vote*.

SIR EDWARD SHERBURNE

1618–1702

477 *Violets in Thaumantia's Bosome*

TWICE happy Violets! that first had Birth
In the warm Spring, when no frosts nip the Earth;
Thrice happy now; since you transplanted are
Unto the sweeter Bosome of my Fair.
And yet poor Flowers! I pitty your hard Fate,
You have but chang'd, not better'd your Estate:
What boots it you t'have scap'd cold Winters breath,
To find, like me, by Flames a sudden death?

Salmacis, &c., 1651

478 *And she washed his Feet with her Teares, and wiped them with the Hairs of her Head*

THE proud *Ægyptian* Queen, her *Roman* Guest,
(T'express her Love in Height of State, and Pleasure)
With Pearl dissolv'd in Gold, did feast,
Both Food, and Treasure.

And now (dear Lord!) thy Lover, on the fair
And silver Tables of thy Feet, behold!
Pearl in her Tears, and in her Hair,
Offers thee Gold.

Salmacis, &c., 1651

478. From the Italian of Giambattista Marino.

ROBERT HEATH

fl. 1650

479 *Seeing her Dancing*

ROBES loosely flowing, and aspect as free,
A careless carriage, deckt with modestie;
A smiling look, but yet severe;
Such comely Graces 'bout her wove,
As she could hardly be perceiv'd to move;
Whilst her silk sailes displaied, she
Swam like a ship with Majestie
As when with stedfast eyes we view the Sun,
We know it goes though see no motion;
So undiscern'd she mov'd, that we
Perceiv'd she stirr'd, but did not see.

Clarastella, 1650

480 *On Clarastella Singing*

YE that in love delight
Approach this sacred Quire, and feast your ears!
Whilst the sweetest *Syren* sings,
Whose musick equals the harmonious spheres,
And perhaps richer pleasure brings!
The dying Swan or *Philomel*
O' th' wood not warbles half so well;
Observe the cadence where each dying sound,
Creates new Echoes to a fifth rebound.

Here's musick to the sight.
She looks and sings with such Majestick grace,
That when I *Clarastella* hear,
She more a woman seems, her voice and face
Taking at once both eye and eare,

That which of these two senses may
Be most refresht, is hard to say.
To glorifie her after death, She'll ne'er
Need Change; She's Angel now, and Heav'n is here.

Clarastella, 1650

481 *On Clarastella walking in her Garden*

SEE how *Flora* smiles to see
This approaching Deitie!
Where each herb looks young and green
In presence of their coming Queen!
Ceres with all her fragrant store,
Could never boast so sweet a flow'r;
While thus in triumph she doth go
The greater Goddess of the two.
Here the Violet bows to greet
Her with homage to her feet;
There the Lilly pales with white
Got by her reflexed light;
Here a Rose in crimson dye
Blushes through her modestie;
There a Pansie hangs his head
'Bout to shrink into his bed,
'Cause so quickly she pass'd by
Not returning suddenly;
Here the Currants red and white
In yon green bush at her sight
Peep through their shady leaves, and cry
Come eat me, as she passes by;
There a bed of Camomile,
When she presseth it doth smell

More fragrant than the perfum'd East,
Or the *Phoenix* spicie nest;
Here the Pinks in rowes do throng
To guard her as she walks along.
There the flexive Turnsole bends
Guided by the rayes she sends
From her bright eyes, as if thence
It suckt life by influence;
Whilst She the prime and chiefest flow'r
In all the Garden by her pow'r
And onely life-inspiring breath
Like the warm Sun redeems from death
Their drooping heads, and bids them live
To tell us She their sweets did give.

Clarastella, 1650

482 *On the unusual cold and rainie weather in the Summer, 1648*

WHY puts our Grandame Nature on
Her winter coat, ere Summer's done?
What, hath she got an ague fit?
And thinks to make us hov'ring sit
Over her lazie Embers? else why should
Old *Hyems* freeze our vernal blood?
Or as we each day, grow older,
Doth the world wax wan and colder?
'Tis so: See how nak'd Charitie
Sterves in this frozen age! whilst we
Have no other heat but glow-worm zeal
Whose warmth we see but cannot feel.

Turnsole: Sunflower.

All chang'd are *Ceres* golden hairs
To Clouded greys and nought appears
In *Flora's* dresse: our hopes do die
And o' th' sudden blasted lie.
Heav'ns glorious lamps do waste away,
The Elements themselves decay,
And the mixt bodies mutinie
By a rebellious sympathie;
Whilst the distemper'd world grows pale
And sickning threatens death to all:
So in an instant waters swept
The old worlds monsters, whilst they wept
Its funeral: but the new world's sins
Are so deep dy'd no flood can rinse.
Nothing but lightning and Heav'ns fire
Can purge our pestilential aire.

Clarastella, 1650

483 *Song in a Siege*

FILL, fill the goblet full with sack!
I mean our tall black-jerkin Jack,
Whose hide is proof 'gainst rabble-Rout,
And will keep all ill weathers out.
What though our plate be coin'd and spent?
Our faces next we'll send to the mint:
And 'fore we'll basely yield the town,
Sack it our selves and drink it down.

Accurst be he doth talk or think
Of treating, or denies to drink,
Such drie hopsucking narrow souls
Taste not the freedome of our bowles.

They only are besieg'd, whilst we
By drinking purchase libertie.
Wine doth enlarge, and ease our minds,
Who freely drinks no thraldome finds.

Let's drink then as we us'd to fight,
As long as we can stand, in spight
Of Foe or Fortune! who can tell?
She with our cups again may swell;
He neither dares to die nor fight,
Whom harmless fears from healths affright:
Then let us drink our sorrows down,
And ourselves up to keep the town.

Clarastella, 1650

484 *To Clarastella on St. Valentines day morning*

HARK how the Lyrick Choristers o' th' wood
Warble their cheerful notes! which understood
Would make us think they woo'd and spake
In pure *Tibullus* phrase, when he did take
His *Lesbia* to him! how they sing
And chirp it merrily
To welcome in that verdant spring
Which makes our blood run high!

Arise then heavy Muse! now winter's done
And the warm pleasant Summer is begun;
Arise! and charge *Aurora* wake,
And weare her best array for this daies sake

Salute her first whom I'd enjoy,
And then let all the nine
To their sweet musick dance and sing
That this day' is Valentine.

Great Bishop! whose more sacred memorie
Crowns this blest day with due solemnitie,
Let me invoke thy holy Shrine
To guide me to another *Valentine*!
Lend me thy urns fair light awhile
With the Morns brighter eies,
To find that happy She, and steal
Upon her by surprise.

Assist me *Jove*! in thy gilt show'rs convey
Me to the bed of my bright *Danae*!
Lest I be blasted or betrai'd
By the quick eyes of some crackt chambermaid,
Got up on purpose to be seen;
And though she stand i' th' way,
Blind me t'all but my *Valentine*!
Till I approach her day!

Or lend me *Gyges* old enchanted ring
That I may walk invisible! and bring
Me thus lockt up in close disguise
To the blest place where this fair beauty lies!
Thus undiscern'd I'll pass the street,
Nor see, nor yet be seen
Of any until we two meet
(My dearest Valentine).

Some draw their *Valentines* by lotterie
Whom they perhaps ne'er saw before, but I
  Make a far wiser choice in mine,
Where *Love* elects discreetly by design:
  Some on their hats in wafer scroll
    Their names have charact'red;
  I on my heart thy name enroll,
    More easie to be read.

See the true windows of the perfum'd East!
Breathing such odours that each sense may feast
  To luxurie! oh, 'twould suffice
To live but one hour in this Paradise!
  Then haste to kisse her balmie hand,
    To kiss her shall I fear?
  I'll gently draw the curtains, and
    Let the bright day appear.

Behold where *Innocence* her self doth lie
Clad in her white array! Fair Deitie!
  I'll onely print upon her dewy lip
One loving kiss and so away will slip.
  She wakes, and blushes on each cheek
    So red, that I may say
  There on each side doth truly break
    The dawning of the day.

Startle not Fairest! It is I am come
Like th' Persian to adore the rising Sun:
  I'm come to view that sight would make
The good old man ev'n for thy onely sake

Wish him alive agen, to see
  Such a fair Saint of 's name,
Whose virtues propagate in thee
  To his eternal fame.

'Tis I am come, who but a Friend before
Am hap'ly now by fate adopted more,
  A brother or what else you deem
To be more neer, or of more high esteem.
  I'm come to joyn in sacrifice
    To our dear *Valentine*;
  Where I must offer to thine eyes,
    Knowing no other Shrine.

Large Hecatombs of kisses I will lay
On th' Altar of thy lips, that men may say
  By their continuance we are true,
And will keep so this year, nor change for new.
  The birds instruct us to do so,
    The season too invites;
  When spring comes they a billing go,
    As we to our delights.

Each am'rous Turtle now his Mate doth chuse,
Whom Nature for that year by pow'rful use
  Taught to be constant: shall not wee
Who love with reason be as firm and free?
  Here then our league let us begin,
    And from this minute count
  Thousands of kisses that within
    This year shall thus amount.

How sweet she breathes! the Zephyre wind that blows
Fresh fragrant odours on the modest Rose
  Sends forth not half so pure a smell
As this which on thy chaster lips doth dwell:
  Here in this holy *Temple* I
    Could fix eternally,
  And pay these vows until I die
    Pitied of none but thee.

Methinks my arms now grasp a treasure more
Worth than both Indies valued double o'er.
  'Tis pitty we should ever part,
I should be poor, if robb'd of thee, my heart:
  The t'other kiss, and though I surfet on
    The sweetness of thy breath,
  The blame shall be on me alone;
    Who'd not die such a death?

Clarastella, 1650

ALEXANDER BROME

1620–1666

485 *Plain Dealing*

WELL, *well*, 'tis true,
  I am now fal'n in Love,
    And 'tis with You:
  And now I plainly see,
While you're *enthron'd* by me above,
You all your *arts* and *pow'rs* improve
  To *Tyrant* over me;
And make *my flames* th' Incentives of *your Scorn*,
While you *rejoyce*, and *feast* your Eyes to see me thus forlorn.

But yet be wise,
And don't believe, that I
Did think your *Eyes*
More bright than *Stars* can be;
Or that your *Face Angels* out-vies
In their *Cælestial* Liveries,
'Twas all but *Poetrie*.
I could have said as much by any *She*,
You are not *beauteous* of *your self*, but are made so by *me*.

Though *we* like Fools,
Fathom the *Earth* and *Skie*,
And drain the *Schools*
For names t' express *you* by:
Out-rant the lowd'st *Hyperboles*
To dub the *Saints*, and *Deities*,
By *Cupid's* Heraldry:
We know you're *Flesh* and *Blood* as well as *Men*,
And when we will can *mortalize*, and make you so agen.

Yet, since my *Fate*
Has drawn me to *this Sin*,
Which I did *hate*,
I'll not my labour lose:
But will *love on*, as I begin,
To th' purpose, now my hand is in,
'Spite of those *Arts* you use;
And let you know, the *World* is not so bare,
There's Things enough to love, besides such *Toyes* as *Ladies* are.

I'll love *good Wine*;
I'll love my *Book* and *Muse*,
Nay all the Nine;
I'll Love my *real Friend*;
I'll Love my *Horse*; and, could I chuse
One, that would not my *Love* abuse,
To *her* my Heart should bend.
I'll love all those, that *laugh*, and those, that *sing*;
I'll love my *Country*, *Prince*, and *Laws*; and those, that love the *King*.

Songs and other Poems, 1668

486 *Love's without Reason*

'TIS not my Ladies face that makes me love her,
Though *beauty* there doth rest,
Enough t' inflame the breast
On one, that never did discover
The *glories* of a face before;
But I that have seen *thousands* more
See nought in hers, but what in others are,
Only because I think she's *fair*, she's *fair*.

'Tis not her *vertues*, nor those vast *perfections*,
That crowd together in her,
Ingage my soul to win her,
For those are only brief *Collections*,
Of what's in man in *folio* writ·
Which by their imitative wit
Women like *Apes* and *Children* strive to do;
But we that have the *substance* slight the *show*.

ALEXANDER BROME

'Tis not her *birth*, her *friends*, nor yet her *treasure*
My free-born soul can hold;
For *chains* are *chains* though gold;
Nor do I *court* her for my pleasure,
Nor for that old *Moralitie*
Do I *love her*, *'cause she loves me*!
For that's no *love* but *gratitude*, and all
Loves that from *fortunes* rise, with *fortunes* fall.

If *friends*, or *birth*, created love within me,
Then *Princes* I'll adore,
And only scorn the *poor*,
If vertue or good parts could win me,
I'll turn *Platonick*, and ne'er vex
My soul with difference of *sex*
And he that loves his *Lady* 'cause she's fair,
Delights his *eye*, so loves himself, nor *her*.

Reason and *Wisdom* are to love high *Treason*,
Nor can be truly love,
Whose *flame's* not far above,
And far beyond his *Wit* or *Reason*,
Then ask no reason for my fires,
For *infinite* are my desires.
Something there is moves me to love, and I
Do know I love, but *know* not *how*, nor *why*.

Songs and other Poems, 1668

487

The Pastoral

On the King's death. Written in 1648

WHERE *Englands Damon* us'd to keep,
 In peace and awe his *flocks*,
Who fed, not fed upon, his sheep,
There *Wolves* and *Tygres* now do prey,
There *Sheep* are slain, and *Goats* do sway,
  There raigns the subtle *Fox*
 While the poor *Lamkins* weep.

The Laurell'd *garland* which before
 Circled his brows about,
The *spotless* coat which once he wore,
The *sheep-hook* which he us'd to sway,
And *pipe* whereon he lov'd to play,
  Are seiz'd on by the *rout*,
 And must be us'd no more.

Poor *Swain*, how thou lament'st to see
 Thy flocks o'er-rul'd by those
That serve thy Cattle all like thee:
Where hateful *vice* usurps the Crown,
And *Loyalty* is trodden down;
  Down scrip and sheep-hook goes,
 When *Foxes* Shepherds be.

Songs and other Poems, 1668

488 *The Riddle*

NO more, no more,
We are already pin'd;
And sore, and poor,
In *body* and in *minde*:
And yet our *sufferings* have been
Less than our *sin*.
Come long-desired *peace* we thee implore,
And let our pains be less, or *power* more.

Lament, Lament,
And let thy *tears* run down,
To see the rent
Between the *Robe* and *Crown*;
Yet both do strive to make it more
Than 'twas before:
War like a serpent has its *head* got in,
And will not end so soon as 't did begin.

One *body* Jars,
And with its self does fight;
War meets with *wars*,
And *might* resisteth *might*;
And both sides say they love the *King*,
And peace will bring:
Yet since these fatal civil broyles begun,
Strange Riddle! both have *conquer'd*, neither *won*.

One *God*, one *King*,
One true *Religion* still;
In every thing
One *Law* both should fulfil;

All these both sides does still pretend
That they defend:
Yet to encrease the *King* and *Kingdoms* woes,
Which side soever wins, good subjects lose.

The *King* doth swear,
That he doth fight for them;
And they declare,
They do the like for him:
Both say they wish and fight for peace,
Yet wars increase:
So between both, before our wars be gone,
Our lives and goods are lost, and we're undone.

Since 'tis our curse,
To fight we know not why;
'Tis worse and worse
The longer thus we lye:
For *War* it self is but a *Nurse*
To make us worse.
Come blessed *peace*, we once again implore,
And let our *pains* be less, or *power* more.

Songs and other Poems, 1668 (written in 1644)

ANDREW MARVELL

1621–1678

489 *A Dialogue between the Resolved Soul, and Created Pleasure*

COURAGE my Soul, now learn to wield
The weight of thine immortal Shield.
Close on thy Head thy Helmet bright.
Ballance thy Sword against the Fight.

See where an Army, strong as fair,
With silken Banners spreads the air.
Now, if thou bee'st that thing Divine,
In this day's Combat let it shine:
And shew that Nature wants an Art
To conquer one resolved Heart.

Pleasure.

Welcome the Creations Guest,
Lord of Earth, and Heavens Heir.
Lay aside that Warlike Crest,
And of Nature's banquet share:
Where the Souls of fruits and flow'rs
Stand prepar'd to heighten yours.

Soul.

I sup above, and cannot stay
To bait so long upon the way.

Pleasure.

On these downy Pillows lye,
Whose soft Plumes will thither fly:
On these Roses strow'd so plain
Lest one Leaf thy Side should strain.

Soul.

My gentler Rest is on a Thought,
Conscious of doing what I ought.

Pleasure.

If thou bee'st with Perfumes pleas'd,
Such as oft the Gods appeas'd,
Thou in fragrant Clouds shalt show
Like another God below.

Soul.

A Soul that knowes not to presume
Is Heaven's and its own perfume.

Pleasure.

Every thing does seem to vie
Which should first attract thine Eye:
But since none deserves that grace,
In this Crystal view *thy* face.

Soul.

When the Creator's skill is priz'd,
The rest is all but Earth disguis'd.

Pleasure.

Hark how Musick then prepares
For thy Stay these charming Aires;
Which the posting Winds recall,
And suspend the Rivers Fall.

Soul.

Had I but any time to lose,
On this I would it all dispose.
Cease Tempter. None can chain a mind
Whom this sweet Chordage cannot bind.

CHORUS.

Earth cannot shew so brave a Sight
As when a single Soul does fence
The Batteries of alluring Sense,
And Heaven views it with delight.
Then persevere: for still new Charges sound:
And if thou overcom'st thou shalt be crown'd.

Pleasure.

All this fair, and soft, and sweet,
  Which scatteringly doth shine,
Shall within one Beauty meet,
  And she be only thine.

Soul.

If things of Sight such Heavens be,
What Heavens are those we cannot see?

Pleasure.

Where so e'er thy Foot shall go
  The minted Gold shall lie;
Till thou purchase all below,
  And want new Worlds to buy.

Soul.

Wer 't not a price who'ld value Gold?
And that's worth nought that can be sold.

Pleasure.

Wilt thou all the Glory have
  That War or Peace commend?
Half the World shall be thy Slave
  The other half thy Friend.

Soul.

What Friends, if to my self untrue?
What Slaves, unless I captive you?

Pleasure.

Thou shalt know each hidden Cause;
  And see the future Time:
Try what depth the Centre draws;
  And then to Heaven climb.

Soul.

None thither mounts by the degree
Of Knowledge, but Humility.

CHORUS.

Triumph, triumph, victorious Soul;
The World has not one Pleasure more:
The rest does lie beyond the Pole,
And is thine everlasting Store.

Miscellaneous Poems, 1681

490 *On a Drop of Dew*

SEE how the Orient Dew,
Shed from the Bosom of the Morn
Into the blowing Roses,
Yet careless of its Mansion new;
For the clear Region where 'twas born
Round in its self incloses:
And in its little Globes Extent,
Frames as it can its native Element.
How it the purple flow'r does slight,
Scarce touching where it lyes,
But gazing back upon the Skies,
Shines with a mournful Light;
Like its own Tear,
Because so long divided from the Sphear.
Restless it roules and unsecure,
Trembling lest it grow impure:
Till the warm Sun pitty its Pain,
And to the Skies exhale it back again.
So the Soul, that Drop, that Ray
Of the clear Fountain of Eternal Day,

Could it within the humane flow'r be seen,
Remembring still its former height,
Shuns the sweet leaves and blossoms green;
And, recollecting its own Light,
Does, in its pure and circling thoughts, express
The greater Heaven in an Heaven less.
In how coy a Figure wound,
Every way it turns away:
So the World excluding round,
Yet receiving in the Day.
Dark beneath, but bright above:
Here disdaining, there in Love.
How loose and easie hence to go:
How girt and ready to ascend.
Moving but on a point below,
It all about does upwards bend.
Such did the Manna's sacred Dew destil;
White, and intire, though congeal'd and chill.
Congeal'd on Earth: but does, dissolving, run
Into the Glories of th' Almighty Sun.

Miscellaneous Poems, 1681

491 *The Coronet*

WHEN for the Thorns with which I long, too long,
With many a piercing wound,
My Saviours head have crown'd,
I seek with Garlands to redress that Wrong:
Through every Garden, every Mead,
I gather flow'rs (my fruits are only flow'rs)
Dismantling all the fragrant Towers
That once adorn'd my Shepherdesses head.

And now when I have summ'd up all my store,
   Thinking (so I my self deceive)
   So rich a Chaplet thence to weave
As never yet the king of Glory wore:
   Alas I find the Serpent old
   That, twining in his speckled breast,
   About the flow'rs disguis'd does fold,
   With wreaths of Fame and Interest.
Ah, foolish Man, that would'st debase with them,
And mortal Glory, Heaven's Diadem!
But thou who only could'st the Serpent tame,
Either his slipp'ry knots at once untie,
And disintangle all his winding Snare:
Or shatter too with him my curious frame
And let these wither, so that he may die,
Though set with Skill and chosen out with Care.
That they, while Thou on both their Spoils dost tread,
May crown thy Feet, that could not crown thy Head.

Miscellaneous Poems, 1681

492 *Bermudas*

WHERE the remote *Bermudas* ride
In th' Oceans bosome unespy'd,
From a small Boat, that row'd along,
The listning Winds receiv'd this Song.
   What should we do but sing his Praise
That led us through the watry Maze,
Unto an Isle so long unknown,
And yet far kinder than our own?
Where he the huge Sea-Monsters wracks,
That lift the Deep upon their Backs.

He lands us on a grassy Stage;
Safe from the Storms, and Prelat's rage.
He gave us this eternal Spring,
Which here enamells every thing;
And sends the Fowls to us in care,
On daily Visits through the Air.
He hangs in shades the Orange bright,
Like golden Lamps in a green Night.
And does in the Pomgranates close,
Jewels more rich than *Ormus* shows.
He makes the Figs our mouths to meet;
And throws the Melons at our feet.
But Apples plants of such a price,
No Tree could ever bear them twice.
With Cedars, chosen by his hand,
From *Lebanon*, he stores the Land.
And makes the hollow Seas, that roar,
Proclaime the Ambergris on shoar.
He cast (of which we rather boast)
The Gospels Pearl upon our Coast.
And in these Rocks for us did frame
A Temple, where to sound his Name.
Oh let our Voice his Praise exalt,
Till it arrive at Heavens Vault:
Which thence (perhaps) rebounding, may
Eccho beyond the *Mexique Bay*.
Thus sung they, in the *English* boat,
An holy and a chearful Note,
And all the way, to guide their Chime,
With falling Oars they kept the time.

Miscellaneous Poems, 1681

493 *A Dialogue between the Soul and Body*

Soul.

O WHO shall, from this Dungeon, raise
A Soul inslav'd so many wayes?
With bolts of Bones, that fetter'd stands
In Feet; and manacled in Hands.
Here blinded with an Eye; and there
Deaf with the drumming of an Ear.
A Soul hung up, as 'twere, in Chains
Of Nerves, and Arteries, and Veins.
Tortur'd, besides each other part,
In a vain Head, and double Heart.

Body.

O who shall me deliver whole,
From bonds of this Tyrannic Soul?
Which, stretcht upright, impales me so,
That mine own Precipice I go;
And warms and moves this needless Frame:
(A Fever could but do the same.)
And, wanting where its spight to try,
Has made me live to let me dye.
A Body that could never rest,
Since this ill Spirit it possest.

Soul.

What Magick could me thus confine
Within anothers Grief to pine?
Where whatsoever it complain,
I feel, that cannot feel, the pain.
And all my Care its self employes,
That to preserve, which me destroys:

Constrain'd not only to indure
Diseases, but, whats worse, the Cure:
And ready oft the Port to gain,
Am Shipwrackt into Health again.

Body.

But Physick yet could never reach
The Maladies Thou me dost teach;
Whom first the Cramp of Hope does Tear:
And then the Palsie Shakes of Fear.
The Pestilence of Love does heat:
Or Hatred's hidden Ulcer eat.
Joy's chearful Madness does perplex:
Or Sorrow's other Madness vex.
Which Knowledge forces me to know;
And Memory will not foregoe.
What but a Soul could have the wit
To build me up for Sin so fit?
So Architects do square and hew,
Green Trees that in the Forest grew.

Miscellaneous Poems, 1681

494 *From the Nymph complaining for the death of her Faun*

THE wanton Troopers riding by
Have shot my Faun and it will dye.
Ungentle men! They cannot thrive
To kill thee. Thou ne'er didst alive
Them any harm: alas nor cou'd
Thy death yet do them any good.
I'm sure I never wisht them ill;
Nor do I for all this; nor will:

But, if my simple Pray'rs may yet
Prevail with Heaven to forget
Thy murder, I will Joyn my Tears
Rather than fail. But, O my fears!

. . . . .

With sweetest milk, and sugar, first
I it at mine own fingers nurst.
And as it grew, so every day
It wax'd more white and sweet than they.
It had so sweet a Breath! And oft
I blusht to see its foot more soft,
And white, (shall I say than my hand?)
Nay, any Ladies of the Land.
It is a wond'rous thing, how fleet
'Twas on those little silver feet.
With what a pretty skipping grace,
It oft would challenge me the Race:
And when 't had left me far away,
'Twould stay, and run again, and stay.
For it was nimbler much than Hinds;
And trod, as on the four Winds.
I have a Garden of my own,
But so with Roses over grown,
And Lillies, that you would it guess
To be a little Wilderness.
And all the Spring time of the year
It onely loved to be there.
Among the beds of Lillyes, I
Have sought it oft, where it should lye;
Yet could not, till it self would rise,
Find it, although before mine Eyes.

For, in the flaxen Lillies shade,
It like a bank of Lillies laid.
Upon the Roses it would feed,
Until its Lips ev'n seem'd to bleed:
And then to me 'twould boldly trip,
And print those Roses on my Lip.
But all its chief delight was still
On Roses thus its self to fill:
And its pure virgin Limbs to fold
In whitest sheets of Lillies cold.
Had it liv'd long, it would have been
Lillies without, Roses within.

. . . . .

Now my Sweet Faun is vanish'd to
Whether the Swans and Turtles go:
In fair *Elizium* to endure,
With milk-white Lambs, and Ermins pure.
O do not run too fast: for I
Will but bespeak thy Grave, and die.
First my unhappy Statue shall
Be cut in Marble; and withal,
Let it be weeping too: but there
Th' Engraver sure his Art may spare;
For I so truly thee bemoane,
That I shall weep though I be Stone:
Until my Tears, still dropping, wear
My breast, themselves engraving there.
There at my feet shalt thou be laid,
Of purest Alabaster made:
For I would have thine Image be
White as I can, though not as Thee.

Miscellaneous Poems, 1681, lines 1–12, 55–92, 105–122

495 *To his Coy Mistress*

HAD we but World enough, and Time,
This coyness Lady were no crime.
We would sit down, and think which way
To walk, and pass our long Loves Day.
Thou by the *Indian Ganges* side
Should'st Rubies find: I by the Tide
Of *Humber* would complain. I would
Love you ten years before the Flood:
And you should if you please refuse
Till the Conversion of the *Jews*.
My vegetable Love should grow
Vaster than Empires, and more slow.
An hundred years should go to praise
Thine Eyes, and on thy Forehead Gaze.
Two hundred to adore each Breast:
But thirty thousand to the rest.
An Age at least to every part,
And the last Age should show your Heart.
For Lady you deserve this State;
Nor would I love at lower rate.

But at my back I alwaies hear
Times winged Charriot hurrying near:
And yonder all before us lye
Desarts of vast Eternity.
Thy Beauty shall no more be found;
Nor, in thy marble Vault, shall sound
My ecchoing Song: then Worms shall try
That long preserv'd Virginity:
And your quaint Honour turn to dust;
And into ashes all my Lust.

The Grave's a fine and private place,
But none I think do there embrace.
 Now therefore, while the youthful hew
Sits on thy skin like morning [dew],
And while thy willing Soul transpires
At every pore with instant Fires,
Now let us sport us while we may;
And now, like am'rous birds of prey,
Rather at once our Time devour,
Than languish in his slow-chapt pow'r.
Let us roll all our Strength, and all
Our sweetness, up into one Ball:
And tear our Pleasures with rough strife,
Thorough the Iron gates of Life.
Thus, though we cannot make our Sun
Stand still, yet we will make him run.

Miscellaneous Poems, 1681

496 *The Gallery*

CLORA come view my Soul, and tell
Whether I have contriv'd it well.
Now all its several lodgings lye
Compos'd into one Gallery;
And the great *Arras*-hangings, made
Of various Faces, by are laid;
That, for all furniture, you'll find
Only your Picture in my Mind.

Here Thou art painted in the Dress
Of an Inhumane Murtheress;
Examining upon our Hearts
Thy fertile Shop of cruel Arts:

[dew]: glew *1681*, dew *Cooke 1726*.

Engines more keen than ever yet
Adorned Tyrants Cabinet;
Of which the most tormenting are
Black Eyes, red Lips, and curled Hair.

But, on the other side, th' art drawn
Like to *Aurora* in the Dawn;
When in the East she slumb'ring lyes,
And stretches out her milky Thighs;
While all the morning Quire does sing,
And *Manna* falls, and Roses spring;
And, at thy Feet, the wooing Doves
Sit perfecting their harmless Loves.

Like an Enchantress here thou show'st,
Vexing thy restless Lover's Ghost;
And, by a Light obscure, dost rave
Over his Entrails, in the Cave;
Divining thence, with horrid Care,
How long thou shalt continue fair;
And (when inform'd) them throw'st away,
To be the greedy Vultur's prey.

But, against that, thou sit'st afloat
Like *Venus* in her pearly Boat.
The *Halcyons*, calming all that's nigh,
Betwixt the Air and Water fly.
Or, if some rolling Wave appears,
A Mass of Ambergris it bears.
Nor blows more Wind than what may well
Convoy the Perfume to the Smell.

These Pictures and a thousand more,
Of Thee, my Gallery do store;
In all the Forms thou can'st invent
Either to please me, or torment:
For thou alone to people me,
Art grown a num'rous Colony;
And a Collection choicer far
Than or *White-hall's*, or *Mantua's* were.

But, of these Pictures and the rest,
That at the Entrance likes me best:
Where the same Posture, and the Look
Remains, with which I first was took.
A tender Shepherdess, whose Hair
Hangs loosely playing in the Air,
Transplanting Flow'rs from the green Hill,
To crown her Head, and Bosome fill.

Miscellaneous Poems, 1681

497 *The Definition of Love*

MY Love is of a birth as rare
As 'tis for object strange and high:
It was begotten by Despair
Upon Impossibility.

Magnanimous Despair alone
Could show me so divine a thing,
Where feeble Hope could ne'er have flown
But vainly flapt its Tinsel Wing.

And yet I quickly might arrive
Where my extended Soul is fixt,
But Fate does Iron wedges drive,
And alwaies crowds it self betwixt.

For Fate with jealous Eye does see
Two perfect Loves; nor lets them close:
Their union would her ruine be,
And her Tyrannick pow'r depose.

And therefore her Decrees of Steel
Us as the distant Poles have plac'd,
(Though Loves whole World on us doth wheel)
Not by themselves to be embrac'd.

Unless the giddy Heaven fall,
And Earth some new Convulsion tear;
And, us to joyn, the World should all
Be cramp'd into a *Planisphere.*

As Lines so Loves *oblique* may well
Themselves in every Angle greet:
But ours so truly *Parallel*,
Though infinite can never meet.

Therefore the Love which us doth bind,
But Fate so enviously debars,
Is the Conjunction of the Mind,
And Opposition of the Stars.

Miscellaneous Poems, 1681

498 *The Picture of little T. C. in a Prospect of Flowers*

SEE with what simplicity
This Nimph begins her golden daies!
In the green Grass she loves to lie,
And there with her fair Aspect tames
The Wilder flow'rs, and gives them names:
But only with the Roses playes;
And them does tell
What Colour best becomes them, and what Smell.

Who can foretell for what high cause
This Darling of the Gods was born!
Yet this is She whose chaster Laws
The wanton Love shall one day fear,
And, under her command severe,
See his Bow broke and Ensigns torn.
Happy, who can
Appease this virtuous Enemy of Man!

O then let me in time compound,
And parly with those conquering Eyes;
Ere they have try'd their force to wound,
Ere, with their glancing wheels, they drive
In Triumph over Hearts that strive,
And them that yield but more despise.
Let me be laid,
Where I may see thy Glories from some shade.

Mean time, whilst every verdant thing
It self does at thy Beauty charm,
Reform the errours of the Spring;

Make that the Tulips may have share
Of sweetness, seeing they are fair;
And Roses of their thorns disarm:
But most procure
That Violets may a longer Age endure.

But O young beauty of the Woods,
Whom Nature courts with fruits and flow'rs,
Gather the Flow'rs, but spare the Buds;
Lest *Flora* angry at thy crime,
To kill her Infants in their prime,
Do quickly make th' Example Yours;
And, ere we see,
Nip in the blossome all our hopes and Thee.

Miscellaneous Poems, 1681

499 *The Mower to the Glo-Worms*

YE living Lamps, by whose dear light
The Nightingale does sit so late,
And studying all the Summer-night,
Her matchless Songs does meditate;

Ye Country Comets, that portend
No War, nor Princes funeral,
Shining unto no higher end
Than to presage the Grasses fall;

Ye Glow-worms, whose officious Flame
To wandring Mowers shows the way,
That in the Night have lost their aim,
And after foolish Fires do stray;

Your courteous Lights in vain you waste,
Since *Juliana* here is come,
For She my Mind hath so displac'd
That I shall never find my home.

Miscellaneous Poems, 1681

500 *The Garden*

HOW vainly men themselves amaze
To win the Palm, the Oke, or Bayes;
And their uncessant Labours see
Crown'd from some single Herb or Tree.
Whose short and narrow verged Shade
Does prudently their Toyles upbraid;
While all Flow'rs and all Trees do close
To weave the Garlands of repose.

Fair Quiet, have I found thee here,
And Innocence thy Sister dear!
Mistaken long, I sought you then
In busie Companies of Men.
Your sacred Plants, if here below,
Only among the Plants will grow.
Society is all but rude,
To this delicious Solitude.

No white nor red was ever seen
So am'rous as this lovely green.
Fond Lovers, cruel as their Flame,
Cut in these Trees their Mistress name.
Little, Alas, they know, or heed,
How far these Beauties Hers exceed!
Fair Trees! wheresoe'er your barkes I wound,
No Name shall but your own be found.

When we have run our Passions heat,
Love hither makes his best retreat.
The *Gods*, that mortal Beauty chase,
Still in a Tree did end their race.
Apollo hunted *Daphne* so,
Only that She might Laurel grow.
And *Pan* did after *Syrinx* speed,
Not as a Nymph, but for a Reed.

What wond'rous Life in this I lead!
Ripe Apples drop about my head;
The Luscious Clusters of the Vine
Upon my Mouth do crush their Wine;
The Nectaren, and curious Peach,
Into my hands themselves do reach;
Stumbling on Melons, as I pass,
Insnar'd with Flow'rs, I fall on Grass.

Mean while the Mind, from pleasure less,
Withdraws into its happiness:
The Mind, that Ocean where each kind
Does streight its own resemblance find;
Yet it creates, transcending these,
Far other Worlds, and other Seas;
Annihilating all that's made
To a green Thought in a green Shade.

Here at the Fountains sliding foot,
Or at some Fruit-trees mossy root,
Casting the Bodies Vest aside,
My Soul into the boughs does glide:

There like a Bird it sits, and sings,
Then whets, and combs its silver Wings;
And, till prepar'd for longer flight,
Waves in its Plumes the various Light.

Such was that happy Garden-state,
While Man there walk'd without a Mate:
After a Place so pure, and sweet,
What other Help could yet be meet!
But 'twas beyond a Mortal's share
To wander solitary there:
Two Paradises 'twere in one
To live in Paradise alone.

How well the skilful Gardner drew
Of flow'rs and herbes this Dial new;
Where from above the milder Sun
Does through a fragrant Zodiack run;
And, as it works, th' industrious Bee
Computes its time as well as we.
How could such sweet and wholsome Hours
Be reckon'd but with herbs and flow'rs!

Miscellaneous Poems, 1681

501 *An Horatian Ode upon Cromwel's Return from Ireland*

THE forward Youth that would appear
Must now forsake his *Muses* dear,
Nor in the Shadows sing
His Numbers languishing.
'Tis time to leave the Books in dust,
And oyl th' unused Armours rust:

Removing from the Wall
The Corslet of the Hall.
So restless *Cromwel* could not cease
In the inglorious Arts of Peace,
But through adventrous War
Urged his active Star.
And, like the three-fork'd Lightning, first
Breaking the Clouds where it was nurst,
Did thorough his own Side
His fiery way divide.
For 'tis all one to Courage high
The Emulous or Enemy;
And with such to inclose
Is more than to oppose.
Then burning through the Air he went,
And Pallaces and Temples rent:
And *Cæsars* head at last
Did through his Laurels blast.
'Tis Madness to resist or blame
The force of angry Heavens flame:
And, if we would speak true,
Much to the Man is due.
Who, from his private Gardens, where
He liv'd reserved and austere,
As if his highest plot
To plant the Bergamot,
Could by industrious Valour climbe
To ruine the great Work of Time,
And cast the Kingdome old
Into another Mold.
Though Justice against Fate complain,
And plead the antient Rights in vain:

But those do hold or break
As Men are strong or weak.
Nature that hateth emptiness,
Allows of penetration less:
And therefore must make room
Where greater Spirits come.
What Field of all the Civil Wars,
Where his were not the deepest Scars?
And *Hampton* shows what part
He had of wiser Art.
Where, twining subtile fears with hope,
He wove a Net of such a scope,
That *Charles* himself might chase
To *Caresbrooks* narrow case.
That thence the *Royal Actor* born
The *Tragick Scaffold* might adorn:
While round the armed Bands
Did clap their bloody hands.
He nothing common did or mean
Upon that memorable Scene:
But with his keener Eye
The Axes edge did try:
Nor call'd the *Gods* with vulgar spight
To vindicate his helpless Right,
But bow'd his comely Head,
Down as upon a Bed.
This was that memorable Hour
Which first assur'd the forced Pow'r.
So when they did design
The *Capitols* first Line,
A bleeding Head where they begun,
Did fright the Architects to run;

And yet in that the *State*
Foresaw its happy Fate.
And now the *Irish* are asham'd
To see themselves in one Year tam'd:
So much one Man can do,
That does both act and know.
They can affirm his Praises best,
And have, though overcome, confest
How good he is, how just,
And fit for highest Trust:
Nor yet grown stiffer with Command,
But still in the *Republick's* hand:
How fit he is to sway
That can so well obey.
He to the *Commons Feet* presents
A *Kingdome*, for his first years rents:
And, what he may, forbears
His Fame to make it theirs:
And has his Sword and Spoyls ungirt,
To lay them at the *Publick's* skirt.
So when the Falcon high
Falls heavy from the Sky,
She, having kill'd, no more does search,
But on the next green Bow to perch;
Where, when he first does lure,
The Falkner has her sure.
What may not then our *Isle* presume
While Victory his Crest does plume!
What may not others fear
If thus he crown each Year!
A *Cæsar* he ere long to *Gaul*,
To *Italy* an *Hannibal*,

And to all States not free
Shall *Clymacterick* be.
The *Pict* no shelter now shall find
Within his party-colour'd Mind;
But from this Valour sad
Shrink underneath the Plad:
Happy if in the tufted brake
The *English Hunter* him mistake;
Nor lay his Hounds in near
The *Caledonian* Deer.
But thou the Wars and Fortunes Son
March indefatigably on;
And for the last effect
Still keep thy Sword erect:
Besides the force it has to fright
The Spirits of the shady Night,
The same *Arts* that did *gain*
A *Pow'r* must it *maintain*.

Miscellaneous Poems, 1681

502 *From A Poem upon the Death of Oliver Cromwell*

I SAW him dead, a leaden slumber lyes,
And mortal sleep over those wakefull eyes:
Those gentle rays under the lids were fled,
Which through his looks that piercing sweetnesse shed;
That port which so majestique was and strong,
Loose and depriv'd of vigour, stretch'd along:
All wither'd, all discolour'd, pale and wan,
How much another thing, no more that man?
Oh! humane glory, vaine, oh! death, oh! wings,
Oh! worthlesse world! oh transitory things!

Yet dwelt that greatnesse in his shape decay'd,
That still though dead, greater than death he lay'd;
And in his alter'd face you something faigne
That threatens death, he yet will live again.
Not much unlike the sacred oak, which shoots
To Heav'n its branches, and through earth its roots:
Whose spacious boughs are hung with trophies round,
And honour'd wreaths have oft the victour crown'd.
When angry Jove darts lightning through the aire,
At mortalls sins, nor his own plant will spare;
(It groanes, and bruises all below that stood
So many yeares the shelter of the wood.)
The tree ere while foreshortned to our view,
When fall'n shews taller yet than as it grew:
So shall his praise to after times encrease,
When truth shall be allow'd, and faction cease,
And his own shadows with him fall; the eye
Detracts from objects than itself more high:
But when death takes them from that envy'd state,
Seeing how little we confess, how greate:
Thee, many ages hence, in martial verse
Shall th' English souldier, ere he charge, rehearse;
Singing of thee, inflame themselves to fight,
And with the name of Cromwell, armyes fright.
As long as rivers to the seas shall runne,
As long as Cynthia shall relieve the sunne,
While stags shall fly unto the forests thick,
While sheep delight the grassy downs to pick,
As long as future time succeeds the past,
Always thy honour, praise and name, shall last.

Miscellaneous Poems, 1681, lines 247–86

503 From '*Last Instructions to a Painter*'

(*i*) *The Dutch in the Medway*

R*UYTER* the while, that had our Ocean curb'd,
Sail'd now among our Rivers undisturb'd:
Survey'd their Crystal Streams, and Banks so green,
And Beauties ere this never naked seen.
Through the vain sedge the bashful *Nymphs* he ey'd;
Bosomes, and all which from themselves they hide.
The Sun much brighter, and the Skies more clear,
He finds the Air, and all things sweeter here.
The sudden change, and such a tempting sight,
Swells his old Veins with fresh Blood, fresh Delight.
Like am'rous Victors he begins to shave,
And his new Face looks in the *English* Wave.
His sporting Navy all about him swim,
And witness their complaisence in their trim.
Their streaming Silks play through the weather fair,
And with inveigling Colours Court the Air.
While the red Flags breathe on their Top-masts high
Terrour and War, but want an Enemy.
Among the Shrowds the Seamen sit and sing,
And wanton Boys on every Rope do cling.
Old *Neptune* springs the Tydes, and Water lent:
(The Gods themselves do help the provident.)
And, where the deep Keel on the shallow cleaves,
With *Trident*'s Leaver, and great Shoulder heaves.
Æolus their Sails inspires with *Eastern* Wind,
Puffs them along, and breathes upon them kind.
With Pearly Shell the *Tritons* all the while
Sound the Sea-march, and guide to *Sheppy Isle*.

So have I seen, in *April's* bud, arise
A Fleet of Clouds, sailing along the Skies:
The liquid Region with their Squadrons fill'd,
The airy Sterns the Sun behind does guild;
And gentle Gales them steer, and Heaven drives,
When, all on sudden, their calm bosome rives
With Thunder and Lightning from each armed Cloud;
Shepherds themselves in vain in bushes shrowd.
Such up the stream the *Belgick* Navy glides,
And at *Sheerness* unloads its stormy sides.

. . . . .

There our sick Ships unrigg'd in Summer lay,
Like molting Fowl, a weak and easie Prey.
For whose strong bulk Earth scarce could Timber find,
The Ocean Water, or the Heavens Wind.
Those Oaken Gyants of the ancient Race,
That rul'd all Seas, and did our Channel grace.
The conscious Stag, so once the Forests dread,
Flies to the Wood, and hides his armless Head.
Ruyter forthwith a Squadron does untack,
They sail securely through the Rivers track.
An *English* Pilot too, (O Shame, O Sin!)
Cheated of Pay, was he that show'd them in.

Lines 523–560; 573–584

(*ii*) *Charles II*

PAINT last the King, and a dead shade of Night,
Only dispers'd by a weak Tapers light;
And those bright gleams that dart along and glare
From his clear Eyes, yet these too dark with Care.

There, as in the calm horrour all alone,
He wakes and muses of th' uneasie Throne:
Raise up a sudden Shape with Virgins Face,
Though ill agree her Posture, Hour, or Place:
Naked as born, and her round Arms behind,
With her own Tresses interwove and twin'd:
Her mouth lockt up, a blind before her Eyes,
Yet from beneath the Veil her blushes rise;
And silent tears her secret anguish speak,
Her heart throbs, and with very shame would break.
The Object strange in him no Terrour mov'd:
He wonder'd first, then pity'd, then he lov'd:
And with kind hand does the coy Vision press,
Whose Beauty greater seem'd by her distress;
But soon shrunk back, chill'd with her touch so cold,
And th' airy Picture vanisht from his hold.
In his deep thoughts the wonder did increase,
And he Divin'd 'twas *England* or the *Peace*.

Miscellaneous Poems, 1681, lines 885–906

THOMAS VAUGHAN

1622–1666

504

The Stone

LORD God! This was a *stone*,
As *hard* as any *One*
Thy *Laws* in *Nature* fram'd:
'Tis now a *springing Well*,
And many *Drops* can tell,
Since it by *Art* was tam'd.

THOMAS VAUGHAN

My God! my *Heart* is so,
'Tis all of *Flint*, and no
Extract of *Teares* will yield:
Dissolve it with thy *Fire*,
That something may *aspire*,
And *grow* up in my *Field*,

Bare Teares I'll not intreat,
But let thy *Spirits Seate*
Upon those *Waters* be,
Then I *new form'd* with *Light*,
Shall move without all *Night*
Of *Excentricity*.

Anthroposophia Theomagica, 1650

HENRY VAUGHAN

1622–1695

505 *To Amoret gone from him*

FANCY, and I, last Evening walkt,
And, *Amoret*, of thee we talkt;
The West just then had stolne the Sun,
And his last blushes were begun:
We sate, and markt how every thing
Did mourne his absence; How the Spring
That smil'd, and curl'd about his beames,
Whilst he was here, now check'd her streames:
The wanton Eddies of her face
Were taught lesse noise, and smoother grace;
And in a slow, sad channell went,
Whisp'ring the banks their discontent:

The carelesse ranks of flowers that spread
Their perfum'd bosomes to his head,
And with an open, free Embrace,
Did entertaine his beamy face;
Like absent friends point to the West,
And on that weake reflection feast.
If Creatures then that have no sense,
But the loose tye of influence,
(Though fate, and time each day remove
Those things that element their love)
At such vast distance can agree,
Why, *Amoret*, why should not wee?

Poems, 1646

506

Regeneration

A WARD, and still in bonds, one day
I stole abroad,
It was high-spring, and all the way
Primros'd, and hung with shade;
Yet, was it frost within,
And surly winds
Blasted my infant buds, and sinne
Like Clouds ecclips'd my mind.

Storm'd thus; I straight perceiv'd my spring
Mere stage, and show,
My walke a monstrous, mountain'd thing
Rough-cast with Rocks, and snow;
And as a Pilgrims Eye
Far from reliefe,
Measures the melancholy skye
Then drops, and rains for griefe,

So sigh'd I upwards still, at last
'Twixt steps, and falls
I reach'd the pinacle, where plac'd
I found a paire of scales,
I tooke them up and layd
In th' one late paines,
The other smoke, and pleasures weigh'd
But prov'd the heavier graines;

With that, some cryed, *Away*; straight I
Obey'd, and led
Full East, a faire, fresh field could spy
Some call'd it, *Jacobs Bed*;
A Virgin-soile, which no
Rude feet e'er trod,
Where (since he stept there,) only go
Prophets, and friends of God.

Here, I repos'd; but scarse well set,
A grove descryed
Of stately height, whose branches met
And mixt on every side;
I entred, and once in
(Amaz'd to see 't,)
Found all was chang'd, and a new spring
Did all my senses greet;

The unthrift Sunne shot vitall gold
A thousand peeces,
And heaven its azure did unfold
Checqur'd with snowie fleeces,

The aire was all in spice
And every bush
A garland wore; Thus fed my Eyes
But all the Eare lay hush.

Only a little Fountain lent
Some use for Eares,
And on the dumbe shades language spent
The Musick of her teares;
I drew her neere, and found
The Cisterne full
Of divers stones, some bright, and round
Others ill-shap'd, and dull.

The first (pray marke,) as quick as light
Danc'd through the flood,
But, th' last more heavy than the night
Nail'd to the Center stood;
I wonder'd much, but tir'd
At last with thought,
My restless Eye that still desir'd
As strange an object brought;

It was a banke of flowers, where I descried
(Though 'twas mid-day,)
Some fast asleepe, others broad-eyed
And taking in the Ray,
Here musing long, I heard
A rushing wind
Which still increas'd, but whence it stirr'd
No where I could not find;

I turn'd me round, and to each shade
Dispatch'd an Eye,
To see, if any leafe had made
Least motion, or Reply,
But while I listning sought
My mind to ease
By knowing, where 'twas, or where not,
It whisper'd *Where I please.*

Lord, then said I, *On me one breath,*
And let me dye before my death!

Cant. Cap. 5. ver. 17.

Arise O North, and come thou South-wind, and blow upon my garden, that the spices thereof may flow out.

Silex Scintillans, 1650

507 *Religion*

MY God, when I walke in those groves,
And leaves thy spirit doth still fan,
I see in each shade that there growes
An Angell taking with a man.

Under a *Juniper*, some house,
Or the coole *Mirtles* canopie,
Others beneath an *Oakes* greene boughs,
Or at some *fountaines* bubbling Eye;

Here *Jacob* dreames, and wrestles; there
Elias by a Raven is fed,
Another time by th' Angell, where
He brings him water with his bread;

In *Abr'hams* Tent the winged guests
(O how familiar then was heaven!)
Eate, drinke, discourse, sit downe, and rest
Untill the Coole, and shady *Even*;

Nay thou thy selfe, my God, in *fire*,
Whirle-winds, and *Clouds*, and the *soft voice*
Speak'st there so much, that I admire
We have no Conf'rence in these daies;

Is the truce broke? or 'cause we have
A mediatour now with thee,
Doest thou therefore old Treaties wave
And by appeales from him decree?

Or is't so, as some green heads say
That now all miracles must cease?
Though thou hast promis'd they should stay
The tokens of the Church, and peace;

No, no; Religion is a Spring
That from some secret, golden Mine
Derives her birth, and thence doth bring
Cordials in every drop, and Wine;

But in her long, and hidden Course
Passing through the Earths darke veines,
Growes still from better unto worse,
And both her taste, and colour staines,

Then drilling on, learnes to encrease
False *Ecchoes*, and Confused sounds,
And unawares doth often seize
On veines of *Sulphur* under ground;

So poison'd, breaks forth in some Clime,
And at first sight doth many please,
But drunk, is puddle, or mere slime
And 'stead of Phisick, a disease;

Just such a tainted sink we have
Like that *Samaritans* dead *Well*,
Nor must we for the Kernell crave
Because most voices like the *shell*.

Heale then these waters, Lord; or bring thy flock,
Since these are troubled, to the springing rock,
Looke downe great Master of the feast; O shine,
And turn once more our *Water* into *Wine*!

Cant. cap. 4. ver. 12.

My sister, my spouse is as a garden Inclosed, as a Spring shut up, and a fountain sealed up.

Silex Scintillans, 1650

508 *The Retreate*

HAPPY those early dayes! when I
Shin'd in my Angell-infancy.
Before I understood this place
Appointed for my second race,
Or taught my soul to fancy ought
But a white, Celestiall thought,
When yet I had not walkt above
A mile, or two, from my first love,
And looking back (at that short space,)
Could see a glimpse of his bright-face;
When on some *gilded Cloud*, or *flowre*
My gazing soul would dwell an houre,

And in those weaker glories spy
Some shadows of eternity;
Before I taught my tongue to wound
My Conscience with a sinfull sound,
Or had the black art to dispense
A sev'rall sinne to ev'ry sense,
But felt through all this fleshly dresse
Bright *shootes* of everlastingnesse.
  O how I long to travell back
And tread again that ancient track!
That I might once more reach that plaine,
Where first I left my glorious traine,
From whence th' Inlightned spirit sees
That shady City of Palme trees;
But (ah!) my soul with too much stay
Is drunk, and staggers in the way.
Some men a forward motion love,
But I by backward steps would move,
And when this dust falls to the urn
In that state I came return.

Silex Scintillans, 1650

509 ## (*Joy of my life!*)

JOY of my life! while left me here,
        And still my Love!
How in thy absence thou dost steere
        Me from above!
        A life well led
        This truth commends,
        With quick, or dead
        It never ends.

Stars are of mighty use: The night
Is dark, and long;
The Road foul, and where one goes right,
Six may go wrong.
One twinkling ray
Shot o'er some cloud,
May clear much way
And guide a crowd.

Gods Saints are shining lights: who stays
Here long must passe
O'er dark hills, swift streames, and steep ways
As smooth as glasse;
But these all night
Like Candles, shed
Their beams, and light
Us into Bed.

They are (indeed,) our Pillar-fires
Seen as we go,
They are that Cities shining spires
We travell to;
A swordlike gleame
Kept man for sin
First *Out*; This beame
Will guide him *In*.

Silex Scintillans, 1650

510 *The Morning-Watch*

O JOYES! Infinite sweetness! with what flowres,
And shoots of glory, my soul breakes, and buds!
All the long houres
Of night, and Rest

Through the still shrouds
Of sleep, and Clouds,
This Dew fell on my Breast;
O how it *Blouds*,
And *Spirits* all my Earth! heark! In what Rings,
And *Hymning Circulations* the quick world
Awakes, and sings;
And rising winds,
And falling springs,
Birds, beasts, all things
Adore him in their kinds.
Thus all is hurl'd
In sacred *Hymnes*, and *Order*, The great *Chime*
And *Symphony* of nature. Prayer is
The world in tune,
A spirit-voyce,
And vocall joyes
Whose *Eccho is* heav'ns blisse.
O let me climbe
When I lye down! The Pious soul by night
Is like a clouded starre, whose beames though said
To shed their light
Under some Cloud
Yet are above,
And shine, and move
Beyond that mistie shroud.
So in my Bed
That Curtain'd grave, though sleep, like ashes, hide
My lamp, and life, both shall in thee abide.

Silex Scintillans, 1650

511 *Peace*

MY Soul, there is a Countrie
  Far beyond the stars,
Where stands a winged sentrie
  All skilfull in the wars,
There above noise, and danger
  Sweet peace sits crown'd with smiles,
And one born in a Manger
  Commands the Beauteous files,
He is thy gracious friend,
  And (O my Soul awake!)
Did in pure love descend
  To die here for thy sake;
If thou canst get but thither,
  There growes the flowre of peace,
The Rose that cannot wither,
  Thy fortresse, and thy ease;
Leave then thy foolish ranges;
  For none can thee secure,
But one, who never changes,
  Thy God, thy life, thy Cure.

Silex Scintillans, 1650

512 (*And do they so?*)

Rom. Cap. 8. ver. 19.

Etenim res Creatæ exerto Capite observantes expectant revelationem Filiorum Dei.

AND do they so? have they a Sense
  Of ought but Influence?
Can they their heads lift, and expect,
    And grone too? why th' Elect

Can do no more: my volumes said
They were all dull, and dead,
They judg'd them senslesse, and their state
Wholly Inanimate.
Go, go; Seal up thy looks,
And burn thy books.

I would I were a stone, or tree,
Or flowre by pedigree,
Of some poor high-way herb, or Spring
To flow, or bird to sing!
Then should I (tyed to one sure state,)
All day expect my date;
But I am sadly loose, and stray
A giddy blast each way;
O let me not thus range!
Thou canst not change.

Sometimes I sit with thee, and tarry
An hour, or so, then vary.
Thy other Creatures in this Scene
Thee only aim, and mean;
Some rise to seek thee, and with heads
Erect peep from their beds;
Others, whose birth is in the tomb,
And cannot quit the womb,
Sigh there, and groan for thee,
Their liberty.

O let not me do lesse! shall they
Watch, while I sleep, or play?
Shall I thy mercies still abuse
With fancies, friends, or newes?

O brook it not! thy blood is mine,
And my soul should be thine;
O brook it not! why wilt thou stop
After whole showres one drop?
Sure, thou wilt joy to see
Thy sheep with thee.

Silex Scintillans, 1650

513 *Corruption*

SURE, It was so. Man in those early days
Was not all stone, and Earth,
He shin'd a little, and by those weak Rays
Had some glimpse of his birth.
He saw Heaven o'er his head, and knew from whence
He came (condemned,) hither,
And, as first Love draws strongest, so from hence
His mind sure progress'd thither.
Things here were strange unto him: Sweat, and till,
All was a thorn, or weed,
Nor did those last, but (like himself,) dyed still
As soon as they did *Seed*.
They seem'd to quarrel with him; for that Act
That fell him, foyl'd them all,
He drew the Curse upon the world, and Crackt
The whole frame with his fall.
This made him long for *home*, as loath to stay
With murmurers, and foes;
He sigh'd for *Eden*, and would often say
Ah! what bright days were those?
Nor was Heav'n cold unto him; for each day
The valley, or the Mountain
Afforded visits, and still *Paradise* lay

In some green shade, or fountain.
Angels lay *Leiger* here; Each Bush, and Cell,
Each Oke, and high-way knew them,
Walk but the fields, or sit down at some *well*,
And he was sure to view them.
Almighty *Love*! where art thou now? mad man
Sits down, and freezeth on,
He raves, and swears to stir nor fire, nor fan,
But bids the thread be spun.
I see, thy Curtains are Close-drawn; Thy bow
Looks dim too in the Cloud,
Sin triumphs still, and man is sunk below
The Center, and his shroud;
All's in deep sleep, and night; Thick darkness lyes
And hatcheth o'er thy people;
But hark! what trumpets that? what Angel cries
Arise! Thrust in thy sickle.

Silex Scintillans, 1650

514 *The World*

I SAW Eternity the other night
Like a great *Ring* of pure and endless light,
All calm, as it was bright,
And round beneath it, Time in hours, days, years
Driv'n by the spheres
Like a vast shadow mov'd, In which the world
And all her train were hurl'd;
The doting Lover in his queintest strain
Did there Complain,
Neer him, his Lute, his fancy, and his flights,
Wits sour delights,

With gloves, and knots the silly snares of pleasure;
        Yet his dear Treasure
All scatter'd lay, while he his eyes did pour
        Upon a flowr.

The darksome States-man, hung with weights and woe,
Like a thick midnight-fog mov'd there so slow
    He did nor stay, nor go;
Condemning thoughts (like sad Ecclipses) scowl
        Upon his soul,
And Clouds of crying witnesses without
    Pursued him with one shout.
Yet digg'd the Mole, and lest his ways be found
        Workt under ground,
Where he did Clutch his prey, but one did see
        That policie;
Churches and altars fed him, Perjuries
        Were gnats and flies,
It rain'd about him blood and tears, but he
        Drank them as free.

The fearfull miser on a heap of rust
Sate pining all his life there, did scarce trust
    His own hands with the dust,
Yet would not place one peece above, but lives
        In feare of theeves.
Thousands there were as frantick as himself
    And hugg'd each one his pelf,
The down-right Epicure plac'd heav'n in sense
        And scornd pretence
While others slipt into a wide Excesse
        Said little lesse;

The weaker sort slight, triviall wares inslave
Who think them brave,
And poor, despised truth sate Counting by
Their victory.

Yet some, who all this while did weep and sing,
And sing, and weep, soar'd up into the *Ring*,
But most would use no wing.
O fools (said I,) thus to prefer dark night
Before true light,
To live in grots, and caves, and hate the day
Because it shews the way,
The way which from this dead and dark abode
Leads up to God,
A way where you might tread the Sun, and be
More bright than he.
But as I did their madness so discusse
One whisper'd thus,
This Ring the Bride-groome did for none provide
But for his bride.

John Cap. 2. ver. 16, 17.

All that is in the world, the lust of the flesh, the lust of the Eyes, and the pride of life, is not of the father, but is of the world.

And the world passeth away, and the lusts thereof, but he that doth the will of God abideth for ever.

Silex Scintillans, 1650

515 *Man*

WEIGHING the stedfastness and state
 Of some mean things which here below reside,
Where birds like watchful Clocks the noiseless date
 And Intercourse of times divide,
Where Bees at night get home and hive, and flowrs
 Early, as well as late,
Rise with the Sun, and set in the same bowrs;

I would (said I) my God would give
The staidness of these things to man! for these
To his divine appointments ever cleave,
 And no new business breaks their peace;
The birds nor sow, nor reap, yet sup and dine,
 The flowres without clothes live,
Yet *Solomon* was never drest so fine.

Man hath still either toyes, or Care,
He hath no root, nor to one place is ty'd,
But ever restless and Irregular
 About this Earth doth run and ride,
He knows he hath a home, but scarce knows where,
 He sayes it is so far
That he hath quite forgot how to go there.

He knocks at all doors, strays and roams,
Nay hath not so much wit as some stones have
Which in the darkest nights point to their homes,
 By some hid sense their Maker gave;
Man is the shuttle, to whose winding quest
 And passage through these looms
God order'd motion, but ordain'd no rest.

Silex Scintillans, 1650

516 *(I walkt the other day)*

I WALKT the other day (to spend my hour,)
Into a field
Where I sometimes had seen the soil to yield
A gallant flowre,
But Winter now had ruffled all the bowre
And curious store
I knew there heretofore.

Yet I whose search lov'd not to peep and peer
I' th' face of things
Thought with my self, there might be other springs
Besides this here
Which, like cold friends, sees us but once a year,
And so the flowre
Might have some other bowre.

Then taking up what I could neerest spie
I digg'd about
That place where I had seen him to grow out,
And by and by
I saw the warm Recluse alone to lie
Where fresh and green
He lived of us unseen.

Many a question Intricate and rare
Did I there strow,
But all I could extort was, that he now
Did there repair
Such losses as befel him in this air
And would ere long
Come forth most fair and young.

This past, I threw the Clothes quite o'er his head,
And stung with fear
Of my own frailty dropt down many a tear
Upon his bed,
Then sighing whisper'd, *Happy are the dead!*
What peace doth now
Rock him asleep below?

And yet, how few believe such doctrine springs
From a poor root
Which all the Winter sleeps here under foot
And hath no wings
To raise it to the truth and light of things,
But is still trod
By ev'ry wandring clod.

O thou! whose spirit did at first inflame
And warm the dead,
And by a sacred Incubation fed
With life this frame
Which once had neither being, forme, nor name,
Grant I may so
Thy steps track here below,

That in these Masques and shadows I may see
Thy sacred way,
And by those hid ascents climb to that day
Which breaks from thee
Who art in all things, though invisibly;
Shew me thy peace,
Thy mercy, love, and ease,

And from this Care, where dreams and sorrows raign
Lead me above
Where Light, Joy, Leisure, and true Comforts move
Without all pain,
There, hid in thee, shew me his life again
At whose dumbe urn
Thus all the year I mourn.

Silex Scintillans, 1650

¶

517 *(They are all gone into the world of light!)*

THEY are all gone into the world of light!
And I alone sit lingring here;
Their very memory is fair and bright,
And my sad thoughts doth clear.

It glows and glitters in my cloudy brest
Like stars upon some gloomy grove,
Or those faint beams in which this hill is drest,
After the Sun's remove.

I see them walking in an Air of glory,
Whose light doth trample on my days:
My days, which are at best but dull and hoary,
Mere glimmering and decays.

O holy hope! and high humility,
High as the Heavens above!
These are your walks, and you have shew'd them me
To kindle my cold love,

Dear, beauteous death! the Jewel of the Just,
Shining no where, but in the dark;
What mysteries do lie beyond thy dust;
Could man outlook that mark!

He that hath found some fledg'd birds nest, may know
At first sight, if the bird be flown;
But what fair Well, or Grove he sings in now,
That is to him unknown.

And yet, as Angels in some brighter dreams
Call to the soul, when man doth sleep:
So some strange thoughts transcend our wonted theams,
And into glory peep.

If a star were confin'd into a Tomb
Her captive flames must needs burn there;
But when the hand that lockt her up, gives room,
She'll shine through all the sphære.

O Father of eternal life, and all
Created glories under thee!
Resume thy spirit from this world of thrall
Into true liberty.

Either disperse these mists, which blot and fill
My perspective (still) as they pass,
Or else remove me hence unto that hill,
Where I shall need no glass.

Silex Scintillans, 1655

518 *The Jews*

WHEN the fair year
Of your deliverer comes,
And that long frost which now benumbs
Your hearts shall thaw; when Angels here

Shall yet to man appear,
And familiarly confer
Beneath the Oke and Juniper:
When the bright *Dove*
Which now these many, many Springs
Hath kept above,
Shall with spread wings
Descend, and living waters flow
To make drie dust, and dead trees grow;

O then that I
Might live, and see the Olive bear
Her proper branches! which now lie
Scattered each where,
And without root and sap decay
Cast by the husband-man away.
And sure it is not far!
For as your fast and foul decays
Forerunning the bright morning-star,
Did sadly note his healing rayes
Would shine elsewhere, since you were blind,
And would be cross, when God was kinde:
So by all signs
Our fulness too is now come in,
And the same Sun which here declines
And sets, will few hours hence begin
To rise on you again, and look
Towards old *Mamre* and *Eshcols* brook.

For surely he
Who lov'd the world so, as to give
His onely Son to make it free,

Whose spirit too doth mourn and grieve
To see man lost, will for old love
From your dark hearts this veil remove.

Faith sojourn'd first on earth in you,
You were the dear and chosen stock:
The Arm of God, glorious and true,
Was first reveal'd to be your rock.

You were the *eldest* childe, and when
Your stony hearts despised love,
The *youngest*, ev'n the Gentiles then
Were chear'd, your jealousie to move.

Thus, Righteous Father! doest thou deal
With Brutish men; Thy gifts go round
By turns, and timely, and so heal
The lost Son by the newly found.

Silex Scintillans, 1655

519 *The dwelling-place*

WHAT happy, secret fountain,
Fair shade, or mountain,
Whose undiscover'd virgin glory
Boasts it this day, though not in story,
Was then thy dwelling? did some cloud
Fix'd to a Tent, descend and shroud
My distrest Lord? or did a star
Beckon'd by thee, though high and far,
In sparkling smiles haste gladly down
To lodge light, and increase her own?

My dear, dear God! I do not know
What lodg'd thee then, nor where, nor how;
But I am sure, thou dost now come
Oft to a narrow, homely room,
Where thou too hast but the least part,
My God, I mean *my sinful heart.*

S. John, chap. I. *ver.* 38, 39.

Then Jesus turned, and saw them following, and saith unto them, what seek ye? They said unto him, Rabbi, (which is to say, being interpreted, Master,) where dwellest thou? He saith unto them, Come and see. They came and saw where he dwelt, and abode with him that day: for it was about the tenth hour.

Silex Scintillans, 1655

520

The Night

John 3. 2.

THROUGH that pure *Virgin-shrine,*
That sacred vail drawn o'er thy glorious noon
That men might look and live as Glow-worms shine,
And face the Moon:
Wise *Nicodemus* saw such light
As made him know his God by night.

Most blest believer he!
Who in that land of darkness and blinde eyes
Thy long expected healing wings could see,
When thou didst rise,
And what can never more be done,
Did at mid-night speak with the Sun!

O who will tell me, where
He found thee at that dead and silent hour!
What hallow'd solitary ground did bear
So rare a flower,
Within whose sacred leafs did lie
The fulness of the Deity.

No mercy-seat of gold,
No dead and dusty *Cherub*, nor carv'd stone,
But his own living works did my Lord hold
And lodge alone;
Where *trees* and *herbs* did watch and peep
And wonder, while the *Jews* did sleep.

Dear night! this worlds defeat;
The stop to busie fools; cares check and curb;
The day of Spirits; my souls calm retreat
Which none disturb!
Christs progress, and his prayer time;
The hours to which high Heaven doth chime.

Gods silent, searching flight:
When my Lords head is fill'd with dew, and all
His locks are wet with the clear drops of night;
His still, soft call;
His knocking time; The souls dumb watch,
When Spirits their fair kindred catch.

Were all my loud, evil days
Calm and unhaunted as is thy dark Tent,
Whose peace but by some *Angels* wing or voice
Is seldom rent;

Christs progress: *Mark, chap.* 1. 35. *S. Luke, chap.* 21. 37.

Then I in Heaven all the long year
Would keep, and never wander here.

But living where the Sun
Doth all things wake, and where all mix and tire
Themselves and others, I consent and run
To ev'ry mire,
And by this worlds ill-guiding light,
Erre more than I can do by night.

There is in God (some say)
A deep, but dazling darkness; As men here
Say it is late and dusky, because they
See not all clear;
O for that night! where I in him
Might live invisible and dim.

Silex Scintillans, 1655

521 *The Water-fall*

WITH what deep murmurs through times silent stealth
Doth thy transparent, cool and watry wealth
Here flowing fall,
And chide, and call,
As if his liquid, loose Retinue staid
Lingring, and were of this steep place afraid,
The common pass
Where, clear as glass,
All must descend
Not to an end:
But quickned by this deep and rocky grave,
Rise to a longer course more bright and brave.

Dear stream! dear bank, where often I
Have sate, and pleas'd my pensive eye,
Why, since each drop of thy quick store
Runs thither, whence it flow'd before,
Should poor souls fear a shade or night,
Who came (sure) from a sea of light?
Or since those drops are all sent back
So sure to thee, that none doth lack,
Why should frail flesh doubt any more
That what God takes, he'll not restore?
O useful Element and clear!
My sacred wash and cleanser here,
My first consigner unto those
Fountains of life, where the Lamb goes?
What sublime truths, and wholesome themes,
Lodge in thy mystical, deep streams!
Such as dull man can never finde
Unless that Spirit lead his minde,
Which first upon thy face did move,
And hatch'd all with his quickning love.
As this loud brooks incessant fall
In streaming rings restagnates all,
Which reach by course the bank, and then
Are no more seen, just so pass men.
O my invisible estate,
My glorious liberty, still late!
Thou art the Channel my soul seeks,
Not this with Cataracts and Creeks.

Silex Scintillans, 1655

522

Quickness

FALSE life! a foil and no more, when
Wilt thou be gone?
Thou foul deception of all men
That would not have the true come on.

Thou art a Moon-like toil; a blinde
Self-posing state;
A dark contest of waves and winde;
A mere tempestuous debate.

Life is a fix'd, discerning light,
A knowing Joy;
No chance, or fit: but ever bright,
And calm and full, yet doth not cloy.

'Tis such a blissful thing, that still
Doth vivifie,
And shine and smile, and hath the skill
To please without Eternity.

Thou art a toilsome Mole, or less
A moving mist,
But life is, what none can express,
A quickness, which my God hath kist.

Silex Scintillans, 1655

523

The Shower

WATERS above! eternal Springs!
The dew, that silvers the *Doves* wings!
O welcom, welcom to the sad:
Give dry dust drink; drink that makes glad!
Many fair *Ev'nings*, many *Flow'rs*
Sweeten'd with rich and gentle showers

Have I enjoy'd, and down have run
Many a fine and shining *Sun*;
But never till this happy hour
Was blest with such an *Evening-shower*!

Thalia Rediviva, 1678

524 *The Revival*

UNFOLD, unfold! take in his light,
Who makes thy Cares more short than night.
The Joys, which with his *Day-star* rise,
He deals to all, but drowsy Eyes:
And what the men of this world miss,
Some *drops* and *dews* of future bliss.
Hark! how his *winds* have chang'd their *note*,
And with warm *whispers* call thee out.
The *frosts* are past, the *storms* are gone:
And backward *life* at last comes on.
The lofty *groves* in express Joyes
Reply unto the *Turtles* voice,
And here in *dust* and *dirt*, O here
The *Lilies* of his love appear!

Thalia Rediviva, 1678

THOMAS STANLEY

1625–1678

525 *On a Violet in her breast*

SEE how this Violet which before
Hung sullenly her drooping head,
As angry at the ground that bore
The purple treasure which she spread,
Doth smilingly erected grow,
Transplanted to those hills of snow.

And whilst the pillows of thy breast
 Do her reclining head sustain,
She swells with pride to be so blest,
 And doth all other flowers disdain,
Yet weeps that dew which kissed her last,
To see her odours so surpast.

Poor flower! how far deceiv'd thou wert,
 To think the riches of the morn,
Of all the sweets she can impart
 Could these or sweeten or adorn,
Since thou from them do'st borrow scent,
And they to thee lend ornament.

Poems and Translations, 1647

526 *The Exequies*

DRAW near
 You lovers that complain
Of Fortune or Disdain,
And to my Ashes lend a Tear;
Melt the hard marble with your grones,
And soften the relentlesse stones,
Whose cold imbraces, the sad Subject hide
Of all Loves cruelties, and Beauties Pride.

No Verse
No Epicedium bring
Nor peacefull Requiem sing,
To charm the terrours of my Herse;
No prophane Numbers must flow near
The sacred silence that dwells here;
Vast Griefs are dumb, softly oh softly mourn,
Lest you disturb the Peace attends my Urn.

Yet strew
Upon my dismall Grave,
Such offerings as you have,
Forsaken Cypresse and sad Yew,
For kinder Flowers can take no Birth
Or growth from such unhappy Earth.
Weep only o'er my Dust, and say, Here lies
To Love and Fate an equall sacrifice.

Poems and Translations, 1647 (text 1651)

527 *Expectation*

CHIDE, chide no more away
The fleeting daughters of the day,
Nor with impatient thoughts out-run
The lazie Sun,
Or think the houres do move too slow;
Delay is kind,
And we too soon shall find
That which we seek, yet fear to know.

The mystick dark decrees
Unfold not of the Destinies,
Nor boldly seek to antedate
The laws of Fate,
Thy anxious search awhile forbeare
Suppresse thy haste,
And know that Time at last
Will crowne thy hope, or fix thy fear.

Poems and Translations, 1647

528

The Repulse

NOT that by this disdain
 I am releas'd,
And free'd from thy tyrannick chain,
 Do I my self think blest;

Nor that thy Flame shall burn
 No more; for know
That I shall into ashes turn
 Before this fire doth so.

Nor yet that unconfin'd
 I now may rove,
And with new beauties please my mind;
 But that thou ne'er didst love:

For since thou hast no part
 Felt of this flame,
I onely from thy tyrant heart
 Repuls'd, not banish'd am.

To lose what once was mine
 Would grieve me more
Than those inconstant sweets of thine
 Had pleas'd my soul before:

Now I have not lost that blisse
 I ne'er possest;
And spite of fate am blest in this,
 That I was never blest.

Poems and Translations, 1647

529 *The Tombe*

WHEN, cruel Fair one, I am slain
By thy disdain,
And, as a Trophy of thy scorn,
To some old tombe am borne,
Thy fetters must their power bequeath
To those of death;
Nor can thy flame immortal burn,
Like monumentall fires within an urn;
Thus freed from thy proud Empire, I shall prove
There is more liberty in Death than Love.

And when forsaken Lovers come,
To see my tombe,
Take heed thou mix not with the crowd
And (as a Victor) proud
To view the spoils thy beauty made
Presse near my shade,
Lest thy too cruel breath or name
Should fan my ashes back into a flame,
And thou, devour'd by this revengeful fire,
His sacrifice, who dy'd as thine, expire.

But if cold Earth, or Marble must
Conceal my dust,
Whilst hid in some dark ruines, I
Dumb and forgotten lie,
The pride of all thy victory
Will sleep with me;

And they who should thy Glory,
Will, or forget, or not believe the story;
Then to increase thy Triumph, let me rest,
Since by thine Eye slain, buried in thy Breast.

Poems and Translations, 1647 (text 1651)

530 *To one that pleaded her own want of merit*

DEAR urge no more that killing cause
Of our divorce;
Love is not fetter'd by such laws,
Nor bows to any force:
Though thou deniest I should be thine,
Yet say not thou deserv'st not to be mine.

Oh rather frown away my breath
With thy disdain,
Or flatter me with smiles to death,
By joy or sorrow slain;
'Tis lesse crime to be kill'd by thee
Than I thus cause of my own death should be.

Thy self of beauty to divest
And me of love,
Or from the worth of thine own breast
Thus to detract, would prove
In us a blindnesse, and in thee
At best a sacrilegious modestie.

But (Dearest) if thou wilt despise
What all admire,
Nor rate thy self at the just price
Of beauty or desire,
Yet meet my flames and thou shalt see
That equall love knows no disparity.

Poems and Translations, 1647

531 *La Belle Confidente*

YOU earthly Souls that court a wanton flame,
Whose pale weak influence
Can rise no higher than the humble name
And narrow laws of Sense,
Learn by our friendship to create
An immaterial fire,
Whose brightnesse Angels may admire,
But cannot emulate.

Sicknesse may fright the roses from her cheek,
Or make the Lilies fade,
But all the subtile wayes that death doth seek
Cannot my love invade:
Flames that are kindled by the eye,
Through time and age expire;
But ours that boast a reach far higher
Can nor decay, nor die.

For when we must resign our vital breath,
Our Loves by Fate benighted,
We by this friendship shall survive in death,
Even in divorce united.

Weak Love through fortune or distrust
In time forgets to burn,
But this pursues us to the Urn,
And marries either's Dust.

Poems and Translations, 1647 (text 1651)

JOHN HALL

1627–1656

532

The Call

ROMIRA, stay,
And run not thus like a young Roe away,
No enemie
Pursues thee (foolish girle) tis onely I,
I'll keep off harms,
If thou'lt be pleas'd to garrison mine arms;
What dost thou fear
I'll turn a Traitour? may these Roses here
To palenesse shred,
And Lilies stand disguised in new Red,
If that I lay
A snare, wherein thou wouldst not gladly stay;
See see the Sunne
Does slowly to his azure Lodging run,
Come sit but here
And presently he'll quit our Hemisphere,
So still among
Lovers, time is too short or else too long;
Here will we spin
Legends for them that have Love Martyrs been,
Here on this plain
We'll talk *Narcissus* to a flowr again;

Come here, and chose
On which of these proud plats thou would repose,
Here maist thou shame
The rusty Violets, with the Crimson flame
Of either cheek,
And Primroses white as thy fingers seek,
Nay, thou maist prove
That mans most Noble Passion is to Love.

Poems, 1646

533 *A Pastorall Hymne*

HAPPY Choristers of Aire,
Who by your nimble flight draw neare
His throne, whose wondrous story
And unconfined glory
Your notes still Caroll, whom your sound
And whom your plumy pipes rebound.

Yet do the lazy Snailes no lesse
The greatnesse of our Lord confesse,
And those whom weight hath chain'd
And to the Earth restrain'd,
Their ruder voices do as well,
Yea and the speechlesse Fishes tell.

Great Lord, from whom each Tree receaves,
Then pays againe as rent, his leaves;
Thou dost in purple set
The Rose and Violet,
And giv'st the sickly Lilly white,
Yet in them all, thy name dost write.

Poems, 1646

ANONYMOUS

534 (*Chloris farewell*)

CHLORIS farewell, I now must go
For if with thee I here do stay
Thine eyes prevaile upon me so,
I shall grow blind and lose my way.

Fame of thy Beauty and thy Youth,
Among the rest me hither brought,
Finding this fame fall short of truth,
Made me stay longer than I thought.

For I'm engag'd by word and oath
A servant to another's will;
Yet for thy love would forfeit both,
Could I be sure to keepe it still.

But what assurance can I take,
When thou fore-knowing this abuse,
For some more worthy Lover's sake,
May'st leave me with so just excuse.

For thou may'st say 'twas not thy fault
That thou didst thus unconstant prove;
Thou wert by my example taught
To breake thy oath, to mend thy love.

No Chloris, no, I will returne
And raise thy story to that height,
That strangers shall at distance burne,
And she distrust me Reprobate.

Then shall my Love this doubt displace,
And gaine such trust, that I may come
And banquet sometimes on thy face,
But make my constant meales at home.

J. Playford, *Musicall Ayres*, 1652

535 *(Tell me you wandering Spirits)*

TELL me you wandering Spirits of the Ayre,
Did not you see a Nymph more bright, more faire
Than beauties darling, or of parts more sweet
Than stolne content; if such a one you meet,
Wait on her hourely, wheresoe'er she flies,
And cry, and cry, *Amintas* for her absence dies.

Go search the Vallies, pluck up every Rose,
You'll finde a scent, a blush of her in those:
Fish, fish, for Pearle, or Corrall, there you'll see
How orientall all her Colours be;
Go call the Echoes to your ayde, and cry,
Cloris, *Cloris*, for that's her name for whom I die.

But stay a while, I have inform'd you ill,
Were she on earth, she had been with me still:
Go fly to Heaven, examine every Sphere,
And try what Star hath lately lighted there;
If any brighter than the Sun you see,
Fall downe, fall downe, and worship it, for that is shee.

J. Playford, *Musicall Ayres*, 1652

536 *An Ode in the praise of Sack*

HEAR me as if thy eares had palate, *Jack*,
   I sing the praise of Sack:
Hence with *Apollo* and the muses nine,
   Give me a cup of wine.
Sack will the soule of Poetry infuse,
   Be that my theam and muse.
But *Bacchus* I adore no Deity,
Nor *Bacchus* neither unlesse Sack he be.

Let us by reverend degrees draw near,
   I feel the Goddesse here.
Loe I, dread Sack, an humble Priest of thine
   First kisse this cup thy shrine.
That with more hallowed lips and inlarg'd soule
   I may receive the whole:
Till *Sibyl*-like full with my God I lye,
And every word I speak be Prophesie.

Come to this Altar you that are opprest,
   Or otherwise distrest,
Here's that will further grievances prevent,
   Without a Parliament:
With fire from hence if once your blood be warm
   Nothing can doe you harme;
When thou art arm'd with Sack, thou canst not feel
Though thunder strike thee; that hath made thee steel.

Art sick man? doe not bid for thy escape
   A cock to *Æsculape*;
If thou wouldst prosper, to this Altar bring
   Thy gratefull offering,

Touch but the shrine, that does the God enclose,
And straight thy feaver goes;
Whilst thou immagin'st this, he's given thee
Not onely health but immortality.

Though thou wert dumb as is the scaly fry
In *Neptunes* royalty:
Drink but as they doe, and new wayes shalt find
To utter thy whole mind;
When Sack more severall language has infus'd
Than Babels builders used:
And whensoever thou thy voyce shalt raise,
No man shall understand but all shall praise.

Hath cruell nature so thy senses bound
Thou canst not judge of sounds?
Lo where yon narrow fountaine scatters forth
Streams of an unknown worth:
The heavenly musick of that murmur there
Would make thee turne all eare;
And keeping time with the harmonious flood,
Twixt every bubble thou shalt cry, good, good.

Has fortune made thee poor, dost thou desire
To heap up glorious mire?
Come to this stream where every drop's a Pearl
Might buy an Earl:
Drench thy selfe soundly here and thou shalt rise
Richer than both the '*Indies.*
So may'st thou still enjoy with full content
Midas his wish without his punishment.

All this can Sack, and more than this Sack can,
   Give me a fickle man
That would be somewhat faine but knows not what,
   There is a cure for that:
Let him quaffe freely of this powerfull flood,
   He shall be what he would.
To all our wishes Sack content does bring,
And but our selves can make us every thing.

Parnassus Biceps, 1656

537 *From A Poem, in defence of the decent Ornaments of Christ-Church*, Oxon, *occasioned by a Banbury brother, who called them Idolatries*

(*i*) *Beauty in Worship*

YOU that prophane our windows with a tongue
Set like some clock on purpose to go wrong;
Who when you were at Service sigh'd, because
You heard the Organs musick not the Dawes:
Pittying our solemn state, shaking the head
To see no ruines from the floor to the lead:
To whose pure nose our Cedar gave offence,
Crying it smelt of Papists frankincense:
Who, walking on our Marbles, scoffing said
'Whose bodies are under these Tombstones laid?'
Counting our Tapers works of darknesse; and
Choosing to see Priests in blue-aprons stand
Rather than in rich Copes which shew the art
Of *Sisera's* prey Imbrodred in each part:
Then when you saw the Altars Bason said
'Why's not the Ewer on the Cupboards head?'

Thinking our very Bibles too prophane,
Cause you ne'er bought such Covers in *Ducklane.*
Loathing all decency, as if you'd have
Altars as foule and homely as a Grave.
Had you one spark of reason, you would finde
Your selves like Idols to have eyes yet blind.
'Tis onely some base niggard Heresie
To think Religion loves deformity.
Glory did never yet make God the lesse,
Neither can beauty defile holinesse.
Whats more magnificent than Heaven? yet where
Is there more love and piety than there?
My heart doth wish (wer't possible) to see
Pauls built with pretious stones and porphery:
To have our Halls and Galleries outshine
Altars in beauty, is to deck our swine
With Orient Pearl, whilst the deserving Quire
Of God and Angels wallow in the mire:
Our decent Copes onely distinction keep
That you may know the Shepheard from the sheep,
As gaudy letters in the Rubrick shew
How you may holi-dayes from lay-dayes know:
Remember *Aarons* Robes and you will say
Ladies at Masques are not so rich as they.
Then are th' Priests words like thunderclaps when he
Is lightning like rayed round with Majesty.
May every Temple shine like those of *Nile,*
And still be free from Rat or Crocodile.
But you will urge both Priest and Church should be
The solemne patternes of humility.
Do not some boast of rags? Cynicks deride
The pomp of Kings but with a greater pride.

Meeknesse consists not in the cloaths but heart,
Nature may be vainglorious well as art;
We may as lowly before God appear
Drest with a glorious pearl as with a tear;
In his high presence where the Stars and Sun
Do but Eclipse there's no ambition.
Colours are here mix'd so, that Rainbows be
(Compared) but clouds without variety.
Art here is Natures envy: this is he,
Not *Paracelsus*, that by Chymistry
Can make a man from ashes, if not dust,
Producing off-springs of his mind not lust.

(ii) The Church-Windows

Shadows do every where for substance passe,
You'd think the sands were in an houre-glasse.
You that do live with Chirurgeons, have you seen
A spring of blood forc'd from a swelling vein?
So from a touch of *Moses* rod doth jump
A Cataract, the rock is made a pump:
At sight of whose o'erflowings many get
Themselves away for fear of being wet.
Have you beheld a sprightfull Lady stand
To have her frame drawn by a painters hand?
Such lively look and presence, such a dresse
King *Pharoahs* Daughters Image doth expresse;
Look well upon her Gown and you will swear
The needle not the pencil hath been there:
At sight of her some gallants do dispute
Whether i' th' Church 'tis lawfull to salute.

Next *Jacob* kneeling, where his Kids-skins such
As it may well cosen old *Isaacs* touch:
A Shepheard seeing how thorns went round about
Abrahams ram, would needs have helpt it out.
Behold the Dove descending to inspire
The Apostles heads with cloven tongues of fire,
And in a superficies there you'll see
The grosse dimensions of profundity:
'Tis hard to judge which is best built and higher
The arch-roofe, in the window or the Quire.

. . . . . .

Here's motion painted too: Chariots so fast
Run, that they're never gone though always past.
The Angels with their Lutes are done so true,
We do not onely look but hearken too,
As if their sounds were painted: thus the wit
Of the pencil hath drawn more than there can sit.
Thus as (in *Archimedes* sphear) you may
In a small glasse the universe survey:
Such various shapes are too ith' Imagry
As age and sex may their own features see.
But if the window cannot shew your face
Look under feet, the Marble is your glasse,
Which too for more than Ornament is there;
The stones may learn your eyes to shed a tear:
Yet though their lively shadows delude sense
They never work upon the conscience;
They cannot make us kneel; we are not such
As think there's balsome in their kisse or touch,
That were grosse superstition we know;
There' is no more power in them than the Popes toe.

The Saints themselves for us can do no good,
Much less their pictures drawn in glass and wood,
They cannot seale, but since they signifie,
They may be worthy of a cast o' th' eye,
Although no worship: that is due alone
Not to the Carpenters but Gods own Sonne.

. . . . . .

Cease then your railings and your dull complaints;
To pull down Galleries and set up Saints
Is no impiety: now we may well
Say that our Church is truely visible:
Those that before our glasse scaffolds prefer,
Would turne our Temple to a Theater.
Windows are Pulpits now; though unlearned, one
May read this Bible's new Edition.
Instead of here and there a verse adorn'd
Round with a lace of paint, fit to be scorn'd
Even by vulgar eyes, each pane presents
Whole chapters with both comment and contents,
The cloudy mysteries of the Gospel here
Transparent as the Christall do appear.
Tis not to see things darkly through a glasse,
Here you may see our Saviour face to face.
And whereas Feasts come seldome, here's descried
A constant Christmas, Easter, Whitsuntide.
Let the deafe hither come; no matter though
Faiths sense be lost, we a new way can shew:
Here we can teach them to believe by the eye,
These silenc'd Ministers do edify:
The Scriptures rayes contracted in a Glasse
Like Emblems do with greater vertue passe.

ANONYMOUS

Look in the book of Martyrs and you'll see
More by the Pictures than the History.
That price for things in colours oft we give
Which we'd not take to have them while they live.
Such is the power of painting that it makes
A loving sympathy twixt men and snakes.
Hence then *Pauls* doctrine may seem more divine;
As Amber through a Glasse doth clearer shine.
Words passe away, as soon as heard are gone;
We read in books what here we dwell upon,
Thus then there's no more fault in Imag'ry
Than there is in the Practice of piety,
Both edifie: what is in letters there
Is writ in plainer Hierogliphicks here.
Tis not a new Religion we have chose;
Tis the same body but in better clothes.
You'll say they make us gaze when we should pray
And that our thoughts do on the figures stray:
If so, you may conclude us beasts; what they
Have for their object is to us the way.
Did any e'er use prospectives to see
No farther than the Glasse: or can there be
Such lazy travellers, so given to sin,
As that they'll take their dwelling at the Inne?
A Christian's sight rests in Divinity,
Signes are but spectacles to help faiths eye,
God is the Center: dwelling on these words,
My muse a Sabbath to my brain affords.
If their nice wits more solemn proof exact,
Know this was meant a Poem not a Tract.

Parnassus Biceps, 1656

538 *Rounds and Catches*

(*i*)[1]

COME, come away, to the Tavern I say,
For now at home 'tis washing day;
Leave your prittle-prattle, and fill us a Pottle,
You are not so wise as *Aristotle*.
Drawer come away, let's make it holy day,
Anon, anon, anon, Sir, what is't you say?

(*ii*)

Have you observ'd the *Wench* in the street,
She's scarce any Hose or Shoes to her feet,
Yet she is very merry, and when she cries she *sings*,
I ha' hot Codlins, hot Codlins;
Or have you ever seen or heard
The mortal with a *Lyon Tawny* beard,
He lives as merrily as any heart can wish,
And still he cryes, buy a Brish, buy a Brish.
Since these are merry, why should we take care,
Musicians like Chameleons must live by the Ayre:
Then let's be Blith and bonny, and no good meeting Baulk,
For when we have no money, we shall finde Chalk.

(*iii*)

Have you any work for a Tinker, Mistris,
Old Brasse, old Pots, or Kettles, I'll mend them all
With a tink terry tink,
And never hurt your Mettles:

1 The first four lines are given in Suckling's *The Sad One*, 4. 4 (1658).

First let me have but a touch of your Ale, 'twill steel me against cold weather,
Or Tinkers Frees, or Vintners Lees, or Tobacco, chuse you whether:
But of your Ale, your nappy Ale, I would I had a Ferkin,
For I am old, and very very cold, and never wear a Jerkin.

(*iv*)

Three blind Mice, three blind Mice,
Dame Julian, Dame Julian,
The Miller and his merry old wife,
She scrap'd her tripe, lick thou the knife.

(*v*)

Wilt thou lend me thy Mare to ride a mile?
No, she's lame going over a Stile.
But if thou wilt her to me spare,
Thou shalt have money for thy Mare.
Oh say ye so, say ye so,
Money will make my Mare to go,
Money will make my Mare to go.

(*vi*)

Why should not we all be merry,
Our Ale is as brown as a Berry?
What then should be the thing,
Should hinder us to sing
Hey down, derry down derry,
Hey down a down hey down derry.

Catch that Catch Can, 1658

539 *An old Souldier of the Queens*

OF an old Souldier of the Queens,
With an old motley coat, and a Maumsie nose,
And an old Jerkin that's out at the elbows,
And an old pair of boots, drawn on without hose
Stuft with rags instead of toes;
And an old Souldier of the Queens,
And the Queens old Souldier.

With an old rusty sword that's hackt with blows,
And an old dagger to scare away the crows,
And an old horse that reels as he goes,
And an old saddle that no man knows,
And an old Souldier of the Queens,
And the Queens old Souldier.

With his old wounds in Eighty Eight,
Which he recover'd, at *Tilbury* fight;
With an old Pasport that never was read,
That in his old travels stood him in great stead;
And an old Souldier of the Queens,
And the Queens old Souldier.

With his old Gun, and his Bandeliers,
And an old head-piece to keep warm his ears,
With an old shirt is grown to wrack,
With a huge Louse, With a great list on his back,
Is able to carry a Pedlar and his Pack;
And an old Souldier of the Queens,
And the Queens old Souldier.

Maumsie: Malmsey.

With an old Quean to lie by his side,
That in old time had been pockifi'd;
He's now rid to *Bohemia* to fight with his foes,
And he swears by his Valour he'll have better cloaths,
Or else he'll lose legs, arms, fingers, and toes,
And he'll come again, when no man knows,
  And an old Souldier of the Queens,
  And the Queen's old Souldier.

Merry Drollery, 1661–9

540 *The Zealous Puritan*

MY Brethren all attend,
  And list to my relation:
This is the day, mark what I say,
  Tends to your renovation;
Stay not among the Wicked,
  Lest that with them you perish,
But let us to *New-England* go,
  And the Pagan People cherish;
    Then for the truths sake come along, come along,
    Leave this place of Superstition:
    Were it not for we, that the Brethren be,
    You would sink into Perdition.

There you may teach our hymns
  Without the Laws controllment:
We need not fear the Bishops there,
  Nor Spiritual-Courts inrollment;
Nay, the Surplice shall not fright us,
  Nor superstitious blindness;

Nor scandals rise when we disguise,
And our Sisters kiss in kindness;
  Then for the truths sake come along, come along,
  Leave this place of Superstition:
  Were it not for we, that the Brethren be,
  You would sink into Perdition.

For Company I fear not,
There goes my Cousin *Hannah*;
And *Ruben*, so persuades to go
My Cousin, *Joyce*, *Susanna*,
With *Abigal* and *Faith*,
And *Ruth*, no doubt, comes after;
And *Sarah* kind, will not stay behind,
My Cousin *Constance* Daughter;
  Then for the truths sake come along, come along,
  Leave this place of Superstition:
  Were it not for we, that the Brethren be,
  You would sink into Perdition.

Now *Tom Tyler* is prepared,
And the Smith as black as a coal;
Ralph Cobbler too with us will go,
For he regards his soul;
And the Weaver, honest *Simon*,
With *Prudence*, *Jacobs* Daughter,
And *Sarah*, she, and *Barbary*
Professeth to come after;
  Then for the truths sake come along, come along,
  Leave this place of Superstition:
  Were it not for we, that the Brethren be,
  You would sink into Perdition.

When we, that are elected,
Arrive in that fair Country,
Even by our faith, as the Brethren saith,
We will not fear our entry;
The Psalms shall be our Musick,
And our time spent in expounding,
Which in our zeal we will reveal
To the brethrens joy abounding;
  Then for the truths sake come along, come along,
  Leave this place of Superstition:
  Were it not for we, that the Brethren be,
  You would sink into Perdition.

Merry Drollery, 1661–9

541 *London sad London*

AN ECCHO

WHAT wants thee, that thou art in this sad taking?
A King.
What made him first remove hence his residing?
Siding.
Did any here deny him satisfaction?
Faction.
Tell me whereon this strength of Faction lyes?
On lyes.
What didst thou do when the King left Parliament?
Lament.
What terms would'st give to gain his Company?
Any.
But how wouldst serve him, with thy best endeavour?
Ever.

Siding: party spirit, factiousness.

ANONYMOUS

What wouldst thou do if here thou couldst behold him?
Hold him.
But if he comes not what becomes of *London*?
Undone.

The Rump, 1662

JOHN BUNYAN

1628–1688

542 (*The Song of the Shepherd in the Valley of Humiliation*)

HE that is down, needs fear no fall,
He that is low, no Pride:
He that is humble, ever shall
Have God to be his Guide.

I am content with what I have,
Little be it, or much:
And, Lord, Contentment still I crave,
Because thou savest such.

Fulness to such a burden is
That go on Pilgrimage:
Here little, and hereafter Bliss,
Is best from Age to Age.

Pilgrim's Progress, Part II, 1684

543 (*The Pilgrim Song*)

WHO would true Valour see,
Let him come hither;
One here will Constant be,
Come Wind, come Weather.

There's no *Discouragement*,
Shall make him once *Relent*,
His first avow'd *Intent*,
To be a Pilgrim.

Who so beset him round,
With dismal *Stories*,
Do but themselves Confound;
His Strength the *more is.*
No *Lyon* can him fright,
He'll with a *Gyant Fight*,
But he will have a right,
To be a Pilgrim.

Hobgoblin, nor foul *Fiend*,
Can *daunt* his Spirit:
He knows, he *at the end*,
Shall Life Inherit.
Then Fancies fly away,
He'll fear not what men say,
He'll labour Night and Day,
To be a Pilgrim.

Pilgrim's Progress, Part II, 1684

544 *(My Little Bird)*

MY little Bird, how canst thou sit;
And sing amidst so many Thorns!
Let me but hold upon thee get,
My Love with Honour thee adorns.

Thou art at present little worth;
Five farthings none will give for thee.
But prethee little Bird come forth,
Thou of more value art to me.

JOHN BUNYAN

'Tis true, it is Sun-shine to day,
To morrow Birds will have a Storm;
My pretty one, come thou away,
My Bosom then shall keep thee warm.

Thou subject art to cold o' nights,
When darkness is thy covering;
At days thy danger 's great by Kites,
How canst thou then sit there and sing?

Thy food is scarce and scanty too,
'Tis Worms and Trash which thou dost eat;
Thy present state I pity do,
Come, I'll provide thee better meat.

I'll feed thee with white Bread and Milk,
And Sugar-plums, if them thou crave;
I'll cover thee with finest Silk,
That from the cold I may thee save.

My Father's Palace shall be thine,
Yea, in it thou shalt sit and sing;
My little Bird, if thou'lt be mine,
The whole year round shall be thy Spring.

I'll teach thee all the Notes at Court;
Unthought of Musick thou shalt play;
And all that thither do resort
Shall praise thee for it ev'ry day.

I'll keep thee safe with Cat and Cur,
No manner o' harm shall come to thee;
Yea, I will be thy Succourer,
My Bosom shall thy Cabbin be.

But lo, behold, the Bird is gone:
These Charmings would not make her yield:
The Child's left at the Bush alone,
The Bird flies yonder o'er the Field.

A Book for Boys and Girls, 1686

CHARLES COTTON

1630–1687

545 *The Retirement. Stanzes Irreguliers. To Mr. Isaak Walton*

FAREWELL thou busie World, and may
We never meet again:
Here I can eat, and sleep, and pray,
And do more good in one short day,
Than he who his whole Age out-wears
Upon thy most conspicuous Theatres,
Where nought but Vice and Vanity do reign.

Good God! how sweet are all things here!
How beautifull the Fields appear!
How cleanly do we feed and lie!
Lord! what good hours do we keep!
How quietly we sleep!
What Peace! What Unanimity!
How innocent from the lewd Fashion,
Is all our bus'ness, all our Conversation!

Oh how happy here's our leisure!
Oh how innocent our pleasure!

544. The moralizing 'Comparison' is omitted.

Oh ye Vallies, oh ye Mountains,
Oh ye Groves and Chrystall Fountains,
How I love at liberty,
By turn to come and visit ye!

O Solitude, the Soul's best Friend,
That man acquainted with himself dost make,
And all his Maker's Wonders to intend;
With thee I here converse at will,
And would be glad to do so still;
For it is thou alone that keep'st the Soul awake.

How calm and quiet a delight
It is alone
To read, and meditate, and write,
By none offended, nor offending none;
To walk, ride, sit, or sleep at one's own ease,
And pleasing a man's self, none other to displease!

Oh my beloved Nymph! fair Dove,
Princess of Rivers, how I love
Upon thy flow'ry Banks to lie,
And view thy Silver stream,
When gilded by a Summer's Beam,
And in it all thy wanton Fry
Playing at liberty,
And with my Angle upon them,
The All of Treachery
I ever learn'd to practise and to try!

Such streams *Rome's* yellow *Tiber* cannot show,
Th' *Iberian Tagus*, nor *Ligurian Po*;
The *Meuse*, the *Danube*, and the *Rhine*,
Are puddle-water all compar'd with thine;

And *Loire's* pure streams yet too polluted are
With thine much purer to compare:
The rapid *Garonne*, and the winding *Seine*,
Are both too mean,
Beloved Dove, with thee
To vie Priority:
Nay, *Tame* and *Isis*, when conjoyn'd, submit,
And lay their Trophies at thy Silver Feet.

Oh my beloved Rocks! that rise
To awe the Earth, and brave the Skies,
From some aspiring Mountain's crown
How dearly do I love,
Giddy with pleasure, to look down,
And from the Vales to view the noble heights above!

Oh my beloved Caves! from Dog-star heats,
And hotter Persecution safe Retreats,
What safety, privacy, what true delight
In the artificial Night
Your gloomy entrails make,
Have I taken, do I take!
How oft, when grief has made me fly
To hide me from Society,
Even of my dearest Friends, have I
In your recesses friendly shade
All my sorrows open laid,
And my most secret woes entrusted to your privacy!

Lord! would men let me alone,
What an over-happy one
Should I think my self to be,
Might I in this desart place,

Which most men by their voice disgrace,
Live but undisturb'd and free!
Here in this despis'd recess
Would I maugre Winter's cold,
And the Summer's worst excess,
Try to live out to sixty full years old,
And all the while
Without an envious eye
On any thriving under Fortune's smile,
Contented live, and then contented die.

Poems, 1689

546 *The New-year. To Mr. W. T.*

HARK, the Cock crows, and yon bright Star,
Tells us the day himself's not far;
And see where, breaking from the night,
He gilds the Western hills with light.
With him old *Janus* does appear,
Peeping into the future Year
With such a look as seems to say
The prospect is not good that way.
Thus do we rise ill sights to see,
And 'gainst our selves to Prophesie,
When the Prophetick fear of things
A more tormenting mischief brings,
More full of Soul-tormenting Gall
Than direst mischiefs can befall.

But stay! but stay! methinks my sight,
Better inform'd by clearer light,
Discerns sereneness in that brow,
That all contracted seem'd but now:
His reverse face may shew distast,

And frown upon the ills are past;
But that which this way looks is clear,
And smiles upon the New-born year.
He looks too from a place so high,
The year lies open to his eye,
And all the moments open are
To the exact discoverer;
Yet more and more he smiles upon
The happy revolution.
Why should we then suspect or fear
The Influences of a year
So smiles upon us the first morn,
And speaks us good so soon as born?

Pox on't! the last was ill enough,
This cannot but make better proof;
Or at the worst, as we brush'd through
The last, why so we may this too;
And then the next in reason shou'd
Be superexcellently good:
For the worst ills we daily see,
Have no more perpetuity
Than the best Fortunes that do fall;
Which also bring us wherewithall
Longer their being to support,
Than those do of the other sort;
And who has one good year in three,
And yet repines at Destiny,
Appears ingrateful in the case,
And merits not the good he has.

Then let us welcome the new guest,
With lusty Brimmers of the best;

Mirth always should good Fortune meet,
And renders e'en disaster sweet:
And though the Princess turn her back,
Let us but line our selves with Sack,
We better shall by far hold out,
Till the next year she face about.

Poems, 1689

547 *Song. Set by Mr. Coleman*

SEE, how like Twilight *Slumber* falls
T' obscure the glory of those balls,
And, as she sleeps,
See how Light creeps
Thorough the Chinks, and Beautifies
The rayie fringe of her fair *Eyes*.

Observe *Loves* feuds, how fast they fly,
To every heart, from her clos'd Eye,
What then will she,
When waking, be?
A glowing Light for all t' admire,
Such as would set the *World* on fire.

Then seal her Eye-lids, gentle *Sleep*,
While cares of her mine open keep;
Lock up, I say,
Those Doors of *Day*,
Which with the *Morn* for Lustre strive,
That I may look on her, and live.

Poems, 1689

548 *Laura Sleeping*

WINDS whisper gently whilst she sleeps,
And fan her with your cooling wings;
Whilst she her drops of Beauty weeps,
From pure, and yet unrivall'd Springs.

Glide over Beauties Field her Face,
To kiss her Lip, and Cheek be bold,
But with a calm, and stealing pace;
Neither too rude; nor yet too cold.

Play in her beams, and crisp her Hair,
With such a gale, as wings soft *Love*,
And with so sweet, so rich an Air,
As breathes from the *Arabian* Grove.

A Breath as hush't as Lovers sigh;
Or that unfolds the Morning door:
Sweet, as the Winds, that gently fly,
To sweep the *Springs* enamell'd Floor.

Murmur soft *Musick* to her Dreams,
That pure, and unpolluted run,
Like to the new-born Christal Streams,
Under the bright enamour'd Sun.

But when she waking shall display
Her light, retire within your bar,
Her Breath is life, her Eyes are day,
And all Mankind her Creatures are.

Poems, 1689

CLEMENT PAMAN

fl. 1660

549 *On Christmas Day to my Heart*

TO Day:
Hark! Heaven sings!
Stretch, tune my Heart
(For hearts have strings
May bear their part)
And though thy Lute were bruis'd i' th' fall;
Bruis'd hearts may reach an humble Partoral.

To Day
Shepheards rejoyce
And Angells do
No more: thy voice
Can reach that too:
Bring then at least thy pipe along
And mingle Consort with the Angells Song.

To day
A shed that 's thatch'd
(Yet straws can sing)
Holds God; God 's match'd
With beasts; Beasts bring
Their song their way; For shame then raise
Thy notes; Lambs bleat and Oxen bellow Praise.

To Day
God honour'd Man
Not Angells: Yet
They sing; And can
Rais'd Man forget?
Praise is our debt to-day, nor shall
Angells (Man's not so poor) discharge it all.

CLEMENT PAMAN

To Day
Then screwe thee high
My Heart: Up to
The Angells key;
Sing Glory; Do;
What if thy stringes all crack and flye?
On such a Ground, Musick 'twill be to dy.

B.M. Add. MS. 18220.

KATHERINE PHILIPS

1631–1664

550 *To my Excellent Lucasia, on our Friendship*

I DID not live until this time
Crown'd my felicity,
When I could say without a crime,
I am not thine, but Thee.

This carcase breath'd, and walkt, and slept,
So that the World believ'd
There was a soul the motions kept;
But they were all deceiv'd.

For as a watch by art is wound
To motion, such was mine:
But never had Orinda found
A soul till she found thine;

Which now inspires, cures and supplies,
And guides my darkened breast:
For thou art all that I can prize,
My Joy, my life, my Rest.

No bridegroom's nor crown-conqueror's mirth
To mine compar'd can be:
They have but pieces of this Earth,
I've all the World in thee.

Then let our flames still light and shine,
And no false fear control,
As innocent as our design,
Immortal as our soul.

Poems, 1667 (text 1678)

551 *Orinda to Lucasia parting, October, 1661, at London*

ADIEU, dear Object of my Love's excess,
And with thee all my hopes of happiness,
With the same fervent and unchangèd heart
Which did its whole self once to thee impart,
(And which, though fortune has so sorely bruis'd,
Would suffer more, to be from this excus'd)
I to resign thy dear converse submit,
Since I can neither keep, nor merit it.
Thou hast too long to me confinèd been,
Who ruin am without, passion within.
My mind is sunk below thy tenderness,
And my condition does deserve it less;
I'm so entangl'd and so lost a thing
By all the shocks my daily sorrows bring,
That wouldst thou for thy old Orinda call,
Thou hardly couldst unravel her at all.
And should I thy clear fortunes interline
With the incessant miseries of mine?

No, no, I never lov'd at such a rate,
To tie thee to the rigours of my fate.
As from my obligations thou art free,
Sure thou shalt be so from my injury.
Though every other worthiness I miss,
Yet I'll at least be generous in this.
I'd rather perish without sigh or groan,
Than thou shouldst be condemn'd to give me one;
Nay, in my soul I rather could allow
Friendship should be a sufferer, than thou:
Go then, since my sad heart has set thee free,
Let all the loads and chains remain on me.
Though I be left the prey of sea and wind,
Thou, being happy, wilt in that be kind;
Nor shall I my undoing much deplore,
Since thou art safe, whom I must value more.
Oh! mayst thou ever be so, and as free
From all ills else, as from my company;
And may the torments thou hast had from it,
Be all that Heaven will to thy life permit.
And that they may thy virtue service do,
Mayst thou be able to forgive them too:
But though I must this sharp submission learn,
I cannot yet unwish thy dear concern.
Not one new comfort I expect to see,
I quit my Joy, Hope, Life, and all but thee;
Nor seek I thence aught that may discompose
That mind where so serene a goodness grows.
I ask no inconvenient kindness now,
To move thy passion, or to cloud thy brow;
And thou wilt satisfy my boldest plea
By some few soft remembrances of me,

Which may present thee with this candid thought,
I meant not all the troubles that I brought.
Own not what Passion rules, and Fate does crush,
But wish thou couldst have done 't without a blush;
And that I had been, ere it was too late,
Either more worthy, or more fortunate.
Ah, who can love the thing they cannot prize?
But thou mayst pity though thou dost despise.
Yet I should think that pity bought too dear,
If it should cost those precious eyes a tear.
  Oh, may no minute's trouble thee possess,
But to endear the next hour's happiness;
And mayst thou when thou art from me remov'd,
Be better pleas'd, but never worse belov'd:
Oh, pardon me for pouring out my woes
In rhyme now, that I dare not do 't in prose.
For I must lose whatever is call'd dear,
And thy assistance all that loss to bear,
And have more cause than e'er I had before,
To fear that I shall never see thee more.

Poems, 1678

JOHN DRYDEN

1631–1700

552 *From 'Astræa Redux'*

(*i*)

NOW with a general Peace the World was blest,
While Ours, a World divided from the rest,
A dreadful Quiet felt, and worser far
Than Armes, a sullen Interval of War:

Thus, when black Clouds draw down the lab'ring Skies,
Ere yet abroad the winged Thunder flies,
An horrid Stillness first invades the ear,
And in that silence We the Tempest fear.
Th' ambitious *Swede* like restless Billows tost
On this hand gaining what on that he lost,
Though in his life he Blood and Ruine breath'd,
To his now guideless Kingdom Peace bequeath'd;
And Heaven, that seem'd regardless of our Fate,
For *France* and *Spain* did Miracles create,
Such mortal Quarrels to compose in Peace
As Nature bred and Int'rest did encrease.
We sigh'd to hear the fair *Iberian* Bride
Must grow a Lilie to the Lilies side,
While Our cross Stars deny'd us *Charles* his bed
Whom Our first Flames and Virgin Love did wed.
For his long absence Church and State did groan;
Madness the Pulpit, Faction seiz'd the Throne:
Experienc'd Age in deep despair was lost
To see the Rebel thrive, the Loyal crost:
Youth that with Joys had unacquainted been
Envy'd gray hairs that once good Days had seen:
We thought our Sires, not with their own content,
Had ere we came to age our Portion spent.
Nor could our Nobles hope their bold Attempt
Who ruined Crowns would Coronets exempt:
For when by their designing Leaders taught
To strike at Pow'r which for themselves they sought,
The vulgar gull'd into Rebellion, arm'd,
Their blood to action by the Prize was warm'd;
The Sacred Purple then and Scarlet Gown,
Like sanguine Dye, to Elephants was shewn.

Thus when the bold *Typhoeus* scal'd the Sky
And forc'd great *Jove* from his own Heaven to fly,
(What King, what Crown from Treasons reach is free,
If *Jove* and *Heaven* can violated be?)
The lesser Gods that shar'd his prosp'rous State
All suffer'd in the Exil'd Thunderer's Fate.
The Rabble now such Freedom did enjoy,
As Winds at Sea, that use it to destroy:
Blind as the *Cyclops*, and as wild as he,
They own'd a lawless savage Libertie,
Like that our painted Ancestors so priz'd
Ere Empire's Arts their Breasts had Civiliz'd.

Lines 1–48

(*ii*)

AND welcom now (*Great Monarch*) to your own;
Behold th' approaching Cliffes of *Albion*;
It is no longer Motion cheats your view,
As you meet it, the Land approacheth you.
The Land returns, and in the white it wears
The marks of Penitence and Sorrow bears.
But you, whose Goodness your Descent doth show,
Your Heav'nly Parentage and Earthly too;
By that same mildness which your Fathers Crown
Before did ravish, shall secure your own.
Not ty'd to rules of Policy, you find
Revenge less sweet than a forgiving mind.
Thus, when th' Almighty would to *Moses* give
A sight of all he could behold and live;
A voice before his Entry did proclaim
Long-Suffring, *Goodness*, *Mercy* in his Name.

Your Pow'r to Justice doth submit your Cause,
Your Goodness only is above the Laws;
Whose rigid Letter, while pronounc'd by you,
Is softer made. So winds that tempests brew
When through Arabian Groves they take their flight
Made wanton with rich Odours, lose their spight.
And as those Lees, that trouble it, refine
The agitated Soul of Generous Wine,
So tears of Joy for your returning spilt,
Work out and expiate our former Guilt.
Methinks I see those Crowds on *Dover's* Strand,
Who in their haste to welcom you to Land
Choak'd up the Beach with their still growing store,
And made a wilder Torrent on the Shore:
While, spurr'd with eager thoughts of past Delight,
Those who had seen you court a second sight;
Preventing still your Steps and making hast
To meet you often whereso-e'er you past.
How shall I speak of that triumphant Day
When you renew'd the expiring Pomp of *May*!
(A month that owns an Interest in your Name:
You and the Flow'rs are its peculiar Claim.)
That Star, that at your Birth shone out so bright,
It stain'd the duller Suns Meridian light,
Did once again its potent Fires renew,
Guiding our Eyes to find and worship you.
 And now times whiter Series is begun,
Which in soft Centuries shall smoothly run;
Those Clouds that overcast your Morn shall fly,
Dispell'd to farthest corners of the Sky.
Our nation, with united Int'rest blest,
Not now content to poize, shall sway, the rest.

Abroad your Empire shall no Limits know,
But like the Sea in boundless Circles flow.
Your much lov'd Fleet shall with a wide Command
Besiege the petty Monarchs of the Land:
And as Old Time his Off-spring swallow'd down,
Our Ocean in its depths all Seas shall drown.
Their wealthy Trade from Pyrate's Rapine free,
Our Merchants shall no more Advent'rers be:
Nor in the farthest East those Dangers fear
Which humble *Holland* must dissemble here.
Spain to your gift alone her *Indies* owes;
For what the Pow'rful takes not he bestows.
And *France* that did an Exiles presence Fear
May justly apprehend you still too near.
At home the hateful names of Parties cease
And factious Souls are weary'd into peace.
The discontented now are only they
Whose Crimes before did your Just Cause betray:
Of those your Edicts some reclaim from sins,
But most your Life and Blest Example wins.
Oh happy Prince whom Heav'n hath taught the way
By paying Vows to have more Vows to pay!
Oh Happy Age! Oh times like those alone,
By Fate reserv'd for great *Augustus* throne!
When the joint growth of Arms and Arts foreshew
The World a Monarch, and that Monarch *You*.

Astræa Redux, lines 250–323, 1660 (text 1688)

553 *From 'To His Sacred Majesty, a Panegyrick on his Coronation, 1661'*

TIME seems not now beneath his years to stoop,
Nor doe his wings with sickly feathers droop:
Soft western winds waft o'er the gaudy spring,
And open'd Scenes of flow'rs and blossoms bring
To grace this happy day, while you appear
Not King of us alone but of the year.
All eyes you draw, and with the eyes the heart,
Of your own pomp your self the greatest part:
Loud shouts the Nations happiness proclaim,
And Heav'n this day is feasted with your Name.

. . . . . .

As flames do on the wings of Incense fly:
Musique herself is lost, in vain she brings
Her choisest notes to praise the best of Kings:
Her melting strains in you a tombe have found
And lye like Bees in their own sweetnesse drowned.
He that brought peace and discord could attone,
His Name is Musick of itself alone.
Now while the sacred oyl anoints your head,
And fragrant scents, begun from you, are spread
Through the large Dome, the peoples joyful Sound
Sent back, is still preserv'd in hallow'd ground:
Which in one blessing mixt descends on you,
As heightned spirits fall in richer dew.
Not that our wishes do increase your store,
Full of your self, you can admit no more:
We add not to your glory, but employ
Our time like Angels in expressing Joy

Nor is it duty or our hopes alone
Create that joy, but full fruition:
We know those blessings which we must possesse
And judge of future by past happinesse. Lines 27–36; 52–72

554 From '*Annus Mirabilis: 1666*'

(*i*) *The Fourth Day's Battle*

THUS re-inforc'd, against the adverse Fleet,
Still doubling ours, brave *Rupert* leads the way;
With the first blushes of the Morn they meet,
And bring night back upon the new-born day.

His presence soon blows up the kindling Fight,
And his loud Guns speak thick like angry men:
It seem'd as Slaughter had been breath'd all night,
And Death new pointed his dull Dart agen.

The *Dutch* too well his mighty Conduct knew,
And matchless Courage since the former Fight!
Whose Navy like a stiff-stretch'd cord did show,
Till he bore in, and bent them into flight.

The wind he shares, while half their Fleet offends
His open side, and high above him shews,
Upon the rest at pleasure he descends,
And, doubly harm'd, he double harms bestows.

Behind, the Gen'ral mends his weary Pace,
And sullenly to his Revenge he sails:
So glides some trodden Serpent on the Grass,
And long behind his wounded Volume trails.

Th' increasing Sound is born to either shore,
And for their stakes the throwing Nations fear:
Their Passion, double with the Cannons roar,
And with warm wishes each Man combats there.

Pli'd thick and close as when the Fight begun,
Their huge unwieldy Navy wasts away;
So sicken waning Moons too near the Sun,
And blunt their Crescents on the edge of day.

And now reduc'd on equal terms to fight,
Their Ships like wasted Patrimonies show;
Where the thin scatt'ring Trees admit the light,
And shun each others Shadows as they grow.

The warlike Prince had sever'd from the rest
Two giant Ships, the pride of all the Main;
Which, with his one, so vigorously he press'd,
And flew so home they could not rise again.

Already batter'd, by his Lee they lay,
In vain upon the passing Winds they call:
The passing Winds through their torn Canvass play,
And flagging Sails on heartless Sailors fall.

Their open'd sides receive a gloomy light,
Dreadful as day let in to shades below:
Without, grim death rides bare-fac'd in their sight,
And urges ent'ring billows as they flow.

When one dire shot, the last they could supply,
Close by the board the Prince's Main-mast bore:
All three now, helpless, by each other lie,
And this offends not, and those fear no more.

So have I seen some fearful Hare maintain
A Course, till tir'd before the Dog she lay,
Who, stretch'd behind her, pants upon the Plain,
Past pow'r to kill as she to get away.

With his loll'd tongue he faintly licks his Prey,
His warm breath blows her flix up as she lies;
She, trembling, creeps upon the ground away,
And looks back to him with beseeching eyes.

The Prince unjustly does his Stars accuse,
Which hinder'd him to push his Fortune on;
For what they to his Courage did refuse,
By mortal Valour never must be done.

This lucky hour the wise *Batavian* takes,
And warns his tatter'd Fleet to follow home:
Proud to have so got off with equal stakes,
Where 'twas a Triumph not to be o'er-come.

The General's force, as kept alive by fight,
Now, not oppos'd, no longer can pursue:
Lasting till Heav'n had done his courage right;
When he had conquer'd he his Weakness knew.

He casts a Frown on the departing Foe,
And sighs to see him quit the watry Field:
His stern fix'd eyes no satisfaction shew,
For all the glories which the Fight did yield.

Stanzas 119–136

(*ii*)

The New London

ME-THINKS already, from this Chymick flame,
I see a city of more precious mold:
Rich as the town which gives the *Indies* name,
With Silver pav'd, and all divine with Gold.

the *Indies*: Mexico.

Already labouring with a mighty fate,
She shakes the Rubbish from her mounting Brow,
And seems to have renew'd her Charters date,
Which Heav'n will to the death of time allow.

More great than human now, and more *August*,
New deified she from her Fires does rise:
Her widening Streets on new Foundations trust,
And, opening, into larger parts she flies.

Before, she like some Shepherdess did shew,
Who sate to bathe her by a River's side;
Not answering to her fame, but rude and low,
Nor taught the beauteous Arts of Modern pride.

Now, like a Maiden Queen, she will behold,
From her high Turrets, hourly Suitors come:
The East with Incense, and the West with Gold,
Will stand, like Suppliants, to receive her Doom.

The silver *Thames*, her own domestick Floud,
Shall bear her Vessels, like a sweeping Train,
And often wind (as of his Mistress proud,)
With longing eyes to meet her Face again.

The wealthy *Tagus*, and the wealthier *Rhine*,
The glory of their Towns no more shall boast,
And *Seine*, that would with *Belgian* Rivers join,
Shall find her Lustre stain'd, and Traffick lost.

The vent'rous Merchant who design'd more far,
And touches on our hospitable Shore,
Charm'd with the Splendour of this Northern Star,
Shall here unlade him, and depart no more.

Our pow'rful Navy shall no longer meet,
The wealth of *France* or *Holland* to invade:
The beauty of this Town without a Fleet,
From all the World shall vindicate her Trade.

And, while this fam'd Emporium we prepare,
The *British* Ocean shall such Triumphs boast,
That those, who now disdain our Trade to share,
Shall rob like Pirates on our wealthy Coast.

Already we have conquer'd half the War,
And the less dang'rous part is left behind:
Our Trouble now is but to make them dare,
And not so great to Vanquish as to Find.

Thus to the Eastern wealth through Storms we go,
But now, the Cape once doubled, fear no more:
A constant Trade-wind will securely blow,
And gently lay us on the Spicy shore.

Annus Mirabilis, Stanzas 293–304, 1667 (text 1668)

555 *Prologue to the University of Oxford, 1673, spoken by Mr. Hart at the acting of the Silent Woman*

WHAT *Greece*, when learning flourish'd, onely knew,
(*Athenian* Judges,) you this day renew.
Here too are Annual Rites to *Pallas* done,
And here Poetique prizes lost or won.
Methinks I see you crown'd with Olives sit,
And strike a sacred Horrour from the Pit.
A Day of Doom is this of your Decree,
Where even the Best are but by Mercy free:
A Day which none but *Johnson* durst have wish'd to see.

Here they who long have known the usefull Stage
Come to be taught themselves to teach the Age.
As your Commissioners our Poets go,
To cultivate the Virtue which you sow;
In your *Lycæum* first themselves refin'd,
And delegated thence to Humane kind.
But as Embassadours, when long from home,
For new Instructions to their Princes come;
So Poets who your Precepts have forgot,
Return, and beg they may be better taught:
Follies and Faults else-where by them are shown,
But by your Manners they correct their own.
Th' illiterate Writer, Emperique like, applies
To Minds diseas'd, unsafe, chance Remedies:
The Learn'd in Schools, where Knowledge first began,
Studies with Care th' Anatomy of Man;
Sees Vertue, Vice, and Passions in their Cause,
And Fame from Science, not from Fortune, draws.
So Poetry, which is in *Oxford* made
An Art, in *London* onely is a Trade.
There haughty Dunces, whose unlearned Pen
Could ne'er spell Grammar, would be reading Men.
Such build their Poems the *Lucretian* way;
So many Huddled Atoms make a Play,
And if they hit in Order by some Chance,
They call that Nature which is Ignorance.
To such a Fame let mere Town-Wits aspire,
And their gay Nonsense their own Citts admire.
Our Poet, could he find Forgiveness here,
Would wish it rather than a *Plaudit* there.
He owns no Crown from those *Prætorian* Bands,
But knows *that* Right is in this Senates Hands.

Not impudent enough to hope your Praise,
Low at the Muses Feet, his Wreath he lays,
And, where he took it up, resigns his Bays.
Kings make their Poets whom themselves think fit.
But 'tis your Suffrage makes Authentique Wit.

(Text 1684)

556 *Prologue to Aureng-Zebe, 1675*

OUR Author by experience finds it true,
'Tis much more hard to please himself than you;
And out of no feign'd Modesty, this day,
Damns his laborious Trifle of a Play;
Not that it's worse than what before he writ,
But he has now another taste of Wit;
And, to confess a Truth (though out of Time,)
Grows weary of his long-loved Mistris Rhyme.
Passion's too fierce to be in Fetters bound,
And Nature flies him like Enchanted Ground:
What Verse can do he has perform'd in this,
Which he presumes the most correct of his;
But spite of all his pride, a secret shame
Invades his Breast at *Shakespear's* sacred name:
Aw'd when he hears his Godlike *Romans* rage,
He in a just despair would quit the Stage;
And to an Age less polish'd, more unskill'd,
Does with disdain the foremost Honours yield.
As with the greater Dead he dares not strive,
He wou'd not match his Verse with those who live:
Let him retire, betwixt two Ages cast,
The first of this, and hindmost of the last.
A losing Gamester, let him sneak away;
He bears no ready Money from the Play.

The Fate which governs Poets, thought it fit,
He shou'd not raise his Fortunes by his Wit.
The Clergy thrive, and the litigious Bar;
Dull Heroes fatten with the Spoils of War:
All Southern Vices, Heav'n be prais'd, are here;
But Wit's a Luxury you think too dear.
When you to cultivate the Plant are loth,
'Tis a shrewd sign 'twas never of your growth:
And Wit in Northern Climates will not blow,
Except, like *Orange-trees*, 'tis hous'd from Snow.
There needs no care to put a Play-house down,
'Tis the most desart place of all the Town:
We and our Neighbours, to speak proudly, are
Like Monarchs, ruin'd with expensive War;
While, like wise *English*, unconcern'd you sit,
And see us play the Tragedy of Wit.

(Text 1676)

557 *From 'Absalom and Achitophel', 1681*

(i)

Shaftesbury

OF these the false *Achitophel* was first,
A Name to all succeeding Ages curst.
For close Designs and crooked Counsels fit,
Sagacious, Bold, and Turbulent of wit,
Restless, unfixt in Principles and Place,
In Pow'r unpleased, impatient of Disgrace;
A fiery Soul, which working out its way,
Fretted the Pigmy Body to decay:
And o'er informed the Tenement of Clay.
A daring Pilot in extremity;
Pleas'd with the Danger, when the Waves went high

He sought the Storms; but, for a Calm unfit,
Would Steer too nigh the Sands to boast his Wit.
Great Wits are sure to Madness near alli'd
And thin Partitions do their Bounds divide;
Else, why should he, with Wealth and Honour blest,
Refuse his Age the needful hours of Rest?
Punish a Body which he coud not please,
Bankrupt of Life, yet Prodigal of Ease?
And all to leave what with his Toil he won
To that unfeather'd two-legg'd thing, a Son:
Got, while his Soul did huddled Notions trie;
And born a shapeless Lump, like Anarchy.
In Friendship false, implacable in Hate,
Resolv'd to Ruine or to Rule the State;
To Compass this the Triple Bond he broke;
The Pillars of the Publick Safety shook,
And fitted *Israel* for a Foreign Yoke;
Then, seiz'd with Fear, yet still affecting Fame,
Usurp'd a Patriot's All-attoning Name.
So easie still it proves in Factious Times
With publick Zeal to cancel private Crimes.
How safe is Treason and how sacred ill,
Where none can sin against the Peoples Will,
Where Crowds can wink; and no offence be known,
Since in anothers guilt they find their own.
Yet, Fame deserv'd, no Enemy can grudge;
The Statesman we abhor, but praise the Judge.
In *Israels* courts ne'er sat an *Abbethdin*
With more discerning Eyes or Hands more clean,
Unbrib'd, unsought, the Wretched to redress;
Swift of Dispatch and easie of Access.
Oh, had he been content to serve the Crown

With Vertues onely proper to the Gown,
Or had the rankness of the Soil been freed
From Cockle that opprest the Noble Seed,
David for him his tuneful Harp had strung,
And Heav'n had wanted one Immortal Song.

Lines 150–197

(ii)

The Malcontents

TO farther this, *Achitophel* Unites
The Malecontents of all the Israelites:
Whose differing Parties he could wisely Join
For several Ends, to serve the same Design.
The Best, and of the Princes some were such,
Who thought the pow'r of Monarchy too much:
Mistaken Men, and Patriots in their Hearts;
Not Wicked, but seduc'd by Impious Arts.
By these the Springs of Property were bent,
And wound so high, they Crack'd the Government.
The next for Interest sought t' embroil the State,
To sell their Duty at a dearer rate;
And make their *Jewish* Markets of the Throne;
Pretending Publick Good, to serve their own.
Others thought Kings an useless heavy Load,
Who Cost too much, and did too little Good.
These were for laying Honest *David* by
On Principles of pure good Husbandry.
With them join'd all th' Haranguers of the Throng
That thought to get Preferment by the Tongue.
Who follow next, a double danger bring,
Not onely hating *David*, but the King;

The *Solymæan* Rout; well Vers'd of old
In Godly Faction, and in Treason bold;
Cowring and Quaking at a Conqu'ror's Sword,
But Lofty to a Lawful Prince Restored;
Saw with Disdain an *Ethnick* Plot begun
And Scorned by *Jebusites* to be Out-done.
Hot *Levites* Headed these; who pull'd before
From th' *Ark*, which in the Judges days they bore,
Resum'd their Cant, and with a Zealous Crie
Pursu'd their old belov'd Theocracie.
Where Sanhedrin and Priest enslav'd the Nation
And justifi'd their Spoils by Inspiration:
For who so fit for Reign as *Aaron's* Race,
If once Dominion they could found in Grace?
These led the Pack; though not of surest scent,
Yet deepest mouth'd against the Government.
A numerous Host of dreaming Saints succeed;
Of the true old Enthusiastick Breed:
'Gainst Form and Order they their Pow'r imploy.
Nothing to Build, and all things to Destroy.
But far more numerous was the Herd of such,
Who think too little, and who talk too much.
These, out of meer instinct, they knew not why,
Adored their Fathers' God, and Property:
And, by the same blind Benefit of Fate,
The Devil and the *Jebusite* did hate:
Born to be sav'd, even in their own despight;
Because they could not help believing right.

Lines 491–540

558 *From 'The Medall', 1682*

Vox Populi

ALMIGHTY crowd, thou shorten'st all dispute;
Power is thy Essence; Wit thy Attribute!
Nor Faith nor Reason make thee at a stay,
Thou leapst o'er all Eternal truths in thy *Pindarique* way!
Athens, no doubt, did righteously decide,
When *Phocion* and when *Socrates* were try'd;
As righteously they did those dooms repent;
Still they were wise, whatever way they went.
Crowds err not, though to both extremes they run;
To kill the Father and recall the son.
Some think the Fools were most as times went then,
But now the World's o'er stock'd with prudent men.
The common Cry is ev'n Religion's Test;
The *Turk's* is, at *Constantinople*, best,
Idols in *India*, Popery at *Rome*,
And our own Worship onely true at home,
And true, but for the time, 'tis hard to know
How long we please it shall continue so;
This side to-day, and that to-morrow burns;
So all are God a'mighties in their turns.
A Tempting Doctrine, plausible and new;
What Fools our Fathers were, if this be true!
Who, to destroy the seeds of Civil War,
Inherent right in Monarchs did declare:
And, that a lawfull Pow'r might never cease,
Secur'd Succession, to secure our Peace.
Thus Property and Sovereign Sway, at last
In equal Balances were justly cast:

But this new *Jehu* spurs the hot mouth'd horse;
Instructs the Beast to know his native force:
To take the Bit between his teeth and fly
To the next headlong Steep of Anarchy.
Too happy *England*, if our good we knew;
Wou'd we possess the freedom we pursue!
The lavish Government can give no more;
Yet we repine; and plenty makes us poor.
God try'd us once; our Rebel-fathers fought:
He glutted 'em with all the Pow'r they sought,
Till, master'd by their own usurping Brave,
The free-born Subject sunk into a Slave.
We loath our Manna, and we long for Quails;
Ah, what is man, when his own wish prevails!
How rash, how swift to plunge himself in ill;
Proud of his Pow'r and boundless in his Will!
That Kings can doe no wrong we must believe;
None can they do, and must they all receive?
Help Heav'n! or sadly we shall see an hour,
When neither wrong nor right are in their pow'r!
Already they have lost their best defence,
The benefit of Laws which they dispence.
No justice to their righteous Cause allow'd;
But baffled by an Arbitrary Crowd;
And Medalls grav'd, their Conquest to record,
The Stamp and Coyn of their adopted Lord.

Lines 91–144

559 *From 'MacFlecknoe', 1682*
The Primacy of Dullness

ALL humane things are subject to decay,
And, when Fate summons, Monarchs must obey:
This *Fleckno* found, who, like *Augustus*, young
Was call'd to Empire and had govern'd long:
In Prose and Verse was own'd, without dispute
Through all the realms of Non-sense, absolute.
This aged Prince now flourishing in Peace,
And blest with issue of a large increase,
Worn out with business, did at length debate
To settle the Succession of the State;
And pond'ring which of all his Sons was fit
To Reign, and wage immortal War with Wit,
Cry'd, 'tis resolv'd; for Nature pleads that He
Should onely rule, who most resembles me:
Shadwell alone my perfect image bears,
Mature in dullness from his tender years;
Shadwell alone of all my Sons is he
Who stands confirm'd in full stupidity.
The rest to some faint meaning make pretence,
But *Shadwell* never deviates into sense.
Some Beams of Wit on other souls may fall,
Strike through and make a lucid intervall;
But *Shadwell's* genuine night admits no ray,
His rising Fogs prevail upon the Day:
Besides, his goodly Fabrick fills the eye
And seems design'd for thoughtless Majesty:
Thoughtless as Monarch Oakes that shade the plain,
And, spread in solemn state, supinely reign.

Lines 1–28

560 *From 'Religio Laici', 1682*

(*i*)

Reason and Revelation

DIM, as the borrow'd beams of Moon and Stars
To *lonely*, *weary*, *wandring* Travellers
Is *Reason* to the *Soul*: And as on high
Those rolling Fires *discover* but the Sky
Not light us *here*; So *Reason's* glimmering Ray
Was lent, not to *assure* our *doubtfull* way,
But *guide* us upward to a *better Day*.
And as those nightly Tapers disappear
When Day's bright Lord ascends our Hemisphere;
So pale grows *Reason* at *Religions* sight;
So *dies*, and so *dissolves* in *Supernatural Light*.
Some few, whose Lamp shone brighter, have been led
From Cause to Cause to *Natures* secret head;
And found that *one first principle* must be;
But *what*, or *who*, that UNIVERSAL HE;
Whether some *Soul* incompassing this Ball,
Unmade, *unmov'd*; yet *making*, *moving All*;
Or various *Atom's*, interfering Dance
Leapt into *Form* (the Noble work of *Chance*,)
Or this great *All* was from *Eternity*;
Not ev'n the *Stagirite* himself could see;
And *Epicurus Guess'd* as well as He.
As *blindly grop'd* they for a *future State*,
As *rashly Judg'd* of *Providence* and *Fate*:
But least of all could their Endeavours find
What most concern'd the good of Humane kind:

For *Happiness* was never to be found;
But vanish'd from 'em, like Enchanted ground.
One thought *Content* the Good to be enjoyed:
This, every little *Accident* destroyed:
The *wiser Madmen* did for *Vertue* toyl,
A Thorny, or at best a barren Soil:
In *Pleasure* some their glutton Souls would steep,
But found their Line too short, the Well too deep,
And leaky Vessels which no *Bliss* cou'd keep.
Thus, *anxious Thoughts* in *endless Circles* roul,
Without a *Centre* where to fix the *Soul*:
In this wilde Maze their vain Endeavours end:
How can the *less* the *Greater* comprehend?
Or *finite Reason* reach *Infinity*?
For what cou'd *Fathom* God were *more* than *He*.

The *Deist* thinks he stands on firmer ground,
Cries εὕρεκα: the mighty Secret's found:
God is that *Spring* of *Good*; *Supreme* and *Best*,
We, made to *serve*, and in that Service *blest*;
If so, some *Rules* of Worship must be given,
Distributed alike to all by Heaven:
Else *God* were *partial*, and to *some* deny'd
The Means His Justice shou'd for *all* provide.
This *general Worship* is to PRAISE, and PRAY:
One part to *borrow* Blessings, one to *pay*:
And when frail Nature slides into *Offence*,
The *Sacrifice* for *Crimes* is *Penitence*.
Yet, since th' Effects of Providence, we find
Are variously dispensed to Humane kind;
That *Vice Triumphs* and *Vertue suffers* here,
(A Brand that Sovereign justice cannot bear;)

Our Reason prompts us to a *future* State,
The *last Appeal* from *Fortune*, and from *Fate*,
Where God's all-righteous ways will be declar'd,
The *Bad* meet *Punishment*, the *Good, Reward.*

Thus Man by his own strength to Heaven wou'd soar:
And wou'd not be Obliged to God for more.
Vain, wretched Creature, how art thou misled
To think thy Wit these God-like notions bred!
These Truths are not the product of thy Mind,
But dropt from Heaven, and of a Nobler kind.
Reveal'd Religion first inform'd thy sight,
And *Reason* saw not till *Faith* sprung the Light.
Hence all thy *Natural Worship* takes the *Source*:
'Tis *Revelation* what thou thinkst *Discourse.*
Else how com'st *Thou* to see these truths so clear,
Which so obscure to *Heathens* did appear?
Not *Plato* these, nor *Aristotle* found.
Nor He whose wisedom *Oracles* renown'd.
Hast thou a Wit so deep, or so sublime,
Or canst thou lower dive, or higher climb?
Canst *Thou*, by *Reason*, more of *God-head* know
Than *Plutarch*, *Seneca*, or *Cicero*?
Those Gyant Wits, in happyer Ages born,
(When *Arms*, and *Arts* did *Greece* and *Rome* adorn,)
Knew no such *Systeme*: no such Piles cou'd raise
Of *Natural Worship*, built on *Pray'r* and *Praise*,
To One sole GOD:
Nor did Remorse, to Expiate Sin, prescribe:
But slew their fellow Creatures for a Bribe:
The guiltless *Victim* groan'd for their Offence;
And *Cruelty* and *Blood*, was *Penitence.*

If *Sheep* and *Oxen* cou'd Attone for Men
Ah! at how cheap a rate the *Rich* might Sin!
And great Oppressours might Heavens Wrath beguile
By offering his own Creatures for a Spoil!

Dar'st thou, poor Worm, offend *Infinity*?
And must the Terms of Peace be given by *Thee*?
Then *Thou* art *Justice* in the *last Appeal*;
Thy easie God instructs Thee to *rebell*:
And, like a King remote, and weak, must take
What Satisfaction *Thou* art pleased to make.

But if there be a *Pow'r* too *Just*, and *strong*
To wink at *Crimes* and bear unpunish'd *Wrong*;
Look humbly upward, see his Will disclose
The *Forfeit* first, and then the *Fine* impose,
A *Mulct thy* poverty cou'd never pay
Had not *Eternal Wisedom* found the way
And with Cœlestial Wealth supply'd thy Store;
His Justice makes the *Fine*, *his Mercy* quits the *Score*.
See God descending in thy Humane Frame;
Th' *offended*, suffering in th' *Offenders* name:
All thy Misdeeds to Him imputed see,
And all his Righteousness devolv'd on thee.

Lines 1–110

(ii)

The Scriptures

IF on the Book itself we cast our view,
Concurrent Heathens prove the Story *True*:
The *Doctrine*, *Miracles*; which must convince,
For *Heav'n* in *Them* appeals to *humane Sense*;

And though they *prove* not, they *Confirm* the Cause,
When what is *Taught* agrees with *Natures Laws*.

Then for the *Style*, *Majestick* and *Divine*,
It speaks no less than God in every Line;
Commanding words; whose *Force* is still the same
As the first *Fiat* that produc'd our Frame.
All Faiths *beside*, or did by *Arms* ascend;
Or *Sense* indulg'd has made *Mankind* their *Friend*;
This *onely* Doctrine does our *Lusts* oppose:
Unfed by Natures Soil, in which it grows;
Cross to our *Interests*, curbing Sense and Sin;
Oppress'd without, and undermin'd within,
It thrives through pain; its own Tormentours tires;
And with a stubborn patience still aspires.
To what can *Reason* such Effects assign,
Transcending *Nature*, but to *Laws Divine*?
Which in that Sacred Volume are contain'd;
Sufficient, clear, and for that use ordained.

Lines 146–167

(iii)

Tradition

OH but, says one, *Tradition* set aside,
Where can we hope for an *unerring Guide*?
For since th' *original* Scripture has been lost,
All Copies *disagreeing*, *maim'd* the *most*,
Or *Christian Faith* can have no *certain* ground
Or *Truth* in *Church Tradition* must be found.

Such an *Omniscient* Church we wish indeed;
'Twere worth *Both Testaments*, and cast in the *Creed*:
But if *this Mother* be a *Guide* so sure

As can all *doubts resolve*, all *truth secure*,
Then her *Infallibility*, as well
Where Copies are *corrupt*, or *lame*, can tell;
Restore *lost Canon* with as little pains,
As *truly explicate* what still *remains*:
Which yet no *Council* dare *pretend* to doe;
Unless like *Esdras*, they could *write* it new:
Strange Confidence, still to *interpret* true,
Yet not be sure that all they have explain'd,
Is in the blest *Original* contain'd.
More Safe, and much more modest 'tis to say
God wou'd not leave Mankind without a way:
And that the *Scriptures*, though not *every where*
Free from Corruption, or intire, or clear,
Are uncorrupt, sufficient, clear, intire,
In all things which our needfull *Faith* require.
If *others* in the *same Glass better* see,
'Tis for *Themselves* they look, but not for *me*:
For MY Salvation must its Doom receive
Not from what OTHERS, but what *I* believe.

Must *all Tradition* then be set aside?
This to affirm were Ignorance or Pride.
Are there not many points, some needfull sure
To saving Faith, that Scripture leaves obscure?
Which every Sect will wrest a several way
(For what *one* Sect interprets, *all* Sects *may*:)
We hold, and say we prove from Scripture plain,
That *Christ* is GOD; the bold *Socinian*
From the *same* Scripture urges he's but MAN.
Now what Appeal can end th' important Suit;
Both parts *talk* loudly, but the *Rule* is *mute*.

Shall I speak plain, and in a Nation free
Assume an honest *Layman's Liberty*?
I think (according to my little Skill,)
To my own Mother-Church submitting still,
That many have been sav'd, and many may,
Who never heard this Question brought in play.
Th' *unletter'd* Christian, who believes in *gross*,
Plods on to *Heaven* and ne'er is at a loss:
For the *Streight-gate* would be made *streighter* yet,
Were *none* admitted there but men of *Wit*.
The few, by Nature form'd, with Learning fraught,
Born to instruct, as others to be taught,
Must Study well the Sacred Page; and see
Which Doctrine, this, or that, does best agree
With the whole *Tenour* of the Work Divine:
And plainlyest points to Heaven's reveal'd Design:
Which Exposition flows from *genuine Sense*;
And which is *forc'd* by *Wit* and *Eloquence*.
Not that Traditions parts are useless here:
When general, old, disinteress'd and clear:
That Ancient Fathers thus expound the Page
Gives *Truth* the reverend Majesty of *Age*,
Confirms its force by biding every *Test*;
For best *Authority's*, next *Rules*, are best.
And still the nearer to the Spring we go
More limpid, more unsoyl'd, the Waters flow.
Thus, *first Traditions* were a proof alone;
Cou'd we be *certain* such they *were*, so *known*:
But since some Flaws in long descent may be,
They make not *Truth* but *Probability*.
Even *Arius* and *Pelagius* durst provoke
To what the *Centuries preceding* spoke.

Such difference is there in an oft-told Tale:
But Truth by its own Sinews will prevail.
Tradition written therefore more commends
Authority, than what from *Voice* descends:
And this, as perfect as its kind can be,
Rouls down to us the Sacred History:
Which, from the *Universal Church* receiv'd,
Is *try'd*, and *after* for its *self* believed.

Lines 276–355

(iv)

Priestcraft and Private Judgement

IN times o'ergrown with Rust and Ignorance,
A gainfull Trade their Clergy did advance:
When want of Learning kept the *Laymen* low,
And none but *Priests* were *Authoriz'd* to *know*;
When what small Knowledge was, in them did dwell;
And he a *God* who cou'd but *Reade* or *Spell*;
Then *Mother Church* did mightily prevail:
She parcel'd out the Bible by *retail*:
But still *expounded* what She *sold* or *gave*;
To keep it in *her Power* to *Damn* or *Save*:
Scripture was *scarce*, and as the Market went,
Poor *Laymen* took *Salvation* on *Content*;
As needy men take Money, good or bad:
God's Word they had not, but the *Priests* they had.

. . . . .

At last, a knowing Age began t' enquire
If *they* the *Book*, or *That* did *them* inspire:
And, making narrower search they found, tho' late,
That what they thought the *Priest's* was *Their Estate*,

Taught by the *Will produc'd*, (the written Word,)
How long they had been *cheated* on *Record*.
Then, every man who saw the title fair,
Claim'd a Child's part, and put in for a Share:
Consulted Soberly his private good;
And sav'd himself as cheap as e'er he cou'd.

'Tis true, my Friend, (and far be Flattery hence)
This good had full as bad a Consequence:
The Book thus put in every vulgar hand,
Which each presum'd he best cou'd understand,
The *Common Rule* was made the *common Prey*;
And at the mercy of the *Rabble* lay.
The tender Page with horney Fists was gaul'd;
And he was gifted most that loudest baul'd;
The *Spirit* gave the *Doctoral Degree,*
And every member of a *Company*
Was of *his Trade* and of the *Bible free.*
Plain *Truths* enough for needfull *use* they found;
But men wou'd still be itching to *expound*;
Each was ambitious of th' obscurest place,
No measure ta'n from *Knowledge,* all from GRACE.
Study and *Pains* were now no more their Care;
Texts were explain'd by *Fasting* and by *Prayer*:
This was the Fruit the *private Spirit* brought;
Occasion'd by *great Zeal* and *little Thought.*
While Crouds unlearn'd, with rude Devotion warm,
About the Sacred Viands buz and swarm,
The *Fly-blown Text* creates a *crawling Brood*;
And turns to *Maggots* what was meant for *Food.*
A Thousand daily Sects rise up, and dye;
A Thousand more the perish'd Race supply:

So all we make of Heavens discover'd Will
Is, not to have it, or to use it ill.
The Danger 's much the same; on several Shelves
If *others* wreck *us* or *we* wreck our *selves.*

What then remains, but, waving each Extreme,
The Tides of Ignorance, and Pride to stem?
Neither so rich a Treasure to forgo;
Nor proudly seek beyond our pow'r to know:
Faith is not built on disquisitions vain;
The things we *must* believe, are *few* and *plain*:
But since men *will* believe more than they *need*;
And every man will make *himself* a Creed,
In doubtfull questions 'tis the safest way
To learn what unsuspected Ancients say:
For 'tis not likely *we* should higher Soar
In search of Heav'n than *all the Church before*:
Nor can we be deceiv'd, unless we see
The *Scripture* and the *Fathers disagree.*
If after all, they stand suspected still,
(For no man's Faith depends upon his Will;)
'Tis some Relief, that points not clearly known,
Without much hazard may be let alone:
And after hearing what our Church can say,
If still our Reason runs another way,
That private Reason 'tis more Just to curb,
Than by Disputes the publick Peace disturb.
For points obscure are of small use to learn:
But *Common quiet* is *Mankind's concern.*

Thus have I made my own Opinions clear:
Yet neither Praise expect, not Censure fear:

And this unpolish'd, rugged Verse I chose;
As fittest for Discourse, and nearest prose:
For while from *Sacred Truth* I do not swerve,
Tom Sternhold's or *Tom Shadwell's Rhimes* will serve.

Lines 370–383; 388–456

561 *To the Memory of Mr. Oldham*

FAREWELL, too little and too lately known,
Whom I began to think and call my own:
For sure our Souls were near alli'd, and thine
Cast in the same poetick mold with mine.
One common Note on either Lyre did strike,
And Knaves and Fools we both abhorr'd alike.
To the same Goal did both our Studies drive:
The last set out the soonest did arrive.
Thus *Nisus* fell upon the slippery place,
Whilst his young Friend perform'd and won the Race.
O early ripe! to thy abundant Store
What could advancing Age have added more?
It might (what Nature never gives the Young)
Have taught the Numbers of thy Native Tongue.
But Satire needs not those, and Wit will shine
Through the harsh Cadence of a rugged Line.
A noble Error, and but seldom made,
When Poets are by too much force betray'd.
Thy gen'rous Fruits, though gather'd ere their prime,
Still shew'd a Quickness; and maturing Time
But mellows what we write to the dull Sweets of Rhyme.

Once more, hail, and farewell! farewell, thou young,
But ah! too short, *Marcellus* of our Tongue!
Thy Brows with Ivy and with Laurels bound;
But Fate and gloomy Night encompass thee around.

(Text 1684)

562 *From 'The Hind and the Panther', 1687*

(i) Private Judgement Condemned

WHAT weight of ancient witness can prevail,
If private reason hold the publick scale?
But, gratious God, how well dost thou provide
For erring judgments an unerring Guide!
Thy throne is darkness in th' abyss of light,
A blaze of glory that forbids the sight;
O teach me to believe Thee thus conceal'd,
And search no farther than Thy self reveal'd;
But her alone for my Directour take
Whom Thou hast promis'd never to forsake!
My thoughtless youth was wing'd with vain desires,
My manhood, long misled by wandring fires,
Follow'd false lights; and when their glimps was gone,
My pride struck out new sparkles of her own.
Such was I, such by nature still I am,
Be Thine the glory and be mine the shame.
Good life be now my task: my doubts are done,
(What more could fright my faith, than Three in One?)
Can I believe eternal God could lye
Disguis'd in mortal mold and infancy?
That the great Maker of the world could dye?
And after that, trust my imperfect sense
Which calls in question his omnipotence?

Can I my reason to my faith compell,
And shall my sight, and touch, and taste rebell?
Superiour faculties are set aside,
Shall their subservient organs be my guide?
Then let the moon usurp the rule of day,
And winking tapers shew the sun his way;
For what my senses can themselves perceive
I need no revelation to believe.

Part I, lines 62–92

(ii) *The Presbyterians*

MORE haughty than the rest, the *wolfish* race
Appear with belly Gaunt and famish'd face:
Never was so deform'd a beast of Grace.
His ragged tail betwixt his leggs he wears
Close clapp'd for shame, but his rough crest he rears,
And pricks up his predestinating ears.
His wild disorder'd walk, his hagger'd eyes,
Did all the bestial citizens surprize.
Though fear'd and hated, yet he ruled awhile,
As Captain or Companion of the spoil.
Full many a year his hatefull head had been
For tribute paid, nor since in *Cambria* seen:
The last of all the Litter scap'd by chance,
And from *Geneva* first infested *France*.
Some Authors thus his Pedigree will trace,
But others write him of an upstart Race:
Because of *Wickliff's* Brood no mark he brings
But his innate Antipathy to Kings.
These last deduce him from th' *Helvetian* kind
Who near the *Leman lake* his Consort lin'd.

That fi'ry *Zuynglius* first th' Affection bred,
And meagre *Calvin* blest the Nuptial Bed.
In *Israel* some believe him whelp'd long since,
When the proud *Sanhedrim* oppress'd the Prince,
Or, since he will be *Jew*, derive him higher,
When *Corah* with his Brethren did conspire,
From *Moyses* Hand the Sov'reign sway to wrest,
And *Aaron* of his Ephod to devest:
Till opening Earth made way for all to pass,
And cou'd not bear the Burd'n of a *class*.

Part I, lines 160–189

(iii) The Church of England

THE *Panther* sure the noblest, next the *Hind*,
And fairest creature of the spotted kind:
Oh, could her in-born stains be wash'd away,
She were too good to be a beast of Prey!
How can I praise, or blame, and not offend,
Or how divide the frailty from the friend?
Her faults and vertues lye so mix'd, that she
Nor wholly stands condemn'd nor wholly free.
Then, like her injured *Lyon*, let me speak,
He cannot bend her, and he would not break.
Unkind already, and estrang'd in part,
The *Wolfe* begins to share her wandring heart.
Though unpolluted yet with actual ill,
She half commits, who sins but in Her will.
If, as our dreaming *Platonists* report,
There could be spirits of a middle sort,
Too black for heav'n, and yet too white for hell,
Who just dropt half-way done, nor lower fell;

So pois'd, so gently she descends from high,
It seems a soft dismission from the skie.
Her house not ancient, whatsoe'er pretence
Her clergy Heraulds make in her defence.
A second century not half-way run
Since the new honours of her blood begun.

Part I, lines 327–350

(*iv*) *The Catholic Church*

ONE in herself, not rent by Schism, but sound,
Entire, one solid shining Diamond,
Not Sparkles shattered into Sects like you,
One is the Church, and must be to be true:
One central principle of unity.
As undivided, so from errours free,
As one in faith, so one in sanctity.
Thus she, and none but she, th' insulting Rage
Of Hereticks oppos'd from Age to Age:
Still when the Giant-brood invades her Throne,
She stoops from Heav'n and meets 'em half way down,
And with paternal Thunder vindicates her Crown.

. . . . . .

Thus one, thus pure, behold her largely spread
Like the fair Ocean from her Mother-Bed;
From East to West triumphantly she rides,
All Shoars are water'd by her wealthy Tides.
The Gospel-sound, diffus'd from Pole to Pole,
Where winds can carry and where waves can roll.
The self same doctrin of the Sacred Page
Convey'd to ev'ry clime, in ev'ry age.

Part II, lines 526–537; 548–555

563 *To my dear Friend, Mr. Congreve, on his Comedy called the Double-Dealer*

WELL then, the promis'd Hour is come at last;
The present Age of Wit obscures the past:
Strong were our Syres, and as they fought they Writ,
Conqu'ring with Force of Arms and Dint of Wit:
Theirs was the Giant Race before the Flood;
And thus, when *Charles* Return'd, our Empire stood.
Like *Janus*, he the stubborn Soil manur'd,
With Rules of Husbandry the Rankness cur'd:
Tam'd us to Manners, when the Stage was rude,
And boistrous *English* Wit with Art indu'd.
Our Age was cultivated thus at length,
But what we gain'd in Skill we lost in Strength.
Our Builders were with Want of Genius curst;
The second Temple was not like the first;
Till you, the best *Vitruvius*, come at length,
Our Beauties equal, but excel our Strength.
Firm *Dorique* Pillars found Your solid Base,
The fair *Corinthian* crowns the higher Space;
Thus all below is Strength, and all above is Grace.
In easie Dialogue is *Fletcher's* Praise:
He mov'd the Mind, but had no Pow'r to raise.
Great *Johnson* did by Strength of Judgment please,
Yet, doubling *Fletcher's* Force, he wants his Ease.
In diff'ring Talents both adorn'd their Age,
One for the Study, t'other for the Stage.
But both to *Congreve* justly shall submit,
One match'd in Judgment, both o'er-match'd in Wit.
In Him all Beauties of this Age we see,

Etherege his Courtship, *Southern's* Purity,
The Satyre, Wit, and Strength of Manly *Wycherly*.
All this in blooming Youth you have Atchiev'd;
Nor are your foil'd Contemporaries griev'd;
So much the Sweetness of your Manners move,
We cannot Envy you, because we Love.
Fabius might joy in *Scipio*, when he saw
A Beardless Consul made against the Law,
And join his Suffrage to the Votes of *Rome*,
Though he with *Hannibal* was overcome.
Thus old *Romano* bow'd to *Raphael's* Fame,
And Scholar to the Youth he taught, became.
O that your Brows my Lawrel had sustain'd,
Well had I been depos'd, if you had reign'd!
The Father had descended for the Son,
For only You are lineal to the Throne.
Thus, when the State one *Edward* did depose,
A greater *Edward* in his Room arose:
But now, not I, but Poetry is curst;
For *Tom* the Second reigns like *Tom* the First.
But let 'em not mistake my Patron's Part
Nor call his Charity their own Desert.
Yet this I Prophesie; Thou shalt be seen,
(Tho' with some short Parenthesis between:)
High on the Throne of Wit; and, seated there,
Nor mine (that's little) but thy Lawrel wear,
Thy first Attempt an early Promise made;
That early Promise this has more than paid.
So bold, yet so judiciously you dare,
That your least Praise, is to be Regular.
Time, Place, and Action may with Pains be wrought,
But Genius must be born, and never can be taught.

This is Your Portion, this Your Native Store:
Heav'n, that but once was Prodigal before,
To *Shakespear* gave as much; she cou'd not give him more.
  Maintain your Post: that's all the Fame you need;
For 'tis impossible you shou'd proceed.
Already I am worn with Cares and Age,
And just abandoning th' ungrateful Stage:
Unprofitably kept at Heav'n's Expence,
I live a Rent-charge on his Providence:
But You, whom ev'ry Muse and Grace adorn,
Whom I foresee to better Fortune born,
Be kind to my Remains; and oh defend,
Against your Judgment, your departed Friend!
Let not th' insulting Foe my Fame pursue;
But shade those Lawrels which descend to You:
And take for Tribute what these Lines express;
You merit more; nor cou'd my Love do less.

The Double-Dealer, 1694

564 *Upon the Death of the Viscount of Dundee*

OH Last and Best of *Scots*! who did'st maintain
Thy Country's Freedom from a Foreign Reign;
New People fill the Land, now thou art gone,
New Gods the Temples, and new Kings the Throne.
Scotland and Thee did each in other live,
Nor wou'dst thou her, nor cou'd she thee survive.
Farewell! who living didst support the State,
And coud'st not fall but with thy Country's Fate.

(Text 1704)

565 *Alexander's Feast; or, The Power of Musique. An Ode in Honour of St. Cecilia's Day: 1697*

'TWAS at the Royal Feast, for *Persia* won,
By *Philip's* Warlike Son:
Aloft in awful State
The God-like Heroe sate
On his Imperial Throne;
His valiant Peers were plac'd around;
Their Brows with Roses and with Myrtles bound.
(So should Desert in Arms be Crown'd:)
The lovely *Thais* by his side,
Sate like a blooming *Eastern* Bride
In Flow'r of Youth and Beauty's Pride.
Happy, happy, happy Pair!
None but the Brave,
None but the Brave,
None but the Brave deserves the Fair.

CHORUS

Happy, happy, happy Pair!
None but the Brave,
None but the Brave,
None but the Brave deserves the Fair.

Timotheus plac'd on high
Amid the tuneful Quire,
With flying Fingers touch'd the Lyre:
The trembling Notes ascend the Sky,
And Heav'nly Joys inspire.
The Song began from *Jove*;

Who left his blissful Seats above,
(Such is the Pow'r of mighty Love.)
A Dragon's fiery Form bely'd the God:
Sublime on Radiant Spires He rode,
When He to fair *Olympia* press'd:
And while He sought her snowy Breast:
Then, round her slender Waist he curl'd,
And stamp'd an Image of himself, a Sov'raign of the World.
The list'ning crowd admire the lofty Sound,
A present Deity, they shout around:
A present Deity, the vaulted Roofs rebound.
With ravish'd Ears
The Monarch hears,
Assumes the God,
Affects to nod,
And seems to shake the Spheres.

CHORUS

With ravish'd Ears
The Monarch hears,
Assumes the God,
Affects to nod,
And seems to shake the Spheres.

The Praise of *Bacchus* then the sweet Musician sung,
Of *Bacchus* ever Fair, and ever Young:
The jolly God in Triumph comes;
Sound the Trumpets; beat the Drums;
Flush'd with a purple Grace
He shows his honest Face:
Now give the Hautboys breath; He comes, He comes.
Bacchus ever Fair and Young
Drinking Joys did first ordain;

Bacchus Blessings are a Treasure;
Drinking is the Soldiers Pleasure;
Rich the Treasure;
Sweet the Pleasure;
Sweet is Pleasure after Pain.

CHORUS

Bacchus *Blessings are a Treasure,*
Drinking is the Soldier's Pleasure;
Rich the Treasure,
Sweet the Pleasure,
Sweet is Pleasure after Pain.

Sooth'd with the Sound the King grew vain;
Fought all his Battails o'er again;
And thrice He routed all his Foes, and thrice he slew the slain.
The Master saw the Madness rise,
His glowing Cheeks, his ardent Eyes;
And while He Heav'n and Earth defy'd,
Chang'd his Hand, and check'd his Pride.
He chose a Mournful Muse,
Soft pity to infuse;
He sung *Darius* Great and Good,
By too severe a Fate,
Fallen, fallen, fallen, fallen,
Fallen from his high Estate,
And weltring in his Blood:
Deserted at his utmost Need
By those his former Bounty fed;
On the bare Earth expos'd He lies,
With not a Friend to close his Eyes.
With down-cast Looks the joyless Victor sate,

Revolving in his alter'd Soul
    The various Turns of Chance below;
And, now and then, a Sigh he stole,
    And Tears began to flow.

CHORUS

Revolving in his alter'd Soul
    The various Turns of Chance below;
And, now and then, a Sigh he stole,
    And Tears began to flow.

The Mighty Master smil'd to see
That Love was in the next Degree;
'Twas but a Kindred-Sound to move,
For Pity melts the Mind to Love.
    Softly sweet, in *Lydian* Measures,
    Soon he sooth'd his Soul to Pleasures.
War, he sung, is Toil and Trouble;
Honour but an empty Bubble.
    Never ending, still beginning,
Fighting still, and still destroying,
    If the World be worth thy Winning,
Think, O think, it worth Enjoying.
    Lovely *Thais* sits beside thee,
    Take the Good the Gods provide thee.
The Many rend the Skies, with loud applause;
So Love was Crown'd, but Musique won the Cause.
    The Prince, unable to conceal his Pain,
            Gaz'd on the Fair
            Who caus'd his Care,
    And sigh'd and look'd, sigh'd and look'd,
    Sigh'd and look'd, and sigh'd again:

At length, with Love and Wine at once oppress'd,
The vanquish'd Victor sunk upon her Breast.

CHORUS

The Prince, unable to conceal his Pain,
Gaz'd on the fair
Who caus'd his Care,
And sigh'd and look'd, sigh'd and look'd,
Sigh'd and look'd, and sigh'd again;
At length, with Love and Wine at once oppress'd,
The vanquish'd Victor sunk upon her Breast.

Now strike the Golden Lyre again;
A lowder yet, and yet a lowder Strain.
Break his Bands of Sleep asunder,
And rouze him, like a rattling Peal of Thunder.
Hark, hark, the horrid Sound
Has rais'd up his Head;
As awak'd from the Dead,
And amaz'd, he stares around.
Revenge, revenge, *Timotheus* cries,
See the Furies arise!
See the Snakes that they rear,
How they hiss in their Hair,
And the Sparkles that flash from their Eyes!
Behold a ghastly Band,
Each a Torch in his Hand!
Those are *Grecian* Ghosts, that in Battail were slain,
And unbury'd remain
Inglorious on the Plain:
Give the Vengeance due
To the Valiant Crew.
Behold how they toss their Torches on high,

How they point to the *Persian* Abodes,
And glitt'ring Temples of their Hostile Gods.
The Princes applaud with a furious Joy;
And the King seized a Flambeau with Zeal to destroy;
Thais led the Way,
To light him to his Prey,
And, like another *Hellen*, fir'd another *Troy*.

CHORUS

And the King seiz'd a Flambeau with Zeal to destroy;
Thais *led the Way,*
To light him to his Prey,
And, like another Hellen, *fir'd another Troy.*

Thus long ago,
Ere heaving Bellows learn'd to blow,
While Organs yet were mute,
Timotheus, to his breathing Flute
And sounding Lyre,
Cou'd swell the Soul to rage, or kindle soft Desire.
At last Divine *Cecilia* came,
Inventress of the Vocal Frame;
The sweet Enthusiast, from her Sacred Store,
Enlarg'd the former narrow Bounds,
And added Length to solemn Sounds,
With Nature's Mother-Wit, and Arts unknown before.
Let old *Timotheus* yield the Prize,
Or both divide the Crown:
He rais'd a Mortal to the Skies;
She drew an Angel down.

GRAND CHORUS

At last Divine Cecilia *came,*
Inventress of the Vocal Frame;

The sweet Enthusiast, from her Sacred Store,
Enlarg'd the former narrow Bounds,
And added Length to solemn Sounds,
With Nature's Mother-Wit, and Arts unknown before.
Let old Timotheus *yield the Prize,*
Or both divide the Crown:
He rais'd a Mortal to the Skies;
She drew an Angel down. (Text 1700)

566 *From 'Virgil's "Aeneid",' 1697*

(*i*)

Dido among the shades

NOT far from these Phœnician Dido stood,
Fresh from her wound, her bosom bathed in blood;
Whom when the Trojan hero hardly knew,
Obscure in shades, and with a doubtful view
(Doubtful as he who sees, through dusky night,
Or thinks he sees, the moon's uncertain light),
With tears he first approached the sullen shade;
And as his love inspired him, thus he said:
'Unhappy queen! then is the common breath
Of rumour true, in your reported death,
And I, alas! the cause?—By Heaven, I vow,
And all the powers that rule the realms below,
Unwilling I forsook your friendly state,
Commanded by the gods, and forced by Fate!
Those gods, that Fate, whose unresisted might
Have sent me to these regions void of light,
Through the vast empire of eternal night!
Nor dared I to presume, that, pressed with grief,
My flight should urge you to this dire relief.

Stay, stay your steps, and listen to my vows!
'Tis the last interview that Fate allows!'
In vain he thus attempts her mind to move
With tears and prayers, and late repenting love.
Disdainfully she looked; then turning round,
She fixed her eyes unmoved upon the ground;
And, what he says and swears, regards no more
Than the deaf rocks, when the loud billows roar:
But whirled away, to shun his hateful sight,
Hid in the forest, and the shades of night:
Then sought Sichæus through the shady grove,
Who answered all her cares, and equalled all her love.

Book 6, lines 610–40

(*ii*)
Marcellus

'SEEK not to know (the ghost replied with tears)
The sorrows of thy sons in future years.
This youth, the blissful vision of a day,
Shall just be shewn on earth, and snatched away.
The gods, too high had raised the Roman state:
Were but their gifts as permanent as great!
What groans of men shall fill the Martian field!
How fierce a blaze his flaming pile shall yield!
What funeral pomp shall floating Tiber see,
When, rising from his bed, he views the sad solemnity!
No youth shall equal hopes of glory give;
No youth afford so great a cause to grieve.
The Trojan honour, and the Roman boast;
Admired when living, and adored when lost!
Mirror of ancient faith in early youth!
Undaunted worth, inviolable truth!

No foe, unpunished, in the fighting field
Shall dare thee, foot to foot, with sword and shield;
Much less in arms oppose thy matchless force,
When thy sharp spurs shall urge thy foaming horse.
Ah! couldst thou break through Fate's severe decree,
A new Marcellus shall arise in thee!
Full canisters of fragrant lilies bring,
Mixed with the purple roses of the spring:
Let me with funeral flowers his body strow;
This gift which parents to their children owe,
This unavailing gift, at least, I may bestow!'

Book 6, lines 1200–26

(*iii*)

Battle of Actium

BETWIXT the quarters, flows a golden sea;
But foaming surges there in silver play.
The dancing dolphins with their tails divide
The glittering waves, and cut the precious tide.
Amid the main, two mighty fleets engage:
Their brazen beaks opposed with equal rage.
Actium surveys the well-disputed prize:
Leucate's watery plain with foamy billows fries.
Young Cæsar, on the stern in armour bright,
Here leads the Romans and their gods to fight:
His beamy temples shoot their flames afar;
And o'er his head is hung the Julian star.
Agrippa seconds him, with prosperous gales,
And, with propitious gods, his foes assails.
A naval crown, that binds his manly brows,
The happy fortune of the fight foreshows.
Ranged on the line opposed, Antonius brings
Barbarian aids, and troops of eastern kings,

The Arabians near, and Bactrians from afar,
Of tongues discordant, and a mingled war:
And, rich in gaudy robes, amidst the strife,
His ill fate follows him—the Egyptian wife.
Moving they fight: with oars and forky prows
The froth is gathered and the water glows.
It seems as if the Cyclades again
Were rooted up, and justled in the main;
Or floating mountains floating mountains meet;
Such is the fierce encounter of the fleet.
Fire-balls are thrown, and pointed javelins fly;
The fields of Neptune take a purple dye.
The queen herself, amidst the loud alarms,
With cymbal tossed, her fainting soldiers warms—
Fool as she was! who had not yet divined
Her cruel fate; nor saw the snakes behind.
Her country gods, the monsters of the sky,
Great Neptune, Pallas, and love's queen, defy.
The dog Anubis barks, but barks in vain,
Nor longer dares oppose the ethereal train.
Mars, in the middle of the shining shield
Is graved, and strides along the liquid field.
The Diræ souse from heaven with swift descent;
And Discord, dyed in blood, with garments rent,
Divides the press: her steps Bellona treads,
And shakes her iron rod above their heads.
  This seen, Apollo, from his Actian height
Pours down his arrows; at whose wingèd flight
The trembling Indians and Egyptians yield,
And soft Sabæans quit the watery field.
The fatal mistress hoists her silken sails,
And shrinking from the fight, invokes the gales.

Aghast she looks, and heaves her breast for breath,
Panting, and pale with fear of future death.
The god had figured her, as driven along
By winds and waves, and scudding through the throng.
Just opposite, sad Nilus opens wide
His arms and ample bosom to the tide,
And spreads his mantle o'er the winding coast;
In which, he wraps his queen and hides the flying host.

Book 8, lines 891–948

567 *From 'To My Honour'd Kinsman, John Driden, of Chesterton, in the County of Huntingdon, Esq.'*

HOW Blessed is He, who leads a Country Life,
Unvex'd with anxious Cares, and void of Strife!
Who studying Peace, and shunning Civil Rage,
Enjoy'd his Youth, and now enjoys his Age:
All who deserve his Love, he makes his own;
And, to be lov'd himself, needs only to be known.
Just, Good, and Wise, contending Neighbours come
From your Award to wait their final Doom;
And, Foes before, return in Friendship home.
Without their Cost, you terminate the Cause;
And save th' Expence of long Litigious Laws:
Where Suits are travers'd; and so little won,
That he who conquers, is but last undone:
Such are not your Decrees; but so design'd,
The Sanction leaves a lasting Peace behind;
Like your own Soul, Serene; a Pattern of your Mind.
Promoting Concord, and composing Strife,
Lord of your self, uncumber'd with a Wife;

Where, for a Year, a Month, perhaps a Night,
Long Penitence succeeds a short Delight:
Minds are so hardly match'd, that ev'n the first,
Though pair'd by Heav'n, in Paradise, were curs'd.
For Man and Woman, though in one they grow,
Yet, first or last, return again to Two.
He to God's Image, She to His was made;
So, farther from the Fount, the Stream at random stray'd.
  How cou'd He stand, when, put to double Pain,
He must a Weaker than himself sustain!
Each might have stood perhaps; but each alone;
Two Wrestlers help to pull each other down.
  Not that my Verse wou'd blemish all the Fair;
But yet, if *some* be Bad, 'tis Wisdom to beware;
And better shun the Bait, than struggle in the Snare.
Thus have you shunn'd, and shun the married State,
Trusting as little as you can to Fate.
  No porter guards the Passage of your Door;
T' admit the Wealthy, and exclude the Poor:
For God, who gave the Riches, gave the Heart
To sanctifie the Whole, by giving Part:
Heav'n, who foresaw the Will, the Means has wrought,
And to the Second Son, a Blessing brought:
The First-begotten had his Father's Share,
But you, like *Jacob*, are *Rebecca's* Heir.
  So may your Stores, and fruitful Fields increase;
And ever be you bless'd, who live to bless.
As *Ceres* sow'd where e'er her Chariot flew;
As Heav'n in Desarts rain'd the Bread of Dew,
So free to Many, to Relations most,
You feed with Manna your own *Israel*-Host.
  With Crowds attended of your ancient Race,

You seek the Champian-Sports, or Sylvan-Chace:
With well-breath'd Beagles, you surround the Wood,
Ev'n then, industrious of the Common Good:
And often have you brought the wily Fox
To suffer for the Firstlings of the Flocks;
Chas'd ev'n amid the Folds; and made to bleed,
Like Felons, where they did the murd'rous Deed.
This fiery Game, your active Youth maintain'd:
Not yet, by years extinguish'd, though restrain'd:
You season still with Sports your serious Hours;
For Age but tastes of Pleasures, Youth devours.
The Hare, in Pastures or in Plains is found,
Emblem of Humane Life, who runs the Round;
And, after all his wand'ring Ways are done,
His Circle fills, and ends where he begun,
Just as the Setting meets the Rising Sun.

. . . . . .

When, often urg'd, unwilling to be Great,
Your Country calls you from your lov'd Retreat,
And sends to Senates, charg'd with Common Care,
Which none more shuns; and none can better bear.
Where cou'd they find another form'd so fit,
To poise, with solid Sense, a spritely Wit!
Were these both wanting, (as they both abound)
Where cou'd so firm Integrity be found?
Well-born and Wealthy; wanting no Support,
You steer betwixt the Country and the Court:
Nor gratifie whate'er the Great desire,
Nor grudging give, what Publick Needs require.
Part must be left, a Fund when Foes invade;
And Part employ'd to roll the Watry Trade;
Ev'n *Canaans* happy Land, when worn with Toil,

Requir'd a Sabbath-Year, to mend the meagre Soil.
  Good senators, (and such are you,) so give,
That Kings may be supply'd, the People thrive;
And He, when Want requires, is truly Wise,
Who slights not Foreign Aids nor over-buys;
But, on our Native Strength, in time of need, relies.

. . . . . .

Our Foes, compell'd by Need have Peace embrac'd;
The Peace both Parties want, is like to last:
Which, if secure, securely we may trade;
Or, not secure, shou'd never have been made.
Safe in our selves, while on our selves we stand,
The Sea is ours, and that defends the Land.
Be, then, the Naval Stores the Nations Care,
New Ships to build, and batter'd to repair.
  Observe the War in ev'ry Annual Course;
What has been done, was done with *British* Force.
Namur Subdu'd, is *England's* Palm alone;
The Rest Besieged; but we Constrain'd the Town:
We saw th' Event that follow'd our Success;
France, though pretending Arms, pursu'd the Peace;
Oblig'd, by one sole Treaty, to restore
What Twenty Years of War had won before.
Enough for *Europe* has our *Albion* fought:
Let us enjoy the Peace our Blood has bought.
When once the *Persian* King was put to Flight,
The weary *Macedons* refus'd to fight:
Themselves their own Mortality confess'd;
And left the son of *Jove*, to quarrel for the rest.
  Ev'n Victors are by Victories undone;
Thus *Hannibal*, with Foreign Laurels won,
To *Carthage* was recall'd, too late to keep his own.

While sore of Battel, while our Wounds are green,
Why shou'd we tempt the doubtful Dye agen?
In Wars renew'd, uncertain of success,
Sure of a Share, as Umpires of the Peace.
A Patriot, both the King and Country serves;
Prerogative, and Privilege preserves:
Of Each, our Laws the certain Limit show;
One must not ebb, nor t' other overflow:
Betwixt the Prince and Parliament we stand;
The Barriers of the State on either Hand:
May neither overflow, for then they drown the Land.
When both are full, they feed our bless'd Abode;
Like those, that water'd once, the Paradise of God.
Some Overpoise of Sway, by Turns they share;
In Peace the People, and the Prince in War:
Consuls of mod'rate Pow'r in Calms were made;
When the *Gauls* came, one sole Dictator sway'd.
Patriots, in Peace, assert the Peoples Right,
With noble Stubbornness resisting Might:
No Lawless Mandates from the Court receive,
Nor lend by Force; but in a Body give.
Such was your gen'rous Grandsire; free to grant
In Parliaments, that weigh'd their Prince's Want:
But so tenacious of the Common Cause,
As not to lend the King against his Laws.
And, in a lothsom Dungeon doom'd to lie,
In Bonds retain'd his Birthright Liberty,
And shamed Oppression, till it set him free.
O true Descendent of a Patriot Line,
Who, while thou shar'st their Lustre, lend'st 'em thine,
Vouchsafe this Picture of thy Soul to see;
'Tis so far Good as it resembles thee:

The Beauties to th' Original I owe;
Which, when I miss, my own Defects I show.
Nor think the Kindred-Muses thy Disgrace;
A poet is not born in ev'ry Race.
Two of a House, few Ages can afford;
One to perform, another to record.
Praise-worthy Actions are by thee embrac'd;
And 'tis my Praise, to make thy Praises last.
For ev'n when Death dissolves our Humane Frame,
The Soul returns to Heav'n, from whence it came;
Earth keeps the Body, Verse preserves the Fame.

The Fables, 1700, lines 1–66; 119–39; 142–209

568 *From 'Sigismonda and Guiscardo'*

Ave atque Vale

THE Messenger dispatch'd, again she view'd
The lov'd Remains, and sighing, thus pursu'd:
Source of my Life, and Lord of my Desires,
In whom I liv'd, with whom my Soul expires;
Poor Heart, no more the Spring of Vital Heat,
Curs'd be the Hands that tore thee from thy Seat!
The Course is finish'd, which thy Fates decreed,
And thou, from thy Corporeal Prison freed:
Soon hast thou reach'd the Goal with mended Pace,
A World of Woes dispatch'd in little space:
Forc'd by thy Worth, thy Foe in Death become
Thy Friend, has lodg'd thee in a costly Tomb;
There yet remain'd thy Fun'ral Exequies,
The weeping Tribute of thy Widows Eyes;

And those, indulgent Heav'n has found the way
That I, before my Death, have leave to pay.
My Father ev'n in Cruelty is kind,
Or Heaven has turn'd the Malice of his Mind
To better Uses than his Hate design'd;
And made th' Insult, which in his Gift appears,
The Means to mourn thee with my pious Tears;
Which I will pay thee down, before I go,
And save my self the Pains to weep below,
If Souls can weep; though once I meant to meet
My Fate with Face unmov'd, and Eyes unwet,
Yet since I have thee here in narrow Room,
My Tears shall set thee first afloat within thy Tomb:
Then (as I know thy Spirit hovers nigh)
Under thy friendly Conduct will I fly
To Regions unexplor'd, secure to share
Thy State; nor Hell shall Punishment appear;
And Heav'n is double Heav'n, if thou art there.

The Fables, 1700, lines 49–680

569 *From 'Cymon and Iphigenia'*

The Power of Love

THE Fool of Nature, stood with stupid Eyes
And gaping Mouth, that testify'd Surprize,
Fix'd on her Face, nor cou'd remove his Sight,
New as he was to Love, and Novice in Delight:
Long mute he stood, and leaning on his Staff,
His Wonder witness'd with an Ideot laugh;
Then would have spoke, but by his glimmering Sense
First found his want of Words, and fear'd Offence:

Doubted for what he was he should be known,
By his Clown-Accent and his Country-Tone.
  Through the rude Chaos thus the running Light
Shot the first Ray that pierc'd the Native Night:
Then Day and Darkness in the Mass were mix'd,
Till gather'd in a Globe, the Beams were fix'd:
Last shone the Sun who, radiant in his Sphere
Illumin'd Heav'n, and Earth, and roll'd around the Year.
So Reason in this Brutal Soul began:
Love made him first suspect he was a Man;
Love made him doubt his broad barbarian Sound;
By Love his want of Words and Wit he found;
That sense of want prepar'd the future way
To Knowledge, and disclos'd the promise of a Day.
  What not his Father's Care, nor Tutor's Art
Cou'd plant with Pains in his unpolish'd Heart,
The best Instructor Love at once inspir'd,
As barren Grounds to Fruitfulness are fir'd;
Love taught him Shame, and Shame with Love at Strife
Soon taught the sweet Civilities of Life.

The Fables, 1700, lines 107–34

570 *Song*

FARWELL ungratefull Traytor,
  Farwell my perjur'd Swain,
Let never injur'd Creature
  Believe a Man again.
The Pleasure of Possessing
Surpasses all Expressing,
But 'tis too short a Blessing,
  And Love too long a Pain.

'Tis easie to deceive us
   In Pity of your Pain,
But when we love you leave us
   To rail at you in vain.
Before we have descry'd it,
There is no Bliss beside it,
But she that once has try'd it
   Will never love again.

The Passion you pretended
   Was only to obtain
But when the Charm is ended
   The Charmer you disdain.
Your Love by ours we measure
Till we have lost our Treasure,
But dying is a Pleasure,
   When Living is a Pain.

The Spanish Friar, 1681

571

A Song

FAIR, sweet and young, receive a prize
   Reserv'd for your Victorious Eyes:
   From Crowds, whom at your Feet you see,
   O pity, and distinguish me;
   As I from thousand Beauties more
Distinguish you, and only you adore.

   Your Face for Conquest was design'd,
   Your ev'ry Motion charms my Mind;
   Angels, when you your Silence break,
   Forget their Hymns to hear you speak;
   But when at once they hear and view,
Are loath to mount, and long to stay with you.

No Graces can your Form improve,
But all are lost, unless you love;
While that sweet Passion you disdain,
Your Veil and Beauty are in vain.
In pity then prevent my Fate,
For after dying all Reprieve 's too late.

Miscellany Poems, 1693

572 *A Song to a Fair Young Lady going out of Town in the Spring*

ASK not the Cause, why sullen Spring
So long delays her flow'rs to bear;
Why warbling Birds forget to sing,
And Winter Storms invert the Year?
Chloris is gone; and Fate provides
To make it *Spring*, where she resides.

Chloris is gone, the Cruel Fair;
She cast not back a pitying Eye:
But left her Lover in Despair,
To sigh, to languish, and to die:
Ah, how can those fair Eyes endure
To give the wounds they will not cure!

Great God of Love, why hast thou made
A Face that can all Hearts command,
That all Religions can invade,
And change the Laws of ev'ry Land?
Where thou hadst plac'd such Pow'r before,
Thou shou'dst have made her Mercy more.

When *Chloris* to the Temple comes,
  Adoring Crowds before her Fall;
She can restore the Dead from Tombs,
  And every Life but mine recall.
I only am by Love design'd
To be the Victim for Mankind.

Miscellany Poems, 1704

NATHANIEL WANLEY

1634–1680

573 *Royall Presents*

THE off'rings of the Easterne kings of old
Unto our lord were Incense, Myrrh and Gold;
Incense because a God; Gold as a king;
And Myrrh as to a dying Man they bring.
Instead of Incense (Blessed Lord) if we
Can send a sigh or fervent Prayer to thee,
Instead of Myrrh if we can but provide
Teares that from penitential eyes do slide,
And though we have no Gold; if for our part
We can present thee with a broken heart
Thou wilt accept: and say those Easterne kings
Did not present thee with more precious things.

Scintillulae Sacrae (Br. Mus. Add. MS. 22472)

574 *The Sigh*

AH! with what freedome could I once have pray'd,
And drench'd in teares my supplications made,
Wing'd 'em with sighs, to send 'em how I strove
By wind or water to my God above;

But now of late methinks I feele
My selfe transforming into steele.
Nothing that's hard but doth impart
Its stubborne hardnesse to my heart.

Ah! with what ardour could I once have heard,
How hath this heart of mine been sweetly stirr'd,
Quick'ned and rais'd to such a lively frame
That I have wondred how and whence it came!
But now alas those dayes are done,
There is more life in stocks or stone;
Nothing more indispos'd can be,
Ah! lead it selfe is light to me.

Ah! when the beames of light on me did shine
How did I gaze on heav'n and thinke it mine.
Then could I spurne at earth as at a toy,
No such poore limits then could bound my Joy;
But ah! how are those white houres fled,
That earth I spurn'd now fills my head,
And I that aim'd than starres more high
Now grov'ling in a dust heape lye.

Ah me! my God, if a deepe sigh or groane
May find thy gracious eare or reach thy throne,
Oh thence dispatch a word, speake till I heare:
Hence-forth be this your posture; AS YOU WERE.

Scintillulae Sacrae (Br. Mus. Add. MS. 22472)

NATHANIEL WANLEY

575 *Humaine Cares*

THESE pretty little birds see how
They skip from bough to bough,
Tuning their sweet melodious notes
Through warbling slender throates,
Nor caring where they next shall feed,
Upon what little worme or seed.

The glitt'ring sparkles of the night
How free they spend their light,
As nimble Fairyes on the ground
They smile and dance the round,
Carelesse where 'tis they shall repaire
That oyle that makes them shine so faire.

The purling waters glide away
And o'er blew pebbles stray,
They leave their fountaines farre behind,
And thousand circles wind
About the Flow'ry meadowes side,
Not doubting but to be supply'd.

The Trees do bud and bloome and grow
And boast their plenty so
As if they fear'd no pilfring hand
Or blustring winds command,
Or nipping frosts should them undresse
And make their leavy glories lesse.

But Man alone, poore foolish man
Who scarce lives out a span,

Is stock'd with cares and Idle feares
For full one hundred yeares,
And as if wanting griefe he must
Go take up sorrow upon trust.

Scintillulae Sacrae (Br. Mus. Add. MS. 22472)

SIR GEORGE ETHEREGE

1635?–1691

576 *Song*

LADIES, though to your Conqu'ring eyes
Love owes his chiefest Victories,
And borrows those bright Arms from you
With which he does the world subdue;
Yet you your selves are not above
The Empire nor the Griefs of Love.

Then wrack not Lovers with disdain,
Lest Love on you revenge their Pain;
You are not free because y'are fair;
The Boy did not his Mother spare.
Beauty 's but an offensive dart;
It is no Armour for the heart.

The Comical Revenge, Act v, Sc. 3, 1664

577 *(Chloris, 'tis not in your power)*

CHLORIS, 'tis not in your power
To say how long our love will last:
It may be, we within this hour,
May lose those joys we now may taste.
The blessed that immortal be
From change in love are only free.

And though you now immortal seem,
Such is th' exactness of your fame:
Those that your beauty so esteem,
Will find it cannot last the same:
 Love from mine eyes has stoln my fire,
 As apt to waste, and to expire.

Then since we mortal Lovers are,
Let's question not how long 'twill last;
But while we love let us take care,
Each minute be with pleasure past:
 It were a madness, to deny
 To live, because w' are sure to die.

Fear not, though love and beauty fail,
My reason shall my heart direct:
Your kindness now will then prevail,
And passion turn into respect:
 Chloris, at worst, you'll in the end
 But change your Lover for a Friend.

New Academy of Compliments, 1671

ANONYMOUS

578 *The Lark*

SWIFT through the yielding Air I glide,
 While nights sable shades abide:
Yet in my flight (though ne'er so fast)
I Tune and Time the wilde winds blast:
And ere the Sun be come about,
Teach the young Lark his Lesson out;
Who early as the Day is born
Sings his shrill Anthem to the rising Morn:

Let never Mortal lose the pains
To imitate my Aiery strains,
Whose pitch too high for humane Ears,
Was set me by the tuneful Spheres.
I carol to the Fairies King,
Wake him a-mornings when I sing:
And when the Sun stoops to the deep,
Rock him again and his fair Queen asleep.

J. Playford, *Select Ayres*, 1669

579 *Beauty extoll'd*

GAZE not on Swans, in whose soft breast
A full-hatch'd Beauty seems to nest,
Nor Snow, which falling from the Sky,
Hovers in its Virginity.

Gaze not on Roses, though new-blown,
Grac'd with a fresh complexion;
Nor Lillies, which no subtle Bee
Hath robb'd by kissing Chymistrie.

Gaze not on that pure milky way,
Where night vies splendour with the day;
Nor pearl, whose Silver Walls confine
The riches of an Indian mine.

For if my Emperess appears,
Swans moulting die, Snow melts to tears;
Roses do blush and hang their heads,
Pale Lillies shrink into their beds.

The milky way rides post to shroud
Its baffl'd glory in a cloud;
And Pearls do climb into her ear,
To hang themselves for envy there.

So have I seen Stars big with light,
Prove lanthorns to the Moon-eyed Night;
Which when *Sol's* Rayes were once display'd,
Sunk in their sockets, and decay'd.

Wits Interpreter, 1671 (1st ed. 1655)

580 *A Messe of Nonsense*

UPON a dark, light, gloomy, sunshine day,
As I in *August* walkt to gather *May*,
It was at noon neer ten a clock at night,
The Sun being set did shine exceeding bright,
I with mine eyes began to hear a noise,
And turn'd my Ears about to see the voice,
When from a cellar seven stories high,
With loud low voice *Melpomene* did cry,
What sober madness hath possest your brains,
And men of no place? shall your easie pains
Be thus rewarded? passing *Smithfield* bars,
Cast up the blear-ey'd eyes down to the stars,
And see the Dragons head in Quartile move,
Now *Venus* is with *Mercury* in love:
Mars patient rages in a fustian fume,
And *Jove* will be reveng'd or quit the room:
Mild *Juno*, beauteous *Saturn*, *Martia* free,
At ten leagues distance now assembled be.
Then shut your eyes and see bright *Iris* mount
Five hundred fathoms deep by just account,
And with a noble ignominious train
Pass flying to the place where *Mars* was slain:
Thus silently she spake, whilst I mine eyes
Fixt on the ground advanced to the skies.

And then not speaking any word reply'd
Our noble family is near ally'd
To that renowned peasant George a Green:
Stout *Wakefield* Pinner, he that stood between
Achilles and the fierce *Eacides*,
And them withstood with most laborious ease,
Yet whilst that *Boreas* and kind *Auster* lie
Together, and at once the same way flie;
And that unmoved wandring fixed star,
That bloody peace foretells, and patient War,
And scares the earth with fiery apparitions,
And plants in men both good and bad conditions;
I ever will with my weak able pen
Subscribe myself your Servant
Francis Ben.

Wits Interpreter, 1671 (1st ed. 1655)

581 *A Devonshire Song*

THOU nere wilt riddle neighbour *John*
Where ich of late have been a;
Why ich have been at Plimouth, mon,
The like hath never been a,
Zich streets, zich men, zich huge zea,
Zich things, zich guns, there rumbling,
Thy zelf like me would bless to zee,
Zich bomination jumbling.

The Town is pitcht with shingle stone,
Do glisten like the ze-a,
The zhops stand ope, and all year long
A Vair I think there be a;
The King zome zwear himself was there,
A man or some such thing a.

Shouldst thou that had no water past
   But thick same in the meer a;
Didst zee the Zea wouldst be agast,
   Vort did zo ztream and rore:
Zo zalt did taste, thy tongue would think
   The vire were in the water;
And 'tus so wide, no land's espy'd,
   Look nere so long thereafter.

The water from the element,
   No man can zee before a,
The Zea was low, yet all anent
   'Twas higher than the Moor a:
'Tis Marle how looking down the cliffe,
   Men do look upward rather,
If these mine eyes had not it zeen,
   Had scarce believ'd my Vather.

Amid the water wooden birds,
   And vlying houses zwim a,
And vull of things as ich have heard,
   And men up to the brim a:
They row unto another world
   And venture to conquer a.
And with their guns voul devellish onds
   They dunder and spit fire a.

Good neighbour *John*, how var is it
   This marle, for ich shall see a.
Ich mope no longer here that's vlat,
   To watch a Zheep or Tree a,

Marle: Marvel.   onds: breaths.

Though it so big as *London* be
Wech ten mile I imagine,
Ich thither Hie, for this place I
Do take it in great dudgeon.

Wits Interpreter, 1671 (1st ed. 1665)

582 *Against Platonick Love*

'TIS true, fair *Celia*, that by thee I live;
That every kiss, and every fond embrace,
Forms a new soul within me, and doth give
A balsam to the wound made by thy face.
Yet still methinks I miss
That bliss,
Which Lovers dare not name,
And only then described is,
When flame doth meet with flame.

Those favours which do bless me every day,
Are yet but empty and Platonical.
Think not to please your servants with half pay.
Good Gamesters never stick to throw at all.
Who can endure to miss
That bliss,
Which Lovers dare not name,
And only then described is,
When flame doth meet with flame.

If all those sweets within you must remain
Unknown and ne'er enjoy'd, like hidden treasure,
Nature as well as I, will lose her name,
And you as well as I your youthful pleasure,

We wrong ourselves to miss
  That bliss,
Which Lovers dare not name,
And only then described is,
When flame doth meet with flame.

Our souls which long have peept at one another
Out of the narrow casements of our eyes,
Shall now by love conducted meet together,
In secret caverns, where all pleasures lies:
  There, there we shall not miss
    That bliss,
  Which Lovers dare not name,
  And only then described is,
  When flame doth meet with flame.

Wits Interpreter, 1671 (1st ed. 1655)

583

Age not to be rejected

AM I despis'd because, you say,
  And I believe, that I am gray?
Know Lady, you have but your day,
And night will come, when men will swear,
Time has spilt snow upon your hair:
Then, when in your glass you seek,
But find no Rose-bud in your cheek;
No, nor the Bed to give a shew,
Where such a rare Carnation grew,
And such a smiling Tulip too,
Ah! then too late, close in your Chamber keeping,
    It will be told
    That you are old
  By those true tears y'are weeping.

Wits Interpreter, 1671 (1st ed. 1655)

584 *Song*

HANG sorrow, cast away care,
    Come let us drink up our Sack;
They say it is good,
        To cherish the blood,
        And eke to strengthen the back;
'Tis wine that makes the thoughts aspire,
        And fills the body with heat,
Beside 'tis good
        If well understood
        To fit a man for the Feat:
Then call,
        And drink up all,
        The Drawer is ready to fill,
A pox of care
        What need we to spare,
        My Father hath made his Will.

Academy of Compliments, 1671

585 (*When Aurelia first I courted*)

WHEN *Aurelia* first I courted,
    She had youth and Beauty too,
Killing pleasures when she sported,
And her Charms were ever new;
Conquering Time doth now deceive her,
Which her Glories did uphold,
All her Arts can ne'er retrieve her,
Poor *Aurelia's* growing old.

The airy Spirits which invited,
Are retir'd, and move no more,
And those eyes are now benighted,
Which were Comets heretofore.
Want of these abate her merits,
Yet I've passion for her name,
Only kind and am'rous Spirits,
Kindle and maintain a flame.

New Academy of Compliments, 1671

586

A Song

CHLORIS, when I to thee present
The cause of all my discontent;
And shew that all the wealth that can
Flow from this little world of man,
Is nought but Constancy and Love,
Why will you other objects prove?

O do not cozen your desires
With common and mechanick fires:
That picture which you see in gold,
In every Shop is to be sold,
And Diamonds of richest prize
Men only value with their eyes.

But look upon my loyal heart,
That knows to value every part:
And loves thy hidden virtue more
Than outward shape, which fools adore:
In that you'll all the treasures find
That can content a noble mind.

Westminster Drolleries, 1671–2

587 *On his Mistris that lov'd Hunting*

LEAVE *Cælia*, leave the woods to chase,
'Tis not a sport, nor yet a place
For one that has so sweet a face.

Nets in thy hand, Nets in thy brow,
In every limb a snare, and thou
Dost lavish them thou car'st not how.

Fond Girle these wild haunts are not best
To hunt: nor is a Savage beast
A fit prey for so sweet a breast.

O do but cast thine eyes behind,
I'll carry thee where thou shalt find
A tame heart of a better kind.

One that hath set soft snares for thee,
Snares where if once thou fettered be,
Thou'lt never covet to be free.

The Dews of *April*, the Winds of *May*
That flow'rs the Meads, and glads the Day
Are not more soft, more sweet than they.

And when thou chancest for to kill,
Thou needst not fear no other ill
Than Turtles suffer when they Bill.

Westminster Drolleries, 1671–2

588 *On his Mistress going from home*

SO does the Sun withdraw his Beames,
From off the Northern coasts and streames;
When Clouds and Frosts ensue,
And leaves the melancholy Slaves

Stupid and dull as near their Graves,
    Till he their joys renew.
Those that in *Greenland* followed Game
Too long, and found when back they came,
Their Shipping gone, believed they must die
Ere Succour came; but yet more blest than I.

How soon our happiness does fly,
Like Sounds, which with their Ecchoes dye,
    And leave us in a Trance,
Bewailing we had e'er enjoy'd
The blessing, since 'tis still destroyed,
    By some unhappy chance.
Why should the spiteful stars agree,
To vex and mock mortality?
For thus, like Traytors which in darkness lie,
W'are only brought into the light to die.

In dreams things are not as they seem.
Else, what's fruition but a dream
    When the possession's past?
Alas: to say we were, we had,
Is poor content, and e'en as bad
As if w' had ne'er had taste.
Fire in great Frosts, small time possest,
Produces pain instead of rest:
So does the short enjoyment of such bliss,
And till restored, continual torment is.

Covent Garden Drollery, 1672

THOMAS TRAHERNE

1637?–1674

589 *The Salutation*

THESE little Limbs,
These Eyes and Hands which here I find,
This panting Heart wherewith my Life begins;
Where have ye been? Behind
What Curtain were ye from me hid so long?
Where was, in what Abyss, my new-made Tongue?

When silent I
So many thousand thousand Years
Beneath the Dust did in a *Chaos* lie,
How could I *Smiles*, or *Tears*,
Or *Lips*, or *Hands*, or *Eyes*, or *Ears* perceive?
Welcome ye Treasures which I now receive.

I that so long
Was *Nothing* from Eternity,
Did little think such Joys as Ear and Tongue
To celebrate or see:
Such Sounds to hear, such Hands to feel, such Feet,
Such Eyes and Objects, on the Ground to meet.

New burnisht Joys!
Which finest Gold and Pearl excell!
Such sacred Treasures are the Limbs of Boys
In which a Soul doth dwell:
Their organized Joints and azure Veins
More Wealth include than the dead World contains.

From Dust I rise
And out of Nothing now awake;
These brighter Regions which salute mine Eyes
A Gift from God I take:
The Earth, the Seas, the Light, the lofty Skies,
The Sun and Stars are mine; if these I prize.

A Stranger here
Strange things doth meet, strange Glory see,
Strange Treasures lodg'd in this fair World appear,
Strange all and New to me:
But that they *mine* should be who Nothing was,
That Strangest is of all; yet brought to pass.

Poems of Felicity (Br. Mus. Burney MS. 392)

590

The Rapture

SWEET Infancy!
O Heavenly Fire! O Sacred Light!
How fair and Bright!
How Great am I
Whom the whole World doth magnify!

O heavenly Joy!
O Great and Sacred Blessedness
Which I possess!
So great a Joy
Who did into my Arms convey?

From God above
Being sent, the Gift doth me enflame
To praise his Name;
The Stars do move,
The Sun doth shine, to shew his Love.

O how Divine
Am I! To all this Sacred Wealth,
This Life and Health,
Who rais'd? Who mine
Did make the same? What hand divine?

Poems of Felicity (Br. Mus. Burney MS. 392)

591 *Solitude*

HOW desolate!
Ah! how forlorn, how sadly did I stand
When in the field my woful State
I felt! Not all the Land,
Not all the Skies,
Tho Heaven shin'd before mine Eyes,
Could Comfort yield in any Field to me,
Nor could my Mind Contentment find or see.

Remov'd from Town,
From People, Churches, Feasts, and Holidays,
The Sword of State, the Mayor's Gown,
And all the Neighb'ring Boys;
As if no Kings
On Earth there were, or living Things,
The silent Skies salute mine Eyes, the Seas
My Soul surround; no Rest I found, or Ease.

My roving Mind
Search'd ev'ry Corner of the spacious Earth,
From Sky to Sky, if it could find,
(But found not) any Mirth:

Not all the Coasts,
Nor all the great and glorious Hosts,
In Heav'n or Earth, did any Mirth afford;
No welcome Good or needed Food, my Board.

I do believe,
The Ev'ning being shady and obscure,
The very Silence did me grieve,
And Sorrow more procure:
A secret Want
Did make me think my Fortune scant.
I was so blind, I could not find my Health,
No Joy mine Eye could there espy, nor Wealth.

Nor could I guess
What kind of thing I long'd for: But that I
Did somewhat lack of Blessedness,
Beside the Earth and Sky,
I plainly found;
It griev'd me much, I felt a Wound
Perplex me sore; yet what my Store should be
I did not know, nothing would shew to me.

Ye sullen Things!
Ye dumb, ye silent Creatures, and unkind!
How can I call you Pleasant Springs
Unless ye ease my Mind!
Will ye not speak
What 'tis I want, nor Silence break?
O pity me, and let me see some Joy;
Some Kindness shew to me, altho a Boy.

They silent stood;
Nor Earth, nor Woods, nor Hills, nor Brooks, nor Skies,
Would tell me where the hidden Good,
Which I did long for, lies:
The shady Trees,
The Ev'ning dark, the humming Bees,
The chirping Birds, mute Springs and Fords, conspire,
While they deny to answer my Desire.

Bells ringing I
Far off did hear; some Country Church they spake;
The Noise re-ecchoing through the Sky
My Melancholy brake;
When 't reacht mine Ear
Some Tidings thence I hop'd to hear:
But not a Bell me News could tell, or shew
My longing Mind, where Joys to find, or know.

I griev'd the more,
'Cause I therby somewhat encourag'd was
That I from thence should learn my Store;
For Churches are a place
That nearer stand
Than any part of all the Land
To Heav'n; from whence some little Sense I might
To help my Mind receive, and find some Light.

They louder sound
Than men do talk, something they should Disclose;
The empty Sound did therefore wound
Because not shew Repose.

It did revive
To think that Men were there alive;
But had my Soul, call'd by the Toll, gone in,
I might have found, to ease my Wound, a Thing.

A little Ease
Perhaps, but that might more molest my Mind;
One flatt'ring Drop would more disease
My Soul with Thirst, and grind
My Heart with grief:
For People can yield no Relief
In publick sort when in that Court they shine,
Except they move my Soul with Love divine.

Th' External Rite,
Altho the face be wondrous sweet and fair,
Can satiate my Appetite
No more than empty Air
Yield solid Food.
Must I the best and highest Good
Seek to possess; or Blessedness in vain
(Tho 'tis alive in some place) strive to gain?

O! what would I
Diseased, wanting, melancholy, give
To find *that* true Felicity,
The place where Bliss doth live?
Those Regions fair
Which are not lodg'd in Sea nor Air,
Nor Woods, nor Fields, nor Arbour yields, nor Springs,
Nor Heavens shew to us below, nor Kings.

I might have gone
Into the City, Market, Tavern, Street,
Yet only chang'd my Station,
And strove in vain to meet
That Ease of Mind
Which all alone I long'd to find:
A common Inn doth no such thing betray,
Nor doth it walk in People's Talk, or Play.

O Eden fair!
Where shall I seek the Soul of Holy Joy,
Since I to find it here despair?
Nor in the shining Day,
Nor in the Shade,
Nor in the Field, nor in a Trade
I can it see. Felicity! Oh, where
Shall I thee find to ease my Mind? Oh, where?

Poems of Felicity (Br. Mus. Burney MS. 392)

592 *On Christmas-Day*

SHALL Dumpish Melancholy spoil my Joys
While Angels sing
And Mortals ring
My Lord and Savior's Praise!
Awake from Sloth, for that alone destroys,
'Tis Sin defiles, 'tis Sloth puts out thy Joys.
See how they run from place to place,
And seek for Ornaments of Grace;
Their Houses deckt with sprightly Green,
In Winter makes a Summer seen;
They Bays and Holly bring
As if 'twere Spring!

Shake off thy Sloth, my drouzy Soul, awake;
With Angels sing
Unto thy King,
And pleasant Musick make;
Thy Lute, thy Harp, or else thy Heart-strings take,
And with thy Musick let thy Sense awake.
See how each one the other calls
To fix his Ivy on the walls,
Transplanted there it seems to grow
As if it rooted were below:
Thus He, who is thy King,
Makes Winter, Spring.

Shall Houses clad in Summer-Liveries
His Praises sing
And laud thy King,
And wilt not thou arise?
Forsake thy Bed, and grow (my Soul) more wise,
Attire thy self in cheerful Liveries:
Let pleasant Branches still be seen
Adorning thee, both quick and green;
And, which with Glory better suits,
Be laden all the Year with Fruits;
Inserted into Him,
For ever spring.

'Tis He that Life and Spirit doth infuse:
Let ev'ry thing
The Praises sing
Of *Christ* the King of Jews;
Who makes things green, and with a Spring infuse
A Season which to see it doth not use:

Old Winter's Frost and hoary hair,
With Garland's crowned, Bays doth wear;
The nipping Frost of Wrath b'ing gone,
To Him the Manger made a Throne,
Due Praises let us sing,
Winter and Spring.

See how, their Bodies clad with finer Cloaths,
They now begin
His Praise to sing
Who purchas'd their Repose:
Wherby their inward Joy they do disclose;
Their Dress alludes to better Works than those:
His gayer Weeds and finer Band,
New Suit and Hat, into his hand
The Plow-man takes; his neatest Shoes,
And warmer Gloves, he means to use:
And shall not I, my King,
Thy Praises sing?

See how their Breath doth smoke, and how they haste
His Praise to sing
With Cherubim;
They scarce a Break-fast taste;
But through the Streets, lest precious Time should waste,
When Service doth begin, to Church they haste.
And shall not I, Lord, come to Thee,
The Beauty of thy Temple see?
Thy Name with Joy I will confess,
Clad in my Saviour's Righteousness;
'Mong all thy Servants sing
To Thee my King.

'Twas thou that gav'st us Cause for fine Attires;
Ev'n thou, O King,
As in the Spring,
Dost warm us with thy fires
Of Love: Thy Blood hath bought us new Desires;
Thy Righteousness doth cloath with new Attires.
Both fresh and fine let me appear
This Day divine, to close the Year;
Among the rest let me be seen
A living Branch and always green,
Think it a pleasant thing
Thy Praise to sing.

At break of Day, O how the Bells did ring!
To thee, my King,
The Bells did ring;
To thee the Angels sing:
Thy Goodness did produce this other Spring,
For this it is they make the Bells to ring:
The sounding Bells do through the Air
Proclaim thy Welcome far and near;
While I alone with Thee inherit
All these Joys, beyond my Merit.
Who would not always sing
To such a King?

I all these Joys, above my Merit, see
By Thee, my King,
To whom I sing,
Entire convey'd to me.
My Treasure, Lord, thou mak'st the People be
That I with pleasure might thy Servants see.

Ev'n in their rude external ways
They do set forth my Savior's Praise,
And minister a Light to me;
While I by them do hear to Thee
  Praises, my Lord and King,
    Whole Churches ring.

Hark how remoter Parishes do sound!
    Far off they ring
    For thee, my King,
  Ev'n round about the Town:
The Churches scatter'd over all the Ground
Serve for thy Praise, who art with Glory crown'd.
  This City is an Engine great
  That makes my Pleasure more compleat;
  The Sword, the Mace, the Magistrate,
  To honor Thee attend in State;
    The whole Assembly sings;
      The Minster rings.

Poems of Felicity (Br. Mus. Burney MS. 392)

593 *Shadows in the Water*

IN unexperienc'd Infancy
  Many a sweet Mistake doth ly:
Mistake tho false, intending true;
A *Seeming* somewhat more than *View*,
  That doth instruct the Mind
  In Things that lie behind,
And many Secrets to us show
Which afterwards we come to know.

Thus did I by the Water's brink
Another World beneath me think;
And while the lofty spacious Skies
Reversed there abus'd mine Eyes,
  I fancy'd other Feet
  Came mine to touch or meet;
As by some Puddle I did play
Another World within it lay.

Beneath the Water People drown'd,
Yet with another Heav'n crown'd,
In spacious Regions seem'd to go
As freely moving to and fro:
  In bright and open Space
  I saw their very face;
Eyes, Hands, and Feet they had like mine;
Another Sun did with them shine.

'Twas strange that People there should walk,
And yet I could not hear them talk:
That through a little wat'ry Chink,
Which one dry Ox or Horse might drink,
  We other Worlds should see,
  Yet not admitted be;
And other Confines there behold
Of Light and Darkness, Heat and Cold.

I call'd them oft, but call'd in vain;
No Speeches we could entertain:
Yet did I there expect to find
Some other World, to please my Mind.

I plainly saw by these
A new *Antipodes*,
Whom, tho they were so plainly seen,
A Film kept off that stood between.

By walking Men's reversed Feet
I chanc'd another World to meet;
Tho it did not to View exceed
A Phantasm, 'tis a World indeed,
Where Skies beneath us shine,
And Earth by Art divine
Another face presents below,
Where People's feet against Ours go.

Within the Regions of the Air,
Compass'd about with Heav'ns fair,
Great Tracts of Land there may be found
Enricht with Fields and fertile Ground;
Where many num'rous Hosts,
In those far distant Coasts,
For other great and glorious Ends,
Inhabit, my yet unknown Friends.

O ye that stand upon the Brink,
Whom I so near me, through the Chink,
With Wonder see: What Faces there,
Whose Feet, whose Bodies, do ye wear?
I my Companions see
In You, another Me.
They seemed Others, but are We;
Our second Selves those Shadows be.

Look how far off those lower Skies
Extend themselves! scarce with mine Eyes
I can them reach, O ye my Friends,
What *Secret* borders on those Ends?
  Are lofty Heavens hurl'd
  'Bout your inferior World?
Are ye the Representatives
Of other People's distant Lives?

Of all the Play-mates which I knew
That here I do the Image view
In other Selves; what can it mean?
But that below the purling Stream
  Some unknown Joys there be
  Laid up in Store for me;
To which I shall, when that thin Skin
Is broken, be admitted in.

Poems of Felicity (Br. Mus. Burney MS. 392)

THOMAS FLATMAN

1637–1688

594 ### *A Thought of Death*

WHEN on my sick Bed I languish,
  Full of sorrow, full of anguish,
Fainting, gasping, trembling, crying,
Panting, groaning, speechless, dying,
My Soul just now about to take her flight
Into the Regions of eternal night;
  Oh tell me you,
That have been long below,
  What shall I do?
What shall I think, when cruel Death appears,
That may extenuate my fears?

Methinks I hear some Gentle Spirit say,
  Be not fearful, come away!
Think with thy self that now thou shalt be free,
And find thy long expected liberty;
Better thou mayst, but worse thou can'st not be
Than in this Vale of Tears, and Misery.
Like *Cæsar*, with assurance then come on,
And unamaz'd attempt the Laurel Crown,
That lies on th' other side Death's *Rubicon*.

Poems, 1686

595 *The Defiance*

BE not too proud, imperious Dame,
  Your charms are transitory things,
May melt, while you at Heaven aim,
  Like *Icarus's* Waxen Wings;
And you a part in his misfortune bear,
Drown'd in a briny Ocean of despair.

You think your beauties are above
  The Poets Brain, and Painters Hand,
As if upon the Throne of Love
  You only should the World command:
Yet know, though you presume your title true,
There are pretenders, that will Rival you.

There's an experienc'd Rebel, Time,
  And in his Squadrons Poverty;
There's Age that brings along with him
  A terrible Artillery:
And if against all these thou keep'st thy Crown,
Th' Usurper Death will make thee lay it down.

Poems, 1686

THOMAS KEN

1637–1711

596 *A Morning Hymn*

AWAKE, my Soul, and with the Sun
Thy daily stage of Duty run,
Shake off dull sloth, and joyful rise,
To pay thy Morning sacrifice.

Thy precious Time misspent, redeem,
Each present Day thy last esteem,
Improve thy Talent with due care,
For the Great Day thyself prepare.

. . . . .

'Wake, and lift up thyself, my Heart,
And with the Angels bear thy part,
Who all night long unwearied sing,
High Praise to the Eternal King.

I wake, I wake, ye Heavenly Choir,
May your devotion me inspire,
That I like you my Age may spend,
Like you may on my God attend.

May I like you in God delight,
Have all day long my God in sight,
Perform like you my Maker's Will,
O may I never more do ill.

Had I your Wings, to Heaven I'd fly,
But God shall that defect supply,
And my Soul wing'd with warm desire,
Shall all day long to Heav'n aspire.

. . . . .

I would not wake, nor rise again,
Ev'n Heaven itself I would disdain,
Wert not Thou there to be enjoy'd,
And I in Hymns to be employ'd.

. . . .

Lord, I my vows to Thee renew,
Disperse my sins as Morning dew,
Guard my first springs of Thought and Will,
And with Thyself my spirit fill.

Direct, control, suggest, this day,
All I design, or do, or say,
That all my Powers, with all their might,
In Thy sole Glory may unite.

Manual for Winchester Scholars, 1712 (first version 1695)

597 *An Evening Hymn*

ALL Praise to Thee, my God, this night,
For all the Blessings of the Light;
Keep me, O keep me, King of Kings,
Beneath Thy own Almighty Wings.

Forgive me, Lord, for Thy dear Son,
The ill that I this day have done;
That with the World, myself and Thee,
I, ere I sleep, at peace may be.

Teach me to live, that I may dread
The Grave as little as my Bed;
To die, that this vile Body may
Rise glorious at the Awful Day.

THOMAS KEN

O! may my Soul on Thee repose,
And may sweet sleep my Eyelids close;
Sleep that may me more vigorous make,
To serve my God when I awake.

When in the night I sleepless lie,
My Soul with Heavenly Thoughts supply;
Let no ill Dreams disturb my Rest,
No powers of darkness me molest.

. . . . .

O when shall I in endless Day,
For ever chase dark sleep away;
And Hymns with the Supernal Choir,
Incessant sing, and never tire?

O may my Guardian, while I sleep,
Close to my Bed his Vigils keep;
His Love angelical instil;
Stop all the avenues of ill.

May he Celestial joy rehearse,
And thought to thought with me converse,
Or in my stead, all the night long,
Sing to my God a grateful Song.

Manual for Winchester Scholars, 1712 (first version 1695)

CHARLES SACKVILLE, EARL OF DORSET

1638–1706

598 *Song; Written at Sea, in the first Dutch War, 1665, the Night before an Engagement*

TO all you ladies now at land
 We men at sea indite;
But first wou'd have you understand
 How hard it is to write;
The Muses now, and Neptune too,
We must implore to write to you,
 With a fa, la, la, la, la.

For tho' the Muses should prove kind,
 And fill our empty brain;
Yet if rough Neptune rouze the wind,
 To wave the azure main,
Our paper, pen, and ink, and we,
Roll up and down our ships at sea,
 With a fa, la, la, la, la.

Then, if we write not by each post,
 Think not we are unkind;
Nor yet conclude our ships are lost
 By Dutchmen, or by wind:
Our tears we'll send a speedier way,
The tide shall bring 'em twice a day,
 With a fa, la, la, la, la.

The king with wonder, and surprize,
 Will swear the seas grow bold;
Because the tides will higher rise,
 Than e'er they us'd of old:

598. Actually written in 1664.

But let him know it is our tears
Bring floods of grief to Whitehall stairs.
  With a fa, la, la, la, la.

Should foggy Opdam chance to know
  Our sad and dismal story;
The Dutch wou'd scorn so weak a foe,
  And quit their fort at Goree:
For what resistance can they find
From men who've left their hearts behind!
  With a fa, la, la, la, la.

Let wind and weather do its worst,
  Be you to us but kind;
Let Dutchmen vapour, Spaniards curse,
  No sorrow we shall find:
'Tis then no matter how things go,
Or who 's our friend, or who 's our foe.
  With a fa, la, la, la, la.

To pass our tedious hours away,
  We throw a merry main;
Or else at serious ombre play;
  But, why should we in vain
Each others ruin thus pursue?
We were undone when we left you.
  With a fa, la, la, la, la.

But now our fears tempestuous grow,
  And cast our hopes away;
Whilst you, regardless of our woe,
  Sit careless at a play:
Perhaps permit some happier man
To kiss your hand, or flirt your fan.
  With a fa, la, la, la, la.

When any mournful tune you hear,
  That dies in ev'ry note;
As if it sigh'd with each man's care,
  For being so remote;
Think then how often love we've made
To you, when all those tunes were play'd.
  With a fa, la, la, la, la.

In justice you cannot refuse,
  To think of our distress;
When we for hopes of honour lose
  Our certain happiness;
All those designs are but to prove
Ourselves more worthy of your love.
  With a fa, la, la, la, la.

And now we've told you all our loves,
  And likewise all our fears;
In hopes this declaration moves
  Some pity from your tears:
Let's hear of no inconstancy,
We have too much of that at sea.
  With a fa, la, la, la, la.

Text from *Works*, 1749

599 (*Phillis for shame let us improve*)

PHILLIS for shame let us improve
  A thousand sev'ral wayes,
These few short Minutes snatchd by Love
  From many tedious days.

Whilst you want courage to despise
The Censures of the Grave;
For all the tyrants in your eyes,
Your heart is but a slave.

My Love is full of noble pride,
And never shall submit,
To let that Fop discretion ride
In triumph over wit.

False friends I have as well as you,
Who daily counsel me,
Fame and ambition to pursue,
And leave off loving thee.

When I the least belief bestow
On what such fools advise:
May I be dull enough to grow
Most miserable wise.

Playford, *Choice Ayres*, 1676

600 *Song*

DORINDA'S sparkling wit, and eyes,
United, cast too fierce a light,
Which blazes high, but quickly dies,
Pains not the heart, but hurts the sight.

Love is a calmer, gentler joy,
Smooth are his looks, and soft his pace;
Her Cupid is a black-guard boy,
That runs his link full in your face.

Text from *Works*, 1749

PHILIP AYRES

1638–1712

601 *On a Fair Beggar*

BAREFOOT and ragged, with neglected Hair,
She whom the Heavens at once made poor and fair,
With humble voice and moving words did stay,
To beg an Alms of all who passed that way.

But thousands viewing her became her Prize,
Willingly yeelding to her conquering Eyes,
And caught by her bright Hairs, whilst careless she
Makes them pay Homage to her Poverty.

So mean a Boon, said I, what can extort
From that fair Mouth, where wanton Love to sport
Amidst the Pearls and Rubies we behold?
Nature on thee has all her Treasures spread,
Do but incline thy rich and pretious Head,
And those fair Locks shall pour down showres of Gold.

Lyric Poems made in Imitation of the Italians, 1687

SIR CHARLES SEDLEY

1639?–1701

602 *(Ah Cloris! that I now could sit)*

AH *Cloris*! that I now could sit
As unconcern'd, as when
Your Infant Beauty cou'd beget
No pleasure, nor no pain.

601. Translated from the Italian of Achillini.

When I the Dawn us'd to admire,
  And prais'd the coming day;
I little thought the growing fire
  Must take my Rest away.

Your Charms in harmless Childhood lay,
  Like metals in the mine,
Age from no face took more away,
  Than Youth conceal'd in thine.

But as your Charms insensibly
  To their perfection prest,
Fond Love as unperceiv'd did flye,
  And in my Bosom rest.

My passion with your Beauty grew,
  And *Cupid* at my heart,
Still as his mother favour'd you,
  Threw a new flaming Dart.

Each glori'd in their wanton part,
  To make a Lover he
Employ'd the utmost of his Art,
  To make a Beauty she.

Though now I slowly bend to love
  Uncertain of my Fate,
If your fair self my Chains approve,
  I shall my freedom hate.

Lovers, like dying men, may well
  At first disorder'd be,
Since none alive can truly tell
  What Fortune they must see.

The Mulberry Garden, Act III, Sc. 2, 1668

603 *A Song to Celia*

NOT *Celia*, that I juster am
  Or better than the rest,
For I would change each Hour like them,
  Were not my Heart at rest.

But I am ty'd to very thee,
  By every Thought I have,
Thy Face I only care to see,
  Thy Heart I only crave.

All that in Woman is ador'd,
  In thy dear self I find,
For the whole Sex can but afford,
  The Handsome and the Kind.

Why then should I seek farther Store,
  And still make Love anew;
When Change it self can give no more,
  'Tis easie to be true.

Miscellaneous Works, 1702

604 *Song*

LOVE still has something of the Sea,
  From whence his Mother rose;
No time his Slaves from Doubt can free,
  Nor give their Thoughts repose:

They are becalm'd in clearest Days,
  And in rough Weather tost;
They wither under cold Delays,
  Or are in Tempests lost.

One while they seem to touch the Port,
Then straight into the Main,
Some angry Wind in cruel sport
The Vessel drives again.

At first Disdain and Pride they fear,
Which if they chance to 'scape,
Rivals and Falsehood soon appear
In a more dreadful shape.

By such Degrees to Joy they come,
And are so long withstood,
So slowly they receive the Sum,
It hardly does them good.

'Tis cruel to prolong a Pain;
And to defer a Joy,
Believe me, gentle *Celemene*,
Offends the winged Boy.

An hundred thousand Oaths your Fears
Perhaps would not remove;
And if I gaz'd a thousand Years
I could no deeper love.

Miscellaneous Works, 1702

605 *Phillis Knotting*

HEARS not my *Phillis*, how the Birds
Their feather'd Mates salute?
They tell their Passion in their Words;
Must I alone be mute?
Phillis, *without Frown or Smile,*
Sat and knotted all the while.

The God of Love in thy bright Eyes
  Does like a Tyrant reign;
But in thy Heart a Child he lyes,
  Without his Dart or Flame.
Phillis, *without Frown or Smile,*
Sat and knotted all the while.

So many Months in Silence past,
  And yet in raging Love,
Might well deserve one Word at last
  My Passion shou'd approve.
Phillis, *without Frown or Smile,*
Sat and knotted all the while.

Must then your faithful Swain expire,
  And not one Look obtain,
Which he, to sooth his fond Desire,
  Might pleasingly explain?
Phillis, *without Frown or Smile,*
Sat and knotted all the while.

Miscellaneous Works, 1702 (first printed 1694)

606

Song

PHILLIS is my only Joy,
  Faithless as the Winds or Seas;
Sometimes coming, sometimes coy,
  Yet she never fails to please;
    If with a Frown
    I am cast down,
    Phillis smiling,
    And beguiling,
Makes me happier than before.

Tho', alas, too late I find,
   Nothing can her Fancy fix;
Yet the Moment she is kind,
   I forgive her all her Tricks;
      Which, tho' I see,
      I can't get free;
      She deceiving,
      I believing;
What need Lovers wish for more?

Miscellaneous Works, 1702

APHRA BEHN

1640–1689

607 *Song. Love Arm'd*

LOVE in Fantastique Triumph satt,
   Whilst Bleeding Hearts around him flow'd,
For whom Fresh paines he did Create,
And strange Tyranick power he show'd;
From thy Bright Eyes he took his fire,
Which round about, in sport he hurl'd;
But 'twas from mine he took desire,
Enough to undo the Amorous World.

From me he took his sighs and tears,
From thee his Pride and Crueltie;
From me his Languishments and Feares,
And every Killing Dart from thee;
Thus thou and I, the God have arm'd,
And set him up a Deity;
But my poor Heart alone is harm'd,
Whilst thine the Victor is, and free.

Poems upon Several Occasions, 1684

HENRY ALDRICH

1647–1710

608

A Catch

IF all be true that I do think
There are *Five Reasons* we should drink;
Good Wine, a Friend, or being Dry,
Or lest we should be by and by;
Or any other Reason why.

H. Playford, *The Banquet of Musick*, Bk. 3, 1689

JOHN WILMOT, EARL OF ROCHESTER

1648–1680

609

The Mistress. A Song

AN Age in her Embraces past,
Would seem a Winter's Day;
Where Life and Light, with envious haste,
Are torn and snatch'd away.

But, oh! how slowly Minutes roul,
When absent from her Eyes,
That fed my Love, which is my Soul;
It languishes and dies.

For then no more a Soul but Shade,
It mournfully does move;
And haunts my Breast, by Absence made
The living Tomb of Love.

You wiser Men despise me not;
Whose Love-sick Fancy raves,
On Shades of Souls, and Heav'n knows what;
Short Ages live in Graves.

Whene'er those wounding Eyes, so full
  Of Sweetness, you did see;
Had you not been profoundly dull,
  You had gone mad like me.

Nor censure us, You who perceive
  My best belov'd and me,
Sigh and lament, complain and grieve,
  You think we disagree,

Alas! 'tis sacred Jealousie,
  Love rais'd to an Extream;
The only Proof 'twixt them and me,
  We love, and do not dream.

Fantastick Fancies fondly move;
  And in frail Joys believe,
Taking false Pleasure for true Love;
  But Pain can ne'er deceive.

Kind jealous Doubts, tormenting Fears,
  And anxious Cares, when past,
Prove our Hearts Treasure fix'd and dear,
  And make us blest at last.

Text from *Poems on Several Occasions*, 1705

610 *A Song*

ABSENT from thee I languish still;
  Then ask me not, When I return?
The straying Fool 'twill plainly kill,
  To wish all Day, all Night to mourn.

Dear; from thine Arms then let me fly,
 That my fantastick Mind may prove,
The Torments it deserves to try,
 That tears my fixt Heart from my Love.

When wearied with a World of Woe,
 To thy safe Bosom I retire,
Where Love and Peace and Truth does flow,
 May I contented there expire.

Lest once more wand'ring from that Heav'n,
 I fall on some base Heart unblest;
Faithless to thee, false, unforgiven,
 And lose my everlasting Rest.

Text from *Poems*, 1705

611 *Love and Life. A Song*

ALL my past Life is mine no more,
 The flying Hours are gone:
Like transitory Dreams giv'n o'er,
Whose Images are kept in store
 By Memory alone.

The Time that is to come is not;
 How can it then be mine?
The present Moment's all my Lot;
And that, as fast as it is got,
 Phillis, is only thine.

Then talk not of Inconstancy,
 False Hearts, and broken Vows;
If I, by Miracle, can be
This live-long Minute true to thee,
 'Tis all that Heav'n allows.

Text from *Poems*, 1705

612 *Upon Drinking in a Bowl*

VULCAN contrive me such a Cup
As *Nestor* us'd of old:
Shew all thy Skill to trim it up;
Damask it round with Gold.

Make it so large, that, fill'd with Sack
Up to the swelling Brim,
Vast Toasts, on the delicious Lake,
Like Ships at Sea, may swim.

Engrave not Battel on his Cheek;
With War I've nought to do:
I'm none of those that took *Mastrick*,
Nor *Yarmouth* Leaguer knew.

Let it no Name of Planets tell,
Fixt Stars, or Constellations:
For I am no Sir *Sidrophel*,
Nor none of his Relations.

But carve thereon a spreading Vine;
Then add two lovely Boys;
Their Limbs in amorous Folds intwine,
The Type of future Joys.

Cupid and *Bacchus* my Saints are;
May Drink and Love still reign:
With Wine I wash away my Cares,
And then to Love again.

Text from *Poems*, 1705

Sir *Sidrophel*: an astrologer in Butler's *Hudibras*.

613 *Constancy. A Song*

I CANNOT change, as others do,
  Though you unjustly scorn:
Since that poor Swain that Sighs for you,
  For you alone was born.
No, *Phillis*, no, your Heart to move
  A surer way I'll try:
And to revenge my slighted Love,
  Will still love on, will still love on, and die.

When, kill'd with Grief, *Amintas* lies;
  And you to mind shall call,
The Sighs that now unpitied rise,
  The Tears that vainly fall.
That welcome Hour that ends this Smart,
  Will then begin your Pain;
For such a faithful tender Heart
  Can never break, can never break in vain.

Text from *Poems*, 1705

614 *Upon Nothing*

NOTHING! thou elder Brother ev'n to Shade,
  Thou hadst a being ere the World was made,
And (well fixt) art alone, of Ending not afraid.

Eer time and place were, time and place were not,
When primitive *Nothing* something streight begot,
Then all proceeded from the great united—What.

Something, the gen'ral Attribute of all,
Sever'd from thee, its sole Original,
Into thy boundless self must undistinguish'd fall.

Yet Something did thy mighty Pow'r command,
And from thy fruitful Emptiness's hand,
Snatch'd Men, Beasts, Birds, Fire, Air, and Land.

Matter, the wickedst Off-spring of thy Race,
By Form assisted, flew from thy embrace,
And Rebel Light obscur'd thy reverend dusky Face.

With Form, and Matter, Time and Place did join,
Body, thy Foe, with thee did Leagues combine,
To spoil thy peaceful Realm, and ruin all thy Line.

But turn-coat Time assists the Foe in vain,
And, brib'd by thee, assists thy short-liv'd Reign,
And to thy hungry Womb drives back thy Slaves again.

Tho' Mysteries are barr'd from Laick Eyes,
And the Divine alone, with Warrant, pries
Into thy Bosom, where the Truth in private lies,

Yet this of thee the Wise may freely say,
Thou from the Virtuous nothing tak'st away,
And to be part with thee the Wicked wisely pray.

Great Negative, how vainly would the Wise
Enquire, define, distinguish, teach, devise,
Didst thou not stand to point their dull Philosophies?

Is, or *is not*, the two great Ends of Fate,
And, true or false, the Subject of Debate,
That perfect, or destroy, the vast Designs of Fate,

When they have rack'd the *Politician's* Breast,
Within thy Bosom must securely rest,
And, when reduc'd to thee, are least unsafe and best.

But, *Nothing*, why does *Something* still permit,
That Sacred Monarchs should at Council sit,
With Persons highly thought at best for nothing fit.

Whilst weighty *Something* modestly abstains
From Princes Coffers, and from Statesmen's Brains,
And Nothing there like stately *Nothing* reigns.

Nothing, who dwell'st with Fools in grave disguise,
For whom they reverend Shapes, and Forms devise,
Lawn Sleeves, and Furs, and Gowns, when they like thee
look wise.

French Truth, *Dutch* Prowess, *Brittish* Policy,
Hibernian Learning, *Scotch* Civility,
Spaniards Dispatch, *Danes* Wit, are mainly seen in thee.

The great Man's Gratitude to his best Friend,
King's Promises, Whores Vows, tow'rds thee they bend,
Flow swiftly into thee, and in thee ever end.

Poems, 1705

615 *An Allusion to Horace. The Tenth Satire of the First Book*

Nempe incomposito dixi pede, &c. . . .

WELL, Sir, 'tis granted, I said D(ryden's) Rhimes,
Were stol'n, unequal, nay dull many times;
What foolish Patron, is there found of his,
So blindly partial, to deny me this?
But that his Plays, embroider'd up and down
With Wit and Learning, justly pleas'd the Town
In the same Paper, I as freely own.
Yet having this allow'd, the heavy Mass,

That stuffs up his loose *Columns*, must not pass:
For by that Rule, I might as well admit,
C(rown's) tedious Sense, for Poetry and Wit.
'Tis therefore not enough, when your false Sense
Hits the false Judgement of an Audience
Of clapping Fools, assembled in vast crowd,
Till the throng'd Play-House crack with the dull load;
Though ev'n that Talent merits in some sort,
That can divert the City and the Court.
Which blund'ring S(ettle), never could attain,
And puzling O(tway), labours at in vain.
But within due proportions circumscribe
What e'er you write, that with a flowing Tide,
The Style may rise, yet in its rise forbear,
With useless Words, t'oppress the Weary'd Ear.
Here be your Language lofty, there more light,
Your Rhetorick with your Poetry unite:
For Elegance sake, sometimes allay the Force
Of *Epithets*, 'twill soften the discourse;
A jest in scorn points out, and hits the thing
More home, than the *Morosest* Satires sting.
Shake-spear and *Johnson* did herein excell,
And might in this be imitated well;
Whom refin'd E(theredge), copies not at all,
But is himself, a sheer Original.
Nor that slow Drudge, in swift *Pindarick* strains,
F(latman), who C(owley) imitates with pains,
And rides a jaded *Muse*, whipt with loose Rains.
When L(ee), makes temp'rate *Scipio*, fret and rave,
And *Hannibal*, a whining Amorous Slave,
I laugh, and wish the hot-brained Fustian-Fool,
In B(usby's) hands, to be well lasht at School.

Of all our Modern Wits none seems to me,
Once to have toucht upon true Comedy,
But hasty S(hadwell), and slow *Wicherley*.
S(hadwell's) unfinish'd works do yet impart,
Great proofs of force of Nature, none of Art;
With just bold strokes he dashes here and there,
Shewing great Mastery with little Care;
And scorns to varnish his good touches o'er,
To make the Fools and Women praise him more.
But *Wicherley*, earns hard what e'er he gains,
He wants no judgement, and he spares no pains;
He frequently excells, and at the least,
Makes fewer faults than any of the best.
Waller, by Nature, for the *Bays* design'd,
With Force and Fire, and fancy unconfin'd,
In *Panegyricks* does excell Mankind.
He best can turn, enforce, and soften things,
To praise great Conquerors, or to flatter Kings.
For pointed Satyrs I would B(uckhurst) choose,
The best good Man, with the worst natur'd Muse.
For Songs and Verses, mannerly, obscene,
That can stir Nature up by spring unseen,
And without forcing blushes please the Queen,
S(edley) has that prevailing, gentle Art,
That can with a resistless Charm impart,
The loosest Wishes to the chastest Heart.
Raise such a Conflict, kindle such a Fire
Betwixt declining Vertue and Desire;
Till the poor vanquish'd Mind dissolves away,
In Dreames all Night, in Sighs and Tears all Day.
D(ryden), in vain try'd this nice way of Wit,
For he to be a tearing *Blade* thought fit,

To give the Ladies a dry Bawdy bob,
And thus he got the name of Poet *Squab.*
But to be just, 'twill to his praise be found,
His Excellencies more than faults abound,
Nor dare I from his sacred Temples tear,
That Laurel which he best deserves to wear.
But does not D(ryden) find even Jonson dull?
Fletcher and *Beaumont* incorrect and full
Of lewd fires as he calls 'em? Shakespeare's stile
Stiff and affected? to his own the while
Allowing all the justness that his Pride
So arrogantly had to them deny'd?
And may not I have leave impartially
To search and censure D(ryden's) works, and try
If these gross faults his choice Pen does commit
Proceed from want of Judgement and of Wit?

Poems, 1685

616 *A Satyr against Mankind*

WERE I, who to my Cost already am,
One of those strange, prodigious Creatures *Man,*
A Spirit free, to chuse for my own Share,
What sort of Flesh and Blood I pleas'd to wear,
I'd be a Dog, a Monkey or a Bear,
Or any thing, but that vain Animal,
Who is so proud of being Rational.
The Senses are too gross; and he'll contrive
A Sixth, to contradict the other Five:
And before certain Instinct, will preferr
Reason, which Fifty times for one does err—
Reason, an *Ignis fatuus* of the Mind,
Which leaves the Light of Nature, Sense, behind.

Pathless, and dangerous, wand'ring ways it takes,
Through Errour's fenny Bogs, and thorny Brakes:
Whilst the misguided Follower climbs with Pain,
Mountains of Whimsies, heapt in his own Brain,
Stumbling from Thought to Thought, falls headlong down
Into Doubt's boundless Sea, where like to drown
Books bear him up a while, and make him try
To swim with Bladders of Philosophy,
In hopes still to o'ertake the skipping Light:
The Vapour dances, in his dazzled sight,
Till spent, it leaves him to Eternal Night.
Then old Age, and Experience, hand in hand,
Lead him to Death, and make him understand,
After a Search so painful, and so long,
That all his Life he has been in the wrong.

. . . .

Which is the basest Creature, Man, or Beast?
Birds feed on Birds, Beasts on each other prey;
But savage Man alone, does Man betray.
Press'd by Necessity, *They* kill for Food;
Man undoes Man, to do himself no good.
With Teeth, and Claws, by Nature arm'd *They* hunt
Nature's allowance, to supply their want:
But Man with Smiles, Embraces, Friendships, Praise,
Inhumanly, his Fellow's Life betrays,
With voluntary Pains, works his Distress;
Not through Necessity, but Wantonness.
For Hunger, or for Love *They* bite or tear,
Whilst wretched Man is still in Arms for Fear:
For Fear he arms, and is of Arms afraid;
From Fear, to Fear, successively betray'd.
Base Fear, the Source whence his best Passions came,

His boasted Honour, and his dear-bought Fame,
The Lust of Pow'r, to which he's such a Slave,
And for the which alone he dares be brave:
To which his various Projects are design'd,
Which makes him gen'rous, affable, and kind:
For which he takes such Pains to be thought Wise,
And screws his Actions, in a forc'd Disguise:
Leads a most tedious Life, in misery,
Under laborious, mean Hypocrisie.
Look to the bottom of his vast Design,
Wherein Man's Wisdom, Pow'r, and Glory join—
The Good he acts, the Ill he does endure,
'Tis all from Fear, to make himself secure.
Meerly for safety, after Fame they thirst;
For all Men would be Cowards if they durst:
And Honesty 's against all common sense—
Men must be Knaves; 'tis in their own Defence,
Mankind's dishonest; if they think it fair,
Amongst known Cheats, to play upon the square,
You'll be undone—
Nor can weak Truth, your Reputation save;
The Knaves will all agree to call you Knave.
Wrong'd shall he live, insulted o'er, opprest,
Who dares be less a Villain than the rest.
Thus here you see what Human Nature craves,
Most Men are Cowards, all Men shou'd be Knaves.
The Difference lies, as far as I can see,
Not in the thing it self, but the degree;
And all the Subject Matter of Debate,
Is only who's a Knave of the first Rate.

Text from *Poems on Several Occasions*, 1705

ANONYMOUS

617 *(I am no subject unto fate)*

I AM no subject unto fate;
The pow'r assum'd I give to you:
Whether returning Love or Hate,
Which falls in storms or gentle dew,

It is my Will which chuseth you;
Though Tyrant, yet, if I'll obey;
Obedience is truly due
To whom I give myself away.

I may be born under a Throne,
A slave, or free, without my Voice;
But Loving, and Religion,
Solely depend on my own choice.

The Worlds dimensions are wide;
My mind not Heaven can confine:
That outward worship is bely'd,
Who inward bows to others shrine.

Force may be called Victory;
Yet only those are overcome,
Who yield unto an Enemy,
That is their certain fate and doom.

Thus fettered I freely love;
My choice doth make the conquest shine:
And 'twill thy power best improve,
That to thy Subject thou incline.

Who wisely Rules, deserves Command;
Then keep thee Loyal next thy Heart;
Elective Monarchs cannot stand,
Nor Loves, without an equal dart.

J. Playford, *Choice Ayres*, 1676

618 *(Happy is the Country Life)*

HAPPY is the Country life
Blest with Content, good Health, and Ease;
Free from factious Noise and Strife,
We only Plot ourselves to please:
Peace of Mind the Days delight,
And Love our welcome Dream at night.

Hail green Fields and shady Woods,
Hail Springs and Streams that still run pure;
Nature's uncorrupted Goods,
Where Virtue only is secure:
Free from Vice, here free from Care,
Age is no pain, and Youth no snare.

J. Playford, *Choice Songs and Ayres*, 1683

JOHN OLDHAM

1653–1683

619 *From A Satyr address'd to a Friend that is about to leave the University, and come abroad in the World*

IF you for Orders, and a Gown design,
Consider only this, dear Friend of mine,
The Church is grown so overstock'd of late,
That if you walk abroad, you hardly meet
More Porters now than Parsons in the street.

At every Corner they are forc'd to ply
For Jobs of hawkering Divinity:
And half the number of the Sacred Herd
Are fain to stroll, and wander unpreferr'd:
 If this, or thoughts of such a weighty Charge
Make you resolve to keep your self at large;
For want of better opportunity,
A School must your next Sanctuary be:
Go, wed some Grammar-Bridewell, and a Wife,
And there beat *Greek*, and *Latin* for your life:
With birchen Scepter there command at will,
Greater than *Busby*'s self, or Doctor *Gill*:
But who would be to the vile Drudg'ry bound
Where there so small encouragement is found?
Where you for recompence of all your pains
Shall hardly reach a common Fidler's gains?
For when you've toil'd, and labour'd all you can,
To dung, and cultivate a barren Brain:
A Dancing-Master shall be better paid,
Tho he instructs the Heels, and you the Head:
To such Indulgence are kind Parents grown,
That nought costs less in breeding than a Son:
Nor is it hard to find a Father now,
Shall more upon a Setting-dog allow:
And with a freer hand reward the Care
Of training up his Spaniel, than his Heir.
 Some think themselves exalted to the Sky,
If they light in some noble Family:
Diet, an Horse, and thirty pounds a year,
Besides th' advantage of his Lordships ear,
The credit of the business, and the State,
Are things that in a Youngster's Sense sound great.

Little the unexperienc'd Wretch does know,
What slavery he oft must undergo:
Who tho in silken Scarf, and Cassock drest,
Wears but a gayer Livery at best:
When Dinner calls, the Implement must wait
With holy Words to consecrate the Meat:
But hold it for a Favour seldom known,
If he be deign'd the Honor to sit down.
Soon as the Tarts appear, Sir *Crape*, withdraw!
Those Dainties are not for a spiritual Maw:
Observe your distance, and be sure to stand
Hard by the Cistern with your Cap in hand:
There for diversion you may pick your Teeth,
Till the kind Voider comes for your Relief:
For meer Board-wages such their Freedom sell,
Slaves to an Hour, and Vassals to a Bell:
And if th' enjoyment of one day be stole,
They are but Pris'ners out upon Parole:
Always the marks of slavery remain,
And they, tho loose, still drag about their Chain.
  And where's the mighty Prospect after all,
A Chaplainship serv'd up, and seven years Thrall?
The menial thing perhaps for a Reward
Is to some slender Benefice preferr'd,
With this Proviso bound, that he must wed
My Ladies antiquated Waiting-Maid,
In Dressing only skill'd, and Marmalade.
  Let others who such meannesses can brook,
Strike Countenance to every Great Man's Look:
Let those that have a mind, turn slaves to eat,
And live contented by another's Plate:
I rate my Freedom higher, nor will I

For Food and Rayment truck my Liberty.
But, if I must to my last shifts be put,
To fill a Bladder, and twelve yards of Gut;
Rather with counterfeited wooden Leg,
And my right Arm tied up, I'll chuse to beg:
I'll rather chuse to starve at large, than be
The gawdiest Vassal to Dependency,
'T has ever been the top of my Desires,
The utmost height to which my wish aspires,
That Heav'n would bless me with a small Estate,
Where I might find a close obscure retreat;
There, free from Noise, and all ambitious ends,
Enjoy a few choice Books, and fewer Friends,
Lord of my self, accountable to none,
But to my Conscience, and my God alone:
There live unthought of, and unheard of, die,
And grudge Mankind my very memory.
But since the Blessing is (I find) too great
For me to wish for, or expect of Fate:
Yet, maugre all the spight of Destiny,
My Thoughts, and Actions are, and shall be free.

Works, 1686

THOMAS D'URFEY

1653?–1723

620 (*Bright was the morning*)

BRIGHT was the morning, and cool the Air
Serene was all the Sky
When on the Waves I left my Fair,
The Center of my Joy;
Heaven and Nature smiling were,
And nothing sad but I;

Each Rosie Field its odour spred
  All fragrant was the shore
Each River God rose from his Bed,
  And sighing own'd her Pow'r;
Curling their Waves, they deck'd their Steeds
  As proud of what they bore.
Glide on ye Waters, bear these Lines,
  And tell her how opprest;
Bear all my Sighs, ye gentle Winds
  And waft them to her Breast.
Tell her if e'er she prove unkind,
  I never shall have rest.

Songs and Poems, 1683 (text from H. Playford, *The Theater of Musick*, 1685)

621 (*Born with the Vices*)

BORN with the Vices of my kind,
  I should inconstant be;
Dear *Celia*, could I rambling find,
  More Beauty than in thee:
The rolling Surges of my Blood,
  By Virtue now grown low;
Should a new Show'r encrease the Flood,
  Too soon would overflow.
But Frailty (when thy Face I see)
  Does modestly retire;
Uncommon must her Graces be,
  Whose Look can bound desire:

621. Compare No. 603 Sedley: *A Song to Celia*.

Not to my Virtue, but thy Pow'r,
This Constancy is due;
When Change itself can give no more,
'Tis easy to be true.

H. Playford, *Banquet of Musick*, Bk. 3, 1689

JOHN NORRIS OF BEMERTON

1657–1711

622 *The Retirement*

WELL, I have thought on't, and I find
This busie world is nonsense all;
I here despair to please my mind,
Her sweetest honey is so mixt with gall.
Come then, I'll try how 'tis to be alone,
Live to my self a while, and be my own.

I've try'd, and bless the happy change;
So happy, I could almost vow
Never from this retreat to range,
For sure I ne'er can be so blest as now.
From all th' allays of bliss I here am free,
I pity others, and none envy me.

Here in this shady lonely grove,
I sweetly think my hours away,
Neither with business vex'd, nor love,
Which in the world bear such tyrannick sway:
No tumults can my close apartment find,
Calm as those seats above, which know no storm nor wind.

Let plots and news embroil the State,
Pray what's that to my books and me?
Whatever be the kingdom's fate,
Here I am sure t' enjoy a monarchy.
Lord of my self, accountable to none,
Like the first man in Paradise, alone.

While the ambitious vainly sue,
And of the partial stars complain,
I stand upon the shore and view
The mighty labours of the distant main,
I'm flush'd with silent joy, and smile to see
The shafts of Fortune still drop short of me.

Th' uneasie pageantry of State,
And all the plagues of thought and sense
Are far remov'd; I'm plac'd by Fate
Out of the road of all impertinence.
Thus, tho my fleeting life runs swiftly on,
'Twill not be short, because 'tis all my own.

Poems, 1684

623 *Hymn to Darkness*

HAIL thou most sacred venerable thing!
  What Muse is worthy thee to sing?
  Thee, from whose pregnant universal womb
All things, even Light thy rival, first did come.
What dares he not attempt that sings of thee,
  Thou first and greatest mystery?
Who can the secrets of thy essence tell?
Thou like the light of God art inaccessible.

Before great Love this monument did raise,
  This ample theatre of praise.
Before the folding circles of the sky
Were tun'd by Him who is all harmony.
Before the morning stars their hymn began,
  Before the councel held for man.
Before the birth of either Time or Place,
Thou reign'st unquestion'd monarch in the empty space.

Thy native lot thou didst to Light resign,
  But still half of the globe is thine.
Here with a quiet, and yet aweful hand,
Like the best emperours thou dost command.
To thee the stars above their brightness owe,
  And mortals their repose below.
To thy protection Fear and Sorrow flee,
And those that weary are of light, find rest in thee.

Tho light and glory be th' Almighty's throne,
  Darkness is His pavilion.
From that His radiant beauty, but from thee
He has His terror and His majesty.
Thus when He first proclaim'd His sacred Law,
  And would His rebel subjects awe,
Like princes on some great solemnity,
H' appear'd in's robes of State, and clad Himself with thee.

The blest above do thy sweet umbrage prize,
  When cloy'd with light, they veil their eyes.
The vision of the Deity is made
More sweet and beatifick by thy shade.

But we poor tenants of this orb below
  Don't here thy excellencies know,
Till Death our understandings does improve,
And then our wiser ghosts thy silent night-walks love.

But thee I now admire, thee would I chuse
  For my religion, or my Muse.
'Tis hard to tell whether thy reverend shade
Has more good votaries or poets made,
From thy dark caves were inspirations given,
  And from thick groves went vows to Heaven.
Hail then thou Muse's and Devotion's spring,
'Tis just we should adore, 'tis just we should thee sing.

Poems, 1684

WALTER POPE

d. 1714

624 *The Old Man's Wish*

IF I live to be old, for I find I go down,
  Let this be my Fate in a country Town;
May I have a warm House with a Stone at the Gate,
And a cleanly young Girl to rub my bald Pate.
  May I govern my Passion with an absolute sway,
  And grow wiser and better as my strength wears away;
  Without Gout or Stone by a gentle Decay.

In a Country Town by a murmuring Brook,
With the Ocean at distance on which I may look;
With a spacious Plain, without Hedge or Stile,
And an easie Pad nag to ride out a Mile.

May I govern my Passion with an absolute sway,
And grow wiser and better as my strength wears away;
Without Gout or Stone by a gentle Decay.

With *Horace* and *Plutarch*, and one or two more,
Of the best Wits that liv'd in the Ages before;
With a dish of Roast Mutton, not Venison nor Teal,
And clean, though coarse, Linnen at every Meal.
May I govern my Passion with an absolute sway,
And grow wiser and better as my strength wears away;
Without Gout or Stone by a gentle Decay.

With a Pudding on *Sunday*, and stout humming Liquor,
And remnants of Latin to welcome the Vicar;
With a hidden Reserve of *Burgundy* Wine,
To drink the King's Health in as oft as I dine.
May I govern my Passion with an absolute sway,
And grow wiser and better as my strength wears away;
Without Gout or Stone by a gentle Decay.

With a Courage undaunted may I face the last day,
And when I am dead, may the better sort say,
(In the Morning when sober, in the Evening when Mellow)
He's gone, and leaves not behind him his Fellow.
May I govern my Passion with an absolute sway,
And grow wiser and better as my strength wears away;
Without Gout or Stone by a gentle Decay.

H. Playford, *The Theater of Musick*, 1685

625 *(Tho' you may boast you're fairer)*

THO' you may boast you're fairer than the rest,
And brag how many Triumphs you have gain'd,
Yet shall your Beauty ne'er my Soul molest,
Since by your Sex I've been so much disdain'd:
He who is often driven to Despair;
Becomes at last regardless of the Fair.

Know *Celia* then, I'll scorn as well as you,
And never more to Woman-kind submit;
Your Tyrant-Graces can't my Heart subdue,
Nor can you conquer with your pow'rful Wit;
I'm now secure from all Love's cruel Harms,
And have prepar'd against them Counter-charms.

They who have follow'd long Love's idle Trade,
And do on all they see dote and admire;
Will, when repuls'd, find Passion quite decay'd,
And so contemn what once they did desire:
This common Tale, alas! few can prevent,
We first must sin, before we can Repent.

H. Playford, *The Theater of Musick*, 1685

626 *(Twas Night)*

TWAS Night, and all the Village wrap'd in Sleep,
When Grief lay hush'd, and Sorrow could not weep;
Ev'n proud Ambition too in quiet lay,
And peaceful Rest did all the World survey:
Only young *Philemon*, whose sad Despair,
Kept him awake, and tortur'd him with Care;
As he upon a River's Bank was laid,
And thus the melancholy Shepherd said:

Break, foolish Heart, and grieve no more,
Thy Sorrows are in vain;
They never can thy Joys restore,
But serve to feed thy Pain:
Those Friends, who when thy Fortune shone,
Were always courting thee,
Now thou art poor, do thee disown,
And scorn thy Company.
Friendship is now become a Trade,
By Fortune bought and sold;
A mere Self-interest is made,
Monopoliz'd by Gold:
Death is the only certain Friend
For all the World's a Cheat;
And he thy Miseries will end,
Tho' they be ne'er so great.
Then farewell World, and worldly Joys,
False Hope and vain Desires;
Which Reason blinds, and Sense destroys,
And only Pride inspires,
Since Virtue, Truth, and Honesty, are flown,
And none but Fortune's Fools are in request;
No more I will my wretched Fate bemoan,
But on this Bank contented ever rest.

H. Playford, *Banquet of Musick*, Bk. I, 1687

627 *(How pleasant is this flowery Plain)*

HOW pleasant is this flowery Plain and Grove!
What perfect scenes of Innocence and Love!
As if the Gods, when all things here below
Were curs'd, reserv'd this place to let us know

ANONYMOUS

How beautiful the World at first was made
Ere Mankind by Ambition was betray'd.
The happy Swain in these enamell'd Fields,
Possesses all the Good that Plenty yields;
Pure without mixture, as it first did come,
From the great Treasury of Nature's Womb;
Free from Disturbance here he lives at ease,
Contented with a little Flock's encrease,
And cover'd with the gentle wings of Peace.
No Fears, no Storms of War his Thoughts molest,
Ambition is a stranger to his Breast;
His Sheep, his Crook, and Pipe, are all his Store,
He needs not, neither does he covet more.
Oft to the silent Groves he does retreat,
Whose Shades defend him from the scorching Heat:
In these Recesses unconcern'd he lyes,
Whilst through the Boughs the whisp'ring *Zephire* flies,
And the Wood Choristers on ev'ry Tree,
Lull him asleep, with their sweet Harmony.
Ah happy Life! Ah blest Retreat,
Void of the Troubles that attend the Great!
From Pride, and courtly Follies, free
From all their gaudy Pomps and Vanity:
No guilty Remorse does their Pleasure annoy,
Nor disturb the Delights of their innocent Joy.
Monarchs, whom Cities and Kingdoms obey,
Are not half so contented, or happy as they.

H. Playford, *Banquet of Musick*, Bk. 1, 1687

628 (*Fair Sylvia*)

FAIR *Sylvia*, cease to blame my Youth,
  For having lov'd before;
So Men, till they have learnt the Truth,
  Strange Deities adore:
My Heart, 'tis true, has often rang'd,
  Like Bees o'er gaudy Flow'rs;
And many thousand Loves has chang'd,
  Till it was fix'd on yours.

But *Sylvia*, when I saw those Eyes,
  'Twas soon determin'd there;
Stars might as well forsake the Skies,
  And vanish in Despair:
When I from this great Rule do err,
  New Beauties to implore;
May I again turn Wanderer,
  And never settle more.

H. Playford, *Banquet of Musick*, Bk. 4, 1689

INDEX OF AUTHORS

References are to the numbers of the poems.

INDEX OF FIRST LINES

INDEX OF FIRST LINES

INDEX OF FIRST LINES

INDEX OF FIRST LINES

INDEX OF FIRST LINES

INDEX OF FIRST LINES

INDEX OF FIRST LINES

INDEX OF FIRST LINES

PRINTED IN GREAT BRITAIN
AT THE UNIVERSITY PRESS, OXFORD
BY VIVIAN RIDLER
PRINTER TO THE UNIVERSITY